CLASSICAL
AMERICAN
PHILOSOPHY

CLASSICAL AMERICAN PHILOSOPHY

ESSENTIAL READINGS
AND
INTERPRETIVE ESSAYS

JOHN J. STUHR

New York   Oxford
OXFORD UNIVERSITY PRESS
1987

Oxford University Press

Oxford New York Toronto
Delhi Bombay Calcutta Madras Karachi
Petaling Jaya Singapore Hong Kong Tokyo
Nairobi Dar es Salaam Cape Town
Melbourne Auckland

and associated companies in
Beirut Berlin Ibadan Nicosia

Library of Congress Cataloging-in-Publication Data
Classical American philosophy.
Includes bibliographies.
1. Philosophy, American. 2. Philosophy.
I. Stuhr, John J.
B935.C48 1987 191 86-18144
ISBN 0-19-504197-6
ISBN 0-19-504198-4

1 3 5 7 9 8 6 4 2

Printed in the United States of America
on acid-free paper

FOR MY PARENTS

PREFACE

This book seeks to present the essential writings of the major figures of classical American philosophy, to provide introductory essays helpful to both beginning and more advanced readers, and to offer suggestions for further reading and study. Ultimately, it aims at contributing to our critical understanding of the American intellectual tradition and spirit, and to our ability to appropriate the insights and dominant commitments of this philosophy in dealing with contemporary issues and problems.

This volume is primarily the result of my experiences in teaching American philosophy and intellectual history to undergraduates. These experiences have yielded several principles that have guided this work. First, I have included significant portions of the work of all of the central classical American philosophers. Peirce, James, and Dewey are standard fare, of course, but Royce, Santayana, and Mead are generally slighted if not wholly omitted. (I have excluded the work of Chauncey Wright, Alfred North Whitehead, C. I. Lewis, and others for reasons of space, but also and mainly because their writings seem less intrinsically connected to and philosophically significant within the classical period and tradition; of course, their work is important and does contain many historical and philosophical points of connection to the major figures and essential writings presented here.)

Second, I have included not simply individually important pieces by these major philosophers, but selections which demonstrate in as much length as possible the range and depth of the authors' views. Obviously, it is difficult to represent the work even of any one of these authors in the relatively few pages of a single volume. Still, I believe that the substantial selections which follow do capture the essential thoughts, concerns, and spirit of each philosopher. (Those collections that seek to cover *all* philosophy in America—early, classical, *and* more contemporary thought—simply cannot include sufficient material by each philosopher unless one is preparing only for a cocktail party.)

Third, I have sought to include selections that are the result of the best editorial work to date. Accordingly, for example, the selections below from the writings of Dewey are reprinted from the definitive Southern Illinois University Press editions of *John Dewey: The Early Works, 1882–1898; John Dewey: The Middle Works, 1899–1924;* and *John Dewey: The Later Works, 1925–1953.* Similarly, the selections from the works of James are reprinted from the definitive Harvard University Press series of *The Works of William James.* The selections from Peirce are reprinted exclusively from Peirce's manuscripts, the Harvard Peirce papers; their presence here marks a great advance over the common Peirce texts, which suffer from editorial rearrangement and fragmentation.

Fourth, I have sought to minimize editorial interference in the selected writings.

Whenever possible, essays, lectures, and book chapters have been presented in their entirety, whole and complete. When this has not been possible (because of space limitations or the nature of the writings themselves), every effort has been made to minimize the imposition of standards and interests other than the author's own. All editorial selectivity has been motivated by the desire to include fundamentally important work, not to alter philosophical form or content.

Finally, I have included introductory, interpretive, critical essays by leading scholars in classical American philosophy. These essays, each of which is original, provide biographical and cultural context, philosophical overview, and critical thoughts about the vision, strengths, difficulties, and contemporary significance of the writings that follow.

Many people have assisted me with this project. Most immediately, I have been aided greatly by Jacquelyn Ann Kegley, Kenneth Laine Ketner, John Lachs, John J. McDermott, and the late David L. Miller. At my request, they contributed introductory essays and advised me on selections and suggestions for further reading. This book would not have been possible without their insights and efforts. In addition to those individuals and publishers who have allowed me to reprint copyrighted material, I owe special thanks to Jo Ann Boydston, Frederick Burkhardt, Frank Oppenheim, Josiah Royce III, and Herman Saatkamp for their help with arrangements for the selections. I am grateful to Cynthia Read at Oxford University Press for early encouragement and unending assistance. Throughout my work, I have been supported by Whitman College—its faculty, administration, and, especially, its students in my American philosophy courses. I have gained much from my teachers at Carleton College and Vanderbilt University. Finally, I want to thank my wife, Eloise, and, above all, my parents, to whom I dedicate this book for creating and nurturing my interest in American philosophy, and for ceaseless support of every sort.

Walla Walla, Wash.   J.J.S.
May 1986

CONTENTS

ACKNOWLEDGMENTS

Selections from the manuscripts of Charles Sanders Peirce are reprinted by permission of the Department of Philosophy of Harvard University (from the annotated xerographic copy of the Harvard Peirce papers at the Institute for Studies in Pragmaticism, Texas Tech University).

Selections from *The Works of William James* are reprinted by permission of Harvard University Press.

Selections from *The Problem of Christianity* and *The Philosophy of Loyalty* are reprinted by permission of Mr. Josiah Royce III.

Selections from *Scepticism and Animal Faith;* from *Obiter Scripta: Lectures, Essays and Reviews;* from *Realms of Being;* from *Winds of Doctrine;* and from *Platonism and the Spiritual Life* are reprinted by permission of the M.I.T. Press.

Selections from *John Dewey: The Early Works, 1882–1898; John Dewey: The Middle Works, 1899–1924;* and *John Dewey: The Later Works, 1925–1953* are reprinted by permission of the Center for Dewey Studies and Southern Illinois University Press.

Selections from *Art as Experience* are reprinted by permission of the Putnam Publishing Group.

Selections from *A Common Faith* are reprinted by permission of Yale University Press.

Selections from *Mind, Self, and Society: From the Standpoint of a Social Behaviorist;* from *Movements of Thought in the Nineteenth Century;* from *The Philosophy of the Act;* and from *The Philosophy of the Present* are reprinted by permission of the University of Chicago Press.

CONTRIBUTORS

Jacquelyn Ann Kegley, who wrote the introduction to Josiah Royce for this volume, is Professor of Philosophy and Chair of the Department of Philosophy and Religious Studies at California State College at Bakersfield. She received her B.A. from Allegheny College, her M.A. from Rice University, and her Ph.D. from Columbia University. She has written many articles and essays on Royce and American philosophy. In addition she has co-authored a text on logic, and has edited three volumes dealing with contemporary problems concerning community, family, education, social services, and technology.

Kenneth Laine Ketner, Charles Sanders Peirce Professor of Philosophy and Director of the Institute for Studies in Pragmaticism at Texas Tech University, wrote the introduction to Peirce. He was educated at Oklahoma State University, UCLA, and the University of California at Santa Barbara, where he received his Ph.D. in philosophy. He has done extensive editorial and bibliographic work on Peirce, and has written books and numerous articles and essays on Peirce, Collingwood, folklore, semiotics, methodology, history and philosophy of science, mathematics, and computing.

John Lachs, author of the introduction to George Santayana, is Professor of Philosophy at Vanderbilt University, where he has received several awards for excellence in teaching. He earned his Ph.D. at Yale University, following his B.A. and M.A. at McGill University. In addition to three books on Santayana, Lachs has written books on Marxist philosophy, Fichte, and social philosophy, and has co-edited an introduction to philosophy. In addition, he has written scores of articles, essays, and reviews on Santayana, American philosophy, philosophy of mind, and moral and political issues.

John J. McDermott, Distinguished Professor of Philosophy and Humanities, Professor and Head of Humanities in Medicine at Texas A&M University, wrote the introduction to William James. He received his Ph.D. from Fordham University, and has received teaching awards at Queens College, CUNY, State University of New York at Stony Brook, and Texas A&M. He is the editor of scholarly editions of the works of Royce, James, and Dewey, and is co-founder and advisory editor of the Harvard University Critical Edition of James's writings. In addition, McDermott is the author of more than fifty essays, two books of philosophical essays on American culture, and is editor of a cultural introduction to philosophy.

The late David L. Miller, Professor of Philosophy at the University of Texas, wrote the introduction to George Herbert Mead. Miller received his Ph.D. from the University of Chicago, and was a former student of Mead. He was a collaborator with the editor of Mead's *The Philosophy of the Act,* edited a volume of Mead's writings, and was the author of a book on Mead's philosophy and numerous essays on Mead's thought and American philosophy. In addition, he was the author of books on individualism, achievement, and the open society, and on science and freedom.

John J. Stuhr, author of the introduction to John Dewey and the general editor of this volume, is Associate Professor and Chair of the Department of Philosophy at Whitman College. He received his B.A. from Carleton College, and his M.A. and Ph.D. from Vanderbilt University. He has received awards for excellence in teaching at Vanderbilt, the University of New England, and Whitman. Stuhr has written extensively on Dewey and classical American philosophy, and is now completing a book on Dewey. In addition, he is the author of essays, articles, and reviews on moral, social, and political issues, the social sciences, and contemporary European thought.

CLASSICAL
AMERICAN
PHILOSOPHY

CLASSICAL AMERICAN PHILOSOPHY

Introduction by John J. Stuhr

This is a book of, and about, the writings of six major American philosophers: Charles Sanders Peirce, William James, Josiah Royce, George Santayana, John Dewey, and George Herbert Mead. Each of these individuals is an original, insightful, and historically important thinker. Each is an essential contributor to the period, perspective, and tradition of classical American philosophy. In addition, each speaks directly, imaginatively, critically, and wisely to our contemporary global society, its distant possibilities for improvement, and its massive, pressing problems.

These problems are clear enough in general outline. Our world is a world of possible nuclear self-destruction, a world in which this unthinkable prospect must not fail to be thought as long as it remains possible. Against this background, wars, invasions, occupations, suppressions, "covert operations," and self-righteous, absolutist international terrorism are the norm. We live in—or, at least, if we are fortunate, near—hunger, malnutrition, disease, deformity, and pain. Our environment, increasingly polluted and plundered, now faces the demands of a rapidly expanding population. Social life is marked by inequity, crime, physical and psychological violence in both individual and institutional forms, and the absence of personal growth, enriching relationships, and genuine community. We see poverty and unfulfillment in the lives of many, and the poverty of fulfillment in the lives of a few others. None of this, of course, is shocking; these facts, at least in the abstract, are commonplace, and they are so horrible, terrifying, and depressing that we have had to become insensitive in some measure to them.

Still, the prospective reader is entitled to a suspicious grin or weary laugh—for this is another book, another book of philosophy, another book of the writings of several dead thinkers. What does it have to offer us as we confront these problems? This is an important question: though it is seldom posed and less frequently addressed, it is *the* pragmatic question *for* (if not *in*) philosophy. It is this question which makes clear the triviality of much contemporary thought—a triviality rooted not in subject matter but in a poverty of approach, form, self-understanding, and, above all, results.[1] The resulting suspicion, scepticism, and smile, however, are well known to the classical American philosophers. Thus, for example, George Santayana begins his *Scepticism and Animal Faith:*

> Here is one more system of philosophy. If the reader is tempted to smile, I can assure him that I smile with him, and that my system . . . differs widely in spirit and pretensions from what usually goes by that name. . . . I am merely attempting to express for the reader the principles to which he appeals when he smiles.[2]

So, too, Dewey confronts our suspicions and sceptical smiles:

> The chief intellectual characteristic of the present age is its despair of any constructive philosophy—not just in its technical meaning, but in the sense of any integrated outlook

and attitude. The developments of the last century have gone so far that we are now aware of the shock and overturn in older beliefs. But the formation of a new, coherent view of nature and man based upon facts consonant with science and actual social conditions is still to be had.[3]

He continues:

> It is in such a context that a thoroughgoing philosophy of experience, framed in light of science and technique, has its significance. For it, the breakdown of traditional ideas is an opportunity. The possibility of producing the kind of experience in which science and the arts are brought unitedly to bear upon industry, politics, religion, domestic life, and human relations in general, is itself something novel. We are not accustomed to it even as an idea. But faith in it is neither a dream nor a demonstrated failure. It is a faith. Realization of the faith so that we may work in larger measure by sight of things achieved, is in the future. . . . A philosophic faith, being a tendency to action, can be tried and tested only in action. I know of no viable alternative in the present day to such a philosophy [of experience] as has been indicated.[4]

The writings that follow are presented in this spirit: they constitute an opportunity, a call to action, and a smile at self-contained intellectual systems, self-certain doctrines, and self-proclaimed absolute truths. Be forewarned, then: classical American philosophy offers no formula for salvation independent of human endeavor in time and nature; no method for infallibility, exactitude, or finality; no claim to truth or account of reality void of intrinsic historical and cultural connection; and no imperative to overcome the finite, unfinished, local, transient, pluralistic character of experience.

The introductory essays below provide the necessary personal, intellectual, and cultural contexts for the writings that follow, and the classical American philosophers speak clearly and effectively for themselves. Accordingly, there is no need for, or value in, an introductory "summary" of this material. On the other hand, a general characterization of its dominant features may be needed as a preliminary to assessing its contemporary value and viability.

Historically, we may identify classical American philosophy with a particular period in America, with particular individuals who influenced and in turn were influenced by each other's thought, and with the particular relation of this philosophy to both earlier and later thought in America. Understood in this manner, classical American philosophy is philosophy in America from approximately 1870 to roughly 1945, from the initial setting forth of pragmatism at the early meetings of the Cambridge "Metaphysical Club" (founded by Peirce, James, and others) to the final work of Dewey after World War II and the deaths of Dewey and Santayana in the early 1950s. In this historical sense, it is a philosophy forged in and through the personal and professional relationships of Peirce, James, Royce, Santayana, Dewey, and Mead, as well as others:[5] their lives overlapped (at, for example, Johns Hopkins, Harvard, Michigan, and Chicago, and at many other places on numerous, briefer occassions); their work and thoughts overlapped even more frequently and importantly, as evidenced by conversations, correspondence, written references, reviews (both positive and negative), and testimonies to the personal importance of the work of one or more of the others. Finally, understood in this historical fashion, classical American philosophy is classically American: it is the critical articulation (in a more complete, consistent, and self-aware manner) of attitudes, outlooks, and forms of life embedded in the culture from and in which it arose.[6] It marks a fruition and unified development of earlier thought, and stands as a point of departure and reference for later philosophic work.

Classical American philosophy may also be characterized in a more thematic or philosophical manner. In this sense, it may be defined by its exponents' common attitudes, purposes, philosophical problems, procedures, terminology, and beliefs. It is in virtue of such a shared complex of features that we identify, understand, and differentiate philosophical developments, movements, and "schools of thought." Such a unity of character, we must recognize, is not a single and simple essence, some necessary and sufficient feature of classical American philosophy, some property present always and only in classical American philosophy. Instead, it is an identifiable configuration, a characteristic shape, a resemblance, an overlapping and interweaving of features (present to differing degrees in the writings of the individual philosophers) that, as a relational whole, pervades and constitutes this philosophy and these philosophers.

What are these defining characteristics and commitments that, as such, must be the basis of claims for the contemporary cultural significance of classical American philosophy? The following themes, briefly listed here but articulated and developed in detail in the writings contained in this volume, appear both central to the classical American philosophical vision, and important for us today:

1. *The rejection of modern philosophy.* Classical American philosophy confronted and largely dismissed the categories, language, and notions central to earlier thought. This thought was fundamentally dualistic: problems arose and positions were articulated and defended in terms of dichotomies such as percept/concept, reason/will, thought/purpose, intellect/emotion, immediate knowledge/inferential knowledge, mind/matter, appearance/reality, experience/nature, belief/action, theory/practice, facts/values, means/ends, divine/human, self/others, individual/community, and so on. Classical American philosophers did not refuse to use these terms; instead, their point was that these notions refer to distinctions made in thought rather than to different kinds of being or levels of existence. That is, these terms have a functional rather than an ontological status: they stand for useful distinctions made within reflection, and not for different kinds of being, discrete and separate prior to reflection. This is crucial because it is bound up with the wholescale rejection of the central problems of modern philosophy, problems which presuppose the above dualistic categories. Classical American philosophers, that is, did not attempt to provide better answers to traditional problems (the "enduring problems" of so many introductory philosophy texts) as much as they sought to dissolve, dismiss, and undercut these problems altogether by denying the metaphysical assumptions which gave rise to them. In doing this, they rejected as well the image of philosophy itself embedded in modern philosophy. Philosophy no longer was to be understood as a purely theoretical quest for eternal truths or knowledge of an ultimate and unchanging reality. Its job no longer was to analyze experience into the real and unreal, the substantial and the insubstantial. Instead, it must be practical, critical, and reconstructive; it must aim at the

successful transformation or amelioration of the experienced problems which call it forth and intrinsically situate it, and its success must be measured in terms of this goal. Thus, for the classical American philosophers, philosophy is primarily an instrument for the ongoing critical reconstruction of daily practice. In a world where daily life is frequently distant from intelligent self-examination and its fruits, a philosophy which removes itself (in subject matter or application) from the genuine problems of life is an unaffordable luxury. Classical American philosophy pursues a different course.

2. *Fallibilism.* For the classical American philosophers, fallibility is an irreducible dimension of the human condition: empirical belief can never be certain, exact, absolute, final. The abandoned "quest for certainty" is replaced by piecemeal, multi-directional efforts to verify and warrant beliefs. The possibility of belief revision is never erased. Fallibilism, however, does not signify a failing or shortcoming. It marks not the absence of omniscience, but the vulnerability of all dogma, the significance of inquiry and experiment, and the future-directed, eventual character of life. It is, for example, in this spirit that Santayana attacks the view of knowledge as certainty, a view central to both traditional metaphysics and scepticism. It is in this spirit that he asks instead for an *honest* philosophy. Similarly, Peirce identifies fallibilism as the spirit of science, and commands us not to block the way of inquiry. In a world saddled with policies and actions rooted in absolutist commitments and ideologies quarantined from examination, fallibilism seems ever more attractive.

3. *Pluralism.* Classical American philosophy is committed to pluralism in its view of reality and human values. Ontologically, experiences occur pluralistically: our transactions with the natural environment are individual and qualitatively unique, though all are equally real. These experiences are irreducibly personal, individual, "owned." We find not experience (in the abstract) but experien*ces* (in the concrete). Morally, values and meanings are genuinely plural: experienced values, no matter how varied and messy, are real insofar as they are experienced. Concern for intellectual neatness aside, experience provides no transcendent position or principle of order for overcoming the varieties of experiences or the experiences of varied values. It is in this spirit that James, perhaps *the* philosopher of pluralism, writes:

> . . . whereas absolutism thinks that . . . substance becomes fully divine only in the form of totality, and is not its real self in any form but the *all*-form, the pluralistic view which I prefer to adopt is willing to believe that there may ultimately never be an all-form at all, that the substance of reality may never get totally collected, that some of it may remain outside of the largest combination of it ever made, and that a distributive form of reality, the *each*-form, is logically as acceptable and empirically as probable as the all-form commonly acquiesced in as so obviously the self-evident thing. . . .
>
> For pluralism, all that we are required to admit as the constitution of reality is what we ourselves find empirically realized in every minimum of finite life.[7]

What we find, for James, are differing experiences, values, and temperaments; accordingly, differing philosophies appear rational—call forth the "sentiment of rationality"— in differing individuals. The search for total, final, literal philosophic agreement, James concludes, *must* fail; a philosophy may not be ultimate and "strait-laced," for "individu-ality outruns all classification."[8] It is in this same light that Santayana contrasts the philosopher's supposed desire for truth with his or her defense of some "vested illusion." In "The Genteel Tradition in American Philosophy," he writes:

> No system would have ever been framed if people had been simply interested in know-ing what is true, whatever it may be. What produces systems is the interest in maintain-ing against all comers that some favourite or inherited idea of ours is sufficient or right. A system may contain an account of many things which, in detail, are true enough; but as a system, covering infinite possibilities that neither our experience nor our logic can prejudge, it must be a work of imagination and a piece of human soliloquy. It may be expressive of human experience, it may be poetical; but how should any one who really coveted truth suppose that it was true?[9]

Local, regional, national, and global differences and conflicts abound. We need a phi-losophy that centrally recognizes those differences and seeks a harmonious pluralism; intellectual attempts to deny, impose on, or transcend this plurality are no longer in-nocuous, if they ever were.

4. *Radical empiricism.* A fundamental aspect of classical American philosophy is its radical view of experience, and its development of the implications of this view. The classical American philosophers reject traditional empiricism because it is not sufficiently empirical, not radically empirical. These concerns are developed most fully by James in *Essays in Radical Empiricism*[10] and by Dewey in "The Need for a Recovery of Philosophy"[11] and *Experience and Nature*:[12] they insist that experience is an active, ongoing affair in which experienc*ing* subject and experienc*ed* object constitute a primal, integral, relational unity. Experience is not an interaction of separate subject and object, a point of connection between a subjective realm of the experiencer and the objective order of nature. Instead, experience is existentially inclusive, continuous, unified: it is that interaction of subject and object which *constitutes* subject and object—as partial features of this active, yet unanalyzed, totality. Experience, then, is not an "interaction" but a "transaction" in which the whole constitutes its interrelated aspects. Experience is primal or pure, and contains no "inner duplicity." Thus, the separation of it into know-ing consciousness and known content can be explained, writes James, "as a particular sort of relation towards one another into which portions of pure experience may enter. The relation itself is a part of pure experience; one of its 'terms' becomes the subject or bearer of the knowledge, the knower, the other becomes the object known."[13] The implications of this view are many and profound. Negatively, radical empiricism is the basis for the rejection of modern philosophy described above: it demonstrates the artifi-ciality of philosophical problems of somehow uniting man and world, experience and nature, self and not-self, mental and physical, and so on. Positively, it points to a new direction for philosophy: philosophy must examine the conditions under which the pre-ceding distinctions are made and applied, and it must critically examine the values served by these distinctions. It is this aim that motivates Dewey, for example, in his writings on ethics, education, politics, and aesthetic and religious experience: today we are in des-

perate need of a philosophy that separates not experience from reality, but rather "blind, slavish, meaningless action" from "action that is free, significant, directed, and responsible."[14]

5. *The continuity of science and philosophy*. The classical American philosophers, especially Peirce, Dewey, and Mead, were greatly influenced by science, and in many ways sought to link philosophy to science. First, classical American philosophers rejected the view of philosophy as "queen of the sciences," as a discipline, in opposition to the sciences, concerned with transcendent reality, ultimate causes, absolute origins, and final, infallible truths. Second, as such, philosophy itself was understood as experimental: pragmatism and instrumentalism are, at base, efforts to connect meaning, truth, and epistemological justification of ideas, beliefs, and theories with the results of experience, experiment, and practice. For example, in "The Experimental Theory of Knowledge," Dewey writes:

> That truth denotes *truths*, that is, specific verifications, combinations of meanings and outcomes reflectively viewed, is, one may say, the central point of the experimental theory. Truth, in general or in the abstract, is a just name for an experienced relation among the things of experience: that sort of relation in which intents are retrospectively viewed from the standpoint of the fulfillment which they secure through their own natural operation or incitement. Thus the experimental theory explains directly and simply the absolutistic tendency to translate concrete true things into the general relationship, Truth, and then to hypostatize this abstraction into identity with real being, Truth *per se* and *in se*, of which all transitory things and events—that is, all experienced realities—are only shadowy futile approximations.[15]

In classical American philosophy, as in the sciences, the results of experimental inquiry are the measure of theory. Here science is understood in terms of a method of inquiry (rather than, for example, a particular subject matter), and, since proper results depend upon proper methods of inquiry, an understanding and critical examination of the nature of inquiry is fundamental. Accordingly, these philosophers were concerned with developing accounts of the nature of scientific method and logical reasoning. The writings below by Peirce, for example, on the nature of science and the theory of science[16] demonstrate the philosophic importance of these issues, as well as his own "saturation" by the spirit of the sciences; and, the influence of this work on the writings of the others demonstrates the centrality of these issues to classical American philosophy as a whole. Third, though scientific in the above senses, classical American philosophy is not reductionistic: the "world" of science is not "more real" than our commonsense, everyday life world; indeed, there is no ontological conflict at all between the objects of scientific activities and the objects of other endeavors. Insisting on radical empiricism, and viewing science as an inquiring (rather than spectating or copying or "mirroring") activity, classical American philosophers reject the premises of efforts to identify the mental with the physical, reduce the experiential to the material, and assimilate the human to the nonhuman. Inquiry into the conditions upon which the occurrence of immediate, qualitative experience depends presupposes, and so cannot call into question, the reality of that experience itself; the object of original experience has been transformed in being made the object of a later knowledge experience (which ignores qualitative features of the object while focusing on its causal relationships), but it has not been replaced or made "less real." Mead makes this clear in "The Nature of Scientific Knowledge,"[17] concluding that "the experimental scientist, apart from some philosophic bias, is not a positivist." In *The Philosophy of The Act,* Mead goes on to demolish popular, naive distinctions (rooted in modern philosophy) between the objective and the subjective, and primary and secondary qualities of existence. The ontological assumptions of science, as evident especially in contemporary physics and chemistry, converge on radical empiricism; Mead writes: "so-called objects which lie beyond the range of possible experience are in reality complex procedures in the control of actual experience."[18] In this age of science and increasing control of nature and society, we do not need a philosophy that seeks to deny or usurp the functions and results of science. Classical American philosophy, by contrast, offers us an understanding of scientific method and insight into the difference between science and pseudoscience, ideology, and dogma. It turns our attention, moreover, to the critical task of evaluating particular uses, users, and results of science.

6. *Pragmatism and meliorism.* Classical American philosophy is pragmatic: its emphasis is on practical results of human activity, and the evaluation of theory by its instrumental function in resolving the problem situation at hand. As such, it is committed not to optimism or pessimism, but to meliorism—the view that human action can improve the human condition. James states this most directly and explicitly, contrasting meliorism with "intellectualism":

> 'Intellectualism' is the belief that our mind comes upon a world complete in itself, and has the duty of ascertaining its contents; but has no power of re-determining its character, for that is already given. . . . It implies the will to insist on a universe of intellectualist constitution, and the willingness to stand in the way of a pluralistic universe's success, such success requiring the good will and active faith, theoretical as well as practical, of all concerned to make it 'come true.' . . .[19]

The reality of this pluralistic or melioristic universe would require human action. James continues:

> The melioristic universe is conceived after a *social* analogy, as a pluralism of independent powers. It will succeed just in proportion as more of these work for its success. If none work, it will fail. If each does his best, it will not fail. Its destiny thus hangs on an *if,* or on a lot of *ifs*—which amounts to saying . . . that, the world being as yet unfinished, its total character can be expressed only by *hypothetical* and not by *categorical* propositions.[20]

This meliorism is clearly evident in Dewey's writings: he is concerned ultimately and in detail with liberating and extending the religious and aesthetic dimensions of experience, with securing effective individuality and community in social life, and with restructuring human relations and institutions so as to foster lifelong growth and education. This melioristic spirit pervades Royce's later writings, which focus on the nature and need for loyalty and community: the moral life requires an ideal to which one is devoted and, above all, the expression of this devotion "in some *sustained and practical way,* by acting steadily."[21] This is an important, politically far-reaching message for individuals accustomed and resigned to the difficulties and institutional roadblocks that face such efforts, for such resignation rapidly turns problematic situations into meta-physically necessary conditions of "fate." Classical American philosophy offers no prom-ise of success, but it directs us to make the effort. Reality, James tells us, is congenial to human powers.[22]

7. *The centrality of community and the social.* It is obvious that we live with others, that our actions are connected to and must take account of others, that we inhabit and form habits in a social environment. For the classical American philosophers, existence is social in a deeper, ontologically more important sense as well: the individual is intrinsi-cally *constituted* by and in his or her social relations; the self is fundamentally a social self. Even James and Santayana, who champion the individual, recognize that cultural conditions enter into the very being of that individual. Mead develops this most fully: the self is "essentially a social structure, and it arises in social experience"; it is thus impossi-ble to conceive of a self arising outside of a social context.[23] Mead continues:

> The unity and structure of the complete self reflects the unity and structure of the social process as a whole; . . . The organization and unification of a social group is identical with the organization and unification of any one of the selves arising within the social process in which that group is engaged, or which it is carrying on.[24]

Mead details how such a self arises in his account (included in the selections below) of language and communication, play, and the generalized other. Practically, two crucial points emerge from this discussion: first, the emergence of the self requires a social process of development—individuality is a social creation, not something innate, fixed, and sure; second, the individual and the social community implicate one another in experience—contrary both to metaphysical schemes which oppose self and society, and to abstract political philosophies, which assume a necessary opposition of private and public interest. These points are central to Dewey's efforts to establish both a new individualism and a genuine public or integrated community of association. And, they emerge powerfully in Royce's accounts of individual and social experience, and the development of local (or "provincial"), national, and international (or "great") commu-nities. We are "saved through the community," through union,[25] Royce writes; individ-ual fulfillment requires not detachment but devotion to communal cause. It is in this context that Royce, during World War I, sought to apply principles drawn from the business of insurance to the actions and associations of nations:

> Were any group of nations to begin in a businesslike and practicable way to do what the individual fellow members of a social order have now the means of doing, namely, to insure against risks of some insurable sort, we should have a good reason to expect that analogous and beneficent indirect workings would ere long follow from even a modest beginning in the art of international insurance.[26]

Despite our own best efforts to "get ahead," our lives often contain little personal fulfillment. Classical American philosophy links the attainment of this individuality with the creation of community and instructs us that the actualization of community requires difficult, imaginative action. Let Santayana have the last word:

> All traditions have been founded on practice: in practice the most ideal of them regain their authority, when practice really deals with reality, and faces the world squarely, in the interests of the whole soul. To bring the whole soul to expression is what all civilization is after. We must be patient, for the task is long; but the fields are always white for the harvest, and the yield cannot be insignificant when labourers go forth into the harvest with the high and diligent spirit which we divine in you.[27]

NOTES

1. See my "Do American Philosophers Exist?: Thoughts on American Philosophy and Culture," *Annals of Scholarship* 2, 4 (1981): 65–90.

2. George Santayana, *Scepticism and Animal Faith* (New York: Dover, 1955), p. v. Included in the selections below, p. 277.

3. John Dewey, "What I Believe" in *John Dewey: The Later Works, 1925–1953*, Vol. 5, Jo Ann Boydston, ed. (Carbondale and Edwardsville, Ill.: Southern Illinois University Press, 1984), pp. 276–277.

4. Ibid., p. 278.

5. Autobiographical writings by all these authors make clear these personal influences. For a brief overview, see Max H. Fisch, "The Classic Period in American Philosophy," in his *Classic American Philosophers* (Englewood Cliffs, N.J.: Prentice-Hall, 1951), pp. 1–8.

6. This point has been made by a number of authors. In addition to the essays by Stuhr and Fisch cited above, see the following: John J. McDermott, *The Culture of Experience: Philosophical Essays in the American Grain* (New York: New York University Press, 1976), pp. 1–20; H. S. Thayer, *Meaning and Action: A Critical History of Pragmatism* (Indianapolis: Hackett, 1981), pp. 432–448; John E. Smith, *The Spirit of American Philosophy* (Albany: State University Press of New York, 1983), pp. 187–206. In addition to these and essays by other authors, many of Santayana's writings on America speak to these issues.

7. William James, *A Pluralistic Universe. The Works of William James*, Frederick Burkhardt, ed. (Cambridge, Mass.: Harvard University Press, 1977), pp. 20, 145.

8. Ibid., p. 7. See also William James, "The Sentiment of Rationality," in *The Will To Believe and Other Essays in Popular Philosophy. The Works of William James*, Frederick Burkhardt, ed., (Cambridge, Mass.: Harvard University Press, 1979), p. 89.

9. George Santayana, "The Genteel Tradition in American Philosophy," in *Winds of Doctrine* (New York: Charles Scribner's Sons, 1913), pp. 198–199.

10. See "A World of Pure Experience," p. 125, below.

11. See "The Need for a Recovery of Philosophy," p. 338, below.

12. See "Experience and Philosophic Method," "Existence as Precarious and Stable," and "Nature, Communication and Meaning," pp. 350, 360, and 364, below.

13. William James, "Does 'Consciousness' Exist?," in *Essays in Radical Empiricism. The Works of William James*, Frederick Burkhardt, ed. (Cambridge, Mass.: Harvard University Press, 1976), pp. 4–5.

14. John Dewey, *Experience and Nature* in *John Dewey: The Later Works, 1925–1953*, Vol. 1, Jo Ann Boydston, ed. (Carbondale and Edwardsville, Ill.: Southern Illinois University, 1981), p. 324. See also John Dewey and Arthur F. Bentley, *Knowing and the Known* (Boston: Beacon Press, 1949), p. 276.

15. John Dewey, "The Experimental Theory of Knowledge," in *John Dewey: The Middle Works, 1899–1924*, Jo Ann Boydston, ed., (Carbondale and Edwardsville, Ill.: Southern Illinois University Press, 1977), pp. 108–109.

16. See pp. 18, 38, 46, and 54, below.

17. George Herbert Mead, "The Nature of Scientific Knowledge," in *The Philosophy of the Act*, Charles W. Morris, ed. (in collaboration with John M. Brewster, Albert M. Dunham, and David L. Miller) (Chicago: The University of Chicago Press, 1938), pp. 45–62. Included in the selections below, pp. 460.

18. Ibid., pp. 291–292.

19. William James, "Faith and the Right to Believe," in *The Writings of William James,* John J. McDermott, ed. (Chicago: The University of Chicago Press, 1977), pp. 735, 737. See also the concluding pages of *A Pluralistic Universe.*

20. James, "Faith and the Right to Believe," op. cit., p. 739.

21. Josiah Royce, *The Philosophy of Loyalty* (New York: Macmillan, 1908), p. 14.

22. William James, "The Sentiment of Rationality," op. cit., p. 73.

23. George Herbert Mead, *Mind, Self, and Society: From the Standpoint of a Social Behaviorist,* Charles W. Morris, ed. (Chicago: The University of Chicago Press, 1934), p. 140. Included in the selections below, p. 447.

24. Ibid., p. 144.

25. Josiah Royce, *The Hope of the Great Community* (New York: Macmillan, 1916), p. 131.

26. Ibid., p. 75.

27. George Santayana, "Tradition and Practice," reprinted in *Santayana on America,* Richard Colton Lyon, ed. (New York: Harcourt, Brace & World, Inc., 1968), p. 35.

CHARLES SANDERS PEIRCE

Introduction by Kenneth Laine Ketner

> . . . if I were asked to nominate the two native Americans of greatest intellectual genius, I think they would both be 19th-century figures—Willard Gibbs and . . . C. S. Peirce.
>
> C. P. Snow[1]

Although now considered by many to be the founder of serious philosophic study in the United States, late in his career, which was a study in extremes of triumph and misery, Peirce sometimes complained, usually without bitterness, that most of his contemporaries did not fully understand or appreciate his work. He was aware that he had something valuable to give mankind, and often felt frustrated that circumstances were preventing him from making that contribution. Today that complaint is still valid, although the flow of scholarship is now in the direction of responding to it. The response will be possible because almost all the books and essays that Peirce wrote, even without support from publishers or universities, have survived and are beginning to appear in convenient editions. In effect, Peirce overcame his lack of resources by writing out his contributions any way he could, sometimes with homemade ink and scrap paper, so that there would be at least one copy of his thoughts which would survive him. In this prologue for a set of materials designed to introduce readers to the work of the man widely considered to be the most original and profound American intellect, let us pursue the question of his complaint from within the context of his era and of ours. As a necessary preparation for that task, we should first quickly review the status of Peirce's writings, both published and unpublished.

He published a great deal during his lifetime, more than received opinion has registered. Perhaps the reason for this misregistration was that many of his publications were unsigned, or appeared in government scientific reports not widely distributed to the public, or in reference works (for example, the thousands of definitions he contributed to *The Century Dictionary*). Recent bibliographic research has identified almost all such items.[2] That he was a severe recluse has been a favored allegation among some students of his life and work. A look at the evidence shows this to be false, for as late as 1906 he wrote published reports of meetings of the National Academy of Sciences that he attended as a member and where he also gave papers. He often expressed pride in the fact that he was elected to the National Academy on the basis of his work in logic, which he understood broadly as the science of scientific method. Another nonreclusive theme one can detect in the same way is the amount of influence Peirce exercised upon others during his lifetime, and the amount of influence others exercised upon him. It is also fashionable to proclaim that Peirce's intellectual ability or output suffered because he lacked a permanent academic chair. Such a position, it is further said, would have provided him with appropriate critical feedback from students and colleagues, which he is supposed to have needed to forestall certain difficulties considered to exist in his works. Yet, by looking over his complete published output one can see that he was constantly, almost until the day he died, responding to and arguing with friends and detractors. Even more pronounced instances of mutual influence are found in his correspondence. Whether there are difficulties in his works is a matter for argumentation, not speculation.

For the most part, Peirce's manuscripts (like his publications, also voluminous) have survived and are widely available for study.[3] Some scholars have described these as fragmentary. It is true that one can find some that fit this category, but one can also find several virtually complete and unified book manuscripts or complete series of lecture notebooks. Furthermore, his system—whether expressed in a series of fragments or in complete essays—is present for examination. At the moment, in addition to Harvard, there are four other centers at which scholars are welcomed to pursue studies of these and related materials.[4] The effort to make Peirce's writings more widely available in conveniently accessible book format began in 1923 and continues today.[5]

From Peirce's vast literary production, which has been estimated to be enough to fill more than one hundred volumes,[6] it is difficult—especially in an introductory anthology—to present a representative selection of Peirce's writings within a narrow scope. That difficulty is increased by the fact that he was a systematic thinker, whose work is poorly appreciated if broken up and perused in isolated chunks. However, clues from study of Peirce's life career suggest a way to organize a set of introductory texts, and these same considerations will begin to suggest an answer to the complaint initially mentioned. In this way we can start to understand why his contemporaries misunderstood him, something that will help us to overcome this barrier insofar as it still affects us.

BIOGRAPHICAL SUMMARY

> A genuine culture was beginning to struggle upward again in the seventies: a Peirce, a Shaler, a Marsh, a Gibbs, a Ryder, a Roebling, a Thomas Eakins, a Richardson, a Sullivan, an Adams, a LaFarge were men that any age might proudly exhibit and make use of. But the procession of American civilization divided and walked around these men.
>
> Lewis Mumford[7]

The first and most important thing one notices by looking carefully at Peirce's total life, especially if one avoids preconceived conclusions about it, is that he was not a philosopher, but was a scientist and mathematician. You, dear reader, at this point might have experienced a voice from your inner dialogue, which said, "That can't possibly be true." If I may join your dialogue, it is clear that the key word of that statement, *"philosophy,"* must be explicated. If we today look back upon a figure from the past, surely we bring our own vocabulary (at least initially) to that task. So the issue amounts to a question about the meaning of the word "philosophy" in our time. It is clear that philosophy today is usually and upon first presumption considered to be a discipline within the humanities, as opposed to being a part of the sciences—let us label this sense as philosophy$_H$. It isn't pertinent whether that widespread public and academic notion is correct. It is relevant that this is the perspective from which most persons would judge the matter now; thus, that is the sense in which the above claim states that Peirce is not a philosopher$_H$. One of the lessons to be gained from reading the intellectual autobiography presented below is that Peirce had concluded that philosophy is (or could easily become) a science that is embedded within a context of other sciences or presuppositions of science; it isn't even the most basic science, a position he reserved for mathematics. This simple fact has been systematically overlooked and ignored by almost all commentators on Peirce, who usually approach his works from the standpoint of philosophy$_H$. To proceed in that manner is to invite a serious misunderstanding of what he believed he had accomplished. Indeed, this simple fact is a convenient touchstone for judging the accuracy of any account of Peirce's works one might encounter. Another barrier has to do with his laboratory cast of mind; a reader who lacks experience with the inner life of a laboratory has a distinct disadvantage to overcome in understanding him.

Perhaps we could identify philosophy in Peirce's sense as philosophy$_S$. This means that he should be compared to scientific philosophers$_S$ such as Aristotle, Bacon, Leibniz, Helmholtz, Mach, or Einstein and contrasted with philosophers$_H$ such as Plato, Ockham, Hegel, James, or Wittgenstein. His boldly announced allegiance to Aristotle as scientist and distaste of the Hellenic tendency to mingle philosophy and practice[8] are very unphilosophic$_H$.

It is not surprising that he would have that outlook, for he was born on September 10, 1839, into the family and extended circle of friends of Benjamin Peirce, professor of mathematics and astronomy at Harvard, an acknowledged leader among American scientists. His father, realizing the son's intellectual gifts, took charge of his early education, submitting him to strict intellectual exercises that especially emphasized rigor, detail, and long perseverance. Charles also made a study of chemistry at a tender age. His graduate degree was in chemistry and throughout his life he often referred to himself simply as a chemist who had in effect been born in a scientific laboratory, for such was the atmosphere of his father's house and social orbit.

When about twelve years old, in his brother's room he came across a copy of Whately's *Logic,* read it, and began his lifelong fascination with that subject, understood as the scientific study of scientific method. After his first degree from Harvard, in 1859, wanting direct experience with the methods of science, he entered the employ of the United States Coast Survey, then the premier government scientific agency. He spent the Civil War years on field surveys in Louisiana or working in Cambridge with his father, the Survey's consulting geometer. In 1865, he made his academic debut with a series of lectures at Harvard entitled "On the Logic of Science."[9] During 1867, he commenced astronomical work at the Harvard Observatory that eventually culminated in *Photometric Researches,* a pioneering attempt at mapping our galaxy, the Milky Way.[10] During the early seventies he was one of the participants in the well-known Metaphysical Club, an informal but serious Cambridge discussion group consisting of

Peirce, James, O. W. Holmes, J. B. Warner, and sometimes Frank Abbot and John Fiske. In November of 1872, his father, now superintendent of the Survey, commissioned him to take charge of its pendulum experiments, by which means one could determine the relative force of gravity at various locations on the globe. With sufficient information of that kind one could more accurately determine the shape of the earth, thus permitting one to make more accurate maps, not to mention increasing knowledge of the value of the force of gravity, which is among the most important physical constants. During the seventies and early eighties, he traveled widely in the United States and in Europe, conducting gravity surveys. In the course of his research, he discovered a serious error in what was then regarded as the best pendulum work in Europe. He defended and sustained his critique at a meeting of the International Geodetic Association in Geneva in 1877. Based on this and related work, he designed the Peirce pendulum, which became the standard apparatus for this kind of research. As a result of these efforts, he became world famous as a mathematical physicist in geodesy.[11]

As a consequence of the need in pendulum research for very accurate measurements, in 1879 he was directed by the Survey to study the possibility of using a wavelength of light as a standard for the length of the meter. This he succeeded in doing shortly thereafter in a "Report on the Spectrum Meter,"[12] tendered to the Survey. Peirce's findings on that topic later contributed to the work of Michelson and Rowland. During 1879 to 1884, while retaining his full-time position with the Survey, Peirce accepted a part-time position as lecturer in logic at the Johns Hopkins University. There he was closely associated with members of the mathematics department under J. J. Sylvester. He was abruptly dismissed from his position in Baltimore, probably because some members of the governing board of Hopkins were told he had taken up residence with Juliette Froissy (who later became his second wife) before concluding his divorce from Melusina Fay (who had deserted him, according to their divorce decree). He returned full time to Survey work, but a number of changes had begun to take place in its policies, perhaps the most important being that its new leaders no longer insisted upon the kind of high standards Peirce brought to his physical and geodetic research. For this and other reasons, Peirce resigned from the Coast Survey in 1891, after first submitting an exhaustive summary report upon his long gravity researches.[13] Perhaps this all too brief account of his scientific accomplishments[14] helps one to understand why in 1895 Peirce remarked that "My philosophy may be described as the attempt of a physicist to make such conjecture as to the constitution of the universe as the methods of science may permit, with the aid of all that has been done by previous philosophers."[15]

While undertaking his astronomical, geodetic, and metrological researches Peirce was also busily involved in helping to create modern symbolic logic. His very important role there has been ill treated, misdescribed, or ignored, as Hilary Putnam has recently explained.[16] His works in this area are well documented in the autobiography reprinted on page 26f, below. Indeed, his researches in formal logic (roughly that part of semeiotic or general logic which he labeled as critic) were important contributions toward a number of contemporary developments, the most notable among which is computer science. In fact, Peirce's legacy to computing may include more than having provided some of its software—it is also likely he contributed somewhat to hardware and to a kind of limitative thesis similar to that advanced by Turing.[17]

The end of his government employment meant a serious loss of income for Peirce, and he spent the nineties attempting to secure an adequate means of support for himself and his chronically ill second wife. He participated in a number of money-making schemes, including projects such as the commercialization of acetylene gas or development of hydroelectrical power. More than once, some well-known businessmen cheated him of his share in such projects. His luck, which favored him in earlier days, had inexorably and irreversibly turned. On March 13, 1897, he wrote the following to his old friend, William James:

> I have learned a great deal about philosophy in the last few years, because they have been very miserable and unsuccessful years—terrible beyond anything the man of ordinary experience can possibly understand or conceive. Thus, I have had a great deal of idleness & time that could not be employed in the duties of ordinary life, deprived of books, of laboratory, everything: and so there was nothing to prevent my elaborating my thoughts, and I have done a great deal of work which has cleared up and arranged my thoughts. Besides this, a new world of which I knew nothing, and of which I cannot find that anybody who has written has really known much, has been disclosed to me, the world of misery. It is absurd to say that Hugo, who has written the least foolishly about it, really knew anything of it. I would like to write a physiology of it. How many days did Hugo ever go at a time without a morsel of food or any idea where food was coming from, my case at this moment for very near three days, and yet that is the most insignificant of the experiences which go to make up misery? Much have I learned of life and of the world, throwing strong lights upon philosophy in these years. Undoubtedly its tendency is to make one value the spiritual more, but not an abstract spirituality. . . . On the other hand, it increases the sense of awe with which one regards Gautama Booda.[18]

This letter led eventually (with background assistance from James) to Peirce being invited to give a series of eight lectures about one year later at the Cambridge Conference, a kind of auxiliary education activity conducted just off Harvard Yard. It is in those 1898 lectures that Peirce first began to set down his mature thought. Surviving correspondence also shows that the Harvard philosophy department was solidly impressed with them, especially Royce and James. Subsequent essays by both men confirm that these lectures and other works by Peirce had a lasting and profound influence upon their own thought, although the Peirce/James debate is one that still continues today. Yet, still no steady employment or other source of adequate income came Peirce's way; eventually he came to spend most of his time on his homestead, Arisbe, near Milford, Pike County, Pennsylvania. He was able to continue publishing articles and book reviews, and occasionally to give lectures—notably his 1903 Lowell lectures,[19] which followed other lectures before the Lowell Institute in 1866 and 1892.[20] But more important, he continued to write essays and even complete whole books, for which he could find no publisher, yet which have survived and will appear in due time.

After the loss in 1910 of his friend and supporter James (in whose honor he informally adopted the additional name "Santiago"—Saint James), full-time misery once again sought him out. He contracted cancer, possibly as a result of being exposed to radiation at the April 1904 National Academy of Science meeting, where "Professor Barker . . . showed one specimen of a salt of uranium . . . [that] shone so brightly as to be visible all over the darkened . . . hall."[21] As the disease reached its terminus, he often asked for pen and paper, writing eventually having become the only way available to him of relieving his pain. At about ten o'clock on the morning of April 19, 1914, he died in the arms of a concerned young neighbor lad who had come to offer assistance.[22]

A SYSTEM OF SCIENCE

> Mr. Charles Peirce has now been for many years the principal representative in this country of a type of investigation in Logic which seems to me, as a student of the subject, to be of very great importance. The general nature of this importance I can best indicate by saying that the study of the methods of science and the comparative study of the types of concepts which have been developed in the various sciences, seem to be at present matters of great theoretical and practical significance.
>
> Josiah Royce[23]

Peirce's system is not a system of philosophy, but is a system of science, the organizing principle of which is method.

> I have now sketched my doctrine of Logical Critic, skipping a good deal. I recognize two other parts of Logic. One which may be called *Analytic* examines the nature of thought, not psychologically, but simply to define what it is to doubt, to believe, to learn, etc., and then to base critic on these definitions is my real method, though in this letter I have taken the third branch of logic *Methodeutic,* which shows how to conduct an inquiry. This is what the greater part of my life has been devoted to, though I base it upon Critic.[24]

Peirce's intellectual career is in effect a lifelong search for a correct account of the nature and function of methods that permit the discovery of truth by those that have the will and capacity to learn from experience, a personality type he designated as scientific intelligence. Moreover, the method whereby Peirce conducted this lifelong effort was itself science, aided by a powerful historical consciousness by means of which he sought in the history of science lessons for his own project. He concluded that scientific intelligences do not begin their activities in an intellectual vacuum—there are presuppositions of science and scientific method. Basically these fall into two large classes: religion and common sense. Peirce distinguished sharply between religion and theory of religion (or theology). Roughly, the difference is parallel to that between someone like Gautama and someone who equates religion to following a creed or living according to a mechani-

cal recipe (the kind of orthodoxy that the early pragmatist Jesus spent his career dis-
claiming). One might say that Gautama or Jesus acted, without thinking or theory or
premeditated recipe, in good ways because their instincts were good. What disturbed
Peirce about theology was that it proposed to give mankind a stone when bread was
needed—the stone of theory, which is not right instinct (which would be the bread of
religion within his system). Within metaphysics he admitted theorizing about religion,
but always insisted that such metaphysics could influence true religion only by a slow,
almost evolutionary process of percolation. Scientific activity is based upon religion, no
matter if the particular scientific intelligence is aware of it or not, because the ideals of
that method presuppose a search for the truth about a reality not yet known. The
influence of Boole is strong here, in a way not yet fully studied.[25]

Common sense is that set of instinctive beliefs that all normal human beings do not
doubt. Peirce considered that these were the result of evolutionary change over millenia.
Like religion, such original beliefs are not theory and, again like religion, there is a place
in his system for theorizing about them (critic, under critical common-sensism), but
again one should not take the theory in place of the fact of the presence and current
nature of such beliefs in all humans. These themes bear a strong resemblance to those
pursued by Wittgenstein in *On Certainty*.

The system proper begins with mathematics. This is the fundament of his entire
intellectual effort. A good way of accurately describing Peirce's career would be to say
that he was a student of the method of mathematics in all its ramifications. He regarded
mathematics as diagrammatic thinking.[26] His treatment of diagrams in this sense arose
from his study of figures like Helmholtz and Listing. Again and again, the general notion
of diagram appeared throughout his system, and it, along with his concept of mathematics, is a central unifying theme. His treatment of method in mathematics makes induction, observation, and experiment basic there, a stance that is in sharp contrast to the
deductivism of today.

His science of philosophy, which in the system of science is called cenoscopy, is
thoroughly based upon his studies of mathematics. A mythical conception of Peirce can
be developed if this important fact is discounted.[27] The first and perhaps most important
application of mathematics to philosophy comes in phaneroscopy (or categoriology).
There Peirce applied the results of his studies of the mathematical graph theory of Euler,
Kempe, Clifford, and Listing.[28] These results led him to a fundamental doctrine, which
he called cenopythagoreanism: namely, that the classification of basic concepts should be
according to their external valency. That notion, taken directly from graph theory within
nineteenth-century topology, became the basis for phaneroscopy and the existential
graph approach to logic.

Now functioning under the control of categories based upon the cenopythagorean
principle, Peirce continued to work out the additional branches of his system. He argued
that logic was the third of the normative sciences, preceded there by aesthetics and
ethics. Again by operating under the inspiration of mathematics, he explicated the
several branches of logic (or semeiotic). There is a contemporary study, called semiotics,
that traces its history to Peirce, but his semeiotic (logic) is radically different from this
phenomenon. Within semeiotic, Peirce included branches for basic definitions (which he

called stecheotic), formal logic (roughly what he designated as critic), and methodology. Perhaps critic is the most difficult to anthologize, for it is principally technical formal logic, the aim of which is to analyze reasoning instead of aiming to create a calculus for reasoning.[29] Methodology, of course, was his ultimate destination, and all that preceded it within the system contributed toward its final explication. The most well-known of Peirce's doctrines, pragmaticism,[30] is a theorem of methodeutic—he often remarked that pragmaticism amounted to little more than a description of a typical (generalized) laboratory experimenter's procedure.[31] After thus securing a methodological base, and only then, did Peirce consider it possible scientifically to undertake philosophy in the central sense, the problems of metaphysics, in other words. Thus, Peirce's Copernican revolution is to make metaphysical philosophy depend upon science, which he understood as reliable methods for seeking truth in all areas of study. That is in opposition to the usual image in which metaphysical philosophy is considered to be prior to science.

ONE HUNDRED FIFTY YEARS LATER

> He is in the very front rank of American thinkers (I, for example, owe more to his writings than to those of anyone but Royce) and his Logic when published will unquestionably (in spite of certain probable obvious oddities) be recognized all over the world as an epoch-making work.
>
> William James[32]

Five years after George Orwell's apocalypse, the one-hundred-fiftieth anniversary of Peirce's birth will be celebrated. As we approach that occasion it is appropriate to ask whether and in what ways Peirce's contributions to mankind have been helpful, or will continue to be helpful, as he thought they would be. This is a large subject and, like other subjects taken up in this introduction, can only be considered briefly.

The contribution that this very book urges upon us is the fact that Peirce's work has deeply influenced every other thinker represented here, some of whom were his pupils in one form or another. And because he and the other five thinkers exemplify the best in America, at least in that period, Peirce has either directly or through these others had a far-reaching impact upon intellectual life in the United States. Opinions of James and Royce about Peirce's importance have appeared above; let us add a sample remark from one more—Dewey:

> The readers who are acquainted with the logical writings of Peirce will note my great indebtedness to him in the general position taken. As far as I am aware, he was the first writer on logic to make inquiry and its methods the primary and ultimate source of logical subject-matter.[33]

But today Peirce's influence is international, not limited by a national boundary. Neither is it limited to mathematics, natural sciences, or philosophy: for instance, the psychiatrist

Walker Percy[34] stated, "I . . . suspect that the state of the behavioral sciences vis-à-vis language is currently in such low spirits, not to say default, that Peirce's time may have come." Perhaps a similar remark is in order for literary criticism and art.[35]

Perhaps one reason for this is the fact that his works address problems with which we still wrestle. Of course, the writings of all thinkers of quality possess this property to some extent, but Peirce's output has it more strongly. Probably this is because he was ahead of his time, this being yet another of the barriers to his works, one that is slowly falling away. There is space to exemplify but one such problem to which his findings may indicate a solution, once his genuine conclusions are better known.

At the International Congress of Mathematicians in 1900, David Hilbert presented a challenging series of questions, the twenty-third of which asked if there was a mechanical way (a precise finite determinate algorithm) that would decisively establish the truth or falsity of any statement within the predicate calculus[36]—a calculus, by the way, that Peirce had helped to develop. In 1936, A. M. Turing showed[37] that if a mechanical algorithm was assumed, then on the most reasonable definition of "mechanical," the answer to Hilbert's question was no. Turing's method was classically Peircean. First, he asked for the meaning of "mechanical," which he produced using the technique Peirce had called pragmaticism and had introduced as the pragmatic maxim in the Metaphysical Club early in the eighteen-seventies in Cambridge, the very technique that had inspired James, Royce, Dewey, and a host of others. The result of Turing's application of pragmaticism (he did not call it that, and may never have known of Peirce) was later named a Turing Machine. Basically, a Turing Machine is not a real machine at all (yet its principles can be instantiated in actual machines), but instead is a way of constructing a kind of general diagram in which later states of modification of the diagram are completely determined or caused by previous states. Thus, it is a machine in the requisite sense: namely, that its rules must funciton to cause it to change its states (change the marks in its diagram) deterministically as opposed to nondeterministically. That is to say, there is no provision in the "machine" for creating, experimenting, or serendipity. Turing was able to show that if "mechanical algorithm" is what one means by the method of mathematics, then that pragmatically implies that there are things such a method cannot produce. Yet these are things (theorems, computations) that human mathematicians can produce through an exercise of their nondeterministic ingenuity, creativity, experimentation, and observation—what Peirce called abduction, induction, and deduction (his general semeiotic or logic of science, in other words). Thus, it seems to me, that Turing's results are very similar to Peirce's results, except expressed in an alternative but equivalent language, or notation (if you will). Peirce took the positive mode and said that mathematics is an experimental, observational, hypothesis-seeking and hypothesis-confirming science, just as all other sciences are, the only difference being that mathematics proceeds with operations upon written or mental diagrams, where "diagram" includes figures as well as algebras. Turing, who took the negative mode, coming from an opposite direction, began by assuming that mathematical method was mechanical and, by using pragmaticism and experiments with diagrams, showed that such an assumption was absurd, thus establishing that mathematical method could not be strictly mechanical. I think the results achieved by both

Peirce and Turing amount to approximately the same thing, and that it would profit us immensely now to return to Peirce's more elaborate and interconnected system of science to pursue further details and ramifications of this matter. There are several other major contemporary issues, ranging from the arts to physics, to which the same assertion could be accurately applied.

A NOTE ON TEXTUAL SOURCES, AND AN OUTLINE OF PEIRCE'S SYSTEM OF SCIENCE

> I have seen a good deal of Charles. S. Peirce, because he has worked for me in my mathematical library, and he is a genius, if there ever was one.
>
> George A. Plimpton[38]

All of the writings of Peirce have been prepared either from original places of publication or from the annotated xerographic copy of the Harvard Peirce papers housed at the Institute for Studies in Pragmaticism at Texas Tech University. Their publication here is by permission of the Department of Philosophy at Harvard University. Extensive references to Peirce's works have been inserted within the "Brief Intellectual Autobiography" in the hope that scholars who want to follow his intellectual career with Peirce himself as a guide will thereby be facilitated. Such insertions (throughout the selections below) are indicated with braces: { }. Editorial emendations to Peirce's papers, to indicate such things as an obviously dropped word or punctuation, are enclosed in brackets: [ ]. Peirce's punctuation, terminology, and spelling have been retained in almost all cases. Nineteenth-century authors were allowed more variation in the latter than is tolerated today. Titles of the selections in almost all cases have been composed by the editor, but by using terminology Peirce favored and in the sequence of his classification of the sciences. Naturally, in order to compress selections for this anthology, it has been necessary to break up otherwise whole essays. Readers are encouraged to seek the full contexts for further study.[39] It is hoped that the obvious disadvantage (incompleteness) of this method of presentation will be overshadowed by its advantage: namely, that perhaps for the first time Peirce's mature writings are presented according to his own scheme of organization, with an introduction that is his intellectual autobiography.

Here is an outline of the selections of Peirce's writings presented in this volume. It is crucial for readers to approach the selections in the order of this system of organization.

I.   A Brief Intellectual Autobiography
II.   Two Influential Early Essays
    A.   Some Consequences of Four Incapacities (Peirce's Anti-Cartesianism)
    B.   How to Make Our Ideas Clear (Introduction of the Pragmatic Maxim)

III.   A System of Science
    A.   The Presuppositions of Science: Common Sense and Religion
    B.   The Nature of Science
    C.   Mathematics: The First Science
    D.   Cenoscopy (Philosophy)
        1.   Phaneroscopy (Phenomenology)
        2.   Normative Sciences
            a.   Esthetics
            b.   Ethics
            c.   Logic as Semeiotic (The Theory of Signs)
                i.   Stecheotic (Basic Definitions)
                ii.   Critic (Theory of Argumentation)
                iii.   Methodeutic (Methodology)
        3.   Metaphysics

NOTES

1. *Saturday Review*, December 13, 1975.

2. Peirce's enormous lifetime publication record is given in *A Comprehensive Bibliography of the Published Works of Charles Sanders Peirce*, 2nd rev. ed., ed. K. L. Ketner (Bowling Green: Philosophy Documentation Center, 1986). This work also indexes a large microfiche edition of Peirce's published works available from the same source. Within that bibliography, works by Peirce are assigned numbers that will often be used here in references or to suggest items for additional study (thus, *P* 373 refers to the definitions he wrote for the *Century*). For some reason, in many essays that discuss Peirce with any detail, there is an almost mechanical claim that Peirce published only one book, *Photometric Researches* (*P* 118). That is disconfirmed by even a cursory glance through *Comprehensive Bibliography,* some early counterexamples being *P* 18, 102, or 161.

3. The great bulk of surviving Peirce manuscripts are in the care of the Department of Philosophy at Harvard University, and are listed (with synopses) in R. S. Robin, *Annotated Catalogue of the Papers of Charles S. Peirce* (Amherst: University of Massachusetts Press, 1967), as supplemented by "The Peirce Papers: A Supplementary Catalogue," by R. S. Robin, *Transactions of the Charles S. Peirce Society* 7 (1971): 37–57. Traditional reference forms for these materials are *MS* and sometimes *L,* for letters, followed by a number assigned by Robin. Microfilms of these manuscripts and of Peirce's professional correspondence have been prepared and may be purchased from the Harvard University Photographic Service.

4. Institute for Studies in Pragmaticism at Texas Tech University; Peirce Edition Project at University of Indiana at Indianapolis; Institut de Recherche en Sciences de la Communication et de l'Education Universitaire de Perpignan; and Philosophisches Seminar Universität Hamburg.

5. Morris Cohen's anthology, *Chance, Love, and Logic* (New York: Harcourt, Brace and Company), appeared in 1923. A much wider undertaking was *The Collected Papers of Charles Sanders Peirce,* an eight-volume set edited by C. Hartshorne and P. Weiss (Vol. 1–6) and A. Burks (Vol. 7–8) (Cambridge, Mass.: Harvard University Press, 1931, 1958). That edition will continue to be valuable for some time, yet its editorial policy of breaking up or rearranging otherwise whole and unified texts may be one source of the false opinion that Peirce was a fragmented or disjointed thinker. Thus, for example, the *Collected Papers* presents the following (Vol. 2, p. 2): "All that you can find in print of my work on logic are simply scattered outcroppings here and there of a rich vein which remains unpublished. Most of it I suppose has been written down; but no human being could ever put together the fragments. I could not myself do so." Peirce, however, continued (although Hartshorne and Weiss did not!): "I could only do it in five or six years of hard work devoted to that alone. Since I am now 63 years old and since all this is matter calculated to make a difference in man's future intellectual development, I can only say that if the *genus homo* is so foolish as not to set me at the task, I shall lean back in my chair and take my ease. I have done a great work wholly without any kind of aid, and now I am willing to undergo the last great effort which must finish me up in order to give men the benefit of what I have done" (published in Eisele, *New Elements,* Vol. 4, p. 162, see below).

The majority of Peirce's extensive (mostly unsigned) book reviews are collected in *Charles Sanders Peirce: Contributions to* The Nation, 3 vols., ed. K. L. Ketner and J. E. Cook (Lubbock: Texas Tech University Press, 1975–1979). His important correspondence with Victoria Lady Welby is published in C. S. Hardwick, ed., *Semiotic and Significs* (Bloomington: Indiana University Press, 1977). Peirce's extensive works within mathematics have been gathered in five books as *The New Elements of Mathematics,* ed. C. Eisele (The Hague: Mouton, 1976). Presently a new critical edition of Peirce's work, based on a chronological plan, is being prepared; three volumes (of a projected twenty-volume set) have appeared as *Writings of Charles S. Peirce,* ed. M. H. Fisch et al. (Bloomington: Indiana University Press, 1982, 1984, 1986). Peirce's important contributions to the history of science have been presented in C. Eisele, ed., *Historical Perspectives on Peirce's Logic of Science: A History of Science* (Berlin: DeGruyter, 1985).

6. *Writings of Peirce,* Vol. 1, p. xi.

7. *The Golden Day: A Study in American Literature and Culture* (Boston: Beacon Press, 1953).

8. *The Collected Papers,* Vol. 1, pars. 616–619.

9. This set of lectures has been reconstructed from manuscript in *Writings of Peirce,* Vol. 1.

10. Victor Lenzen, "Charles S. Peirce as Astronomer," in E. Moore and R. Robin, eds., *Studies in the Philosophy of Charles S. Peirce* (Amherst: University of Massachusetts Press, 1964), pp. 33–50.

11. Victor Lenzen, "Charles S. Peirce as Mathematical Geodesist," *Transactions of the Charles S. Peirce Society* 8 (1972): 90–105.

12. *MSS* 1072–75.

13. Victor Lenzen, "An Unpublished Scientific Monograph by C. S. Peirce," *Transactions of the Charles S. Peirce Society* 5 (1969): 5–24.

14. For additional details, see: Carolyn Eisele, *Studies in the Scientific and Mathematical Philosophy of Charles S. Peirce,* ed. R. M. Martin (The Hague: Mouton, 1979).

15. *MS* 867. See also Victor Lenzen, "Charles S. Peirce as a Mathematical Physicist," *Transactions of the Charles S. Peirce Society* 11 (1975): 159–166.

16. Hilary Putnam, "Peirce the Logician," *Historia Mathematica* 9 (1982): 290–301.

17. Kenneth Laine Ketner, "The Early History of Computer Design: Charles Sanders Peirce and Marquand's Logical Machines," *The Princeton University Library Chronicle* 45 (1984): 186–224.

18. Peirce to James, William James papers, Houghton Library, Harvard University, published by permission of Harvard University.

19. *Comprehensive Bibliography, P* 1005.

20. Ibid., *P* 17 and *P* 471.

21. *Charles Sanders Peirce: Contributions to* The Nation, Vol. 3, p. 165.

22. Victor Lenzen, "Reminiscences of a Mission to Milford," *Transactions of the Charles S. Peirce Society* 1 (1965): 3–11.

23. *MS L* 75c, 1902.

24. *New Elements of Mathematics.* Vol. 3, p. 207.

25. *Contributions to* The Nation, Vol. 3, pp. 197–199, 206–208.

26. Kenneth Laine Ketner, "Peirce on Diagrammatic Thought," in K. Oehler, ed., *Zeichen und Realität* (Tübingen: Stauffenburg Verlag), pp. 305–319.

27. Kenneth Laine Ketner, "Who was Charles Sanders Peirce?" *Krisis* 1 (1983): 10–18.

28. Compare *MS* 482 or *Collected Papers,* Vol. 4 pars. 350f., although in the latter the editors got the diagrams mixed up—compare *MS* 479.

29. For a good selection of papers on critic, see *Collected Papers,* Vol. 3.

30. Originally Peirce had used "pragmatism" to identify this doctrine, but shortly after the turn of the century, he announced that he wished his own approach to be known as "pragmaticism," a word (he said) that was ugly enough to be safe from kidnappers—see *Collected Papers,* Vol. 5, par. 414. Peirce held very strict views on terminology in all sciences, including philosophy: see Kenneth Laine Ketner, "Peirce's Ethics of Terminology," *Transactions of the Charles S. Peirce Society* 17 (1981): 327–347.

31. Compare *Comprehensive Bibliography, P* 1078, *MSS* 320, 322, and *L* 427.

32. *MS L* 75c, 1902.

33. John Dewey, *Logic, The Theory of Inquiry* (New York: Henry Holt, 1938), p. 9n.

34. Walker Percy, *The Message in the Bottle: How Queer Man Is, How Queer Language Is, and What One Has to Do With the Other* (New York: Farrar, Strauss, & Giroux, 1975), p. 159.

35. See: Joel Weinsheimer, "The Realism of C. S. Peirce, or How Homer and Nature Can Be the Same," *American Journal of Semiotics* 2 (1983): 225–264; Frances Williams Scott, "Process from the Peircean Point of View: Some Applications to Art," *American Journal of Semiotics* 2 (1983): 157–174.

36. J. E. Hopcroft, "Turing Machines," *Scientific American* 250 (1984): 86f.

37. "On Computable Numbers, with an Application to the Entscheidungsproblem," *Proceedings of the London Mathematical Society* 42 (1937): 230–265. For a fascinating biography of Turing (including a nontechnical discussion of Turing machines), see Andrew Hodges, *Alan Turing: The Enigma* (New York: Simon and Schuster, 1983).

38. *MS L* 75c, 1902.

39. See *Suggestions for Further Reading,* pp. 91–92 below. Works about Peirce are also listed in *Compre-hensive Bibliography,* and an update of the large secondary literature is given in C. J. W. Kloesel, "Bibliogra-phy of Charles Peirce, 1976 through 1980," *The Monist* 65 (1982): 246–276 (reissued in E. Freeman, ed., *The Relevance of Peirce* [LaSalle: Open Court, 1983]).

The following are also highly recommended: H. G. Herzberger, "Peirce's Remarkable Theorem," in L. Sumner, J. Slater, and F. Wilson, eds., *Pragmatism and Purpose* (Toronto: University of Toronto Press, 1981), pp. 41–58; K. Oehler, section on Peirce in *Die Welt als Zeichen* (Berlin: Severin und Siedler, 1981); *Peirce Studies* 1, "Studies in Peirce's Semiotic" (Bloomington: Indiana University Press, 1979); *Peirce Studies* 2, "Peirce's Conception of God: A Developmental Study," by D. M. Orange (Bloomington: Indiana University Press, 1984); Josiah Royce, *The Problem of Christianity,* ed. of 1968, ed. J. E. Smith (Chicago: University of Chicago Press, 1913), esp. pp. 275f.; David Savan, "The Unity of Peirce's Thought," in *Pragmatism and Purpose,* pp. 3–14; Thomas A. Sebeok and Jean Umiker-Sebeok, *"You Know My Method"*: *A Juxtaposition of Charles S. Peirce and Sherlock Holmes* (Bloomington: Gaslight Publications, 1980).

A Brief Intellectual Autobiography

Charles Santiago Sanders Peirce[1] (b. 1839), son of the mathematician Benjamin P., brought up in a circle of physicists and naturalists, and specially educated as a chemist, derived his first introduction to philosophy from the K.d.r.V. and other celebrated German works, and only later made acquaintance with English, Greek, and Scholastic philosophy. Accepting unreservedly Kant's opinion that the metaphysical conceptions are merely the logical conceptions differently applied, he inferred that logic ought to be studied in the spirit of the exact sciences, and regarded Kant's table of Functions of Judgment as culpably superficial. He also thought that Kant's reply to the question how are synthetical judgments *a posteriori* possible was altogether insufficient, and that an exact inquiry into it would probably throw some light upon judgments *a priori*. Appointed in 1864 Lecturer on Logic {*P* 16} in Harvard University, he divided all reasoning into, 1st, the deductive, including all necessary inference together with all probable inference to which the calculus of probabilities is properly applicable (rejecting inverse probabilities not founded on positive information), 2nd, the inductive, including all experimental testing of hypotheses (for he considers a physical experiment to be in a general sense of the same nature as a geometrical reasoning, which is performed by internal experimentation) but excluding, 3rd, the "abductive," or the process of forming and accepting on probation, a hypothesis by which to explain surprising facts. He put forth a "critic," or mathematical deduction of the validity of these modes of reasoning, founded upon the principle that nothing is subject to logical (any more than to ethical) criticism except so far as it is subject to self-control. What one does not in the least doubt one should not pretend to doubt; but a man should train himself to doubt. His account of validity of induction is that its premises do not lend the slightest probability to its conclusion, but that we are justified in provisionally accepting the conclusion by the postulate that any error in that conclusion will ultimately be corrected by the further application of the same method. This postulate will only be true if the inductive conclusion be understood to be limited to a "possible experience" (a Kantian conception

modified) of future similar experiments. But he already held it to be impossible to conceive anything otherwise than as an object of possible experience, and that of the kind that "experiment," or purposive arrangement of conditions, may bring; and in 1877, in two articles in the *Revue philosophique* {*P* 129, 162}, he put forth the doctrine he called *Pragmatism,* namely, that every concept (as distinguished from a generalized sensation, such as 'red') is equivalent to a conditional purpose, should one have certain desires and certain types of experience, to act in a certain general way. In 1867, he published in the 'Proceedings of the American Academy of Arts and Sciences' of Boston, five papers {*P* 30–34} in which he professed to limit himself to incontrovertible assertions. In one of these, 'On the Classification of Arguments' {*P* 31} (partly repeating a paper he had distributed {*P* 18} the year before) he undertook to reduce all inference to *substitution* (an idea adopted afterwards by Taine and Jevons) without, however, maintaining that substitution was an elementary operation; and indeed he subsequently showed that the substitution of B for A is never logically justified unless it be justifiable first to insert B and unless it be subsequently justifiable to omit A. This paper also studied the relation between particular judgments and negative judgments. Another of the papers of 1867 proposed a new list of categories {*P* 32}, which will be given below.

In 1868[2] he contributed three papers {*P* 26, 27, 41} to W. T. Harris's 'Journal of Speculative Philosophy' in which he endeavored to prove and to trace the consequences of certain propositions in epistemology tending toward the recognition of the reality of continuity and of generality and going to show the absurdity of individualism and of egoism. In 1870, he published, in the Memoirs of the American Academy of Arts and Sciences, an extension of the Boolian algebra of logic {*P* 52} to render it applicable to the logic of relations, and developed this branch of logic somewhat further than DeMorgan had done. Especially he demonstrated that all relations between four or more correlates are reducible to compounds of triadic relations, while triadic relations can never be defined in terms of dyadic relations

From *MS L* 107, 1904.

exclusively. In the North American Review for October 1871, in a review of Frazer's edition of Berkeley's Works {*P* 60}, he argued in favor of Scotistic realism.

In 1877–8 he published a series of articles in the Popular Science Monthly {*P* 107, 119–123} (two of them appeared also in the Revue Philosophique {*P* 129, 162}) in which he enounced the principle he called *pragmatism,* that is, that every concept (in contrast to qualities of feeling, images, experiences, etc.) is definable in terms of a possible purpose of conduct under hypothetical general conditions, and that from this can be deduced the best rule for rendering ideas clear, namely, "Consider what effects that *might conceivably* have practical bearings we conceive the object of our conception to have; then, our concept of those effects *is* the *whole* concept in question." But since P not only admits the difference between a commensurable and an incommensurable length, but has specially insisted upon abnumerable (abzählbar) multitudes (this had better be translated *Menge* though incorrectly, because students of philosophy would not know the correct term *Mächtigkeit*) it is evident that he understands "conceivably practical bearings" in a peculiarly wide sense. In the same articles he discussed the "uniformity of nature" {*P* 122} and undertook to demonstrate that while it afforded opportunities for inductive reasonings, it does not constitute the general ground of validity of such reasonings. He also argued that as a fact there appears to be as little orderliness in the universe {*P* 122} as we can conceive that a universe should have, and further that the degrees of orderliness of the universe is relative to the mind that contemplates it, consisting merely in the breadth (Umfang) of that mind's interests. In 1880–3, while lecturing on logic in the Johns Hopkins University, he developed in several papers in the American Journal of Mathematics, a theory of necessary reasoning {*P* 167}, a paper on the logic of number {*P* 187} in which he distinguished between finite and infinite collections in substantially the same way that Dedekind did six years later, and by means of the conception of correspondence, which is Gauss's conception of the *Abbild* (employed also by P in his Quincuncial Projection of the Spheroid {*P* 135, also 183} of 1879), he deduced the validity of the Fermatian inference {also *P* 187} (sometimes unsuitably termed mathematical induction). He also produced a general algebra of logic {*P* 296} in which subscript

letters are attached to letters on the line signifying relations, these subscripts indicating individual correlates, while the letters Σ and Π with the same subscripts show whether the individuals are to be selected universally or existentially, that is, by the interpreter of the proposition or by the utterer of it. He further produced an algebra of dyadic relations {?*P* 268} to which the third volume of Schröder's Algebra der Logik {*O* 435(I), *O* 468(II), *O* 610(III)} is devoted; but P is not so entirely satisfied with that method as Schröder was. {cf. *P* 620, 637, 627, 449} He also distributed a brochure entitled 'A Brief Description of the Algebra of Relatives' {*P* 220}. Closely connected with this is his edition of his father's book called "Linear Associative Algebra."[3] To a volume of papers by his students entitled 'Studies in Logic' {*P* 268} (Boston, 1883), some of them contributions of prime importance, he contributed a note on the algebra of dyadic relations, and a discussion of the validity and rules of scientific induction. He rests this wholly on the principles of the calculus of probabilities, yet denies that the inductive argument lends the slightest probability to the conclusion, and refutes the principle of inverse probabilities as applied by Laplace without statistical information. He makes the justification of induction to consist in the fact that if the conclusion is erroneous, the same method, persisted in further, will bring a correction of it. In 1884, he presented to the United States National Academy of Sciences, a memoir {*P* 303} in collaboration with his student, J. Jastrow, describing experiments which show that there is no Differenz-Schwelle in sensation, or that if there be it is almost incredibly small. The philosophical interest of this consists in part in its bearing upon *Synechism,* or the principle of universal continuity, which does not mean that there is no discontinuity, which is involved in all existence. It was also shown by these experiments that a perception might be so slight (*petite,* Leibniz), that the greatest effort of attention under the most exceptionally favorable circumstances would fail to make the subject aware of it, so that he could answer the question which of two alternative characters it had, and yet if the subject was required to answer at random, in 60 percent of the cases his answer agreed with the objective fact. Upon this phenomenon, P, in 1887, in a communication {*P* 352} to the American Society for Psychical Research, based an attack upon the book called 'Phantasms of the Living,' and was drawn into a considerable controversy with Mr. E. W. Gurney, which is printed in the Proceedings of that Society {O 353, P 354, O 381, also P 640}. The same year he contributed a paper {P 347–8} on the evidences of immortality to the volume 'Science and Immortality,' Edited by S. J. Barrows, Boston: 1887, in which he expressed the opinion that current views of cosmology, especially those of Spencer, were unsound in being too thoroughly mechanical. {cf. P 474, 525} But he thought there was no extant evidence for immortality unless the catholic miracles be admitted to be such. In 1891–3, in the 'Monist' {P 439, 474, 477, 480, 521, 525}, he outlined a hypothesis capable of being subjected to inductive tests, which hypothesis, called *tychism*, was that the laws of nature, although real, are results of a process of evolution, and as such are not yet and never will be exactly fulfilled by the facts, which depart from the laws in the same way, although vastly less than, observations do. He had intended to complete this series of papers by one or more concerning *Synechism*, but was not encouraged to do so. In 1896 in two articles {P 620, 637} in the 'Monist' reviewing Schroeder's Algebra der Logik, he described a logical method called *entitative graphs*, using diagrams instead of algebraic symbols. He also considered the foundations of the logico-mathematical doctrine of multitude, the so-called 'cardinal numbers' of G. Cantor, and proved that every multitude is exceeded by another multitude and that the infinite multitudes form a single simple wohl-geordnet series, or as he would say in English, a simple Cantorian series. Beyond that series the individual members of collections lose their separate identities in consequence of becoming essentially indefinite, and the multitude passes into continuity. In 1901 in a review {P 802} of the first three chapters of Pearson's 'Grammar of Science,' in the Popular Science Monthly, P argued for the reality of natural law and against the doctrine that we reason from 'first impressions of sense.' In 1903, in connection with a course of lectures {P 1005} on Logic before the Lowell Institute in Boston, he wrote a 'Syllabus of Logic', {MS 478; P 1035} but it was only in part printed owing to the small fund for the purpose. In the same year he gave a course of lectures {P 1004} in Harvard University on *Pragmatism*. In 1905 he expects to publish one article (and hopes that more may be accepted) in the 'Monist' on Pragmatism. {More were published: P 1077–

80, 1124, 1126, 1128, 1171, 1193.} P wrote all the philosophical definitions in the Century Dictionary {P 373}, and some of these relating to logic in Baldwin's Dictionary {P 761–78, 806–970}.

Although Peirce is much given to raising doubts about his own philosophy, yet the alterations it has undergone since 1866, except for the introduction of the problematical tychism and a few minor corrections (of which the most important relate to the precise nature, definitions, and grounds of validity of induction and abduction), and an increasing insistence on the exclusion of psychological premisses from logic, consist in the extension of his inquiries to new problems and the greater fullness of his positions. In order to understand his doctrine, which has little in common with those of modern schools, it is necessary to know, first of all, how he classifies the sciences. He divides all science into Science of Research, Science of Review (comprising such works as those of Comte and Spencer, and the doctrine of the classification of the sciences itself), and Practical Science. That of the third branch, though elaborately worked out, need not detain us; and that of the second has not engaged his attention. The classification of Science of Research is shown in outline in the following scheme.

MATHEMATICS
PHILOSOPHY
    Phenomenology, or Ideoscopy {Phaneros-copy}
    Normative Science
        Esthetics
        Ethics
        Logic {Semeiotic}
            Speculative Grammar {Stechiotic}
            Critic
            Methodeutic {Speculative Rhetoric}
    Metaphysics
IDIOSCOPY (Bentham), or SPECIAL SCIENCE
    Physics
        Nomological Physics, i.e. Physical Geometry, Dynamics, General Physics, etc.
        Classificatory Physics, Chemistry, Crystallography, Biology, etc.
        Descriptive Physics, Geognosy, Astronomy, etc.
    Psychics
        Nomological Psychics, i.e. General Psychology, Psychical Chrononomy, etc.
        Classificatory Psychics, Special Psychology, Linguistics, Ethnology, etc.

Descriptive Psychics, History, Criticism, etc.

This classification (which has been worked out in minute detail) is to be regarded as simply Comte's classification, corrected. That is to say, the endeavor has been so to arrange the scheme that each science ought to make appeal, for its *general principles*, exclusively to the sciences placed above it, while for instances and special facts, it will find the sciences below it more serviceable. Mathematics merely traces out the consequences of hypotheses without caring whether they correspond to anything real or not. It is purely deductive, and all necessary inference is mathematics, pure or applied. Its hypotheses are suggested by any of the other sciences, but its assumption of them is not a scientific act. Philosophy merely analyzes the experience common to all men. The truth of this experience is not an object of any science because it cannot really be doubted. All so-called 'logical' analysis, which is the method of philosophy, ought to be regarded as philosophy, pure or applied. Idioscopy is occupied with the discovery and examination of phenomena, aided by mathematics and philosophy. It is extremely doubtful which of its two wings should be placed first. The three main branches of philosophy are distinguished as follows. Phenomenology considers the phenomenon in general, whatever comes before the mind in any way, and without caring whether it be fact or fiction, discovers and describes the elements which will invariably be present in it, that is, the categories. Normative science considers the phenomenon only so far as it can be controlled, compares purpose with performance, and ascertains the general principles of the relation between them. Metaphysics is still more special only considering the phenomenon in so far as it is a sign of what is real. [The first of] the three branches of normative science, or the science of the phenomenon in so far as it is controllable, philosophical esthetics (which becomes something very different from the study which the noun usually designates) [,] studies the characters which will belong to the phenomenon so far as it is controllable, that is, the characters of what is aimed at. Thus, the question, What is the *summum bonum*, is regarded as an esthetical question. If pleasure be defined as that quality of feeling which is common and peculiar to all experiences that we desire, P is inclined to deny that there is any such thing as pleasure, and to think that that which is common and peculiar to such experiences is an intellectual

character, the realization of the ideal, or reasonableness. Ethics studies in the controllable phenomenon the act and process of controlling it. This study is the very heart of normative science, and emphasizes more strongly than the others that dichotomy which is the constitutive characteristic of normative science. For it is the study of the controlled and the uncontrolled as they appear in effort and resistance. This abstract ethics which can derive no principle from metaphysics or from psychology can plainly have little in common with ordinary ethics. Logic is of a much more special kind for it studies the relation of the phenomenon to the essential character of the phenomenon as controllable, that is, its reasonableness, or embodying an idea. That which embodies an idea is a sign, and it is best to make logic the science of the general properties of signs. Since P maintains that every thought, percept, image, feeling, etc. is a sign [,] ordinary logic, so far as it can be separated from metaphysics and psychology will be included in the abstract logic. Finally, under the head of metaphysics will be included, not merely ontology, but also whatever philosophy can determine respecting causation, the freedom of the will, the connection of mind and matter, optimism or pessimism, immortality, theology, time and space, etc.

Peirce's studies of philosophy have mostly been concerned with phenomenology,[4] logic, and some parts of metaphysics. In phenomenology, he is of opinion that there are two sets of categories, a long list and a short one; and he admits that there may possibly be still others. Though he devoted two years to the study of the long list, he attained no satisfactory results. The shorter list is called by [the] easily remembered designation of the *ceno-pythagorean categories*. These are *Firstness, Secondness,* and *Thirdness. Firstness* is the mode or element of being by which any subject is such as it is, *positively* and regardless of everything else; or rather, the category is not bound down to this particular conception but is the element which is characteristic and peculiar in this definition and is a prominent ingredient in the ideas of quality, qualitativeness, absoluteness, originality, variety, chance, possibility, form, essence, feeling, etc. *Secondness* is that mode or element of being by which any subject is such as it is in a second subject regardless of any third; or rather, the category is the leading and characteristic element in this definition, which is prominent in the ideas of dyadic relativity or relation, action, effort, existence, individuality, opposition, negation, dependence, blind force. Secondness has two grades, the *genuine* and the *degenerate* (just as a pair of rays is called a "degenerate" conic) and this is true in several ways. Every genuine secondness has two correlative aspects, of which one is more active or first, the other more passive or second; and these two together make a total secondness between two correlative subjects. There is a long chapter of these dichotomic distinctions of secondness. *Thirdness* is that mode or element of being whereby a subject is such as it is to a second and for a third; or rather it is the characteristic ingredient of this definition, which is prominent in the ideas of instrument, organon, method, means, mediation, betweenness, representation, communication, community, composition, generality, regularity, continuity, totality, system, understanding, cognition, abstraction, etc. That the three categories are independent of one another is proved as follows. Secondness involves Firstness, but it is discriminated from it by the circumstances that we may consider non-relative characters of subjects neglecting their dyadic relations. But a dyadic relation cannot be a result of non-relative characters, since if it were so there would be, besides the possession of non-relative characters of two objects, some connection between these facts; and this would be itself a dyadic relation. So Thirdness involves Secondness and thereby involves Firstness too; but it can be discriminated from Secondness by the circumstance that Secondness may occur either with or without Thirdness. Thirdness cannot be reduced to Secondness and Firstness, since if this were possible every triadic relation could be expressed in terms of dyadic relations and of non-relative attributions. Now no triadic relation can be so expressed, for it would appear in such expression as a composite relation formed of dyadic relations. Now composition is itself a triadic relation. On the other hand, there is no independent Fourthness or more complex mode or element of being; since it is easily demonstrable that every tetradic relation consists in a compound of triadic relations. Thirdness is subject to two grades of degeneracy. All genuine thirdness has a mental character.

Logic is by P. made synonymous with semeiotic, the pure theory of signs, in general. Its first part, speculative grammar {cf. *New Elements of Mathematics,* Vol. 3, pp. 207–210}, corresponding to stecheology (Elementarlehre), classifies and describes signs. A sign is anything, A, in a relation, *r,* to something, B, its *object,* this relation, *r,* consisting in fitness to determine something so as to produce something, C, the *interpretant* of the sign, which shall be in the relation *r* to B, or at least in some analogous relation. Thus, the sign involves the idea of a possible endless series of interpretations. In what relation this entire series, taken as a whole, stands to the object, B, depends upon circumstances.

NOTES

1. {Two informative variant beginnings from *MS L* 107}:

Peirce, Charles Santiago Sanders, b. Cambridge, Mass. 1839 Sep. 10, son of Benjamin P, the leading American mathematician of his day, and his wife Sarah Hunt Mills P. dau. of U.S. Senator Mills (the predecessor of Webster) who died early in Northampton, Mass. where he had established a noted law school. C.S.P. took the degrees of A.B. (1859), A.M., and S.B. in chemistry in Harvard. From Boyhood he has been devoted to Logic, considered as the theory of reasoning, especially in science, and of logical analysis. Moved chiefly by his desire to obtain an intimate knowledge of scientific reasoning, he made original investigations in the history of the pronounciation of English (N.A. Rev. 1864) {*P* 13}, Multiple Algebra (Proc. A.A.A.S. 1875–7 and Am. J. of Math. 1882), Colors (Am. J. Sci. and A. 1877) {*P* 100}, the Doctrine of Chances (N.A. Rev. {*P* 21}, and Pop. Sci. Monthly, 1878), Certain Phenomena of diffraction Spectra {*P* 134} (Am. J. Math.), and as an officer of the U.S. Geod. Survey of gravity.

Charles Santiago Sanders Peirce (b. 1839) son of the mathematician Benjamin P., reared in circle of physicists and naturalists, and specially educated as a chemist, laid the foundation of his philosophical conceptions in a study of the K.d.r.V. Accepting unreservedly Kant's opinion that metaphysical conceptions can only be the conceptions of formal logic in different application, he was struck with the want of thoroughness of Kant's study of formal logic, and undertook a reexamination of the subject. In 1864, he was appointed lecturer on logic in Harvard University, and devoted his lectures to the criticism of the reasoning of physicists, as he did a course in 1866 before the Lowell Institute in Boston. In 1867 he published a classification of reasonings (in which he reduced all reasoning to substitution, an idea afterward followed out by Taine), a New List of Categories (Firstness, Secondness, Thirdness), an improvement of Boole's algebra of logic, etc. He had, by his studies of physical reasoning, already been led to question the rejection by modern philosophers of any mode of real being other than individual existence and actual happening; and studies of Aquinas,

Scotus, Ockham, etc. led him to a rejection of nominalism expressed in three papers in the Journal of Speculative Philosophy (Vol II) and in the North American Review for October 1871 (Review of Frazer's Berkeley). In 1870, he produced a memoir on the application of Boole's principles to the logic of relations; and the study of this branch of logic profoundly modified his conceptions of logic.

2. {From a variant passage} In 1868 he contributed three papers to W. T. Harris's 'Journal of Speculative Philosophy' in which he insisted that while it is necessary to be deliberate, circumspect, and critical in adopting any opinion, and to be upon the alert for symptoms of error in our belief yet that which we do not geniunely doubt cannot possibly be subjected to any real criticism, and that which we never have doubted neither has nor needs any logical support. For instance, to say that a mathematical demonstration rests upon or appeals to a logical principle is meaningless except in the sense that a certain similarity or affinity of form may be traced between the demonstration and the principle. For the demonstration being evident, it can no more be supported by a principle of logic than the principles of logic can be supported by the demonstration. Hence, philosophy can have no other starting point than the total of beliefs which we bring to it. Moreover, it cannot [ever] be good logic to suppose any principle to be first or ultimate. For that is to suppose it inexplicable, while no hypothesis is acceptable for any other reason than that it explains the known facts. Resting on these principles, he offered various proofs of the following propositions; 1st, that we have no power of immediate introspection. That every experience has a double aspect is a datum of perception; and this double aspect is well explained in all its features by the theory that we are conscious. But that we are conscious is an inference, not a datum of perception. 2nd, there is no cognition which is logically first, but every cognition is logically determined by previous cognitions. 3rd, all cognition is of the nature of a sign, and must be interpreted in a subsequent cognition to be a cognition at all. In this absolutely present instant there is no cognitive consciousness. 4th, of the absolutely incognizable there is no conception of any description. Upon these four propositions he based a doctrine of *Synechism,* or principle of the universality of the law of continuity, carrying with it a return to scholastic realism. From the same propositions he deduced the different modes of validity of the different kinds of logical inference.

3. {From a variant page}
His father had in 1870 distributed a work called 'Linear Associative Algebra.' In 1882, the son edited a new edition of that work {*P* 188} in which he showed its connection with the logic of relations. C. S. Peirce regards universal science, or Cenoscopy (Bentham's word), as consisting of Mathematics, which merely studies hypotheses without any concern for their truth, and Philosophy, which studies whatever can be inferred from ordinary experience.

4. {From a variant} As to phenomenology, he is of opinion that there are at least two sets of categories. After devoting two years to the study of one of these, which corresponds with Hegel's categories, he became discouraged by the difficulty of attaining any satisfactory approach to certainty, and abandoned the subject. On the other hand, he has found another set, corresponding to Hegel's three stages, more easy to investigate and extremely useful. He calls these the *cenopythagorean categories.* They are three in number, *Firstness, Secondness,* and *Thirdness. Firstness,* or the mode of being of that which is such as it is regardless of anything else, as exemplified by simple Qualities of feeling; *Secondness,* or the mode of being of that which is such as it is relatively to a second object but regardless of any third; and *Thirdness,* or that which is such as it is in bringing a second into relation to a third. That thirdness cannot be reduced to any combination of secondnesses follows at once from the fact that combination is itself a triadic relation; so that a combination of secondnesses would itself involve an irreducible thirdness. On the other hand, [there] can be no irreducible Fourthness or mode of being defined by a relation between more than three correlates, since it is easily shown that every such relation is definable as a triadic relation among triadic relations. The most characteristic form of thirdness is that of a *sign:* and it is shown that every cognition is of the nature of a sign. Every sign has an object, which may be regarded either as it is immediately represented in the sign to be and as it is in its own firstness. It is equally essential to the function of a sign that it should determine an *Interpretant,* or a second correlate related to the object of the sign as the sign is itself related to that object; and this interpretant may be regarded as the sign represents it to be, as it is in its pure secondness to the object, and as it is in its own firstness. Upon these considerations are founded six trichotomic divisions of signs (of which only two were recognized in 1867). For in the first place a sign may, in its own firstness, either be a mere idea or quality of feeling, or it may be a 'sinsign,' that is, an individual existent (and P. holds, with Hegel, that existence consists in the blind reaction of the existent with the rest of the universe in which it exists), or it may (like a word) be a general type ('legisign') to which existents may conform. In the second place a sign may, in its secondness to its object as represented (according to the statement of 1867, which may have indirectly influenced Stout's psychological division of signs) either, as an 'Icon,' be related to that object by virtue of a character which belongs to the sign in its own Firstness, and which equally would belong to it though the object did not exist, or, as an 'Index,' may be related to its object by a real secondness, such as a physical connection, to it, or it may, as a 'Symbol,' be related to its object only because it will be represented in its interpretant as so related, as is the case with any word or other conventional sign, or any general type of image regarded as a schema of a concept.

Some Consequences of Four Incapacities

Descartes is the father of modern philosophy, and the spirit of Cartesianism—that which principally distinguishes it from the scholasticism which it displaced—may be compendiously stated as follows:

1. It teaches that philosophy must begin with universal doubt; whereas scholasticism had never questioned fundamentals.

2. It teaches that the ultimate test of certainty is to be found in the individual consciousness; whereas scholasticism had rested on the testimony of sages and of the Catholic Church.

3. The multiform argumentation of the middle ages is replaced by a single thread of inference depending often upon inconspicuous premises.

4. Scholasticism had its mysteries of faith, but undertook to explain all created things. But there are many facts which Cartesianism not only does not explain, but renders absolutely inexplicable, unless to say that "God makes them so" is to be regarded as an explanation.

In some, or all of these respects, most modern philosophers have been, in effect, Cartesians. Now without wishing to return to scholasticism, it seems to me that modern science and modern logic require us to stand upon a very different platform from this.

1. We cannot begin with complete doubt. We must begin with all the prejudices which we actually have when we enter upon the study of philosophy. These prejudices are not to be dispelled by a maxim, for they are things which it does not occur to us *can* be questioned. Hence this initial scepticism will be a mere self-deception, and not real doubt; and no one who follows the Cartesian method will ever be satisfied until he has formally recovered all those beliefs which in form he has given up. It is, therefore, as useless a preliminary as going to the North Pole would be in order to get to Constantinople by coming down regularly upon a meridian. A person may, it is true, in the course of his studies, find reason to doubt what he began by believing; but in that case he doubts because he has a positive reason for it, and not on account of the Cartesian maxim. Let us not pretend to doubt in philosophy what we do not doubt in our hearts.

2. The same formalism appears in the Cartesian criterion, which amounts to this: "Whatever I am clearly convinced of, is true." If I were really convinced, I should have done with reasoning, and should require no test of certainty. But thus to make single individuals absolute judges of truth is most pernicious. The result is that metaphysicians will all agree that metaphysics has reached a pitch of certainty far beyond that of the physical sciences;—only they can agree upon nothing else. In sciences in which men come to agreement, when a theory has been broached, it is considered to be on probation until this agreement is reached. After it is reached, the question of certainty becomes an idle one, because there is no one left who doubts it. We individually cannot reasonably hope to attain the ultimate philosophy which we pursue; we can only seek it, therefore, for the *community* of philosophers. Hence, if disciplined and candid minds carefully examine a theory and refuse to accept it, this ought to create doubts in the mind of the author of the theory himself.

3. Philosophy ought to imitate the successful sciences in its methods, so far as to proceed only from tangible premises which can be subjected to careful scrutiny, and to trust rather to the multitude and variety of its arguments than to the conclusiveness of any one. Its reasoning should not form a chain which is no stronger than its weakest link, but a cable whose fibres may be ever so slender, provided they are sufficiently numerous and intimately connected.

4. Every unidealistic philosophy supposes some absolutely inexplicable, unanalyzable ultimate; in short, something resulting from mediation itself not susceptible of mediation. Now that anything *is* thus inexplicable can only be known by reasoning from signs. But the only justification of an inference from signs is that the conclusion explains the fact. To suppose the fact absolutely inexplicable, is not to explain it, and hence this supposition is never allowable.

In the last number of this journal will be found a piece entitled "Questions concerning certain Faculties claimed for Man," which has been written in this spirit of opposition to Cartesianism. That criticism of certain faculties re-

From *The Journal of Speculative Philosophy,* Vol. 2, 1868, pp. 140–141.

sulted in four denials, which for convenience may here be repeated:

1. We have no power of Introspection, but all knowledge of the internal world is derived by hypothetical reasoning from our knowledge of external facts.
2. We have no power of Intuition, but every cognition is determined logically by previous cognitions.
3. We have no power of thinking without signs.

4. We have no conception of the absolutely incognizable.

These propositions cannot be regarded as certain; and, in order to bring them to a further test, it is now proposed to trace them out to their consequences. We may first consider the first alone; then trace the consequences of the first and second; then see what else will result from assuming the third also; and, finally, add the fourth to our hypothetical premises. . . .

How to Make Our Ideas Clear

I

Whoever has looked into a modern treatise on logic of the common sort, will doubtless remember the two distinctions between *clear* and *obscure* conceptions, and between *distinct* and *confused* conceptions. They have lain in the books now for nigh two centuries, unimproved and unmodified, and are generally reckoned by logicians as among the gems of their doctrine.

A clear idea is defined as one which is so apprehended that it will be recognized wherever it is met with, and so that no other will be mistaken for it. If it fails of this clearness, it is said to be obscure.

This is rather a neat bit of philosophical terminology; yet, since it is clearness that they were defining, I wish the logicians had made their definition a little more plain. Never to fail to recognize an idea, and under no circumstances to mistake another for it, let it come in how recondite a form it may, would indeed imply such prodigious force and clearness of intellect as is seldom met with in this world. On the other hand, merely to have such an acquaintance with the idea as to have become familiar with it, and to have lost all hesitancy in recognizing it in ordinary cases, hardly seems to deserve the name of clearness of apprehension, since after all it only amounts to a subjective feeling of mastery which may be entirely mistaken. I take it, however, that when the logicians speak of "clearness," they mean nothing more than such a familiarity with an idea, since they regard the quality as but a small merit, which needs to be supplemented by another, which they call *distinctness*.

A distinct idea is defined as one which contains nothing which is not clear. This is technical language; by the *contents* of an idea logicians understand whatever is contained in its definition. So that an idea is *distinctly* apprehended, according to them, when we can give a precise definition of it, in abstract terms. Here the professional logicians leave the subject; and I would not have troubled the reader with what they have to say, if it were not such a striking example of how they have been slumbering through ages of intellectual activity, listlessly disregarding the enginery of modern thought, and never dreaming of applying its lessons to the improvement of logic. It is easy to show that the doctrine that familiar use and abstract distinctness make the perfection of apprehension has its only true place in philosophies which have long been extinct; and it is now time to formulate the method of attaining to a more perfect clearness of thought, such as we see and admire in the thinkers of our own time.

When Descartes set about the reconstruction of philosophy, his first step was to (theoretically) permit skepticism and to discard the practice of the schoolmen of looking to authority as the ultimate source of truth. That done, he sought a more natural fountain of true principles, and professed to find it in the human mind; thus passing, in the directest way, from the method of authority to that of apriority, as described in my first paper. {See pp. 81–84,

From *The Popular Science Monthly*, Vol. 12, 1878, pp. 286ff.

below.} Self-consciousness was to furnish us with our fundamental truths, and to decide what was agreeable to reason. But since, evidently, not all ideas are true, he was led to note, as the first condition of infallibility, that they must be clear. The distinction between an idea *seeming* clear and really being so, never occurred to him. Trusting to introspection, as he did, even for a knowledge of external things, why should he question its testimony in respect to the contents of our own minds? But then, I suppose, seeing men, who seemed to be quite clear and positive, holding opposite opinions upon fundamental principles, he was further led to say that clearness of ideas is not sufficient, but that they need also to be distinct, i.e., to have nothing unclear about them. What he probably meant by this (for he did not explain himself with precision) was, that they must sustain the test of dialectical examination; that they must not only seem clear at the outset, but that discussion must never be able to bring to light points of obscurity connected with them.

Such was the distinction of Descartes, and one sees that it was precisely on the level of his philosophy. It was somewhat developed by Leibnitz. This great and singular genius was as remarkable for what he failed to see as for what he saw. That a piece of mechanism could not do work perpetually without being fed with power in some form was a thing perfectly apparent to him; yet he did not understand that the machinery of the mind can only transform knowledge, but never originate it, unless it be fed with facts of observation. He thus missed the most essential point of the Cartesian philosophy, which is, that to accept propositions which seem perfectly evident to us is a thing which, whether it be logical or illogical, we cannot help doing. Instead of regarding the matter in this way, he sought to reduce the first principles of science to formulas which cannot be denied without self-contradiction, and was apparently unaware of the great difference between his position and that of Descartes. So he reverted to the old formalities of logic, and, above all, abstract definitions played a great part in his philosophy. It was quite natural, therefore, that on observing that the method of Descartes labored under the difficulty that we may seem to ourselves to have clear apprehensions of ideas which in truth are very hazy, no better remedy occurred to him than to require an abstract definition of every important term. Accordingly, in adopting the distinction of *clear* and *distinct* notions, he described the latter quality as the clear apprehen-

sion of everything contained in the definition; and the books have ever since copied his words. There is no danger that his chimerical scheme will ever again be overvalued. Nothing new can ever be learned by analyzing definitions. Nevertheless, our existing beliefs can be set in order by this process, and order is an essential element of intellectual economy, as of every other. It may be acknowledged, therefore, that the books are right in making familiarity with a notion the first step toward clearness of apprehension, and the defining of it the second. But in omitting all mention of any higher perspicuity of thought, they simply mirror a philosophy which was exploded a hundred years ago. That much-admired "ornament of logic"—the doctrine of clearness and distinctness—may be pretty enough, but it is high time to relegate to our cabinet of curiosities the antique *bijou,* and to wear about us something better adapted to modern uses.

The very first lesson that we have a right to demand that logic shall teach us is, how to make our ideas clear; and a most important one it is, depreciated only by minds who stand in need of it. To know what we think, to be masters of our own meaning, will make a solid foundation for great and weighty thought. It is most easily learned by those whose ideas are meagre and restricted; and far happier they than such as wallow helplessly in a rich mud of conceptions. A nation, it is true, may, in the course of generations, overcome the disadvantage of an excessive wealth of language and its natural concomitant, a vast, unfathomable deep of ideas. We may see it in history, slowly perfecting its literary forms, sloughing at length its metaphysics, and, by virtue of the untirable patience which is often a compensation, attaining great excellence in every branch of mental acquirement. The page of history is not yet unrolled which is to tell us whether such a people will or will not in the long-run prevail over one whose ideas (like the words of their language) are few, but which possesses a wonderful mastery over those which it has. For an individual, however, there can be no question that a few clear ideas are worth more than many confused ones. A young man would hardly be persuaded to sacrifice the greater part of his thoughts to save the rest; and the muddled head is the least apt to see the necessity of such a sacrifice. Him we can usually only commiserate, as a person with a congenital defect. Time will help him, but intellectual maturity with regard to clearness comes rather late, an unfortunate arrangement of Nature, inasmuch as clearness is of less use to a man settled in life, whose errors have in great measure had their effect, than it would be to one whose path lies before him. It is terrible to see how a single unclear idea, a single formula without meaning, lurking in a young man's head, will sometimes act like an obstruction of inert matter in an artery, hindering the nutrition of the brain, and condemning its victim to pine away in the fullness of his intellectual vigor and in the midst of intellectual plenty. Many a man has cherished for years as his hobby some vague shadow of an idea, too meaningless to be positively false; he has, nevertheless, passionately loved it, has made it his companion by day and by night, and has given to it his strength and his life, leaving all other occupations for its sake, and in short has lived with it and for it, until it has become, as it were, flesh of his flesh and bone of his bone; and then he has waked up some bright morning to find it gone, clean vanished away like the beautiful Melusina of the fable, and the essence of his life gone with it. I have myself known such a man; and who can tell how many histories of circle-squarers, metaphysicians, astrologers, and what not, may not be told in the old German story?

II

The principles set forth in the first of these papers lead, at once, to a method of reaching a clearness of thought of a far higher grade than the "distinctness" of the logicians. We have there found that the action of thought is excited by the irritation of doubt, and ceases when belief is attained; so that the production of belief is the sole function of thought. All these words, however, are too strong for my purpose. It is as if I had described the phenomena as they appear under a mental microscope. Doubt and Belief, as the words are commonly employed, relate to religious or other grave discussions. But here I use them to designate the starting of any question, no matter how small or how great, and the resolution of it. If, for instance, in a horse-car, I pull out my purse and find a five-cent nickel and five coppers, I decide, while my hand is going to the purse, in which way I will pay my fare. To call such a question Doubt, and my decision Belief, is certainly to use words very disproportionate to the occasion. To speak of such a doubt as causing an irritation which needs to be appeased, suggests a temper which is uncomfortable to the verge of insanity. Yet, looking at the mat-

ter minutely, it must be admitted that, if there is the least hesitation as to whether I shall pay the five coppers or the nickel (as there will be sure to be, unless I act from some previously contracted habit in the matter), though irritation is too strong a word, yet I am excited to such small mental activity as may be necessary to deciding how I shall act. Most frequently doubts arise from some indecision, however momentary, in our action. Sometimes it is not so. I have, for example, to wait in a railway-station, and to pass the time I read the advertisements on the walls, I compare the advantages of different trains and different routes which I never expect to take, merely fancying myself to be in a state of hesitancy, because I am bored with having nothing to trouble me. Feigned hesitancy, whether feigned for mere amusement or with a lofty purpose, plays a great part in the production of scientific inquiry. However the doubt may originate, it stimulates the mind to an activity which may be slight or energetic, calm or turbulent. Images pass rapidly through consciousness, one incessantly melting into another, until at last, when all is over—it may be in a fraction of a second, in an hour, or after long years—we find ourselves decided as to how we should act under such circumstances as those which occasioned our hesitation. In other words, we have attained belief.

In this process we observe two sorts of elements of consciousness, the distinction between which may best be made clear by means of an illustration. In a piece of music there are the separate notes, and there is the air. A single tone may be prolonged for an hour or a day, and it exists as perfectly in each second of that time as in the whole taken together; so that, as long as it is sounding, it might be present to a sense from which everything in the past was as completely absent as the future itself. But it is different with the air, the performance of which occupies a certain time, during the portions of which only portions of it are played. It consists in an orderliness in the succession of sounds which strike the ear at different times; and to perceive it there must be some continuity of consciousness which makes the events of a lapse of time present to us. We certainly only perceive the air by hearing the separate notes; yet we cannot be said to directly hear it, for we hear only what is present at the instant, and an orderliness of succession cannot exist in an instant. These two sorts of objects, what we are *immediately* conscious of and what we are *mediately* conscious of, are found in all consciousness. Some elements (the sensations) are completely present at every instant so long as they last, while others (like thought) are actions having beginning, middle, and end, and consist in a congruence in the succession of sensations which flow through the mind. They cannot be immediately present to us, but must cover some portion of the past or future. Thought is a thread of melody running through the succession of our sensations.

We may add that just as a piece of music may be written in parts, each part having its own air, so various systems of relationship of succession subsist together between the same sensations. These different systems are distinguished by having different motives, ideas, or functions. Thought is only one such system, for its sole motive, idea, and function, is to produce belief, and whatever does not concern that purpose belongs to some other system of relations. The action of thinking may incidentally have other results; it may serve to amuse us, for example, and among *dilettanti* it is not rare to find those who have so perverted thought to the purposes of pleasure that it seems to vex them to think that the questions upon which they delight to exercise it may ever get finally settled; and a positive discovery which takes a favorite subject out of the arena of literary debate is met with ill-concealed dislike. This disposition is the very debauchery of thought. But the soul and meaning of thought, abstracted from the other elements which accompany it, though it may be voluntarily thwarted, can never be made to direct itself toward anything but the production of belief. Thought in action has for its only possible motive the attainment of thought at rest; and what ever does not refer to belief is no part of the thought itself.

And what, then, is belief? It is the demicadence which closes a musical phrase in the symphony of our intellectual life. We have seen that it has just three properties: First, it is something that we are aware of; second, it appeases the irritation of doubt; and, third, it involves the establishment in our nature of a rule of action, or, say for short, a *habit*. As it appeases the irritation of doubt, which is the motive for thinking, thought relaxes, and comes to rest for a moment when belief is reached. But, since belief is a rule for action, the application of which involves further doubt and further thought, at the same time that it is a stopping-place, it is also a new starting-place for thought. That is why I have permitted myself to call it thought at rest, although thought is essentially an action. The *final* upshot of thinking is the exercise of volition, and of this

thought no longer forms a part; but belief is only a stadium of mental action, an effect upon our nature due to thought, which will influence future thinking.

The essence of belief is the establishment of a habit, and different beliefs are distinguished by the different modes of action to which they give rise. If beliefs do not differ in this respect, if they appease the same doubt by producing the same rule of action, then no mere differences in the manner of consciousness of them can make them different beliefs, any more than playing a tune in different keys is playing different tunes. Imaginary distinctions are often drawn between beliefs which differ only in their mode of expression;—the wrangling which ensues is real enough, however. To believe that any objects are arranged as in Fig. 1, and to believe that they are arranged in Fig. 2, are one and the same belief; yet it is conceivable that a man should assert one proposition

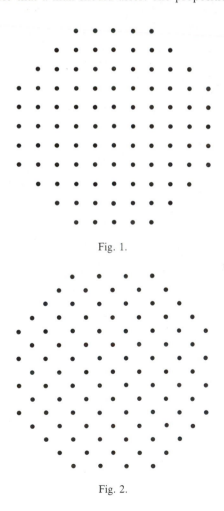

Fig. 1.

Fig. 2.

and deny the other. Such false distinctions do as much harm as the confusion of beliefs really different, and are among the pitfalls of which we ought constantly to beware, especially when we are upon metaphysical ground. One singular deception of this sort, which often occurs, is to mistake the sensation produced by our unclearness of thought for a character of the object we are thinking. Instead of perceiving that the obscurity is purely subjective, we fancy that we contemplate a quality of the object which is essentially mysterious; and if our conception be afterward presented to us in a clear form we do not recognize it as the same, owing to the absence of the feeling of unintelligiblity. So long as this deception lasts, it obviously puts an impassable barrier in the way of perspicuous thinking; so that it equally interests the opponents of rational thought to perpetuate it, and its adherents to guard against it.

Another such deception is to mistake a mere difference in the grammatical construction of two words for a distinction between the ideas they express. In this pedantic age, when the general mob of writers attend so much more to words than to things, this error is common enough. When I just said that thought is an *action,* and that it consists in a *relation,* although a person performs an action but not a relation, which can only be the result of an action, yet there was no inconsistency in what I said, but only a grammatical vagueness.

From all these sophisms we shall be perfectly safe so long as we reflect that the whole function of thought is to produce habits of action; and that whatever there is connected with a thought, but irrelevant to its purpose, is an accretion to it, but no part of it. If there be a unity among our sensations which has no reference to how we shall act on a given occasion, as when we listen to a piece of music, why we do not call that thinking. To develop its meaning, we have, therefore, simply to determine what habits it produces, for what a thing means is simply what habits it involves. Now, the identity of a habit depends on how it might lead us to act, not merely under such circumstances as are likely to arise, but under such as might possibly occur, no matter how improbable they may be. What the habit is depends on *when* and *how* it causes us to act. As for the *when,* every stimulus to action is derived from perception; as for the *how,* every purpose of action is to produce some sensible result. Thus, we come down to what is tangible and practical, as the root of every real distinction of thought, no matter how subtle it may be;

and there is no distinction of meaning so fine as to consist in anything but a possible difference of practice.

To see what this principle leads to, consider in the light of it such a doctrine as that of transubstantiation. The Protestant churches generally hold that the elements of the sacrament are flesh and blood only in a tropical sense; they nourish our souls as meat and the juice of it would our bodies. But the Catholics maintain that they are literally just that; although they possess all the sensible qualities of wafer-cakes and diluted wine. But we can have no conception of wine except what may enter into a belief, either—

1. That this, that, or the other, is wine; or,
2. That wine possesses certain properties.

Such beliefs are nothing but self-notifications that we should, upon occasion, act in regard to such things as we believe to be wine according to the qualities which we believe wine to possess. The occasion of such action would be some sensible perception, the motive of it to produce some sensible result. Thus our action has exclusive reference to what affects the senses, our habit has the same bearing as our action, our belief the same as our habit, our conception the same as our belief; and we can consequently mean nothing by wine but what has certain effects, direct or indirect, upon our senses; and to talk of something as having all the sensible characters of wine, yet being in reality blood, is senseless jargon. Now, it is not my object to pursue the theological question; and having used it as a logical example I drop it, without caring to anticipate the theologian's reply. I only desire to point out how impossible it is that we should have an idea in our minds which relates to anything but conceived sensible effects of things. Our idea of anything *is* our idea of its sensible effects; and if we fancy that we have any other we deceive ourselves, and mistake a mere sensation accompanying the thought for a part of the thought itself. It is absurd to say that thought has any meaning unrelated to its only function. It is foolish for Catholics and Protestants to fancy themselves in disagreement about the elements of the sacrament, if they agree in regard to all their sensible effects, here or hereafter.

It appears, then, that the rule for attaining the third grade of clearness of apprehension is as follows: Consider what effects, which might conceivably have practical bearings, we conceive the object of our conception to have. Then, our conception of these effects is the whole of our conception of the object. . . .

The Presuppositions of Science: Common Sense and Religion

PROLOGUE

I have a difficult task before me to render these four lectures profitable to you. It would be less so if you came without a single idea on the subject. But everybody, every butcher and baker, has ideas of logic and [has] even used the technical terminology of the subject. He says he deals in articles of "prime necessity." Perhaps he would be surprised to learn that the phrase "prime necessity" was invented by logicians to express a logical conception which has now become in common mouths very vague, it is true; but which still has a little of the original concept in a vague form clinging to it.

If I had a class in logic to conduct for a year, I should harp still, as I used to do at the Johns Hopkins, upon the maieutic character of my office,—which means that I should do all I could to make my hearers think for themselves, by which I earned the gratitude of men who are useful to mankind. I should insist that they must not suppose that my opinions were bound to be correct, but must work out their own ways of thinking. But now that there are but four lectures, and all falling in one week, the case is otherwise. I must beg you to remember that comprehension comes first and criticism later. It will be as much as you can possibly do in this week with diligent endeavors, to understand what I mean by logic and what the general outline of my system is. In order to do as much as that you must endeavor to take up a sympathetic attitude,—to try to catch what it is that I am driving at, and to store up in your minds an outline of my theory which you will subject to criticism in the months to come.

In order that you may understand me, that you may for this one week put yourselves, as far as you can, in my intellectual shoes,—leaving yourselves to decide only after you have worn them for awhile whether they really fit or not,— [. . .] I am going to begin by telling you something about my classification of the sciences; because it will aid you in the difficult task of imbibing my notion of the kind of science that I hold logic to be.

COMMON SENSE

Among the advantages which our humble cousins whom it pleases us to refer to as "the lower animals" enjoy over some of our own family is that they *never* reason about vitally important topics, and never have to lecture nor to listen to lectures about them. Docilely allowing themselves to be guided by their instincts into almost every detail of life, they live exactly as their Maker intended them to live. The result is, that they very rarely fall into error of any kind, and *never* into a vital one. What a contrast to our lives! Truly, that Reason upon which we so plume ourselves, though it may answer for little things, yet for great decisions is hardly surer than a toss-up.

The mental qualities we most admire in human Kind, the maiden's delicacy, the mother's devotion, manly courage, are merely instincts and inheritances from the biped who did not yet speak; while the characters that are most contemptible, such as, backbiting, Treachery, hypocrisy, thieving, will be found if the students of the psychology of criminals are to be trusted, to be effects of reasoning. Undoubtedly we are compelled to reason a little, unless we can hire servants to do it for us. Accounts have to be kept either by ourselves or by our clerks. Logic is computation, said Hobbes; and those who have deepest delved in that dreary discipline testify that all reasoning whatever involves mathematics, and laugh over the fallacies of those who attempt to reason unmathematically. Now tell me, is mathematics an occupation for a gentleman and an athlete? Is not such drudgery fit only for the lower classes? One may well be struck with pity for the masses of population concentrated in New York and living under such unnatural conditions that they are forced to think mathematically. However, it is not as if they had the tender nurture of a cultured modern Harvard, that great eleemosynary institu-

The Prologue is from *MS* 1334, Lecture I to the Adirondack Summer School, 1905. The sections "Common Sense" and "Religion" are from *MS* 435, Lecture I, "On Detached Ideas in General, and on Vitally Important Topics as such," 1898. The subsection "Faith" is from *MS L* 463, Peirce to Welby, December 23, 1908. The subsection "Science Presupposes God" is from *MS* 436, Lecture I, 1898. None of these lectures were delivered.

tion that Massachusetts has established to the end that the *élite* of her youths may be aided to earning comfortable incomes and living softly cultured lives. The brains of those New York plebeians are coarse, strong, laboring brains, who don't know what it is to be free from mathematics. Their conceptions are crude and vulgar enough, but their vigor of reasoning would surprise you. I have seen my [private] scholars there wrestle with problems that I would no more venture to allow the exquisitely polished intellects of a modern university to attack than I would venture to toss a cannon-ball into an eggshell cup.

I intend to call upon you for no reasoning in these lectures more complicated than one of Hegel's dilemmas. For all reasoning is mathematical and requires effort; and I mean to shun the guilt of overstraining anybody's powers. That is why I have selected a subject for my lectures which is not at all in my line, but which I hope may prove to be to your taste.

I entitle the whole course Detached Ideas on Topics of Vital Importance. In this introductory lecture I shall submit to your judgment some reflections about Detached Ideas in general, and about Vitally important Topics in general.

On vitally important topics reasoning is out of place. The very theory of reasoning, were we resolutely to attack it without any dread of mathematics, would furnish us conclusive reasons for limiting the applicability of reasoning to unimportant matters; so that, unless a problem is insignificant in importance compared with the aggregate of analogous problems, reasoning itself pronounces that there is a fallacy in submitting the question to reason, at all. That must remain merely an assertion, mathematics being *taboo*. But possibly before the course is complete, you may [be] able to get a glimpse of the general drift of the demonstration of it. Let the assertion go at present for what it is worth.

In regard to the greatest affairs of life, the wise man follows his heart and does not trust his head. This should be the method of every man, no matter how powerful his intellect. More so still, perhaps, if mathematics is too difficult for him, that is to say, if he is unequal to any intricate reasoning whatsoever. Would not a man physically puny be a fool not to recognize it, and to allow an insane megalomania to induce him to enter a match game of football? But the slightest of physical frames might as well attempt to force back a locomotive engine, as for the mightiest of mental gi-

ants to try to regulate his life advantageously by a purely reasoned out theory.

Common sense, which is the resultant of the traditional experience of mankind, witnesses unequivocally that the heart is more than the head, and is in fact everything in our highest concerns, thus agreeing with my unproved logical theorem; and those persons who think that sentiment has no part in common sense forget that the dicta of common sense are objective facts, not the way some dyspeptic may feel, but what the healthy, natural, normal democracy thinks. And yet when you open the next new book on the philosophy of religion that comes out, the chances are that it will be written by an intellectualist who in his preface offers you his metaphysics as a guide for the soul, talking as if philosophy were one of our deepest concerns. How can the writer so deceive himself?

If, walking in a garden on a dark night, you were suddenly to hear the voice of your sister crying to you to rescue her from a villain, would you stop to reason out the metaphysical question of whether it were possible for one mind to cause material waves of sound and for another mind to perceive them? If you did, the problem might probably occupy the remainder of your days. In the same way, if a man undergoes any religious experience and hears the call of his Saviour, for him to halt till he has adjusted a philosophical difficulty would seem to be an analogous sort of thing, whether you call it stupid or whether you call it disgusting. If on the other hand, a man has had no religious experience, then any religion not an affectation is as yet impossible for him; and the only worthy course is to wait quietly till such experience comes. No amount of speculation can take the place of experience.

Pray pardon my hopping about from one branch of my discourse to another and back again with no more apparent purpose than a robin redbreast or a Charles Lamb. Because it would hardly be logically consistent for me to arrange my matter with scrupulously logical accuracy when the very thing I am driving at is that logic and reasoning are only of secondary importance. There are two psychological or anthropological observations about our reasoning powers which it is convenient to insert here.

One is that powers of reasoning in any but the most rudimentary way are a somewhat uncommon gift, about as uncommon as a talent for music. Indeed, a much smaller number of persons actually attain to any proficiency in reasoning. But then the exercise of intricate ratiocination requires great energy and prolonged effort, while musical practice is nearly unmixed pleasure, I suppose, for those who do it well. Moreover, owing to several peculiar circumstances, good instruction in reasoning is exceedingly rare. As for what is taught in the colleges under the name of logic, oh dear, perhaps the less said the better. It is true that mathematics teaches one branch of reasoning. That is, indeed, its chief value in education. But how few teachers understand the logic of mathematics! And how few understand the psychology of the puzzled pupil! The pupil meets with a difficulty in Euclid. Two to one the reason is that there is a logical flaw. The boy, however, is conscious only of a mysterious hindrance. What his difficulty is he cannot tell the teacher; the teacher must teach him. Now the teacher probably never really saw the true logic of the passage. But he thinks he does because, owing to long familiarity, he has lost the sense of coming up against an invisible barrier that the boy feels. Had the teacher ever really conquered the logical difficulty himself, of course he would recognize just what it was, and thus would fulfill the first condition, at least, of being helpful. But not having conquered the difficulty, but only having worn out the sense of difficulty by familiarity, he simply cannot understand why the boy should feel any difficulty; and all he can do is to exclaim, "Oh, these stupid, stupid boys!" As if a physician should exclaim, "Oh, these horrid patients, they won't get well!" But suppose, by some extraordinary conjunction of the planets, a really good teacher of reasoning were to be appointed, what would be his first care? It would be to guard his scholars from that malady with which logic is usually infested, so that unless it runs off them like water from a duck, it is sure to make them the very worst of reasoners, namely, unfair reasoners, and what is worse unconsciously unfair, for the rest of their lives. The good teacher will therefore take the utmost pains to prevent the scholars getting puffed up with their logical acquirements. He will wish to impregnate them with the right way of looking at reasoning before they shall be aware that they have learned anything; and he will not mind giving considerable time to that, for it is worth a great deal. But now come the examiner and the pupil himself. They want *results,* tangible to them. The teacher is dismissed as a failure, or, if he is allowed another chance, he will take good care to reverse the method of his teaching and give them *results,*—especially, as that is the lazy way. These are some of the causes of there

being so few strong reasoners in the world. But allowing for the influence of such causes as well as we can, the fact still remains that comparatively few persons are originally possessed of any but the feeblest modicum of this talent. What is the significance of that? Is it not a plain sign that the faculty of reasoning is not of the first importance to success in life? For were it so, its absence would cause the individual to postpone marriage and so affect his procreation; and thus natural selection would operate to breed the race for vigorous reasoning powers, and they would become common. And the study of characters confirms this conclusion. For though the men who are most extraordinarily successful evidently do reason deeply about the details of their business, yet no ordinary degrees of good success are influenced,—otherwise than perhaps favorably,—by any lack of great reasoning power. We all know highly successful men, lawyers, editors, scientific men,—not to speak of artists—whose great deficiency in this regard is only revealed by some unforeseen accident.

The other observation I desired to make about the human reason is that we find people mostly modest enough about qualities which really go to making fine men and women,—the courageous man not usually vaunting his courage, nor the modest woman boasting of her modesty, nor the loyal vain of their good faith: the things they are vain about are some insignificant gifts of beauty, or skill of some kind. But beyond all, with the exception of those who, being trained in logic, follow its rules and thus do not trust their direct reasoning powers at all, everybody else ridiculously overrates his own logic, and if he really has superior powers of reason is usually so consumed by conceit, that it is far from rare to see a young man completely ruined by it; so that one is sometimes tempted to think, and perhaps truly, that it conduces not only to a man's success from a worldly point of view but to his attaining any real elevation of character to be all but a fool in this regard, provided only he be perfectly aware of his own deficiency.

But however unimportant logical vigor may be there are a few careers which a man who is deficient in mathematics would do well to avoid. He had better not cherish much ambition in the direction of philosophy. As *professor* of philosophy he might pass muster. Several very useful German books remind us of this. But he will not be of much service to philosophy itself. It is true that as this subject has hitherto been treated, its reasonings have been of the very simplest. And though they may cease to be so simple after the logic of relatives shall have been digested and assimilated, yet that will not happen for a good many years. There are, however, two peculiarities of metaphysics which are of decisive importance in this connection.

Permit me here to interrupt what I am saying in order to explain to you, once for all, the senses which I attach to the words philosophy and metaphysics. I define *philosophy* as that branch of science which is founded in the main upon such experience as is familiar to every man, and which experience, owing to its extreme familiarity, no man ever did or ever will really doubt, so that the conclusions of philosophy *ought* to carry,—and *would,* I suppose, carry were it only investigated according [to] a really scientific method,—a degree of certitude, a sort of necessity, which can belong to none of the sciences which rest upon special, or recondite, experiences. I define philosophy in this way because the division of sciences according to the departments of experience with which they deal gives more natural groups than any other principle of division except that according to their abstractness, which is Comte's principle followed also by Spencer. But this latter principle is, taken by itself, insufficient and too vague; and besides the two substantially agree in their results. We must not indeed forbid to a science, especially not to philosophy, resort to any premises or methods whatsoever. Philosophy may adduce as data results of special sciences. But it is distinguished from other sciences in resting mainly upon familiar experiences. That gives it its character, its abstractness, its universality, and the sort of necessity which marks it. Above it in Comte's scale, as I would reform that scale, stands only pure abstract mathematics, which makes no inquiry at all into what is the fact, but studies only hypotheses. When all the possible hypotheses of mathematics shall be seen to form a continuum, or cosmos, as they are already beginning to do, then mathematics will stand out as the queen of the sciences, to which all the others even philosophy are but adjuvant. For it will contain the ideal essence of them all, but purified from brute existence and rounded out into the perfection they do not attain.

*   *   *

Conservatism, true conservatism, which is sentimental conservatism, and by those who have no powers of observation to see what sort of men conservatives are, is often called stupid conservatism, an epithet far more applicable to the false conservatism that looks to see on which side bread is buttered,—true conservatism, I say, means not trusting to reasonings about questions of vital importance but rather to hereditary instincts and traditional sentiments. Place before the conservative arguments to which he can find no adequate reply and which go, let us say, to demonstrate that wisdom and virtue call upon him to offer to marry his own sister, and though he be unable to answer the arguments, he will not act upon their conclusion, because he believes that tradition and the feelings that tradition and custom have developed in him are safer guides than his own feeble ratiocination. Thus, true conservatism is sentimentalism. Of course, sentiment lays no claim to infallibility, in the sense of *theoretical infallibility,* a phrase that logical analysis proves to be a mere jingle of words with a jungle of contradictory meanings. The conservative need not forget that he might have been born a Brahmin with a traditional sentiment in favor of *suttee,*—a reflection that tempts him to become a radical. But still, on the whole, he thinks his wisest plan is to reverence his deepest sentiments as his highest and ultimate authority, which is regarding them as *for him practically infallible,*—that is, to say infallible in the only sense of the word in which *infallible* has any consistent meaning.

The opinion prevalent among radicals that conservatives, and sentimentalists generally, are fools is only a cropping-out of the tendency of men to conceited exaggeration of their reasoning powers. Uncompromising radical though I be upon some questions, inhabiting all my life in an atmosphere of science, and not reckoned as particularly credulous, I must confess that the conservative sentimentalism I have defined recommends itself to my mind as eminently sane and wholesome. Commendable as it undoubtedly is to reason out matters of detail, yet to allow mere reasonings and reason's self-conceit to overslaw,[1] the normal and manly sentimentalism which ought to lie at the cornerstone of all our conduct seems to me to be foolish and despicable.

Philosophy after all is, at its highest valuation, nothing more than a branch of science, and as such is not a matter of vital importance; and those who represent it as being so are simply offering us a stone when we ask for bread. Mind, I do not deny that a philosophical or other scientific error may be fraught with disastrous consequences for the whole people. It might conceivably bring about the extirpation of the human race. Importance in that sense it might have in any degree. Nevertheless, in no case is it of *vital* importance.

A great calamity the error may be, *qua* event, in the sense in which an earthquake, or the impact of a comet, or the extinction of the sun would be an important event, and consequently, if it happens to lie in the line of my duty or of yours to investigate any philosophical question and to publish the more or less erroneous results of our investigations, I hope we shall not fail to do so, if we can. Certainly, any task which lies before us to be done has its importance. But there our responsibility ends. Nor is it the philosophy itself, *qua* cognition, that is vital, so much as it is our playing the part that is allotted to us.

You will observe that I have not said a single word in disparagement of the philosophy of religion, in general, which seems to me a most interesting study, at any rate, and possibly likely to lead to some useful result. Nor have I attacked any sect of that philosophy. It is not the philosophy which I hold to be baleful, but the representing it to be of vital importance, as if any genuine religion could come from the head instead of from the heart.

Somewhat allied to the philosophy of religion is the science of ethics. It is equally useless. Now books of casuistry, indeed, using the word "casuistry" not in any technical sense, but merely to signify discussions of what ought to be done in various difficult situations, might be made at once extremely entertaining and positively useful. But casuistry is just what the ordinary treatises upon ethics do not touch, at least not seriously. They chiefly occupy themselves with reasoning out the basis of morality and other questions secondary to that. Now what's the *use* of prying into the philosophical basis of morality? We all know what morality is: it is behaving as you were brought up to behave, that is, to think you ought to be punished for not behaving. But to believe in thinking as you have been brought up to think defines *conservatism*. It needs no reasoning to perceive that morality is conservatism. But conservatism again means, as you will surely agree, not trusting to one's reasoning powers. To be a moral man is to obey the traditional maxims of your community without hesitation or discussion. Hence, ethics, which is reasoning out an explanation of morality is,—I will not say immoral, [for] that would be going too far,—composed of the very substance of im-

morality. If you ever happen to be thrown in with an unprofessional thief, the only very bad kind of thief, so as to be able to study his psychological peculiarities, you will find that two things characterize him; first, an even more immense conceit in his own reasoning powers than is common, and second, a disposition to reason about the basis of morals.

Ethics, then, even if not a positively dangerous study, as it sometimes proves, is as useless a science as can be conceived. But it must be said, in favor of ethical writers, that they are commonly free from the nauseating custom of boasting of the utility of their science.

RELIGION

Among vitally important truths there is one which I verily verily believe,—and which men of infinitely deeper insight than mine have believed,—to be solely supremely important. It is that vitally important facts are of all truths the veriest trifles. For the only vitally important matter is *my* concern, business, and duty,—or yours. Now you and I,—what are, we? Mere cells of the social organism. Our deepest sentiment pronounces the verdict of our own insignificance. Psychological analysis shows that there is nothing which distinguishes my personal identity except my faults and my limitations,—or if, you please my blind will, which it is my highest endeavor to annihilate. Not in the contemplation of "topics of vital importance" but in those universal things with which philosophy deals, the factors of the universe, is man to find his highest occupation. To pursue "topics of vital importance" as the first and best can lead only to one or other of two terminations,—either on the one hand what is called I hope not justly, Americanism, the worship of business, the life in which the fertilizing stream of genial sentiment dries up or shrinks to a rill of comic tit-bits, or else on the other hand, to monasticism, sleepwalking in this world with no eye nor heart except for the other. Take for the lantern of your footsteps the cold light of reason and regard your business, your duty, as the highest thing, and you can only rest in one of those goals or the other. But suppose you embrace, on the contrary, a conservative sentimentalism, modestly rate your own reasoning powers at the very mediocre price they would fetch if put up at auction, and *then* what do you come to? Why, *then,* the very first command that is laid upon you, your quite highest business and duty, becomes, as everybody knows, to recognize a higher busi-

ness than your business, *not* merely an avoca-
tion after the daily task of your vocation is
performed, but a generalized conception of
duty which completes your personality by
melting it into the neighboring parts of the universal cosmos. If this sounds unintelligible, just
take for comparison the first good mother of a
family that meets your eye, and ask whether
she is not a sentimentalist, whether you would
wish her to be otherwise, and lastly whether
you can find a better formula in which to outline the universal features of her portrait than
that I have just given. I dare say you can improve upon that; but you will find one element
of it is correct,—especially if your understanding is aided by the logic of relatives,—and that
is that the supreme commandment of the
Buddhisto-christian religion is, to generalize,
to complete the whole system even until continuity results and the distinct individuals weld
together. Thus, it is that while reasoning and
the science of reasoning strenuously proclaim
the subordination of reasoning to sentiment,
the very supreme commandment of sentiment
is that man should generalize, or what the logic
of relatives shows to be the same thing [,]
should become welded into the universal continuum, which is what true reasoning consists
in. But this does not reinstate reasoning [,] for
this generalization should come about, not
merely in man's cognitions, which are but the
superficial film of his being, but objectively, in
the deepest emotional springs of his life. In
fulfilling this command, man prepares himself
for transmutation into a new form of life, the
joyful Nirvana in which the discontinuities of
his will shall have all but disappeared.

Do you know what it was that was at the
root of the barbarism of the Plantagenet period and paralyzed awakening science from the
days of Roger Bacon to those of Francis Bacon? We plainly trace it in the history, the
writings, the monuments of that age. It was the
exaggerated interest men took in matters of
vital importance.

Do you know what it is in Christianity that
when recognized makes our religion an agent
of reform and progress? It is its marking duty
at its proper finite figure. Not that it dimin-
ishes in any degree its vital importance, but
that behind the outline of that huge mountain
it enables us to descry a silvery peak rising into
the calm air of eternity.

The generalization of sentiment can take
place on different sides. Poetry is one sort of
generalization of sentiment, and in so far is the
regenerative metamorphosis of sentiment. But

poetry remains on one side ungeneralized, and
to that is due its emptiness. The complete generalization, the complete regeneration of sentiment is religion, which is poetry, but poetry
completed.

That is about what I had to say to you about
topics of vital importance. To sum it up, all
sensible talk about vitally important topics
must be commonplace, all reasoning about
them unsound, and all study of them narrow
and sordid.

Faith

Dear Lady Welby, for the past week all my time
and all my energy have been taken up with what
we Yankees (i.e. the stock of those who came
over to Massachusetts before 1645,—I forget
the exact date,) call "chores." I believe that in
standard English the word is lost. It means the
menial offices of every day in a household, especially, a primitive household,—the hewing of
wood and the drawing of water and the like.

I now return to the expression of my abhor-
rence of the doctrine that any proposition whatever is infallibly true. Unless truth be recognized as *public*,—as that of which *any* person
would come to be convinced if he carried his
inquiry, his sincere search for immovable belief, far enough,—then there will be nothing to
prevent each one of us from adopting an utterly futile belief of his own which all the rest
will disbelieve. Each one will set himself up as
a little prophet; that is, a little "crank," a half-
witted victim of his own narrowness.

But if Truth be something public, it must
mean that to the acceptance of which as a basis
of conduct any person you please would ultimately come if he pursued his inquiries far
enough;—yes, every rational being, however
prejudiced he might be at the outset. For
Truth has that compulsive nature which Pope
well expressed:

The eternal years of God are her's.

But, you will say, I am setting up this very
proposition as infallible truth. Not at all; it is a
mere definition. I do not say that it is infallibly
true that there is any belief to which a person
would come if he were to carry his inquiries far
enough. I only say that that alone is what I call
Truth. I cannot infallibly know that there is
any Truth.

You say there is a certain "Faith" the object
of which is absolutely "certain." Will you have
the goodness to tell me what you mean by

"certain"? Does it mean anything more than that you personally are obstinately resolved upon sticking to the proposition, *ruat caelum?* It reminds me of an anecdote that was told me in 1859 by a southern darky. "You know," says he, "massa, that General Washington and General Jackson was great friends, dey was (the fact being that the latter was an irreconcilable opponent of the former, but did not become a figure in national politics until after Washington had retired from public life). Well, one day Gen'l. Washington, he said to Gen'l. Jackson, "Gen'l, how tall should you think that horse of mine was?" "I don't know, General," says General Jackson, "how tall is he, General Washington?" "Why," says General Washington, "he is sixteen feet high." "Feet, General Washington," say Gen'ral Jackson, "feet, General Washington? You means *hands,* Gen'ral!" "Did I say *feet,* General Jackson," said General Washington. "Do you mean to say that I said my horse was sixteen *feet* high?" "You certainly said so, General Washington." "Very well, then, Gen'ral Jackson, if I *said* feet, *if* I said feet, then I sticks to it!" Is your "sublime faith" any more "sublime" than that? How?

Now I will tell you the meaning that *I* would, in my turn, attach to the word faith. The New Testament word is πιστις, which means, in its most proper sense, *trust;* i.e. belief in something not as having any knowledge or approach to knowledge about the matter of belief, but "implicit belief," as the catholics say, i.e. belief in it derived from one's belief that a witness who testifies to it would not so testify if it were not so. Hence, the latest writers of classical Greek, such as Plato and Isocrates, and the earliest writers of common Greek, such as Aristotle, use it for any mediate belief, any belief well founded on another belief. That is, these writers apply πιστις to an assured belief. They also apply it to an *assurance* of any belief. But the English word "faith" could not be used so without great violence to usage which would be entirely unwarranted by any need. I think that what the word is needed to express, and what it might be restricted to express without too great violence to usage is *that belief which the believer does not himself recognize,* or rather (since that cannot properly be called belief), that which he is prepared to conform his conduct to, without recognizing what it is to which he is conforming his conduct. For example, if I do not know what Liddell & Scott say is the meaning of πιστις but am convinced that whatever they

may say is its meaning really is so, I have a *faith* that it is so. A person who says "Oh, I could not believe that this life is our only life; for if I did I should be so miserable that I should suicide forthwith," I say that he has a *Faith* that things are not intolerably bad for any individual or at any rate are not so for *him.* Every true man of science, i.e. every man belonging to a social group all the members of which sacrifice all the ordinary motives of life to their desire to make their beliefs concerning one subject conform to verified judgments of perception together with sound reasoning, and who therefore really believes the universe to be governed by reason, or in other words by God,—but who does not explicitly recognize that he believes in God,—has Faith in God, according to my use of the term Faith. For example, I knew a scientific man who devoted his last years to reading theology in hopes of coming to a belief in God, but who never could in the least degree come to a consciousness of having the least belief of the sort, yet passionately pursued that very mistaken means of attaining his heart's supreme desire. He, according to me, was a shining example of Faith in God. For to believe in reasoning about phenomena is to believe that they are governed by reason, that is, by God. That to my mind is a high and wholesome belief. One is often in a situation in which one is obliged to assume, i.e. to go upon, a proposition which one ought to recognize as extremely doubtful. But in order to conduct oneself with vigorous consistency one must dismiss doubts on the matter from consideration. There is a vast difference between *that* and any holding of the proposition for certain. To hold a proposition to be certain is to puff oneself up with the vanity of perfect knowledge. It leaves no room for Faith. It is not absolutely certain that twice two is four. It is humanly certain that no conception of God can be free from all error. I once made a careful study of Dr. Schaff's three solid volumes on "The Creeds of Christendom." I found not one that said one word about the principle of love, although that seems to be the leading element of christian faith. In order to find out, if I could, the reason for this passing strange omission, I made a study of the circumstances which determined the formulation of each Symbolum, and ascertained that, with the possible exception of what we erroneously call "The Apostle's Creed," concerning whose origin we have no definite information, but which is no exception as regards the information in question, and certainly does not breathe the spirit of such early documents as the Διδαχη,[2] every one sprang from the *odium theologicum* and the desire to have some certain person excommunicated, with the evident wish that he might be damned. Theology arises from discontent with religious Faith,—which implies a lack of such Faith, and with a desire to substitute for that a scientific anatomy and physiology of God, which, rightly considered, is blasphemous and antireligious. It is also in most striking disaccord with the spirit of the son of Mary.

Your pleading that I should not use such a phrase as "attractive fancy" and I suppose you might feel so about the phrase "strictly hypothetical God" seems to show that I quite failed to convey my own sense of the value of the Neglected Argument,[3] in that it does not lead to any theology at all, but only to what *I* mean by a purely religious *Faith,* which will have already taken deep root before the subject of it thinks of it at all as a belief. Writing this is like having to explain a joke.

* * *

. . . By the way, when I was speaking of creeds, I might have mentioned . . . that I say the creed in church with the rest. By doing so I only signify, as I presume the majority do,—I hope they do;—my willingness to put aside, most heartily, anything that tends to separate me from my fellow christians. For the very ground of my criticism of creeds is that every one of them was originally designed to produce such a separation, contrary to the notions of him who said "He that is not against me is for me." By the way, I have been reading, with much study, the book of W. B. Smith entitled *Der vorchristliche Jesus,* which I have little doubt is sound in the main; and I think probably christianity was a higher development out of Buddhism, modified by Jewish belief in a living god . . . .

Science Presupposes God

I would have liked to have made all this quite plain, so that you could have perceived its exact truth as evident. But it happens that no dificult reasoning can be made evident and exact without mathematics; and I regret that however victorious Harvard may be in contests of atheletics, the vigor of mind requisite for diagrammatic reasoning is wanting here. I regret it, because what I say to you, put in the rough and apparently arbitrary and maimed

way in which I am driven to hinting it, seems at once commonplace and enigmatic, the taste of which is like sugar and salt. But there is one great comfort for us all. It is that the historical development of man has now reached a stage at which all our intellectual feebleness will be made up, in two or three centuries [,] because the race which is wanting in vigor of thought is now sure to be supplanted by a race that can reason mathematically without being overcome by that tired feeling. Perhaps it will be the Japanese who are certainly superior to us in every respect except brute vigor, and to whom, therefore, we ought to be very willing to surrender our empire. At any rate, we must either quit or work, in whichever way the current of civilization finds the path of least resistance.

It was over the door of Plato's Academy that was put up the notice "No admission for the αγεωμετητης."[4] Ah! Were it only from the Academy that he was debarred. He is utterly cut off from all contemplation of the rational. His reason is embryological. Between him and all the perfections which the Cosmos approaches or suggests, a dense fog obstructs all vision. He is bound down to his five senses and to the day's happenings, like a poor dog. And to think that emancipation from all this is possible by a sufficient effort, but that the man cannot screw his courage up to making that effort!

It is true that there is no treatise on the parts of mathematics which are valuable not as a utensil but as the crown of a freeman's education. I would not for the world say anything in disparagement of Schröder's Logik. Yet I cannot but think there is room for a brief presentation of the Logic of Relatives and of Exact Logic generally, subjective and objective, which shall be less mechanical and fatiguing and shall better display its living ideas and connections with philosophy and with life. I wrote such a book myself with the utmost care and no economy of pains. I was well pleased with it myself. But the publishers told me it would not pay, especially as I was not a university professor; and so I put the MS to another use; that of lighting fires.

Thus, in every way I am driven to see that this country will have nothing intellectual that is beautiful and finished. It wants only sporadic ideas on vitally important topics; and that is why I am inflicting upon you this wretched desultory sermonizing for which I am no more fitted than I am for rowing stroke in the Varsity crew. I can only say that if anybody wishes to have his eyes opened to a cosmos of thought of such wonderful beauty that merely as a poem the delight of it would a thousand times repay the effort of finding it, and which in addition to that appears to be the very Key that unlocks the secret of the physical and psychical universe, if he will come to me prepared, not for brilliant *aperçus* but for thorough work, I can help him to it. When I have said that, well knowing that the news will be received with incredulity, I have gone as far as duty requires. How bleak a climate America with its vitally important topics is for vitally unimportant but cosmically vital ideas, I have often thought when I have vainly tried to get into print a just word of praise for the solid work of some American thinker.

NOTES

1. {See *The Century Dictionary:* "overslaugh"— to oppress or hinder}
2. {*The Didache*}
3. {See below, pp. 88–89.}
4. {The Greek means "ignorant of mathematics."}

The Nature of Science

My classification of the sciences will give you a first inkling of my notion of the position that logic holds among the sciences.

This classification adopts the general idea of the classification called Comte's. When I speak of it as "the classification called Comte's," I must state that of my own knowledge, I know no reason for not simply calling it Comte's classification. But Dr. Robert Flint and other writers aver very solemnly, "If that classification possess any merits they must be ascribed to Dr. Burdin, who conceived it, and to Saint-Simon, who first received and published it; not to Comte, although he showed how much could be made of it." Notwithstanding the scoundrelly character of the clerical profession in times past, I cannot believe that Dr. Flint would use such language without conclusive proof of its truth, convincing to every mind. I am sorry that I cannot quite suppress a lingering suggestion of doubt in my mind owing to the unspeakable mendacity of the cloth in times too recent. I certainly cannot for an instant believe that Comte was a conscious plagiarist.

This scheme, as you know, arranges what are called by Comte the "abstract sciences" in a ladder, with the idea that each derives its principles from the discoveries of the more abstract science that occupies the rung above, while all are at the same time pressing upwards in the endeavor to become more "abstract." Since Comte first set forth that scheme, many others have been proposed; but among the score or more which have seemed to me to be at all deserving of study, including all that are widely known, I have not found one which was not manifestly founded upon that which goes by Comte's name; and if my own has no other distinction it shall have that of honestly owning a filiation to a system of philosophy to which I am profoundly opposed,—a filiation of which too many of its offspring seem to be basely ashamed to own.

This, however, is not the only peculiarity of my classification. In order to make it useful I wished it to be a natural classification, that is, I wished it to embody the chief facts of relationships between the sciences so far as they present themselves to scientific and observational study. Now to my apprehension, it is only natural experiential objects that lend themselves to such a natural classification. I do not think, for example, that we can make a natural classification of plane curves or of any other mere possibilities. We do classify them, or rather, divide them, according to their *orders* and *classes* or their so-called *deficiencies*. But this is a mere enumeration of the logically possible cases. It embodies no positive information. It cannot therefore serve the same purpose as a natural classification. My notion is that what we call "natural classification" is, from the nature of things limited to natural objects. Now the vast majority of classifications of the sciences are classifications of *possible* sciences, which are certainly not natural objects. What is a science as a natural object? It is the actual

From *MS* 1334, Adirondack Summer School Lectures, 1905.

living occupation of an actual group of living men. It is in that sense only that I presume to attempt any classification of the sciences. A very considerable proportion of all the so-called classifications of the sciences are classifications of *scientia,* or επιστήμαι, in the ancient sense of perfect knowledge. Others are classifications not of sciences but of the objects of systemetized knowledge.

But what I mean by a "science," both for the purpose of this classification and in general, is the life devoted to the pursuit of truth according to the best known methods on the part of a group of men who understand one another's ideas and works as no outsider can. It is not what they have already found out which makes their business a science; it is that they are pursuing a branch of truth according, I will not say, to the best methods that are known at the time. I do not call the solitary studies of a single man a science. It is only when a group of men, more or less in intercommunication, are aiding and stimulating one another by their understanding of a particular group of studies as outsiders cannot understand them, that I call their life a science. It is not necessary that they should all be at work upon the same problem, or that all should be fully acquainted with all that it is needful for another of them to know; but their studies must be so closely allied that any one of them could take up the problem of any other after some months of special preparation and that each should understand pretty minutely what it is that each one's of the others work consists in; so that any two of them meeting together shall be thoroughly conversant with each other's ideas and the language he talks and should feel each other to be brethern. In particular, one thing which commonly unites them is their common skill, unpossessed by outsiders, in the use of certain instruments, and their common skill in performing certain kinds of work. The men of that group have dealings with the men of another group whose studies are more abstract, to whom they go for information about principles that the men of the second group understand better, but which the men of the first group need to apply. At the same time the men of this first group will probably have far more skill in their special applications of these principles than have the members of the second group who understand better the principles themselves. Thus the astronomer resorts to the student of optics, who understands the principles of optics better than he does. But he understands the applications of those principles to astronomical instruments and to work with

them far better than the pure optical student does. One group may be in such wise dependent upon several other groups. Now I do not pretend that all the ramifications of dependence of one science upon another can be fully represented by any scheme of arrangement of the names of those sciences, even if we limit the kind of dependence that we seek to represent to dependence for *principles.* But I do undertake to represent somewhat vaguely the dependence *for principles* only of each science and each group of sciences upon others after the manner of Comte, or Charles Burdin, or whoever it was that made that wonderful discovery.

All human lives separate themselves and segregate themselves into three grand groups whose members understand one another in a general way, but can['t] for the life of them understand sympathetically the pursuits and aims of the others. The first group consists of the devotees of enjoyment who devote themselves to carving their bread and eating as fine bread as they can and who seek the higher enjoyments of themselves and their fellows. This is the largest and most necessary class. The second group despise such a life and cannot fully understand it. Their notion of life is to accomplish results. They build up great concerns, they go into politics, not as the heeler[1] does, for a living, but in order to wield the forces of state, they undertake reforms of one and another kind. This group makes civilization. The men of the third group who are comparatively few cannot conceive at all a life for enjoyment and look down upon a life of action. Their purpose is to worship God in the development of ideas and of truth. These are the men of science. They again segregate themselves into three great groups distinguished by their different conceptions of the purpose of science. There are those who look upon themselves as the tutors and superiors of the doers. Science to their minds tells how the world's work is to be done; and the sciences they cultivate are the Practical Sciences. But in order to develope any practical science, a man must have the equivalent of a digest of science [,] a systematized account of all human knowledge. Therefore there must be a second class of men whose purpose it is to produce such digests, one working upon one part of it and another upon another. For these men, science is what Coleridge defined it as being, organized knowledge. This very business I am engaged in, of classifying the sciences is a necessary part of this work of systematizing and digesting human knowledge. I have called such sciences the Sciences of Review, and also Tactics, or *Taxospude,* the endeavor to arrange science. The third great division of science I call *heuretics* or *heurospude,* the endeavor to discover. It is true that all scientific men are engaged upon nothing else than the endeavor to discover. This is true of *taxospudists* and the *prattospudists* as much as of the *heurospudists.* But the difference is that the prattospudists endeavor to discover for the ultimate purpose of doing, and the *taxospudists* endeavor to discover for the purpose of applying knowledge in any way, be it in action or more especially in cognition. But the *heurospudists* look upon discovery as making acquaintance with God and as the very purpose for which the human race was created. Indeed as the very purpose of God in creating the world at all. They think it a matter of no consequence whether the human race subsists and enjoys or whether it be exterminated, as [in] time it very happily will be, as soon as it has subserved its purpose of developing a new type of mind that can love and worship God better.

You must not think that I mean to say in any wooden sense that God's notion in creating the world was to have somebody to admire him. We cannot possibly put ourselves in God's shoes, even so far as to say in any definite, wooden sense that *God is.* I only mean that the purpose of creation as it must appear to us in our highest approaches to an understanding of it, is to make an answering mind. It is God's movement toward self reproduction. And when I say that *God is,* I mean that the conception of a God is the highest flight toward an understanding of the original of the whole physico-psychical universe that we can make. It has the advantage over the agnostics and other views of offering to our apprehension an object to be loved. Now the *heurospudist* has an imperative need of finding in nature an object to love. His science cannot subsist without it. For science to him must be worship in order not to fall down before the feet of some idol of human workmanship. Remember that the human race is but an ephemeral thing. In a little while it will be altogether done with and cast aside. Even now it is merely dominant on one small planet of one insignificant star, while all that our sight embraces on a starry night is to the universe far less than a single cell of the brain is to the whole man.

NOTE

1. {Slang for "hack politician"; see *The Century Dictionary.*}

Mathematics, The First Science

MATHEMATICS

Mathematics is the science which draws necessary conclusions. Such was the definition first given by my father, Benjamin Peirce, in 1870. At that day the new mathematics was in its early infancy and the novelty of this definition was disconcerting even to the most advanced mathematicians; but today no competent man would adopt a definition decidedly opposed to that. The only fault I should find with it is that if we conceive a science, not as a body of ascertained truth, but, as the living business which a group of investigators are engaged upon, which I think is the only sense which gives a natural classification of sciences, then we must include under mathematics everything that is an indispensable part of the mathematician's business; and therefore we must include the *formulation* of his hypotheses as well as the tracing out of their consequences. Certainly, into that work of formulation the mathematicians put an immense deal of intellectual power and energy.

Moreover, the hypotheses of the mathematician are of a peculiar nature. The mathematician does not in the least concern himself about their truth. They are often designed to represent *approximately* some state of things which he has some reason to believe is real-

The section "Mathematics" is from *MS* 459, The Lowell Lectures, 1903. The section "Diagrams" is from *MS* 293, ca. 1906. The section "Diagram Observation" is from *MS* 15, "On Quantity," ca. 1895. The section "Two Kinds of Deduction" is from *MS L* 224, Peirce to William James, December 25, 1909.

ized; but he does not regard it as his business to find out whether this be true or not; and he generally knows very well that his hypothesis only approximates to a representation of that state of things. The substance of the mathematician's hypothesis is therefore a creature of his imagination. Yet nothing can be more unlike a poet's creation. The reason is that the poet is interested in his images solely on account of their own beauty or interest as images, while the mathematician is interested in his hypotheses solely on account of the ways in which necessary inferences can be drawn from them. He consequently makes them perfectly definite in all those respects which could affect the ways in which parts of them could or [could] not be taken together so as to lead to necessary consequences. If he leaves the hypotheses determinate in any other respects, they are hypotheses of *applied* mathematics. The pure mathematician generalizes his hypotheses so as to make them applicable to all conceivable states of things in which precisely analogous conclusions could be drawn. In view of this I would define Pure Mathematics as the science of pure hypotheses perfectly definite in respects which can create or destroy forms of necessary consequences from them and entirely indeterminate in other respects.

I am confident that this definition will be accepted by mathematicians as, at least, substantially accurate.

As for the old definition that mathematics is the science of quantity, it first appears, I believe, in Boëthius, about A.D. 500 when mathematics was at its lowest ebb; and at that time three words that occur in it had entirely different meanings from those they now carry. Those three words are *Mathematics, Science,* and *Quantity*. First, under mathematics [were] then included only four sciences called Arithmetic, Astronomy, Geometry, and Music. But by arithmetic was not meant anything now called by that name; for our arithmetic was called *logistic* and was not included in mathematics. Secondly, by *science* was then meant *comprehension* through principles, which we now call *philosophy,* a thing which a modern mathematician would not touch with a nine foot pole. Thirdly, by *quantity* was meant simply things *measurable*. Therefore, the true meaning of that phrase Mathematics is the science of quantity was that four branches of learning, of which all but geometry are now utterly forgotten, constituted the philosophy of measurement. You see it is one of the many cases in which a phrase has quite survived its meaning. The relation of Quantity to Mathematics is, in fact this, that it is found that in one way or another the conception of quantity has an important bearing upon almost every branch of mathematics, as it has upon logic itself. But it is by no means the principal subject of all branches of mathematics. Thus the theory of Linear Perspective is a branch of Mathematics. Yet it is properly and primarily not concerned with quantity; and if it is made to appear so, it is badly taught.

Some very eminent and profound mathematicians go so far as to say that Mathematics is a branch of Logic. Dedekind is one of these, whose little book published by the Open Court Company under the title of Essays on Number I beg leave to recommend to your study. But Mathematics is not Logic for the reason that the mathematician deals exclusively with assumptions for whose truth he in no wise makes himself responsible, while logic deals with positive truth. The mathematician's interest in reasoning is to get at the conclusion in the speediest way consistent with certainty. The logician, on the contrary, does not care particularly what the conclusion is. His interest lies in picking the reasoning to pieces and discovering the principles upon which its leading to truth depends. As far as necessary inference is concerned, the mathematician and the logician meet upon a common highway. But they face in contrary directions.

Still, the mere fact that mathematicians of high rank consider mathematics as a branch of logic may serve as sufficient justification for my devoting a part of this course to the examination of mathematics.

There is no science more infested with a vermin of ignorant pretenders than logic; and there is one simple question by which they can commonly be detected. Ask your pretended logician whether there are any necessary reasonings of an essentially different character from mathematical reasonings. If he says no, you may hope he knows something about logic; but if he says "yes," he is contradicting a well-established truth universally admitted by sound logicians. If you ask for a sample, it will be found to be a very simple mathematical reasoning *blurred* by being confusedly apprehended. For a necessary reasoning is one which *would* follow under all circumstances, whether you are talking of the real world or the world of the Arabian Nights' or what. And that precisely defines mathematical reasoning. It is true that a *distinctively* mathematical reasoning is one that is so intricate that we need some kind of a diagram to follow it out. But something of the nature of a diagram, be it only an imaginary skeleton proposition, or even a mere noun with the ideas of its application and signification is needed in all necessary reasoning. Indeed one may say that something of this kind is needed in all reasoning whatsoever, although in induction it is the real experiences that serves as diagram.

One of the most striking characters of pure mathematics,—of course you will understand that I speak only of mathematics in its present condition, and only occasionally and with much diffidence speculate as to what the mathematics of the future may be,—but one of [the] characters of latter day pure mathematics is that all its departments are so intimately related that one cannot treat of any one as it should be treated without considering all the others. We see the same thing in several other advanced sciences. But so far as it is possible to break mathematics into departments, we observe that in each department there is a certain set of alternatives to which every question relates. Thus, in projective geometry, which is the whole geometry that is allied to perspective *without measurement,* namely, the geometry of planes, their intersections and envelopes, and the intersections and envelopes of intersections and envelopes, the question always is whether a figure lies in another figure or not, whether a point one way described lies on a point another way described, whether a point lies on a line or not, whether three lines coincide or not. Here there are two alternatives. In other departments, the alternatives are all the integer numbers; in still others, the alternatives are all the analytical numbers, etc. The set of alternatives to which a branch of mathematics constantly refers may be considered as a system of values; and in that sense, mathematics seems always to deal with quantity. It would seem that if any lines of demarcation are to be drawn between different mathematical theories they must be according to the number of alternatives in the set of alternatives to which it refers; but I am bound to say that this is a notion personal to myself,—and that I have my doubts as to its worth as the basis of a complete classification of mathematics. We may, however, accept it in so far as it shows that the simplest possible kind of mathematics will be that all whose questions relate to which one of a single set of two alternatives is to be admitted. Now in Existential Graphs, all questions relate to whether a graph is true or false; and we may conceive that every proposition has one or other of two values, the *infinite* value of being true, and the *zero* value of being false. We have, therefore, in Existential Graphs an exposition of this simplest possible form of mathematics. It is Applied Mathematics, because we have given definite logical significations to the graphs. But if we were to define the graphs solely by means of the five fundamental rules of their transformation, allowing them to mean whatever they might mean while preserving those rules, we should then see in them the Pure Mathematics of two values, the simplest of all possible mathematics.

Were we to follow out the same principle, we should divide all mathematics according to the number of alternatives in the set of alternatives to which it constantly refers and also to the number of different sets of alternatives to which it refers. Perhaps that would give as natural a classification of pure mathematical inquiries as any that could at this time be proposed. At any rate, we may so far safely trust to it, to conclude that the very first thing to be inquired into in order to comprehend the nature of mathematics, is the matter of *number.*

Certainly, of all mathematical ideas, next after the idea of two alternatives, the most ubiquitous is the idea of whole numbers. Dr. Georg Cantor is justly recognized as the author of two important doctrines, that of *Cardinal Numbers* and that of *Ordinal Numbers.* But I protest against his use of the term *Cardinal Number.* What he calls cardinal number is not number at all. A cardinal number is one of the vocables used primarily in the experiment called counting a collection, and used secondarily as an appellative of that collection. But what Cantor means by a cardinal number is the *zeroness, oneness, twoness, threeness,* etc.—in short the *multitude* of the collection. I shall always use the word *multitude* to mean the *degree of maniness* of a collection. By *ordinal numbers* Cantor means certain symbols invented by him to denote the place of an object in a series in which each object has another next after it. The character of being in a definite place in such a series may be called the *posteriority* of the object.

Since I have alluded to Cantor, for whose work I have a profound admiration, I had better say that what I have to tell you about Multitude is not in any degree borrowed from him. My studies of the subject began before his, and were nearly completed before I was aware of his work, and it is my independent development substantially agreeing in its results with his, of which I intend to give a rough sketch.

And since I have recommended Dedekind's work, I will say that it amounts to a very able and original development of ideas which I had published six years previously. Schröder in the third volume of his logic shows how Dedekind's development might be made to conform more closely to my conceptions. That is interesting; but Dedekind's development has its own independent value. I even incline to think that it follows a comparatively better way. For I am not so much in love with my own system as the late Professor Schröder was. I may add that quite recently Mr. Whitehead and the Hon. Bertrand Russell have treated of the subject; but they seem merely to have put truths already known into a uselessly technical and pedantic form.

DIAGRAMS

In order to expound my proposition that all necessary reasoning is diagrammatic, it is requisite that I explain exactly what I mean by a Diagram, a word which I employ in a wider sense than is usual. A Diagram, in my sense, is in the first place a Token, or singular Object used as a Sign; for it is essential that it should be capable of being perceived and observed. It is, however, what is called a General sign; that is, it denotes a general Object. It is, indeed, constructed with that intention, and thus represents the Object of that intention. Now the Object of an intention, purpose, or desire is always General. The Diagram represents a definite Form of Relation. This Relation is usually one which actually exists, as in a map, or is intended to exist, as in a Plan. But this is so far from being essential to the Diagram as such, that if details are added to represented existential or experiential peculiarities, such additions are distinctly of an undiagrammatic nature. The pure Diagram is designed to represent and to render intelligible, the Form of Relation merely. Consequently, Diagrams are restricted to the representation of a certain class of relations; namely, those that are intelligible. We may make a diagram of the Battle of Gettysburgh, because in a certain [sense], it may thus be rendered comprehensible. But we do not make a diagram simply to represent the relation of killer to killed, though it would not be impossible to represent this relation in a Graph-Instance; and the reason we do not is that there is little or nothing in that relation that is rationally comprehensible. It is known as a fact, and that is all. I believe I may venture to affirm that an intelligible relation, that is, a relation of thought, is created only by the act of representing it. I do not mean to say that if we should some day find out the metaphysical nature of the relation of killing, that intelligible relation would thereby be created. For if such be the nature of killing, such it always was, from the date of a certain "difficulty" and consurrection in a harvest field. No; for the intelligible relation has been signified, though not read by man, since the first killing was done, if not long before. The thought of God,—if the anthropomorhism is too distasteful to you, you can say the thought in the universe,—had represented it. At any rate, a Diagram is clearly in every case a sign of an ordered Collection or Plural,—or, more accurately, of the ordered Plurality or Multitude, or of an Order in Plurality. Now a Plural,—say, for example, Alexander, Hannibal, Caesar, and Napoleon,—seems unquestionably to be an *ens rationis,* that is to be created by the very representation of it; and Order appears to be of the same nature; that is, to be an Aspect, or result of taking account of things in a certain way. But these are subtle points; and I should like to give the question maturer consideration before risking much on the correctness of my solution. No such doubt bedims our perception that it is as an Icon that the Diagram represents the definite Form of intelligible relation which constitutes its Object, that is, that it represents that Form by a more or less vague resemblance thereto. There is not usually much vagueness, but I use that word because the Diagram does not itself define just how far the likeness extends, and in some characteristic cases such definition would be impossible, although the Form of Relation is in itself Definite, since it is General. It is, however, a very essential feature of the Diagram *per se* that while it is as a whole an Icon, it yet contains parts which are capable of being recognized and distinguished by the affixion to each of a distinct Semantic Index (or Indicatory Seme, if you prefer this phrase). Letters of the alphabet commonly fulfil this office. How characteristic these Indices are of the Diagram is shown by the fact that though in one form or another they are indispensable in using the diagram, yet they are seldom wanted for the general enunciation of the proposition which the Diagram is used for demonstrating. That which is most of all requisitionable from a definition of an artificial contrivance such as a Diagram is, is that it should state what the Definition does and what it is for; so that these points must now be touched upon even at the risk that this Definition of a Diagram might be threatened with danger to its absolute preeminence over all others, of what sort soever, that ever have been or ever shall be given, in respect to the chief grace of definitions, that of Brevity. That which every sign does is to determine its Interpretant. The responsive Interpretant, or Signification, of one kind of signs is a vague presentation, of another kind is an Action, while of a third it is involved in a Habit and is General in its nature. It is to this third class that a Diagram belongs. It has to be interpreted according to Conventions embodied in Habits. One contemplates the Diagram, and one at once prescinds from the accidental characters that have no significance. They disappear altogether from one's understanding of the Diagram; and although they be of a sort which no visible thing be without (I am supposing the diagram to be of the visual kind), yet their [disappearance] is only an understood disappearance and does not prevent the features of the Diagram, now become a Schema, from being subjected to the scrutiny of observation. By what psychical apparatus this may get effected the logician does not inquire. It suffices for him, that one can contemplate the Diagram and perceive that it has certain features which would always belong to it however its insignificant features might be changed. What is true of the geometrical diagram drawn on paper would be equally true of the same Diagram when put on the blackboard. The assurance is the same as that of any description of what we see before our eyes. But the action of the Diagram does not stop here. It has the same percussive action on the Interpreter that any other Experience has. It does not stimulate any immediate counter-action, nor does it, in its function as a Diagram, contribute particularly to any expectation. As Diagram, it excites curiosity as to the effect of a transformation of it. . . .

DIAGRAM OBSERVATION

. . . Modern exact logic shows that every operation of deductive reasoning consists of four steps as follows:

1st, a diagram, or visual image, whether composed of lines, like a geometrical figure, or an array of signs, like an algebraical formula, or of a mixed nature, like a graph, is constructed, so as to embody in iconic form, the state of things asserted in the premise (there will be but one premise, after all that is known

and is pertinent is collected into one copulative proposition).

2nd, Upon scrutiny of this diagram, the mind is led to suspect that the sort of information sought may be discovered, by modifying the diagram in a certain way. This experiment is tried.

3rd. The results of the experiment are carefully *observed*. This is genuine experiential observation, even though the diagram exists only in the imagination; for after it has once been created, though the reasoner has power to change it, he has no power to make the creation already past and done different from what it is. It is, therefore, just as real an object as if drawn on paper. Included in this observation is the analysis of what is seen and the representation of it in general language. What is so observed is a new relation between the parts of the diagram not mentioned in the precept by which it was constructed.

4th, By repeating the experiment, or by the similarity of the experiment to many others which have often been repeated without varying the result, the reasoner infers inductively, with a degree of probability practically amounting to certainty, that every diagram constructed according to the same precept would present the same relation of parts which has been observed in the diagram experimented upon. . . .

TWO KINDS OF DEDUCTION

In my opinion, excepting Metaphysics there is no science that is more in need of the science of Logic than Psychology proper is. On the other hand, I found Logic largely on a study which I call Phaneroscopy, which is the keen observation of and generalization from the direct Perception of what we are immediately aware of. I find there are three kinds of possible warrant for a Belief. Here is this distressing number 3 again, against which you seem to have sworn eternal enmity, but which *will* turn up again and again. I don't think you are willing to believe that space has three dimensions, are you? None of the 3 warrants is Positively Infallible although one of them is so in a Pickwickian sense. The first kind of warrant consists in the reasoner's being *disposed to believe* in his proposition. This goes toward warranting the belief, since the very undertaking to find out a truth one does not directly perceive assumes that things conform in a measure to what our reason thinks they should. In other words our Reason is akin to the Reason that governs the universe, we must assume that or despair of finding out anything. Now despair is always illogical; and we are warranted in thinking so, since otherwise all reasoning will be in vain. If it be so, a strong inward impulse to Believe a given proposition tends to show that proposition to be true; and if it be not so, we never can discover what we don't directly perceive, do what we may.

Dec. 28. I have been suffering horribly for 2 days and am now like a drowned rat. Juliette was also ill all last night and it sometimes seems all but hopeless to keep her alive through the winter if it is going to keep on as it has begun with 50°F only attainable for a couple of hours. My ink will freeze in a few days I hear and then what shall I do, I wonder. The second warrant is in case one's inference is from some state of things capable of expression in a proposition (generally a copulative proposition of some complexity) and when every state of things not denied by this proposition is a state of things in which the conclusion is true. Such inference is Deduction, or Necessary Inference. There are two kinds of Deduction; and it is truly significant that it should have been left for me to discover this. I first found, and subsequently *proved* {See P 296}, that every Deduction involves the observation of a Diagram (whether Optical, Tactical, or Acoustic) and having drawn the diagram (for I myself always work with Optical Diagrams) one finds the conclusion to be represented by it. Of course, a diagram is required to comprehend any assertion. My two genera of Deductions are 1st those in which any Diagram of a state of things in which the premisses are true represents the conclusion to be true and such reasoning I call *Corollarial* because all the corollaries that different editors have added to Euclid's Elements are of this nature. 2nd Kind. To the Diagram of the truth of the Premisses something else has to be added, which is usually a mere May-be and then the conclusion appears. I call this *Theorematic* reasoning because all the most important theorems are of this nature.

A very good example of this is the Ten Point Theorem whose diagram I have here drawn [Fig. 1]. If rays be drawn on a plane (or great circles on a hemisphere) so that three rays meet in one point, *O,* of the plane and on each of these rays two points, *A* and *a* on one, *B* and *b,* on another and *C* and *c* on the third; and if then from each of these six points two rays be drawn to 2 and the points on different rays through *O;* so that the new rays may be

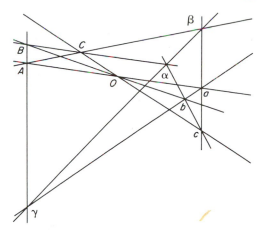

Fig. 1. Ten Point Theorem.

lettered *AB, AC, BC, ab, bc, ca,* there will be for each of the 3 rays through *O,* two of the six rays last drawn that do not pass through lettered points on that rays, but these two rays will cut each other and their three intersections; that is the intersection of *BC* and *bc,* which I mark, α, and the intersection of *CA* and *ca* which I mark, β, and the intersection of *AB* and *ab* which I mark γ *will lie on one ray!* Now for more than two centuries, if not for three in all, the greatest mathematicians have tried to prove *that* by the diagram required to exhibit it *alone,* and have tried in vain. But it is readily proved in several ways by additions to the diagram; as for example by imagining the ray *OBb* to be the shadow on projection of a ray through *O* but not on the plane of *AOCac.* It then becomes evident, from the fact that two flats of dimensions *M* and *N* lying in in a flat of dimensions *P* not greater than *M + N* necessarily have a flat of dimensions *M + N − P* in common. Thus 2 planes in a flat of 3 dimensions have 2 + 2 − 3 = 1 or a ray in common.

The 3rd kind of warrant is that which justifies the use of a method of inference provided it be carried out to the end consistently. There are 3 kinds of inference of this kind. They are all inferences from random samples. The strongest is that which is a sample (that is, a collection) of units. In that case, the theory of errors is applicable. The second kind is where there are no definite multitudes but where, as the sample is enlarged, the inference becomes stronger and stronger. The third kind which is the weakest of all forms of Induction is where the only defence is that if the conclusion is false, its falsity will *sometime* be detected if the method of inference be persisted in long enough. For example, if we infer from the fact that so closely as we have been able to measure, the sum of the angles of a triangle is 180°, therefore it is exactly so, the only warrant for this inference is that if we go on making our errors of measurement less and less, then if the sum be not exactly 180°, we shall ultimately find out that it is more or less if we persist in making the measurements. No inductive inference can be weaker than that and have any warrant at all.

Cenoscopy (Philosophy)

CENOSCOPY (PHILOSOPHY)

We now come to what particularly concerns us, *Cenoscopy,* or *Philosophy.* You will observe that I make this a branch of science upon which all special science including psychology depends, while the empirical philosophers generally, Comte, followed by his imitators Spencer and Fiske (and all their violent opposition to him only make their dependency more), as well as Wundt and many others, make philosophy to depend upon the special sciences. I do not however so totally disagree with them as would appear at first glance. On the contrary, I quite acknowledge that there is such a science as they call positive philosophy or Synthetic Philosophy or Cosmic Philosophy [or] by some other such name. That science stands in my opinion at the head of the Sciences of Review. But all these philosophers make one of the most disastrous mistakes possible in confounding this science with Cenoscopy, which must not depend upon the special sciences inasmuch as they, on the contrary, need to depend upon it.

The reason that I hold this unification of widely separated sciences to be so disastrous is that it leads to the most important questions, especially logical questions, never receiving any serious consideration at any time. One branch of cenoscopy is logic, and one branch of logic is methodeutic which should investigate the general principles upon which scientific studies should be carried on. But under the plan of these philosophers, logic is to be founded upon the study of all the other sciences. That is to say you are first to make your researches and after that inquire how they ought to be made, locking the barn door after the horse is already stolen. To be sure, those philosophers maintain that two sciences can be reciprocally dependent upon each other. But the question of whether they can be so dependent or not, than which no question is of greater importance to the well-being of science, never receives at their hands any serious study. The question is asked in the vaguest terms, without any exact determination of what kind of dependence is referred to; and is answered on the basis of a loose analogy to cases in which when the number of observations exceeds the number required to draw a conclusion the conclusion is utilized to correct the observations. They do not analyze the conditions under which such a thing is possible. For the reason that under their method they first assume an answer to it without any serious examination; and then having acted upon that hasty answer throughout, it has naturally lost all practical importance, and so never does get any serious consideration. If they were to analyze the case which they fancy sustains their notion of reciprocal dependence, they would see that, far from sustaining that idea, it is quite opposed to it. A student of one subject[,] say[,] Dr. A[,] may go to a student of another subject, say[,] Dr. B, and ask him a question and make use of his answer; and subsequently Dr. B who gave the answer may ask a question of Dr. A, and if it be a wholly independent question there is no reason why he should not derive solid information from him. But the idea that Doctors A and B can each supply the other with the very same information or with information virtually the same is ridiculous. I maintain that no two sciences can depend each upon results of the other for principles without which it cannot exist as a science. Now all the special sciences,—in particular, dynamics[,] the most fundamental of the physical sciences[,] and the science of association[,] the

From *MS* 1334, Adirondack Summer School Lectures, 1905.

most fundamental of the psychical sciences,—depend for their existence as sciences upon principles which only the metaphysician can properly discuss. To show how differently the ultra empiricists think, I will quote a sentence from the second edition of Wundt's 'System der Philosophie.' He says: "Ich muss zugeben: wenn man es als ein Axiom betrachtet, metaphysiche Systeme Müssten unabhangig von allen Einflüssen des Einzelwissens, sozusagen durch eine wissenschaftliche *generatio aequivoca,* entstehen, so lasst sich gegen jene Meinung nicht viel einwenden. In der That glaube ich dass es einen Unterschied macht, wo man anfangt, und wo man aufhört. Da ich von den Naturwissenschaften ausgegangen und dann durch die Beschäftigung mit empirische Psychologie zur Philosophie gekommen bin, so wurde es mir unmöglich erscheinen anders zu philosophiren als nach eine Methode, die dieser Folge der Probleme enspricht."[1] It is that slur about the *generatio aequivoca* that I wish to call attention which implies that a doctrine which is not based upon a result of one of the *Einzelwissenschfaten,* or Special Sciences, has no basis at all. Now all such results depend upon logical principles without which no special science would have any credibility. It would therefore follow that logical principles are based on nothing at all, and that the special sciences which are based on those baseless principles have no solid basis, were it not that Wundt thinks that Logic and the Special Sciences, like two lying witnesses in court, sustain each other's credit. But according to me there are certain principles that no man doubts,—that *you* do not doubt in the least degree. Very vague, I confess, or rather insist, that they are; but still not entirely nonsensical; and that it is upon these principles of Common Sense that Logic and all Cenoscopy must rest; and since they are absolutely indubitable there can be no consistent dissatisfaction with them. These are not results of any special science, but on the contrary, antecede all scientific research and are taken for granted by all scientists. For scientific men are not sophists and wranglers over nothing, but are eminently men of Common Sense, that is of Human Instinct, beyond the gates of which it is impossible for men to push their criticism. I could not ask for more convincing support of this Common Sensism than is furnished by the ultra-empiricist Ernst Mach in his book "Die Mechanik in ihrer Entwickelung historisch-kritisch dargestellt."

NOTE

1. {I must admit: if one regards it as an axiom that metaphysical systems ought to arise independently of all influences of special sciences, so to speak by means of a scientific *generatio aequivoca* [equivocal or indeterminate generation], then there can be little objection to that opinion. In fact I believe that it makes a difference where one begins and one stops. Since I started out with the natural sciences, and then came to philosophy through my concern with empirical psychology, it seems impossible to me to philosophize other than according to a method which corresponds to this series of problems.}

Phaneroscopy (Phenomenology)

PHANEROSCOPY (PHENOMENOLOGY)

My views of Cenoscopy are, no doubt, immature. I have only been working on the problem some forty odd years and what can be expected from an infant: give me a hundred years more of vigor, be it in this body you see before you, or in that of some young man who will take up the work and find a successor, and we shall have something better than vague guessing. The division ought to be into three parts: *Phaneroscopy,* or *Protoscopy, Deuteroscopy,* and *Tritoscopy.*

Phaneroscopy is the description of the *phaneron;* and by the *phaneron* I mean the collective total of all that is in any way or in any sense present to the mind quite regardless of whether it corresponds to any real thing or

This section is from the following: *MS* 1334, Adirondack Summer School Lectures, 1905; *MS* 293, Prolegomena to an Apology for Pragmaticism, ca. 1903; *MS* 478, Syllabus of a Course of Lectures at the Lowell Institute beginning Nov. 23, 1903; and *The Century Dictionary Supplement,* pp. 217, 475, 981, 1189, and 1344.

not. If you ask present *when,* and to *whose* mind, I reply that I leave these questions unanswered, never having entertained a doubt that those features of the phaneron that I have found in my own mind are present at all times and to all minds. So far as I have developed this science of phaneroscopy it is occupied with the formal elements of the phaneron. I know that there is another series of elements imperfectly represented by Hegel's categories. But I have been unable to give any satisfactory account of them.

*   *   *

The System of Existential Graphs the development of which has only been begun by a solitary student, furnishes already the best diagram of the contents of the logical Quasi-mind that has ever yet been found and promises much future perfectionment. Let us call the collective whole of all that could ever be present to the mind in any way or in any sense, the *Phaneron.* Then the substance of every Thought (and of much beside Thought proper) will be a Constituent of the Phaneron. The Phaneron being itself far too elusive for direct observation, there can be no better method of studying it than through the Diagram of it which the System of Existential Graphs puts at our disposition. We have already tasted the first-fruits of this method, we shall soon gather more, and I, for my part, am in confident hope that by-and-by (not in my brief time) a rich harvest may be garnered by this means.

What, in a general way, does the Diagram of Existential Graphs represent the mode of structure of the Phaneron to be like? The question calls for a comparison, and in answering it a little flight of fancy will be in order. It represents the structure of the Phaneron to be quite like that of a chemical compound. In the imagined representation of the Phaneron (for we shall not, as yet, undertake actually to construct such a Graph), in place of the ordinary spots, which are Graphs not *represented* as compound, we shall have Instances of the absolutely Indecomposable Elements of the Phaneron (supposing it has any ultimate constituents, which, of course, remains to be seen, until we come to the question of their Matter; and as long as we are, as at present, discoursing only of their possible Forms, their being may be presumed), which [are] close enough analogues of the Atoms in the Chemical Graph of "Rational Formula." Each Elementary Graph, like each chemical element, has its definite Valency,—the number

of Pegs {i.e. loose ends, compare free ions in chemistry.} on the periphery of its Instance,— and the Lines of Identity (which never branch) will be quite analogous to the chemical bonds. This is resemblance enough. It is true that in Existential Graphs we have the Cuts, to which nothing in the chemical Graph corresponds. Not yet, at any rate. We are now just beginning to rend away the veil that has hitherto enshrouded the constitution of the proteid bodies; but whatever I may conjecture as to those vast super-molecules, some containing fifteen thousand molecules, whether it seems probable on chemical grounds, or not, that they contain groups of opposite polarity from the residues outside those groups, and whether or not similar polar submolecules appear within the complex inorganic acids, it is certainly too early to take those into account in helping the exposition of the constitution of the phaneron. Were such ideas as solid as they are, in fact, vaporous, they ought to be laid aside until we have first thoroughly learned all the lessons of that analogy between the constitution of the phaneron and that of chemical bodies which consists in both the one and the other being composed of elements of definite valency.

In all natural classifications, without exception, distinctions of form, once recognized, take precedence over differences of matter. Who would now throw Iron, with its valency, perhaps, of eight, as used to be done, into the same class with Manganese, of valency seven, Chromium, with its valency of six (though these three all belong to the even fourth series), and Aluminum with valency three and in the odd series three, rather than with Nickel and Cobalt, and even along with Ruthenium, Rhodium, and Palladium of the sixth series, and with the tenth-series Osmium, Iridium, and Platinum? Or who would for one instant liken ordinary alcohol to methyl ether (which has the same Material composition) instead of with the alcoholates? The same precedence of Form over Matter is seen in the classification of psychical products. Some of Rafael's greatest pictures,—the Christ bearing the cross, for example,—are suffused with a brick red tinge, intended, I doubt not, to correct for the violet blueness of the deep shade of the chapels in which they were meant to be hung. But who would classify Rafael's paintings according to their predominant tinges instead of according to the nature of the composition, or the stages of Rafael's development? There is no need of insisting upon a matter so obvious. Besides there is a rational explanation of the precedence of Form over Matter in natural classifications. For such classifications are intended to render the composition of the entire classified collection rationally intelligible,—no matter what else they may be intended to show; and Form is something that the mind can "take in," assimilate, and comprehend; while Matter is always foreign to it, and though recognizable, is incomprehensible. The reason of this, again, is plain enough: Matter is that by virtue of which an object gains Existence, a fact known only by an Index, which is connected with the object only by brute force; while Form, being that by which the object is such as it is, is comprehensible. It follows that, assuming that there are any indecomposable constituents of the Phaneron, since each of these has a definite Valency, or number of Pegs to its Graph-Instance, this is the only Form, or, at any rate, the only intelligible Form, the Element of the Phaneron can have, the Classification of Elements of the Phaneron must, in the first place, be classified according to their Valency, just as are the chemical elements.

We call a Spot a Medad, Monad, Dyad, Triad, Tetrad, or by some other such name, according as its Valency, or the number of its Pegs, is 0, 1, 2, 3, 4, etc. It is to be remarked that a Graph not only has attachments to other Graphs through its Pegs and through Lines of Identity, but is also attached to the Area on which it is scribed, this Area being a Sign of a logical Universe. But it is not the same kind of attachment, since the Entire Graph of the Area is after a fashion *predicated* of that Universe, while the Lines of Identity represent Individual Subjects of which the two connected Spots are predicated either being regarded as determining the other. There would therefore be a confusion of thought in adding one to the number of Pegs and calling the sum the Valency. It would rather be the sum of two different categories of Valency. But in the case of the Medad, where there is no Peg, the possibility of scribing the Graph upon an Area is the only Valency the Spot has,—the only circumstance that brings it and other thoughts together. For this reason, we can, without other than a Verbal inconsistency, due to the incompleteness of our Terminology, speak of a Medad as a Monad. For some purposes, it is indispensable so to regard it.

* * *

In classification generally, it may fairly be said to be established, if it ever was doubted,

that Form, in the sense of structure is of far higher significance than Material. Valency is the basis of all external structure; and where indecomposability precludes internal structure,—as in the classification of elementary concepts,—valency ought to be made the first consideration. I term [this] the doctrine of *cenopythagoreanism.*

* * *

Now, before we go on to further conventions, let us [see to] what the three already admitted lead. The different figures are all supposed to be scribed on the *recto* {page}, and we will agree that the universe of discourse shall consist of all human persons now living on the earth.

Fig. 1.

The dot of Fig. 1 denotes then some person now living on the globe to whom the description witch applies; so that the whole asserts that a witch now lives on earth.

Fig. 2.

The dot of Fig. 2, which denotes some person now living who is described as a witch and as rich; so that the whole asserts that some rich witch exists, or some witch is rich.

Fig. 3.

The line of Fig. 3 is a continuum of contiguous dots, and contiguity signifies identity; so that the heavy line asserts the identity of the individuals denoted by its extremities; and the whole is equivalent to Fig. 2, asserting that some rich person is a witch. Any sign scribed on this system (which by the way is called the *System of Existential Graphs,* but must on no account be confounded with the System of En-titative Graphs expressed in Vol. VII of the *Monist*), and which expresses an assertion is called [a] *graph,* or, more accurately, an *existential graph,* whether it is disconnected or joined to other graphs. The term graph is taken in the sense of a type; and that which is actually on the paper is a *graph-instance.* But the word "scribe" is taken in such a sense that to put a graph-instance on any area is accurately described as "scribing the graph" of which it is an instance on the same area.

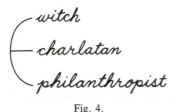

Fig. 4.

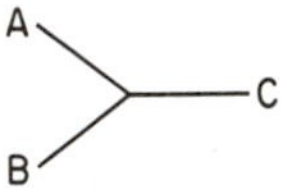

Fig. 5.

Fig. 4 introduces a point of branching of a line of identity, which is an instance of the graph of ter-identity, so that Fig. 5 means A is identical at once with B and with C. Fig. 4 asserts that some philanthropist is at once a witch and a charlatan, or there is a person who reunites the three characters of witch, charlatan, and philanthropist.

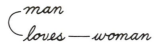

Fig. 6.

Fig. 6 asserts that some man loves a woman [.]

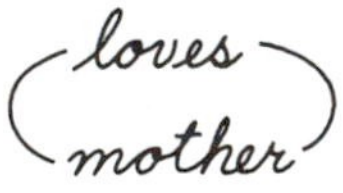

Fig. 7.

Fig. 7 asserts that some mother loves somebody of whom she is the mother.

Fig. 8.

Fig. 8 asserts that somebody steals something from a person and gives it back. (Here the universe embraces things as well as persons.)

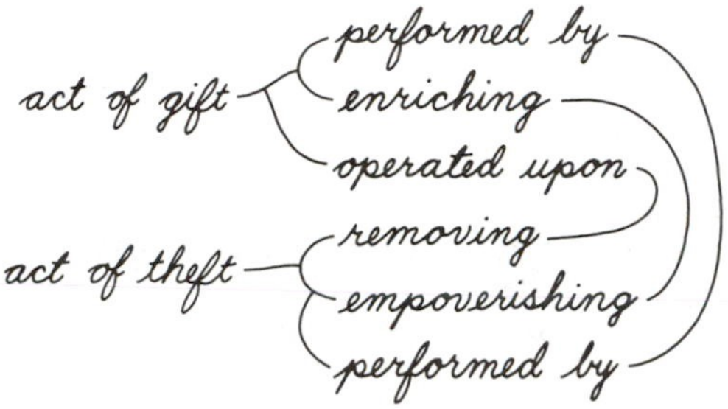

Fig. 9.

Fig. 9 asserts the same thing, but in such a way that the only triadic graph instances are those of teridentity, by introducing acts into the universe. It is, however, easy to see that there is here no genuine reduction of the triadic relations of giving and stealing into dyadic relations with the relation of teridentity. I will leave the precise formulation of the reason why it is not so, as a highly instructive exercise to be performed by you, dear reader. I shall thus be doing something in return for your amiability in wading through this screed slough. Above all, do not imagine that I am insincere in these expressions.

The conventions so far adopted enable us to translate and analyze but a very limited range of signs; and it would [be] rash in the extreme to adopt any generalization simply because it was sustained by these few instances. Yet by examining how certain points stand now, and holding our results over to be modified when the system is further developed, we shall be able to divide our difficulties and so conquer them with greater facility. In the first place, it is none too early to say a word or two in explanation of the purpose of this diagrammatization of the course of logical thinking. This system follows pretty closely in the footsteps of the logical algebras, and especially in that of the "Universal Algebra of

Logic" {e.g., *P* 167}, to which it might serve as an illuminative introduction, although it fulfills the principal common purpose of them and of it better, on the whole, than either of them do. It must not be supposed that the principal purpose even of the algebras is to furnish a method for passing from premisses to necessary conclusions. When a person first makes the acquaintance of Boolian algebra, never having heard of such a thing before, the fact that it works out the conclusions of complicated premisses semi-automatically strikes him as all but magical. This is natural; especially, as the person is likely to be pretty young; and thus he naturally gets the idea that the system is mainly, if not wholly, a calculus in the most wooden sense. But in truth there is nothing that ought to be surprising in the matter, and the same power will necessarily be possessed by any mode of exact and analytical expression of propositions: for any such mode there must be a code of permissible transformations that can be applied to produce any necessary conclusions from the first assumptions and will never give rise to anything but such a conclusion. Still less was any system of mine designed to be employed as a pasigraphy, although I dare say a superior pasigraphy could be developed upon the basis of existential graphs. The chief purpose which governed the construction of the algebras and still more exclusively that of existential graphs has been the facilitation of logical analysis, and the resolution of problems in logic.

For example, one of the puzzling problems of logic is how concepts can be combined. If two concepts, A and B, are to be compounded, there must, it would seem, be needed a combining concept C,—a sort of cement joined at once to A and to B. But then the question recurs, How is C to be compounded with A, and how with B? But the System of Existential Graphs at once solves the enigma. If the two bonds of Fig. 6 were broken, its meaning would be "Something is a man; something is a woman; something loves something." When the bonds are joined these indefinite somethings explain each other. The compound states that the something that loves something is the something that is a man, while the something that that something loves is the something that is a woman. The two explicit indefinites mutually define each other. The expression "explicit indefinite" calls for a word of explanation. Any idea that can be diagrammatized by our first three conventions is indefinite in countless ways. That is, countless

questions might be asked as to what they refer to, and would remain unanswered in the idea itself. But the thought is not directed to them all. On the other hand the concept of "something" not only leaves a possible question as to what it refers to unanswered, but itself thinks of that question. That is what I call an "explicit indefinite." It is expressed by the loose end of a line of identity. If we convert any ordinary point of a line of identity on the recto into a point of teridentity by starting there a new branch of the line, then if the end of the new branch be left loose, we shall thus diagrammatize the operation of thought by which an implicit indefiniteness is made explicit.

After the bonds of Fig. 6 are both broken, the three resulting graphs are still united by virtue of all being attached to the same recto; so that the copulate judgment is diagrammatized, "There is a man, and something loves something, and there is a woman." But the mode of this composition does not differ in principle from the way by which, in the unseparated Fig. 6, the ideas of man and woman are joined. They are joined by their explicit indefinite being defined by the two explicit indefinites of "Something loves something." But this is precisely the thought expressed by a blank space of the recto which extends up to two loose ends of lines of identity, except that in the interpretations of the latter graph, "loves" is to be replaced by "is coexistent with." In this way we see that Fig. 6 with broken bonds expresses the thought "Some man is coexistent with something that loves something coexistent with a woman." That this analysis is correct will become evident if you reflect that the recto denotes the universe and that the placing of a dot upon the recto asserts that the something that dot denotes exists in the universe. Hence, if two separate dots are scribed on the recto, the whole expresses that the individuals those dots denote both exist in the same universe, that is, that they coexist. Indeed, we may once for all lay down the principle that any supposed analysis that can be represented in existential graphs as being an analysis must be a true analysis, provided the representation in existential graphs involves no iteration. The reason for this exception is that iteration is a device whereby two graphs may be combined without their combination being diagrammatized as such. This is the key of the problem about giving, as the reader has perhaps discovered. It appears, then, that, so far as we have as yet gone, all combination of concepts takes place by the mutual definition of indefinites; and it will be interesting to note whether or not this formula will require modification for cases not yet considered.

We have thus made a hopeful beginning in the task of constructing a system for diagrammatizing intellectual cognition. Before penetrating further we desiderate some synopsis, some forecast, of what lies before us. The domain of ideas (I purposely employ a vague term) and the domain of signs seem to coincide. Since, therefore, signs are considerably more tangible and overt to examination than ideas otherwise are, I will sketch out such a classification of signs as I can make in advance. Of course, having only studied signs during one brief life-time, I cannot know very much about them. I know, however, enough to see that the sketch of classification that I am about to give stands in some need of being more detailed, and to see how it could be carried into more detail. But I am restrained from doing this by the reflexion that if distinctions are made too fine and too numerous the mind cannot steadily retain a firm grasp of them. I proceed upon a principle adopted in advance of any particular examination of the different kinds of signs, and which is of such a nature as to be capable of giving a more or less detailed classification within almost any limits. But let it not be forgotten that I am only attempting such a classification as can be made almost entirely in advance of any acquaintance with signs.

I consider the essential structure of a sign. It has an Object and an Interpretant; or rather, more closely viewed, it has two Objects and three Interpretants. So then, three divisions of signs will be according to the mode of being of the sign, according to the nature of the Immediate Object, and according to the nature of [the] Immediate Interpretant. The Dynamical Object and the Dynamical Interpretant exist independently of the Sign; and therefore each affords two divisions of Signs, the one according to the mode of being of the Dynamical Correlate, the other according to the manner in which the Dynamical Object determines the Sign or the manner in which the Dynamical Interpretant is determined by the Sign. As for the Final Interpretant, that seems to necessitate three divisions of Signs, because besides its own various possible natures, and its dynamical relation to the sign, the Final Interpretant has a purposive relation to the Sign. Thus, in all, I make ten different divisions of signs.

I make each of these divisions a trichotomy,

and my reason for doing so, though the exposition of it is somewhat long, seems to me to be at every step as plain and commonsensible as anything could be. Yet some of those who have heard me develope it have, by some perverse ingenuity (as it appears to me), persuaded themselves that it is most abstruse, if not mystical, or even utterly unintelligible. My own candid opinion is that these men, whose intellectual insight I otherwise most warmly respect, have in this been thrown into a panic or other mental spasm on detecting in my plain pointings out of truth that anybody ought to see, some threatened danger to their darling theory of the universe. In my opinion, however, it is logic that ought to determine metaphysics, and not metaphysics logic. I should be glad to learn what my present readers think of my reasons.

I invite you, Reader, to turn your attention to a subject which, at first sight, seems to have as little to do with signs as anything could. It is what I call the *Phaneron,* meaning the totality of all that is before or in your mind, or mine, or any man's, in any sense in which that expression is ever used. There can be no psychological difficulty in determining whether anything belongs to the Phaneron, or not; for whatever seems to be before the mind *ipso facto* is so, in my sense of the phrase. I invite you to consider, not everything in the Phaneron, but only its indecomposable elements, that is, those that are logically indecomposable, or indecomposable to direct inspection. I wish to make out a classification, or division, of these indecomposable elements; that is, I want to sort them into their different kinds according to their real characters. I have some acquaintance with two different such classifications, both quite true; and there may be others. Of these two I know of, one is as division according to the Form or Structure of the elements, the other according to their Matter. The two most passionately laborious years of my life were exclusively devoted to trying to ascertain something for certain about the latter; but I abandoned the attempt, as beyond my powers, or, at any rate, unsuited to my genius. I had not neglected to examine what others had done but could not persuade myself that they had been more successful than I. Fortunately, however, all taxonomists of every department have found classifications according to structure to be the most important.

A reader may very intelligently ask, How is it possible for an indecomposable element to have any differences of structure? Of internal logical structure it would be clearly impossible. But of external structure, that is to say, structure of its possible compounds, limited differences of structure are possible; witness the chemical elements, of which the "groups," or vertical columns of Mendeleef's table, are universally and justly recognized as ever so much more important than the "series," or horizontal ranks in the same table. These columns are characterized by their several valencies, thus:

He, Ne, A, Kr, are medads (μηα none + the patronymic − ιαης);

H, L, Na, K, Cu, Rb, Ag, Cs, -, -, Au, are monads;

G, Mg, Ca, Zn, Sr, Cd, Ba, -, -, Hg, Rd, are dyads;

B, Al, Sc, Ga, Y, In, La, -, Yb, Tl, Act, are triads;

C, Si, Ti, Ge, Zr, Sn, Ce, -, -, Pb, Th, are tetrads;

N, P, V, As, Cb, Sb, Pr, -, Ta, Bi, Po, are properly pentads (as PCl_5, though owing to the junction of two pegs they often appear as triads[;] their pentad character is particularly required to explain certain phenomena of albumins);

O, S, Se, Cr, Se, Mo, Te, Nd, -, W, -, U, are properly hexads (though by junction of bonds they usually appear as dyads);

F, Cl, Mn, Br, -, I, are properly heptads (usually appearing as monads); Fe, Co, Ni, Ru, Rh, Pd, -, -, -, Os, Ir, Pt, are octads;

(Sm, Eu, Gd, Er, Tb, Bz, Cl, are not yet placed in the table.)

So, then, since elements may have structure through valency, I invite the reader to join me in a direct inspection of the valency of elements of the Phaneron. Why do I seem to see my reader draw back? Does he fear to be compromised by my bias, due to preconceived views? Oh, very well; yes, I do bring some convictions to the inquiry. But let us begin by subjecting these to criticism, postponing actual observation until all preconceptions are disposed of, one way or the other.

First, then, let us ask whether or not valency is the sole formal respect in which elements of the Phaneron can possibly vary. But seeing that the possibility of such a ground of division is dependent upon the possibility of multivalence, while the possibility of a division according to valency can in no wise be regarded as a result of relations between bonds, it follows that any division by variations of such relations must be taken as secondary to the division ac-

cording to valency, if such divisions there be. Now (my logic here may be puzzling, but it is correct), since my ten trichotomies of signs, should they prove to be independent of one another (which is, to be sure, logically improbable), would suffice to furnish us classes of signs to the number of

$$3^{10} = (3^2)^5 = (10 - 1)^5 = \begin{aligned} &10^5 - 5 \cdot 10^4 \\ &+10 \cdot 10^3 - 10 \cdot 10^2 \\ &+5 \cdot 10 - 1 \\ &= 50000 \\ &+ 9000 \\ &+ 49 \\ &= 59049 \end{aligned}$$

(*Voila* a lesson in vulgar arithmetic thrown in to boot!) which calculation rather threatens a multitude of classes too great to be conveniently carried in one's head, rather than a group inconveniently small, we shall, I think, do well to postpone preparations for further divisions until there be some prospect of such a thing being wanted.

If, then, there be any formal division of elements of the Phaneron, there must be a division according to valency; and we may expect medads, monads, dyads, triads, tetrads, etc. Some of these, however, can be antecedently excluded, as impossible; although it is important to remember that these divisions are not exactly like the corresponding divisions of Existential Graphs, which have relation only to explicit indefinites. In the present application, a medad must mean an indecomposable idea altogether severed logically from every other; a monad will mean an element which, except that it is thought as applying to some subject, has no other characters than these which are complete in it without any reference to anything else; a dyad will be an elementary idea of something that would possess such characters as it does possess relatively to something else but regardless of any third object of any category[;] a triad would be an elementary idea of something which should be such as it were relatively to two others in different ways, but regardless of any fourth, and so on. Some of these, I repeat, are plainly impossible. A medad would be a flash of mental "heat-lightning" absolutely instantaneous, Thunderless, unremembered, and altogether without effect.

It can further be said in advance, not, indeed, purely *a priori* but with the degree of apriority that is proper to {signs} logic, namely, as a necessary deduction from the fact that there are signs, that there must be an elementary triad. For were every element of the Phaneron a monad or a dyad, without the relative of teridentity (which is, of course, a triad) it is evident that no triad could ever be built up. Now the relation of every sign to its Object and Interpretant is plainly a triad. A triad might be built of of pentads or of any higher perissid elements in many ways. But it can be proved,—and really with extreme simplicity, though the statement of the general proof is confusing,—that no [indecomposable] element can have a higher valency than three.[1]

* * *

Phenomenology is that branch of science which is treated in Hegel's *Phanomenologie des Geistes* (a work far too inaccurate to be recommended to any but mature scholars, though perhaps the most profound ever written) in which the author seeks to make out what are the elements or, if you please, the kinds of elements, that are invariably present in whatever is, in any sense, in mind. According to the present writer, these *universal categories* are three. Since all three are invariably present, a pure idea of any one, absolutely distinct from the others, is impossible; indeed, anything like a satisfactorily clear discrimination of them is a work of long and active meditation. They may be termed *Firstness, Secondness,* and *Thirdness.*

Firstness is that which is such as it is positively and regardless of anything else.

Secondness is that which is as it is in a *second* something's being as it is, regardless of any third.

Thirdness is that whose being consists in its bringing about a secondness.

There is no Fourthness that does not merely consist in Thirdnesses.

Of these three, Secondness is the easiest to comprehend, being the element that the rough-and-tumble of this world renders most prominent. We talk of *hard* facts. That hardness, that compulsiveness of experience, is Secondness. A door is slightly ajar. You try to open it. Something prevents. You put your shoulder against it, and experience a sense of effort and a sense of resistance. These are not two forms of consciousness; they are two aspects of one two-sided consciousness. It is inconceivable that there should be any effort without resistance, or any resistance without a contrary effort. This double-sided consciousness is Secondness. All consciousness, all being awake, consists in a sense of reaction between *ego* and *non-ego*, al-

though the sense of effort be absent. It is a peculiarity of Secondness that in whatever field it presents itself there are two forms in which it may present itself; and these two forms differ in the Secondness being more thoroughly genuine in the one than in the other. Thus, reaction with a sense of striving, which we regard as brought on by ourselves, is volition. The Secondness there is strong. But in perception there is a sense of reaction without striving, which we think of as belonging to the outward thing. It is, as we may say, a *degenerate*[2] form of Secondness. The idea of Secondness seems here to be unnecessarily imported into the phenomenon, which might have been regarded as a mere dream, or rather as the quality of our being, without being materially different, except in the absence of the element of Secondness. Secondness cannot be thus eliminated from the phenomenon of volition. So both volition and perception can be exercized upon our own consciousness, giving rise to the conception [of] an Internal world,—which is nothing but consciousness with a Secondness imported into it,—and an External world. We not only thus experience Secondness, but we attribute it to outward things; which we regard as so many individual objects, or quasi selves, reacting on one another. Secondness only is while it actually is. The same thing can never happen twice. As Heraclitus said, one cannot cross the same river twice.[3] ποταμγαρ ο υΚεθη εμβηυα τ αυτ ῳ.

For an example of Firstness, look at anything red. That redness is positively what it is. Contrast may heighten our consciousness of it; but the redness is not relative to anything; it is absolute, or positive. If one imagines or remembers red, his imagination will be either vivid or dim, but that will not, in the least, affect the quality of the redness, which may be brilliant or dull, in either case. The vividness is the degree of our consciousness of it, its reaction on us. The quality in itself has no vividness or dimness. In itself, then, it cannot be consciousness. It is, indeed, itself, a mere possibility. Now consciousness is either awake (more or less) or it has no being at all. Possibility, the mode of being of Firstness, is the embryo of being. It is not nothing. It is not existence. We not only have an immediate acquaintance with Firstness in the qualities of feelings and sensations, but we attribute it to outward things. We think that a piece of iron has a quality in it that a piece of brass has not, which *consists* in the steadily continuing *possibility* of its being attracted by a magnet. In fact, it seems undeniable that there really are such possibilities, and that though they are not existences, they are not *nothing*. They are possibilities, and nothing more. But whether this be admitted or not, it is undeniable that such elements are in the objects as we commonly conceive them; and that is all that concerns phenomenology. Firstness is too simple to have any degenerate form.

Thirdness is found wherever one thing brings about a Secondness between two things. In all such cases, it will be found that Thought plays a part. By thought is meant something like the meaning of a word, which may be "embodied," that is, may govern, this or that, but it is not confined to any existent. Thought is often supposed to be something in consciousness; but on the contrary, it is impossible ever actually to be directly conscious of thought. It is something to which consciousness will conform, as a writing may conform to it. Thought is rather of the nature of a habit, which determines the suchness of that which may come into existence, when it does come into existence. Of such a habit one may be conscious of a symptom; but to speak of being directly conscious of a habit, as such, is nonsense. In a still fuller sense, Thirdness consists in the formation of a habit. In any succession of events that have occurred there must be some kind of regularity. Nay, there must be regularities strictly exceeding all multitude. But as soon as time adds another event to the series, a great part of those regularities will be broken, and so on indefinitely. If, however, there be a regularity that never will be and never would be broken, that has a mode of being consisting in this destiny or determination of the nature of things that the endless future shall conform to it. That is what we call a *law*. Whether any such law be discoverable or not, it is certain we have the idea of such a thing, and should there be such a *law*, it would evidently have a *reality, consisting in* the fact that predictions based on it would be borne out by actual events. Nobody can doubt that we know laws upon which we can base predictions to which actual events still in the womb of the future will conform to a marked extent, if not perfectly. To deny reality to such laws is to quibble about words. Many philosophers say they are "mere symbols." Take away the word *mere,* and this is true. They are symbols; and symbols being the only things in the universe that have any importance, the word "mere" is a great impertinence. In short, wherever there is thought there is Thirdness. It is genuine Thirdness that gives thought its characteristic, although Thirdness consists in nothing but one thing's bringing two into Second-

ness. In whatever field we find Thirdness, we find it occurring in three forms, whereof two are related to one another somewhat as the degenerate and genuine forms of Secondness, while the third has a living character that the others want.

In order to understand logic, it is necessary to get as clear notions as possible of these three categories and to gain the ability to recognize them in the different conceptions with which logic deals.

* * *

cenopythagorean (sen″ō-pi-thag-ō-rē′an), a. (Gr. Καιθνος, recent, new, + E. *Pythagorean.*) Of or pertaining to a modern doctrine which resembles Pythagoreanism in accepting universal categories that are related to and are named after numbers.

Cenopythagorean phenomenology, universal phenomenology as it is understood by those who recognize the categories of *firstness, secondness,* and *thirdness*

firstness, n. 2. In the phenomenology of C.S. Peirce, the mode of being of that which is whatever it is regardless of anything else. This is true only of qualities of feeling, such as red or scarlet, and of such qualities of a similar nature as we suppose things to possess. Thus, although hardness consists in resistance to being scratched by a second thing, yet our ordinary common-sense conception is that a hard body possesses in itself a quality which it retains although it never comes into contact with another, and that this quality, which it possesses regardless of anything else and would possess though all of the universe never existed, is the cause of the difficulty of scratching it. The mode of being of such an internal quality is *firstness*. That which has firstness can have no parts, because the being of an object which has parts consists in the being of the parts, which are none of them the whole. Any analysis of the constituents of a quality is a description of something found to be true of whatever possesses that quality. But a quality of feeling, as it is in its mode of being as a quality, has no parts.

secondness . . . , n. 2. (a) The mode of being of an object which is such as it is by virtue of being connected with or related to another object or objects, regardless of any triadic relation. (b) The mode of connection or relation of such an object with such another. (c) In a looser sense, the secundal, or relative, character which belongs to an individual object, as having such a mode of being.

thirdness . . . n. 2. The mode of being of that which is such as it is by virtue of a triadic relation which is incapable of being defined in terms of dyadic relations.

NOTES

1. {In a very important manuscript of 1897 (as yet unpublished), entitled "On Logical Graphs" (*MS* 482), Peirce gave a mathematical account of what might be called Valency Analysis (VA). In late manuscripts (the preceding one, for example) and letters, he often referred to this or its results, even in the last year of his life describing it as his "most lucid and interesting paper" (*MS L* 477). Working from within mathematical topology and early graph theory, in this MS Peirce gave a very general definition of a logical graph, then used those ideas to develop two graphical logic systems, the Entitative and the Existential. The latter system soon showed itself to be the most generally useful. However, while Peirce's graphical logic has been well discussed, the underlying ideas associated with VA have not. Moreover, VA is important for understanding his later work in general. So here is a quick summary of the results of Peirce's Valency Analysis.

The quickest access to it is by way of relations. Here is a dyadic relation: The fire caused an explosion. If we think of this relation independently of the things it relates, we might express it as "_____ caused _____." We thereby generalize the subjects of the causal relation. Peirce went one step further (in *MS* 482 and elsewhere) by also generalizing the relation proper. One can think of his move here as a "black box" step. Thus, our example becomes

where the dark dot is the relation, the content of which is no longer known. Its two arms, or "loose ends," are the things (unspecified) that are related by the black box. Such a diagram allows one to see only the "external form" of the original relation. Here are drawings of a monad, a triad, a tetrad, and a pentad treated in that same fashion.

The valency of any combination of the above kind of graphs is determined simply by counting the number of loose ends. For instance, the valency of the above entire line of graphs is 13.

The outer tips of loose ends represent places where connections with tips of other loose ends may occur. To connect two loose ends is to bond or compose. Composition in this system ALWAYS occurs using TWO AND ONLY TWO loose ends (compare Peirce's discussion, above, of "explicit indefiniteness"). Now, in any graph that has at least one bond, the overall valency will be given by this rule:

Valency of the overall graph is equal to the sum of the valencies of the component graphs imagined without bonds minus two times the number of bonds.

Here are two examples, drawn with "+" (to aid you in visualizing) at the places where two loose ends have been bonded; the third example is drawn without an aid.

It follows as a corollary of this rule that no oddly valent graph can be composed exclusively of evenly valent graphs. Since the above rule is true of all graphs in VA, if we assumed that an oddly valent graph was made entirely of evenly valent graphs, we would get the absurd consequence that an oddly valent graph has a valency equal to the sum of only even numbers minus an even number (two times any number gives an even number). So the corollary holds that no odd graph can be made only from even graphs. This means that within this system, triads cannot be composed of dyads only. Notice also that, by definition, monads are indecomposable into more elementary things. If a monad bonds with another monad, a graph of zero valency (a medad) results. If a dyad bonds with a monad, a monad is produced. If a dyad bonds with another dyad, another dyad results; or from one dyad a medad may be produced. A triad may produce a monad if two of its loose ends are bonded. Two triads and two bonds will produce a dyad. Three triads and three bonds will produce a triad. But more important, two triads and one bond will produce a tetrad. And in general, tetrads and higher relations may be composed from $N - 2$ triads. Thus, a pentad may be composed of $5 - 2$, or 3, triads and 2 bonds; an octad may be composed of $8 - 2$, or 6, triads and 5 bonds.

These results, if applied to relations in general, suggest the general formal properties of Peirce's categories: (a) Firsts (monads), Seconds (dyads), and Thirds (triads) are unique (not derived from something more elementary within the system of VA); (b) Thirds are not reducible to Seconds (a slightly more general form of the corollary of the valency rule); Firsts, Seconds, and Thirds are complete, in the sense that with them the external form of all relations can in principle be derived (compare the rule that allows tetrads and higher relations to be made from combinations of a more elementary form, the triad); (c) Firsts and Seconds are contained within Thirds (in that triads may be bonded in ways to produce monads or dyads or triads).

The system of VA was widely applied by Peirce in his later work, much as a mathematical physicist might apply any mathematical hypothesis considered possibly relevant to some particular problem under study. Failure to take note of VA can produce some serious misunderstandings of Peirce. For instance, semioticists often display Peirce's notion of a sign relation with a triangle (where O, R, and I are the Object, Representamen, and Interpretant, respectively):

Peirce would have rejected this, for it displays a sign relation (the overall diagram) as composed entirely of dyads (as if it were reducible to an appropriate collection of efficient causal relations). One of the most important doctrines of his semeiotic is that signs are irreducible triadic relations. A more appropriate diagram for the sign relation "R represents O to I" would be (where S is the sign relation triad proper):

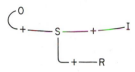

It seems to me that once one gives Peirce the applied system of VA, his position is logically reasonably tight. Probably the place his approach is most vulnerable to attack is the point at which his mathematical hypothesis is first applied to philosophical subject matter. Of course, Peirce was a man who regarded philosophy as a science in which such hypotheses were tested, and ultimately confirmed or disconfirmed.}

2. This term is borrowed from the geometers who speak of a pair of complanar rays as a "degenerate conic." That is, the idea of their being a conic is unnecessarily imported.

3. These cannot be the very words of Heraclitus. But I have taken one of the more epigrammatic of half a dozen versions. The one most likely to be the correct quotation is too tame.

Normative Science

NORMATIVE SCIENCE

There arose in the Lyceum after the death of Aristotle [a question] as to whether Logic was a Speculative or Practical Science, an Art, or an Organon. It is not worth while to explain the meanings of these terms. The dispute, like many others, continued long after its meaning had been forgotten; and to this day Normative Sciences are frequently confounded with Practical Sciences. They are, however, properly speaking pure sciences, although practical studies are joined to them, so that in part they are truly Practical Sciences. But the normative science proper is not a practical science but is a study in the pure interest of theory. The conception of a family of sciences of their description is, I believe, due to Herbart, together with the word *normative*.

If we are to admit only two normative sciences, the first of these, which for convenience we call *ethics* relating to *control of the existent,* or say to *actualization,* and the second to *thought,* then that first ethics must have two sections, the one on the ultimate aim, or *summum bonum,* which will be the same as esthetics, if esthetics is not to be confined to sensuous beauty, but is to relate to the admirable and adorable generally, while the other, which may be called *critical ethics* treats of the conditions of conformity to the ideal.

If a new word must be made to designate that first section, I will suggest that *axiagastics* be the name of the science of the worthy of adoration. For I hold that the science must consist in the analysis of that which is admirable without any ulterior reason for being admirable, or in other words the analysis of what it is that excites that feeling akin to worship that fills one's whole life in the contemplation of an idea that excites this feeling. We must suppose that primitive or barbarous

From *MS* 1334, Adirondack Summer School Lectures, 1905.

people hardly have this idea, since hardly any word in any language (as far as I know) expresses it. The French *beau* approximates it but is poor and cold. The primitive man found too much reason to think of the divine *not* as something to be passionately loved, but as something to be feared. Only the Greek αγαμαι is an exception[,] a glorious verb expressing how the common people in primitive times looked up to their leaders with passionate admiration and devotion[.] [It] comes the nearest to expressing the idea. Repeating the root, although the linguists do not say they are the same, I make the word *axiagastics,* for the science of that which is worthy to be admired and adored. But I am not thoroughly persuaded that Baumgarten's word *esthetics* will be too unwarrantably wrenched in being given this meaning.

Critical ethics will be the science of the general conditions of control; and it is easy to see that it comes chiefly to the doctrine of *self-control.*

Logic takes its start in that. It is but an application of ethics to thought. For *reasoning* differs from the formation of a new belief by the action of the association of ideas only by being a deliberate, controlled, piece of conduct.[1]

However, the one sole way to success in logic is to regard it as a science of signs; and I defined it in 1867 as the theory of the relation of symbols to their objects. Further experience has convinced me that the best plan is to consider logic as embracing more than that, and [as] the general theory of signs of all kinds, not merely in their relation to their objects but in every way.

This way of looking upon logic is the one salvation for the science. You will object. You will say, "What[,] have not these signs got to be understood by some mind?" I reply, yes, undoubtedly. But when you speak vaguely of some mind's understanding them, you mingle confusedly many circumstances, some of them essential, but furnishing no science until they are separated and each is definitely recognized in its precise functions and the merely accidental circumstances cleared away. What is thinking? It can only take place in signs. What is it to understand a sign? It is merely that the sign is interpreted in a sign in your minds. The whole function of the mind is to make a sign interpret itself in another sign and ultimately perhaps in an action or in an emotion. But the emotion is an idle thing unless it leads to an action. The action is an idle thing unless it produces a result which agrees with a sign through a sign. The whole problem is of signs; and if a

mind has to be taken into account, it should be considered in its relation to signs.

There will be no preparation for understanding these lectures, which, judging by great psychologists, are not easy to understand, and I may say I am sure they are quite impossible to understand from the psychological standpoint since they turn principally upon elements of experience that the psychologist takes pains to shut out from view,—I say there is no better preparation than that of spending an hour more or less, remembering for how very short a time attention can be on the stretch without relaxation, in spending then the remnants of an hour most of it given to rest and to bringing attention back, in thinking how thought is a discourse of the self that has been to the critical self that is coming. "I says to myself," say the wise unlearned. Thought is nothing but a tissue of signs. The objects concerning which thought is occupied are signs. To try to strip off the signs and get down to the very meaning itself is like trying to peel an onion and get down to the very onion itself. "You may get down, however, to actions," say some of the pragmatists. I beg their pardon. You may get down to resolutions to act. But they are not actions but signs of actions. Get down to the very actions themselves and you can no longer find in them the meanings of the signs. Let us talk about yonder chair. "Chair" is a word. It is a sign. The *Vorstellung* chair is a sign. What will you have[?] Get down to the very impressions of sense, and there is no chair there. The life we lead is a life of signs. Sign under sign endlessly. In one of my early papers, in the second volume of the Journal of Speculative Philosophy {*P* 26}, I compared the case to the dipping of an ivory object {a triangle arranged thus ▽} down into water. There will be at any instant, as the dipping proceeds, a water line, or locus which is at once occupied by air, water, and ivory. No matter at how early an instant in the dipping process we snap our mental camera, there will have been [a] line already. Where there has been no line already there is no line, but only a point.

Some men, like our dear James and like Thomas Davidson, the founder of this school, think that this [is] absurd. They think there must be a first line. That is, against the testimony of the sense or imagination they invoke logic. Well, we say to them, put the argument, if there be one into any syllogistic form. They are unable to do so. Very well, we say, if it cannot be put into any of the recognized forms of syllogism, tell us under what new form of reasoning you can put the argument that makes the testimony of fact absurd,—that makes it absurd that Achilles shall overtake the tortoise,—for that is the same thing. They are unable to do that. Then, we say do you mean to say that the real Achilles will not overtake the real tortoise is a fact? No, they admit that he will. So then, we say, we and all mathematicians, who are the only exact reasoners see no absurdity at all in this. But you have an inscrutable logic which cannot be reduced to any principle, which requires you from true premises to insist upon what you yourselves admit to be a false conclusion. What is logic *for,* if not to prevent the passage from true premises to false conclusions? To this, they have nothing to say, but they go their way still insisting that it is absurd that Achilles should overtake the tortoise. "Absurd," we call after them in a last appeal, ["]should mean contrary to reason, and you are unable to formulate this reason. Why not give up this logic and adopt that of all mathematicians?["] More ineradicable with them than reason itself is that tendency of theirs to consider the general, the law, as an existent thing. I do not see what remains to us, to whom the whole matter is perfectly clear, but to say that they are minds congenitally incapable of a necessary form of thought. Certainly a logic which leads one from true premises to admittedly false conclusions appears to us to be a poor form of logic; and when that logic is unable to formulate itself we are tempted to call it mental incapacity. Yet they base their whole philosophy [upon] this unhesitatingly. I for my part prefer to cast my lot with the mathematicians, whose logic does not kick up such capers, and is able to give an account of itself. "Well," says James, "I hate logic." I reply that I am sorry, but a philosophy ought not to be based upon that sentiment.

But though these gentlemen are unable to formulate their own logic, we have no diffi-culty at all in formulating it for them. They sometimes think that it is continuity only that they object to. They are mistaken. Continuity is not necessarily involved in what they pronounce absurd. What they find absurd is the endless. The very idea of the future, as endless, is to them absurd, though they may not at once see that it is. In short, though they think in signs like the rest of us, they do not really think in general signs, but only in such imperfect interpretations of them as can be made into images and slight inhibited efforts.

* * *

Having thus given you a preliminary idea of my point of view in the study of logic, I am going to impart to you a little of my doctrine . . . . For what I have been talking to you is not cenoscopy at all. It is taxospude.

NOTE

1. {From a variant page at *MS* 1334:42} Ethics is the Science of self-control. It has only two parts, according to me; for I turn the whole question of the *summum bonum* over to *axiagastics,* called *Esthetics,* thus making ethics to depend upon esthetics as many others have done. That leaves two things for ethics itself to do. The first is to describe the operation of self-control, not psychologically, that is, not as a student of the law of thinking ought to describe it, but as it presents itself as a problem to the psychologist to explain it. The other part of ethics, I call critical ethics. It is not far from what is called casuistry, except that unlike that it does not consist in dealing with cases. It tells to what conditions conduct must conform in order to be right. Logic is an application of ethics, just as ethics is an application of *axiagastics*[.] For the difference between reasoning and the creation of a new belief by the association of ideas is that reasoning is *self-controlled thought,* or thought *tamed and trained.*

Esthetics

What does right reasoning consist in? It consists in such reasoning as shall be conducive to our ultimate aim. What, then, is our ultimate aim? Perhaps it is not necessary that the logician should answer this question. Perhaps it might be possible to deduce the correct rules of reasoning from the mere assumption that we have some ultimate aim. But I cannot see how this could be done. If we had, for example, no other aim than the pleasure of the

From *MS* 449, Lowell Lectures, "Second Draught," 1903.

moment, we should fall back into the same absence of any logic that the fallacious argument would lead to. We should have no ideal of reasoning, and consequently no norm. It seems to me that the logician ought to recognize what our ultimate aim is. It would seem to be the business of the moralist to find this out, and that the logician has to accept the teaching of ethics in this regard. But the moralist, as far as I can make it out, merely tells us that we have a power of self-control, that no narrow or selfish aim can ever prove satisfactory, that the only satisfactory aim is the broadest, highest, and most general possible aim; and for any more definite information, as I conceive the matter, he has to refer us to the esthetician, whose business it is to say what is the state of things which is most admirable in itself regardless of any ulterior reason. So, then, we appeal to the esthete to tell us what it is that is admirable without any reason for being admirable beyond its inherent character. Why, that, he replies is the beautiful. Yes, we urge, such is the name that you give to it but what *is it?* What is this character? If he replies that it consists in a certain quality of feeling, a certain *bliss,* I for one decline altogether to accept the answer as sufficient. I should say to him, My dear Sir, if you can prove to me that this quality of feeling that you speak of does, as a fact, attach to what you call the beautiful, or that which would be admirable without any reason for being so, I am willing enough to believe you; but I cannot without strenuous proof admit that any particular quality of feeling is admirable without a reason. For it is too revolting to be believed unless one is forced to believe it. A fundamental question like this, however practical the issues of it may be, differs entirely from any ordinary practical question, in that whatever is accepted as good in itself must be accepted without compromise. In deciding any special question of conduct it is often quite right to allow weight to different conflicting considerations and calculate their resultant. But it is quite different in regard to that which is to be [the] aim of all endeavor. The object admirable that is admirable *per se* must, no doubt, be general. Every ideal is more or less general. It may be a complicated state of things. But it must be a *single* ideal; it must have *unity,* because it is an idea and unity is essential to every idea and every ideal. Objects of utterly disparate kinds may, no doubt, be admirable, because some special reason may make each one of them so. But

when it comes to the ideal of the admirable, in itself, its very nature of its being is to be a precise idea; and if somebody tells me it is either this, or that, or that other, I say to him, It is clear you have no *idea* of what precisely it is. But an ideal must be capable of being embraced in a unitary idea, or it is no ideal at all. Therefore, there can be no compromises between different considerations here. The admirable ideal cannot be too extremely admirable. The more thoroughly it has whatever character is essential to it, the more admirable it must be. Now what would the doctrine that that which is admirable in itself is a quality of feeling, come to if taken in all its purity and carried to its furthest extreme,—which should be the extreme of admirableness? It would amount to saying that the one ultimately admirable object is the unrestrained gratification of a desire, regardless of what the nature of that desire may be. Now that is too shocking. It would be the doctrine that all the higher modes of consciousness with which we are acquainted in ourselves, such as love and reason, are good only so far as they subserve the lowest of all modes of consciousness. It would be the doctrine that this vast universe of Nature which we contemplate with such awe is good only to produce a certain quality of feeling. Certainly, I must be excused for not admitting that doctrine unless it be proved with the utmost evidence. So, then, what proof is there that it is true? The only reason for it that I have been able to learn is that *gratification, pleasure,* is the only conceivable result that is satisfied with itself; and therefore since we are seeking for that which is *fine* and *admirable* without any reason beyond itself, *pleasure, bliss,* is the only object which can satisfy the conditions. This is a respectable argument. It deserves consideration. Its premiss, that pleasure is the only conceivable result that is perfectly self-satisfied, must be granted. Only, in these days of evolutionary ideas which are traceable to the French Revolution as their instigator, and still further back to Galileo's experiment at [the] leaning tower of Pisa, and still further back to all the stands that have been made by Luther and even by Robert of Lincoln against attempts to bind down human Reason to any prescriptions fixed in advance,—in these days, I say, when these ideas of progress and growth have themselves grown up so as [to] occupy our minds as they now do, how can we be expected [to] allow the assumption to pass that the admirable in itself is any stationary result? The explanation of the circumstance that the only result that is satisfied with itself is a quality of feeling is that reason always looks forward to an endless future and expects endlessly to improve its results. Consider, for a moment, what Reason, as well as we can today conceive it, really is. I do not mean man's faculty which is so called from its embodying in some measure Reason, or Νους, as something manifesting itself in the mind, in the history of mind's development, and in nature. What is this reason? In the first place, it is something that never can have been completely embodied. The most insignificant of general ideas always involves conditional predictions or requires for its fulfillment that events should come to pass, and all that ever can have come to pass must fall short of completely fulfilling its requirements. A little example will serve to illustrate what I am saying. Take any general term whatever. I say of a stone that it is *hard*. That means that so long as the stone remains hard, every essay to scratch it by the moderate pressure of a knife will surely fail. To call the stone *hard* is to predict that no matter how often you try the experiment, it will fail every time. That innumerable series of conditional predictions is involved in the meaning of this lowly adjective. Whatever may have been done will not begin to exhaust its meaning. At the same time, the very being, of the General, of Reason, is of such a mode that this being *consists* in the Reason's actually governing events. Suppose a piece of carborundum has been made and has subsequently been dissolved in aqua regia without anybody at any time, so far as I know, ever having tried to scratch it with a knife. Undoubtedly, I may have good reason, nevertheless, to call it hard; because some actual fact has occurred such that Reason compels me to call it so, and a general idea of all the facts of the case can only be formed if I do call it so. In this case, my calling it hard is an actual event which is governed by that law of hardness of the piece of carborundum. But if there were no actual fact whatsoever which was meant by saying that the piece of carborundum was hard, there would be not the slightest meaning in the word hard as applied to it. The very being of the general, of reason, *consists* in its governing individual events. So, then, the essence of Reason is such that its being never can have been completely perfected. It always must be in a state of incipiency, of growth. It is like the character of a man which consists in the ideas that he will conceive and in the efforts that he will make, and which only develops as the occasions actually arise. Yet in all his life long no son of Adam has ever fully manifested what there was in him. So, then, the development of Reason requires as a part of it the occurrence of more individual events than ever can occur. It requires too all the coloring of all qualities of feeling, including pleasure in its proper place among the rest. This development of Reason consists, you will observe in embodiment, that is, in manifestation. The creation of the universe, which did not take place during a certain busy week, in the year 4004 B.C. but is going on today and never will be done, is this very developement of Reason. I do not see how one can have a more satisfying ideal of the admirable than the development of reason so understood. The one thing whose admirableness is not due to an ulterior Reason is Reason itself comprehended in all its fullness, so far as we can comprehend it. Under this conception, the ideal of conduct will be to execute our little function in the operation of the creation by giving a hand toward rendering the world more reasonable whenever, as the slang is, it is "up to us," to do so. In logic, it will be observed that knowledge is reasonableness; and the ideal of reasoning will be to follow such methods as must develope knowledge the most speedily. . . .

Ethics

In order that my use of terms, notations, etc., may be understood, I explain that my conscience imposes upon me the following rules.

Were I to make the smallest pretension to dictate the conduct of others in this matter, I should be reproved by [the] first of these rules.

From "The Ethics of Terminology," *Syllabus of Certain Topics of Logic* (P 1035). (Boston: Mudge, 1903).

Yet if I were to develop the reasons the force of which I feel myself, I presume they would have weight with others.

Those reasons would embrace, in the first place, the consideration that the woof and warp of all thought and all research is symbols, and the life of thought and science is the life inherent in symbols; so that it is wrong to say that a good language is *important* to good thought, merely; for it is of the essence of it. Next would come the consideration of the increasing value of precision of thought as it advances. Thirdly, the progress of science cannot go far except by collaboration; or, to speak more accurately, no mind can take one step without the aid of other minds. Fourthly, the health of the scientific communion requires the most absolute mental freedom. Yet the scientific and philosophical worlds are infested with pedants and pedagogues who are continually endeavoring to set up a sort of magistrature over thoughts and other symbols. It thus becomes one of the first duties of one who sees what the situation is, energetically to resist everything like arbitrary dictation in scientific affairs, and above all, as to the use of terms and notations. At the same time, a general agreement concerning the use of terms and of notations,—not too rigid, yet prevailing, with most of the co-workers in regard to most of the symbols, to such a degree that there shall be some small number of different systems of expression that have to be mastered,—is indispensable. Consequently, since this is not to be brought about by arbitrary dictation, it must be brought about by the power of rational principles over the conduct of men.

Now what rational principle is there which will be perfectly determinative as to what terms and notations shall be used, and in what senses, and which at the same time possesses the requisite power to influence all right-feeling and thoughtful men?

In order to find the answer to that question, it is necessary to consider, first, what would be the character of an ideal philosophical terminology and system of logical symbols; and secondly, to inquire what the experience of those branches of science has been that have encountered and conquered great difficulties of nomenclature, etc., in regard to the principles which have proved efficacious, and in regard to unsuccessful methods of attempting to produce uniformity.

As to the ideal to be aimed at, it is, in the first place, desirable for any branch of science that it should have a vocabulary furnishing a family of cognate words for each *scientific* meaning, unless its different meanings apply to objects of different categories that can never be mistaken for one another. To be sure, this requisite might be understood in a sense which would make it utterly impossible. For every symbol is a living thing, in a very strict sense that is no mere figure of speech. The body of the symbol changes slowly, but its meaning inevitably grows, incorporates new elements and throws off old ones. But the effort of all should be to keep the *essence* of every scientific term unchanged and exact; although absolute exactitude is not so much as conceivable. Every symbol is, in its origin, either an image of the idea signified, or a reminiscence of some individual occurrence, person or thing, connected with its meaning, or is a metaphor. Terms of the first and third origins will inevitably be applied to different conceptions; but if the conceptions are strictly analogous in their principal suggestions, this is rather helpful than otherwise, provided always that the different meanings are remote from one another, both in themselves and in the occasions of their occurrence. Science is continually gaining new conceptions; and every new *scientific* conception should receive a new word, or better, a new family of cognate words. The duty of supplying this word naturally falls upon the person who introduces the new conception; but it is a duty not to be undertaken without a thorough knowledge of the principles and a large acquaintance with the details and history of the special terminology in which it is to take a place, nor without a sufficient comprehension of the principles of word-formation of the national language, nor without a proper study of the laws of symbols, in general. That there should be two different terms of identical scientific value may or may not be an inconvenience, according to circumstances. Different systems of expression are often of the greatest advantage.

The ideal terminology will differ somewhat for different sciences. The case of philosophy is very peculiar in that it has positive need of popular words in popular sense,—not as its own language (as it has too usually used those words), but as objects of its study. It thus has a peculiar need of a language distinct and detached from common speech, such a language as Aristotle, the scholastics, and Kant endeavored to supply, while Hegel endeavored to destroy it. It is good economy for philosophy to provide itself with a vocabulary so outlandish that loose thinkers shall not be tempted to borrow its words. Kant's adjectives "objective" and "subjective" proved not to be barbarous enough, by half, long to retain their usefulness in philosophy, even if there had been no other objection to them. The first rule of good taste in writing is to use words whose meanings will not be misunderstood; and if a reader does not know the meaning of the words, it is infinitely better that he should know he does not know it. This is particularly true in logic, which wholly consists, one might almost say, in exactitude of thought.

The sciences which have had to face the most difficult problems of terminology have unquestionably been the classificatory sciences of physics, chemistry and biology. The nomenclature of chemistry is, on the whole, good. In their dire need, the chemists assembled in congress, and adopted certain rules for forming names of substances. Those names are well-known, but they are hardly used. Why not? Because the chemists were not psychologists, and did not know that a congress is one of the most impotent of things, even less influential by far than a dictionary. The problem of the biological taxonomists has, however, been incomparably more difficult; and they have solved it (barring small exceptions) with brilliant success. How did they accomplish this? Not by appealing to the power of congresses, but by appealing to the power of the idea of right and wrong. For only make a man *really see* that a certain line of conduct is wrong, and he *will* make a strong endeavor to do the right thing,—be he thief, gambler, or even a logician or moral philosopher. The biologists simply talked to one another, and made one another see that when a man has introduced a conception into science, it naturally becomes both his privilege and his duty to assign to that conception suitable scientific expressions; and that when a name has been conferred upon a conception by him to whose labors science is indebted for that conception, it becomes the duty of all,—a duty to the discoverer, and a duty to science,—to accept his name, unless it should be of such a nature that the adoption of it would be unwholesome for science; that should the discoverer fail in his duty, either by giving no name or an utterly unsuitable one, then, after a reasonable interval, whoever first has occasion to employ a name for that conception must invent a suitable one; and others ought to follow him; but that whoever deliberately uses a word or other symbol in any other sense than that which was conferred upon it by its sole right-ful creator commits a shameful offence against the inventor of the symbol and against science, and it becomes the duty of the others to treat the act with contempt and indignation.

As fast as the students of any branch of philosophy educate themselves to a genuine scientific love of truth to the degree to which the scholastic doctors were moved by it, suggestions similar to those above will suggest themselves; and they will consequently form a technical terminology. In logic, a terminology more than passably good has been inherited by us from the scholastics. This scholastic terminology has passed into English speech more than into any other modern tongue, rendering it the most logically exact of any. This has been accompanied by the inconvenience that a considerable number of words and phrases of scientific logic have come to be used with a laxity quite astounding. Who, for example, among the dealers in Quincy Hall who talks of "articles of *prime necessity*," would be able to say what that phrase "prime necessity" strictly means? He could not have sought out a more technical phrase. There are dozens of other loose expressions of the same provenance.

Having thus given some idea of the nature of the reasons which weigh with me, I proceed to state the rules which I find to be binding upon me in this field.

1st, To take pains to avoid following any recommendation of an arbitrary nature as to the use of philosophical terminology.

2nd, To avoid using words and phrases of vernacular origin as technical terms of philosophy.

3rd, To use the scholastic terms in their anglicised forms for philosophical conceptions, so far as they are strictly applicable; and never to use them in other than their proper senses.

4th, For ancient philosophical conceptions overlooked by the scholastics, to imitate, as well as I can, the ancient expression.

5th, For precise philosophical conceptions introduced into philosophy since the middle ages, to use the anglicised form of the original expression, if not positively unsuitable, but only in its precise original sense.

6th, For philosophical conceptions which vary by a hair's breadth from those for which suitable terms exist, to invent terms with a due regard for the usages of philosophical terminology and those of the English language but yet with a distinctly technical appearance. Before proposing a term, notation, or other symbol, to consider maturely whether it perfectly suits the conception and will lend itself to every occasion, whether it interferes with any existing term, and whether it may not create an inconvenience by interfering with the expression of some conception that may hereafter be introduced into philosophy. Having once introduced a symbol, to consider myself almost as much bound by it as if it had been introduced by somebody else; and after others have accepted it, to consider myself more bound to it than anybody else.

7th, To regard it as needful to introduce new systems of expression when new connections of importance between conceptions come to be made out, or when such systems can, in any way, positively subserve the purposes of philosophical study.

Stecheotic (Basic Definitions)

A *Sign,* or *Representamen,* is a First, which stands in such a genuine triadic relation to a Second, called its *Object,* as to be capable of determining a Third, called its *Interpretant,* to assume the same triadic relation to its Object in which it stands itself to the same Object. The triadic relation is *genuine,* that is, its three members are bound together by it in a way that does not consist in any complexus of dyadic relations. That is the reason the Interpretant, or Third, cannot stand in a mere dyadic relation to the Object, but must stand in such a relation to it as the Representamen itself does. Nor can the triadic relation in which the Third stands be merely similar to that in which the First stands, for this would make the relation of the Third to the First a degenerate Secondness merely. The Third must indeed stand in such a relation, and thus must be capable of determining a Third of its own; but besides that, it must have a second triadic relation in which the Representamen, or rather the relation thereof to its Object, shall be its own (the Third's) Object, and must be capable of determining a Third to this relation. All this must equally be true of the Third's Thirds and so on endlessly; and this, and more, is involved in the familiar idea of a Sign; and as the term Representamen is here used, nothing more is implied. A *Sign* is a Representamen with a mental Intepretant. Possibly there may be Representamens that are not Signs. Thus, if a sunflower, in turning towards the sun, becomes by that very act fully capable, without further condition, of reproducing a sunflower which turns in precisely corresponding ways toward the sun, and of doing so with the same reproductive power, the sunflower would become a Representamen of the sun. But *thought* is the chief, if not the only, mode of representation.

Representamens are divided by two trichotomies. The first and most fundamental is that any Representamen is either an *Icon,* an *Index,* or a *Symbol.* Namely, while no Representamen actually functions as such until it actually determines an Interpretant, yet it becomes a Representamen as soon as it is fully capable of doing this; and its Representative Quality is not necessarily dependent upon its ever actually determining an Interpretant, nor even upon its actually having an Object.

An *Icon* is a Representamen whose Representative Quality is a Firstness of it as a First. That is, a quality that it has *qua* thing renders it fit to be a representamen. Thus, anything is fit to be a *Substitute* for anything that it is like. (The conception of "substitute" involves that of a purpose, and thus of genuine thirdness.) Whether there are other kinds of substitutes or not we shall see. A Representamen by Firstness alone can only have a similar Object. Thus, a Sign by Contrast, denotes its object only by virtue of a contrast, or Secondness, between two qualities. A Sign by Firstness is an image of its object and, more strictly speaking, can only be an *idea.* For it must produce an Interpretant idea; and an external object excites an idea by a reaction upon the brain. But most strictly speaking, even an idea, except in the sense of a possibility, or Firstness, cannot be an Icon. A possibility alone is an Icon purely by virtue of its quality; and its object can only be a Firstness. But a Sign may be *iconic,* that is, may represent its object mainly by its similarity, no matter what its mode of being. If a substantive be wanted, an iconic representamen may be termed a *hypoicon.*

From *MS* 478, "Speculative Grammar," 1903.

Any material image, as a painting, is largely conventional in its mode of representation; but in itself, without legend or label it may be called a *hypoicon*. Hypoicons may [be] roughly divided according to the mode of Firstness of which they partake. Those which partake the simple qualities, or First Firstnesses, are *images;* those which represent the relations, mainly dyadic, or so regarded, of the parts of one thing by analogous relations in their own parts, are *diagrams;* those which represent the representative character of a representamen by representing a parallelism in something else, are *metaphors.*

An *Index* is a Representamen whose Representative Firstness consists in a genuine Secondness, or existential relation to its Object. Thus the shout of a driver, "Hi, there!," (the very event, when it takes place) considered as simply calling attention to him is an Index. So, the veering of a weather-cock is an Index of the veering of the wind which produces it. It follows from the definition that an Index and its Object must alike be existent individual Seconds or Secondnesses, things or facts. The object directly indicated must actually be there and then. A *Subindex,* or *hyposeme* is a sign which denotes its object principally because it is actually connected with it, without necessarily being strictly an individual Index. Thus, a proper name, a personal, demonstrative, or relative pronoun is not an individual or existing thing, but it represents its object by virtue, chiefly, of being actually connected with it. An Index may have a Hypoicon as a constituent part of it. Thus, a weather-cock shows the direction of the wind iconically; but it shows that it is the wind's direction, and that as a matter of present fact, as an *index,* almost free from any conventional admixture.

A *Symbol* is a Representamen whose Representative character consists precisely in its being a rule that will determine its Interpretant. All words, sentences, books, and other conventional signs are Symbols. We speak of writing or pronouncing the word "man"; but it is only a *replica,* or embodiment of the word, that is pronounced or written. The word itself has no existence although it has a real being, *consisting in* the fact that existents *will* conform to it. It is a general mode of succession of three sounds or representamens of sounds, which becomes a sign only in the fact that a habit, or acquired law, will cause replicas of it to be interpreted as meaning a law or men. The word and its meaning are both general rules; but the word alone of the two prescribes

the qualities of its replicas in themselves. Otherwise the "word" and its "meaning" do not differ, unless some special sense be attached to "meaning."

A Symbol is a law, or regularity of the indefinite future. Its Interpretant must be of the same description; and so must be also its complete immediate Object, or meaning.[1] But a law necessarily governs, or "is embodied in" individuals, and prescribes some of their qualities. Consequently, a constituent of a Symbol may be an Index, and a constituent may be an Icon. A man walking with a child points his arm up into the air and says, "There is a balloon." The pointing arm is an essential part of the symbol without which the latter would convey no information. But if the child asks, ["]What is a ballon,["] and the man replies, "It is something like a great big soap bubble," he makes the image a part of the symbol. Thus, while the complete object of a symbol, that is to say, its meaning, is of the nature of a law, it must *denote* an individual, and must *signify* a character. A *genuine* symbol is a Symbol that has a general meaning. There are two kinds of degenerate symbols, the *Singular Symbol* whose Object is an existent individual, and which signifies only such characters as that individual may realize; and the *Abstract Symbol,* whose only Object is a character.

Although the immediate Interpretant of an Index must be an Index, yet since its Object may be the Object of a Singular Symbol, the Index may have such a Symbol for its indirect Interpretant. Even a genuine Symbol may be an imperfect Interpretant of it. So an *icon* may have a degenerate Index, or an Abstract Symbol for an indirect Interpretant, and a genuine Index of Symbol for an imperfect Interpretant.

The second trichotomy of representamens is into 1st, simple signs, substitutive signs, or *sumisigns;* 2nd, double signs, informational signs, quasi-propositions, or *dicisigns;* 3rd, triple signs, rationally persuasive signs, *arguments,* or *suadisigns.* Of these three classes, the one whose nature is, by all odds, the easiest to comprehend, is the second, that of quasi-propositions, despite the fact that the question of the essential nature of the "judgment" is today quite the most vexed of all questions of logic. The truth is that *all* these classes are of very intricate natures; but the problem of the day is needlessly complicated by the attention of most logicians, instead of extending to propositions in general, being confined to "judgments," or acts of mental acceptance of propositions, which not only involve characters, additional to those of propo-, sitions in general,—characters required to differentiate them as propositions of a particular kind,—but which further involve, beside the mental proposition itself, the peculiar act of assent. The problem is difficult enough, when we merely seek to analyze the essential nature of the *Dicisign,* in general, that is, the kind of sign that *conveys* information, in contradistinction to a sign from which information may be derived.[2]

The readiest characteristic test showing whether a sign is a Dicisign or not, is that a Dicisign is either true or false, but does not directly furnish reasons for its being so. This shows that a Dicisign must profess to refer or relate to something as having a real being independently of the representation of it as such, and further that this reference or relation must not be shown as rational, but must appear as a blind Secondness. But the only kind of sign whose object is necessarily existent is the genuine Index. This Index might, indeed, be a part of a Symbol; but in that case the relation would appear as rational. Consequently a Dicisign necessarily represents itself to be a genuine Index, and to be nothing more. At this point let us discard all other considerations, and see what sort of sign a sign must be that in any way represents itself to be a genuine Index of its Object, and nothing more. Substituting for "represents __ to be" a clearer interpretation, the statement is that the Dicisign's Interpretant represents an identity of the Dicisign with a genuine Index of the Dicisign's real Object. That is, the Interpretant represents a real existential relation, or genuine Secondness, as subsisting between the Dicisign and its real Object. But the Interpretant of a Sign can represent no other Object than that of the Sign itself. Hence this same existential relation must be an Object of the Dicisign, if the latter have any real Object. This represented existential relation, in being an Object of the Dicisign, makes that real Object, which is correlate of this relation also an Object of the Dicisign.

This latter Object may be distinguished as the *Primary Object,* the other being termed the *Secondary Object.* The Dicisign, in so far as it is the relate of the existential relation which is the Secondary Object of the Dicisign, can evidently not be the entire Dicisign. It is at once a part of the Object and a part of the Interpretant of the Dicisign. Since the Dicisign is represented in its Interpretant to be an Index of a complexus as such, it must be represented in that same Interpretant to be composed of two parts, corresponding respectively to its Object and to itself. That is to say, in order to understand the Dicisign, it must be regarded as composed of two such parts whether it be in itself so composed or not. It is difficult to see how this can be, unless it really have two such parts; but perhaps this may be possible. Let us consider these two represented parts separately. The part which is represented to represent the Primary Object, since the Dicisign is represented to be an Index of its Object, must be represented as an Index, or some representamen of an Index, of the Primary Object. The part which is represented to represent a part of the Dicisign is represented as at once part of the Interpretant and part of the Object. It must, therefore, be represented as such a sort of Representamen (or to represent such a sort), as can have its Object and its Interpretant the same. Now, a Symbol cannot even have itself as its Object; for it is a law governing its Object. For example, if I say "This proposition conveys information about itself," or "Let the term 'sphynx' be a general term to denote anything of the nature of a symbol that is applicable to every 'sphynx' and to nothing else," I shall talk unadulterated nonsense. But a Representamen mediates between its Interpretant and its Object, and that which cannot be the Object of the Representamen cannot be the Object of the Interpretant. Hence, *a fortiori,* it is impossible that a Symbol should have its Object as its Interpretant. An Index can very well represent itself. Thus, every number has a double; and thus the entire collection of even numbers is an Index of the entire collection of numbers, and so this collection of even numbers contains an Index of itself. But it is impossible for an Index to be its own Interpretant, since an Index is nothing but an individual existence in a Secondness with something; and it only becomes an Index by being capable of being represented by some Representamen as being in that relation. Could this Interpretant be itself there would be no difference between an Index and a Second. An Icon, however, is strictly a possibility, involving a possibility, and thus the possibility of its being represented as a possibility is the possibility of the involved possibility. In this kind of Representamen alone, then, the Interpretant may be the Object. Consequently, that constituent of the Dicisign, which is represented in the Interpretant as being a part of the Object, must be represented by an Icon or by a Representamen of an Icon. The Dicisign, as it must be understood in order to be understood at all, must contain those two parts. But the Dicisign is represented to be an Index of the Object, in that the latter involves something corresponding to these parts; and it is this Secondness that the Dicisign is represented to be the Index of. Hence the Dicisign must exhibit a connection between these parts of itself, and must represent this connection to correspond to a connection in the object between the Secundal Primary Object and the Firstness indicated by the part corresponding to the Dicisign.

We conclude, then, that, if we have succeeded in threading our way through the maze of these abstractions, a Dicisign, defined as a Representamen whose Interpretant represents it as an Index of its Object, must have the following characters:

1st, It must, in order to be understood, be considered as containing two parts. Of these, the one, which may be called the *Subject,* is or represents an Index of a Second existing independently of its being represented, while the other, which may be called the *Predicate,* is or represents an Icon of a firstness.

2nd, These two parts must be represented as connected; and that in such a way that if the Dicisign has any Object, it must be an Index of a Secondness subsisting between the Real Object represented in one represented part of the Dicisign to be indicated and a Firstness represented in the other represented part of the Dicisign to be Iconized. . . .

Deduction is that kind of argument which arbitrarily assumes a hypothesis, and whether it be realized or not has no bearing on the reasoning; but the hypothesis must be of a general nature (for it will amount to the same thing if it refers to familiar ideas of a general nature); and it then not only *asserts* but *shows,* i.e. puts the Interpreter into a condition to assent to, concerning that purely hypothetical universe (as for the purposes of Deduction it always is) a proposition termed the *Conclusion,* which is really the Interpretant of the Symbol.

Abduction is that kind of argument, which sets out from a *surprising* experience, that is an experience contrary to an active or passive belief. This comes in the form of a perceptual judgment, or some proposition referring to such a judgment, and a new formula becomes necessary in order to generalize experience. But now the interpretant of the Abduction represents it to be *like,* that is to say, an Icon of, a replica of a Symbol. In common language, it seems to see a possible explanation of

the surprising fact, and thereby accepts this Symbol, in the form of a proposition, as *Likely.* This does not mean *Probable* in the technical sense. That is to say, it is not such a probability as might safely be the basis for underwriters, if they had a sufficiently large number of cases to go upon. It merely means that the truth being like that proposition, the proposition is accepted in the Interrogative Mood,—a mood existing in Universal Grammar, whether it exists in any language or not. It is concluded to be a good question to ask. This is what is called *making an explanatory hypothesis.* The majority of logicians do not include it among arguments, but only as an adjuvant to arguments. But this is an error of classification. Every such adjuvant of an argument is *ipso facto* an argument. It tends toward a conclusion. Those same writers very likely recognize Abduction in another part of their book as *generalization.* But the two are merely varieties of one class of symbols.

Abduction is the first step in the whole process of reasoning. Its conclusion becomes a premiss for Deduction which, colligating this with pre-accepted propositions, produces quasi predictions as to the course of future experience,—that is, what would be predictions in the usual sense, if the conclusion of the abduction were fully believed. They may properly be termed *Predictions,* although not assertory predictions. In fact, no prediction can quite amount, in sound logic, to a Prophecy, regarding itself as infallible. The action of Induction is not carried on in pure thought. It consists in taking one's instruments and making experiments, and in concluding from the results of these to what extent it will be safe to rely upon the hypothesis. This mode of thought regards the conclusion of the Abduction as a pure dream. For one can reason deductively just the same concerning the so-called imaginaries, that is, the unfounded dreams of mathematicians as concerning existences. Yet it must be something very different from a dream, in that, either in the hypothesis itself, or in the pre-known truths brought to bear upon it, there must be a *Universal* proposition, or Rule. Take the "immediate inference," which is as truly a deduction, as any other, from "There is a woman whom any Spaniard there may be adores," to "Any Spaniard there may be stands to some woman or other in the relation of adoring her." This inference may be drawn by a "rule of thumb"; that is, a habit may act to cause a feeling of confidence in the conclusion, without any deliberation or control. This, however, may happen even if the inference is not of the kind termed "immediate" (that is, a deduction from a relatively simple premiss, not a copulative proposition). But such inference, not being self-controlled, is not *Reasoning*. Yet even in that case, the habit is a universal rule in itself, although its operation may be hindered sometimes. But if the inference is drawn deliberately, the reasoner will consider that if the woman can be specified in advance of knowing what Spaniard is to be adduced, it can only make it easier to find such a woman if the Spaniard is fixed upon first; or in some other way, the case will be brought under a known or evident universal truth. Thus, the argument sets out from a law represented to be known actually to hold throughout the universe of the hypothesis, and in the conclusion interprets the effect of this law. As Prof. Mitchell[3] profoundly said, the whole operation virtually consists in *erasure*.

Deduction has two markedly different kinds; *necessary inference* and *inference of a probability*. What is called "probable inference" is not necessarily *probable deduction,* but includes all inference not necessary. Probable deduction is necessary inference concerning probability, in the strict statistical sense. What makes it very distinct from necessary inference proper is that while the latter has no concern with the realization of its hypothesis, and reasons about its premisses as expressing a conceivable state of things, regardless of actual existence, probability, on the other hand, is essentially limited to the *course of experience*. In the realm of Firstness, Probability has no meaning. True there is a doctrine of "geometrical probability," but it is only a particular way of viewing problems in geometrical integration. The conception of probability, which is lugged into it, has no particular relevancy to it, further than that it may be suggestive in regard to this problem, as it may in regard to many others. But while probability *supposes* a course of actual experiences, this supposition is itself entirely arbitrary, so far as concerns the reasoning.

Deduction produces from the conclusion of Abduction predictions as to what would be found true in experience in case that conclusion were realized. Now comes the work of Induction, which is not to be done while lolling in an easy chair, since it consists in actually going to work and making the experiments, hence going on to settle a general conclusion as to how far the hypothesis holds good.

If, from a replica of a proposition, some-thing be erased, such that, if the blank, or blanks, so left were filled, each with a proper name, then the general symbol of which this blank form is a replica is termed by the present writer a *rheme* (the word is taken from the use of ρημα in Plato, Aristotle, Dionysius the Thracian, and many others to denote a verb. . . . This shows just how far the present writer has warped the original meaning.) A rheme is either a *medad* (a patronymic formed by the writer from μηδεν), a *monad,* a *dyad,* a *triad,* a *polyad,* etc. according as the number of blanks is 0, 1, 2, 3, or more than two. Any symbol which may be a direct constituent of a proposition is called a *term* (*terminus,* Boëthius). The logicians usually say that a categorical proposition has "two terms," its *subject* and its *predicate,* wherein, by a carelessness of expression, or by copying Aristotle,[4] they stumble upon the truth. Their usual *doctrine* is (though often not directly stated in one sentence), that such a proposition has three terms, the subject, the predicate, and *copula* (Abelard). The correct designation of the subject and predicate, in accord with their doctrine, is the *extremes,* which is translated from the same Greek word as *term* (ορος). The ordinary doctrine makes the copula the only verb, and all other terms to be either proper names or general class-names; because this gives the simplest and most satisfactory account of the proposition. It happens to be true that in the overwhelming majority of languages there are no general class names and adjectives that are not conceived as parts of some verb (even when there really is no such verb) and consequently nothing like a copula is required in forming sentences in such languages. The author (though with no pretension to being a linguist), has fumbled the grammars of many languages in the search for a language constructed at all in the way in which the logicians go out of their way to teach that all men think (for even if they do so, that has really nothing to do with logic). The only such tongue that he has succeeded in finding is the Basque, which seems to have but two or three verbs, all the other principal words being conceived as nouns. Every language must have proper names; and there is no verb wrapped up in a proper name. Therefore, there would seem to be a direct suggestion there of a true common noun or adjective. But, notwithstanding that suggestion, almost every family of man thinks of general words as parts of verbs. This seems to refute the logicians' psychology.

A proper name, when one meets with it for the first time, is existentially connected with some percept or other equivalent individual knowledge of the individual it names. It is *then,* and then only, a genuine Index. The next time one meets with it, one regards it as an Icon of that Index. The habitual acquaintance with it having been acquired, it becomes a Symbol whose Interpretant represents it as an Icon of an Index of the Individual named.

If you look into a textbook of chemistry for a definition of *lithium,* you may be told that it is that element whose atomic weight is 7 very nearly. But if the author has a more logical mind he will tell you that if you search among minerals that are vitreous, translucent, grey or white, very hard, brittle, and insoluble, for one which imparts a crimson tinge to an unluminous flame, this mineral being triturated with lime or witherite rats-bane, and then fused, can be partly dissolved in muriatic acid; and if this solution be evaporated, and the residue be extracted with sulphuric acid, and duly purified, it can be converted by ordinary methods into a chloride, which being obtained in the solid state, fused, and electrolyzed with half a dozen powerful cells, will yield a globule of a pinkish silvery metal that will float on gasolene; and the material of *that* is a specimen of lithium. The peculiarity of this definition,—or rather this precept that is more serviceable than a definition,—is that it tells you that what the word lithium denotes by prescribing what you are to *do* in order to gain a perceptual acquaintance with the object of the word. Every subject of a proposition, unless it is either an Index (like the environment of the interlocutors, or something attracting attention in that environment, as the pointing finger of the speaker) or a Subindex (like a proper name, personal pronoun or demonstrative) must be a *Precept,* or Symbol, not only describing to the Interpreter what is to be done, by him or others or both, in order to obtain an Index of an individual (whether a unit or a single set of units) of which the proposition is represented as meant to be true, but also assigning a designation to that individual, or, if it is a set, to each single unit of the set. Until a better designation is found, such a term may be called a Precept. Thus, the Subject of the proposition, 'Whatever Spaniard there may be adores some woman' may best be regarded as, "Take any individual, A, in the universe, and then there will be some individual, B, in the universe, such that A and B in this order form a dyad of which what follows is true," the

Predicate being "——is either not a Spaniard or else adores a woman that is ——."

Any term fit to be the subject of a proposition may be termed an *Onome.* A *Categoreumatic Term* (Duns Scotus, but probably earlier) is any term fit to be the subject or predicate of a proposition. A *Syncategoreumatic Term* or *Syncathegreuma (Summulae)* is a Symbol going to make up a *Categoreumatic Term.* The copula seems to fall between two stools, being neither categoreumatic nor syncategoreumatic.

Arguments can only be Symbols, not Indices nor Icons. An argument is either a *Deduction,* an *Induction,* or an *Abduction.*

As to these words, *deducere,* in Latin, means rather to lead away or aside than to lead down; and if the word is applied to argumentation, which is not very common, it is rather the premisses that are *deduced* to their conclusion than the conclusion that is deduced from premisses. The term *deductio* was used by Boethius; but only for a quite special, and obscurely explained mode of reasoning which Aristotle calls απαγωγη. It was very little used in logic until we find Hamilton in 1837 (*Lectures on Metaph,* xxxvii) and Whewell in the same year (*Hist of Inductive Science*) speaking of *deduction* and *deductive reasoning* as a great branch of reasoning opposed to induction, and speaking as if this were a familiar use of words. In the few logical books that the present writer has been able to consult, he has not found the term *deduction* thus used at an earlier date. It is certain, that it is a peculiarly English term; and the use of it can only be traced to the peculiar sense given in English to the word *deduce.* In Latin, *deducere* means to lead away or aside rather than to lead down, and if it is applied to reasoning at all (which does not very often happen) it is the premisses which are deduced to the conclusion, not the conclusion from the premisses. In Old French *deduvie* is not very far removed in meaning from *seduvie;* and later it has been applied to any kind of serial sequence, especially a chronological sequence. But in English, from pre-Elizabethan times, *deduce* has been used to denote the recognition of the effect of a rule in particular cases. Both Hamilton and Whewell were strongly influenced by Kant; and Kant regards all necessary reasoning as the application of a general rule to a particular case. That must have made both those writers more ready to take up a floating usage of speech which contrasted Deduction with Induction. It happens that this English sense of deduction has some affinity with the use of the word by Boethius, as remarked by Adamson; but that may be reckoned to be fortuitous.

The term *Induction* (L *inductio*) was introduced into logic, in the same sense it bears today, by Cicero. The word is constructed after the model of the equivalent Greek επαγωει which was used by Socrates, though not in the whole breadth of its Aristotelian meaning.

NOTES

1. There are two ways in which a Symbol may have a real Existential Thing as its real Object. First, the thing may conform to it, whether accidentally or by virtue of the Symbol having the virtue of a growing habit; and secondly, by the Symbol having an Index as a part of itself. But the immediate object of a symbol can only be a symbol and if it has in its own

nature another kind of object, this must be by an *endless series.*

2. To explain the judgment in terms of the "proposition" is to explain it by that which is essentially intelligible. To explain the proposition in terms of the "judgment" is to explain the self-intelligible in terms of a psychical act, which is the most obscure of phenomena or facts.

3. Because Mitchell happened to be a student under a master at the time he produced his paper "On a New Algebra of Logic," that work has been spoken of in a tone unfit to be used toward so masterly a performance. Barring the *Analytics* of Aristotle and Boole's *Laws of Thought*, I never read anything else on necessary inference so rich in instructive suggestions. What I have gained from the study of it is inestimable. {See Mitchell in *P* 268.}

4. "Οϱον δὲ ϰαλῶ εἰς ὃν διαλεται ἡ πϱότασις, οιον τό τε ϰατηγοϱουμενον ϰαι τὸ ϰαθ οὐ ϰατηγοϱειτας, says Aristotle 24b.16. {I call that a term into which the premise is resolved, that is, both the predicate and that of which it is being predicated, 'being' being added and 'not being' being removed, or vice versa.}

Critic (Theory of Argumentation)

All necessary reasoning is diagrammatic; and the assurance furnished by all other reasoning must be based upon necessary reasoning. In this sense, all reasoning depends directly or indirectly upon diagrams. Only it is necessary to distinguish reasoning, properly so called, where the acceptance [of the] conclusion in the sense in which it is drawn, is seen *evidently* to be justified, from cases in which a rule of inference is followed because it has been found to work well, which I call following a rule of thumb, and accepting a conclusion without seeing why further than that the impulse to do so seems irresistible. In both those cases, there might be a sound argument to defend the acceptance of the conclusion; but to accept the conclusion without any criticism or supporting argument is not what I call reasoning. For example, a person having been accustomed to considering finite collections only might contract a habit of using the syllogism of transposed quantity, of which the following is an instance.

Every Hottentot kills a Hottentot
No Hottentot is killed by more than one Hottentot
Therefore every Hottentot is killed by a Hottentot.

Later forgetting why this necessarily follows for finite collections (if he ever did understand it), this person might by mere force of habit apply the same kind of reasoning to endless generations or other infinite [classes]; or he might apply it to a finite class, but with so little understanding that only luck would prevent his applying it to infinite collections. Such a case is an application of a rule of thumb and is not reasoning. Many persons are deceived by the catch about Achilles and the Tortoise; and I knew one extremely bright man who could not, for the life of him, perceive any fault in this reasoning:

> *It either rains or it doesn't rain:*
> *It rains;*
> *Therefore, it doesn't rain.*

Such people appear to mistake the rule of thumb for reasoning.

Descartes, in one of his letters, is quite explicit that his *Je pense, donc je suis* is not a syllogism with a suppressed premiss. I infer, then, that he thought it not impossible that an imaginary being should think (i.e. be conscious)

From *MS* 293, "Prolegomena to an Apology for Pragmaticism," 1906.

albeit he had no real existence. Of course, there would be a fallacy here, but not one that Descartes might not easily fall into. In the same fallacious manner, I suppose he said, It would be quite possible antecedently that I had never existed. But when he tried to suppose, not of a being in general, who might be imaginary, but of himself, that *he* was conscious without existing, he found *that* quite impossible; while yet he had no reason or principle that could serve as major premiss in the argument. This confused inability to suppose his being false, as long as he *thought,* was not, in my terminology, Reasoning, because Reasoning renders the truth of its conclusion plain and comprehensible, and does not, like the plagiaristic formula of Descartes, stumble in the dark against an invisible wall of inability to conceive something.

In order to expound fully my proposition that all necessary reasoning is diagrammatic, I ought to explain exactly what I mean by a Diagram. But at present it would be extremely difficult to do quite that. At a later place in this paper I will endeavour to do so; but just now, I think it will better meet the reader's needs to give an exposition that shall cover the main points, and to leave the others, whose needfulness is only perceived after deep study, to follow when the need of them comes out.

To begin with, then, a Diagram is an Icon of a set of rationally related objects. By *rationally* related, I mean that there is between them, not merely one of those relations which we know by experience, but know not how to comprehend, but one of those relations which anybody who reasons at all must have an inward acquaintance with. This is not a sufficient definition, but just now I will go no further, except that I will say that the Diagram not only represents the related correlates, but also, and much more definitely represents the relations between them, as so many objects of the Icon. Now necessary reasoning makes its conclusion *evident.* What is this "Evidence"? It consists in the fact that the truth of the conclusion is *perceived,* in all its generality, and in the generality the how and why of the truth is perceived. What sort of a Sign can communicate this Evidence? No index, surely, can it be; since it is by brute force that the Index thrusts its Object into the Field of Interpretation, the consciousness, as if disdaining gentle "evidence." No Symbol can do more than apply a "rule of thumb" resting as it does entirely on Habit (including under this term natural disposition); and a Habit is no evidence. I suppose it would be the general opinion of logicians, as it certainly was long mine,

that the Syllogism is a Symbol, because of its Generality. But there is an inaccurate analysis and confusion of thought at the bottom of that view; for so understood it would fail to furnish Evidence. It is true that ordinary Icons,—the only class of Signs that remains for necessary inference,—merely suggest the possibility of that which they represent, being percepts *minus* the insistency and percussivity of percepts. In themselves, they are mere Semes, predicating of nothing, not even so much as interrogatively. It is, therefore, a very extraordinary feature of Diagrams that they *show,*—as literally *show* as a Percept shows the Perceptual Judgment to be true,—that a consequence does follow, and more marvellous yet, that it *would* follow under all varieties of circumstances accompanying the premisses. It is not, however, the statical Diagram-icon that directly shows this; but the Diagram-icon having been constructed with an Intention, involving a Symbol of which it is the Interpretant (as Euclid, for example, first enounces in general terms the proposition he intends to prove, and then proceeds to draw a diagram, usually a figure, to exhibit the antecedent condition thereof) which Intention, like every other, is General as to its Object, in the light of this Intention determines an Initial Symbolic Interpretant. Meantime, the Diagram remains in the field of perception of imagination; and so the Iconic Diagram and its Initial Symbolic Interpretant taken together constitute what we shall not too much wrench Kant's term in calling a *Schema,* which is on the one side an object capable of being observed while on the other side it is General. (Of course, I always use 'general' in the usual sense of general as to its object. If I wish to say that a sign is general as to its matter, I call it a Type, or Typical.) Now let us see how the Diagram entrains its consequence. The Diagram sufficiently partakes of the percussivity of a Percept to determine, as its Dynamic, or Middle, Interpretant, a state [of] activity in the Interpreter, mingled with curiosity. As usual, this mixture leads to Experimentation. It is the normal Logical effect; that is to say, it not only happens in the cortex of the human brain, but must plainly happen in every Quasi-mind in which Signs of all kinds have a vitality of their own. Now, sometimes in one way, sometimes in another, we need not pause to enumerate the ways, certain modes of transformation of Diagrams of the system of diagrammatization used have become recognized as permissible. Very likely the recognition descends from some former Induction, remarkably strong owing to the cheapness of mere mental experimentation. Some circumstance connected with the purpose which first prompted the construction of the diagram contributes to the determination of the permissible transformation that actually gets performed. The Schema *sees,* as we may say, that the transformate Diagram is substantially contained in the transformand Diagram, and in the significant features to it, regardless of the accidents,—as, for example, the Existential Graph that remains after a deletion from the Phemic Sheet is contained in the Graph originally there, and would do so whatever colored ink were employed. The transformate Diagram is the Eventual, or Rational, Interpretant of the transformand Diagram, at the same time being a new Diagram of which the Initial Interpretant, or signification, is the Symbolic statement, or statement in general terms, of the Conclusion. By this labyrinthine path, and by no other, is it possible to attain to Evidence; and 'Evidence belongs to every Necessary Conclusion.

There are at least two other entirely different lines of argumentation each very nearly, and perhaps quite, as conclusive as the above, though less instructive, to prove that all necessary reasoning is by diagrams. One of these shows that every step of such an argumentation can be represented, but usually much more analytically, by Existential Graphs. Now to say that the graphical procedure is more analytical than another is to say that it demonstrates what the other virtually assumes without proof. Hence, the Graphical method, which is diagrammatic is the sounder form of the same argumentation. The other proof consists in taking up, one by one, each form of necessary reasoning, and showing that the diagrammatic exhibition of it does it perfect justice.

Let us now consider non-necessary reasoning. This divides itself, according to the different ways in which it may be valid, into three classes: probable deduction; experimental reasoning, which I now call Induction; and processes of thought capable of producing no conclusion more definite than a conjecture, which I now call Abduction. I examined this subject in an essay in the volume of 'Studies in Logic by Members of the Johns Hopkins University,' published in 1883; and have since made three independent and laborious investigations of the question of validity, and others connected with it. As my latest work has been written out for the press and may some time be printed, I will limit what I say here as much as possible. The general principle of the validity of Induction is correctly stated in the Johns Hopkins Essay, but is too narrowly defined. All the forms of reasoning there principally considered come under the class of Inductions, as I now define it. Much could now be added to the Essay. The validity of Induction consists in the fact that it proceeds according to a method which though it may give provisional results that are incorrect will yet, if steadily pursued, eventually correct any such error. The two propositions that all Induction possesses this kind of validity, and that no Induction possesses any other kind that is more than a further determination of this kind, are both susceptible of demonstration by necessary reasoning. The demonstrations are given in my Johns Hopkins paper; and although the description of the mode of validity there is too narrow, yet it covers the strongest inductions and most of the reasonings generally recognized as Inductions. It is characteristic of the present state of logic that no attempt has been made to refute the demonstrations, but the old talk conclusively refuted by me goes on just the same. To say that the validity of Induction rests on Necessary Reasoning is as much as to say that Induction separated from the deduction of its validity does not make it evident that its conclusion has the kind of justification to which it lays claim. This being the case, it is not surprising that Induction, separated from the deduction of its validity, makes no essential use of diagrams. But instead of experimenting on Diagrams it experiments upon the very Objects concerning which it reasons. That is to say, it does so in an easily extended sense of the term "experiment", the sense in which I commonly employ the word in the critical part of logic.

The third mode of non-necessary reasoning, if we are to count the deduction of probabilities as a class, though it ought not to be reckoned such, is Abduction. Abduction is no more nor less than guessing, a faculty attributed to Yankees.[1]

NOTE

1. In point of fact, the three most remarkable, because most apparently unfounded, guesses I know of were made by Englishmen. They were Bacon's guess that heat was a mode of motion, Dalton's of chemical atoms, and Young's (or was it Wallaston's) that violet, *green* (and not yellow, as the painters

said) and red were the fundamental colors. Such validity as this has consists in the generalization that no new truth is ever otherwise reached while some new truths are thus reached. This is a result of Induction; and therefore in a remote way Abduction rests upon diagrammatic reasoning.

Methodeutic (Methodology)

If the settlement of opinion is the sole object of inquiry, and if belief is of the nature of a habit, why should we not attain the desired end, by taking any answer to a question which we may fancy, and constantly reiterating it to ourselves, dwelling on all which may conduce to that belief, and learning to turn with contempt and hatred from anything which might disturb it? This simple and direct method is really pursued by many men. I remember once being entreated not to read a certain newspaper lest it might change my opinion upon free-trade. "Lest I might be entrapped by its fallacies and misstatements," was the form of expression. "You are not," my friend said, "a special student of political economy. You might, therefore, easily be deceived by fallacious arguments upon the subject. You might, then, if you read this paper, be led to believe in protection. But you admit that free-trade is the true doctrine; and you do not wish to believe what is not true." I have often known this system to be deliberately adopted. Still oftener, the instinctive dislike of an undecided state of mind, exaggerated into a vague dread of doubt, makes men cling spasmodically to the views they already take. The man feels that, if he only holds to his belief without wavering, it will be entirely satisfactory. Nor can it be denied that a steady and immovable faith yields great peace of mind. It may, indeed, give rise to inconveniences, as if a man should resolutely continue to believe that fire would not burn him, or that he would be eternally damned if he received his *ingesta* otherwise than through a stomach-pump. But then the man who adopts this method will not allow that its inconveniences are greater than its advantages. He will say, "I hold steadfastly to the truth, and the truth is always wholesome." And in many cases it may very well be that the pleasure he derives from his calm faith overbalances any inconveniences resulting from its deceptive character. Thus, if it be true that death is annihilation, then the man who believes that he will certainly go straight to heaven when he dies, provided he have fulfilled certain simple observances in this life, has a cheap pleasure which will not be followed by the least disappointment. A similar consideration seems to have weight with many persons in religious topics, for we frequently hear it said, "Oh, I could not believe so-and-so, because I should be wretched if I did." When an ostrich buries its head in the sand as danger approaches, it very likely takes the happiest course. It hides the danger, and then calmly says there is no danger; and, if it feels perfectly sure there is none, why should it raise its head to see? A man may go through life, systematically keeping out of view all that might cause a change in his opinions, and if he only succeeds—basing his method, as he does, on two fundamental psychological laws—I do not see what can be said against his doing so. It would be an egotistical impertinence to object that his procedure is irrational, for that only amounts to saying that his method of settling belief is not ours. He does not propose to himself to be rational, and, indeed, will often talk with scorn of man's weak and illusive reason. So let him think as he pleases.

But this method of fixing belief, which may be called the method of tenacity, will be unable to hold its ground in practice. The social impulse is against it. The man who adopts it will find that other men think differently from him, and it will be apt to occur to him, in some saner moment, that their opinions are quite as good as his own, and this will shake his confidence in his belief. This conception, that another man's thought or sentiment may be equivalent to one's own, is a distinctly new step, and a highly important one. It arises from an impulse too strong in man to be suppressed, without danger of destroying the human spe-

From "Illustrations of the Logic of Science: First Paper—The Fixation of Belief," *Popular Science Monthly,* vol. 12, 1878, pp. 7f.

cies. Unless we make ourselves hermits, we shall necessarily influence each other's opinions; so that the problem becomes how to fix belief, not in the individual merely, but in the community.

Let the will of the state act, then, instead of that of the individual. Let an institution be created which shall have for its object to keep correct doctrines before the attention of the people, to reiterate them perpetually, and to teach them to the young; having at the same time power to prevent contrary doctrines from being taught, advocated, or expressed. Let all possible causes of a change of mind be removed from men's apprehensions. Let them be kept ignorant, lest they should learn of some reason to think otherwise than they do. Let their passions be enlisted, so that they may regard private and unusual opinions with hatred and horror. Then, let all men who reject the established belief be terrified into silence. Let the people turn out and tar-and-feather such men, or let inquisitions be made into the manner of thinking of suspected persons, and, when they are found guilty of forbidden beliefs, let them be subjected to some signal punishment. When complete agreement could not otherwise be reached, a general massacre of all who have not thought in a certain way has proved a very effective means of settling opinion in a country. If the power to do this be wanting, let a list of opinions be drawn up, to which no man of the least independence of thought can assent, and let the faithful be required to accept all these propositions, in order to segregate them as radically as possible from the influence of the rest of the world.

This method has, from the earliest times, been one of the chief means of upholding correct theological and political doctrines, and of preserving their universal or catholic character. In Rome, especially, it has been practised from the days of Numa Pompilius to those of Pius Nonus. This is the most perfect example in history; but wherever there is a priesthood—and no religion has been without one—this method has been more or less made use of. Wherever there is an aristocracy, or a guild, or any association of a class of men whose interests depend or are supposed to depend on certain propositions, there will be inevitably found some traces of this natural product of social feeling. Cruelties always accompany this system; and when it is consistently carried out, they become atrocities of the most horrible kind in the eyes of any rational man. Nor should this occasion surprise, for the officer of a society does not feel justified in surrendering the interests of that society for the sake of mercy, as he might his own private interests. It is natural, therefore, that sympathy and fellowship should thus produce a most ruthless power.

In judging this method of fixing belief, which may be called the method of authority, we must, in the first place, allow its immeasurable mental and moral superiority to the method of tenacity. Its success is proportionately greater; and, in fact, it has over and over again worked the most majestic results. The mere structures of stone which it has caused to be put together—in Siam, for example, in Egypt, and in Europe—have many of them a sublimity hardly more than rivaled by the greatest works of Nature. And, except the geological epochs, there are no periods of time so vast as those which are measured by some of these organized faiths. If we scrutinize the matter closely, we shall find that there has not been one of their creeds which has remained always the same; yet the change is so slow as to be imperceptible during one person's life, so that individual belief remains sensibly fixed. For the mass of mankind, then, there is perhaps no better method than this. If it is their highest impulse to be intellectual slaves, then slaves they ought to remain.

But no institution can undertake to regulate opinions upon every subject. Only the most important ones can be attended to, and on the rest men's minds must be left to the action of natural causes. This imperfection will be no source of weakness so long as men are in such a state of culture that one opinion does not influence another—that is, so long as they cannot put two and two together. But in the most priestridden states some individuals will be found who are raised above that condition. These men possess a wider sort of social feeling; they see that men in other countries and in other ages have held to very different doctrines from those which they themselves have been brought up to believe; and they cannot help seeing that it is the mere accident of their having been taught as they have, and of their having been surrounded with the manners and associations they have, that has caused them to believe as they do and not far differently. And their candor cannot resist the reflection that there is no reason to rate their own views at a higher value than those of other nations and other centuries; and this gives rise to doubts in their minds.

They will further perceive that such doubts as

these must exist in their minds with reference to every belief which seems to be determined by the caprice either of themselves or of those who originated the popular opinions. The willful adherence to a belief, and the arbitrary forcing of it upon others, must, therefore, both be given up, and a new method of settling opinions must be adopted, which shall not only produce an impulse to believe, but shall also decide what proposition it is which is to be believed. Let the action of natural preferences be unimpeded, then, and under their influence let men, conversing together and regarding matters in different lights, gradually develop beliefs in harmony with natural causes. This method resembles that by which conceptions of art have been brought to maturity. The most perfect example of it is to be found in the history of metaphysical philosophy. Systems of this sort have not usually rested upon any observed facts, at least not in any great degree. They have been chiefly adopted because their fundamental propositions seemed "agreeable to reason." This is an apt expression; it does not mean that which agrees with experience, but that which we find ourselves inclined to believe. Plato, for example, finds it agreeable to reason that the distances of the celestial spheres from one another should be proportional to the different lengths of strings which produce harmonious chords. Many philosophers have been led to their main conclusions by considerations like this; but this is the lowest and least developed form which the method takes, for it is clear that another man might find Kepler's theory, that the celestial spheres are proportional to the inscribed and circumscribed spheres of the different regular solids, more agreeable to *his* reason. But the shock of opinions will soon lead men to rest on preferences of a far more universal nature. Take, for example, the doctrine that man only acts selfishly—that is, from the consideration that acting in one way will afford him more pleasure than acting in another. This rests on no fact in the world, but it has had a wide acceptance as being the only reasonable theory.

This method is far more intellectual and respectable from the point of view of reason than either of the others which we have noticed. But its failure has been the most manifest. It makes of inquiry something similar to the development of taste; but taste, unfortunately, is always more or less a matter of fashion, and accordingly metaphysicians have never come to any fixed agreement, but the pendulum has swung backward and forward between a more material and a more spiritual

philosophy, from the earliest times to the latest. And so from this, which has been called the *a priori* method, we are driven, in Lord Bacon's phrase, to a true induction. We have examined into this *a priori* method as something which promised to deliver our opinions from their accidental and capricious element. But development, while it is a process which eliminates the effect of some casual circumstances, only magnifies that of others. This method, therefore, does not differ in a very essential way from that of authority. The government may not have lifted its finger to influence my convictions; I may have been left outwardly quite free to choose, we will say, between monogamy and polygamy, and, appealing to my conscience only, I may have concluded that the latter practice is in itself licentious. But when I come to see that the chief obstacle to the spread of Christianity among a people of as high culture as the Hindoos has been a conviction of the immorality of our way of treating women, I cannot help seeing that, though governments do not interfere, sentiments in their development will be very greatly determined by accidental causes. Now, there are some people, among whom I must suppose that my reader is to be found, who, when they see that any belief of theirs is determined by any circumstance extraneous to the facts, will from that moment not merely admit in words that that belief is doubtful, but will experience a real doubt of it, so that it ceases to be a belief.

To satisfy our doubts, therefore, it is necessary that a method should be found by which our beliefs may be caused by nothing human, but by some external permanency—by something upon which our thinking has no effect. Some mystics imagine that they have such a method in a private inspiration from on high. But that is only a form of the method of tenacity, in which the conception of truth as something public is not yet developed. Our external permanency would not be external, in our sense, if it was restricted in its influence to one individual. It must be something which affects, or might affect, every man. And, though these affections are necessarily as various as are individual conditions, yet the method must be such that the ultimate conclusion of every man shall be the same. Such is the method of science. Its fundamental hypothesis, restated in more familiar language, is this: There are real things, whose characters are entirely independent of our opinions about them; those realities affect our senses according to regular laws, and, though our sensations are as different as our relations to the objects, yet, by taking advantage of the laws of perception, we can ascertain by reasoning how things really are, and any man, if he have sufficient experience and reason enough about it, will be led to the one true conclusion. The new conception here involved is that of reality. It may be asked how I know that there are any realities. If this hypothesis is the sole support of my method of inquiry, my method of inquiry must not be used to support my hypothesis. The reply is this: 1. If investigation cannot be regarded as proving that there are real things, it at least does not lead to a contrary conclusion; but the method and the conception on which it is based remain ever in harmony. No doubts of the method, therefore, necessarily arise from its practice, as is the case with all the others. 2. The feeling which gives rise to any method of fixing belief is a dissatisfaction at two repugnant propositions. But here already is a vague concession that there is some *one* thing to which a proposition should conform. Nobody, therefore, can really doubt that there are realities, or, if he did, doubt would not be a source of dissatisfaction. The hypothesis, therefore, is one which every mind admits. So that the social impulse does not cause me to doubt it. 3. Everybody uses the scientific method about a great many things, and only ceases to use it when he does not know how to apply it. 4.

Experience of the method has not led me to doubt it, but, on the contrary, scientific investigation has had the most wonderful triumphs in the way of settling opinion. These afford the explanation of my not doubting the method or the hypothesis which it supposes; and not having any doubt, nor believing that anybody else whom I could influence has, it would be the merest babble for me to say more about it. If there be anybody with a living doubt upon the subject, let him consider it.

To describe the method of scientific investigation is the object of this series of papers. At present I have only room to notice some points of contrast between it and other methods of fixing belief.

This is the only one of the four methods which presents any distinction of a right and a wrong way. If I adopt the method of tenacity and shut myself out from al¹ influences, whatever I think necessary to doing this is necessary according to that method. So with the method of authority: the state may try to put down heresy by means which, from a scientific point of view, seem very ill-calculated to accomplish its purposes; but the only test *on that method* is what the state thinks, so that it cannot pursue the method wrongly. So with the *a priori* method. The very essence of it is to think as one is inclined to think. All metaphysicians will be sure to do that, however they may be inclined to judge each other to be perversely wrong. . . .

Metaphysics

METAPHYSICS

We have seen that logic requires that the more abstract sciences should be developed earlier than the more concrete ones. For the more concrete sciences require as fundamental principles the results of the more abstract sciences, while the latter only make use of the results of the former as data; and if one fact is wanting, some other will generally serve to support the same generalization.

But notwithstanding this, there is one highly abstract science which is in a deplorably backward condition. I mean Metaphysics. There is and can be no doubt that this immature condition of Metaphysics has very greatly hampered the progress of one of the two great branches of special science, I mean the Moral or Psychical Sciences. Most immediately has it checked the development of psychology; while the backward state of psychology has been a great disadvantage to all the other psychical sciences, such as linguistics, anthropology, social science, etc. To my mind it is equally clear that defective and bad metaphysics has been almost as injurious to the physical sciences, and is the

---

The section "Metaphysics" is from *MS* 940, "The Logic of Events," 1898. The section "Answers to Questions Concerning My Belief in God" is from *MS* 845 of that title, 1905.

real reason why all that depends upon the science of the constitution of matter, even physiology, is more or less rolling in the trough of the sea in rudderless fashion. The common opinion has been that Metaphysics is backward because it is intrinsically beyond the reach of human cognition. But that, I think I can clearly discern, is a complete mistake. Why should metaphysics be so difficult? Because it is abstract? But the abstracter a science is, the easier it is, both as a general rule of experience and as a corollary from logical principles. Mathematics, which is far more abstract than metaphysics, is certainly far more developed than any special science; and the same is true, though less tremendously so, of logic. But it will be said that metaphysics is inscrutable because its objects are not open to observation. This is doubtless true of some systems of metaphysics, though not to the extent that it is supposed to be true. The things that any science discovers are beyond the reach of direct observation. We cannot see energy, nor the attraction of gravitation, nor the flying molecules of gases, nor the luminiferous ether, nor the forests of the carbonaceous era, nor the explosions in nerve-cells. It is only the premisses of science, not its conclusions, which are directly observed. But metaphysics, even bad metaphysics, really rests on observations, whether consciously or not; and the only reason that this is not universally recognized is that it rests upon Kinds of phenomena with which every man's experience is so saturated that he usually pays no particular attention to them. The data of metaphysics are not less open to observation, but immeasurably more so, than the data, say, of the very highly developed science of astronomy, to make any important addition to whose observations requires an expenditure of many tens of thousands of dollars. No, I think we must abandon the idea that metaphysics is backward owing to any intrinsic difficulty of it.

In my opinion the chief cause of its backward condition is that its leading professors have been theologians. Were they simply Christian ministers the effect of intrusting very important scientific business to their hands would be quite as bad as if the same number of Wall Street promoters and Broad Street brokers were appointed to perform the task. The unfitness in the one case, as in the other, would consist in those persons having no idea of any broader interests than the personal interests of some person or collection of persons. Both classes are practical men. Now it is quite impossible for a practical man to comprehend what science is about unless he becomes as a little child and is born again. Scientific men are made out of youths who during the plastic period of life are set to study science for a number of years. Most of these develop into mere teachers; only a minority imbibe the spirit of science. The practical man has a definite job which he sets himself to accomplish. For that purpose he has to adopt some consistent plan which must be based upon a theory, and to that theory he must be wedded before the work begins. Even if his practical problem is no more serious than playing a game of whist, when there are only three rounds of a hand to be played, he must go upon the supposition that the cards lie so that he can win the odd trick. If he is a judge presiding over the hearing of a cause, that cause must be decided somehow, no matter how defective the evidence may be; and consequently he is constrained to lay down a rule for the burden of proof. But the idea of science is to pile the ground before the foot of the outworks of truth with the carcasses of this generation, and perhaps of others to come after it, until some future generation, by treading on them, can storm the citadel. The difference comes to this, that the practical man stakes everything he cares for upon the hazard of a die, and must believe with all the force of his manhood that the object for which he strives is good and that the theory of his plan is correct; while the scientific man is above all things desirous of learning the truth and, in order to do so, ardently desires to have his present provisional beliefs, and all his beliefs are merely provisional, swept away, and will work hard to accomplish that object. This is the reason that a good practical man cannot do the best scientific work. The temperaments requisite for the two kinds of business are altogether contrary to one another. This is above all true of the practical teacher [who] has no calling for his work unless he thoroughly believes that he is already in possession of all-important truth, with which he seeks by every physiological means to imbue other minds, so that they shall be unable to give it up. But a scientific man who has any such immovable beliefs to which he regards himself as religiously bound to be loyal, cannot at the same time desire to have his beliefs altered. In other words he cannot wish to learn the truth. Hence, I say that had the business of metaphysics been intrusted to ordinary parish priests it would have been performed unscientifically enough. But what has in fact been its fate has been far more tragic, in that it has been given over not to parish priests but to the caste of theologians. How much theologians may have contributed to the cause of Christianity, how far their writings and performances may have [been] the instruments of bringing home to men's hearts the truth of the Gospel of Love, or how far, on the other hand, they may have subserved the agencies that work to make Christians forget that truth, it is not in my province to inquire. I once bought and read through Dr. Schaff's three volumes upon the *Creeds of Christendom* for the purpose of ascertaining whether the theologians, who composed them, had ever once, from the first to the last, inserted a single clause in one of them by way of recognition of the principle of love; and I found that such a thing had never been done. But then we must remember that, that principle being fully admitted by all Christians, its insertion would not have served to damn anybody. Now the principal business of theologians is to make men feel the enormity of the slightest departure from the metaphysics they assume to be connected with the standard faith. Upon their religious side, however, I will not pretend to any opinion about the influence of theologians. But since theology pretends to be a science, they must also be judged as scientific men. And in that regard I must say that another so deplorably corrupt an influence as theirs upon the morals of science I do not believe has ever been operative. Theology, I am persuaded, derives its initial impulse from a religious wavering; for there is quite as much, or more, that is mysterious and calculated to awaken scientific curiosity, in the intercourse of men with one another as in their intercourse with God, and it [is] a problem quite analogous to that of theology. Yet we do not find that theologians have cared much for those problems. They have taken human conversation as a matter of course, with rather a remarkable absence of all curiosity about it. But, as far as I can penetrate into the motive of theology, it begins in an effort of men who have joined the Christian army and sworn fidelity to it to silence the suggestions of their hearts that they renounce their allegiance. How far it is successful in that purpose I will not inquire. But nothing can be more unscientific than the attitude of minds who are trying to confirm themselves in early beliefs. The struggle of the scientific man is to try to see the errors of his beliefs,—if he can be said to have any beliefs. The logic which observational science uses, is not like the logic

that the books teach, quite independent of the motive and spirit of the reasoner. There is an ethics indisolubly bound up with it,—an ethics of fairness and impartiality—and a writer, who teaches, by his example, to find arguments for a conclusion which he wishes to believe saps the very foundations of science by trifling with its morals. To sum up, the case is this:

We should expect to find metaphysics, judging from its position in the scheme of the sciences, to be somewhat more difficult than logic, but still on the whole one of the simplest of sciences, as it is one whose main principles must be settled before very much progress can be gained either in psychics or in physics.

Historically we are astonished to find that it has been a mere arena of ceaseless and trivial disputation. But we also find that it has been pursued in a spirit the very contrary of that of wishing to learn the truth, which is the most essential requirement of the logic of science; and it is worth trying whether by proceeding modestly recognizing in metaphysics an observational science, and applying to it the universal methods of such science, without caring one straw what kind of conclusions we reach or what their tendencies may be, but just honestly applying induction and hypothesis we cannot gain some ground for hoping that the disputes and obscurities of the subject may at last disappear.

ANSWERS TO QUESTIONS CONCERNING MY BELIEF IN GOD

The questions can be answered without very long explanations. "Do you believe in the existence of a Supreme Being?" Hume, in his "Dialogues Concerning Natural Religion," justly points out that the phrase "supreme being" is not an equivalent of "God," since it neither implies infinity nor any of the other attributes of God, excepting only Being and Supremacy. This is important; and another distinction between the two designations is still more so. Namely, "God" is a vernacular word, and like all such words, but more than almost any, is *vague*. No words are so well-understood as vernacular words, in one way; yet they are invariably vague; and of many of them it is true that, let the logician do his best to substitute precise equivalents in their places, still the vernacular words alone, for all their vagueness, answer the principal purposes. This is emphatically the case with the very vague word "God," which is not made less vague by saying that it imports "infinity," etc., since those attributes are at least as vague. I shall, therefore, if you please, substitute "God," for "Supreme Being" in the question.

I will also take the liberty of substituting "reality" for "existence." This is perhaps over-scrupulosity; but I myself always use *exist* in its strict philosophical sense of "react with the other like things in the environment." Of course, in that sense, it would be fetichism to say that God "exists." The word "reality," on the contrary, is used in ordinary parlance in its correct philosophical sense. It is curious that its legal meaning, in which we speak of "real estate," is the earliest, occurring early in the XIIth century. Albertus Magnus, who as a high ecclesiastic, must have had to do with such matters, imported it into philosophy. But it did not become at all common until Duns Scotus, in the latter part of the XIIIth century began to use it freely. I define the *real* as that which holds its characters on such a tenure that it makes not the slightest difference what any man or men may have *thought* them to be, or ever will have *thought* them to be, here using thought to include, imagining, opining, and willing (as long as forcible *means* are not used); but the real thing's characters will remain absolutely untouched. Of any kind of figment, this is not true. So, then, the question being whether I believe in the reality of God, I answer, Yes. I further opine that pretty nearly everybody more or less believes this, including many of the scientific men of my generation who are accustomed to think the belief is entirely unfounded. The reason they fall into this extraordinary error about their own belief is that they precide (or render precise) the conception, and in doing so, inevitably change it; and such precise conception is easily shown not to be warranted, even if it cannot be quite refuted. Every concept that is vague is liable to be self-contradictory in those respects in which it is vague. *No* concept, not even those of mathematics, is absolutely precise; and some of the most important for everyday use are extremely vague. Nevertheless, our instinctive beliefs involving such concepts are far more trustworthy than the best established results of science, if these be precisely understood. For instance, we all think that there is an element of order in the universe. Could any laboratory experiments render that proposition more certain than instinct or common sense leaves it? It is ridiculous to broach such a question. But when anybody undertakes to say *precisely* what that order consists in, he will quickly find he outruns all logical warrant. Men who are given to defining too much, inevitably run themselves into confusion in dealing with the vague concepts of common sense.

They generally make the matter worse by erroneous, not to say absurd, notions of the function of reasoning. Every race of animals is provided with instincts well-adapted to its needs, and especially to strengthening the stock. It is wonderful how unerring these instincts are. Man is no exception in this respect; but man is so continually getting himself into novel situations that he needs, and is supplied with, a subsidiary faculty of *reasoning* for bringing instinct to bear upon situations to which it does not directly apply. This faculty is a very imperfect one in respect to fallibility; but then it is only needed to bridge short gaps. Every step has to be reviewed and criticized; and indeed this is so essential that it is best to call an uncriticized step of inference by another name. If one does not at all know how one's belief comes about, it cannot be called even by the name of inference. If, with St. Augustine, we draw the inference "I think; therefore, I am," but when asked how we justify this inference, can only say that we are *compelled to think* that, since we think, we are. This uncriticized inference ought not to be called reasoning, which at the very least conceives its inference to be one of a general class of possible inferences on the same model, and all equally valid. But one must go back and criticize the premises and the *principles* that guide the drawing of the conclusions. If it could be made out that all the ultimate (or first) premises, were percepts; and that all the ultimate logical principles were as clear as the principle of contradiction, then one might say that one's conclusion was *perfectly* rational. Strictly speaking, it would not be quite so, because it is quite possible for perception itself to deceive us, and it is much more possible for us to be mistaken about the indubitableness of logical principles. But as a matter of fact, as far as logicians have hitherto been able to push their analyses, we have *in no single case,* concerning a matter of *fact,* as distinguished from a matter of mathematical conditional possibility, been able to reach this point. We are in every case either forced by such inexorable critic, sooner or later to declare, "such and such a proposition or mode of inference I *cannot doubt;* it seems perfectly clear that it is so, but I can't say *why,*" or else the critic himself tires before this criticism has been pushed to its very end.

If you absolutely cannot doubt a proposition,—cannot bring yourself, upon deliberation, to entertain the least suspicion of the truth of it, it is plain that there is no room to desire anything more. Many and many a philosopher seems to think that taking a piece of paper and writing down "I doubt that" is doubting it, or that it is a thing he can do in a minute as soon as he decides what he wants to doubt. Descartes convinced himself that the safest way was to "begin" by doubting everything, and accordingly he tells us he straightway did so, except only his *je pense,* which he borrowed from St. Augustine. Well I guess not; for genuine doubt does not talk of *beginning* with doubting. The pragmatist knows that doubt is an art which has to be acquired with difficulty; and his genuine doubts will go much further than those of any Cartesian. What he does not doubt, about ordinary matters of everybody's life, he is apt to find that no well-matured man doubts. They are part of our instincts. Instincts are now known not to be nearly so unchangeable as used to be supposed; and the present "mutation"-theory, which I have *always* insisted must be the way in which species have arisen, is, I am confident, the first beginning of the correct theory, and shows that it is no disproof of the instinctive character of a belief that it relates to concepts which the primitive man cannot be supposed to have had. Now, this is no confirmation of what one does not doubt. For what one does not doubt cannot be rendered more satisfactory than it already is. Yet while I may entertain, as far as I can search my mind, no perceptible doubt whatever of any one of a hundred propositions, I may suspect that, among so many, some one that is not true may have slipped in; and if so, the marvellous inerrancy of instinct may perhaps add a little to my *general* confidence in the whole lot. However, I am far from insisting upon the point. I think the consideration is better adapted to helping us to detect the counterfeit paper doubts, of which so many are in circulation.

All the instinctive beliefs, I notice, are vague. The moment they are precided, the pragmatist will begin to doubt them.

The fourth part of the first book of Hume's *Treatise of Human Nature* affords a strong argument for the correctness of my view that reason is a mere succedaneum to be used where instinct is wanting, by exhibiting the intensely ridiculous way in which a man winds himself up in silly paper doubts if he undertakes to throw common sense, i.e. instinct, overboard and be perfectly rational. Bradley's *Appearance and Reality* is another example of the same thing, although Bradley is at the opposite

pole from Hume in what he *does* admit. But Bradley is in no way as good a case as Hume. Hume endeavours to modify his conclusion by not stating it in the extreme length to which it ought to carry him. But a careful reader will see that if he proves anything at all by all his reasoning it is that reasoning, as such, is *ipso facto* and essentially illogical, "illegitimate," and unreasonable. And the reason it is so, is that either it is bad reasoning, or rests on doubtful premisses, or else that those premisses have not been thoroughly criticized. Of course not. The moment you come to a proposition which is perfectly satisfactory, so that you can entertain not the smallest suspicion of it, this fact debars you from making any genuine criticism of it. So that what Hume's argument would lead him to is that reasoning is "illegitimate" because its premisses are perfectly satisfactory. He candidly confesses that they are satisfactory to himself. But he seems to be dissatisfied with himself for being satisfied. It is easy to see, however, that he pats himself on the back, and is very well satisfied. Bradley's position is equally ridiculous. Another circumstance which goes toward confirming my view that instinct is the great internal source of all wisdom and of all knowledge is that all the "triumphs of science," of which that poor old XIX th century used to be so vain, have been confined to two directions. They either consist in physical,—that is, ultimately, dynamical,—explanations of phenomena, or else in explaining things on the basis of our common sense knowledge of human nature. Now dynamics is nothing but an elaboration of common sense; its experiments are mere imaginary experiments. So it all comes down to common-sense in these two branches, of which the one is founded on those instincts about physical forces that are required for the feeding-impulse, and the other on those instincts about our fellows that are requisite to the satisfaction of the reproductive impulse. Thus, then, all science is nothing but an outgrowth from those two instincts.

You will see that all I have been saying is not preparatory to any argument for the reality of God. It is intended as an apology for resting the belief upon instinct as the very bed-rock on which all reasoning must be built.

I have often occasion to walk, at night, for about a mile over an entirely untravelled road, much of it between open fields without a house in sight. The circumstances are not favorable to severe study, but are so to calm meditation. If the sky is clear, I look at the stars in the silence, thinking how each successive increase in the aperture of a telescope makes many more of them visible than all that had been visible before. The fact that the heavens do not show a sheet of light proves that there are vastly more dark bodies, say planets, than there are suns. They must be inhabited, and most likely millions of them with beings much more intelligent than we are. For on the whole, the solar system seems one of the simplest; and presumably under more complicated phenomena greater intellectual power will be developed. What must be the social phenomena of such a world! How extraordinary are the minds even of the lower animals. We cannot appreciate our own powers any more than a writer can appreciate his own stlye, or a thinker the peculiar quality of his own thought. I don't mean that a Dante did not know that he expressed himself with fewer words than other men do, but he could not admire himself as we admire him; nor can we wonder at human intelligence as we do at that of wasps. Let a man drink in such thoughts as come to him in contemplating the physico-psychical universe of mind which coincides with the universe of matter. The idea of there being a God over it all of course will be often suggested; and the more he considers it, the more he will be enwrapt with Love of this idea. He will ask himself whether or not there really is a God. If he allows instinct to speak, and searches his own heart, he will at length find that he cannot help believing it. I cannot tell how every man will think. I know the majority of men, especially educated men, are so full of pedantries,—especially the male sex,—that they cannot think straight about these things. But I can tell how a man must think if he is a pragmatist. Now the shower of communications that I have been getting during the last two months causes me to share the expectation that I find so many good judges are entertaining, that pragmatism is going to be the dominant philosophical opinion of the XX th century.

Pragmatism, as it was originally defined by me, is the doctrine that the *entire* intellectual purport of a concept consists in the sum of all the conceivable conditional resolutions as to conduct to which it would give rise under the different conceivable circumstances and under the different conceivable motives. But so many of those who have been attracted by the doctrine wish to include, as part of the meaning, sensations, while still calling themselves pragmatists, and some of them wish to limit it to what *will* happen, that I now recommend that the word be understood in the general sense of those who think they belong to the same school of thought as those who are now commonly called pragmatists. I continue to hold my original opinion which I now call *pragmaticism*. It is perfectly understood, the world over, that I am the father of the whole movement. I am confident that when the matter is thoroughly sifted it will be found that sensation has nothing to do with the intellectual purport, and that it is absolutely necessary to admit the conceivable general conditional resolutions.

I must point out some of the doctrines that are involved in pragmaticism. The entire intellect of the middle ages from about the end of the second crusade when Aristotle's Analytics became known in Western Europe, say A.D. 1149,—though perhaps I ought to go back to the days when those two great beings Gerbert (i.e. Herbert) and Theophane, the daughter, played their parts upon the stage of Europe,—down to the fall of Constantinople in A.D. 1453, when the Humanists began to be influential, was concentrated upon the question of the reality of generals, and the questions connected with that. At first, Nominalism had the upper hand, and Abelard was its *fin fleur*. Then, deeper studies brought a limited and carefully defined Realism,—the doctrine that *some* generals are real. In the hands of Duns Scotus, and his contemporaries toward the end of the XIII th century, this doctrine became so extraordinarily elaborated, that Ockham, moved partly by political and ecclesiastical motives, undertook to revive nominalism. Hobbes and Leibniz were students of Ockham (though in the later philosophy of Leibniz there is much that is profoundly inconsistent with nominalism, especially his principle of Continuity). Berkeley may have dipped into Ockham. At any rate, he was influenced by Hobbes. Hume's philosophy resulted from the study of Berkeley. Upon them came Gay and Hartley, who however paid no particular attention to the nominalistic philosophy. Upon them James Mill built his philosophy. John Stuart Mill, Bain, Grote, and others were direct pupils of James Mill, who also influenced his intensely nominalistic friend Bentham. Thus, all that English philosophy (really Scotch, but what we call Scotch Philosophy is opposed to it) was the school of Ockham. But in the Middle Ages, when the study of philosophy was carried on in oral disputations, conducted under a strict system of rules, called the Obligations, so that disputants were kept strictly to the point, and were obliged squarely to meet *all* their opponents arguments, in a way now, alas, utterly obsolete, under that system the Ockhamists were beaten out of their boots, so that when the Humanists came, they found the Scotists,—the Dunses, as they were called,—in control of the universities. Now these Dunses had a complete disdain for elegance. They looked upon study as a study of the truth, according to scientific methods. They thought elegance was merely turning the minds of young men to trifles. In short, the Dunses were obscurantists. It is interesting to see that in these days the word "dunce,"—i.e. Duns,— did not at all convey the notion of stupidity or want of intellect. Quite the contrary, a dunce was a person who was so deep and subtle in his thought that no ordinary person could cope with him; but he was a person who knew no Greek, who read and wrote the most unreadable books, and who held elegant literature in contempt. The humanists were, some of them, bright minds; but they never deeply studied philosophy, being wholly engaged in literature. They hated the Dunses, and very naturally embraced the simpler doctrine of Ockham, while declining to dispute or argue about it. Through the reformation and also because scholasticism had exhausted all its important problems and had come to be occupied with nonsense, the humanists gained a complete victory, and got control of the universities. Thus, it resulted that all modern philosophy is nominalistic. Even Hegel is to my mind a nominalist; Kant is decidedly and prominently so. Yet the only real discussion of the question had gone the other way.

Writing to my brother, I can permit myself to say that my strongest philosophical works were a paper of May 14, 1867, *On a New List of Categories* and a paper which appeared some time in 1868 called *Some Consequences of Four Incapacities,* in which I declared for scholastic realism. I argued it at more length in the North American Review for October 1871, in a review of Frazer's edition of Berkeley. Next after these, in strength, were my two connected papers of November 1877, *The Fixation of Belief,* and Jan 1878 (first written in French on a voyage from Hoboken to Plymouth in September 1877) *How to Make our Ideas Clear,* in which I enunciated the principle of pragmaticism. I have done a great deal of better work; but none of it has been printed. There is a pretty good article of Jan 1901 on *Pearson's Grammar of Science,* which attacks nominalism. In the *Monist* articles I am now writing I am greatly hampered for want of space and by the necessity of making myself understood by a somewhat large public. F.E. Abbot made a very clear defence of Realism in

the introduction to his book *Scientific Theism,* 1885. There are lots of philosophers who call themselves scholastic realists, but who are hardly so, such as Royce. As Abbot well says, every scientific man who believes the laws of nature represent any truth of nature and are not mere *arbitrary* arrangements of facts is, in so far, a Realist. It is plain that pragmaticism involves scholastic realism, since it makes all intellectual purport, and therefore, the meaning of reality itself, to consist in what *would be,* under conceivable conditions most of which can never be actualized. It thus involves making real being to include more than *existence.* Now that is precisely the point in dispute between Realists and Nominalists. "A real possibility," says the nominalist "is nonsense. For that is *possible* which we do not know is not true." The realist says that there is, besides, a real possibility and real necessity (not mere compulsion, but rational necessity, as in the laws of nature). I *can* open my window, if I find the air stuffy in my study. I really *can.* That is a positive objective possibility. I discussed Necessitarianism in the *Monist* of April 1892 and July 1893. It is a pity my best articles cannot be reprinted in one volume. It is perfectly heart-breaking to hear people tell me to my face, as they do, that they are perfectly unintelligible. If they were collected in a volume, philosophers would in some future generation get the benefit of them. If ever I get the chance to publish them, I have half a mind to write a mystifying preface to the effect that I have been a rummager, and that these doctrines are not mine at all, that I have simply phrased them. That is true; for they are God's truth. In that way, I may be able to point out their merits from a disinterested standpoint.

You will perceive that, according to pragmatism, our meaning is always more or less vague, and the more so the more the meaning approximates to what we see out of our eyes. A highly precise (i.e. "abstract") character, like the hardness of the diamond, is tolerably precisely conceived. And yet which of these four things is what we *mean* by the word hardness (as applied to a diamond more than to carborundum), leaving the other three as *properties* of hard things? 1. The possibility of scratching carborundum with a diamond. 2. The possibility of passing an edge of carborundum with great pressure over the face of a diamond without making a scratch. 3. The impossibility of drawing the edge of a diamond heavily over the face of a crystal of carborundum without scratching it. 4. The impossibility of scratching a diamond by drawing an edge of carborundum over its face. But now let us turn to the most familiar object there is, the material universe. You cannot define it or describe it, or do anything but just talk of IT. *It* is raining here. *It* is plain to be seen, but hard to express. Of course *grammatically* the "it" does not refer to the universe. But that is at the bottom of such impersonals. We also call it, *The Truth*, where the definite article shows we mean the universe.

If a pragmaticist is asked what he means by the word "God," he can only say that just as long acquaintance with a man of great character may deeply influence one's whole manner of conduct, so that a glance at his portrait may make a difference, just as almost living with Dr. Johnson enabled poor Boswell to write an immortal book and a really sublime book, just as long study of the works of Aristotle may make him an acquaintance, so if contemplation and study of the physico-psychical universe can imbue a man with principles of conduct analogous to the influence of a great man's works or conversation, then that analogue of a mind,—for it is impossible to say that *any* human attribute is *literally* applicable,—is what he means by "God." Of course, various great theologians explain that one cannot attribute *reason* to God, nor perception (which always involves an element of surprise, and of learning what one did not know), and, in short, that his "mind" is necessarily so unlike ours, that some,—though wrongly,—high in the church say that it is only negatively, as being entirely different from everything else, that we can attach any meaning to the Name. This is not so; because the discoveries of science, their enabling us to *predict* what will be the course of nature, is proof conclusive, that, though we cannot think any

thought of God's, we can catch a fragment of His Thought, as it were.

Now such being the pragmaticist's answer to the question what he means by the word "God," the question whether there really *is* such a being is the question whether all physical science is merely the figment,—the arbitrary figment,—of the students of nature, and further whether the *one* lesson the Gautama Boodha, Confucius, Socrates, and all who from any point of view have had their ways of conduct determined by meditation upon the physico-psychical universe, be only their arbitrary notion or be the Truth, behind the appearances which the frivolous man does not think of; and whether the superhuman courage which such contemplation has conferred upon priests who go to pass their lives with lepers and refuse all offers of rescue is mere silly fanaticism, the passion of a baby, or whether it is a strength derived from the power of the truth. Now the only guide to the answer to this question lies in the power of the passion of love which more or less overmasters every agnostic scientist and everybody who seriously and deeply considers the universe. But whatever there may be of *argument* in all this is as nothing, the merest nothing, in comparison to its force as an appeal to one's own instinct, which is to argument what substance is to shadow, what bed-rock is to the built foundations of a cathedral.

Caldecott's *Philosophy of Religion* explains 13 different *types* of reasons for believing in God, with different varieties of several of them. I have examined them all with care, and think each one proves *something*. But I do not think their conclusions always have much to do with *religion*.

Suggestions for Further Reading

Works by Peirce

Charles Sanders Peirce: Contributions to The Nation. Three volumes. Edited by K. L. Ketner and J. E. Cook. Lubbock: Texas Tech University Press, 1975–1979.

The Collected Papers of Charles Sanders Peirce. Eight volumes. Edited by C. Hartshorne and P. Weiss (vol. 1–6), and A. Burks (vol. 7–8). Cambridge, Mass.: Harvard University Press, 1935, 1958.

Dictionary of Philosophy and Psychology. Edited by James Mark Baldwin. Two volumes. New York: Macmillan, 1901, 1902. (Peirce made many contributions, identifed in the *Comprehensive Bibliography.*)

Historical Perspectives on Peirce's Logic of Science: A History of Science. Edited by C. Eisele. Berlin: Mouton-DeGruyter, 1985.

The New Elements of Mathematics. Edited by C. Eisele. The Hague: Mouton, 1976.

Semiotic and Significs. Edited by C. S. Hardwick. Bloomington: Indiana University Press, 1977.

Writings of Charles S. Peirce. Twenty volumes projected; two volumes have appeared. Edited by M. H. Fisch et al. Bloomington: Indiana University Press, 1982, 1984.

Anthologies

Chance, Love and Logic. Edited by Morris Cohen. New York: Century, 1923, 1980.
Charles S. Peirce: Selected Writings. Edited by Philip P. Weiner. (Original title: *Values in a Universe of Chance.*) New York: Dover, 1961.
Philosophical Writings of Peirce. Edited by Justus Buchler. New York: Dover, 1940.

Essential Works on Peirce

Carolyn Eisele. *Studies in the Scientific and Mathematical Philosophy of Charles S. Peirce.* Edited by R. M. Martin. The Hague: Mouton, 1979.
Joseph L. Esposito. *Evolutionary Metaphysics: The Development of Peirce's Theory of Categories.* Athens: Ohio University Press, 1980.
Max H. Fisch. *Peirce, Semeiotic, and Pragmatism: Essays by Max H. Fisch.* Edited by K. Ketner and C. Kloesel. Bloomington: Indiana University Press, 1986.
Christopher Hookway, *Peirce.* London: Routledge and Kegan Paul, 1986.
Kenneth L. Ketner, editor. *A Comprehensive Bibliography of the Published Works of Charles Sanders Peirce.* Second ed. rev., Bowling Green, KY: Philosophy Documentation Center, 1986.
Kenneth L. Ketner, editor. *Proceedings of the C. S. Peirce Bicentennial International Congress.* Lubbock: Texas Tech University, 1981.
R. S. Robin. *Annotated Catalogue of the Papers of Charles S. Peirce.* Amherst: University of Massachusetts Press, 1967. This is supplemented by Robin's "The Peirce Papers: A Supplementary Catalogue," *Transactions of the Charles S. Peirce Society,* Vol. 7, 1971, pp. 37–57.
Don D. Roberts. *The Existential Graphs of Charles S. Peirce.* The Hague: Mouton, 1973.

WILLIAM JAMES

Introduction by John J. McDermott

The thought of William James is the vestibule to the speculative break-throughs of the twentieth century. He anticipates the directions of modern physics, psychoanalysis and depth psychology, modern art, and the emphasis on relations rather than on objects or substances. James is a process philosopher, by which we mean that he assesses the journey, the flow, to be more important than the outcome or the product.

A contemporary of Henri Bergson, whom he influenced, and a goad to the subsequent work of John Dewey and Alfred North Whitehead, James was also a decisive factor in the thought of Niels Bohr, Edmund Husserl, Miguel de Unamuno, Maria Montessori, and a countless host of lesser figures. Long an underground thinker, William James rivals Emerson as a writer who is read widely by nonprofessional philosophers. The appeal of the writings of William James transcends disciplinary boundaries, for commentators on science, psychology, art, politics, ethics, and religion find his works as stimulating as do philosophers. In fact, the work of William James is never subject to such artificial discipline boundaries as that found in a typical university curriculum. He wrote for reflective people, no matter their occupation or persuasion. As such, James is the thinker who most appeals to the average person seeking wisdom and depth in his or her own, personal experiences.

Nonetheless, James's thought is not without its technical virtuosity and requires more than a casual reading or scanning to reveal its profounder import. In this volume we have presented the major highlights of James's positions on psychology, ethics, metaphysics, and the theory of knowledge. The selections have been taken from the ongoing critical edition of *The Works of William James* as published by Harvard University Press. These texts have been scrupulously edited and represent James's final thought on each issue. The limits of space do not allow us to present James's rich views on religion, psychical research, and his prescient commentary on European-American culture as found in his *Letters*.[1]

Before detailing the major lineaments of James's thought, it will be helpful to our understanding if we discuss his cultural and family context. The biographical details of the life of a major thinker is always of some assistance in enabling us to grasp the issues, the responses, and the omissions found in the work. In the case of William James, the details are of paramount importance, for his life and his work were entwined in an unusually intimate way.[2] Without attempting any psychobiography and without any speculation as to hidden meanings or hidden interpersonal relationships, we can still provide a portrait of James as an engaged, sometimes depressed and yet always alert person.

William James was the son of Henry James, Sr., and Mary Robertson Walsh, both of Scottish-Irish Protestant lineage. William was the oldest of five children and felt the burden of making a career worthy of the expectations of his father, who, ironically, never had one himself. Having a comfortable inheritance and having had his leg amputated as a youth, Henry James, Sr., concentrated on talking and writing imposing, verbose, and little-read theological books. He was a friend and confidant of the great literary figures in the American nineteenth century, for example, Margaret Fuller, Ralph Waldo Emerson, Bronson Alcott, Henry David Thoreau, James Russell Lowell, and Nathaniel Hawthorne. The family was inundated by ideas and was taken on frequent trips to Europe, where they received tutoring, especially in languages. The second son in the family was Henry James, Jr., the justly famous writer.[3] Two other sons, Garth Wilkinson and Robertson, lived star-crossed lives, mostly because of their experience in the American Civil War, a painful odyssey in which neither William nor Henry participated. The fifth child was Alice James, who suffered from neurasthenia until her death, from cancer, in 1892. She left behind a brilliant diary and many elegant letters. Trapped in a male-dominated family, her considerable literary talents found little room for public expression and she remained a victim throughout her life.[4]

Returning now to the life of William James, it is important to focus on his early years, from his birth in 1842 until 1870, when he reached an emotional crossroad at the age of twenty-eight. James was privately educated and in fact had no college degree, although he studied at Harvard College periodically. He did manage to sit for the examination required for a medical degree, which he received in 1869, while promising never to practice, for he regarded the state of nineteenth-century medicine as largely humbug. Nonetheless, he read widely and in several languages, especially French and German. In 1867, he began publishing unsigned reviews of some of the books he was reading. It was at this time, however, that James was under a cloud of depression and was suffering from deep feelings of insecurity and inadequacy.

Sometime toward the end of the decade, James underwent a frightening personal experience, called in nineteenth-century parlance a vastation. Taken from the work of the mystic-philosopher Emanuel Swedenborg, a vastation refers to the projecting of the inner self outward, usually in a grotesque form. Notably, this experience of William James was strikingly similar to one had by his father at approximately the same age in his own life. James records this experience surreptitiously, as though it came to him by an unknown French correspondent. We now know that it is an autobiographical report from William James and we offer it here in full.

> Whilst in this state of philosophic pessimism and general depression of spirits about my prospects, I went one evening into a dressing-room in the twilight to procure some article that was there; when suddenly there fell upon me without any warning, just as if it came out of the darkness, a horrible fear of my own existence. Simultaneously there arose in my mind the image of an epileptic patient whom I had seen in the asylum, a black-haired youth with greenish skin, entirely idiotic, who used to sit all day on one of the benches, or rather shelves against the wall, with his knees drawn up against his chin, and the coarse gray undershirt, which was his only garment, drawn over them inclosing his entire figure. He sat there like a sort of sculptured Egyptian cat or Peruvian mummy, moving nothing but his black eyes and looking absolutely non-human. This image and my fear entered into a species of combination with each other. *That shape am I,* I felt, potentially. Nothing that I possess can defend me against that fate, if the hour for it

should strike for me as it struck for him. There was such a horror of him, and such a perception of my own merely momentary discrepancy from him, that it was as if something hitherto solid within my breast gave way entirely, and I became a mass of quivering fear. After this the universe was changed for me altogether. I awoke morning after morning with a horrible dread at the pit of my stomach, and with a sense of the insecurity of life that I never knew before, and that I have never felt since. It was like a revelation; and although the immediate feelings passed away, the experience has made me sympathetic with the morbid feelings of others ever since. It gradually faded, but for months I was unable to go out into the dark alone.

In general I dreaded to be left alone. I remember wondering how other people could live, how I myself had ever lived, so unconscious of that pit of insecurity beneath the surface of life. My mother in particular, a very cheerful person, seemed to me a perfect paradox in her unconsciousness of danger, which you may well believe I was very careful not to disturb by revelations of my own state of mind. I have always thought that this experience of melancholia of mine had a religious bearing. . . . I mean that the fear was so invasive and powerful that if I had not clung to scripture-texts like 'The eternal God is my refuge,' etc., 'Come unto me, all ye that labor and are heavy-laden,' etc., 'I am the resurrection and the life,' etc. I think I should have grown really insane.[5]

The key line here is *"That shape am I,* I felt, potentially." James, early on, became convinced of the diaphanous and utterly fragile character of the classically alleged, rock-bottom personal self. With exquisite originality James diagnoses the fabric of self-consciousness only to discover that it is neither a redoubt nor a bunker. He doubts the existence of the traditional "soul" and opts rather for a more free-flowing movement between the focus of one's own self and the fringe that we visit. These visits to the fringe turn up radically different versions of our own selves, for, it turns out, we are actually multiple selves. The fundamental question that nags James at this time has to do with whether we have any control over the making of our own self. In early 1870, James makes an entry in his diary that reveals his pervasive dubiety about his ability to transcend the jejune character of ordinary life, with its routine and often hypocritical demands. Although he does not admit his suicidal tendency until a subsequent entry, James in February of 1870, depressed by the death of his young and beautiful cousin Minny Temple, drew a tombstone in his diary and dallied with his own demise. The text reads as follows:

Feb. 1, 1870

. . . Today I about touched bottom, and perceive plainly that I must face the choice with open eyes: shall I frankly throw the moral business overboard, as one unsuited to my innate aptitudes, or shall I follow it, and it alone, making everything else merely stuff for it? I will give the latter alternative a fair trial. Who knows but the moral interest may become developed . . . Hitherto I have tried to fire myself with the moral interest, as an aid in the accomplishing of certain utilitarian ends.[6]

James hereby laments the bland nineteenth-century Protestant ethic that suffuses his life. Proper manners, career, and systemic hypocrisy are the constant accompaniments of his consciousness and his conscience. In that both his reading and the turbulence of his interior life taught him that there must be more, evermore, James casts a wistful glance at suicide but then, fortunately, begins to read the works of the philosopher Charles Renouvier, for whom the will is not so much an agent of approbation as it is an agent of change. In April of 1870, James makes a diary entry that is to be decisive for both his life and his thought.

April 30, 1870

I think that yesterday was a crisis in my life. I finished the first part of Renouvier's second "Essais" and see no reason why his definition of Free Will—"the sustaining of a thought *because I choose to* when I might have other thoughts"—need be the definition of an illusion. At any rate, I will assume for the present—until next year—that it is no illusion. My first act of free will shall be to believe in free will. For the remainder of the year, I will abstain from the mere speculation and contemplative *Grublei* in which my nature takes most delight, and voluntarily cultivate the feeling of moral freedom, by reading books favorable to it, as well as by acting. After the first of January, my callow skin being somewhat fledged, I may perhaps return to metaphysical study and skepticism without danger to my powers of action. For the present then remember: care little for speculation; much for the *form* of my action; recollect that only when habits of order are formed can we advance to really interesting fields of action—and consequently accumu-late grain on grain of willful choice like a very miser; never forgetting how one link dropped undoes an indefinite number. *Principiis obsta*—Today has furnished the excep-tionally passionate initiative which Bain posits as needful for the acquisition of habits. I will see to the sequel. Not in maxims, not in *Anschauungen,* but in accumulated *acts* of thought lies salvation. *Passer outre.* Hitherto, when I have felt like taking a free initia-tive, like daring to act originally, without carefully waiting for contemplation of the external world to determine all for me, suicide seemed the most manly form to put my daring into; now, I will go a step further with my will, not only act with it, but believe as well; believe in my individual reality and creative power. My belief, to be sure, *can't* be optimistic—but I will posit life (the real, the good) in the self-governing *resistance* of the ego to the world. Life shall [be built in] doing and suffering and creating.[7]

When one comes to know James's thought, this text reads like an early blueprint of all of his later intellectual concerns. We sort out only the major contention, namely, that the human will is cognitive. The first act of the will, with no rational guarantees pro-vided, is to believe that the will is free. By this James does not mean free to assume that what we believe is necessarily true. Rather, the will is free to believe in possibilities underwent until the crush of empirical facticity rejects the belief. No optimism here, for James stresses the hazards of taking a chance, a risk, a gamble on the future of experi-ence. Yet, were we to hang back, we would never know the possible paths extant, many of which are blocked from our view by the dominance of rote, habit, custom and ill-advised authority.

The concluding sentence of this diary entry is crucial to James's project, for he affirms the creative and constitutive activity of the self. He is aware of the presence of self-deception, setback, and foolhardy risk. Still, he reaches for the aggressive and chance-ridden character of moving out, moving into the unknown, for the personal alternative of acceptance of the religious, ethical, and social status quo is stultifying and depressing.

After his recovery, James began to plot his belated future. Throughout the 1870s he wrote book reviews, most of them also unsigned. The year 1878, however, was to be dramatically auspicious. In that year, he wrote and published his first detailed essays and he promised to deliver a textbook in psychology to the well-respected publisher Henry Holt. James had been teaching physiology and psychology at Harvard since 1873 and was now willing to structure his thoughts in a systematic way. Perhaps most important in his journey, James married Alice Howe Gibbens in 1878, thereby assuring him of both roots and sustenance away from the demands and carping of his paternal home. The next twelve years were to be very productive for James and they culminated in the publication of his magisterial two-volume work *The Principles of Psychology,* a book still regarded as the greatest work in the history of psychology and one of the classic written works in the history of the English language.

William James was to continue publishing until his death in 1910 at the age of sixty-eight. When finished, his collected works of published and unpublished writings will approximate twenty volumes. It would be impossible and improper for an introduction of this kind to probe all of the themes and arguments in such an extensive set of writings. All the more true is this in that an understanding of James's thought requires an acquaintance with his philosophical peers and his polemical opponents. His letters and writings bristle with praise, condemnation, and rhetorical questioning of the great minds of the European-American period from 1870 until 1910. Central to his concerns was the thought of Herbert Spencer, whom he loathed, Darwin, Shadworth Hodgson, Henri Bergson, and his friendly foil, colleague, and neighbor, Josiah Royce. Familiar to James was the thought of all the experimental psychologists and most of the philosophers of the nineteenth century. There were omissions, however, for he did not have a serious acquaintance with the work of Marx, Nietzsche, or Kierkegaard. Still, he was the first major thinker to realize the signal contribution and the rich intellectual future of the work of John Dewey and, long before any one else, James knew of the genius of Charles Sanders Peirce.

The bold and innovative thought of William James was not without its critics, primarily those of the incipient analytical philosophical persuasion, especially as found in the critiques of G. E. Moore and Bertrand Russell, both of which were dramatically wrong-headed and shallow.[8] James was not without responsibility for the rising tide of criticism directed to his work, for he often published his public lectures without recasting them with regard to the more critical and dubious philosophical reader. James was a flamboyant, witty, and brilliant lecturer whose prose style was often elegant at the expense of conceptual detail. Put differently, most of James's published works, especially those which are famous as, for example, *The Will to Believe, The Varieties of Religious Experience, Pragmatism,* and *A Pluralistic Universe,* are virtuoso performances in a prose that delights, tantalizes, and is often telescoped as to the assumptions and arguments at work behind the scene.

The present setting of this introduction does not have the girth sufficient to unravel all of James's assumptions active in his writing. Still, we can point to three texts that serve as mooring points for an understanding of his philosophical position, one which is demonstrated over and again in both his published work and in his unpublished papers. The first of these texts is from his early period as found in the essay "The Sentiment of Rationality," first published in 1879. The remaining two texts are to be found in his *Pragmatism,* published in 1907, although they represent cameo versions of two seemingly contradictory positions long at war in his thought throughout his reflective life.

The opening text reads as follows:

> If we survey the field of history and ask what feature all great periods of revival, of expansion of the human mind, display in common, we shall find, I think, simply this: that each and all of them have said to the human being, "The inmost nature of the reality is congenial to *powers* which you possess."[9]

This text shows James to be a pragmatic idealist, that is, a position which admits to the existence of the world in its sheer physicality but at the same time affirms the source of meaning for that world to be dependent on the creative imagination of the human mind. Reality is not a surd, having no internal coherence. The coherence, however, does not flash out as an obvious and intractable set of laws, as Aristotle would have it. Reality is not given, final, and complete to the human mind. Rather, it is "congenial" to our understanding and our principles of organization. Reality is not permanently opaque and unintelligible, as philosophical nihilism contends. To the contrary, the human mind and reality enter into a relationship in which the "powers" of human imagination and the "energies" of human activity act as a constituting source for meaning. Such meaning is never complete, for the "inmost nature of reality" is only "congenial" to our powers and, therefore, never fully explicated.

Following James, the history of human language and civilization is equivalent to the evolving meaning of reality. As with DNA, this process is open-ended and is laced with chance as a permanent strand in the relationship between the physical world and the human mind. James sees no possibility of reality ever being grasped whole and entire. He offers two reasons for this never-ending pluralism. First, nature itself is subject to multiple permutations that violate its own history and, second, each human perspective is precisely that, a perspective, and cannot be exactly dovetailed with the perspectives of other human beings. Consequently, James holds that the world is intelligible, but not in any final way. He describes reality as a pluriverse or a multiverse, riven with chance, mishap, and always denying any intellectual or conceptual closure.[10] In a notebook entry of 1903, James states his aversion to philosophical closure.

> What, on pragmatist terms, does 'nature itself' signify? To my mind it signifies the non-artificial; the artificial having certain definite aesthetic characteristics which I dislike, and can only apperceive in others as matters of personal taste,—to me bad taste. All neat schematisms with permanent and absolute distinctions, classifications with absolute pretensions, systems with pigeon-holes, etc., have this character. All 'classic,' clean, cut and dried, 'noble,' fixed, 'eternal,' *Weltanschauungen* seem to me to violate the character with which life concretely comes and the expression which it bears of being, or at least of involving, a muddle and a struggle, with an 'ever not quite' to all our formulas, and novelty and possibility forever leaking in.[11]

William James's stress on "novelty," "possibility," and an "ever not quite" to all of our judgments has always irritated professional philosophers, known for their drive toward clarity and even closure. James is unquestionably an antifoundationalist philosopher, by which we mean that he opposes the effort, begun by René Descartes in the seventeenth century, to place philosophical inquiry on a footing that is absolutely secure, one that rivals the alleged certitude of mathematics. To be an antifoundationalist and an anti-Cartesian is now quite acceptable in contemporary philosophy, but it was the early pragmatists Chauncey Wright, Charles Sanders Peirce, and William James who were the first to challenge the arrogance of claims for absolute philosophical certitude. Yet, despite his proclivity for chance, novelty, and a permanent pluralism in our understanding of the world, James was not naive about the obduracy of nature and about the way in which nature has its own meaning, independent of the way in which we perceive it. In his *Pragmatism*, published in 1907, James issues a warning to those who fail to match conceptions with the way in which reality "concretely comes."

> *Woe to him whose beliefs*
> *play fast and loose with*
> *the order which realities*
> *follow in his experience;*
> *they will lead him nowhere*
> *or else make false connexions.*[12]

In order to explicate this text, some background information and analysis is essential. Before publishing *Pragmatism*, James had published a series of essays, in 1904–1905, subsequently collected posthumously in 1912 as *Essays in Radical Empiricism*. As early as 1897, in a preface to his *Will to Believe*, James had described his philosophical position as radical empiricism.

> Were I obliged to give a short name to the attitude in question, I should call it that of *radical empiricism*. . . . I say "empiricism" because it is contented to regard its most assured conclusions concerning matters of fact as hypotheses liable to modification in the course of future experience; and I say "radical," because it treats the doctrine of monism itself as an hypothesis. . . .

> He who takes for his hypothesis the notion that it [pluralism] is the permanent form of the world is what I call a radical empiricist. For him the crudity of experience remains an eternal element thereof. There is no possible point of view from which the world can appear an absolutely single fact.[13]

Again, in 1909, in another preface, James lays out the characteristics of radical empiricism.

> Radical empiricism consists first of a postulate, next of a statement of fact, and finally of a generalized conclusion.
> The postulate is that the only things that shall be debatable among philosophers shall be things definable in terms drawn from experience. [Things of an unexperienceable

nature may exist *ad libitum,* but they form no part of the material for philosophic debate.]

The statement of fact is that the relations between things, conjunctive as well as disjunctive, are just as much matters of direct particular experience, neither more so nor less so, than the things themselves.

The generalized conclusion is that therefore the parts of experience hold together from next to next by relations that are themselves parts of experience. The directly apprehended universe needs, in short, no extraneous transempirical connective support, but possesses in its own right a concatenated or continuous structure.[14]

Returning to the text from *Pragmatism* cited above, we can now see how James telescopes his deeper meanings, for nothing less than a grasp of his radical empiricism enables us to appreciate his warning. "Woe to him" (or her) refers to any attempt to forge or make relations that are in stark opposition to the way in which reality sets up.

Such an effort has the extremely baleful consequence of failing to "make connexions," that is, failing to hook into the flow of both consciousness and nature. James holds that objects are mock-ups, pockets, boxes of relations that are snipped and packaged for reasons of utility. Our task is to acknowledge these "substantive states," these "perches" in the stream, while yet regarding them as functional, placeholders, and pregnant with "connections" that transcend them. If we do not take these perches, these gatherings into consideration, then we may as well confuse water with stone and wood with cloth. On the other hand, if we allow ourselves only a literal reading of the flow, we become trapped as merely a definer, categorizer, and obsequious servant of the way in which the world has been passed down to us, in all of its obviousness, banality, and rigidity. Thus, the second text in *Pragmatism* states:

> In our cognitive as well as in our active life we are creative. We *add* both to the subject and to the predicate part of reality. The world stands really malleable, waiting to receive its final touches at our hand. Like the kingdom of heaven, it suffers violence willingly. Man *engenders* truths upon it.[15]

This text is extraordinary, especially given the warning by James, discussed above. Here we have in an unvarnished way James's doctrine of the Promethean self. The text itself is exquisite. Notice the emphasis on the "hands." Reality does not come ready-made. It is true that for James, reality has its own relational network, its own obduracy. Yet, reality is malleable, pliant, awaiting our touch, our presence, our organization. The fabric known as the world results from the raw physicality of nature and the probing, constituting presence of the human imagination. Consequently, science is not final or absolute. Science functions more like a prose poem, gathering, relating, searching, and structuring, temporarily. It is the world which we come to know, more or less. It is the world with which we transact, for better or for worse. Yet, without human imagination, cognition, and construction, there would be no world, no relations, no metaphors, and, finally, no meaning.

This tension between the world as given, present, set up, in business, and our version of the world, splayed out over many disciplines, patterns, and charts, is precisely the center of James's philosophy. Human life cannot make a world out of whole cloth, *ab ovo*. Still, the world is meaningless without human articulation of its meaning, a meaning that is inseparable from how we came to mean the world. The problem, of course, is that the human version of the world is conflicted, for there is more than one of us. James was not sufficiently sophisticated about the social conditioning that pervades our personal world view. This sense of the social context for individual versions of experience was to be explored in depth by his successors, John Dewey and George Herbert Mead, as well as by his European counterparts, Karl Marx, Wilhelm Dilthey, and the twentieth-century founders of the sociology of knowledge, especially Karl Mannheim. Despite his comparative unawareness of the immediate social contexting of the individual self, James was aware of the pluralism of approaches to constructing a meaningful world, as witness his statement in *Pragmatism*:

> Ought not the existence of the various types of thinking which we have reviewed, each so splendid for certain purposes, yet all conflicting still, and neither one of them able to support a claim of absolute veracity, to awaken a presumption favorable to the pragmatistic view that all our theories are *instrumental,* are mental modes of *adaptation* to reality, rather than revelations or gnostic answers to some divinely instituted world-enigma? . . . Certainly the restlessness of the actual theoretic situation, the value for some purposes of each thought-level, and the inability of either to expel the others decisively, suggest this pragmatistic view.[16]

James's pluralistic approach to inquiry is distinctively American in that it allows everyone to have his or her say before the inquiry is put to rest, and even a reopening of the discussion awaits the slightest hint of new information, data, or perspective. For example in his essay "The Sentiment of Rationality," published in 1879, James stresses the role of temperament as crucial to one's philosophical approach. In the absence of a full selection of this essay, I offer the reader two long representative texts. First:

> . . . All those data that cannot be analytically identified with the attribute invoked as universal principle, remain as independent kinds or natures, associated empirically with the said attribute but devoid of rational kinship with it.
>
> Hence the unsatisfactoriness of all our speculations. On the one hand, so far as they retain any multiplicity in their terms, they fail to get us out of the empirical sand-heap world; on the other, so far as they eliminate multiplicity the practical man despises their empty barrenness. The most they can say is that the elements of the world are such and such, and that each is identical with itself wherever found; but the question Where is it found? the practical man is left to answer by his own wit. Which, of all the essences, shall here and now be held the essence of this concrete thing, the fundamental philosophy never attempts to decide. We are thus led to the conclusion that the simple classification of things is, on the one hand, the best possible theoretic philosophy, but is, on the other, a most miserable and inadequate substitute for the fulness of the truth. It is a monstrous abridgment of life, which, like all abridgments is got by the absolute loss and casting out of real matter. This is why so few human beings truly care for philosophy. The particular determinations which she ignores are the real matter exciting needs, quite as potent and authoritative as hers. What does the moral enthusiast care for philosophi-

cal ethics? Why does the *Aesthetik* of every German philosopher appear to the artist as an abomination of desolation?

Second, the conclusion of the essay:

> To sum up: No philosophy will permanently be deemed rational by all men which (in addition to meeting logical demands) does not to some degree pretend to determine expectancy, and in a still greater degree make a direct appeal to all those powers of our nature which we hold in highest esteem. Faith, being one of these powers, will always remain a factor not to be banished from philosophic constructions, the more so since in many ways it brings forth its own verification. In these points, then, it is hopeless to look for literal agreement amongst mankind.
>
> The ultimate philosophy, we may therefore conclude, must not be too strait-laced in form, must not in all its parts divide heresy from orthodoxy by too sharp a line. There must be left over and above the propositions to be subscribed *ubique, semper, et ab omnibus,* another realm into which the stifled soul may escape from pedantic scruples and indulge its own faith at its own risks; and all that can here be done will be to mark out distinctly the questions which fall within faith's sphere.[17]

It is clear that for James, openness to experience, to novelty, to surprise is a cardinal tenet of the philosophical enterprise. Inquiry which proceeds from narrow, a priori assumptions is anathema in James's search for truth, meaning, and insight.

The selections that follow illustrate James's basic philosophical, moral, and personal approaches to the major questions that confront us as human beings. The order of these selections is not chronological but rather first introduces the reader to James's psychology, metaphysics, and pragmatic epistemology and then proceeds to the earlier moral writings. The rationale for this ordering is that the later thought of James is assumed by him in the earlier writings, which are only intelligible given the overall published agenda. Similarly, this discussion of the selections follows no chronology but rather seeks to help the reader obtain apertures into the seminal thought of William James.

Dividing the world into the "tough-minded" and the "tender-minded," as he does in *Pragmatism,* reveals James's thought as a mixture of both.

THE TENDER-MINDED	THE TOUGH-MINDED
Rationalistic (going by 'principles'),	Empiricist (going by 'facts'),
Intellectualistic,	Sensationalistic,
Idealistic,	Materialistic,
Optimistic,	Pessimistic,
Religious,	Irreligious,
Free-willist,	Fatalistic,
Monistic,	Pluralistic,
Dogmatical.	Sceptical.[18]

If we were to apply these tables to James, we would find that he is "tender-minded," to wit: Idealistic, Optimistic, Religious and Free-willist. We would find that he is also "tough-minded," to wit: Empiricist, Sensationalistic, and Pluralistic. To resolve this opposition, James invokes the sentiment of rationality, by which he means to stress the inordinate importance of how we "feel" about things, others, and the world as a factor in how we "think" about the same concerns.

The "Dilemma of Determinism" published in 1884, is a tour de force, one of James's most brilliant essays. The upshot of his position is that even if it turns out that all is determined, it would make no difference in any past experience, all of which were had under the guise of free will. Second, if all were to be determined from here on, there is considerable doubt as to whether we could or would live under such a rubric, leading James to conclude that, whatever the ultimate course may be, it is our decision *here* and *now* that "gives the palpitating reality to our moral life."

Another selection comes from James's classic chapter on "The Stream of Thought,"[19] from *The Principles of Psychology,* published in 1890. This chapter is a reworking of an important essay written by James in 1884, "On Some Omissions of Introspective Psychology."[20] At that time, James isolated two major approaches to epistemological certitude, that is, to a viable theory of knowledge. Both of these approaches were considered by James in a broad and nontechnical fashion, given that he was more interested in his resolution than in their proposals. In short, never trust a great, imaginative thinker to yield an accurate version of other great thinkers. That task is for the historians of ideas. Still, James is prescient when he cites the following problems at work in the Associationist and Idealist epistemologies, respectively.

First, James praises Associationism for its emphasis on particulars and on the role of the body in the knowing activity. Descended from Locke, the Associationists held that the mind was literally a responder to single bodily sensations and was able to associate a parallel set of ideas to the set of sensations had. James, however, denied that any such activity takes place in the human mind. In a chapter in the *Principles* entitled "The Methods and Snares of Psychology," James decries the naivete of the Associationist position.

> As each object may come and go, be forgotten and then thought of again, it is held that the thought of it has a precisely similar independence, self-identity, and mobility. The thought of the object's recurrent identity is regarded as the identity of its recurrent thought; and the perceptions of multiplicity, of coexistence, of succession, are severally conceived to be brought about only through a multiplicity, a coexistence, a succession, of perceptions. The continuous flow of the mental stream is sacrificed, and in its place an atomism, a brickbat plan of construction, is preached, for the existence of which no good introspective grounds can be brought forward, and out of which presently grow all sorts of paradoxes and contradictions, the heritage of woe of students of the mind.
>
> These words are meant to impeach the entire English psychology derived from Locke and Hume, and the entire German psychology derived from Herbart, as far as they both treat 'ideas' as separate subjective entities that come and go.[21]

James's basic critique of the Associationist doctrine is that it does not provide for any continuity in our experience, holding rather to a relationship of mere contiguity or next-by-next. The second position that James analyzes does provide continuity, for all experience is unintelligible unless it is grasped as an aspect of the Absolute Mind. Referring to this viewpoint as British Idealism, James criticizes its inability to account for particulars and the comparative absence of bodily sensations in the act of knowing. James waged a lifelong debate on the plausibility of the Idealist position with two of its most brilliant exponents, F. H. Bradley and Josiah Royce. The fundamental issue is whether one has to forgo experiential continuity in order to experience particulars or whether one has to forgo particulars in order to posit a general coherence in the way particular experiences hang together.

In his 1884 essay "On Some Omissions of Introspective Psychology" and again in his chapter "The Stream of Thought" in *The Principles of Psychology* of 1890, James rejects both positions in favor of a claim that we experience relations between objects as well as the objects themselves, thereby providing both the experience of particulars and the experience of continuity. He writes, "If there be such things as feelings at all, *then so surely as relations between objects exist* [in the nature of things], *so surely, and more surely, do feelings exist to which these relations are known.*" And, further, "we ought to say a feeling of *and,* a feeling of *if,* a feeling of *by,* quite as readily as we say a feeling of *blue* or a feeling of *cold.*"[22] James's contention that we have an affective grasp of relations leads him to diagnose the activity of consciousness as a flow, a stream, rather than as a container or a box. The selection below on "The Stream of Thought" provides a rich description of the activity of consciousness. A subsequent selection on "The World of Pure Experience" attempts to show that mind and body are not ultimately separate but only separate by name or by function. The flow of consciousness is whole and continuous, whereas our conceptual formulations tend to break it up into definitions, names, nouns, and other assorted categories.

It is true, of course, that to survive, human beings need placeholders, perches, moving points in the flow, which act as redoubts, way stations, and abodes. Were they not present, we would be carried in the stream as flotsam, rudderless. The task then is twofold: (1) forge those moorings that are most propitious and advantageous for our human needs and (2) avoid becoming trapped and mired such that we confuse our own temporary bunker with the entire fabric of possibility. The remaining three selections below address this issue head on. In "What Pragmatism Means," James stresses the importance of consequences as the source of evaluation of our acts and our beliefs. He urges us to liberate ourselves from a rote acceptance of dogmatic claims by opening ourselves to the call of experience, especially in its novel forms. In order for this to become a living attitude for us, we must forsake absolute certitude and beliefs that admit of no exception and generate intolerance rather than understanding for competing positions. In "The Moral Philosopher and the Moral Life," James stresses the importance of the strenuous mood, one which is forever seeking new possibilities, new vistas, and a wider range of choices.

The last selection to be considered is "The Will to Believe," James's best-known, most controversial, and most misunderstood essay. James is *not* saying that if one believes strongly enough, the belief will come true. He is saying that belief enables us to test hypotheses out of the range of our ordinary experience. If these hypotheses, when they unearth the data of new experience, prove to be inept, incomplete, or simply wrong, then they should be abandoned. We cannot know the worth of a belief until it is pressed forward into the crucible of new experience. James holds that the willingness to risk belief in possibilities that are often scoffed or mocked by common sense generates an energy that frequently leads to paths of insight otherwise closed off from us. This perpetual searching, this strenuous mood, pervades James's life and thought.

After the publication of *The Principles of Psychology*, James turned his attention to more directly philosophical works and he both lectured and published extensively until his death in 1910. His last book was entitled *A Pluralistic Universe*, in which he plumbed the reaches of extrasensory perception, the widest range of human consciousness, and wondered again about life after death. These were existentially appropriate themes at this time, for James was suffering from arteriosclerosis. In current terminology, he badly needed a heart bypass operation, obviously unavailable at the time. Instead, he went to Europe with his wife, Alice, and met his brother Henry while seeking some form of a cure through the mineral springs of the Continent or galvanic shock treatments. None of these nostrums worked and James returned home to die on Friday, August 26, 1910. Sixty-eight years of age, James nonetheless died prematurely. Had Kant or Dewey or Whitehead or Santayana died at that age, much of their work would have been undone. The autopsy revealed "acute enlargement of the heart."[23] Despite the voluminous work that James had published, he was frustrated that he had not finished his major treatise on philosophy. On July 26, 1910, exactly one month before his death, James stated that this manuscript would not be finished. "Call it 'a beginning of an introduction to philosophy.' Say that I hope by it to round out my system, which is now too much like an arch built on only one side."[24] The manuscript was published posthumously as *Some Problems of Philosophy* and presented sufficient insight to make us greatly lament that he never finished this intended major work.

The selections in this volume reveal classical American philosophy at its best. The selections from James are especially rich in wisdom and beauty of prose style. The reader is encouraged to proceed on to a full reading of James's *Works,* now excellently edited and easily available. James is an unusual philosophical writer in that he reverses the usual response of the reader. Most philosophy, at first reading, is impenetrable and pockmarked with the jargon and technical phrasing of the period. Slowly, the reader becomes acquainted with these prose shortcuts and then sufficiently sophisticated to make his or her way through the text. On reading James, however, the first response is one of elation at the apparent simplicity and elegance of the literary style. It is only after several readings that the philosophical depth and complexity begin to emerge, much to the delight of the reader, who, first seduced, is now educated.

I leave the reader with two short texts from the writings of William James. The first is as follows: "It is, in short, the re-instatement of the vague and the inarticulate to its proper place in our mental life which I am so anxious to press on the attention."[25] The quest is clear: avoid a life lived by formulas, by definitions, and seek instead the fringe, the novel, the unspoken, the secret and the hidden recesses of being, which speak only to those who know how to listen.

The second text was written in 1876 and is found in a brief letter to *The Nation,* entitled "The Teaching of Philosophy in Our Colleges." At that time, James wrote: "one can never deny that philosophic study means the habit of always seeing an alternative, of not taking the usual for granted, of making conventionalities fluid again, of imagining foreign states of mind."[26] This request of James is not easy to fulfill. Each of us has our bedrock. Each of us is frightened of new ideas, new perspectives, new values, and new beliefs. The opponent to a liberal education praises the encrusted, the habitual, and the socially acceptable. Yet human life has moved forward by taking chances. We have no guarantee that the alternatives to our present beliefs, habits, and values are better. They may be injurious. But, then, they may be enriching. How do we know what to do unless we try? Seek, then, an alternative and test it against the penalty and possibility of experience. Such is the philosophical message of William James.

NOTES

1. A basic bibliography of the writings of William James: *The Works of William James,* ed. Frederick Burkhardt (Cambridge, Mass.: Harvard University Press, 1975–). *Pragmatism,* 1975, Introduction by H. Standish Thayer. *The Meaning of Truth,* 1975, Introduction by H. Standish Thayer. *Essays in Radical Empiricism,* 1976, Introduction by John J. McDermott. *A Pluralistic Universe,* 1977, Introduction by Richard Bernstein. *The Will to Believe,* 1979, Introduction by Edward H. Madden. *Essays in Philosophy,* 1978, Introduction by John J. McDermott. *Some Problems of Philosophy,* 1979, Introduction by Peter H. Hare. *The Principles of Psychology,* 3 vols., 1981, Introduction by Gerald E. Myers and Rand B. Evans. *Essays in Religion and Morality,* 1982, Introduction by John J. McDermott. *Talks to Teachers on Psychology,* 1983, Introduction by Gerald E. Myers. *Essays in Psychology,* 1983, Introduction by William R. Woodward. *Psychology: Briefer Course,* 1984, Introduction by Michael M. Sokal. *The Varieties of Religious Experience,* 1985, Introduction by John E. Smith. *Essays in Psychical Research,* forthcoming, Introduction by Robert A. McDermott. Further volumes representing James's unpublished papers.
Leading commentaries are noted in the suggestions for further reading, pp. 176–177.
2. The life of William James has received unusually close attention. In addition to his *Letters* and the works by Allen, Myers, and Perry, cited in the "Suggestions for Further Reading," see: Howard M. Feinstein, *Becoming William James* (Ithaca: Cornell University Press, 1984). The entire family is brilliantly limned, with accompanying texts, in F. O. Matthiessen, *The James Family* (New York: Alfred A. Knopf, 1947).
3. Cf. Leon Edel, *Henry James,* 5 vols. (New York: J.B. Lippincott Company, 1953–1972). Also see *Henry James—Letters,* 4 vols., Leon Edel, ed. (Cambridge, Mass.: Harvard University Press, 1974–1984).
4. Cf. *The Diary of Alice James,* ed. by Leon Edel (New York: Dodd, Mead and Company, 1964). Also Jean Strouse, *Alice James—A Biography* (Boston: Houghton-Mifflin & Company, 1980).
5. *The Works of William James—The Varieties of Religious Experience,* pp. 134–135.
6. "Diary" in *The Writings of William James,* ed. John J. McDermott (Chicago: The University of Chicago Press, 1977), p. 7.
7. Ibid., pp. 7–8.
8. For the relevant texts in the ongoing critique of James's thought, especially his pragmatism, see *Pragmatic Philosophy,* ed. Amelie Rorty (New York: Doubleday and Company, 1966).
9. "The Sentiment of Rationality," in *The Works of William James—The Will to Believe,* p. 73.
10. *The Works of William James—A Pluralistic Universe,* passim.
11. Ralph Barton Perry, *The Thought and Character of William James,* 2 vols. (Boston: Little, Brown and Company, 1935), p. 700.
12. *The Works of William James—Pragmatism,* p. 99.
13. *The Works of Williams James—The Will to Believe,* pp. 5–6.
14. *The Works of William James—The Meaning of Truth,* pp. 6–7.
15. *The Works of William James—Pragmatism,* p.123.
16. Ibid., p. 94.
17. "The Sentiment of Rationality," in *The Works of William James—The Will to Believe,* pp. 61, 89.
18. *The Works of William James—Pragmatism,* p. 13.
19. When James published his shorter version of *The Principles of Psychology* under the title of *Psychology: Briefer Course,* he renamed this chapter "The Stream of Consciousness," a title that has become tremendously famous as it has been allied with the literary work of Marcel Proust, James Joyce, and many other writers of the twentieth century.

20. "On Some Omissions of Introspective Psychology," in *The Works of William James—Essays in Psychology,* pp. 142–167.

21. *The Works of William James—The Principles of Psychology,* pp. 194–195.

22. Ibid., p. 238. (Also included in the selections in this volume; see below, pp. 116–117).

23. For the record of James's wife, Alice, in her diary for these last days of his life, see Gay Wilson Allen, *William James: A Biography* (New York: The Viking Press, 1967), pp. 490–493.

24. Ibid., p. 469.

25. *The Works of William James—Psychology: Briefer Course,* p. 150.

25. "The Teaching of Philosophy," *The Works of William James—Essays in Philosophy,* p. 4.

The Stream of Thought

We now begin our study of the mind from within. Most books start with sensations, as the simplest mental facts, and proceed synthetically, constructing each higher stage from those below it. But this is abandoning the empirical method of investigation. No one ever had a simple sensation by itself. Consciousness, from our natal day, is of a teeming multiplicity of objects and relations, and what we call simple sensations are results of discriminative attention, pushed often to a very high degree. It is astonishing what havoc is wrought in psychology by admitting at the outset apparently innocent suppositions, that nevertheless contain a flaw. The bad consequences develop themselves later on, and are irremediable, being woven through the whole texture of the work. The notion that sensations, being the simplest things, are the first things to take up in psychology is one of these suppositions. The only thing which psychology has a right to postulate at the outset is the fact of thinking itself, and that must first be taken up and analyzed. If sensations then prove to be amongst the elements of the thinking, we shall be no worse off as respects them than if we had taken them for granted at the start.

The first fact for us, then, as psychologists, is that thinking of some sort goes on. I use the word thinking . . . for every form of consciousness indiscriminately. If we could say in English 'it thinks,' as we say 'it rains,' or 'it blows,' we should be stating the fact most simply and with the minimum of assumption. As we cannot, we must simply say that *thought goes on.*

FIVE CHARACTERS IN THOUGHT

How does it go on? We notice immediately five important characters in the process, of which it shall be the duty of the present chapter to treat in a general way:

1) Every thought tends to be part of a personal consciousness.

2) Within each personal consciousness thought is always changing.

3) Within each personal consciousness thought is sensibly continuous.

4) It always appears to deal with objects independent of itself.

5) It is interested in some parts of these objects to the exclusion of others, and welcomes or rejects—*chooses* from among them, in a word—all the while.

In considering these five points successively, we shall have to plunge *in medias res* as regards our vocabulary, and use psychological terms which can only be adequately defined in later chapters of the book. But everyone knows what the terms mean in a rough way; and it is only in a rough way that we are now to take them. This chapter is like a painter's first charcoal sketch upon his canvas, in which no niceties appear.

1) *Thought tends to Personal Form*

When I say *every thought is part of a personal consciousness,* 'personal consciousness' is one of the terms in question. Its meaning we know so long as no one asks us to define it, but to give an accurate account of it is the most difficult of philosophic tasks. This task we must confront in the next chapter; here a preliminary word will suffice.

In this room—this lecture-room, say—there are a multitude of thoughts, yours and mine, some of which cohere mutually, and some not. They are as little each-for-itself and reciprocally independent as they are all-belonging-together. They are neither: no one of them is separate, but each belongs with certain others and with none beside. My thought belongs with my other thoughts, and your thought with your other thoughts. Whether anywhere in the room there be a mere thought, which is nobody's thought, we have no means of ascertaining, for we have no experience of its like. The only states of consciousness that we naturally deal with are found in personal consciousnesses, minds, selves, concrete particular I's and you's.

Each of these minds keeps its own thoughts to itself. There is no giving or bartering between them. No thought even comes into direct *sight* of a thought in another personal consciousness than its own. Absolute insulation, ir-

From *The Works of William James—The Principles of Psychology,* 3 vols., ed., Frederick Burkhardt, (Cambridge, Mass.: Harvard University Press, 1981), pp. 219–240, 262–278.

reducible pluralism, is the law. It seems as if the elementary psychic fact were not *thought* or *this thought* or *that thought,* but *my thought,* every thought being *owned.* Neither contemporaneity, nor proximity in space, nor similarity of quality and content are able to fuse thoughts together which are sundered by this barrier of belonging to different personal minds. The breaches between such thoughts are the most absolute breaches in nature. Everyone will recognize this to be true, so long as the existence of *something* corresponding to the term 'personal mind' is all that is insisted on, without any particular view of its nature being implied. On these terms the personal self rather than the thought might be treated as the immediate datum in psychology. The universal conscious fact is not 'feelings and thoughts exist,' but 'I think' and 'I feel.' No psychology, at any rate, can question the *existence* of personal selves. The worst a psychology can do is so to interpret the nature of these selves as to rob them of their worth. A French writer, speaking of our ideas, says somewhere in a fit of anti-spiritualistic excitement that, misled by certain peculiarities which they display, we 'end by personifying' the procession which they make,—such personification being regarded by him as a great philosophic blunder on our part. It could only be a blunder if the notion of personality meant something essentially different from anything to be found in the mental procession. But if that procession be itself the very 'original' of the notion of personality, to personify it cannot possibly be wrong. It is already personified. There are no marks of personality to be gathered *aliunde,* and then found lacking in the train of thought. It has them all already; so that to whatever farther analysis we may subject that form of personal selfhood under which thoughts appear, it is, and must remain, true that the thoughts which psychology studies do continually tend to appear as parts of personal selves.

I say 'tend to appear' rather than 'appear' on account of those facts of sub-conscious personality, automatic writing, etc., of which we studied a few in the last chapter. The buried feelings and thoughts proved now to exist in hysterical anæsthetics, in recipients of post-hypnotic suggestion, etc., themselves are parts of *secondary personal selves.* These selves are for the most part very stupid and contracted, and are cut off at ordinary times from communication with the regular and normal self of the individual; but still they form

conscious unities, have continuous memories, speak, write, invent distinct names for themselves, or adopt names that are suggested; and, in short, are entirely worthy of that title of secondary personalities which is now commonly given them. According to M. Janet these secondary personalities are always abnormal, and result from the splitting of what ought to be a single complete self into two parts, of which one lurks in the background whilst the other appears on the surface as the only self the man or woman has. For our present purpose it is unimportant whether this account of the origin of secondary selves is applicable to all possible cases of them or not, for it certainly is true of a large number of them. Now although the *size* of a secondary self thus formed will depend on the number of thoughts that are thus split-off from the main consciousness, the *form* of it tends to personality, and the later thoughts pertaining to it remember the earlier ones and adopt them as their own. M. Janet caught the actual moment of inspissation (so to speak) of one of these secondary personalities in his anaesthetic somnambulist Lucie. He found that when this young woman's attention was absorbed in conversation with a third party, her anæsthetic hand would write simple answers to questions whispered to her by himself. "Do you hear?" he asked. "*No,*" was the unconsciously written reply. "But to answer you must hear." "*Yes, quite so.*" "Then how do you manage?" "*I don't know.*" "There must be someone who hears me." "*Yes.*" "Who?" "*Someone other than Lucie.*" "Ah! another person. Shall we give her a name?" "*No.*" "Yes, it will be more convenient." "*Well, Adrienne, then.*" "Once baptized, the subconscious personage," M. Janet continues, "grows more definitely outlined and displays better her psychological characters. In particular she shows us that she is conscious of the feelings excluded from the consciousness of the primary or normal personage. She it is who tells us that I am pinching the arm or touching the little finger in which Lucie for so long has had no tactile sensations."

In other cases the adoption of the name by the secondary self is more spontaneous. I have seen a number of incipient automatic writers and mediums as yet imperfectly 'developed,' who immediately and of their own accord write and speak in the name of departed spirits. These may be public characters, as Mozart, Faraday, or real persons formerly known to the subject, or altogether imaginary beings. Without prejudicing the question of real 'spirit-control' in the more developed sorts of trance-utterance, I incline to think that these (often deplorably unintelligent) rudimentary utterances are the work of an inferior fraction of the subject's own natural mind, set free from control by the rest, and working after a set pattern fixed by the prejudices of the social environment. In a spiritualistic community we get optimistic messages, whilst in an ignorant Catholic village the secondary personage calls itself by the name of a demon, and proffers blasphemies and obscenities, instead of telling us how happy it is in the summer-land.

Beneath these tracts of thought, which, however rudimentary, are still organized selves with a memory, habits, and sense of their own identity, M. Janet thinks that the facts of catalepsy in hysteric patients drive us to suppose that there are thoughts quite unorganized and impersonal. A patient in cataleptic trance (which can be produced artificially in certain hypnotized subjects) is without memory on waking, and seems insensible and unconscious as long as the cataleptic condition lasts. If, however, one raises the arm of such a subject it stays in that position, and the whole body can thus be moulded like wax under the hands of the operator, retaining for a considerable time whatever attitude he communicates to it. In hysterics whose arm, for example, is anæsthetic, the same thing may happen. The anæsthetic arm may remain passively in positions which it is made to assume; or if the hand be taken and made to hold a pencil and trace a certain letter, it will continue tracing that letter indefinitely on the paper. These acts, until recently, were supposed to be accompanied by no consciousness at all: they were physiological reflexes. M. Janet considers with much more plausibility that feeling escorts them. The feeling is probably merely that of the position or movement of the limb, and it produces no more than its natural effects when it discharges into the motor centres which keep the position maintained, or the movement incessantly renewed. Such thoughts as these, says M. Janet, "are known by *no one,* for disaggregated sensations reduced to a state of mental dust are not synthetized in any personality." He admits, however, that these very same unutterably stupid thoughts tend to develop memory,—the cataleptic ere long moves her arm at a bare hint; so that they form no important exception to the law that all thought tends to assume the form of personal consciousness.

2) *Thought is in Constant Change*

I do not mean necessarily that no one state of mind has any duration—even if true, that would be hard to establish. The change which I have more particularly in view is that which takes place in sensible intervals of time; and the result on which I wish to lay stress is this, that *no state once gone can recur and be identical with what it was before.* Let us begin with Mr. Shadworth Hodgson's description:

> "I go straight to the facts, without saying I go to perception, or sensation, or thought, or any special mode at all. What I find, when I look at my consciousness at all, is, that what I cannot divest myself of, or not have in consciousness, if I have any consciousness at all, is a sequence of different feelings. I may shut my eyes and keep perfectly still, and try not to contribute anything of my own will; but whether I think, or do not think, whether I perceive external things or not, I always have a succession of different feelings. Anything else that I may have also, of a more special character, comes in as parts of this succession. Not to have the succession of different feelings is not to be conscious at all. . . . The chain of consciousness is a sequence of *differents.*"

Such a description as this can awaken no possible protest from anyone. We all recognize as different great classes of our conscious states. Now we are seeing, now hearing; now reasoning, now willing; now recollecting, now expecting; now loving, now hating; and in a hundred other ways we know our minds to be alternately engaged. But all these are complex states. The aim of science is always to reduce complexity to simplicity; and in psychological science we have the celebrated 'theory of *ideas*' which, admitting the great difference among each other of what may be called concrete conditions of mind, seeks to show how this is all the resultant effect of variations in the *combination* of certain simple elements of consciousness that always remain the same. These mental atoms or molecules are what Locke called 'simple ideas.' Some of Locke's successors made out that the only simple ideas were the sensations strictly so called. Which ideas the simple ones may be does not, however, now concern us. It is enough that certain philosophers have thought they could see under the dissolving-view-appearance of the mind elementary facts of *any* sort that remained unchanged amid the flow.

And the view of these philosophers has been called little into question, for our common experience seems at first sight to corroborate it entirely. Are not the sensations we get from the same object, for example, always the same? Does not the same piano-key, struck with the same force, make us hear in the same way? Does not the same grass give us the same feeling of green, the same sky the same feeling of blue, and do we not get the same olfactory sensation no matter how many times we put our nose to the same flask of cologne? It seems a piece of metaphysical sophistry to suggest that we do not; and yet a close attention to the matter shows that *there is no proof that the same bodily sensation is ever got by us twice.*

What is got twice is the same OBJECT. We hear the same *note* over and over again; we see the same *quality* of green, or smell the same objective perfume, or experience the same *species* of pain. The realities, concrete and abstract, physical and ideal, whose permanent existence we believe in, seem to be constantly coming up again before our thought, and lead us, in our carelessness, to suppose that our 'ideas' of them are the same ideas. When we come, some time later, to the chapter on Perception, we shall see how inveterate is our habit of not attending to sensations as subjective facts, but of simply using them as stepping-stones to pass over to the recognition of the realities whose presence they reveal. The grass out of the window now looks to me of the same green in the sun as in the shade, and yet a painter would have to paint one part of it dark brown, another part bright yellow, to give its real sensational effect. We take no heed, as a rule, of the different way in which the same things look and sound and smell at different distances and under different circumstances. The sameness of the *things* is what we are concerned to ascertain; and any sensations that assure us of that will probably be considered in a rough way to be the same with each other. This is what makes off-hand testimony about the subjective identity of different sensations well-nigh worthless as a proof of the fact. The entire history of Sensation is a commentary on our inability to tell whether two sensations received apart are exactly alike. What appeals to our attention far more than the absolute quality or quantity of a given sensation is its *ratio* to whatever other sensations we may have at the same time. When everything is dark a somewhat less dark sensation makes us see an object white. Helmholtz calculates that the white marble painted in a picture representing an architectural view by moonlight is, when seen by daylight, from ten to twenty thousand times brighter than the real moonlit marble would be.

Such a difference as this could never have been *sensibly* learned; it had to be inferred from a series of indirect considerations. There are facts which make us believe that our sensibility is altering all the time, so that the same object cannot easily give us the same sensation over again. The eye's sensibility to light is at its maximum when the eye is first exposed, and blunts itself with surprising rapidity. A long night's sleep will make it see things twice as brightly on wakening, as simple rest by closure will make it see them later in the day. We feel things differently according as we are sleepy or awake, hungry or full, fresh or tired; differently at night and in the morning, differently in summer and in winter; and above all things differently in childhood, manhood, and old age. Yet we never doubt that our feelings reveal the same world, with the same sensible qualities and the same sensible things occupying it. The difference of the sensibility is shown best by the difference of our emotion about the things from one age to another, or when we are in different organic moods. What was bright and exciting becomes weary, flat, and unprofitable. The bird's song is tedious, the breeze is mournful, the sky is sad.

To these indirect presumptions that our sensations, following the mutations of our capacity for feeling, are always undergoing an essential change, must be added another presumption, based on what must happen in the brain. Every sensation corresponds to some cerebral action. For an identical sensation to recur it would have to occur the second time *in an unmodified brain.* But as this, strictly speaking, is a physiological impossibility, so is an unmodified feeling an impossibility; for to every brain-modification, however small, must correspond a change of equal amount in the feeling which the brain subserves.

All this would be true if even sensations came to us pure and single and not combined into 'things.' Even then we should have to confess that, however we might in ordinary conversation speak of getting the same sensation again, we never in strict theoretic accuracy could do so; and that whatever was true of the river of life, of the river of elementary feeling, it would certainly be true to say, like Heraclitus, that we never descend twice into the same stream.

But if the assumption of 'simple ideas of sensation' recurring in immutable shape is so easily shown to be baseless, how much more baseless is the assumption of immutability in the larger masses of our thought!

For there it is obvious and palpable that our state of mind is never precisely the same. Every thought we have of a given fact is, strictly speaking, unique, and only bears a resemblance of kind with our other thoughts of the same fact. When the identical fact recurs, we *must* think of it in a fresh manner, see it under a somewhat different angle, apprehend it in different relations from those in which it last appeared. And the thought by which we cognize it is the thought of it-in-those-relations, a thought suffused with the consciousness of all that dim context. Often we are ourselves struck at the strange differences in our successive views of the same thing. We wonder how we ever could have opined as we did last month about a certain matter. We have outgrown the possibility of that state of mind, we know not how. From one year to another we see things in new lights. What was unreal has grown real, and what was exciting is insipid. The friends we used to care the world for are shrunken to shadows; the women, once so divine, the stars, the woods, and the waters, how now so dull and common! the young girls that brought an aura of infinity, at present hardly distinguishable existences; the pictures so empty; and as for the books, what *was* there to find so mysteriously significant in Goethe, or in John Mill so full of weight? Instead of all this, more zestful than ever is the work, the work; and fuller and deeper the import of common duties and of common goods.

But what here strikes us so forcibly on the flagrant scale exists on every scale, down to the imperceptible transition from one hour's outlook to that of the next. Experience is remoulding us every moment, and our mental reaction on every given thing is really a resultant of our experience of the whole world up to that date. The analogies of brain-physiology must again be appealed to to corroborate our view.

Our earlier chapters have taught us to believe that, whilst we think, our brain changes, and that, like the aurora borealis, its whole internal equilibrium shifts with every pulse of change. The precise nature of the shifting at a given moment is a product of many factors. The accidental state of local nutrition or blood-supply may be among them. But just as one of them certainly is the influence of outward objects on the sense-organs during the moment, so is another certainly the very special susceptibility in which the organ has been left at that moment by all it has gone through in the past. Every

brain-state is partly determined by the nature of this entire past succession. Alter the latter in any part, and the brain-state must be somewhat different. Each present brain-state is a record in which the eye of Omniscience might read all the foregone history of its owner. It is out of the question, then, that any total brain-state should identically recur. Something like it may recur; but to suppose *it* to recur would be equivalent to the absurd admission that all the states that had intervened between its two appearances had been pure nonentities, and that the organ after their passage was exactly as it was before. And (to consider shorter periods) just as, in the senses, an impression feels very differently according to what has preceded it; as one color succeeding another is modified by the contrast, silence sounds delicious after noise, and a note, when the scale is sung up, sounds unlike itself when the scale is sung down; as the presence of certain lines in a figure changes the apparent form of the other lines, and as in music the whole æsthetic effect comes from the manner in which one set of sounds alters our feeling of another; so, in thought, we must admit that those portions of the brain that have just been maximally excited retain a kind of soreness which is a condition of our present consciousness, a codeterminant of how and what we now shall feel.

Ever some tracts are waning in tension, some waxing, whilst others actively discharge. The states of tension have as positive an influence as any in determining the total condition, and in deciding what the *psychosis* shall be. All we know of submaximal nerve-irritations, and of the summation of apparently ineffective stimuli, tends to show that *no* changes in the brain are physiologically ineffective, and that presumably none are bare of psychological result. But as the brain-tension shifts from one relative state of equilibrium to another, like the gyrations of a kaleidoscope, now rapid and now slow, is it likely that its faithful psychic concomitant is heavier-footed than itself, and that it cannot match each one of the organ's irradiations by a shifting inward iridescence of its own? But if it can do this, its inward iridescences must be infinite, for the brain-redistributions are in infinite variety. If so coarse a thing as a telephone-plate can be made to thrill for years and never reduplicate its inward condition, how much more must this be the case with the infinitely delicate brain?

I am sure that this concrete and total manner of regarding the mind's changes is the only true manner, difficult as it may be to carry it out in detail. If anything seems obscure about it, it will grow clearer as we advance. Meanwhile, if it be true, it is certainly also true that no two 'ideas' are ever exactly the same, which is the proposition we started to prove. The proposition is more important theoretically than it at first sight seems. For it makes it already impossible for us to follow obediently in the footprints of either the Lockian or the Herbartian school, schools which have had almost unlimited influence in Germany and among ourselves. No doubt it is often *convenient* to formulate the mental facts in an atomistic sort of way, and to treat the higher states of consciousness as if they were all built out of unchanging simple ideas. It is convenient often to treat curves as if they were composed of small straight lines, and electricity and nerve-force as if they were fluids. But in the one case as in the other we must never forget that we are talking symbolically, and that there is nothing in nature to answer to our words. *A permanently existing 'idea' or 'Vorstellung' which makes its appearance before the footlights of consciousness at periodical intervals, is as mythological an entity as the Jack of Spades.*

What makes it convenient to use the mythological formulas is the whole organization of speech, which, as was remarked a while ago, was not made by psychologists, but by men who were as a rule only interested in the facts their mental states revealed. They only spoke of their states as *ideas of this or of that thing.* What wonder, then, that the thought is most easily conceived under the law of the thing whose name it bears! If the thing is composed of parts, then we suppose that the thought of the thing must be composed of the thoughts of the parts. If one part of the thing have appeared in the same thing or in other things on former occasions, why then we must be having even now the very same 'idea' of that part which was there on those occasions. If the thing is simple, its thought is simple. If it is multitudinous, it must require a multitude of thoughts to think it. If a succession, only a succession of thoughts can know it. If permanent, its thought is permanent. And so on *ad libitum.* What after all is so natural as to assume that one object, called by one name, should be known by one affection of the mind? But, if language must thus influence us, the agglutinative languages, and even Greek and Latin with their declensions, would be the better guides. Names did not appear in them inal-

terable, but changed their shape to suit the context in which they lay. It must have been easier then than now to conceive of the same object as being thought of at different times in non-identical conscious states.

This, too, will grow clearer as we proceed. Meanwhile a necessary consequence of the belief in permanent self-identical psychic facts that absent themselves and recur periodically is the Humian doctrine that our thought is composed of separate independent parts and is not a sensibly continuous stream. That this doctrine entirely misrepresents the natural appearances is what I next shall try to show.

3) *Within each personal consciousness, thought is sensibly continuous*

I can only define 'continuous' as that which is without breach, crack, or division. I have already said that the breach from one mind to another is perhaps the greatest breach in nature. The only breaches that can well be conceived to occur within the limits of a single mind would either be *interruptions, time*-gaps during which the consciousness went out altogether to come into existence again at a later moment; or they would be breaks in the *quality,* or content, of the thought, so abrupt that the segment that followed had no connection whatever with the one that went before. The proposition that within each personal consciousness thought feels continuous means two things:

1. That even where there is a time-gap the consciousness after it feels as if it belonged together with the consciousness before it, as another part of the same self;

2. That the changes from one moment to another in the quality of the consciousness are never absolutely abrupt.

The case of the time-gaps, as the simplest, shall be taken first. And first of all, a word about time-gaps of which the consciousness may not itself be aware.

. . . we saw that such time-gaps existed, and that they might be more numerous than is usually supposed. If the consciousness is not aware of them, it cannot feel them as interruptions. In the unconsciousness produced by nitrous oxide and other anæsthetics, in that of epilepsy and fainting, the broken edges of the sentient life may meet and merge over the gap, much as the feelings of space of the opposite margins of the 'blind spot' meet and merge over that objective interruption to the sensitiveness of the eye. Such consciousness as this, whatever it be for the onlooking psychologist, is for itself unbroken. It *feels* unbroken; a waking day of it is sensibly a unit as long as that day lasts, in the sense in which the hours themselves are units, as having all their parts next each other, with no intrusive alien substance between. To expect the consciousness to feel the interruptions of its objective continuity as gaps, would be like expecting the eye to feel a gap of silence because it does not hear, or the ear to feel a gap of darkness because it does not see. So much for the gaps that are unfelt.

With the felt gaps the case is different. On waking from sleep, we usually know that we have been unconscious, and we often have an accurate judgment of how long. The judgment here is certainly an inference from sensible signs, and its ease is due to long practice in the particular field. The result of it, however, is that the consciousness is, *for itself*, not what it was in the former case, but interrupted and discontinuous, in the mere time-sense of the words. But in the other sense of continuity, the sense of the parts being inwardly connected and belonging together because they are parts of a common whole, the consciousness remains sensibly continuous and one. What now is the common whole? The natural name for it is *myself, I,* or *me.*

When Paul and Peter wake up in the same bed, and recognize that they have been asleep, each one of them mentally reaches back and makes connection with but *one* of the two streams of thought which were broken by the sleeping hours. As the current of an electrode buried in the ground unerringly finds its way to its own similarly buried mate, across no matter how much intervening earth; so Peter's present instantly finds out Peter's past, and never by mistake knits itself on to that of Paul. Paul's thought in turn is as little liable to go astray. The past thought of Peter is appropriated by the present Peter alone. He may have a *knowledge,* and a correct one too, of what Paul's last drowsy states of mind were as he sank into sleep, but it is an entirely different sort of knowledge from that which he has of his own last states. He *remembers* his own states, whilst he only *conceives* Paul's. Remembrance is like direct feeling; its object is suffused with a warmth and intimacy to which no object of mere conception ever attains. This quality of warmth and intimacy and immediacy is what Peter's *present* thought also possesses for itself. So sure as this present is me, is mine, it says, so sure is anything else that comes with the same warmth and intimacy and immediacy, me and

mine. What the qualities called warmth and intimacy may in themselves be will have to be matter for future consideration. But whatever past feelings appear with those qualities must be admitted to receive the greeting of the present mental state, to be owned by it, and accepted as belonging together with it in a common self. This community of self is what the time-gap cannot break in twain, and is why a present thought, although not ignorant of the time-gap, can still regard itself as continuous with certain chosen portions of the past.

Consciousness, then, does not appear to itself chopped up in bits. Such words as 'chain' or 'train' do not describe it fitly as it presents itself in the first instance. It is nothing jointed; it flows. A 'river' or a 'stream' are the metaphors by which it is most naturally described. *In talking of it hereafter, let us call it the stream of thought, of consciousness, or of subjective life.*

But now there appears, even within the limits of the same self, and between thoughts all of which alike have this same sense of belonging together, a kind of jointing and separateness among the parts, of which this statement seems to take no account. I refer to the breaks that are produced by sudden *contrasts in the quality* of the successive segments of the stream of thought. If the words 'chain' and 'train' had no natural fitness in them, how came such words to be used at all? Does not a loud explosion rend the consciousness upon which it abruptly breaks, in twain? Does not every sudden shock, appearance of a new object, or change in a sensation, create a real interruption, sensibly felt as such, which cuts the conscious stream across at the moment at which it appears? Do not such interruptions smite us every hour of our lives, and have we the right, in their presence, still to call our consciousness a continuous stream?

This objection is based partly on a confusion and partly on a superficial introspective view.

The confusion is between the thoughts themselves, taken as subjective facts, and the things of which they are aware. It is natural to make this confusion, but easy to avoid it when once put on one's guard. The things are discrete and discontinuous; they do pass before us in a train or chain, making often explosive appearances and rending each other in twain. But their comings and goings and contrasts no more break the flow of the thought that thinks them than they break the time and the space in which they lie. A silence may be broken by a thunder-clap, and we may be so stunned and confused for a moment by the shock as to give no instant account to ourselves of what has happened. But that very confusion is a mental state, and a state that passes us straight over from the silence to the sound. The transition between the thought of one object and the thought of another is no more a break in the *thought* than a joint in a bamboo is a break in the wood. It is a part of the *consciousness* as much as the joint is a part of the *bamboo*.

The superficial introspective view is the overlooking, even when the things are contrasted with each other most violently, of the large amount of affinity that may still remain between the thoughts by whose means they are cognized. Into the awareness of the thunder itself the awareness of the previous silence creeps and continues; for what we hear when the thunder crashes is not thunder *pure,* but thunder-breaking-upon-silence-and-contrasting-thunder-breaking-upon-silence-and-contrasting-with-it. Our feeling of the same objective thunder, coming in this way, is quite different from what it would be were the thunder a continuation of previous thunder. The thunder itself we believe to abolish and exclude the silence; but the *feeling* of the thunder is also a feeling of the silence as just gone; and it would be difficult to find in the actual concrete consciousness of man a feeling so limited to the present as not to have an inkling of anything that went before. Here, again, language works against our perception of the truth. We name our thoughts simply, each after its thing, as if each knew its own thing and nothing else. What each really knows is clearly the thing it is named for, with dimly perhaps a thousand other things. It ought to be named after all of them, but it never is. Some of them are always things known a moment ago more clearly; others are things to be known more clearly a moment hence. Our own bodily position, attitude, condition, is one of the things of which *some* awareness, however inattentive, invariably accompanies the knowledge of whatever else we know. We think; and as we think we feel our bodily selves as the seat of the thinking. If the thinking be *our* thinking, it must be suffused through all its parts with that peculiar warmth and intimacy that make it come as ours. Whether the warmth and intimacy be anything more than the feeling of the same old body always there, is a matter for the next chapter to decide. *Whatever* the content of the ego may be, it is habitually felt *with* everything else by us humans, and must form a *liaison*

between all the things of which we become successively aware.

On this gradualness in the changes of our mental content the principles of nerve-action can throw some more light. When studying . . . the summation of nervous activities, we saw that no state of the brain can be supposed instantly to die away. If a new state comes, the inertia of the old state will still be there and modify the result accordingly. Of course we cannot tell, in our ignorance, what in each instance the modifications ought to be. The commonest modifications in sense-perception are known as the phenomena of contrast. In æsthetics they are the feelings of delight or displeasure which certain particular orders in a series of impressions give. In thought, strictly and narrowly so called, they are unquestionably that consciousness of the *whence* and the *whither* that always accompanies its flows. If recently the brain-tract a was vividly excited, and then b, and now vividly c, the total present consciousness is not produced simply by c's excitement, but also by the dying vibrations of a and b as well. If we want to represent the brain-process we must write it thus: abc—three different processes coexisting, and correlated with them a thought which is no one of the three thoughts which they would have produced had each of them occurred alone. But whatever this fourth thought may exactly be, it seems impossible that it should not be something *like* each of the three other thoughts whose tracts are concerned in its production, though in a fast-waning phase.

It all goes back to what we said in another connection only a few pages ago (p. 111). As the total neurosis changes, so does the total psychosis change. But as the changes of neurosis are never absolutely discontinuous, so must the successive psychoses shade gradually into each other, although their *rate* of change may be much faster at one moment than at the next.

This difference in the rate of change lies at the basis of a difference of subjective states of which we ought immediately to speak. When the rate is slow we are aware of the object of our thought in a comparatively restful and stable way. When rapid, we are aware of a passage, a relation, a transition *from* it, or *between* it and something else. As we take, in fact, a general view of the wonderful stream of our consciousness, what strikes us first is this different pace of its parts. Like a bird's life, it seems to be made of an alternation of flights and perchings. The rhythm of language expresses this, where every thought is expressed in a sentence, and every sentence closed by a period. The resting-places are usually occupied by sensorial imaginations of some sort, whose peculiarity is that they can be held before the mind for an indefinite time, and contemplated without changing; the places of flight are filled with thoughts of relations, static or dynamic, that for the most part obtain between the matters contemplated in the periods of comparative rest.

Let us call the resting-places the 'substantive parts,' and the places of flight the 'transitive parts,' of the stream of thought. It then appears that the main end of our thinking is at all times the attainment of some other substantive part than the one from which we have just been dislodged. And we may say that the main use of the transitive parts is to lead us from one substantive conclusion to another.

Now it is very difficult, introspectively, to see the transitive parts for what they really are. If they are but flights to a conclusion, stopping them to look at them before the conclusion is reached is really annihilating them. Whilst if we wait till the conclusion *be* reached, it so exceeds them in vigor and stability that it quite eclipses and swallows them up in its glare. Let anyone try to cut a thought across in the middle and get a look at its section, and he will see how difficult the introspective observation of the transitive tracts is. The rush of the thought is so headlong that it almost always brings us up at the conclusion before we can arrest it. Or if our purpose is nimble enough and we do arrest it, it ceases forthwith to be itself. As a snowflake caught in the warm hand is no longer a flake but a drop, so, instead of catching the feeling of relation moving to its term, we find we have caught some substantive thing, usually the last word we were pronouncing, statically taken, and with its function, tendency, and particular meaning in the sentence quite evaporated. The attempt at introspective analysis in these cases is in fact like seizing a spinning top to catch its motion, or trying to turn up the gas quickly enough to see how the darkness looks. And the challenge to *produce* these psychoses, which is sure to be thrown by doubting psychologists at anyone who contends for their existence, is as unfair as Zeno's treatment of the advocates of motion, when, asking them to point out in what place an arrow *is* when it moves, he argues the falsity of their thesis from their inability to make to so preposterous a question an immediate reply.

The results of this introspective difficulty are baleful. If to hold fast and observe the transitive parts of thought's stream be so hard, then the great blunder to which all schools are liable must be the failure to register them, and the undue emphasizing of the more substantive parts of the stream. Were we not ourselves a moment since in danger of ignoring any feeling transitive between the silence and the thunder, and of treating their boundary as a sort of break in the mind? Now such ignoring as this has historically worked in two ways. One set of thinkers have been led by it to *Sensationalism.* Unable to lay their hands on any coarse feelings corresponding to the innumerable relations and forms of connection between the facts of the world, finding no *named* subjective modifications mirroring such relations, they have for the most part denied that feelings of relation exist; and many of them, like Hume, have gone so far as to deny the reality of most relations *out* of the mind as well as in it. Substantive psychoses, sensations and their copies and derivatives, juxtaposed like dominoes in a game, but really separate, everything else verbal illusion,—such is the upshot of this view. The *Intellectualists,* on the other hand, unable to give up the reality of relations *extra mentem,* but equally unable to point to any distinct substantive feelings in which they were known, have made the same admission that the feelings do not exist. But they have drawn an opposite conclusion. The relations must be known, they say, in something that is no feeling, no mental modification continuous and consubstantial with the subjective tissue out of which sensations and other substantive states are made. They are known, these relations, by something that lies on an entirely different plane, by an *actus purus* of Thought, Intellect, or Reason, all written with capitals and considered to mean something unutterably superior to any fact of sensibility whatever.

But from our point of view both Intellectualists and Sensationalists are wrong. If there be such things as feelings at all, *then so surely as relations between objects exist in rerum naturâ, so surely, and more surely, do feelings exist to which these relations are known.* There is not a conjunction or a preposition, and hardly an adverbial phrase, syntactic form, or inflection of voice, in human speech, that does not express some shading or other of relation which we at some moment actually feel to exist between the larger objects of our thought. If we speak objectively, it is the real relations that appear revealed; if we speak subjectively, it is the stream of consciousness that matches each of them by an inward coloring of its own. In either case the relations are numberless, and no existing language is capable of doing justice to all their shades.

We ought to say a feeling of *and,* a feeling of *if,* a feeling of *but,* and a feeling of *by,* quite as readily as we say a feeling of *blue* or a feeling of *cold.* Yet we do not: so inveterate has our habit become of recognizing the existence of the substantive parts alone, that language almost refuses to lend itself to any other use. The Empiricists have always dwelt on its influence in making us suppose that where we have a separate name, a separate thing must needs be there to correspond with it; and they have rightly denied the existence of the mob of abstract entities, principles, and forces, in whose favor no other evidence than this could be brought up. But they have said nothing of that obverse error . . . of supposing that where there is *no* name no entity can exist. All *dumb* or anonymous psychic states have, owing to this error, been coolly suppressed; or, if recognized at all, have been named after the substantive perception they led to, as thoughts 'about' this object or 'about' that, the stolid word *about* engulfing all their delicate idiosyncrasies in its monotonous sound. Thus the greater and greater accentuation and isolation of the substantive parts have continually gone on.

Once more take a look at the brain. We believe the brain to be an organ whose internal equilibrium is always in a state of change—the change affecting every part. The pulses of change are doubtless more violent in one place than in another, their rhythm more rapid at this time than at that. As in a kaleidoscope revolving at a uniform rate, although the figures are always rearranging themselves, there are instants during which the transformation seems minute and interstitial and almost absent, followed by others when it shoots with magical rapidity, relatively stable forms thus alternating with forms we should not distinguish if seen again; so in the brain the perpetual rearrangement must result in some forms of tension lingering relatively long, whilst others simply come and pass. But if consciousness corresponds to the fact of rearrangement itself, why, if the rearrangement stop not, should the consciousness ever cease? And if a lingering rearrangement brings with it one kind of consciousness, why should not a swift rearrangement bring another kind of consciousness as peculiar as the rearrangement itself? The lingering consciousnesses, if of simple objects, we call 'sensa-

tions' or 'images,' according as they are vivid or faint; if of complex objects, we call them 'percepts' when vivid, 'concepts' or 'thoughts' when faint. For the swift consciousnesses we have only those names of 'transitive states,' or 'feelings of relation,' which we have used. As the brain-changes are continuous, so do all these consciousnesses melt into each other like dissolving views. Properly they are but one protracted consciousness, one unbroken stream.

4) *Human thought appears to deal with objects independent of itself; that is, it is cognitive, or possesses the function of knowing*

For Absolute Idealism, the infinite Thought and its objects are one. The Objects are, through being thought; the eternal Mind is, through thinking them. Were a human thought alone in the world there would be no reason for any other assumption regarding it. Whatever it might have before it would be its vision, would be there, in *its* 'there,' or then, in *its* 'then'; and the question would never arise whether an extra-mental duplicate of it existed or not. The reason why we all believe that the objects of our thoughts have a duplicate existence outside, is that there are *many* human thoughts, each with the *same* objects, as we cannot help supposing. The judgment that *my* thought has the same object as *his* thought is what makes the psychologist call my thought cognitive of an outer reality. The judgment that my own past thought and my own present thought are of the same object is what makes *me* take the object out of either and project it by a sort of triangulation into an independent position, from which it may *appear* to both. *Sameness* in a multiplicity of objective appearances is thus the basis of our belief in realities outside of thought. . . . we shall have to take up the judgment of sameness again.

To show that the question of reality being extra-mental or not is not likely to arise in the absence of repeated experiences of the *same,* take the example of an altogether unprecedented experience, such as a new taste in the throat. Is it a subjective quality of feeling, or an objective quality felt? You do not even ask the question at this point. It is simply *that taste.* But if a doctor hears you describe it, and says: "Ha! Now you know what *heartburn* is," then it becomes a quality already existent *extra mentem tuam,* which you in turn have come upon and learned. The first spaces, times, things, qualities, experienced by the child probably appear, like the first heartburn, in this absolute way, as simple *beings,* neither in nor out of thought. But later, by having other thoughts than this present one, and making repeated judgments of sameness among their objects, he corroborates in himself the notion of realities, past and distant as well as present, which realities no one single thought either possesses or engenders, but which all may contemplate and know. This, as was stated in the last chapter, is the *psychological* point of view, the relatively uncritical non-idealistic point of view of all natural science, beyond which this book cannot go. A mind which has become conscious of its own cognitive function, plays what we have called 'the psychologist' upon itself. It not only knows the things that appear before it; it knows that it knows them. This stage of reflective condition is, more or less explicitly, our habitual adult state of mind.

It cannot, however, be regarded as primitive. The consciousness of objects must come first. We seem to lapse into this primordial condition when consciousness is reduced to a minimum by the inhalation of anæsthetics or during a faint. Many persons testify that at a certain stage of the anæsthetic process objects are still cognized whilst the thought of self is lost. Professor Herzen says:

> During the syncope there is absolute psychic annihilation, the absence of all consciousness; then at the beginning of coming to, one has at a certain moment a vague, limitless, infinite feeling—a sense of *existence in general* without the least trace of distinction between the me and the not-me.

Dr. Shoemaker of Philadelphia describes during the deepest conscious stage of ether-intoxication a vision of

> two endless parallel lines in swift longitudinal motion . . . on a uniform misty background . . . together with a constant sound or whirr, not loud but distinct . . . which seemed to be connected with the parallel lines. . . . These phenomena occupied the whole field. There were present no dreams or visions in any way connected with human affairs, no ideas or impressions akin to anything in past experience, no emotions, of course no idea of personality. There was no conception as to what being it was that was regarding the two lines, or that there existed any such thing as such a being; the lines and waves were all.

Similarly a friend of Mr. Herbert Spencer, quoted by him in *Mind* (vol. III, p. 556),

speaks of "an undisturbed empty quiet everywhere, except that a stupid presence lay like a heavy intrusion *somewhere*—a blotch on the calm." This sense of objectivity and lapse of subjectivity, even when the object is almost indefinable, is, it seems to me, a somewhat familiar phase in chloroformization, though in my own case it is too deep a phase for any articulate after-memory to remain. I only know that as it vanishes I seem to wake to a sense of my own existence as something additional to what had previously been there.

Many philosophers, however, hold that the reflective consciousness of the self is essential to the cognitive function of thought. They hold that a thought, in order to know a thing at all, must expressly distinguish between the thing and its own self. This is a perfectly wanton assumption, and not the faintest shadow of reason exists for supposing it true. As well might I contend that I cannot dream without dreaming that I dream, swear without swearing that I swear, deny without denying that I deny, as maintain that I cannot know without knowing that I know. I may have either acquaintance-with, or knowledge-about, an object O without thinking about myself at all. It suffices for this that I think O, and that it exist. If, in addition to thinking O, I also think that I exist and that I know O, well and good; I then know one more thing, a fact about O, of which I previously was unmindful. That, however, does not prevent me from having already known O a good deal. O *per se,* or O *plus* P, are as good objects of knowledge as O *plus me* is. The philosophers in question simply substitute one particular object for all others, and call it *the* object *par excellence.* It is a case of the 'psychologist's fallacy'. *They* know the object to be one thing and the thought another; and they forthwith foist their own knowledge into that of the thought of which they pretend to give a true account. To conclude, then, *thought may, but need not, in knowing, discriminate between its object and itself.*

We have been using the word Object. *Something must now be said about the proper use of the term Object in Psychology.*

In popular parlance the word object is commonly taken without reference to the act of knowledge, and treated as synonymous with individual subject of existence. Thus if anyone ask what is the mind's object when you say 'Columbus discovered America in 1492,' most people will reply 'Columbus,' or 'America,' or, at most, 'the discovery of America.' They will name a substantive kernel or nucleus of the consciousness, and say the thought is 'about' that,—as indeed it is,—and they will call that your thought's 'object.' Really that is usually only the grammatical object, or more likely the grammatical subject, of your sentence. It is at most your 'fractional object'; or you may call it the 'topic' of your thought, or the 'subject of your discourse.' But the *Object* of your thought is really its entire content or deliverance, neither more nor less. It is a vicious use of speech to take out a substantive kernel from its content and call that its object; and it is an equally vicious use of speech to add a substantive kernel not articulately included in its content, and to call that its object. Yet either one of these two sins we commit, whenever we content ourselves with saying that a given thought is simply 'about' a certain topic, or that that topic is its 'object.' The object of my thought in the previous sentence, for example, is strictly speaking neither Columbus, nor America, nor its discovery. It is nothing short of the entire sentence, 'Columbus-discovered-America-in-1492.' And if we wish to speak of it substantively, we must make a substantive of it by writing it out thus with hyphens between all its words. Nothing but this can possibly name its delicate idiosyncrasy. And if we wish to *feel* that idiosyncrasy we must reproduce the thought as it was uttered, with every word fringed and the whole sentence bathed in that original halo of obscure relations, which, like an horizon, then spread about its meaning.

Our psychological duty is to cling as closely as possible to the actual constitution of the thought we are studying. We may err as much by excess as by defect. If the kernel or 'topic,' Columbus, is in one way less than the thought's object, so in another way it may be more. That is, when named by the psychologist, it may mean much more than actually is present to the thought of which he is a reporter. Thus, for example, suppose you should go on to think: 'He was a daring genius!' An ordinary psychologist would not hesitate to say that the object of your thought was still 'Columbus.' True, your thought is *about* Columbus. It 'terminates' in Columbus, leads from and to the direct idea of Columbus. But for the moment it is not fully and immediately Columbus, it is only 'he,' or rather 'he-was-a-daring-genius'; which, though it may be an unimportant difference for conversational purposes, is, for introspective psychology, as great a difference as there can be.

The object of every thought, then, is neither more nor less than all that the thought thinks, exactly as the thought thinks it, however complicated the matter, and however symbolic the manner of the thinking may be. It is needless to say that memory can seldom accurately reproduce such an object, when once it has passed from before the mind. It either makes too little or too much of it. Its best plan is to repeat the verbal sentence, if there was one, in which the object was expressed. But for inarticulate thoughts there is not even this resource, and introspection must confess that the task exceeds her powers. The mass of our thinking vanishes for ever, beyond hope of recovery, and psychology only gathers up a few of the crumbs that fall from the feast.

The next point to make clear is that, *however complex the object may be, the thought of it is one undivided state of consciousness.* As Thomas Brown says:

> I have already spoken too often to require again to caution you against a mistake, into which, I must confess, that the terms, which the poverty of our language obliges us to use, might, of themselves, very naturally lead you:—the mistake of supposing, that the most complex states of mind are not truly, in their very essence, as much one and indivisible, as those which we term simple—the complexity and seeming coexistence which they involve being relative to our feeling only, not to their own absolute nature. I trust I need not repeat to you, that, in itself, every notion, however seemingly complex, is, and must be, truly simple—being one state, or affection, of one simple substance, mind. Our conception of a whole army, for example, is as truly this one mind existing in this one state, as our conception of any of the individuals that compose an army: Our notion of the abstract numbers, eight, four, two, is as truly one feeling of the mind, as our notion of simple unity.

The ordinary associationist-psychology supposes, in contrast with this, that whenever an object of thought contains many elements, the thought itself must be made up of just as many ideas, one idea for each element, and all fused together in appearance, but really separate. The enemies of this psychology find (as we have already seen) little trouble in showing that such a bundle of separate ideas would never form one thought at all, and they contend that an Ego must be added to the bundle to give it unity, and bring the various ideas into relation with each other. We will not discuss the ego just yet, but it is obvious that if things are to be thought in relation, they must be thought together, and in one *something,* be that something ego, psychosis, state of consciousness, or whatever you please. If not thought with each other, things are not thought in relation at all. Now most believers in the ego make the same mistake as the associationists and sensationists whom they oppose. Both agree that the elements of the subjective stream are discrete and separate and constitute what Kant calls a 'manifold.' But while the associationists think that a 'manifold' can form a single knowledge, the egoists deny this, and say that the knowledge comes only when the manifold is subjected to the synthetizing activity of an ego. Both make an identical hypothesis; but the egoist, finding it won't express the facts, adds another hypothesis to correct it. Now I do not wish just yet to 'commit myself' about the existence or non-existence of the ego, but I do contend that we need not invoke it for this particular reason— namely, because the manifold of ideas has to be reduced to unity. *There is no manifold of coexisting ideas;* the notion of such a thing is a chimera. *Whatever things are thought in relation are thought from the outset in a unity, in a single pulse of subjectivity, a single psychosis, feeling, or state of mind.*

The reason why this fact is so strangely garbled in the books seems to be what . . . I called the psychologist's fallacy. We have the inveterate habit, whenever we try introspectively to describe one of our thoughts, of dropping the thought as it is in itself and talking of something else. We describe the things that appear to the thought, and we describe other thoughts *about* those things—as if these and the original thought were the same. If, for example, the thought be 'the pack of cards is on the table,' we say, "Well, isn't it a thought of the pack of cards? Isn't it of the cards as included in the pack? Isn't it of the table? And of the legs of the table as well? The table has legs—how can you think the table without virtually thinking its legs? Hasn't our thought then, all these parts—one part for the pack and another for the table? And within the pack-part a part for each card, as within the table-part a part for each leg? And isn't each of these parts an idea? And can our thought, then, be anything but an assemblage or pack of ideas, each answering to some element of what it knows?"

Now not one of these assumptions is true. The thought taken as an example is, in the first place, not of 'a pack of cards.' It is of 'the-pack-of-cards-is-on-the-table,' an entirely different subjective phenomenon, whose Object implies the pack, and every one of the cards in it, but whose conscious constitution bears very little resemblance to that of the thought of the pack *per se.* What a thought *is,* and what it may be developed into, or explained to stand for, and be equivalent to, are two things, not one.

An analysis of what passes through the mind as we utter the phrase *the pack of cards is on the table* will, I hope, make this clear, and may at the same time condense into a concrete example a good deal of what has gone before.

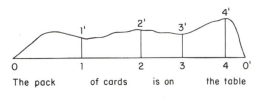

Fig. 1. The Stream of Consciousness.

It takes time to utter the phrase. Let the horizontal line in Fig. 1 represent time. Every part of it will then stand for a fraction, every point for an instant, of the time. Of course the thought has *time-parts.* The part 2–3 of it, though continuous with 1–2, is yet a different part from 1–2. Now I say of these time-parts that we cannot take any one of them so short that it will not after some fashion or other be a thought of the whole object 'the pack of cards is on the table.' They melt into each other like dissolving views, and no two of them feel the object just alike, but each feels the total object in a unitary undivided way. This is what I mean by denying that in the thought any parts can be found corresponding to the object's parts. Time-parts are not such parts.

Now let the vertical dimensions of the figure stand for the objects or contents of the thoughts. A line vertical to any point of the horizontal, as 1–1', will then symbolize the object in the mind at the instant 1; a space above the horizontal, as 1–1'–2'–2, will symbolize all that passes through the mind during the time 1–2 whose line it covers. The entire diagram from o to o' represents a finite length of thought's stream.

Can we now define the psychic constitution of each vertical section of this segment? We can, though in a very rough way. Immediately after o, even before we have opened our mouths to speak, the entire thought is present to our mind in the form of an intention to utter that sentence. This intention, though it has no simple name, and though it is a transitive state immediately displaced by the first word, is yet a perfectly determinate phase of thought, unlike anything else. . . .Again, immediately before o′, after the last word of the sentence is spoken, all will admit that we again think its entire content as we inwardly realize its completed deliverance. All vertical sections made through any other parts of the diagram will be respectively filled with other ways of feeling the sentence's meaning. Through 2, for example, the cards will be the part of the object most emphatically present to the mind; through 4, the table. The stream is made higher in the drawing at its end than at its beginning, because the final way of feeling the content is fuller and richer than the initial way. As Joubert says, "we only know just what we meant to say, after we have said it." And as M. V. Egger remarks, "before speaking, one barely knows what one intends to say, but afterwards one is filled with admiration and surprise at having said and thought it so well."

This latter author seems to me to have kept at much closer quarters with the facts than any other analyst of consciousness. But even he does not quite hit the mark, for, as I understand him, he thinks that each word as it occupies the mind *displaces* the rest of the thought's content. He distinguishes the 'idea' (what I have called the total *object* or meaning) from the consciousness of the words, calling the former a very feeble state, and contrasting it with the liveliness of the words, even when these are only silently rehearsed. "The feeling," he says, "of the words makes ten or twenty times more noise in our consciousness than the sense of the phrase, which for consciousness is a very slight matter." And having distinguished these two things, he goes on to separate them in time, saying that the idea may either precede or follow the words, but that it is a 'pure illusion' to suppose them simultaneous. Now I believe that in all cases where the words are *understood,* the total idea may be and usually is present not only before and after the phase has been spoken, but also whilst each separate word is uttered. It is the overtone, halo, or fringe of the word, *as spoken in that sentence.* It is never absent; no word in an understood sentence comes to consciousness as a mere noise. We feel its meaning as it passes; and although our object differs from one moment to another as to its verbal kernel or nucleus, yet it is *similar* throughout the entire segment of the stream. The same object is known everywhere, now from the point of view, if we may so call it, of this word, now

from the point of view of that. And in our feeling of each word there chimes an echo or foretaste of every other. The consciousness of the 'Idea' and that of the words are thus consubstantial. They are made of the same 'mind-stuff,' and form an unbroken stream. Annihilate a mind at any instant, cut its thought through whilst yet uncompleted, and examine the object present to the cross-section thus suddenly made; you will find, not the bald word in process of utterance, but that word suffused in verbal thought, will usually be some word. A series of sections 1–1′, taken at the moments 1, 2, 3, would then look like this:

The pack of cards
is on the table

Fig. 2. The pack of cards is on the table.

The pack of cards
is on the table

Fig. 3. The pack of cards is on the table.

The pack of cards
is on the table

Fig. 4. The pack of cards is on the table.

The horizontal breadth stands for the entire object in each of the figures: the height of the curve above each part of that object marks the relative prominence of that part in the thought. At the moment symbolized by the first figure *pack* is the prominent part: in the third figure it is *table,* etc.

We can easily add all these plane sections together to make a solid, one of whose solid dimensions will represent time, whilst a cut across this at right angles will give the thought's content at the moment when the cut is made. Let it be the thought. 'I am the same I that I was yesterday.' If at the fourth moment of time we annihilate the thinker and examine how the last pulsation of his consciousness was made, we find that it was an awareness of the whole content with *same* most prominent, and the other parts of the thing known relatively less distinct. With each prolongation of the scheme in the time-direction, the summit of the curve of section would come further towards the end of the sentence. If we make a solid wooden frame with the sentence written on its front, and the time-scale on one of its sides, if we spread flatly a sheet of India rubber over its top, on which rectangular co-ordinates are painted, and slide a smooth ball under the rubber in the direction from o to 'yesterday,' the bulging of the membrane along this diagonal at successive moments will symbolize the changing of the thought's content in a way plain enough, after what has been said, to call for no more explana-

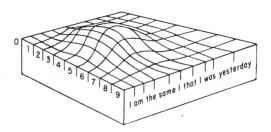

Fig. 5. I am the same I that I was yesterday.

tion. Or to express it in cerebral terms, it will show the relative intensities, at successive moments, of the several nerve-processes to which the various parts of the thought-object correspond.

The last peculiarity of consciousness to which attention is to be drawn in this first rough description of its stream is that

5) *It is always interested more in one part of its object than in another, and welcomes and rejects, or chooses, all the while it thinks*

The phenomena of selective attention and of deliberative will are of course patent examples of this choosing activity. But few of us are aware how incessantly it is at work in operations not ordinarily called by these names. Accentuation and Emphasis are present in every perception we have. We find it quite impossible to disperse our attention impartially over a number of impressions. A monotonous succession of sonorous strokes is broken up into rhythms, now of one sort, now of another, by the different accent which we place on different strokes. The simplest of these rhythms is the double one, tick-tóck, tick-tóck, tick-tóck.

Dots dispersed on a surface are perceived in rows and groups. Lines separate into diverse figures. The ubiquity of the distinctions, *this* and *that, here* and *there, now* and *then,* in our minds is the result of our laying the same selective emphasis on parts of place and time.

But we do far more than emphasize things, and unite some, and keep others apart. We actually *ignore* most of the things before us. Let me briefly show how this goes on.

To begin at the bottom, what are our very senses themselves but organs of selection? Out of the infinite chaos of movements, of which physics teaches us that the outer world consists, each sense-organ picks out those which fall within certain limits of velocity. To these it responds, but ignores the rest as completely as if they did not exist. It thus accentuates particular movements in a manner for which objectively there seems no valid ground; for, as Lange says, there is no reason whatever to think that the gap in Nature between the highest sound-waves and the lowest heat-waves is an abrupt break like that of our sensations; or that the difference between violet and ultra-violet rays has anything like the objective importance subjectively represented by that between light and darkness. Out of what is in itself an undistinguishable, swarming *continuum,* devoid of distinction or emphasis, our senses make for us, by attending to this motion and ignoring that, a world full of contrasts, of sharp accents, of abrupt changes, of picturesque light and shade.

If the sensations we receive from a given organ have their causes thus picked out for us by the conformation of the organ's termination, Attention, on the other hand, out of all the sensations yielded, picks out certain ones as worthy of its notice and suppresses all the rest. Helmholtz's work on Optics is little more than a study of those visual sensations of which common men never become aware— blind spots, *muscæ volitantes,* after-images, irradiation, chromatic fringes, marginal changes of color, double images, astigmatism, movements of accommodation and convergence, retinal rivalry, and more besides. We do not even know without special training on which of our eyes an image falls. So habitually ignorant are most men of this that one may be blind for years of a single eye and never know the fact.

Helmholtz says that we notice only those sensations which are signs to us of *things.* But what are things? Nothing, as we shall abundantly see, but special groups of sensible qualities, which happen practically or æsthetically to interest us, to which we therefore give substantive names, and which we exalt to this exclusive status of independence and dignity. But in itself, apart from my interest, a particular dust-wreath on a windy day is just as much of an individual thing, and just as much or as little deserves an individual name, as my own body does.

And then, among the sensations we get from each separate thing, what happens? The mind selects again. It chooses certain of the sensations to represent the thing most *truly,* and considers the rest as its appearances, modified by the conditions of the moment. Thus my table-top is named *square,* after but one of an infinite number of retinal sensations which it yields, the rest of them being sensations of two acute and two obtuse angles; but I call the latter *perspective* views, and the four right angles the *true* form of the table, and erect the attribute squareness into the table's essence, for æsthetic reasons of my own. In like manner, the real form of the circle is deemed to be the sensation it gives when the line of vision is perpendicular to its centre—all its other sensations are signs of this sensation. The real sound of the cannon is the sensation it makes when the ear is close by. The real color of the brick is the sensation it gives when the eye looks squarely at it from a near point, out of the sunshine and yet not in the gloom; under other circumstances it gives us other color-sensations which are but signs of this—we then see it looks pinker or blacker than it really is. The reader knows no object which he does not represent to himself by preference as in some typical attitude, of some normal size, at some characteristic distance, of some standard tint, etc., etc. But all these essential characteristics, which together form for us the genuine objectivity of the thing and are contrasted with what we call the subjective sensations it may yield us at a given moment, are mere sensations like the latter. The mind chooses to suit itself, and decides what particular sensation shall be held more real and valid than all the rest.

Thus perception involves a twofold choice. Out of all present sensations, we notice mainly such as are significant of absent ones; and out of all the absent associates which these suggest, we again pick out a very few to stand for the objective reality *par excellence.* We could have no more exquisite example of selective industry.

That industry goes on to deal with the things thus given in perception. A man's empirical thought depends on the things he has experienced, but what these shall be is to a large extent determined by his habits of attention. A thing may be present to him a thousand times, but if he persistently fails to notice it, it cannot be said to enter into his experience. We are all seeing flies, moths, and beetles by the thousand, but to whom, save an entomologist, do they say anything distinct? On the other hand, a thing met only once in a lifetime may leave an indelible experience in the memory. Let four men make a tour in Europe. One will bring home only picturesque impressions—costumes and colors, parks and views and works of architecture, pictures and statues. To another all this will be non-existent; and distances and prices, populations and drainage-arrangements, door- and window-fastenings, and other useful statistics will take their place. A third will give a rich account of the theatres, restaurants, and public balls, and naught beside; whilst the fourth will perhaps have been so wrapped in his own subjective broodings as to tell little more than a few names of places through which he passed. Each has selected, out of the same mass of presented objects, those which suited his private interest and has made his experience thereby.

If, now, leaving the empirical combination of objects, we ask how the mind proceeds *rationally* to connect them, we find selection again to be omnipotent. In a future chapter we shall see that all Reasoning depends on the ability of the mind to break up the totality of the phenomenon reasoned about, into parts, and to pick out from among these the particular one which, in our given emergency, may lead to the proper conclusion. Another predicament will need another conclusion, and require another element to be picked out. The man of genius is he who will always stick in his bill at the right point, and bring it out with the right element—'reason' if the emergency be theoretical, 'means' if it be practical—transfixed upon it. I here confine myself to this brief statement, but it may suffice to show that Reasoning is but another form of the selective activity of the mind.

If now we pass to its æsthetic department, our law is still more obvious. The artist notoriously selects his items, rejecting all tones, colors, shapes, which do not harmonize with each other and with the main purpose of his work. That unity, harmony, 'convergence of characters,' as M. Taine calls it, which gives to works of art their superiority over works of nature, is wholly due to *elimination*. Any natural subject will do, if the artist has wit enough to pounce upon some one feature of it as characteristic, and suppress all merely accidental items which do not harmonize with this.

Ascending still higher, we reach the plane of Ethics, where choice reigns notoriously supreme. An act has no ethical quality whatever unless it be chosen out of several all equally possible. To sustain the arguments for the good course and keep them ever before us, to stifle our longing for more flowery ways, to keep the foot unflinchingly on the arduous path, these are characteristic ethical energies. But more than these; for these but deal with the means of compassing interests already felt by the man to be supreme. The ethical energy *par excellence* has to go farther and choose which *interest* out of several, equally coercive, shall become supreme. The issue here is of the utmost pregnancy, for it decides a man's entire career. When he debates, Shall I commit this crime? choose that profession? accept that office, or marry this fortune?—his choice really lies between one of several equally possible future Characters. What he shall *become* is fixed by the conduct of this moment. Schopenhauer, who enforces his determinism by the argument that with a given fixed character only one reaction is possible under given circumstances, forgets that, in these critical ethical moments, what consciously *seems* to be in question is the complexion of the character itself. The problem with the man is less what act he shall now choose to do, than what being he shall now resolve to become.

Looking back, then, over this review, we see that the mind is at every stage a theatre of simultaneous possibilities. Consciousness consists in the comparison of these with each other, the selection of some, and the suppression of the rest by the reinforcing and inhibiting agency of attention. The highest and most elaborated mental products are filtered from the data chosen by the faculty next beneath, out of the mass offered by the faculty below that, which mass in turn was sifted from a still larger amount of yet simpler material, and so on. The mind, in short, works on the data it receives very much as a sculptor works on his block of stone. In a sense the statue stood there from eternity. But there were a thousand different ones beside it, and the sculptor alone is to thank for having extricated this one from the rest. Just so the world of each of us, how-soever different our several views of it may be, all lay embedded in the primordial chaos of sensations, which gave the mere *matter* to the thought of all of us indifferently. We may, if we like, by our reasonings unwind things back to that black and jointless continuity of space and moving clouds of swarming atoms which science calls the only real world. But all the while the world *we* feel and live in will be that which our ancestors and we, by slowly cumulative strokes of choice, have extricated out of this, like sculptors, by simply rejecting certain portions of the given stuff. Other sculptors, other statues from the same stone! Other minds, other worlds from the same monotonous and inexpressive chaos! My world is but one in a million alike embedded, alike real to those who may abstract them. How different must be the worlds in the consciousness of ant, cuttle-fish, or crab!

But in my mind and your mind the rejected portions and the selected portions of the original world-stuff are to a great extent the same. The human race as a whole largely agrees as to what it shall notice and name, and what not. And among the noticed parts we select in much the same way for accentuation and preference or subordination and dislike. There is, however, one entirely extraordinary case in which no two men ever are known to choose alike. One great splitting of the whole universe into two halves is made by each of us; and for each of us almost all of the interest attaches to one of the halves; but we all draw the line of division between them in a different place. When I say that we all call the two halves by the same names, and that those names are '*me*' and '*not-me*' respectively, it will at once be seen what I mean. The altogether unique kind of interest which each human mind feels in those parts of creation which it can call *me* or *mine* may be a moral riddle, but it is a fundamental psychological fact. No mind can take the same interest in his neighbor's *me* as in his own. The neighbor's me falls together with all the rest of things in one foreign mass, against which his own *me* stands out in startling relief. Even the trodden worm, as Lotze somewhere says, contrasts his own suffering self with the whole remaining universe, though he have no clear conception either of himself or of what the universe may be. He is for me a mere part of the world; for him it is I who am the mere part. Each of us dichotomizes the Kosmos in a different place.

A World of Pure Experience

It is difficult not to notice a curious unrest in the philosophic atmosphere of the time, a loosening of old landmarks, a softening of oppositions, a mutual borrowing from one another on the part of systems anciently closed, and an interest in new suggestions, however vague, as if the one thing sure were the inadequacy of the extant school-solutions. The dissatisfaction with these seems due for the most part to a feeling that they are too abstract and academic. Life is confused and superabundant, and what the younger generation appears to crave is more of the temperament of life in its philosophy, even tho it were at some cost of logical rigor and of formal purity. Transcendental idealism is inclining to let the world wag incomprehensibly, in spite of its Absolute Subject and his unity of purpose. Berkeleyan idealism is abandoning the principle of parsimony and dabbling in panpsychic speculations. Empiricism flirts with teleology; and, strangest of all, natural realism, so long decently buried, raises its head above the turf, and finds glad hands outstretched from the most unlikely quarters to help it to its feet again. We are all biased by our personal feelings, I know, and I am personally discontented with extant solutions, so I seem to read the signs of a great unsettlement, as if the upheaval of more real conceptions and more fruitful methods were imminent, as if a true landscape might result, less clipped, straight-edged and artificial.

If philosophy be really on the eve of any considerable rearrangement, the time should be propitious for anyone who has suggestions of his own to bring forward. For many years past my mind has been growing into a certain type of *weltanschauung*. Rightly or wrongly, I have got to the point where I can hardly see things in any other pattern. I propose, therefore, to describe the pattern as clearly as I can consistently with great brevity, and to throw my description into the bubbling vat of publicity where, jostled by rivals and torn by critics, it will eventually either disappear from notice, or else, if better luck befal it, quietly subside to the profundities, and serve as a possible ferment of new growths or a nucleus of new crystallization.

I. RADICAL EMPIRICISM

I give the name of 'radical empiricism' to my *weltanschauung*. Empiricism is known as the opposite of rationalism. Rationalism tends to emphasize universals and to make wholes prior to parts in the order of logic as well as in that of being. Empiricism, on the contrary, lays the explanatory stress upon the part, the element, the individual, and treats the whole as a collection and the universal as an abstraction. My description of things, accordingly, starts with the parts and makes of the whole a being of the second order. It is essentially a mosaic philosophy, a philosophy of plural facts, like that of Hume and his descendants, who refer these facts neither to substances in which they inhere nor to an absolute mind that creates them as its objects. But it differs from the humian type of empiricism in one particular which makes me add the epithet radical.

To be radical, an empiricism must neither admit into its constructions any element that is not directly experienced, nor exclude from them any element that is directly experienced. For such a philosophy, *the relations that connect experiences must themselves be experienced relations, and any kind of relation experienced must be accounted as 'real' as anything else in the system*. Elements may indeed be redistributed, the original placing of things getting corrected, but a real place must be found for every kind of thing experienced, whether term or relation, in the final philosophic arrangement.

Now, ordinary empiricism, in spite of the fact that conjunctive and disjunctive relations present themselves as being fully coordinate parts of experience, has always shown a tendency to do away with the connexions of things, and to insist most on the disjunctions. Berkeley's nominalism, Hume's statement that whatever things we distinguish are as "loose and separate" as if they had no manner of connexion, James Mill's denial that similars have anything 'really' in common, the resolution of the causal tie into habitual sequence, John Mill's account of both physical things and selves as composed of discontinuous possibilities, and the general pulverization of all expe-

From *The Works of William James—Essays in Radical Empiricism,* ed., Frederick Burkhardt (Cambridge, Mass.: Harvard University Press, 1976), pp. 21–44.

rience by association and the mind-dust theory, are examples of what I mean.

The natural result of such a world-picture has been the efforts of rationalism to correct its incoherencies by the addition of trans-experiential agents of unification, substances, intellectual categories and powers, or selves; whereas, if empiricism had only been radical and taken everything that comes without disfavor, conjunction as well as separation, each at its face-value, the results would have called for no such artificial correction. *Radical empiricism,* as I understand it, *does full justice to conjunctive relations,* without, however, treating them as rationalism always tends to treat them, as being true in some supernal way, as if the unity of things and their variety belonged to different orders of truth, and vitality altogether.

II. CONJUNCTIVE RELATIONS

Relations are of different degrees of intimacy. Merely to be 'with' one another in a universe of discourse is the most external relation that terms can have, and seems to involve nothing whatever as to farther consequences. Simultaneity and time-interval come next, and then space-adjacency and distance. After them, similarity and difference, carrying the possibility of many inferences. Then relations of activity, tying terms into series involving change, tendency, resistance, and the causal order generally. Finally, the relation experienced between terms that form states of mind, and are immediately conscious of continuing each other. The organization of the self as a system of memories, purposes, strivings, fulfilments or disappointments, is incidental to this most intimate of all relations, the terms of which seem in many cases actually to compenetrate and suffuse each other's being.

Philosophy has always turned on grammatical particles. With, near, next, like, from, towards, against, because, for, through, my—these words designate types of conjunctive relation arranged in a roughly ascending order of intimacy and inclusiveness. *A priori,* we can imagine a universe of withness but no nextness; or one of nextness but no likeness, or of likeness with no activity, or of activity with no purpose, or of purpose with no ego. These would be universes, each with its own grade of unity. The universe of human experience is, by one or another of its parts, of each and all these grades. Whether or not it possibly enjoys some still more absolute grade of union does not appear upon the surface.

Taken as it does appear, our universe is to a large extent chaotic. No one single type of connexion runs through all the experiences that compose it. If we take space-relations, they fail to connect minds into any regular system. Causes and purposes obtain only among special series of facts. The self-relation seems extremely limited and does not link two different selves together. *Prima facie,* if you should liken the universe of absolute idealism to an aquarium, a crystal globe in which goldfish are swimming, you would have to compare the empiricist universe to something more like one of those dried human heads with which the Dyaks of Borneo deck their lodges. The skull forms a solid nucleus; but innumerable feathers, leaves, strings, beads, and loose appendices of every description float and dangle from it, and save that they terminate in it, seem to have nothing to do with one another. Even so my experiences and yours float and dangle, terminating, it is true, in a nucleus of common perception, but for the most part out of sight and irrelevant and unimaginable to one another. This imperfect intimacy, this bare relation of *withness* between some parts of the sum total of experience and other parts, is the fact that ordinary empiricism over-emphasizes against rationalism, the latter always tending to ignore it unduly. Radical empiricism, on the contrary, is fair to both the unity and the disconnexion. It finds no reason for treating either as illusory. It allots to each its definite sphere of description, and agrees that there appear to be actual forces at work which tend, as time goes on, to make the unity greater.

The conjunctive relation that has given most trouble to philosophy is *the co-conscious transition,* so to call it, by which one experience passes into another when both belong to the same self. About the facts there is no question. My experiences and your experiences are 'with' each other in various external ways, but mine pass into mine, and yours pass into yours in a way in which yours and mine never pass into one another. Within each of our personal histories, subject, object, interest and purpose *are continuous or may be continuous.* Personal histories are processes of change in time, and *the change itself is one of the things immediately experienced.* 'Change' in this case means continuous as opposed to discontinuous transition. But continuous transition is one sort of a conjunctive relation; and to be a radical empiricist means to hold fast to this conjunctive relation of all others, for this is the strategic point, the position through which, if a hole be made, all the corruptions of dialectics and all the metaphysical fictions pour into our philosophy. The holding fast to this relation means taking it at its face-value, neither less nor more; and to take it at its face-value means first of all to take it just as we feel it and not to confuse ourselves with abstract talk *about* it, involving words that drive us to invent secondary conceptions in order to neutralize their suggestions and to make our actual experience again seem rationally possible.

What I do feel simply when a later moment of my experience succeeds an earlier one is that tho they are two moments, the transition from the one to the other is *continuous*. Continuity here is a definite sort of experience; just as definite as is the *discontinuity-experience* which I find it impossible to avoid when I seek to make the transition from an experience of my own to one of yours. In this latter case I have to get on and off again, to pass from a thing lived to another thing only conceived, and the break is positively experienced and noted. Tho the functions exerted by my experience and by yours may be the same (*e.g.,* the same objects known and the same purposes followed), yet the sameness has in this case to be ascertained expressly (and often with difficulty and uncertainty) after the break has been felt; whereas in passing from one of my own moments to another the sameness of object and interest is unbroken, and both the earlier and the later experience are of things directly lived.

There is no other *nature*, no other whatness than this absence of break and this sense of continuity in that most intimate of all conjunctive relations, the passing of one experience into another when they belong to the same self. And this whatness is real empirical 'content' just as the whatness of separation and discontinuity is real content in the contrasted case. Practically to experience one's personal continuum in this living way is to know the originals of the ideas of continuity and of sameness, to know what the words stand for concretely, to own all that they can ever mean. But all experiences have their conditions; and over-subtle intellects, thinking about the facts here, and asking how they are possible, have ended by substituting a lot of static objects of conception for the direct perceptual experiences. "Sameness," they have said, "must be a stark numerical identity; it can't run on from next to next. Continuity can't mean mere absence of gap; for if you say two things are in immediate contact, *at* the contact how can they

be two? If, on the other hand, you put a relation of transition between them, that itself is a third thing, and needs to be related or hitched to its terms. An infinite series is involved," and so on. The result is that from difficulty to difficulty, the plain conjunctive experience has been discredited by both schools, the empiricists leaving things permanently disjoined, and the rationalists remedying the looseness by their absolutes or substances, or whatever other fictitious agencies of union they may have employed. From all which artificiality we can be saved by a couple of simple reflections: first, that conjunctions and separations are, at all events, co-ordinate phenomena which, if we take experiences at their face-value, must be accounted equally real; and second, that if we insist on treating things as really separate when they are given as continuously joined, invoking, when union is required, transcendental principles to overcome the separateness we have assumed, then we ought to stand ready to perform the converse act. We ought to invoke higher principles of *dis*union also, to make our merely experienced *dis*junctions more truly real. Failing thus, we ought to let the originally given continuities stand on their own bottom. We have no right to be lopsided or to blow capriciously hot and cold.

III. THE COGNITIVE RELATION

The first great pitfall from which such a radical standing by experience will save us is an artificial conception of the *relations between knower and known*. Throughout the history of philosophy the subject and its object have been treated as absolutely discontinuous entities; and thereupon the presence of the latter to the former, or the 'apprehension' by the former of the latter, has assumed a paradoxical character which all sorts of theories had to be invented to overcome. Representative theories put a mental 'representation,' 'image,' or 'content' into the gap, as a sort of intermediary. Common-sense theories left the gap untouched, declaring our mind able to clear it by a self-transcending leap. Transcendentalist theories left it impossible to traverse by finite knowers, and brought an absolute in to perform the saltatory act. All the while, in the very bosom of the finite experience, every conjunction required to make the relation intelligible is given in full. Either the knower and the known are:

(1) the self-same piece of experience taken twice over in different contexts; or they are

(2) two pieces of *actual* experience belonging to the same subject, with definite tracts of conjunctive transitional experience between them; or

(3) the known is a *possible* experience either of that subject or another, to which the said conjunctive transitions *would* lead, if sufficiently prolonged.

To discuss all the ways in which one experience may function as the knower of another, would be incompatible with the limits of this essay. I have treated of type 1, the kind of knowledge called perception, in an article in the *Journal of Philosophy,* for September 1, 1904, called 'Does "consciousness" exist?' This is the type of case in which the mind enjoys direct 'acquaintance' with a present object. In the other types the mind has 'knowledge-about' an object not immediately there. Of type 2, the simplest sort of conceptual knowledge, I have given some account in two articles, published respectively in *Mind,* Vol. X., p. 27, 1885, and in the *Psychological Review,* Vol. II., p. 105, 1895. Type 3 can always formally and hypothetically be reduced to type 2, so that a brief description of that type will now put the present reader sufficiently at my point of view, and make him see what the actual meanings of the mysterious cognitive relation may be.

Suppose me to be sitting here in my library at Cambridge, at ten minutes' walk from 'Memorial Hall,' and to be thinking truly of the latter object. My mind may have before it only the name, or it may have a clear image, or it may have a very dim image of the hall, but such an intrinsic difference in the image makes no difference in its cognitive function. Certain *extrinsic* phenomena, special experiences of conjunction, are what impart to the image, be it what it may, its knowing office.

For instance, if you ask me what hall I mean by my image, and I can tell you nothing; or if I fail to point or lead you towards the Harvard Delta; or if, being led by you, I am uncertain whether the Hall I see be what I had in mind or not; you would rightly deny that I had 'meant' that particular hall at all, even tho my mental image might to some degree have resembled it. The resemblance would count in that case as coincidental merely, for all sorts of things of a kind resemble one another in this world without being held for that reason to take cognizance of one another.

On the other hand, if I can lead you to the hall, and tell you of its history and present uses; if in its presence I feel my idea, however imperfect it may have been, to have led hither and to be now *terminated;* if the associates of the image and of the felt hall run parallel, so that each term of the one context corresponds serially, as I walk, with an answering term of the other; why then my soul was prophetic, and my idea must be, and by common consent would be, called cognizant of reality. That percept was what I *meant,* for into it my idea has passed by conjunctive experiences of sameness and fulfilled intention. Nowhere is there jar, but every later moment continues and corroborates an earlier one.

In this continuing and corroborating, taken in no transcendental sense, but denoting definitely felt traditions, *lies all that the knowing of a percept by an idea can possibly contain or signify.* Wherever such transitions are felt, the first experience *knows* the last one. Where they do not, or where even as possibles they cannot, intervene, there can be no pretence of knowing. In this latter case the extremes will be connected, if connected at all, by inferior relations—bare likeness or succession, or by 'withness' alone. Knowledge of sensible realities thus comes to life inside the tissue of experience. It is *made;* and made by relations that unroll themselves in time. Whenever certain intermediaries are given, such that, as they develope towards their terminus, there is experience from point to point of one direction followed, and finally of one process fulfilled, the result is that *their starting-point thereby becomes a knower and their terminus an object meant or known.* That is all that knowing (in the simple case considered) can be known-as, that is the whole of its nature, put into experiential terms, Whenever such is the sequence of our experiences we may freely say that we had the terminal object 'in mind' from the outset, even altho *at* the outset nothing was there in us but a flat piece of substantive experience like any other, with no self-transcendency about it, and no mystery save the mystery of coming into existence and of being gradually followed by other pieces of substantive experience, with conjunctively transitional experiences between. That is what we *mean* here by the object's being 'in mind.' Of any deeper more real way of its being in mind we have no positive conception, and we have no right to discredit our actual experience by talking of such a way at all.

I know that many a reader will rebel at this. "Mere intermediaries," he will say, "even tho they be feelings of continuously growing fulfilment, only *separate* the knower from the known, whereas what we have in knowledge is a kind of immediate touch of the one by the other, an 'apprehension' in the etymological sense of the word, a leaping of the chasm as by lightning, an act by which two terms are smitten into one over the head of their distinctness. All these dead intermediaries of yours are out of each other, and outside of their termini still."

But do not such dialectic difficulties remind us of the dog dropping his bone and snapping at its image in the water? If we knew any more real kind of union *aliunde,* we might be entitled to brand all our empirical unions as a sham. But unions by continuous transition are the only ones we know of, whether in this matter of a knowledge-about that terminates in an acquaintance, whether in personal identity, whether in logical predication through the copula 'is,' or elsewhere. If anywhere there were more absolute unions, they could only reveal themselves to us by just such conjunctive results. These are what the unions are *worth,* these are all that *we can ever practically mean* by union, by continuity. Is it not time to repeat what Lotze said of substances, that to *act like* one is to *be* one? Should we not say here that to be experienced as continuous is to be really continuous, in a world where experience and reality come to the same thing? In a picture gallery a painted hook will serve to hang a painted chain by, a painted cable will hold a painted ship. In a world where both the terms and their distinctions are affairs of experience, conjunctions that are experienced must be at least as real as anything else. They will be 'absolutely' real conjunctions, if we have no transphenomenal absolute ready, to derealize the whole experienced world by, at a stroke. If, on the other hand, we had such an absolute, not one of our opponents' theories of knowledge could remain standing any better than ours could; for the distinctions as well as the conjunctions of experience would impartially fall its prey. The whole question of how 'one' thing can know 'another' would cease to be a real one at all in a world where otherness itself was an illusion.

So much for the essentials of the cognitive relation where the knowledge is conceptual in type, or forms knowledge 'about' an object. It consists in intermediary experiences (possible, if not actual) of continuously developing progress, and, finally, of fulfilment, when the sensible percept which is the object is reached. The percept here not only *verifies* the concept, proves its function of knowing that percept to be true, but the percept's existence as the ter-

minus of the chain of intermediaries *creates* the function. Whatever terminates that chain was, because it now proves itself to be, what the concept 'had in mind.'

The towering importance for human life of this kind of knowing lies in the fact that an experience that knows another can figure as its *representative,* not in any quasi-miraculous 'epistemological' sense, but in the definite practical sense of being its *substitute* in various operations, sometimes physical and sometimes mental, which lead us to its associates and results. By experimenting on our ideas of reality, we may save ourselves the trouble of experimenting on the real experiences which they severally mean. The ideas form related systems, corresponding point for point to the systems which the realities form; and by letting an ideal term call up its associates systematically, we may be led to a terminus which the corresponding real term would have led to in case we had operated on the real world. This brings us to the general question of substitution, and some remarks on that subject seem to be the next thing in order.

IV. SUBSTITUTION

In Taine's brilliant book on 'Intelligence,' substitution was for the first time named as a cardinal logical function, tho of course the facts had always been familiar enough. What, exactly, in a system of experiences, does the 'substitution' of one of them for another mean?

According to my view, experience as a whole is a process in time, whereby innumerable particular terms lapse and are superseded by others that follow upon them by transitions which, whether disjunctive or conjunctive in content, are themselves experiences, and must in general be accounted at least as real as the terms which they relate. What the nature of the event called 'superseding' signifies, depends altogether on the kind of transition that obtains. Some experiences simply abolish their predecessors without continuing them in any way. Others are felt to increase or to enlarge their meaning, to carry out their purpose, or to bring us nearer to their goal. They 'represent' them, and may fulfil their function better than they fulfilled it themselves. But to 'fulfil a function' in a world of pure experience can be conceived and defined in only one possible way. In such a world transitions and arrivals (or terminations) are the only events that happen, tho they happen by so many sorts of path.

The only function that one experience can perform is to lead into another experience; and the only fulfillment we can speak of is the reaching of a certain experienced end. When one experience leads to (or can lead to) the same end as another, they agree in function. But the whole system of experiences as they are immediately given presents itself as a quasi-chaos through which one can pass out of an initial term in many directions and yet end in the same terminus, moving from next to next by a great many possible paths.

Either one of these paths might be a functional substitute for another, and to follow one rather than another might on occasion be an advantageous thing to do. As a matter of fact, and in a general way, the paths that run through conceptual experiences, that is, through 'thoughts' or 'ideas' that 'know' the things in which they terminate, are highly advantageous paths to follow. Not only do they yield inconceivably rapid transitions; but, owing to the 'universal' character which they frequently possess, and to their capacity for association with one another in great systems, they outstrip the tardy consecutions of the things themselves, and sweep us on towards our ultimate termini in a far more labor-saving way than the following of trains of sensible perception ever could. Wonderful are the new cuts and the short-circuits the thought-paths make. Most thought-paths, it is true, are substitutes for nothing actual; they end outside the real world altogether, in wayward fancies, utopias, fictions or mistakes. But where they do re-enter reality and terminate therein, we substitute them always; and with these substitutes we pass the greater number of our hours.

This notion of the purely substitutional or conceptual physical world brings us to the most critical of all the steps in the development of a philosophy of pure experience. The paradox of self-transcendency in knowledge comes back upon us here, but I think that our notions of pure experience and of substitution, and our radically empirical view of conjunctive transitions, are *denkmittel* that will carry us safely through the pass.

V. WHAT OBJECTIVE REFERENCE IS

Whosoever feels his experience to be something substitutional even while he has it, may be said to have an experience that reaches beyond itself. From inside of its own entity it says 'more,' and postulates reality existing elsewhere. For the transcendentalist, who holds knowing to consist in a *salto mortale* across an 'epistemological chasm,' such an idea presents no difficulty; but it seems at first sight as if it might be inconsistent with an empiricism like our own. Have we not explained that conceptual knowledge is made such wholly by the existence of things that fall outside of the knowing experience itself—by intermediary experiences and by a terminus that fulfils? Can the knowledge be there before these elements that constitute its being have come? And, if knowledge be not there, how can objective reference occur?

The key to this difficulty lies in the distinction between knowing as verified and completed, and the same knowing as in transit and on its way. To recur to the Memorial Hall example lately used, it is only when our idea of the Hall has actually terminated in the percept that we know 'for certain' that from the beginning it was truly cognitive of *that*. Until established by the end of the process, its quality of knowing that, or indeed of knowing anything, could still be doubted; and yet the knowing really was there, as the result now shows. We were *virtual* knowers of the Hall long before we were certified to have been its actual knowers, by the percept's retroactive validating power. Just so we are 'mortal' all the time, by reason of the virtuality of the inevitable event which will make us so when it shall have come.

Now the immensely greater part of all our knowing never gets beyond this virtual stage. It never is completed or nailed down. I speak not merely of our ideas of imperceptibles like ether-waves or dissociated 'ions,' or of 'ejects' like the contents of our neighbors' minds; I speak also of ideas which we might verify if we would take the trouble, but which we hold for true altho unterminated perceptually, because nothing says 'no' to us, and there is no contradicting truth in sight. *To continue thinking unchallenged is, ninety-nine times out of a hundred, our practical substitute for knowing in the completed sense.* As each experience runs by cognitive transition into the next one, and we nowhere feel a collision with what we elsewhere count as truth or fact, we commit ourselves to the current as if the port were sure. We live, as it were, upon the front edge of an advancing wave-crest, and our sense of a determinate direction in falling forward is all we cover of the future of our path. It is as if a differential quotient should be conscious and treat itself as an adequate substitute for a traced-out curve. Our experience, *inter alia,* is of variations of rate and of direction, and lives in these transitions more than in the journey's end. The experiences of tendency are sufficient to act upon—what more could we have *done* at those moments even if the later verification comes complete?

This is what, as a radical empiricist, I say to the charge that the objective reference which is so flagrant a character of our experiences involves a chasm and mortal leap. A positively conjunctive transition involves neither chasm nor leap. Being the very original of what we mean by continuity, it makes a continuum wherever it appears. I know full well that such brief words as these will leave the hardened transcendentalist unshaken. Conjunctive experiences *separate* their terms, he will still say: they are third things interposed, that have themselves to be conjoined by new links, and to invoke them makes our trouble infinitely worse. To 'feel' our motion forward is impossible. Motion implies terminus; and how can terminus be felt before we have arrived? The barest start and sally forwards, the barest tendency to leave the instant, involves the chasm and the leap. Conjunctive transitions are the most superficial of appearances, illusions of our sensibility which philosophical reflection pulverizes at a touch. Conception is our only trustworthy instrument, conception and the absolute working hand in hand. Conception disintegrates experience utterly, but its disjunctions are easily overcome again when the absolute takes up the task.

Such transcendentalists I must leave, provisionally at least, in full possession of their creed. I have no space for polemics in this essay, so I shall simply formulate the empiricist doctrine as my hypothesis, leaving it to work or not work as it may.

Objective reference, I say then, is an incident of the fact that so much of our experience comes as an insufficient and consists of process and transition. Our fields of experience have no more definite boundaries than have our fields of view. Both are fringed forever by a *more* that continuously developes, and that continuously supersedes them as life proceeds. The relations, generally speaking, are as real here as the terms are, and the only complaint of the transcendentalist's with which I could at all sympathize would be his charge that, by first making knowledge to consist in external relations as I have done, and by then confessing that nine-tenths of the time these are not actually but only virtually there, I have knocked the solid bottom out of the whole business, and palmed off a substitute of knowledge for the genuine thing. Only the admission, such a critic might say, that our ideas are self-transcendent and 'true' already, in advance of the experiences that are to terminate them, can bring solidity back to knowledge in a world like this, in which transitions and terminations are only by exception fulfilled.

This seems to me an excellent place for applying the pragmatic method. What would the self-transcendency affirmed to exist in advance of all experiential mediation or termination, be *known-as*? What would it practically result in for *us,* were it true?

It could only result in our orientation, in the turning of our expectations and practical tendencies into the right path; and the right path here, so long as we and the object are not yet face to face (or can never get face to face, as in the case of ejects), would be the path that led us into the object's nearest neighborhood. Where direct acquaintance is lacking, 'knowledge-about' is the next best thing, and an acquaintance with what actually lies about the object, and is most closely related to it, puts such knowledge within our grasp. Ether-waves and your anger, for example, are things in which my thoughts will never *perceptually* terminate, but my concepts of them lead me to their very brink, to the chromatic fringes and to the hurtful words and deeds which are their really next effects.

Even if our ideas did in themselves possess the postulated self-transcendency, it would still remain true that their putting us into possession of such effects *would be the sole cash-value of the self-transcendency for us.* And this cash-value, it is needless to say, is *verbatim et literatim* what our empiricist account pays in. On pragmatist principles therefore, a dispute over self-transcendency is a pure logomachy. Call our concepts of ejective things self-transcendent or the reverse, it makes no difference, so long as we don't differ about the nature of that exalted virtue's fruits—fruits for us, of course, humanistic fruits.

If an absolute were proved to exist for other reasons, it might well appear that *his* knowledge is terminated in innumerable cases where ours is still incomplete. That, however, would be a fact indifferent to our knowledge. The latter would grow neither worse nor better, whether we acknowledged such an absolute or left him out.

So the notion of a knowledge still *in transitu* and on its way joins hands here with that notion of a 'pure experience' which I tried to explain in my recent article entitled 'Does "consciousness" exist?' The instant field of the present is always experience in its 'pure' state, plain unqualified actuality, a simple *that,* as yet undifferentiated into thing and thought, and only virtually classifiable as objective fact or as someone's opinion about fact. This is as true when the field is conceptual as when it is perceptual. 'Memorial Hall' is 'there' in my idea as much as when I stand before it. I proceed to act on its account in either case. Only in the later experience that supersedes the present one is this *naïf* immediacy retrospectively split into two parts, a 'consciousness' and its 'content,' and the content corrected or confirmed. While still pure, or present, any experience—mine, for example, of what I write about in these very lines—passes for 'truth.' The morrow may reduce it to 'opinion.' The transcendentalist in all his particular knowledges is as liable to this reduction as I am: his absolute does not save him. Why, then, need he quarrel with an account of knowledge that insists on naming this effect? Why not treat the working of the idea from next to next as the essence of its self-transcendency? Why insist that knowing is a static relation out of time when it practically seems so much a function of our active life? For a thing to be valid, says Lotze, is the same as to make itself valid. When the whole universe seems only to be making itself valid and to be still incomplete (else why its ceaseless changing?) why, of all things, should knowing be exempt? Why should it not be making itself valid like everything else? That some parts of it may be already valid or verified beyond dispute, the empirical philosopher, of course, like anyone else, may always hope.

VI. THE CONTERMINOUSNESS OF DIFFERENT MINDS

With transition and prospect thus enthroned in pure experience, it is impossible to subscribe to the idealism of the english school. Radical empiricism has, in fact, more affinities with natural realism than with the views of Berkeley or of Mill, and this can be easily shown.

For the berkeleyan school, ideas (the verbal equivalent of what I term experiences) are discontinuous. The content of each is wholly immanent, and there are no transitions with which they are consubstantial and through which their beings may unite. Your Memorial Hall and mine, even when both are percepts,

are wholly out of connexion with each other. Our lives are a congeries of solipsisms, out of which in strict logic only a God could compose a universe even of discourse. No dynamic currents run between my objects and your objects. Never can our minds meet in the *same.*

The incredibility of such a philosophy is flagrant. It is 'cold, strained, and unnatural' in a supreme degree; and it may be doubted whether even Berkeley himself, who took it so religiously, really believed, when walking through the streets of London, that his spirit and the spirits of his fellow wayfarers had absolutely different towns in view.

To me the decisive reason in favor of our minds meeting in *some* common objects at least is that, unless I make that supposition, I have no motive for assuming that your mind exists at all. Why do I postulate your mind? Because I see your body acting in a certain way. Its gestures, facial movements, words and conduct generally, are 'expressive,' so I deem it actuated as my own is, by an inner life like mine. This argument from analogy is my *reason,* whether an instinctive belief runs before it or not. But what is 'your body' here but a percept in *my* field? It is only as animating *that* object, *my* object, that I have any occasion to think of you at all. If the body that you actuate be not the very body that I see there, but some duplicate body of your own with which that has nothing to do, we belong to different universes, you and I, and for me to speak of you is folly. Myriads of such universes even now may coexist, irrelevant to one another; my concern is solely with the universe with which my own life is connected.

In that perceptual part of *my* universe which I call *your* body, your mind and my mind meet and may be called conterminous. Your mind actuates that body and mine sees it; my thoughts pass into it as into their harmonious cognitive fulfillment; your emotions and volitions pass into it as causes into their effects.

But that percept hangs together with all our other physical percepts. They are of one stuff with it; and if it be our common possession, they must be so likewise. For instance, your hand lays hold of one end of a rope and my hand lays hold of the other end. We pull against each other. Can our two hands be mutual objects in this experience, and the rope not be mutual also? What is true of the rope is true of any other percept. Your objects are over and over again the same as mine. If I ask you *where* some object of yours is, our old Memorial Hall, for example, you point to *my*

Memorial Hall with *your* hand which *I* see. If you alter an object in your world, put out a candle, for example, when I am present, *my* candle *ipso facto* goes out. It is only as altering my objects that I guess you to exist. If your objects do not coalesce with my objects, if they be not identically where mine are, they must be proved to be positively somewhere else. But no other location can be assigned for them, so their place must be what it seems to be, the same.

Practically, then, our minds meet in a world of objects which they share in common, which would still be there, if one or several of the minds were destroyed. I can see no formal objection to this supposition's being literally true. On the principles which I am defending, a 'mind' or 'personal consciousness' is the name for a series of experiences run together by certain definite transitions, and an objective reality is a series of similar experiences knit by different transitions. If one and the same experience can figure twice, once in a mental and once in a physical context (as I have tried, in my article on 'Consciousness,' to show that it can), one does not see why it might not figure thrice, or four times, or any number of times, by running into as many different mental contexts, just as the same point, lying at their intersection, can be continued into many different lines. Abolishing any number of contexts would not destroy the experience itself or its other contexts, any more than abolishing some of the point's linear continuations would destroy the others, or destroy the point itself.

I well know the subtle dialectic which insists that a term taken in another relation must needs be an intrinsically different term. The crux is always the old greek one, that the same man can't be tall in relation to one neighbor, and short in relation to another, for that would make him tall and short at once. In this essay I cannot stop to refute this dialectic, so I pass on, leaving my flank for the time exposed. But if my reader will only allow that the same '*now*' both ends his past and begins his future; or that, when he buys an acre of land from his neighbor, it is the same acre that successively figures in the two estates; or that when I pay him a dollar, the same dollar goes into his pocket that came out of mine; he will also in consistency have to allow that the same object may conceivably play a part in, as being related to the rest of, any number of otherwise entirely different minds. This is enough for my present point: the common-sense notion of minds sharing the same object offers no special

logical or epistemological difficulties of its own; it stands or falls with the general possibility of things being in conjunctive relation with other things at all.

In principle, then, let natural realism pass for possible. Your mind and mine *may* terminate in the same percept, not merely against it, as if it were a third external thing, but by inserting themselves into it and coalescing with it, for such is the sort of conjunctive union that appears to be experienced when a perceptual terminus 'fulfils.' Even so, two hawsers may embrace the same pile, and yet neither one of them touch any other part, except that pile, of what the other hawser is attached to.

It is therefore not a formal question, but a question of empirical fact solely, whether, when you and I are said to know the 'same' Memorial Hall, our minds do terminate at or in a numerically identical percept. Obviously, as a plain matter of fact, they do *not*. Apart from color-blindness and such possibilities, we see the Hall in different perspectives. You may be on one side of it and I on another. The percept of each of us, as he sees the surface of the Hall, is moreover only his provisional terminus. The next thing beyond my percept is not your mind, but more percepts of my own into which my first percept developes, the interior of the Hall, for instance, or the inner structure of its bricks and mortar. If our minds were in a literal sense *con*terminous, neither could get beyond the percept which they had in common, it would be an ultimate barrier between them—unless indeed they flowed over it and became 'coconscious' over a still larger part of their content, which (thought-transference apart) is not supposed to be the case. In point of fact the ultimate common barrier can always be pushed, by both minds, farther than any actual percept of either, until at last it resolves itself into the mere notion of imperceptibles like atoms or ether, so that, where we do terminate in percepts, our knowledge is only speciously completed, being, in theoretic strictness, only a virtual knowledge of those remoter objects which conception carries out.

Is natural realism, permissible in logic, refuted then by empirical fact? Do our minds have no object in common after all?

Yes, they certainly have *space* in common. On pragmatic principles we are obliged to predicate sameness wherever we can predicate no assignable point of difference. If two named things have every quality and function indiscernible, and are at the same time in the same place, they must be written down as numerically one thing under two different names. But there is no test discoverable, so far as I know, by which it can be shown that the place occupied by your percept of Memorial Hall differs from the place occupied by mine. The percepts themselves may be shown to differ; but if each of us be asked to point out where his percept is, we point to an identical spot. All the relations, whether geometrical or causal, of the Hall originate or terminate in that spot wherein our hands meet, and where each of us begins to work if he wishes to make the Hall change before the other's eyes. Just so it is with our bodies. That body of yours which you actuate and feel from within must be in the same spot as the body of yours which I see or touch from without. 'There' for me means where I place my finger. If you do not feel my finger's contact to be 'there' in *my* sense, when I place it on your body, where then do you feel it? Your inner actuations of your body meet my finger *there:* it is *there* that you resist its push, or shrink back, or sweep the finger aside with your hand. Whatever farther knowledge either of us may acquire of the real constitution of the body which we thus feel, you from within and I from without, it is in that same place that the newly conceived or perceived constituents have to be located, and it is *through* that space that your and my mental intercourse with each other has always to be carried on, by the mediation of impressions which I convey thither, and of the reactions thence which those impressions may provoke from you.

In general terms, then, whatever differing contents our minds may eventually fill a place with, the place itself is a numerically identical content of the two minds, a piece of common property in which, through which, and over which they join. The receptacle of certain of our experiences being thus common, the experiences themselves might some day become common also. If that day ever did come, our thoughts would terminate in a complete empirical identity, there would be an end, so far as *those* experiences went, to our discussions about truth. No points of difference appearing, they would have to count as the same.

VII. CONCLUSION

With this we have the outlines of a philosophy of pure experience before us. At the outset of my essay, I called it a mosaic philosophy. In actual mosaics the pieces are held together by their bedding, for which bedding the substances, transcendental egos, or absolutes of other philosophies may be taken to stand. In radical empiricism there is no bedding; it is as if the pieces clung together by their edges, the transitions experienced between them forming their cement. Of course such a metaphor is misleading, for in actual experience the more substantive and the more transitive parts run into each other continuously, there is in general no separateness needing to be overcome by an external cement; and whatever separateness is actually experienced is not overcome, it stays and counts as separateness to the end. But the metaphor serves to symbolize the fact that experience itself, taken at large, can grow by its edges. That one moment of it proliferates into the next by transitions which, whether conjunctive or disjunctive, continue the experiential tissue, cannot, I contend, be denied. Life is in the transitions as much as in the terms connected; often, indeed, it seems to be there more emphatically, as if our spurts and sallies forward were the real firing-line of the battle, were like the thin line of flame advancing across the dry autumnal field which the farmer proceeds to burn. In this line we live prospectively as well as retrospectively. It is 'of' the past, inasmuch as it comes expressly as the past's continuation; it is 'of' the future in so far as the future, when it comes, will have continued *it*.

These relations of continuous transition experienced are what make our experiences cognitive. In the simplest and completest cases the experiences are cognitive of one another. When one of them terminates a previous series of them with a sense of fulfilment, it, we say, is what those other experiences 'had in view.' The knowledge, in such a case, is verified, the truth is 'salted down.' Mainly, however, we live on speculative investments, or on our prospects only. But living on things *in posse* is as good as living in the actual, so long as our credit remains good. It is evident that for the most part it is good, and that the universe seldom protests our drafts.

In this sense we at every moment can continue to believe in an existing *beyond*. It is only in special cases that our confident rush forward gets rebuked. The beyond must of course always in our philosophy be itself of an experiential nature. If not a future experience of our own or a present one of our neighbor, it must be a thing in itself in Dr. Prince's and Professor Strong's sense of the term—that is, it must be an experience *for* itself whose relation to other things we translate into the action of molecules, ether-waves, or whatever else the physical symbols may be. This opens the chapter of the relations of radical empiricism to panpsychism, into which I cannot enter now.

The beyond can in any case exist simultaneously—for it can be experienced *to have existed* simultaneously—with the experience that practically postulates it by looking in its direction, or by turning or changing in the direction of which it is the goal. Pending that actuality of union, in the virtuality of which the 'truth,' even now, of the postulation consists, the beyond and its knower are entities split off from each other. The world is in so far forth a pluralism of which the unity is not fully experienced as yet. But, as fast as verifications come, trains of experience, once separate, run into one another; and that is why I said, earlier in my essay, that the unity of the world is on the whole undergoing increase. The universe continually grows in quantity by new experiences that graft themselves upon the older mass; but these very new experiences often help the mass to a more consolidated form.

These are the main features of a philosophy of pure experience. It has innumerable other aspects and arouses innumerable questions, but the points I have touched on seem enough to make an entering wedge. In my own mind such a philosophy harmonizes best with a radical pluralism, with novelty and indeterminism, moralism and theism, and with the 'humanism' lately sprung upon us by the Oxford and the Chicago schools. I cannot, however, be sure that all these doctrines are its necessary and indispensable allies. It presents so many points of difference, both from the common sense and from the idealism that have made our philosophic language, that it is almost as difficult to state it as it is to think it out clearly, and if it is ever to grow into a respectable system, it will have to be built up by the contributions of many co-operating minds. It seems to me, as I said at the outset of this essay, that many minds are, in point of fact, now turning in a direction that points toward radical empiricism. If they are carried farther by my words, and if then they add their stronger voices to my feebler one, the publication of this essay will have been worth while.

What Pragmatism Means

Some years ago, being with a camping party in the mountains, I returned from a solitary ramble to find everyone engaged in a ferocious metaphysical dispute. The *corpus* of the dispute was a squirrel—a live squirrel supposed to be clinging to one side of a tree-trunk; while over against the tree's opposite side a human being was imagined to stand. This human witness tries to get sight of the squirrel by moving rapidly round the tree, but no matter how fast he goes, the squirrel moves as fast in the opposite direction, and always keeps the tree between himself and the man, so that never a glimpse of him is caught. The resultant metaphysical problem now is this: *Does the man go round the squirrel or not?* He goes round the tree, sure enough, and the squirrel is on the tree; but does he go round the squirrel? In the unlimited leisure of the wilderness, discussion had been worn threadbare. Everyone had taken sides, and was obstinate; and the numbers on both sides were even. Each side, when I appeared, therefore appealed to me to make it a majority. Mindful of the scholastic adage that whenever you meet a contradiction you must make a distinction, I immediately sought and found one, as follows: "Which party is right," I said, "depends on what you *practically mean* by 'going round' the squirrel. If you mean passing from the north of him to the east, then to the south, then to the west, and then to the north of him again, obviously the man does go around him, for he occupies these successive positions. But if on the contrary you mean being first in front of him, then on the right of him, then behind him, then on his left, and finally in front again, it is quite as obvious that the man fails to go round him, for by the compensating movements the squirrel makes, he keeps his belly turned towards the man all the time, and his back turned away. Make the distinction, and there is no occasion for any farther dispute.

From *The Works of William James—Pragmatism,* ed. Frederick Burkhardt (Cambridge, Mass.: Harvard University Press, 1975), pp. 27–44.

You are both right and both wrong according as you conceive the verb 'to go round' in one practical fashion or the other."

Altho one or two of the hotter disputants called my speech a shuffling evasion, saying they wanted no quibbling or scholastic hair-splitting, but meant just plain honest English 'round,' the majority seemed to think that the distinction had assuaged the dispute.

I tell this trivial anecdote because it is a peculiarly simple example of what I wish now to speak of as *the pragmatic method*. The pragmatic method is primarily a method of settling metaphysical disputes that otherwise might be interminable. Is the world one or many?—fated or free?—material or spiritual?—here are notions either of which may or may not hold good of the world; and disputes over such notions are unending. The pragmatic method in such cases is to try to interpret each notion by tracing its respective practical consequences. What difference would it practically make to anyone if this notion rather than that notion were true? If no practical difference whatever can be traced, then the alternatives mean practically the same thing, and all dispute is idle. Whenever a dispute is serious, we ought to be able to show some practical difference that must follow from one side or the other's being right.

A glance at the history of the idea will show you still better what pragmatism means. The term is derived from the same Greek word πρᾶγμα, meaning action, from which our words 'practice' and 'practical' come. It was first introduced into philosophy by Mr. Charles Peirce in 1878. In an article entitled 'How to Make Our Ideas Clear,' in the 'Popular Science Monthly' for January of that year, Mr. Peirce, after pointing out that our beliefs are really rules for action, said that, to develope a thought's meaning, we need only determine what conduct it is fitted to produce: that conduct is for us its sole significance. And the tangible fact at the root of all our thought-distinctions, however subtle, is that there is no one of them so fine as to consist in anything but a possible difference of practice. To attain perfect clearness in our thoughts of an object, then, we need only consider what conceivable effects of a practical kind the object may involve—what sensations we are to expect from it, and what reactions we must prepare. Our conception of these effects, whether immediate or remote, is then for us the whole of our conception of the object, so far as that conception has positive significance at all.

This is the principle of Peirce, the principle of pragmatism. It lay entirely unnoticed by anyone for twenty years, until I, in an address before Professor Howison's philosophical union at the university of California, brought it forward again and made a special application of it to religion. By that date (1898) the times seemed ripe for its reception. The word 'pragmatism' spread, and at present it fairly spots the pages of the philosophic journals. On all hands we find the 'pragmatic movement' spoken of, sometimes with respect, sometimes with contumely, seldom with clear understanding. It is evident that the term applies itself conveniently to a number of tendencies that hitherto have lacked a collective name, and that it has 'come to stay '

To take in the importance of Peirce's principle, one must get accustomed to applying it to concrete cases. I found a few years ago that Ostwald, the illustrious Leipzig chemist, had been making perfectly distinct use of the principle of pragmatism in his lectures on the philosophy of science, tho he had not called it by that name.

"All realities influence our practice," he wrote me, "and that influence is their meaning for us. I am accustomed to put questions to my classes in this way: In what respects would the world be different if this alternative or that were true? If I can find nothing that would become different, then the alternative has no sense."

That is, the rival views mean practically the same thing, and meaning, other than practical, there is for us none. Ostwald in a published lecture gives this example of what he means. Chemists have long wrangled over the inner constitution of certain bodies called 'tautomerous.' Their properties seemed equally consistent with the notion that an instable hydrogen atom oscillates inside of them, or that they are instable mixtures of two bodies. Controversy raged; but never was decided. "It would never have begun," says Ostwald, "if the combatants had asked themselves what particular experimental fact could have been made different by one or the other view being correct. For it would then have appeared that no difference of fact could possibly ensue; and the quarrel was as unreal as if, theorizing in primitive times about the raising of dough by yeast, one party should have invoked a 'brownie,' while another insisted on an 'elf' as the true cause of the phenomenon."

It is astonishing to see how many philosophical disputes collapse into insignificance the moment you subject them to this simple test of tracing a concrete consequence. There can *be* no difference anywhere that doesn't *make* a difference elsewhere—no difference in abstract truth that doesn't express itself in a difference in concrete fact and in conduct consequent upon that fact, imposed on somebody, somehow, somewhere and somewhen. The whole function of philosophy ought to be to find out what definite difference it will make to you and me, at definite instants of our life, if this world-formula or that world-formula be the true one.

There is absolutely nothing new in the pragmatic method. Socrates was an adept at it. Aristotle used it methodically. Locke, Berkeley and Hume made momentous contributions to truth by its means. Shadworth Hodgson keeps insisting that realities are only what they are 'known-as.' But these forerunners of pragmatism used it in fragments: they were preluders only. Not until in our time has it generalized itself, become conscious of a universal mission, pretended to a conquering destiny. I believe in that destiny, and I hope I may end by inspiring you with my belief.

Pragmatism represents a perfectly familiar attitude in philosophy, the empiricist attitude, but it represents it, as it seems to me, both in a more radical and in a less objectionable form than it has ever yet assumed. A pragmatist turns his back resolutely and once for all upon a lot of inveterate habits dear to professional philosophers. He turns away from abstraction and insufficiency, from verbal solutions, from bad *a priori* reasons, from fixed principles, closed systems, and pretended absolutes and origins. He turns towards concreteness and adequacy, towards facts, towards action, and towards power. That means the empiricist temper regnant, and the rationalist temper sincerely given up. It means the open air and possibilities of nature, as against dogma, artificiality and the pretence of finality in truth.

At the same time it does not stand for any special results. It is a method only. But the general triumph of that method would mean an enormous change in what I called in my last lecture the 'temperament' of philosophy. Teachers of the ultra-rationalistic type would be frozen out, much as the courtier type is frozen out in republics, as the ultramontane type of priest is frozen out in protestant lands. Science and metaphysics would come much nearer together, would in fact work absolutely hand in hand.

Metaphysics has usually followed a very primitive kind of quest. You know how men have always hankered after unlawful magic, and you know what a great part, in magic, *words* have always played. If you have his name, or the formula of incantation that binds him, you can control the spirit, genie, afrite, or whatever the power may be. Solomon knew the names of all the spirits, and having their names, he held them subject to his will. So the universe has always appeared to the natural mind as a kind of enigma, of which the key must be sought in the shape of some illuminating or powerbringing word or name. That word names the universe's *principle,* and to possess it is, after a fashion, to possess the universe itself. 'God,' 'Matter,' 'Reason,' 'the Absolute,' 'Energy,' are so many solving names. You can rest when you have them. You are at the end of your metaphysical quest.

But if you follow the pragmatic method, you cannot look on any such word as closing your quest. You must bring out of each word its practical cash-value, set it at work within the stream of your experience. It appears less as a solution, then, than as a program for more work, and more particularly as an indication of the ways in which existing realities may be *changed.*

Theories thus become instruments, not answers to enigmas, in which we can rest. We don't lie back upon them, we move forward, and, on occasion, make nature over again by their aid. Pragmatism unstiffens all our theories, limbers them up and sets each one at work. Being nothing essentially new, it harmonizes with many ancient philosophic tendencies. It agrees with nominalism for instance, in always appealing to particulars; with utilitarianism in emphasizing practical aspects; with positivism in its disdain for verbal solutions, useless questions, and metaphysical abstractions.

All these, you see, are *anti-intellectualist* tendencies. Against rationalism as a pretension and a method, pragmatism is fully armed and militant. But, at the outset, at least, it stands for no particular results. It has no dogmas, and no doctrines save its method. As the young Italian pragmatist Papini has well said, it lies in the midst of our theories, like a corridor in a hotel. Innumerable chambers open out of it. In one you may find a man writing an atheistic volume; in the next someone on his knees praying for faith and strength; in a third a chemist investigating a body's properties. In a fourth a system of idealistic metaphysics is being excogitated; in a fifth the impossibility of metaphysics is being shown. But they all own the corridor, and all must pass through it if they want a practicable way of getting into or out of their respective rooms.

No particular results then, so far, but only an attitude of orientation, is what the pragmatic method means. *The attitude of looking away from first things, principles, 'categories,' supposed necessities; and of looking towards last things, fruits, consequences, facts.*

So much for the pragmatic method! You may say that I have been praising it rather than explaining it to you, but I shall presently explain it abundantly enough by showing how it works on some familiar problems. Meanwhile the word pragmatism has come to be used in a still wider sense, as meaning also a certain *theory of truth*. I mean to give a whole lecture to the statement of that theory, after first paving the way, so I can be very brief now. But brevity is hard to follow, so I ask for your redoubled attention for a quarter of an hour. If much remains obscure, I hope to make it clearer in the later lectures.

One of the most successfully cultivated branches of philosophy in our time is what is called inductive logic, the study of the conditions under which our sciences have evolved. Writers on this subject have begun to show a singular unanimity as to what the laws of nature and elements of fact mean, when formulated by mathematicians, physicists and chemists. When the first mathematical, logical and natural uniformities, the first *laws,* were discovered, men were so carried away by the clearness, beauty and simplification that resulted, that they believed themselves to have deciphered authentically the eternal thoughts of the Almighty. His mind also thundered and reverberated in syllogisms. He also thought in conic sections, squares and roots and ratios, and geometrized like Euclid. He made Kepler's laws for the planets to follow; he made velocity increase proportionally to the time in falling bodies; he made the law of the sines for light to obey when refracted; he established the classes, orders, families and genera of plants and animals, and fixed the distances between them. He thought the archetypes of all things, and devised their variations; and when we rediscover any one of these his wondrous institutions, we seize his mind in its very literal intention.

But as the sciences have developed farther, the notion has gained ground that most, perhaps all, of our laws are only approximations. The laws themselves, moreover, have grown so numerous that there is no counting them; and so many rival formulations are proposed in all the branches of science that investigators have become accustomed to the notion that no theory is absolutely a transcript of reality, but that any one of them may from some point of view be useful. Their great use is to summarize old facts and to lead to new ones. They are only a man-made language, a conceptual shorthand, as someone calls them, in which we write our reports of nature; and languages, as is well known, tolerate much choice of expression and many dialects.

Thus human arbitrariness has driven divine necessity from scientific logic. If I mention the names of Sigwart, Mach, Ostwald, Pearson, Milhaud, Poincaré, Duhem, Ruyssen, those of you who are students will easily identify the tendency I speak of, and will think of additional names.

Riding now on the front of this wave of scientific logic Messrs. Schiller and Dewey appear with their pragmatistic account of what truth everywhere signifies. Everywhere, these teachers say, 'truth' in our ideas and beliefs means the same thing that it means in science. It means, they say, nothing but this, *that ideas (which themselves are but parts of our experience) become true just in so far as they help us to get into satisfactory relation with other parts of our experience,* to summarize them and get about among them by conceptual short-cuts instead of following the interminable succession of particular phenomena. Any idea upon which we can ride, so to speak; any idea that will carry us prosperously from any one part of our experience to any other part, linking things satisfactorily, working securely, simplifying, saving labor; is true for just so much, true in so far forth, true *instrumentally*. This is the 'instrumental' view of truth taught so successfully at Chicago, the view that truth in our ideas means their power to 'work,' promulgated so brilliantly at Oxford.

Messrs. Dewey, Schiller and their allies, in reaching this general conception of all truth, have only followed the example of geologists, biologists and philologists. In the establishment of these other sciences, the successful stroke was always to take some simple process actually observable in operation—as denudation by weather, say, or variation from parental type, or change of dialect by incorporation of new words and pronunciations—and then to generalize it, making it apply to all times, and produce great results by summating its effects through the ages.

The observable process which Schiller and Dewey particularly singled out for generalization is the familiar one by which any individual settles into *new opinions*. The process here is always the same. The individual has a stock of old opinions already, but he meets a new experience that puts them to a strain. Somebody contradicts them; or in a reflective moment he discovers that they contradict each other; or he hears of facts with which they are incompatible; or desires arise in him which they cease to satisfy. The result is an inward trouble to which his mind till then had been a stranger, and from which he seeks to escape by modifying his previous mass of opinions. He saves as much of it as he can, for in this matter of belief we are all extreme conservatives. So he tries to change first this opinion, and then that (for they resist change very variously), until at last some new idea comes up which he can graft upon the ancient stock with a minimum of disturbance of the latter, some idea that mediates between the stock and the new experience and runs them into one another most felicitously and expediently.

This new idea is then adopted as the true one. It preserves the older stock of truths with a minimum of modification, stretching them just enough to make them admit the novelty, but conceiving that in ways as familiar as the case leaves possible. An *outrée* explanation, violating all our preconceptions, would never pass for a true account of a novelty. We should scratch round industriously till we found something less excentric. The most violent revolutions in an individual's beliefs leave most of his old order standing. Time and space, cause and effect, nature and history, and one's own biography remain untouched. New truth is always a go-between, a smoother-over of transitions. It marries old opinion to new fact so as ever to show a minimum of jolt, a maximum of continuity. We hold a theory true just in proportion to its success in solving this 'problem of maxima and minima.' But success in solving this problem is eminently a matter of approximation. We say this theory solves it on the whole more satisfactorily than that theory; but that means more satisfactorily to ourselves, and individuals will emphasize their points of satisfaction differently. To a certain degree, therefore, everything here is plastic.

The point I now urge you to observe particularly is the part played by the older truths. Failure to take account of it is the source of much of the unjust criticism leveled against pragmatism. Their influence is absolutely controlling. Loyalty to them is the first principle—in most cases it is the only principle; for by far the most usual way of handling phenomena so novel that they would make for a serious rearrangement of our preconceptions is to ignore them altogether, or to abuse those who bear witness for them.

You doubtless wish examples of this process of truth's growth, and the only trouble is their superabundance. The simplest case of new truth is of course the mere numerical addition of new kinds of facts, or of new single facts of old kinds, to our experience—an addition that involves no alteration in the old beliefs. Day follows day, and its contents are simply added. The new contents themselves are not true, they simply *come* and *are*. Truth is *what we say about* them, and when we say that they have come, truth is satisfied by the plain additive formula.

But often the day's contents oblige a rearrangement. If I should now utter piercing shrieks and act like a maniac on this platform, it would make many of you revise your ideas as to the probable worth of my philosophy. 'Radium' came the other day as part of the day's content, and seemed for a moment to contradict our ideas of the whole order of nature, that order having come to be identified with what is called the conservation of energy. The mere sight of radium paying heat away indefinitely out of its own pocket seemed to violate that conservation. What to think? If the radiations from it were nothing but an escape of unsuspected 'potential' energy, pre-existent inside of the atoms, the principle of conservation would be saved. The discovery of 'helium' as the radiation's outcome, opened a way to this belief. So Ramsay's view is generally held to be true, because, altho it extends our old ideas of energy, it causes a minimum of alteration in their nature.

I need not multiply instances. A new opinion counts as 'true' just in proportion as it gratifies the individual's desire to assimilate the novel in his experience to his beliefs in stock. It must both lean on old truth as grasp new fact; and its success (as I said a moment ago) in doing this, is a matter for the individual's appreciation. When old truth grows, then, by new truth's addition, it is for subjective reasons. We are in the process and obey the reasons. That new idea is truest which performs most felicitously its function of satisfying our double urgency. It makes itself true, gets itself classed as true, by the way it works; grafting itself then upon the ancient body of truth, which thus grows much as a tree grows by the activity of a new layer of cambium.

Now Dewey and Schiller proceed to generalize this observation and to apply it to the most ancient parts of truth. They also once were plastic. They also were called true for human reasons. They also mediated between still earlier truths and what in those days were novel observations. Purely objective truth, truth in whose establishment the function of giving human satisfaction in marrying previous parts of experience with newer parts played no role whatever, is nowhere to be found. The reasons why we call things true is the reason why they *are* true, for 'to be true' *means* only to perform this marriage-function.

The trail of the human serpent is thus over everything. Truth independent; truth that we *find* merely; truth no longer malleable to human need; truth incorrigible, in a word; such truth exists indeed superabundantly—or is supposed to exist by rationalistically minded thinkers; but then it means only the dead heart of the living tree, and its being there means only that truth also has its paleontology and its 'prescription,' and may grow stiff with years of veteran service and petrified in men's regard by sheer antiquity. But how plastic even the oldest truths nevertheless really are has been vividly shown in our day by the transformation of logical and mathematical ideas, a transformation which seems even to be invading physics. The ancient formulas are reinterpreted as special expressions of much wider principles, principles that our ancestors never got a glimpse of in their present shape and formulation.

Mr. Schiller still gives to all this view of truth the name of 'Humanism,' but, for this doctrine too, the name of pragmatism seems fairly to be in the ascendant, so I will treat it under the name of pragmatism in these lectures.

Such then would be the scope of pragmatism—first, a method; and second, a genetic theory of what is meant by truth. And these two things must be our future topics.

What I have said of the theory of truth will, I am sure, have appeared obscure and unsatisfactory to most of you by reason of its brevity. I shall make amends for that hereafter. In a lecture on 'common sense' I shall try to show what I mean by truths grown petrified by antiquity. In another lecture I shall expatiate on the idea that our thoughts become true in proportion as they successfully exert their go-between function. In a third I shall show how

hard it is to discriminate subjective from objective factors in Truth's development. You may not follow me wholly in these lectures; and if you do, you may not wholly agree with me. But you will, I know, regard me at least as serious, and treat my effort with respectful consideration.

You will probably be surprised to learn, then, that Messrs. Schiller's and Dewey's theories have suffered a hailstorm of contempt and ridicule. All rationalism has risen against them. In influential quarters Mr. Schiller, in particular, has been treated like an impudent schoolboy who deserves a spanking. I should not mention this, but for the fact that it throws so much sidelight upon that rationalistic temper to which I have opposed the temper of pragmatism. Pragmatism is uncomfortable away from facts. Rationalism is comfortable only in the presence of abstractions. This pragmatist talk about truths in the plural, about their utility and satisfactoriness, about the success with which they 'work,' etc., suggests to the typical intellectualist mind a sort of coarse lame second-rate make-shift article of truth. Such truths are not real truth. Such tests are merely subjective. As against this, objective truth must be something non-utilitarian, haughty, refined, remote, august, exalted. It must be an absolute correspondence of our thoughts with an equally absolute reality. It must be what we *ought* to think, unconditionally. The conditioned ways in which we *do* think are so much irrelevance and matter for psychology. Down with psychology, up with logic, in all this question!

See the exquisite contrast of the types of mind! The pragmatist clings to facts and concreteness, observes truth at its work in particular cases, and generalizes. Truth, for him, becomes a class-name for all sorts of definite working-values in experience. For the rationalist it remains a pure abstraction, to the bare name of which we must defer. When the pragmatist undertakes to show in detail just *why* we must defer, the rationalist is unable to recognize the concretes from which his own abstraction is taken. He accuses us of *denying* truth; whereas we have only sought to trace exactly why people follow it and always ought to follow it. Your typical ultra-abstractionist fairly shudders at concreteness: other things equal, he positively prefers the pale and spectral. If the two universes were offered, he would always choose the skinny outline rather than the rich thicket of reality. It is so much purer, clearer, nobler.

I hope that as these lectures go on, the concreteness and closeness to facts of the pragmatism which they advocate may be what approves itself to you as its most satisfactory peculiarity. It only follows here the example of the sister-sciences, interpreting the unobserved by the observed. It brings old and new harmoniously together. It converts the absolutely empty notion of a static relation of 'correspondence' (what that may mean we must ask later) between our minds and reality, into that of a rich and active commerce (that anyone may follow in detail and understand) between particular thoughts of ours, and the great universe of other experiences in which they play their parts and have their uses.

But enough of this at present? The justification of what I say must be postponed. I wish now to add a word in further explanation of the claim I made at our last meeting, that pragmatism may be a happy harmonizer of empiricist ways of thinking, with the more religious demands of human beings.

Men who are strongly of the fact-loving temperament, you may remember me to have said, are liable to be kept at a distance by the small sympathy with facts which that philosophy from the present-day fashion of idealism offers them. It is far too intellectualistic. Old fashioned theism was bad enough, with its notion of God as an exalted monarch, made up of a lot of unintelligible or preposterous 'attributes'; but, so long as it held strongly by the argument from design, it kept some touch with concrete realities. Since, however, darwinism has once for all displaced design from the minds of the 'scientific,' theism has lost that foothold; and some kind of an immanent or pantheistic deity working *in* things rather than above them is, if any, the kind recommended to our contemporary imagination. Aspirants to a philosophic religion turn, as a rule, more hopefully nowadays towards idealistic pantheism than towards the older dualistic theism, in spite of the fact that the latter still counts able defenders.

But, as I said in my first lecture, the brand of pantheism offered is hard for them to assimilate if they are lovers of facts, or empirically minded. It is the absolutistic brand, spurning the dust and reared upon pure logic. It keeps no connexion whatever with concreteness. Affirming the Absolute Mind, which is its substitute for God, to be the rational presupposition of all particulars of fact, whatever they may be, it remains supremely indifferent to what the particular facts in our world actu-

ally are. Be they what they may, the Absolute will father them. Like the sick lion in Esop's fable, all footprints lead into his den, but *nulla vestigia retrorsum*. You cannot redescend into the world of particulars by the Absolute's aid, or deduce any necessary consequences of detail important for your life from your idea of his nature. He gives you indeed the assurance that all is well with *Him,* and for his eternal way of thinking; but thereupon he leaves you to be finitely saved by your own temporal devices.

Far be it from me to deny the majesty of this conception, or its capacity to yield religious comfort to a most respectable class of minds. But from the human point of view, no one can pretend that it doesn't suffer from the faults of remoteness and abstractness. It is eminently a product of what I have ventured to call the rationalistic temper. It disdains empiricism's needs. It substitutes a pallid outline for the real world's richness. It is dapper; it is noble in the bad sense, in the sense in which to be noble is to be inapt for humble service. In this real world of sweat and dirt, it seems to me that when a view of things is 'noble,' that ought to count as a presumption against its truth, and as a philosophic disqualification. The prince of darkness may be a gentleman, as we are told he is, but whatever the God of earth and heaven is, he can surely be no gentleman. His menial services are needed in the dust of our human trials, even more than his dignity is needed in the empyrean.

Now pragmatism, devoted tho she be to facts, has no such materialistic bias as ordinary empiricism labors under. Moreover, she has no objection whatever to the realizing of abstractions, so long as you get about among particulars with their aid and they actually carry you somewhere. Interested in no conclusions but those which our minds and our experiences work out together, she has no *a priori* prejudices against theology. *If theological ideas prove to have a value for concrete life, they will be true, for pragmatism, in the sense of being good for so much. For how much more they are true, will depend entirely on their relations to the other truths that also have to be acknowledged.*

What I said just now about the Absolute of transcendental idealism is a case in point. First, I called it majestic and said it yielded religious comfort to a class of minds, and then I accused it of remoteness and sterility. But so far as it affords such comfort, it surely is not sterile; it has that amount of value; it performs a concrete function. As a good pragmatist, I myself ought to call the Absolute true 'in so far forth,' then; and I unhesitatingly now do so.

But what does *true in so far forth* mean in this case? To answer, we need only apply the pragmatic method. What do believers in the Absolute mean by saying that their belief affords them comfort? They mean that since in the Absolute finite evil is 'overruled' already, we may, therefore, whenever we wish, treat the temporal as if it were potentially the eternal, be sure that we can trust its outcome, and, without sin, dismiss our fear and drop the worry of our finite responsibilty. In short, they mean that we have a right ever and anon to take a moral holiday, to let the world wag in its own way, feeling that its issues are in better hands than ours and are none of our business.

The universe is a system of which the individual members may relax their anxieties occasionally, in which the don't-care method is also right for men, and moral holidays in order— that, if I mistake not, is part, at least, of what the Absolute is 'known-as,' that is the great difference in our particular experiences which his being true makes for us, that is part of his cash-value when he is pragmatically interpreted. Farther than that the ordinary lay-reader in philosophy who thinks favorably of absolute idealism does not venture to sharpen his conceptions. He can use the Absolute for so much, and so much is very precious. He is pained at hearing you speak incredulously of the Absolute, therefore, and disregards your criticisms because they deal with aspects of the conception that he fails to follow.

If the Absolute means this, and means no more than this, who can possibly deny the truth of it? To deny it would be to insist that men should never relax, and that holidays are never in order.

I am well aware how odd it must seem to some of you to hear me say that an idea is 'true' so long as to believe it is profitable to our lives. That it is *good,* for as much as it profits, you will gladly admit. If what we do by its aid is good, you will allow the idea itself to be good in so far forth, for we are the better for possessing it. But is it not a strange misuse of the word 'truth,' you will say, to call ideas also 'true' for this reason?

To answer this difficulty fully is impossible at this stage of my account. You touch here upon the very central point of Messrs. Schiller's, Dewey's and my own doctrine of truth, which I cannot discuss with detail until my sixth lecture. Let me now say only this, that truth is *one*

species of good, and not, as is usually supposed, a category distinct from good, and co-ordinate with it. *The true is the name of whatever proves itself to be good in the way of belief, and good, too, for definite, assignable reasons.* Surely you must admit this, that if there were *no* good for life in true ideas, or if the knowledge of them were positively disadvantageous and false ideas the only useful ones, then the current notion that truth is divine and precious, and its pursuit a duty, could never have grown up or become a dogma. In a world like that, our duty would be to *shun* truth, rather. But in this world, just as certain foods are not only agreeable to our taste, but good for our teeth, our stomach and our tissues; so certain ideas are not only agreeable to think about, or agreeable as supporting other ideas that we are fond of, but they are also helpful in life's practical struggles. If there be any life that it is really better we should lead, and if there be any idea which, if believed in, would help us to lead that life, then it would be really *better for us* to believe in that idea, *unless, indeed, belief in it incidentally clashed with other greater vital benefits.*

'What would be better for us to believe'! This sounds very like a definition of truth. It comes very near to saying 'what we *ought* to believe': and in *that* definition none of you would find any oddity. Ought we ever not to believe what it is *better for us* to believe? And can we then keep the notion of what is better for us, and what is true for us, permanently apart?

Pragmatism says no, and I fully agree with her. Probably you also agree, so far as the abstract statement goes, but with a suspicion that if we practically did believe everything that made for good in our own personal lives, we should be found indulging all kinds of fancies about this world's affairs, and all kinds of sentimental superstitions about a world hereafter. Your suspicion here is undoubtedly well founded, and it is evident that something happens when you pass from the abstract to the concrete, that complicates the situation.

I said just now that what is better for us to believe is true *unless the belief incidentally clashes with some other vital benefit.* Now in real life what vital benefits is any particular belief of ours most liable to clash with? What indeed except the vital benefits yielded by *other beliefs* when these prove incompatible with the first ones? In other words, the greatest enemy of any one of our truths may be the rest of our truths. Truths have once for all this desperate instinct of self-preservation and of desire to extinguish whatever contradicts them. My belief in the Absolute, based on the good it does me, must run the gauntlet of all my other beliefs. Grant that it may be true in giving me a moral holiday. Nevertheless, as I conceive it,—and let me speak now confidentially, as it were, and merely in my own private person,—it clashes with other truths of mine whose benefits I hate to give up on its account. It happens to be associated with a kind of logic of which I am the enemy, I find that it entangles me in metaphysical paradoxes that are inacceptable, etc., etc. But as I have enough trouble in life already without adding the trouble of carrying these intellectual inconsistencies, I personally just give up the Absolute. I just *take* my moral holidays; or else as a professional philosopher, I try to justify them by some other principle.

If I could restrict my notion of the Absolute to its bare holiday-giving value, it wouldn't clash with my other truths. But we cannot easily thus restrict our hypotheses. They carry supernumerary features, and these it is that clash so. My disbelief in the Absolute means then disbelief in those other supernumerary features, for I fully believe in the legitimacy of taking moral holidays.

You see by this what I meant when I called pragmatism a mediator and reconciler and said, borrowing the word from Papini, that she 'unstiffens' our theories. She has in fact no prejudices whatever, no obstructive dogmas, no rigid canons of what shall count as proof. She is completely genial. She will entertain any hypothesis, she will consider any evidence. It follows that in the religious field she is at a great advantage both over positivistic empiricism, with its anti-theological bias, and over religious rationalism, with its exclusive interest in the remote, the noble, the simple, and the abstract in the way of conception.

In short, she widens the field of search for God. Rationalism sticks to logic and the empyrean. Empiricism sticks to the external senses. Pragmatism is willing to take anything, to follow either logic or the senses, and to count the humblest and most personal experiences. She will count mystical experiences if they have practical consequences. She will take a God who lives in the very dirt of private fact—if that should seem a likely place to find him.

Her only test of probable truth is what works best in the way of leading us, what fits every part of life best and combines with the collectivity of experience's demands, nothing being omitted. If theological ideas should do this, if the notion of God, in particular, should prove to do it, how could pragmatism possibly deny God's existence? She could see no meaning in treating as 'not true' a notion that was pragmatically so successful. What other kind of truth could there be, for her, than all this agreement with concrete reality?

In my last lecture I shall return again to the relations of pragmatism with religion. But you see already how democratic she is. Her manners are as various and flexible, her resources as rich and endless, and here conclusions as friendly as those of mother nature.

The Moral Philosopher and the Moral Life

The main purpose of this paper is to show that there is no such thing possible as an ethical philosophy dogmatically made up in advance. We all help to determine the content of ethical philosophy so far as we contribute to the race's moral life. In other words, there can be no final truth in ethics any more than in physics, until the last man has had his experience and said his say. In the one case as in the other, however, the hypotheses which we now make while waiting, and the acts to which they prompt us, are among the indispensable conditions which determine what they "say" shall be.

First of all, what is the position of him who seeks an ethical philosophy? To begin with, he must be distinguished from all those who are satisfied to be ethical sceptics. He *will* not be a sceptic; therefore so far from ethical scepticism being one possible fruit of ethical philosophizing, it can only be regarded as that residual

From *The Works of William James—The Will to Believe*. Frederick Burkhardt, ed. Cambridge, Mass: Harvard University Press, 1979, pp. 141–162.

alternative to all philosophy which from the outset menaces every would-be philosopher who may give up the quest discouraged, and renounce his original aim. That aim is to find an account of the moral relations that obtain among things, which will weave them into the unity of a stable system, and make of the world what one may call a genuine universe from the ethical point of view. So far as the world resists reduction to the form of unity, so far as ethical propositions seem unstable, so far does the philosopher fail of his ideal. The subject-matter of his study is the ideals he finds existing in the world; the purpose which guides him is this ideal of his own, of getting them into a certain form. This ideal is thus a factor in ethical philosophy whose legitimate presence must never be overlooked; it is a positive contribution which the philosopher himself necessarily makes to the problem. But it is his only positive contribution. At the outset of his inquiry he ought to have no other ideals. Were he interested peculiarly in the triumph of any one kind of good, he would *pro tanto* cease to be a judicial investigator, and become an advocate for some limited element of the case.

There are three questions in ethics which must be kept apart. Let them be called respectively the *psychological* question, the *metaphysical* question, and the *casuistic* question. The psychological question asks after the historical *origin* of our moral ideas and judgments; the metaphysical question asks what the very *meaning* of the words "good," "ill," and "obligation" are; the casuistic question asks what is the *measure* of the various goods and ills which men recognize, so that the philosopher may settle the true order of human obligations.

I

The psychological question is for most disputants the only question. When your ordinary doctor of divinity has proved to his own satisfaction that an altogether unique faculty called "conscience" must be postulated to tell us what is right and what is wrong; or when your popular-science enthusiast has proclaimed that "apriorism" is an exploded superstition, and that our moral judgments have gradually resulted from the teaching of the environment, each of these persons thinks that ethics is settled and nothing more is to be said. The familiar pair of names, Intuitionist and Evolutionist, so commonly used now to

connote all possible differences in ethical opinion, really refer to the psychological question alone. The discussion of this question hinges so much upon particular details that it is impossible to enter upon it at all within the limits of this paper. I will therefore only express dogmatically my own belief, which is this—that the Benthams, the Mills, and the Bains have done a lasting service in taking so many of our human ideals and showing how they must have arisen from the association with acts of simple bodily pleasures and reliefs from pain. Association with many remote pleasures will unquestionably make a thing significant of goodness in our minds; and the more vaguely the goodness is conceived of, the more mysterious will its source appear to be. But it is surely impossible to explain all our sentiments and preferences in this simple way. The more minutely psychology studies human nature, the more clearly it finds there traces of secondary affections, relating the impressions of the environment with one another and with our impulses in quite different ways from those mere associations of coexistence and succession which are practically all that pure empiricism can admit. Take the love of drunkenness; take bashfulness, the terror of high places, the tendency to sea-sickness, to faint at the sight of blood, the susceptibility to musical sounds; take the emotion of the comical, the passion for poetry, for mathematics, or for metaphysics—no one of these things can be wholly explained by either association or utility. They *go with* other things that can be so explained, no doubt; and some of them are prophetic of future utilities, since there is nothing in us for which some use may not be found. But their origin is in incidental complications to our cerebral structure, a structure whose original features arose with no reference to the perception of such discords and harmonies as these.

Well, a vast number of our moral perceptions also are certainly of this secondary and brain-born kind. They deal with directly felt fitnesses between things, and often fly in the teeth of all the prepossessions of habit and presumptions of utility. The moment you get beyond the coarser and more commonplace moral maxims, the Decalogues and Poor Richard's Almanacs, you fall into schemes and positions which to the eye of commonsense are fantastic and over-strained. The sense for abstract justice which some persons have is as excentric a variation, from the natural-history point of view, as is the passion for music or for the higher philosophical consistencies which consumes the soul of others. The feeling of the inward dignity of certain spiritual attitudes, as peace, serenity, simplicity, veracity; and of the essential vulgarity of others, as querulousness, anxiety, egoistic fussiness, etc.—are quite inexplicable except by an innate preference of the more ideal attitude for its own pure sake. The nobler thing *tastes* better, and that is all that we can say. "Experience" of consequences may truly teach us what things are *wicked,* but what have consequences to do with what is *mean* and *vulgar?* If a man has shot his wife's paramour, by reason of what subtle repugnancy in things is it that we are so disgusted when we hear that the wife and the husband have made it up and are living comfortably together again? Or if the hypothesis were offered us of a world in which Messrs. Fourier's and Bellamy's and Morris's utopias should all be outdone, and millions kept permanently happy on the one simple condition that a certain lost soul on the far-off edge of things should lead a life of lonely torture, what except a specific and independent sort of emotion can it be which would make us immediately feel, even though an impulse arose within us to clutch at the happiness so offered, how hideous a thing would be its enjoyment when deliberately accepted as the fruit of such a bargain? To what, once more, but subtle brain-born feelings of discord can be due all these recent protests against the entire race-tradition of retributive justice?—I refer to Tolstoï with his ideas of non-resistance, to Mr. Bellamy with his substitution of oblivion for repentance (in his novel of Dr. Heidenhain's Process), to M. Guyau with his radical condemnation of the punitive ideal. All these subtleties of the moral sensibility go as much beyond what can be ciphered out from the "laws of association" as the delicacies of sentiment possible between a pair of young lovers go beyond such precepts of the "etiquette to be observed during engagement" as are printed in manuals of social form.

No! Purely inward forces are certainly at work here. All the higher, more penetrating ideals are revolutionary. They present themselves far less in the guise of effects of past experience than in that of probable causes of future experience, factors to which the environment and the lessons it has so far taught us must learn to bend.

This is all I can say of the psychological question now. In the last chapter of a recent work I have sought to prove in a general way the existence, in our thought, of relations which do not merely repeat the couplings of experience. Our ideals have certainly many sources. They are not all explicable as signifying corporeal pleasures to be gained, and pains to be escaped. And for having so constantly perceived this psychological fact, we must applaud the intuitionist school. Whether or not such applause must be extended to that school's other characteristics will appear as we take up the following questions.

The next one in order is the metaphysical question, of what we mean by the words "obligation," "good," and "ill."

II

First of all, it appears that such words can have no application or relevancy in a world in which no sentient life exists. Imagine an absolutely material world, containing only physical and chemical facts, and existing from eternity without a God, without even an interested spectator: would there be any sense in saying of that world that one of its states is better than another? Or if there were two such worlds possible, would there be any rhyme or reason in calling one good and the other bad—good or bad positively, I mean, and apart from the fact that one might relate itself better than the other to the philosopher's private interests? But we must leave these private interests out of the account, for the philosopher is a mental fact, and we are asking whether goods and evils and obligations exist in physical facts *per se.* Surely there is no *status* for good and evil to exist in, in a purely insentient world. How can one physical fact, considered simply as a physical fact, be "better" than another? Betterness is not a physical relation. In its mere material capacity, a thing can no more be good or bad than it can be pleasant or painful. Good for what? Good for the production of another physical fact, do you say? But what in a purely physical universe demands the production of that other fact? Physical facts simply *are* or *are not;* and neither when present or absent, can they be supposed to make demands. If they do, they can only do so by having desires; and then they have ceased to be purely physical facts, and have become facts of conscious sensibility. Goodness, badness, and obligation must be *realized* somewhere in order really to exist; and the first step in ethical philosophy is to see that no merely inorganic "nature of things" can realize them. Neither moral relations nor the moral law can swing *in vacuo.* Their only habitat can be a mind which feels them; and no world composed of merely physical facts can possibly be a world to which ethical propositions apply.

The moment one sentient being, however, is made a part of the universe, there is a chance for goods and evils really to exist. Moral relations now have their *status,* in that being's consciousness. So far as he feels anything to be good, he *makes it good.* It *is* good, for him; and being good for him, is absolutely good, for he is the sole creator of values in that universe, and outside of his opinion things have no moral character at all.

In such a universe as that it would of course be absurd to raise the question of whether the solitary thinker's judgments of good and ill are true or not. Truth supposes a standard outside of the thinker to which he must conform; but here the thinker is a sort of divinity, subject to no higher judge. Let us call the supposed universe which he inhabits a *moral solitude.* In such a moral solitude it is clear that there can be no outward obligation, and that the only trouble the god-like thinker is liable to have will be over the consistency of his own several ideals with one another. Some of these will no doubt be more pungent and appealing than the rest, their goodness will have a profounder, more penetrating taste; they will return to haunt him with more obstinate regrets if violated. So the thinker will have to order his life with them as its chief determinants, or else remain inwardly discordant and unhappy. Into whatever equilibrium he may settle, though, and however he may straighten out his system, it will be a right system; for beyond the facts of his own subjectivity there is nothing moral in the world.

If now we introduce a second thinker with his likes and dislikes into the universe, the ethical situation becomes much more complex, and several possibilities are immediately seen to obtain.

One of these is that the thinkers may ignore each other's attitude about good and evil altogether, and each continue to indulge his own preferences, indifferent to what the other may feel or do. In such a case we have a world with twice as much of the ethical quality in it as our moral solitude, only it is without ethical unity. The same object is good or bad there, according as you measure it by the view which this one or that one of the thinkers takes. Nor can you find any possible ground in such a world for saying that one

thinker's opinion is more correct than the other's, or that either has the truer moral sense. Such a world, in short, is not a moral universe but a moral dualism. Not only is there no single point of view within it from which the values of things can be unequivocally judged, but there is not even a demand for such a point of view, since the two thinkers are supposed to be indifferent to each other's thoughts and acts. Multiply the thinkers into a pluralism, and we find realized for us in the ethical sphere something like that world which the antique sceptics conceived of—in which individual minds are the measures of all things, and in which no one "objective" truth, but only a multitude of "subjective" opinions, can be found.

But this is the kind of world with which the philosopher, so long as he holds to the hope of a philosophy, will not put up. Among the various ideals represented, there must be, he thinks, some which have the more truth or authority; and to these the others *ought* to yield, so that system and subordination may reign. Here in the word "ought" the notion of *obligation* comes emphatically into view, and the next thing in order must be to make its meaning clear.

Since the outcome of the discussion so far has been to show us that nothing can be good or right except so far as some consciousness feels it to be good or thinks it to be right, we perceive on the very threshold that the real superiority and authority which are postulated by the philosopher to reside in some of the opinions, and the really inferior character which he supposes must belong to others, cannot be explained by any abstract moral "nature of things" existing antecedently to the concrete thinkers themselves with their ideals. Like the positive attributes good and bad, the comparative ones better and worse must be *realized* in order to be real. If one ideal judgment be objectively better than another, that betterness must be made flesh by being lodged concretely in someone's actual perception. It cannot float in the atmosphere, for it is not a sort of meteorological phenomenon, like the aurora borealis or the zodiacal light. Its *esse* is *percipi,* like the *esse* of the ideals themselves between which it obtains. The philosopher, therefore, who seeks to know which ideal ought to have supreme weight and which one ought to be subordinated, must trace the *ought* itself to the *de facto* constitution of some existing consciousness, behind which, as one of the data of the universe, he as a purely ethical philosopher is unable to go. This consciousness must make the one ideal right by feeling it to be right, the other wrong by feeling it to be wrong. But now what particular consciousness in the universe *can* enjoy this prerogative of obliging others to conform to a rule which it lays down?

If one of the thinkers were obviously divine, while all the rest were human, there would probably be no practical dispute about the matter. The divine thought would be the model, to which the others should conform. But still the theoretic question would remain, What is the ground of the obligation, even here?

In our first essays at answering this question, there is an inevitable tendency to slip into an assumption which ordinary men follow when they are disputing with one another about questions of good and bad. They imagine an abstract moral order in which the objective truth resides; and each tries to prove that this pre-existing order is more accurately reflected in his own ideas than in those of his adversary. It is because one disputant is backed by this overarching abstract order that we think the other should submit. Even so, when it is a question no longer of two finite thinkers, but of God and ourselves—we follow our usual habit, and imagine a sort of *de jure* relation, which antedates and overarches the mere facts, and would make it right that we should conform our thoughts to God's thoughts, even though he made no claim to that effect, and though we preferred *de facto* to go on thinking for ourselves.

But the moment we take a steady look at the question, *we see not only that without a claim actually made by some concrete person there can be no obligation, but that there is some obligation wherever there is a claim.* Claim and obligation are, in fact, coextensive terms; they cover each other exactly. Our ordinary attitude of regarding ourselves as subject to an overarching system of moral relations, true "in themselves," is therefore either an out-and-out superstition, or else it must be treated as a merely provisional abstraction from that real Thinker in whose actual demand upon us to think as he does our obligation must be ultimately based. In a theistic-ethical philosophy that thinker in question is, of course, the Deity to whom the existence of the universe is due.

I know well how hard it is for those who are accustomed to what I have called the superstitious view, to realize that every *de facto* claim creates in so far forth an obligation. We inveterately think that something which we call the "validity" of the claim is what gives to it its obligatory character, and that this validity is something outside of the claim's mere existence as a matter of fact. It rains down upon the claim, we think, from some sublime dimension of being, which the moral law inhabits, much as upon the steel of the compass-needle the influence of the Pole rains down from out of the starry heavens. But again, how can such an inorganic abstract character of imperativeness, additional to the imperativeness which is in the concrete claim itself, *exist?* Take any demand, however slight, which any creature, however weak, may make. Ought it not, for its own sole sake, to be satisfied? If not, prove why not. The only possible kind of proof you could adduce would be the exhibition of another creature who should make a demand that ran the other way. The only possible reason there can be why any phenomenon ought to exist is that such a phenomenon actually is desired. Any desire is imperative to the extent of its amount; it *makes* itself valid by the fact that it exists at all. Some desires, truly enough, are small desires; they are put forward by insignificant persons; and we customarily make light of the obligations which they bring. But the fact that such personal demands as these impose small obligations does not keep the largest obligations from being personal demands.

If we must talk impersonally, to be sure we can say that "the universe" requires, exacts, or makes obligatory such or such an action, whenever it expresses itself through the desires of such or such a creature. But it is better not to talk about the universe in this personified way, unless we believe in a universal or divine consciousness which actually exists. If there be such a consciousness, then its demands carry the most of obligation simply because they are the greatest in amount. But it is even then not *abstractly* right that we should respect them. It is only *concretely* right—or right after the fact, and by virtue of the fact, that they are actually made. Suppose we do not respect them, as seems largely to be the case in this queer world. That ought not to be, we say; that is wrong. But in what way is this fact of wrongness made more acceptable or intelligible when we imagine it to consist rather in the laceration of an *à priori* ideal order than in the disappointment of a living personal God? Do we, perhaps, think that we cover God and protect him and make his impotence over us less ultimate, when we back him up with this *à priori* blanket from which he may draw some warmth of further appeal? But the only force of appeal to *us,* which either a living God or an abstract ideal order can wield, is found in the "everlasting ruby vaults" of our own human hearts, as they happen to beat responsive and not irresponsive to the claim. So far as they do feel it when made by a living consciousness, it is life answering to life. A claim thus livingly acknowledged is acknowledged with a solidity and fulness which no thought of an "ideal" backing can render more complete; while if, on the other hand, the heart's response is withheld, the stubborn phenomenon is there of an impotence in the claims which the universe embodies, which no talk about an eternal nature of things can gloze over or dispel. An ineffective *à priori* order is as impotent a thing as an ineffective God; and in the eye of philosophy, it is as hard a thing to explain.

We may now consider that what we distinguished as the metaphysical question in ethical philosophy is sufficiently answered, and that we have learned what the words "good," "bad," and "obligation" severally mean. They mean no absolute natures, independent of personal support. They are objects of feeling and desire, which have no foothold or anchorage in Being, apart from the existence of actually living minds.

Wherever such minds exist, with judgments of good and ill, and demands upon one another, there is an ethical world in its essential features. Were all other things, gods and men and starry heavens, blotted out from this universe, and were there left but one rock with two loving souls upon it, that rock would have as thoroughly moral a constitution as any possible world which the eternities and immensities could harbor. It would be a tragic constitution, because the rock's inhabitants would die. But while they lived, there would be real good things and real bad things in the universe; there would be obligations, claims, and expectations; obediences, refusals, and disappointments; compunctions and longings for harmony to come again, and inward peace of conscience when it was restored; there would, in short, be a moral life, whose active energy would have no limit but the intensity of interest in each other with which the hero and heroine might be endowed.

We, on this terrestrial globe, so far as the visible facts go, are just like the inhabitants of such a rock. Whether a God exist, or whether no God exist, in yon blue heaven above us

bent, we form at any rate an ethical republic here below. And the first reflection which this leads to is that ethics have as genuine and real a foothold in a universe where the highest consciousness is human, as in a universe where there is a God as well. "The religion of humanity" affords a basis for ethics as well as theism does. Whether the purely human system can gratify the philosopher's demand as well as the other is a different question, which we ourselves must answer ere we close.

III

The last fundamental question in Ethics was, it will be remembered, the *casuistic* question. Here we are, in a world where the existence of a divine thinker has been and perhaps always will be doubted by some of the lookers-on, and where, in spite of the presence of a large number of ideals in which human beings agree, there are a mass of others about which no general consensus obtains. It is hardly necessary to present a literary picture of this, for the facts are too well known. The wars of the flesh and the spirit in each man, the concupiscences of different individuals pursuing the same unshareable material or social prizes, the ideals which contrast so according to races, circumstances, temperaments, philosophical beliefs, etc.—all form a maze of apparently inextricable confusion with no obvious Ariadne's thread to lead one out. Yet the philosopher, just because he is a philosopher, adds his own peculiar ideal to the confusion (with which if he were willing to be a sceptic he would be passably content), and insists that over all these individual opinions there is a *system of truth* which he can discover if he only takes sufficient pains.

We stand ourselves at present in the place of that philosopher, and must not fail to realize all the features that the situation comports. In the first place we will not be sceptics; we hold to it that there is a truth to be ascertained. But in the second place we have just gained the insight that that truth cannot be a self-proclaiming set of laws, or an abstract "moral reason," but can only exist in act, or in the shape of an opinion held by some thinker really to be found. There is, however, no visible thinker invested with authority. Shall we then simply proclaim our own ideals as the lawgiving ones? No; for if we are true philosophers we must throw our own spontaneous ideals, even the dearest, impartially in with that total mass of ideals which are fairly to be judged. But how then can we as philosophers ever find a test; how avoid complete moral scepticism on the one hand, and on the other escape bringing a wayward personal standard of our own along with us, on which we simply pin our faith?

The dilemma is a hard one, nor does it grow a bit more easy as we revolve it in our minds. The entire undertaking of the philosopher obliges him to seek an impartial test. That test, however, must be incarnated in the demand of some actually existent person; and how can he pick out the person save by an act in which his own sympathies and prepossessions are implied?

One method indeed presents itself, and has as a matter of history been taken by the more serious ethical schools. If the heap of things demanded proved on inspection less chaotic than at first they seemed, if they furnished their own relative test and measure, then the casuistic problem would be solved. If it were found that all goods *qua* goods contained a common essence, then the amount of this essence involved in any one good would show its rank in the scale of goodness, and order could be quickly made; for this essence would be *the* good upon which all thinkers were agreed, the relatively objective and universal good that the philosopher seeks. Even his own private ideals would be measured by their share of it, and find their rightful place among the rest.

Various essences of good have thus been found and proposed as bases of the ethical system. Thus, to be a mean between two extremes; to be recognized by a special intuitive faculty; to make the agent happy for the moment; to make others as well as him happy in the long run; to add to his perfection or dignity; to harm no one; to follow from reason or flow from universal law; to be in accordance with the will of God; to promote the survival of the human species of this planet—are so many tests, each of which has been maintained by somebody to constitute the essence of all good things or actions so far as they are good.

No one of the measures that have been actually proposed has, however, given general satisfaction. Some are obviously not universally present in all cases—*e.g.,* the character of harming no one, or that of following a universal law; for the best course is often cruel; and many acts are reckoned good on the sole condition that they be exceptions, and serve not as examples of a universal law. Other characters, such as following the will of God, are unascertainable and vague. Others again,

like survival, are quite indeterminate in their consequences, and leave us in the lurch where we most need their help: a philosopher of the Sioux Nation, for example, will be certain to use the survival-criterion in a very different way from ourselves. The best, on the whole, of these marks and measures of goodness seems to be the capacity to bring happiness. But in order not to break down fatally, this test must be taken to cover innumerable acts and impulses that never *aim* at happiness; so that, after all, in seeking for a universal principle we inevitably are carried onward to the *most* universal principle—that *the essence of good is simply to satisfy demand.* The demand may be for anything under the sun. There is really no more ground for supposing that all our demands can be accounted for by one universal underlying kind of motive than there is ground for supposing that all physical phenomena are cases of a single law. The elementary forces in ethics are probably as plural as those of physics are. The various ideas have no common character apart from the fact that they are ideals. No single abstract principle can be so used as to yield to the philosopher anything like a scientifically accurate and genuinely useful casuistic scale.

A look at another peculiarity of the ethical universe, as we find it, will still farther show us the philosopher's perplexities. As a purely theoretic problem, namely, the casuistic question would hardly ever come up at all. If the ethical philosopher were only asking after the best *imaginable* system of goods he would indeed have an easy task; for all demands as such are *prima facie* respectable, and the best simply imaginary world would be one in which every demand was gratified as soon as made. Such a world would, however, have to have a physical constitution entirely different from that of the one which we inhabit. It would need not only a space, but a time, "of n-- dimensions," to include all the acts and experiences incompatible with one another here below, which would then go on in conjunction— such as spending our money, yet growing rich; taking our holiday, yet getting ahead with our work; shooting and fishing, yet doing no hurt to the beasts; gaining no end of experience, yet keeping our youthful freshness of heart; and the like. There can be no question that such a system of things, however brought about, would be the absolutely ideal system; and that if a philosopher could create universes *à priori,* and provide all the mechanical conditions, that

is the sort of universe which he should unhesitatingly create.

But this world of ours is made on an entirely
different pattern, and the casuistic question
here is most tragically practical. The actually
possible in this world is vastly narrower than
all that is demanded; and there is always a
pinch between the ideal and the actual which
can only be got through by leaving part of the
ideal behind. There is hardly a good which we
can imagine except as competing for the possession of the same bit of space and time with
some other imagined good. Every end of desire that presents itself appears exclusive of
some other end of desire. Shall a man drink
and smoke, *or* keep his nerves in condition?—
he cannot do both. Shall he follow his fancy
for Amelia, *or* for Henrietta?—both cannot be
the choice of his heart. Shall he have the dear
old Republican party, *or* a spirit of unsophisti-
cation in public affairs?—he cannot have both,
etc. So that the ethical philosopher's demand
for the right scale of subordination in ideals is
the fruit of an altogether practical need. Some
part of the ideal must be butchered, and he
needs to know which part. It is a tragic situation, and no mere speculative conundrum,
with which he has to deal.

Now *we* are blinded to the real difficulty of
the philosopher's task by the fact that we are
born into a society whose ideals are largely
ordered already. If we follow the ideal which is
conventionally highest, the others which we
butcher either die and do not return to haunt
us; or if they come back and accuse us of
murder, everyone applauds us for turning to
them a deaf ear. In other words, our environment encourages us not to be philosophers but
partisans. The philosopher, however, cannot,
so long as he clings to his own ideal of objectivity, rule out any ideal from being heard. He is
confident, and rightly confident, that the simple
taking counsel of his own intuitive preferences
would be certain to end in a mutilation of the
fulness of the truth. The poet Heine is said to
have written "Bunsen" in the place of "Gott"
in his copy of that author's work entitled "God
in History," so as to make it read "Bunsen in
der Geschichte." Now, with no disrespect to
the good and learned Baron, is it not safe to say
that any single philosopher, however wide his
sympathies, must be just such a Bunsen in der
Geschichte of the moral world, so soon as he
attempts to put his own ideas of order into that
howling mob of desires, each struggling to get
breathing-room for the ideal to which it clings?
The very best of men must not only be insensible, but be ludicrously and peculiarly insensible, to many goods. As a militant, fighting free-
handed that the goods to which he *is* sensible
may not be submerged and lost from out of life,
the philosopher, like every other human being,
is in a natural position. But think of Zeno and
of Epicurus, think of Calvin and of Paley, think
of Kant and Schopenhauer, of Herbert Spencer
and John Henry Newman, no longer as one-
sided champions of special ideals, but as schoolmasters deciding what all must think—and what
more grotesque topic could a satirist wish for on
which to exercise his pen? The fabled attempt
of Mrs. Partington to arrest the rising tide of the
North Atlantic with her broom was a reasonable spectacle compared with their effort to
substitute the content of their clean-shaven systems for that exuberant mass of goods with
which all human nature is in travail, and groan-
ing to bring to the light of day. Think, furthermore, of such individual moralists, no longer as
mere schoolmasters, but as pontiffs armed with
the temporal power, and having authority in
every concrete case of conflict to order which
good shall be butchered and which shall be suffered to survive—all the notion really turns one
pale. All one's slumbering revolutionary instincts waken at the thought of any single moralist wielding such powers of life and death.
Better chaos forever than an order based on
any closet-philosopher's rule, even though he
were the most enlightened possible member of
his tribe. No! if the philosopher is to keep his
judicial position, he must never become one of
the parties to the fray.

What can he do, then, it will now be asked,
except to fall back on scepticism and give up
the notion of being a philosopher at all? But
do we not already see a perfectly definite path
of escape which is open to him just because he
is a philosopher, and not the champion of one
particular ideal? Since everything which is demanded is by that fact a good, must not the
guiding principle for ethical philosophy (since
all demands conjointly cannot be satisfied in
this poor world) be simply to satisfy at all
times *as many demands as we can?* That act
must be the best act, accordingly, which makes
for the *best whole,* in the sense of awakening
the least sum of dissatisfactions. In the casuistic scale, therefore, those ideals must be written highest which *prevail at the least cost,* or by
whose realization the least possible number of
other ideals are destroyed. Since victory and
defeat there must be, the victory to be philosophically prayed for is that of the more inclu-

sive side—of the side which even in the hour of triumph will to some degree do justice to the ideals in which the vanquished party's interests lay. The course of history is nothing but the story of men's struggles from generation to generation to find the more and more inclusive order. *Invent some manner* of realizing your own ideals which will also satisfy the alien demands—that and that only is the path of peace! Following this path, society has shaken itself into one sort of relative equilibrium after another by a series of social discoveries quite analogous to those of science. Polyandry and polygamy and slavery, private warfare and liberty to kill, judicial torture and arbitrary royal power have slowly succumbed to actually aroused complaints; and though someone's ideals are unquestionably the worse off for each improvement, yet a vastly greater total number of them find shelter in our civilized society than in the older savage ways. So far then, and up to date, the casuistic scale is made for the philosopher already far better than he can ever make it for himself. An experiment of the most searching kind has proved that the laws and usages of the land are what yield the maximum of satisfaction to the thinkers taken all together. The presumption in cases of conflict must always be in favor of the conventionally recognized good. The philosopher must be a conservative, and in the construction of his casuistic scale must put the things most in accordance with the customs of the community on top.

And yet if he be a true philosopher he must see that there is nothing final in any actually given equilibrium of human ideals, but that, as our present laws and customs have fought and conquered other past ones, so they will in their turn be overthrown by any newly discovered order which will hush up the complaints that they still give rise to, without producing others louder still. "Rules are made for man, not man for rules"—that one sentence is enough to immortalize Green's *Prolegomena to Ethics.* And although a man always risks much when he breaks away from established rules and strives to realize a larger ideal whole than they permit, yet the philosopher must allow that it is at all times open to anyone to make the experiment, provided he fear not to stake his life and character upon the throw. The pinch is always here. Pent in under every system of moral rules are innumerable persons whom it weighs upon, and goods which it represses; and these are always rumbling and grumbling in the background, and ready for any issue by which they may get free.

See the abuses which the institution of private property covers, so that even to-day it is shamelessly asserted among us that one of the prime functions of the national government is to help the adroiter citizens to grow rich. See the unnamed and unnamable sorrows which the tyranny, on the whole so beneficent, of the marriage-institution brings to so many, both of the married and the unwed. See the wholesale loss of opportunity under our *régime* of so-called equality and industrialism, with the drummer and the counter-jumper in the saddle, for so many faculties and graces which could flourish in the feudal world. See our kindliness for the humble and the outcast, how it wars with that stern weeding-out which until now has been the condition of every perfection in the breed. See everywhere the struggle and the squeeze; and everlastingly the problem how to make them less. The anarchists, nihilists, and free-lovers; the free-silverites, socialists, and single-tax men; the free-traders and civil-service reformers; the prohibitionists and anti-vivisectionists; the radical darwinians with their idea of the suppression of the weak—these and all the conservative sentiments of society arrayed against them, are simply deciding through actual experiment by what sort of conduct the maximum amount of good can be gained and kept in this world. These experiments are to be judged, not *à priori*, but by actually finding, after the fact of their making, how much more outcry or how much appeasement comes about. What closet-solutions can possibly anticipate the result of trials made on such a scale? Or what can any superficial theorist's judgment be worth, in a world where every one of hundreds of ideals has its special champion already provided in the shape of some genius expressly born to feel it, and to fight to death in its behalf? The pure philosopher can only follow the windings of the spectacle, confident that the line of least resistance will always be towards the richer and the more inclusive arrangement, and that by one tack after another some approach to the kingdom of heaven is incessantly made.

IV

All this amounts to saying that, so far as the casuistic question goes, ethical science is just like physical science, and instead of being deducible all at once from abstract principles, must simply bide its time, and be ready to revise its conclusions from day to day. The presumption of course, in both sciences, always is that the vulgarly accepted opinions are true, and the right casuistic order that which public opinion believes in; and surely it would be folly quite as great, in most of us, to strike out independently and to aim at originality in ethics as in physics. Every now and then, however, someone is born with the right to be original, and his revolutionary thought or action may bear prosperous fruit. He may replace old "laws of nature" by better ones; he may, by breaking old moral rules in a certain place, bring in a total condition of things more ideal than would have followed had the rules been kept.

On the whole, then, we must conclude that no philosophy of ethics is possible in the old-fashioned absolute sense of the term. Everywhere the ethical philosopher must wait on facts. The thinkers who create the ideals come he knows not whence, their sensibilities are evolved he knows not how; and the question as to which of two conflicting ideals will give the best universe then and there, can be answered by him only through the aid of the experience of other men. I said some time ago, in treating of the "first" question, that the intuitional moralists deserve credit for keeping most clearly to the psychological facts. They do much to spoil this merit on the whole, however, by mixing with it that dogmatic temper which, by absolute distinctions and unconditional "thou shalt nots," changes a growing, elastic, and continuous life into a superstitious system of relics and dead bones. In point of fact, there are no absolute evils, and there are no non-moral goods; and the *highest* ethical life—however few may be called to bear its burdens—consists at all times in the breaking of rules which have grown too narrow for the actual case. There is but one unconditional commandment, which is that we should seek incessantly, with fear and trembling, so to vote and to act as to bring about the very largest total universe of good which we can see. Abstract rules indeed can help; but they help the less in proportion as our intuitions are more piercing, and our vocation is the stronger for the moral life. For every real dilemma is in literal strictness a unique situation; and the exact combination of ideals realized and ideals disappointed which each decision creates is always a universe without a precedent, and for which no adequate previous rule exists. The philosopher, then, *quâ* philosopher, is no better able to determine the best universe in the concrete emergency than other men. He sees, indeed, somewhat better than most men what the question always is—not a question of this good

or that good simply taken, but of the two total universes with which these goods respectively belong. He knows that he must vote always for the richer universe, for the good which seems most organizable, most fit to enter into complex combinations, most apt to be a member of a more inclusive whole. But which particular universe this is he cannot know for certain in advance; he only knows that if he makes a bad mistake the cries of the wounded will soon inform him of the fact. In all this the philosopher is just like the rest of us non-philosophers; so far as we are just and sympathetic instinctively, and so far as we are open to the voice of complaint. His function is in fact indistinguishable from that of the best kind of statesman at the present day. His books upon ethics, therefore, so far as they truly touch the moral life, must more and more ally themselves with a literature which is confessedly tentative and suggestive rather than dogmatic—I mean with novels and dramas of the deeper sort, with sermons, with books on statecraft and philanthropy and social and economical reform. Treated in this way ethical treatises may be voluminous and luminous as well; but they never can be *final,* except in their abstractest and vaguest features; and they must more and more abandon the old-fashioned, clear-cut, and would-be "scientific" form.

V

The chief of all the reasons why concrete ethics cannot be final is that they have to wait on methaphysical and theological beliefs. I said some time back that real ethical relations existed in a purely human world. They would exist even in what we called a moral solitude if the thinker had various ideals which took hold of him in turn. His self of one day would make demands on his self of another; and some of the demands might be urgent and tyrannical, while others were gentle and easily put aside. We call the tyrannical demands *imperatives.* If we ignore these we do not hear the last of it. The good which we have wounded returns to plague us with interminable crops of consequential damages, compunctions, and regrets. Obligation can thus exist inside a single thinker's consciousness; and perfect peace can abide with him only so far as he lives according to some sort of a casuistic scale which keeps his more imperative goods on top. It is the nature of these goods to be cruel to their rivals. Nothing shall avail when weighed in the balance against them. They call out all the mercilessness in our disposition, and do not easily forgive us if we are so soft-hearted as to shrink from sacrifice in their behalf.

The deepest difference, practically, in the moral life of man is the difference between the easy-going and the strenuous mood. When in the easy-going mood the shrinking from present ill is our ruling consideration, the strenuous mood, on the contrary, makes us quite indifferent to present ill, if only the greater ideal be attained. The capacity for the strenuous mood probably lies slumbering in every man, but it has more difficulty in some than in others in waking up. It needs the wilder passions to arouse it, the big fears, loves, and indignations; or else the deeply penetrating appeal of some one of the higher fidelities, like justice, truth or freedom. Strong relief is a necessity of its vision; and a world where all the mountains are brought down and all the valleys are exalted is no congenial place for its habitation. This is why in a solitary thinker this mood might slumber on forever without waking. His various ideals, known to him to be mere preferences of his own, are too nearly of the same denominational value: he can play fast or loose with them at will. This too is why, in a merely human world without a God, the appeal to our moral energy falls short of its maximal stimulating power. Life, to be sure, is even in such a world a genuinely ethical symphony; but it is played in the compass of a couple of poor octaves, and the infinite scale of values fails to open up. Many of us, indeed—like Sir James Stephen in those eloquent *Essays by a Barrister*—would openly laugh at the very idea of the strenuous mood being awakened in us by those claims of remote posterity which constitute the last appeal of the religion of humanity. We do not love these men of the future keenly enough; and we love them perhaps the less the more we hear of their evolutionized perfection, their high average longevity and education, their freedom from war and crime, their relative immunity from pain and zymotic disease, and all their other negative superiorities. This is all too finite, we say; we see too well the vacuum beyond. It lacks the note of infinitude and mystery, and may all be dealt with in the don't-care mood. No need of agonizing ourselves or making others agonize for these good creatures just at present.

When, however, we believe that a God is there, and that he is one of the claimants, the infinite perspective opens out. The scale of the symphony is incalculably prolonged. The more imperative ideals now begin to speak with an altogether new objectivity and significance, and to utter the penetrating, shattering, tragi-

cally challenging note of appeal. They ring out like the call of Victor Hugo's alpine eagle, "qui parle au précipice et que le gouffre entend," and the strenuous mood awakens at the sound. It saith among the trumpets, ha, ha! it smelleth the battle afar off, the thunder of the captains and the shouting. Its blood is up; and cruelty to the lesser claims, so far from being a deterrent element, does but add to the stern joy with which it leaps to answer to the greater. All through history, in the periodical conflicts of puritanism with the don't-care temper, we see the antagonism of the strenuous and genial moods, and the contrast between the ethics of infinite and mysterious obligation from on high, and those of prudence and the satisfaction of merely finite need.

The capacity of the strenuous mood lies so deep down among our natural human possibilities that even if there were no metaphysical or traditional grounds for believing in a God, men would postulate one simply as a pretext for living hard, and getting out of the game of existence its keenest possibilities of zest. Our attitude towards concrete evils is entirely different in a world where we believe there are none but finite demanders, from what it is in one where we joyously face tragedy for an infinite demanders' sake. Every sort of energy and endurance, of courage and capacity for handling life's evils, is set free in those who have religious faith. For this reason the strenuous type of character will on the battle-field of human history always outwear the easy-going type, and religion will drive irreligion to the wall.

It would seem, too—and this is my final conclusion—that the stable and systematic moral universe for which the ethical philosopher asks is fully possible only in a world where there is a divine thinker with all-enveloping demands. If such a thinker existed, his way of subordinating the demands to one another would be the finally valid casuistic scale; his claims would be the most appealing; his ideal universe would be the most inclusive realizable whole. If he now exist, then actualized in his thought already must be that ethical philosophy which we seek as the pattern which our own must evermore approach. In the interest of our own ideal of systematically unified moral truth, therefore, we, as would-be philosophers, must postulate a divine thinker, and pray for the victory of the religious cause. Meanwhile, exactly what the thought of the infinite thinker may be is hidden from us even were we sure of his existence; so that our postulation of him after all serves only to let loose in us the strenuous mood. But this is what it does in all men, even those who have no interest in philosophy. The ethical philosopher, therefore, whenever he ventures to say which course of action is the best, is on no essentially different level from the common man. "See, I have set before thee this day life and good, and death and evil; therefore, choose life that thou and thy seed may live"—when this challenge comes to us, it is simply our total character and personal genius that are on trial; and

if we invoke any so-called philosophy, our choice and use of that also are but revelations of our personal aptitude or incapacity for moral life. From this unsparing practical ordeal no professor's lectures and no array of books can save us. The solving word, for the learned and the unlearned man alike, lies in the last resort in the dumb willingnesses and unwillingnesses of their interior characters, and nowhere else. It is not in heaven, neither is it beyond the sea; but the word is very nigh unto thee, in thy mouth and in thy heart, that thou mayest do it.

The Dilemma of Determinism

A common opinion prevails that the juice has ages ago been pressed out of the free-will controversy, and that no new champion can do more than warm up stale arguments which everyone has heard. This is a radical mistake. I know of no subject less worn out, or in which inventive genius has a better chance of breaking open new ground—not, perhaps, of forcing a conclusion or of coercing assent, but of deepening our sense of what the issue between the two parties really is, of what the ideas of fate and to free-will imply. At our very side almost, in the past few years, we have seen falling in rapid succession from the press works that present the alternative in entirely novel lights. Not to speak of the English disciples of Hegel, such as Green and Bradley; not to speak of Hinton and Hodgson, nor of Hazard here—we see in the writings of Renouvier, Fouillée, and Delbœuf how completely changed and refreshed is the form of all the old disputes. I cannot pretend to vie in orginality with any of the old disputes. I cannot pretend to vie in originality with any of the masters I have named, and my ambition limits itself to just one little point. If I can make two of the necessarily implied corollaries of determinism clearer to you than they have been made before, I shall have made it possible for you to decide for or against that doctrine with a better understanding of what you are about. And if you prefer not to decide at all, but to remain doubters, you will at least see more plainly what the subject of your hesitation is. I thus disclaim openly on the threshold all pre-

tension to prove to you that the freedom of the will is true. The most I hope is to induce some of you to follow my own example in assuming it true, and acting as if it were true. If it be true, it seems to me that this is involved in the strict logic of the case. Its truth ought not to be forced willy-nilly down our indifferent throats. It ought to be freely espoused by men who can equally well turn their backs upon it. In other words, our first act of freedom, if we are free, ought in all inward propriety to be to affirm that we are free. This should exclude, it seems to me, from the free-will side of the equation all hope of a coercive demonstration—a demonstration which I, for one, am perfectly contented to go without.

With thus much understood at the outset, we can advance. But not without one more point understood as well. The arguments I am about to urge all proceed on two suppositions: first, when we make theories about the world and discuss them with one another, we do so in order to attain a conception of things which shall give us subjective satisfaction; and, second, if there be two conceptions, and the one seems to us, on the whole, more rational than the other, we are entitled to suppose that the more rational one is the truer of the two. I hope that you are all willing to make these suppositions with me; for I am afraid that if there be any of you here who are not, they will find little edification in the rest of what I have to say. I cannot stop to argue the point; but I myself believe that all the magnificent achieve-

From *The Works of William James—The Will to Believe,* ed. Frederick Burkhardt (Cambridge, Mass.: Harvard University Press, 1979), pp. 114–40.

ments of mathematical and physical science—our doctrines of evolution, of uniformity of law, and the rest—proceed from our indomitable desire to cast the world into a more rational shape in our minds than the shape into which it is thrown there by the crude order of our experience. The world has shown itself, to a great extent, plastic to this demand of ours for rationality. How much farther it will show itself plastic no one can say. Our only means of finding out is to try; and I, for one, feel as free to try conceptions of moral as of mechanical or of logical rationality. If a certain formula for expressing the nature of the world violates my moral demand, I shall feel as free to throw it overboard, or at least to doubt it, as if it disappointed my demand for uniformity of sequence, for example; the one demand being, so far as I can see, quite as subjective and emotional as the other is. The principle of causality, for example—what is it but a postulate, an empty name covering simply a demand that the sequence of events shall some day manifest a deeper kind of belonging of one thing with another than the mere arbitrary juxtaposition which now phenomenally appears? It is as much an altar to an unknown god as the one that Saint Paul found at Athens. All our scientific and philosophic ideals are altars to unknown gods. Uniformity is as much so as is free-will. If this be admitted, we can debate on even terms. But if anyone pretends that while freedom and variety are, in the first instance, subjective demands, necessity and uniformity are something altogether different, I do not see how we can debate at all.

To begin, then, I must suppose you acquainted with all the usual arguments on the subject. I cannot stop to take up the old proofs from causation, from statistics, from the certainty with which we can foretell one another's conduct, from the fixity of character, and all the rest. But there are two *words* which usually encumber these classical arguments, and which we must immediately dispose of if we are to make any progress. One is the eulogistic word *freedom,* and the other is the opprobrious word *chance.* The word "chance" I wish to keep, but I wish to get rid of the word "freedom." Its eulogistic associations have so far overshadowed all the rest of its meaning that both parties claim the sole right to use it, and determinists to-day insist that they alone are freedom's champions. Old-fashioned determinism was what we may call *hard* determinism. It did not shrink from such words as fatality,

bondage of the will, necessitation, and the like. Nowadays, we have a *soft* determinism which abhors harsh words, and, repudiating fatality, necessity, and even predetermination, says that its real name is freedom; for freedom is only necessity understood, and bondage to the highest is identical with true freedom. Even a writer as little used to making capital out of soft words as Mr. Hodgson hesitates not to call himself a "free-will determinist."

Now, all that is a quagmire of evasion under which the real issue of fact has been entirely smothered. Freedom in all these senses presents simply no problem at all. No matter what the soft determinist mean by it—whether he mean the acting without external constraint, whether he mean the acting rightly, or whether he mean the acquiescing in the law of the whole—who cannot answer him that sometimes we are free and sometimes we are not? But there *is* a problem, an issue of fact and not of words, an issue of the most momentous importance, which is often decided without discussion in one sentence—nay, in one clause of a sentence—by those very writers who spin out whole chapters in their efforts to show what "true" freedom is; and that is the question of determinism, about which we are to talk to-night.

Fortunately, no ambiguities hang about this word or about its opposite, indeterminism. Both designate an outward way in which things may happen, and their cold and mathematical sound has no sentimental associations that can bribe our partiality either way in advance. Now, evidence of an external kind to decide between determinism and indeterminism is, as I intimated a while back, strictly impossible to find. Let us look at the difference between them and see for ourselves. What does determinism profess?

It professes that those parts of the universe already laid down absolute appoint and decree what the other parts shall be. The future has no ambiguous possibilities hidden in its womb: the part we call the present is compatible with only one totality. Any other future complement than the one fixed from eternity is impossible. The whole is in each and every part, and welds it with the rest into an absolute unity, an iron block, in which there can be no equivocation or shadow of turning.

"With Earth's first Clay They did the Last Man knead,
And there of the Last Harvest sow'd the Seed;
    And the first Morning of Creation wrote
What the Last Dawn of Reckoning shall read."

Indeterminism, on the contrary, says that the parts have a certain amount of loose play on one another, so that the laying down of one of them does not necessarily determine what the other shall be. It admits that possibilities may be in excess of actualities, and that things not yet revealed to our knowledge may really in themselves be ambiguous. Of two alternative futures which we conceive, both may now be really possible; and the one become impossible only at the very moment when the other excludes it by becoming real itself. Indeterminism thus denies the world to be one unbending unit of fact. It says there is a certain ultimate pluralism in it; and, so saying, it corroborates our ordinary unsophisticated view of things. To that view, actualities seem to float in a wider sea of possibilities from out of which they are chosen; and, *somewhere,* indeterminism says, such possibilities exist, and form a part of truth.

Determinism, on the contrary, says they exist *nowhere,* and that necessity on the one hand and impossibility on the other are the sole categories of the real. Possibilities that fail to get realized are, for determinism, pure illusions: they never were possibilities at all. There is nothing inchoate, it says, about this universe of ours, all that was or is or shall be actual in it having been from eternity virtually there. The cloud of alternatives our minds escort this mass of actuality withal is a cloud of sheer deceptions, to which "impossibilities" is the only name that rightfully belongs.

The issue, it will be seen, is a perfectly sharp one, which no eulogistic terminology can smear over or wipe out. The truth *must* lie with one side or the other, and its lying with one side makes the other false.

The question relates solely to the existence of possibilities, in the strict sense of the term, as things that may, but need not, be. Both sides admit that a volition, for instance, has occurred. The indeterminists say another volition might have occurred in its place: the determinists swear that nothing could possibly have occurred in its place. Now can science be called in to tell us which of these two point-blank contradicters of each other is right? Science professes to draw no conclusions but such as are based on matters of fact, things that have actually happened; but how can any amount of assurance that something actually happened give us the least grain of information as to whether another thing might or might not have happened in its place? Only facts can be proved by other facts. With things that are possibilities and not facts,

facts have no concern. If we have no other evidence than the evidence of existing facts, the possibility-question must remain a mystery never to be cleared up.

And the truth is that facts practically have hardly anything to do with making us either determinists or indeterminists. Sure enough, we make a flourish of quoting facts this way or that; and if we are determinists, we talk about the infallibility with which we can predict one another's conduct; while if we are indeterminists, we lay great stress on the fact that it is just because we cannot foretell one another's conduct, either in war or statecraft or in any of the great and small intrigues and businesses of men, that life is so intensely anxious and hazardous a game. But who does not see the wretched insufficiency of this so-called objective testimony on both sides? What fills up the gaps in our minds is something not objective, not external. What divides us into possibility men and anti-possibility men is different faiths or postulates—postulates of rationality. To this man the world seems more rational with possibilities in it—to that man more rational with possibilities excluded; and talk as we will about having to yield to evidence, what makes us monists or pluralists, determinists or indeterminists, is at bottom always some sentiment like this.

The stronghold of the deterministic sentiment is the antipathy to the idea of chance. As soon as we begin to talk indeterminism to our friends, we find a number of them shaking their heads. This notion of alternative possibility, they say, this admission that any one of several things may come to pass, is, after all, only a round-about name for chance; and chance is something the notion of which no sane mind can for an instant tolerate in the world. What is it, they ask, but barefaced crazy unreason, the negation of intelligibility and law? And if the slightest particle of it exist anywhere, what is to prevent the whole fabric from falling together, the stars from going out, and chaos from recommencing her topsy-turvy reign?

Remarks of this sort about chance will put an end to discussion as quickly as anything one can find. I have already told you that "chance" was a word I wished to keep and use. Let us then examine exactly what it means, and see whether it ought to be such a terrible bugbear to us. I fancy that squeezing the thistle boldly will rob it of its sting.

The sting of the word "chance" seems to lie

in the assumption that it means something positive, and that if anything happens by chance, it must needs be something of an intrinsically irrational and preposterous sort. Now chance means nothing of the kind. It is a purely negative and relative term, giving us no information about that of which it is predicated, except that it happens to be disconnected with something else—not controlled, secured, or necessitated by other things in advance of its own actual presence. As this point is the most subtle one of the whole lecture, and at the same time the point on which all the rest hinges, I beg you to pay particular attention to it. What I say is that it tells us nothing about what a thing may be in itself to call it "chance." It may be a bad thing, it may be a good thing. It may be lucidity, transparency, fitness incarnate, matching the whole system of other things, when it has once befallen, in an unimaginably perfect way. All you mean by calling it "chance" is that this is not guaranteed, that it may also fall out otherwise. For the system of other things has no positive hold on the chance-thing. Its origin is in a certain fashion negative; it escapes, and says, Hands off! coming, when it comes as a free gift, or not at all.

This negativeness, however, and this opacity of the chance-thing when thus considered *ab extra,* or from the point of view of previous things or distant things, do not preclude its having any amount of positiveness and luminosity from within, and at its own place and moment. All that its chance-character asserts about it is that there is something in it really of its own, something that is not the unconditional property of the whole. If the whole wants this property, the whole must wait till it can get it, if it be a matter of chance. That the universe may actually be a sort of joint-stock society of this sort, in which the sharers have both limited liabilities and limited powers, is of course a simple and conceivable notion.

Nevertheless, many persons talk as if the minutest dose of disconnectedness of one part with another, the smallest modicum of independence, the faintest tremor of ambiguity about the future, for example, would ruin everything, and turn this goodly universe into a sort of insane sand-heap or nulliverse, no universe at all. Since future human volitions are as a matter of fact the only ambiguous things we are tempted to believe in, let us stop for a moment to make ourselves sure whether their independent and accidental character need be fraught with such direful consequences to the universe as these.

What is meant by saying that my choice of which way to walk home after the lecture is ambiguous and matter of chance as far as the present moment is concerned? It means that both Divinity Avenue and Oxford Street are called; but that only one, and that one *either* one, shall be chosen. Now, I ask you seriously to support that this ambiguity of my choice is real; and then to make the impossible hypothesis that the choice is made twice over, and each time falls on a different street. In other words, imagine that I first walk through Divinity Avenue, and then imagine that the powers governing the universe annihilate ten minutes of time with all that it contained, and set me back at the door of this hall just as I was before the choice was made. Imagine then that, everything else being the same, I now make a different choice and traverse Oxford Street. You, as passive spectators, look on and see the two alternative universes—one of them with me walking through Divinity Avenue in it, the other with the same me walking through Oxford Street. Now, if you are determinists you believe one of these universes to have been from eternity impossible: you believe it to have been impossible because of the intrinsic irrationality or accidentality somewhere involved in it. But looking outwardly at these universes, can you say which is the impossible and accidental one, and which the rational and necessary one? I doubt if the most iron-clad determinist among you could have the slightest glimmer of light on this point. In other words, either universe *after the fact* and once there would, to our means of observation and understanding, appear just as rational as the other. There would be absolutely no criterion by which we might judge one necessary and the other matter of chance. Suppose now we relieve the gods of their hypothetical task and assume my choice, once made, to be made forever. I go through Divinity Avenue for good and all. If, as good determinists, you now begin to affirm, what all good determinists punctually do affirm, that in the nature of things I *couldn't* have gone through Oxford Street—had I done so it would have been chance, irrationality, insanity, a horrid gap in nature—I simply call your attention to this, that your affirmation is what the Germans call a *Machtspruch,* a mere conception fulminated as a dogma and based on no insight into details. Before my choice, either street seemed as natural to you as to me. Had I happened to take Oxford Street, Divinity Avenue would have figured in your philosophy as the gap in nature; and you would have so proclaimed it with the best deterministic conscience in the world.

But what a hollow outcry, then, is this against a chance which, if it were present to us, we could by no character whatever distinguish from a rational necessity! I have taken the most trivial of examples, but no possible example could lead to any different result. For what are the alternatives which, in point of fact, offer themselves to human volition? What are those futures that now seem matters of chance? Are they not one and all like the Divinity Avenue and Oxford Street of our example? Are they not all of them *kinds* of things already here and based in the existing frame of nature? Is anyone ever tempted to produce an *absolute* accident, something utterly irrelevant to the rest of the world? Do not all the motives that assail us, all the futures that offer themselves to our choice, spring equally from the soil of the past; and would not either one of them, whether realized through chance or through necessity, the moment it was realized, seem to us to fit that past, and in the completest and most continuous manner to interdigitate with the phenomena already there?

The more one thinks of the matter, the more one wonders that so empty and gratuitous a hubbub as this outcry against chance should have found so great an echo in the hearts of men. It is a word which tells us absolutely nothing about what chances, or about the *modus operandi* of the chancing; and the use of it as a war-cry shows only a temper of intellectual absolutism, a demand that the world shall be a solid block, subject to one control—which temper, which demand, the world may not be bound to gratify at all. In every outwardly verifiable and practical respect, a world in which the alternatives that now actually distract *your* choice were decided by pure chance would be by *me* absolutely undistinguished from the world in which I now live. I am, therefore, entirely willing to call it, so far as your choices go, a world of chance for me. To *yourselves,* it is true, those very acts of choice, which to me are so blind, opaque, and external, are the opposites of this, for you are within them and effect them. To you they appear as decisions; and decisions, for him who makes them, are altogether peculiar psychic facts. Self-luminous and self-justifying at the living moment at which they occur, they appeal to no outside moment to put its stamp upon them or make them continuous with the rest of nature. Themselves it is rather who seem to make nature continuous; and in their strange and intense function of granting consent to one possibility and withholding it from another, to transform an equivocal and double future into an inalterable and simple past.

But with the psychology of the matter we have no concern this evening. The quarrel which determinism has with chance fortunately has nothing to do with this or that psychological detail. It is a quarrel altogether metaphysical. Determinism denies the ambiguity of future volitions, because it affirms that nothing future can be ambiguous. But we have said enough to meet the issue. Indeterminate future volitions *do* mean chance. Let us not fear to shout it from the house-tops if need be; for we now know that the idea of chance is, at bottom, exactly the same thing as the idea of gift—the one simply being a disparaging, and the other a eulogistic, name for anything on which we have no effective *claim.* And whether the world be the better or the worse for having either chances or gifts in it will depend altogether on *what* these uncertain and unclaimable things turn out to be.

And this at last brings us within sight of our subject. We have seen what determinism means: we have seen that indeterminism is rightly described as meaning chance; and we have seen that chance, the very name of which we are urged to shrink from as from a metaphysical pestilence, means only the negative fact that no part of the world, however big, can claim to control absolutely the destinies of the whole. But although, in discussing the word "chance," I may at moments have seemed to be arguing for its real existence, I have not meant to do so yet. We have not yet ascertained whether this be a world of chance or no; at most, we have agreed that it seems so. And I now repeat what I said at the outset, that, from any strict theoretical point of view, the question is insoluble. To deepen our theoretic sense of the *difference* between a world of chances in it and a deterministic world is the most I can hope to do; and this I may now at last begin upon, after all our tedious clearing of the way.

I wish first of all to show you just what the notion that this is a deterministic world implies. The implications I call your attention to are all bound up with the fact that it is a world in which we constantly have to make what I shall, with your permission, call judgments of regret. Hardly an hour passes in which we do not wish that something might be otherwise; and happy indeed are those of us whose hearts have never echoed the wish of Omar Khayyam.

"That we might catch ere closed the Book of Fate,
  And make The Writer on a fairer leaf
Inscribe our names, or quite obliterate!

"Ah Love! could you and I with Fate conspire
To grasp this sorry Scheme of Things entire,
  Would not we shatter it to bits—and then
Re-mould it nearer to the Heart's Desire!"

Now, it is undeniable that most of these regrets are foolish, and quite on a par in point of philosophic value with the criticisms on the universe of that friend of our infancy, the hero of the fable "The Atheist and the Acorn,"

"Fool! had that bough a pumpkin bore,
Thy whimsies would have worked no more," etc.

Even from the point of view of our own ends, we should probably make a botch of remodelling the universe. How much more then from the point of view of ends we cannot see! Wise men therefore regret as little as they can. But still some regrets are pretty obstinate and hard to stifle—regrets for acts of wanton cruelty or treachery, for example, whether performed by others or by ourselves. Hardly anyone can remain *entirely* optimistic after reading the confession of the murderer at Brockton the other day: how, to get rid of the wife whose continued existence bored him, he inveigled her into a desert spot, shot her four times, and then, as she lay on the ground and said to him, "You didn't do it on purpose, did you, dear?" replied, "No, I didn't do it on purpose," as he raised a rock and smashed her skull. Such an occurrence, with the mild sentence and self-satisfaction of the prisoner, is a field for a crop of regrets, which one need not take up in detail. We feel that, although a perfect mechanical fit to the rest of the universe, it is a bad moral fit, and that something else would really have been better in its place.

But for the deterministic philosophy the murder, the sentence, and the prisoner's optimism were all necessary from eternity; and nothing else for a moment had a ghost of a chance of being put into their place. To admit such a chance, the determinists tell us, would be to make a suicide of reason; so we must steel our hearts against the thought. And here our plot thickens, for we see the first of those difficult implications of determinism and monism which it is my purpose to make you feel. If

this Brockton murder was called for by the rest of the universe, if it had to come at its preappointed hour, and if nothing else would have been consistent with the sense of the whole, what are we to think of the universe? Are we stubbornly to stick to our judgment of regret, and say, though it *couldn't* be, yet it *would* have been a better universe with something different from this Brockton murder in it? That, of course, seems the natural and spontaneous thing for us to do; and yet it is nothing short of deliberately espousing a kind of pessimism. The judgment of regret calls the murder bad. Calling a thing bad means, if it means anything at all, that the thing ought not to be, that something else ought to be in its stead. Determinism, in denying that anything else can be in its stead, virtually defines the universe as a place in which what ought to be is impossible—in other words, as an organism whose constitution is afflicted with an incurable taint, an irremediable flaw. The pessimism of a Schopenhauer says no more than this—that the murder is a symptom; and that it is a vicious symptom because it belongs to a vicious whole, which can express its nature no otherwise than by bringing forth just such a symptom as that at this particular spot. Regret for the murder must transform itself, if we are determinists and wise, into a larger regret. It is absurd to regret the murder alone. Other things being what they are, *it* could not be different. What we should regret is that whole frame of things of which the murder is one member. I see no escape whatever from this pessimistic conclusion, if, being determinists, our judgment of regret is to be allowed to stand at all.

The only deterministic escape from pessimism is everywhere to abandon the judgment of regret. That this can be done, history shows to be not impossible. The devil, *quoad existentiam,* may be good. That is, although he be a *principle* of evil, yet the universe, with such a principle in it, may practically be a better universe than it could have been without. On every hand, in a small way, we find that a certain amount of evil is a condition by which a higher form of good is bought. There is nothing to prevent anybody from generalizing this view, and trusting that if we could but see things in the largest of all ways, even such matters as this Brockton murder would appear to be paid for by the uses that follow in their train. An optimism *quand même,* a systematic and infatuated optimism like that ridiculed by Voltaire in his *Candide,* is one of the possible ideal ways in which a man may train himself to look on life. Bereft of dogmatic hardness and lit up with the expression of a tender and pathetic hope, such an optimism has been the grace of some of the most religious characters that ever lived.

"Throb thine with Nature's throbbing breast,
And all is clear from east to west."

Even cruelty and treachery may be among the absolutely blessed fruits of time, and to quarrel with any of their details may be blasphemy. The only real blasphemy, in short, may be that pessimistic temper of the soul which lets it give way to such things as regrets remorse, and grief.

Thus, our deterministic pessimism may become a deterministic optimism at the price of extinguishing our judgments of regret.

But does not this immediately bring us into a curious logical predicament? Our determinism leads us to call our judgments of regret wrong, because they are pessimistic in implying that what is impossible yet ought to be. But how then about the judgments of regret themselves? If they are wrong, other judgments, judgments of approval presumably, ought to be in their place. But as they are necessitated, nothing else *can* be in their place; and the universe is just what it was before—namely, a place in which what ought to be appears impossible. We have got one foot out of the pessimistic bog, but the other one sinks all the deeper. We have rescued our actions from the bonds of evil, but our judgments are now held fast. When murders and treacheries cease to be sins, regrets are theoretic absurdities and errors. The theoretic and the active life thus play a kind of see-saw with each other on the ground of evil. The rise of either sends the other down. Murder and treachery cannot be good without regret being bad: regret cannot be good without treachery and murder being bad. Both, however, are supposed to have been foredoomed; so something must be fatally unreasonable, absurd, and wrong in the world. It must be a place of which either sin or error forms a necessary part. From this dilemma there seems at first sight no escape. Are we then so soon to fall back into the pessimism from which we thought we had emerged? And is there no possible way by which we may, with good intellectual consciences, call the cruelties and the treacheries, the reluctances and the regrets, *all* good together?

Certainly there is such a way, and you are probably most of you ready to formulate it yourselves. But, before doing so, remark how inevitably the question of determinism and indeterminism slides us into the question of optimism and pessimism, or, as our fathers called it, "the question of evil." The theological form of all these disputes is the simplest and the deepest, the form from which there is the least escape—not because, as some have sarcastically said, remorse and regret are clung to with a morbid fondness by the theologians as spiritual luxuries, but because they are existing facts of the world, and as such must be taken into account in the deterministic interpretation of all that is fated to be. If they are fated to be error, does not the bat's wing of irrationality still cast its shadow over the world?

The refuge from the quandary lies, as I said, not far off. The necessary acts we erroneously regret may be good, and yet our error in so regretting them may be also good, on one simple condition; and that condition is this: The world must not be regarded as a machine whose final purpose is the making real of any outward good, but rather as a contrivance for deepening the theoretic consciousness of what goodness and evil in their intrinsic natures are. Not the doing either of good or of evil is what nature cares for, but the knowing of them. Life is one long eating of the fruit of the tree of *knowledge*. I am in the habit, in thinking to myself, of calling this point of view the *gnostical* point of view. According to it, the world is neither an optimism nor a pessimism, but a *gnosticism*. But as this term may perhaps lead to some misunderstandings, I will use it as little as possible here, and speak rather of *subjectivism*, and the *subjectivistic* point of view.

Subjectivism has three great branches—we may call them scientificism, sentimentalism, and sensualism, respectively. They all agree essentially about the universe, in deeming that what happens there is subsidiary to what we think or feel about it. Crime justifies its criminality by awakening our intelligence of that criminality, and eventually our remorses and regrets; and the error included in remorse and regrets, the error of supposing that the past could have been different, justifies itself by its use. Its use is to quicken our sense of *what* the irretrievably lost is. When we think of it as that which might have been ("the saddest words of tongue or pen"), the quality of its worth speaks to us with a wilder sweetness;

and, conversely, the dissatisfaction wherewith we think of what seems to have driven it from its natural place gives us the severer pang. Admirable artifice of nature! we might be tempted to exclaim—deceiving us in order the better to enlighten us, and leaving nothing undone to accentuate to our consciousness the yawning distance of those opposite poles of good and evil between which creation swings.

We have thus clearly revealed to our view what may be called the dilemma of determinism, so far as determinism pretends to think things out at all. A merely mechanical determinism, it is true, rather rejoices in not thinking them out. It is very sure that the universe must satisfy its postulate of a physical continuity and coherence, but it smiles at anyone who comes forward with a postulate of moral coherence as well. I may suppose, however, that the number of purely mechanical or hard determinists among you this evening is small. The determinism to whose seductions you are most exposed is what I have called soft determinism—the determinism which allows considerations of good and bad to mingle with those of cause and effect in deciding what sort of a universe this may rationally be held to be. The dilemma of this determinism is one whose left horn is pessimism and whose right horn is subjectivism. In other words, if determinism is to escape pessimism, it must leave off looking at the goods and ills of life in a simple objective way, and regard them as materials, indifferent in themselves, for the production of consciousness, scientific and ethical, in us.

To escape pessimism is, as we all know, no easy task. Your own studies have sufficiently shown you the almost desperate difficulty of making the notion that there is a single principle of things, and that principle absolute perfection, rhyme together with our daily vision of the facts of life. If perfection be the principle, how comes there any imperfection here? If God be good, how came he to create—or, if he did not create, how comes he to permit—the devil? The evil facts must be explained as seeming: the devil must be whitewashed, the universe must be disinfected, if neither God's goodness nor his unity and power are to remain impugned. And of all the various ways of operating the disinfection, and making bad seem less bad, the way of subjectivism appears by far the best.

For, after all, is there not something rather absurd in our ordinary notion of external things being good or bad in themselves? Can murders and treacheries, considered as mere outward happenings, or motions of matter, be bad without anyone to feel their badness? And could paradise properly be good in the absence of a sentient principle by which the goodness was perceived? Outward goods and evils seem practically indistinguishable except in so far as they result in getting moral judgments made about them. But then the moral judgments seem the main thing, and the outward facts mere perishing instruments for their production. This is subjectivism. Everyone must at some time have wondered at that strange paradox of our moral nature, that, though the pursuit of outward good is the breath of its nostrils, the attainment of outward good would seem to be its suffocation and death. Why does the painting of any paradise or utopia, in heaven or on earth, awaken such yawnings for nirvana and escape? The white-robed harp-playing heaven of our sabbath-schools, and the ladylike tea-table elysium represented in Mr. Spencer's *Data of Ethics,* as the final consummation of progress, are exactly on a par in this respect—lubberlands, pure and simple, one and all. We look upon them from this delicious mess of insanities and realities, strivings and deadnesses, hopes and fears, agonies and exultations, which forms our present state, and *tedium vitæ* is the only sentiment they awaken in our breasts. To our crepuscular natures, born for the conflict, the Rembrandtesque moral chiaroscuro, the shifting struggle of the sunbeam in the gloom, such pictures of light upon light are vacuous and expressionless, and neither to be enjoyed nor understood. If *this* be the whole fruit of the victory, we say; if the generations of mankind suffered and laid down their lives; if prophets confessed and martyrs sang in the fire, and all the sacred tears were shed for no other end than that a race of creatures of such unexampled insipidity should succeed, and protract in *sæcula sæculorum* their contented and inoffensives lives—why, at such a rate, better lose than win the battle, or at all events better ring down the curtain before the last act of the play, so that a business that began so importantly may be saved from so singularly flat a winding-up.

All this is what I should instantly say, were I called on to plead for gnosticism; and its real friends, of whom you will presently perceive I am not one, would say without difficulty a great deal more. Regarded as a stable finality, every outward good becomes a mere weariness to the flesh. It must be menaced, be occasionally lost, for its goodness to be fully felt as such. Nay, more than occasionally lost. No one knows the worth of innocence till he knows it is gone forever, and that money cannot buy it back. Not the saint, but the sinner that repenteth, is he to whom the full length and breadth, and height and depth, of life's meaning is revealed. Not the absence of vice, but vice there, and virtue holding her by the throat, seems the ideal human state. And there seems no reason to suppose it not a permanent human state. There is a deep truth in what the school of Schopenhauer insists on—the illusoriness of the notion of moral progress. The more brutal forms of evil that go are replaced by others more subtle and more poisonous. Our moral horizon moves with us as we move, and never do we draw nearer to the far-off line where the black waves and the azure meet. The final purpose of our creation seems most plausibly to be the greatest possible enrichment of our ethical consciousness, through the intensest play of contrasts and the widest diversity of characters. This of course obliges some of us to be vessels of wrath, whilst it calls others to be vessels of honor. But the subjectivist point of view reduces all these outward distinctions to a common denominator. The wretch languishing in the felon's cell may be drinking draughts of the wine of truth that will never pass the lips of the so-called favorite of fortune. And the peculiar consciousness of each of them is an indispensable note in the great ethical concert which the centuries as they roll are grinding out of the living heart of man.

So much for subjectivism! If the dilemma of determinism be to choose between it and pessimism, I see little room for hesitation from the strictly theoretical point of view. Subjectivism seems the more rational scheme. And the world may, possibly, for aught I know, be nothing else. When the healthy love of life is on one, and all its forms and its appetites seem so unutterably real; when the most brutal and the most spiritual things are lit by the same sun, and each is an integral part of the total richness—why, then it seems a grudging and sickly way of meeting so robust a universe to shrink from any of its facts and wish them not to be. Rather take the strictly dramatic point of view, and treat the whole thing as a great unending romance which the spirit of the universe, striving to realize its own content, is eternally thinking out and representing to itself.

No one, I hope, will accuse me, after I have said all this, of underrating the reasons in favor of subjectivism. And now that I proceed to say

why those reasons, strong as they are, fail to convince my own mind, I trust the presumption may be that my objections are stronger still.

I frankly confess that they are of a practical order. If we practically take up subjectivism in a sincere and radical manner and follow its consequences, we meet with some that make us pause. Let a subjectivism begin in never so severe and intellectual a way, it is forced by the law of its nature to develop another side of itself and end with the corruptest curiosity. Once dismiss the notion that certain duties are good in themselves, and that we are here to do them, no matter how we feel about them; once consecrate the opposite notion that our performances and our violations of duty are for a common purpose, the attainment of subjective knowledge and feeling, and that the deepening of these is the chief end of our lives—and at what point on the downward slope are we to stop? In theology, subjectivism develops as its "left wing" antinomianism. In literature, its left wing is romanticism. And in practical life it is either a nerveless sentimentality or a sensualism without bounds.

Everywhere it fosters the fatalistic mood of mind. It makes those who are already too inert more passive still; it renders wholly reckless those whose energy is already in excess. All through history we find how subjectivism, as soon as it has a free career, exhausts itself in every sort of spiritual, moral, and practical license. Its optimism turns to an ethical indifference, which infallibly brings dissolution in its train. It is perfectly safe to say now that if the hegelian gnosticism, which has begun to show itself here and in Great Britain, were to become a popular philosophy, as it once was in Germany, it would certainly develop its left wing here as there, and produce a reaction of disgust. Already I have heard a graduate of this very school express in the pulpit his willingness to sin like David, if only he might repent like David. You may tell me he was only sowing his wild, or rather his tame, oats; and perhaps he was. But the point is that in the subjectivistic or gnostical philosophy oat-sowing, wild or tame, becomes a systematic neccessity and the chief function of life. After the pure and classic truths, the exciting and rancid ones must be experienced; and if the stupid virtues of the philistine herd do not then come in and save society from the influence of the children of light, a sort of inward putrefaction becomes its inevitable doom.

Look at the last runnings of the romantic

school, as we see them in that strange contemporary Parisian literature, with which we of the less clever countries are so often driven to rinse out our minds after they have become clogged with the dulness and heaviness of our native pursuits. The romantic school began with the worship of subjective sensibility and the revolt against legality of which Rousseau was the first great prophet; and through various fluxes and refluxes, right wings and left wings, it stands to-day with two men of genius, M. Renan and M. Zola, as it principal exponents—one speaking with its masculine, and the other with what might be called its feminine, voice. I prefer not to think now of less noble members of the school, and the Renan I have in mind is of course the Renan of latest dates. As I have used the term gnostic, both he and Zola are gnostics of the most pronounced sort. Both are athirst for the facts of life, and both think the facts of human sensibility to be of all facts the most worthy of attention. Both agree, moreover, that sensibility seems to be there for no higher purpose—certainly not, as the Philistines say, for the sake of bringing mere outward rights to pass and frustrating outward wrongs. One dwells on the sensibilities for their energy, the other for their sweetness; one speaks with a voice of bronze, the other with that of an Æolian harp; one ruggedly ignores the distinction of good and evil, the other plays the coquette between the craven unmanliness of his Philosophic Dialogues and the butterfly optimism of his *Souvenirs de jeunesse*. But under the pages of both there sounds incessantly the hoarse bass of *vanitas vanitatum, omnia vanitas,* which the reader may hear, whenever he will, between the lines. No writer of this French romantic school has a word of rescue from the hour of satiety with the things of life—the hour in which we say, "I take no pleasure in them"—or from the hour of terror at the world's vast meaningless grinding, if perchance such hours should come. For terror and satiety are facts of sensibility like any others; and at their own hour they reign in their own right. The heart of the romantic utterances, whether poetical, critical, or historical, is this inward remedilessness, what Carlyle calls this far-off whimpering of wail and woe. And from this romantic state of mind there is absolutely no possible *theoretic* escape. Whether, like Renan, we look upon life in a more refined way, as a romance of the spirit; or whether, like the friends of Mr. Zola, we pique ourselves on our "scientific" and "analytic" character, and prefer to be cynical, and call the world a "roman experimental" on

an infinite scale—in either case the world appears to us potentially as what the same Carlyle once called it, a vast, gloomy, solitary Golgotha and mill of death.

The only escape is by the practical way. And since I have mentioned the nowadays much-reviled name of Carlyle, let me mention it once more, and say it is the way of his teaching. No matter for Carlyle's life, no matter for a great deal of his writing. What was the most important thing he said to us? He said: "Hang your sensibilities! Stop your snivelling complaints, and your equally snivelling raptures! Leave off your general emotional tomfoolery, and get to WORK like men!" But this means a complete rupture with the subjectivist philosophy of things. It says conduct, and not sensibility, is the ultimate fact for our recognition. With the vision of certain works to be done, of certain outward changes to be wrought or resisted, it says our intellectual horizon terminates. No matter how we succeed in doing these outward duties, whether gladly and spontaneously, or heavily and unwillingly, do them we somehow must; for the leaving of them undone is perdition. No matter how we feel; if we are only faithful in the outward act and refuse to do wrong, the world will in so far be safe, and we quit of our debt towards it. Take, then, the yoke upon our shoulders; bend our neck beneath the heavy legality of its weight; regard something else than our feeling as our limit, our master, and our law; be willing to live and die in its service—and, at a stroke, we have passed from the subjective into the objective philosophy of things, much as one awakens from some feverish dream, full of bad lights and noises, to find one's self bathed in the sacred coolness and quiet of the air of the night.

But what is the essence of this philosophy of objective conduct, so old-fashioned and finite, but so chaste and sane and strong, when compared with its romantic rival? It is the recognition of limits, foreign and opaque to our understanding. It is the willingness, after bringing about some external good, to feel at peace; for our responsibility ends with the performance of that duty, and the burden of the rest we may lay on higher powers.

> *"Look to thyself, O Universe!*
> *Thou art better, and not worse,"*

we may say in that philosophy, the moment we have done our stroke of conduct, however small. For in the view of that philosophy the universe belongs to a plurality of semi-independent forces, each one of which may help or hinder, and be helped or hindered by, the operations of the rest.

But this brings us right back, after such a long détour, to the question of indeterminism and to the conclusion of all I came here to say to-night. For the only consistent way of representing a pluralism and a world whose parts may affect one another through their conduct being either good or bad is the indeterministic way. What interest, zest, or excitement can there be in achieving the right way, unless we are enabled to feel that the wrong way is also a possible and a natural way—nay, more, a menacing and an imminent way? And what sense can there be in condemning ourselves for taking the wrong way, unless we need have done nothing of the sort, unless the right way was open to us as well? I cannot understand the willingness to act, no matter how we feel, without the belief that acts are really good and bad. I cannot understand the belief that an act is bad, without regret at its happening. I cannot understand regret without the admission of real, genuine possibilities in the world. Only *then* is it other than a mockery to feel, after we have failed to do our best, that an irreparable opportunity is gone from the universe, the loss of which it must forever after mourn.

If you insist that this is all superstition, that possibility is in the eye of science and reason impossibility, and that if I act badly 'tis that the universe was foredoomed to suffer this defect, you fall right back into the dilemma, the labyrinth, of pessimism and subjectivism, from out of whose toils we have just wound our way.

Now, we are of course free to fall back, if we please. For my own part, though, whatever difficulties may beset the philosophy of objective right and wrong, and the indeterminism it seems to imply, determinism, with its alternative of pessimism or romanticism, contains difficulties that are greater still. But you will remember that I expressly repudiated awhile ago the pretension to offer any arguments which could be coercive in a so-called scientific fashion in this matter. And I consequently find myself, at the end of this long talk, obliged to state my conclusions in an altogether personal way. This personal method of appeal seems to be among the very conditions of the problem; and the most anyone can do is to confess as candidly as he can the grounds for the faith that is in him, and leave his example to work on others as it may.

Let me, then, without circumlocution say just this. The world is enigmatical enough in all conscience, whatever theory we may take up towards it. The indeterminism I defend, the free-will theory of popular sense based on the judgment of regret, represents that world as vulnerable, and liable to be injured by certain of its parts if they act wrong. And it represents their acting wrong as a matter of possibility or accident, neither inevitable nor yet to be infallibly warded off. In all this, it is a theory devoid either of transparency or of stability. It gives us a pluralistic, restless universe, in which no single point of view can ever take in the whole scene; and to a mind possessed of the love of unity at any cost, it will, no doubt, remain forever inacceptable. A friend with such a mind once told me that the thought of my universe made him sick, like the sight of the horrible motion of a mass of maggots in their carrion bed.

But whilst I freely admit that the pluralism and the restlessness are repugnant and irrational in a certain way, I find that every alternative to them is irrational in a deeper way. The indeterminism with its maggots, if you please to speak so about it, offends only the native absolutism of my intellect—an absolutism which, after all, perhaps, deserves to be snubbed and kept in check. But the determinism with its necessary carrion, to continue the figure of speech, and with no possible maggots to eat the latter up, violates my sense of moral reality through and through. When, for example, I imagine such carrion as the Brockton murder, I cannot conceive it as an act by which the universe, as a whole, logically and necessarily expresses its nature without shrinking from complicity with such a whole. And I deliberately refuse to keep on terms of loyalty with the universe by saying blankly that the murder, since it does flow from the nature of the whole, is not carrion. There are *some* instinctive reactions which I, for one, will not tamper with. The only remaining alternative, the attitude of gnostical romanticism, wrenches my personal instincts in quite as violent a way. It falsifies the simple objectivity of their deliverance. It makes the goose-flesh the murder excites in me a sufficient reason for the perpetration of the crime. It tranforms life from a tragic reality into an insincere melodramatic exhibition, as foul or as tawdry as anyone's diseased curiosity pleases to carry it out. And with its consecration of the "roman naturaliste" state of mind, and its enthronement of the baser crew of Parisian *littérateurs* among the eternally indispensable organs by which the infinite spirit of things attains to that subjective illumination which is the task of its life, it leaves me in presence of a sort of subjective carrion considerably more noisome than the objective carrion I called it in to take away.

No! better a thousand times, than such systematic corruption of our moral sanity, the plainest pessimism, so that it be straightforward; but better far than that the world of chance. Make as great an uproar about chance as you please, I know that chance means pluralism and nothing more. If some of the members of the pluralism are bad, the philosophy of pluralism, whatever broad views with a clean breast of affection and an unsophisticated moral sense. And if I still wish to think of the world as a totality, it lets me feel that a world with a *chance* in it of being altogether good, even if the chance never come to pass, is better than a world with no such chance at all. That "chance" whose very notion I am exhorted and conjured to banish from my view of the future as the suicide of reason concerning it, that "chance" is—what? Just this—the chance that in moral respects the future may be other and better than the past has been. This is the only chance we have any motive for supposing to exist. Shame, rather, on its repudiation and its denial! For its presence is the vital air which lets the world live, the salt which keeps it sweet.

And here I might legitimately stop, having expressed all I care to see admitted by others to-night. But I know that if I do stop here, misapprehensions will remain in the minds of some of you, and keep all I have said from having its effect; so I judge it best to add a few more words.

In the first place, in spite of all my explanations, the word "chance" will still be giving trouble. Though you may yourselves be adverse to the deterministic doctrine, you wish a pleasanter word than "chance" to name the opposite doctrine by; and you very likely consider my preference for such a word a perverse sort of a partiality on my part. It certainly *is* a bad word to make converts with; and you wish I had not thrust it so butt-foremost at you— you wish to use a milder term.

Well, I admit there may be just a dash of perversity in its choice. The spectacle of the mere word-grabbing game played by the soft determinists has perhaps driven me too violently the other way; and, rather than be found wrangling with them for the good words, I am willing to take the first bad one which comes

along, provided it be unequivocal. The question is of things, not of eulogistic names for them; and the best word is the one that enables men to know the quickest whether they disagree or not about the things. But the word "chance," with its singular negativity, is just the word for this purpose. Whoever uses it instead of "freedom," squarely and resolutely gives up all pretence to control the things he says are free. For *him,* he confesses that they are no better than mere chance would be. It is a word of *impotence,* and is therefore the only sincere word we can use, if, in granting freedom to certain things, we grant it honestly, and really risk the game. "Who chooses me must give me and forfeit all he hath." Any other word permits of quibbling, and lets us, after the fashion of the soft determinists, make a pretence of restoring the caged bird to liberty with one hand, whilst with the other we anxiously tie a string to its leg to make sure it does not get beyond our sight.

But now you will bring up your final doubt. Does not the admission of such an unguaranteed chance or freedom preclude utterly the notion of a Providence governing the world? Does it not leave the fate of the universe at the mercy of the chance-possibilities, and so far insecure? Does it not, in short, deny the craving of our nature for an ultimate peace behind all tempests, for a blue zenith above all clouds?

To this my answer must be very brief. The belief in free-will is not in the least incompatible with the belief in Providence, provided you do not restrict the Providence to fulminating nothing for *fatal* decrees. If you allow him to provide possibilities as well as actualities to the universe, and to carry on his own thinking in those two categories just as we do ours, chances may be there, uncontrolled even by him, and the course of the universe be really ambiguous; and yet the end of all things may be just what he intended it to be from all eternity.

An analogy will make the meaning of this clear. Suppose two men before a chessboard— the one a novice, the other an expert player of the game. The expert intends to beat. But he cannot foresee exactly what any one actual move of his adversary may be. He knows, however, all the *possible* moves of the latter; and he knows in advance how to meet each of them by a move of his own which leads in the direction of victory. And the victory infallibly arrives after no matter how devious a course, in the one predestined form of check-mate to the novice's king.

Let now the novice stand for us finite free agents, and the expert for the infinite mind in which the universe lies. Suppose the latter to be thinking out his universe before he actually creates it. Suppose him to say, I will lead things to a certain end, but I will not *now* decide on all the steps thereto. At various points, ambiguous possibilities shall be left open, *either* of which, at a given instant, may become actual. But whichever branch of these bifurcations become real, I know what I shall do at the *next* bifurcation to keep things from drifting away from the final result I intend.

The creator's plan of the universe would thus be left blank as to many of its actual details, but all possibilities would be marked down. The realization of some of these would be left absolutely to chance; that is, would only be determined when the moment of realization came. Other possibilities would be *contingently* determined; that is, their decision would have to wait till it was seen how the matters of absolute chance fell out. But the rest of the plan, including its final upshot, would be rigorously determined once for all. So the creator himself would not need to know *all* the details of actuality until they came; and at any time his own view of the world would be a view partly of facts and partly of possibilities, exactly as ours is now. Of one thing, however, he might be

certain; and that is that his world was safe, and that no matter how much it might zigzag he could surely bring it home at last.

Now, it is entirely immaterial, in this scheme, whether the creator leave the absolute chance-possibilities to be decided by himself, each when its proper moment arrives, or whether, on the contrary, he alienate this power from himself, and leave the decision out and out to finite creatures such as we men are. The great point is that the possibilities are really *here*. Whether it be we who solve them, or he working through us, at those soul-trying moments when fate's scales seem to quiver, and good snatches the victory from evil or shrinks nerveless from the fight, is of small account, so long as we admit that the issue is decided nowhere else than *here* and *now*. *That* is what gives the palpitating reality to our moral life and makes it tingle, as Mr. Mallock says, with so strange and elaborate an excitement. This reality, this excitement, are what the determinisms, hard and soft alike, suppress by their denial that *anything* is decided here and now, and their dogma that all things were foredoomed and settled long ago. If it be so, may you and I have been foredoomed to the error of continuing to believe in liberty. It is fortunate for the winding up of controversy that in every discussion with determinism this *argumentum ad hominem* can be its adversary's last word.

The Will to Believe

In the recently published *Life* by Leslie Stephen of his brother, Fitzjames, there is an account of a school to which the latter went when he was a boy. The teacher, a certain Mr. Guest, used to converse with his pupils in this wise: "Gurney, what's the difference between justification and sanctification?—Stephen, prove the Omnipotence of God!" etc. In the midst of our Harvard freethinking and indifference we are prone to imagine that here at your good old orthodox College conversation continues to be somewhat upon this order; and to show you that we at Harvard have not lost all interest in these vital subjects, I have brought with me to-night something like a sermon on justification by faith to read to you—I mean an essay in justification *of*

faith, a defence of our right to adopt a believing attitude in religious matters, in spite of the fact that our merely logical intellect may not have been coerced. "The Will to Believe," accordingly, is the title of my paper.

I have long defended to my own students the lawfulness of voluntarily adopted faith; but as soon as they have got well imbued with the logical spirit, they have as a rule refused to admit my contention to be lawful philosophically, even though in point of fact they were personally all the time chock-full of some faith or other themselves. I am all the while, however, so profoundly convinced that my own position is correct, that your invitation has seemed to me a good occasion to make my

From *The Works of William James—The Will to Believe,* ed. Frederick Burkhardt (Cambridge, Mass.: Harvard University Press, 1979, pp. 13–33.

statements more clear. Perhaps your minds will be more open than those with which I have hitherto had to deal. I will be as little technical as I can, though I must begin by setting up some technical distinctions that will help us in the end.

I

Let us give the name of *hypothesis* to anything that may be proposed to our belief; and just as the electricians speak of live and dead wires, let us speak of any hypothesis as either *live* or *dead*. A live hypothesis is one which appeals as a real possibility to him whom it is proposed. If I ask you to believe in the Mahdi, the notion makes no electric connection with your nature—it refuses to scintillate with any credibility at all. As an hypothesis it is completely dead. To an Arab, however (even if he be not one of the Mahdi's followers), the hypothesis is among the mind's possibilities: it is alive. This shows that deadness and liveness in an hypothesis are not intrinsic properties, but relations to the individual thinker. They are measured by his willingness to act. The maximum of liveness in an hypothesis means willingness to act irrevocably. Practically, that means belief; but there is some believing tendency wherever there is willingness to act at all.

Next, let us call the decision between two hypotheses an *option*. Options may be of several kinds. They may be—1, *living* or *dead*; 2, *forced* or *avoidable*; 3, *momentous* or *trivial*; and for our purposes we may call an option a *genuine* option when it is of the forced, living and momentous kind.

1. A living option is one in which both hypotheses are live ones. If I say to you: "Be a theosophist or be a mahomedan," it is probably a dead option, because for you neither hypothesis is likely to be alive. But if I say "Be an agnostic or be a Christian," it is otherwise: trained as you are, each hypothesis makes some appeal, however small, to your belief.

2. Next, if I say to you: "Choose between going out with your umbrella or without it," I do not offer you a genuine option, for it is not forced. You can easily avoid it by not going out at all. Similarly, if I say "Either love me or hate me," "Either call my theory true or call it false," your option is avoidable. You may remain indifferent to me, neither loving nor hating, and you may decline to offer any judgment as to my theory. But if I say, "Either accept this truth or go without it," I put on you

a forced option, for there is no standing place outside of the alternative. Every dilemma based on a complete logical disjunction, with no possibility of not choosing, is an option of this forced kind.

3. Finally, if I were Dr. Nansen and proposed to you to join my North Pole expedition, your option would be momentous; for this would probably be your only similar opportunity, and your choice now would either exclude you from the North Pole sort of immortality altogether or put at least the chance of it into your hands. He who refuses to embrace a unique opportunity loses the prize as surely as if he tried and failed. *Per contra,* the option is trivial when the opportunity is not unique, when the stake is insignificant, or when the decision is reversible if it later prove unwise. Such trivial options abound in the scientific life. A chemist finds an hypothesis live enough to spend a year in its verification: he believes in it to that extent. But if his experiments prove inconclusive either way, he is quit for his loss of time, no vital harm being done.

It will facilitate our discussion if we keep all these distinctions well in mind.

II

The next matter to consider is the actual psychology of human opinion. When we look at certain facts, it seems as if our passional and volitional nature lay at the root of all our convictions. When we look at others, it seems as if they could do nothing when the intellect had once said its say. Let us take the latter facts up first.

Does it not seem preposterous on the very face of it to talk of our opinions being modifiable at will? Can our will either help or hinder our intellect in its perceptions of truth? Can we, by just willing it, believe that Abraham Lincoln's existence is a myth, and that the portraits of him in *McClure's Magazine* are all of someone else? Can we, by any effort of our will, or by any strength of wish that it were true, believe ourselves well and about when we are roaring with rheumatism in bed, or feel certain that the sum of the two one-dollar bills in our pocket must be a hundred dollars? We can *say* any of these things, but we are absolutely impotent to believe them, and of just such things is the whole fabric of the truths that we do believe in made up—matters of fact, immediate or remote, as Hume said, and relations between ideas, which are either there or not there for us if we see them so, and which if not there cannot be put there by any action of our own.

In Pascal's *Thoughts* there is a celebrated passage known in literature as Pascal's wager. In it he tries to force us into Christianity by reasoning as if our concern with truth resembled our concern with the stakes in a game of chance. Translated freely his words are these: You must either believe or not believe that God is—which will you do? Your human reason cannot say. A game is going on between you and the nature of things which at the day of judgment will bring out either heads or tails. Weigh what your gains and your losses would be if you should stake all you have on heads, or God's existence: If you win in such case, you gain eternal beatitude; if you lose, you lose nothing at all. If there were an infinity of chances, and only one for God in this wager, still you ought to stake your all on God; for though you surely risk a finite loss by this procedure, any finite loss is reasonable, even a certain one is reasonable, if there is but the possibility of infinite gain. Go, then, and take holy water, and have masses said; belief will come and stupefy your scruples—*Cela vous fera croire et vous abêtira*. Why should you not? At bottom, what have you to lose?

You probably feel that when religious faith expresses itself thus, in the language of the gaming-table, it is put to its last trumps. Surely Pascal's own personal belief in masses and holy water had far other springs; and this celebrated page of his is but an argument for others, a last desperate snatch at a weapon against the hardness of the unbelieving heart. We feel that a faith in masses and holy water adopted wilfully after such a mechanical calculation would lack the inner soul of faith's reality; and if we were ourselves in the place of the Deity, we should probably take particular pleasure in cutting off believers of this pattern from their infinite reward. It is evident that unless there be some pre-existing tendency to believe in masses and holy water, the option offered to the will by Pascal is not a living option. Certainly no Turk ever took to masses and holy water on its account; and even to us Protestants these means of salvation seem such foregone possibilities that Pascal's logic, invoked for them specifically, leave us unmoved. As well might the Mahdi write to us, saying "I am the Expected One whom God has created in his effulgence. You shall be infinitely happy if you confess me; otherwise you shall be cut off from the light of the sun. Weigh, then, your infinite gain if I am genuine against your finite sacrifice if I am not!" His logic would be that of Pascal; but he would vainly use it on us, for the hypothesis he offers us is dead. No tendency to act on it exists in us to any degree.

The talk of believing by our volition seems, then, from one point of view, simply silly. From another point of view it is worse than silly, it is vile. When one turns to the magnificent edifice of the physical sciences, and sees how it was reared; what thousands of disinterested moral lives of men lie buried in its mere foundations; what patience and postponement, what choking down of preference, what submission to the icy laws of outer fact are wrought into its very stones and mortar; how absolutely impersonal it stands in its vast augustness—then how besotted and contemptible seems every little sentimentalist who comes blowing his voluntary smoke-wreaths, and pretending to decide things from out of his private dream! Can we wonder if those bred in the rugged and manly school of science should feel like spewing such subjectivism out of their mouths? The whole system of loyalties which grow up in the schools of science go dead against its toleration; so that it is only natural that those who have caught the scientific fever should pass over to the opposite extreme, and write sometimes as if the incorruptibly truthful intellect ought positively to prefer bitterness and unacceptableness to the heart in its cup.

> *"It fortifies my soul to know*
> *That, though I perish, Truth is so—"*

sings Clough, whilst Huxley exclaims: "My only consolation lies in the reflection that, however bad our posterity may become, so long as they hold by the plain rule of not pretending to believe what they have no reason to believe because it may be to their advantage so to pretend [the word 'pretend' is surely here redundant], they will not have reached the lowest depths of immorality." And that delicious *enfant terrible* Clifford writes: "Belief is desecrated when given to unproved and unquestioned statements, for the solace and private pleasure of the believer . . . . Whoso would deserve well of his fellows in this matter will guard the purity of his belief with a very fanaticism of jealous care, lest at any time it should rest on an unworthy object, and catch a stain which can never be wiped away . . . . If [a] belief has been accepted on insufficient evidence [even though the belief be true, as Clifford on the same page explains], the pleasure is a stolen one . . . . It is sinful, because it is stolen in defiance of our duty to mankind. That duty is to guard ourselves from such beliefs as from a pestilence, which may shortly master our own body and then spread to the rest of the town . . . . It is wrong always, everywhere, and for anyone, to believe anything upon insufficient evidence."

III

All this strikes one as healthy, even when expressed, as by Clifford, with somewhat too much of robustious pathos in the voice. Freewill and simple wishing do seem, in the matter of our credences, to be only fifth wheels to the coach. Yet if anyone should thereupon assume that intellectual insight is what remains after wish and will and sentimental preference have taken wing, or that pure reason is what then settles our opinions, he would fly quite as directly in the teeth of the facts.

It is only our already dead hypotheses that our willing nature is unable to bring to life again. But what has made them dead for us is for the most part a previous action of our willing nature of an antagonistic kind. When I say "willing nature," I do not mean only such deliberate volitions as may have set up habits of belief that we cannot now escape from—I mean all such factors of belief as fear and hope, prejudice and passion, imitation and partisanship, the circumpressure of our caste and set. As a matter of fact we find ourselves believing, we hardly know how or why. Mr. Balfour gives the name of "authority" to all those influences, born of the intellectual climate, that make hypotheses possible or impossible for us, alive or dead. Here in this room, we all of us believe in molecules and the conservation of energy, in democracy and necessary progress, in Protestant Christianity and the duty of fighting for "the doctrine of the immortal Monroe," all for no reasons worthy of the name. We see into these matters with no more inner clearness, and probably with much less, than any disbeliever in them might possess. His unconventionality would probably have some grounds to show for its conclusions; but for us, not insight, but the *prestige* of the opinions, is what makes the spark shoot from them and light up in our sleeping magazines of faith. Our reason is quite satisfied, in nine hundred and ninety-nine cases out of every thousand of us, if it can find a few arguments that will do to recite in case our credulity is criticized by someone else. Our faith is faith in someone else's faith, and in the greatest matters this is most the case. Our belief in truth itself, for instance, that there is a truth, and that our minds and it are made for each other—what is it but a passionate affirmation of desire, in which our social system backs us up? We want to have a truth; we want to believe that our experiments and studies and discussions must put us in a continually better and better position towards it; and on this line we agree to fight out our thinking lives. But if a pyrrhonistic sceptic asks us *how we know* all this, can our logic find a reply? No! Certainly it cannot. It is just one volition against another—we willing to go in for life upon a trust or assumption which he, for his part, does not care to make.

As a rule we disbelieve all facts and theories for which we have no use. Clifford's cosmic emotions find no use for Christian feelings. Huxley belabors the bishops because there is no use for sacerdotalism in his scheme of life. Newman, on the contrary, goes over to Romanism, and finds all sorts of reasons good for staying there, because a priestly system is for him an organic need and delight. Why do so few "scientists" even look at the evidence for telepathy, so called? Because they think, as a leading biologist, now dead, once said to me, that even if such a thing were true, scientists ought to band together to keep it suppressed and concealed. It would undo the uniformity of Nature and all sorts of other things without which scientists cannot carry on their pursuits. But if this very man had been showing something which as a scientist he might *do* with telepathy, he might not only have examined the evidence, but even have found it good enough. This very law which the logicians would impose upon us—if I may give the name of logicians to those who would rule out our willing nature here—is based on nothing but their own natural wish to exclude all elements for which they, in their professional quality of logicians, can find no use.

Evidently, then, our non-intellectual nature does influence our convictions. There are passional tendencies and volitions which run before and others which come after belief, and it is only the latter that are too late for the fair; and they are not too late when the previous passional work has been already in their own direction. Pascal's argument, instead of being powerless, then seems a regular clincher, and is the last stroke needed to make our faith in masses and holy water complete. The state of things is evidently far from simple; and pure insight and logic, whatever they might do ideally, are not the only things that really do produce our creeds.

IV

Our next duty, having recognized this mixed-up state of affairs, is to ask whether it be simply reprehensible and pathological, or whether, on the contrary, we must treat it as a normal element in making up our minds. The thesis I defend is, briefly stated, this: *Our passional nature not only lawfully may, but must, decide an option between propositions, whenever it is a genuine option that cannot by its nature be decided on intellectual grounds; for to say, under such circumstances, "Do not decide, but leave the question open," is itself a passional decision—just like deciding yes or no—and is attended with the same risk of losing the truth.* The thesis thus abstractly expressed will, I trust, soon become quite clear. But I must first indulge in a bit more of preliminary work.

V

It will be observed that for the purposes of this discussion we are on "dogmatic" ground—ground, I mean, which leaves systematic philosophical scepticism altogether out of account. The postulate that there is truth, and that it is the destiny of our minds to attain it, we are deliberately resolving to make, though the sceptic will not make it. We part company with him, therefore, absolutely, at this point. But the faith that truth exists, and that our minds can find it, may be held in two ways. We may talk of the *empiricist* way and of the *absolutist* way of believing in truth. The absolutists in this matter say that we not only can attain to knowing truth, but we can *know when* we have attained to knowing it; whilst the empiricists think that although we may attain it, we cannot infallibly know when. To *know* is one thing, and to know for certain *that* we know is another. One may hold to the first being possible without the second; hence the empiricists and the absolutists, although neither of them is a sceptic in the usual philosophic sense of the term, show very different degrees of dogmatism in their lives.

If we look at the history of opinions, we see that the empiricist tendency has largely prevailed in science, whilst in philosophy the absolutist tendency has had everything its own way. The characteristic sort of happiness, indeed, which philosophies yield has mainly consisted in the conviction felt by each successive school or system that by it bottom-certitude had been attained. "Other philosophies are collections of opinions, mostly false; *my* philosophy gives standing-ground forever"—who does not recognize in this the key-note of every system worthy of the name? A system, to be a system at all, must come as a *closed* system, reversible in this or that detail, perchance, but in its essential features never!

Scholastic orthodoxy, to which one must always go when one wishes to find perfectly clear statement, has beautifully elaborated this absolutist conviction in a doctrine which it calls that of "objective evidence." If, for example, I am unable to doubt that I now exist before you, that two is less than three, or that if all men are mortal then I am mortal too, it is because these things illumine my intellect irresistibly. The final ground of this objective evidence possessed by certain propositions is the *adæquatio intellectûs nostri cum rê.* The certitude it brings involves an *aptitudinem ad extorquendum certum assensum* on the part of the truth envisaged, and on the side of the subject, a *quietem in cognitione,* when once the object is mentally received, that leaves no possibility of doubt behind; and in the whole transaction nothing operates but the *entitas ipsa* of the object and the *entitas ipsa* of the mind. We slouchy modern thinkers dislike to talk in Latin—indeed, we dislike to talk in set terms at all; but at bottom our own state of mind is very much like this whenever we uncritically abandon ourselves: You believe in objective evidence, and I do. Of some things we feel that we are certain: we know, and we know that we do know. There is something that gives a click inside of us, a bell that strikes twelve, when the hands of our mental clock have swept the dial and meet over the meridian hour. The greatest empiricists among us are only empiricists on reflection: when left to their instincts, they dogmatize like infallible popes. When the Cliffords tell us how sinful it is to be Christians on such "insufficient evidence" insufficiency is really the last thing they have in mind. For them the evidence is absolutely sufficient, only it makes the other way. They believe so completely in an anti-christian order of the universe that there is no living option: Christianity is a dead hypothesis from the start.

VI

But now, since we are all such absolutists by instinct, what in our quality of students of philosophy ought we to do about the fact? Shall we espouse and indorse it? Or shall we treat it as a weakness of our nature from which we must free ourselves, if we can?

I sincerely believe that the latter course is the only one we can follow as reflective men. Objective evidence and certitude are doubtless very fine ideals to play with, but where on this moonlit and dream-visited planet are they found? I am, therefore, myself a complete empiricist so far as my theory of human knowledge goes. I live, to be sure, by the practical faith that we must go on experiencing and thinking over our experience, for only thus can our opinions grow more true; but to hold any one of them—I absolutely do not care which—as if it never could be re-interpretable or corrigible, I believe to be a tremendously mistaken attitude, and I think that the whole history of philosophy will bear me out. There is but one indefectibly certain truth, and that is the truth that pyrrhonistic scepticism itself leaves standing—the truth that the present phenomenon of consciousness exists. That, however, is the bare starting-point of knowledge, the mere admission of a stuff to be philosophized about. The various philosophies are but so many attempts at expressing what this stuff really is. And if we repair to our libraries what disagreement do we discover! Where is a certainly true answer found? Apart from abstract propositions of comparison (such as two and two are the same as four), propositions which tell us nothing by themselves about concrete reality, we find no proposition ever regarded by anyone as evidently certain that has not either been called a falsehood, or at least had its truth sincerely questioned by someone else. The transcending of the axioms of geometry, not in play but in earnest, by certain of our contemporaries (as Zöllner and Charles H. Hinton), and the rejection of the whole aristotelian logic by the Hegelians, are striking instances in point.

No concrete test of what is really true has ever been agreed upon. Some make the criterion external to the moment of perception, putting it either in revelation, the *consensus gentium,* the instincts of the heart, or the systematized experience of the race. Others make the perceptive moment its own test— Descartes, for instance, with his clear and distinct ideas guaranteed by the veracity of God; Reid with his "common-sense"; and Kant with his forms of synthetic judgment *a priori.* The inconceivability of the opposite; the capacity to be verified by sense; the possession of complete organic unity or self-relation, realized when a thing is its own other—are standards which, in turn, have been used. The much lauded objective evidence is never triumphantly there; it is a mere aspiration or *Grenzbegriff,* marking the infinitely remote ideal of our thinking life. To claim that certain truths now possess it, is simply to say that when you think them true and they *are* true, then their evidence is objective, otherwise it is not. But practically one's conviction that the evidence one goes by is of the real objective brand, is only one more subjective opinion added to the lot. For what a contradictory array of opinions have objective evidence and absolute certitude been claimed! The world is rational through and through—its existence is an ultimate brute fact; there is a personal God—a personal God is inconceivable; there is an extra-mental physical world immediately known—the mind can only know its own ideas; a moral imperative exists—obligation is only the resultant of desires; a permanent spiritual principle is in everyone—there are only shifting states of mind; there is an endless chain of causes—there is an absolute first cause; an eternal necessity—a freedom; a purpose—no purpose; a primal One—a primal Many; a universal continuity—an essential discontinuity in things; an infinity—no infinity. There is this—there is that; there is indeed nothing which someone has not thought absolutely true, whilst his neighbor deemed it absolutely false; and not an absolutist among them seems ever to have considered that the trouble may all the time be essential, and that the intellect, even with truth directly in its grasp, may have no infallible signal for knowing whether it be truth or no. When, indeed, one remembers that the most striking practical application to life of the doctrine of objective certitude has been the conscientious labors of the Holy Office of the Inquisition, one feels less tempted than ever to lend the doctrine a respectful ear.

But please observe, now, that when as empiricists we give up the doctrine of objective certitude, we do not thereby give up the quest or hope of truth itself. We still pin our faith on its existence, and still believe that we gain an ever better position towards it by systematically continuing to roll up experiences and think. Our great difference from the scholastic lies in the way we face. The strength of his system lies in the principles, the origin, the *terminus a quo* of his thought; for us the strength is in the outcome, the upshot, the *ter-*

minus ad quem. Not where it comes from but what it leads to is to decide. It matters not to an empiricist from what quarter an hypothesis may come to him: he may have acquired it by fair means or by foul; passion may have whispered or accident suggested it; but if the total drift of thinking continues to confirm it, that is what he means by its being true.

VII

One more point, small but important, and our preliminaries are done. There are two ways of looking at our duty in the matter of opinion— ways entirely different, and yet ways about whose difference the theory of knowledge seems hitherto to have shown very little concern. *We must know the truth;* and *we must avoid error*—these are our first and great commandments as would-be knowers; but they are not two ways of stating an identical commandment, they are two separable laws. Although it may indeed happen that when we believe the truth *A,* we escape as an incidental consequence from believing the falsehood *B,* it hardly ever happens that by merely disbelieving *B* we necessarily believe *A.* We may in escaping *B* fall into believing other falsehoods, *C* or *D,* just as bad as *B;* or we may escape *B* by not believing anything at all, not even *A.*

Believe truth! Shun error!—these, we see, are two materially different laws; and by choosing between them we may end by colouring differently our whole intellectual life. We may regard the chase for truth as paramount, and the avoidance of error as secondary; or we may, on the other hand, treat the avoidance of error as more imperative, and let truth take its chance. Clifford, in the instructive passage which I have quoted, exhorts us to the latter course. Believe nothing, he tells us, keep your mind in suspense forever, rather than by closing it on insufficient evidence incur the awful risk of believing lies. You, on the other hand, may think that the risk of being in error is a very small matter when compared with the blessings of real knowledge, and be ready to be duped many times in your investigation rather than postpone indefinitely the chance of guessing true. I myself find it impossible to go with Clifford. We must remember that these feelings of our duty about either truth or error are in any case only expressions of our passional life. Biologically considered, our minds are as ready to grind out falsehood as veracity, and he who says "Better go without belief forever than believe a lie!" merely shows his

own preponderant private horror of becoming a dupe. He may be critical of many of his desires and fears, but this fear he slavishly obeys. He cannot imagine anyone questioning its binding force. For my own part, I have also a horror of being duped; but I can believe that worse things than being duped may happen to a man in this world: so Clifford's exhortation has to my ears a thoroughly fantastic sound. It is like a general informing his soldiers that it is better to keep out of battle forever than to risk a single wound. Not so are victories either over enemies or over nature gained. Our errors are surely not such awfully solemn things. In a world where we are so certain to incur them in spite of all our caution, a certain lightness of heart seems healthier than this excessive nervousness on their behalf. At any rate, it seems the fittest thing for the empiricist philosopher.

VIII

And now, after all this introduction, let us go straight at our question. I have said, and now repeat it, that not only as a matter of fact do we find our passional nature influencing us in our opinions, but that there are some options between opinions in which this influence must be regarded both as an inevitable and as a lawful determinant of our choice.

I fear here that some of you my hearers will begin to scent danger, and lend an inhospitable ear. Two first steps of passion you have indeed had to admit as necessary—we must think so as to avoid dupery, and we must think so as to gain truth; but the surest path to those ideal consummations, you will probably consider, is from now onwards to take no farther passional step.

Well, of course I agree as far as the facts will allow. Wherever the option between losing truth and gaining it is not momentous, we can throw the chance of *gaining truth* away, and at any rate save ourselves from any chance of *believing falsehood,* by not making up our minds at all till objective evidence has come. In scientific questions, this is almost always the case; and even in human affairs in general, the need of acting is seldom so urgent that a false belief to act on is better than no belief at all. Law courts, indeed, have to decide on the best evidence attainable for the moment, because a judge's duty is to make law as well as to ascertain it, and (as a learned judge once said to me) few cases are worth spending much time over: the great thing is to have them decided on *any* acceptable principle, and got out of the way. But in our dealings with objective nature we obviously are recorders, not makers, of the truth; and decisions for the mere sake of deciding promptly and getting on to the next business would be wholly out of place. Throughout the breadth of physical nature facts are what they are quite independently of us, and seldom is there any such hurry about them that the risks of being duped by believing a premature theory need be faced. The questions here are always trivial options, the hypotheses are hardly living (at any rate not living for us spectators), the choice between believing truth or falsehood is seldom forced. The attitude of sceptical balance is therefore the absolutely wise one if we would escape mistakes. What difference, indeed, does it make to most of us whether we have or have not a theory of the Röntgen rays, whether we believe or not in mind-stuff, or have a conviction about the causality of conscious states? It makes no difference. Such options are not forced on us. On every account it is better not to make them, but still keep weighing reasons *pro et contra* with an indifferent hand.

I speak, of course, here of the purely judging mind. For purposes of discovery such indifference is to be less highly recommended, and science would be far less advanced than she is if the passionate desires of individuals to get their own faiths confirmed had been kept out of the game. See for example the sagacity which Spencer and Weismann now display. On the other hand, if you want an absolute duffer in an investigation, you must, after all, take the man who has no interest whatever in its results: he is the warranted incapable, the positive fool. The most useful investigator, because the most sensitive observer, is always he whose eager interest in one side of the question is balanced by an equally keen nervousness lest he become deceived. Science has organized this nervousness into a regular *technique,* her so-called method of verification; and she has fallen so deeply in love with the method that one may even say she has ceased to care for truth by itself at all. It is only truth as technically verified that interests her. The truth of truths might come in merely affirmative form, and she would decline to touch it. Such truth as that, she might repeat with Clifford, would be stolen in defiance of her duty to mankind. Human passions, however, are stronger than technical rules. "Le cœur a ses raisons," as Pascal says, "que la raison ne connaît point"; and however indifferent to all but the bare rules of the game the umpire, the abstract intellect, may be, the concrete players who furnish him the materials to judge of are usually, each one of them, in love with some pet "live hypothesis" of his own. Let us agree, however, that wherever there is no forced option, the dispassionately judicial intellect with no pet hypothesis, saving us, as it does, from dupery at any rate, ought to be our ideal.

The question next arises: Are there not somewhere forced options in our speculative questions, and can we (as men who may be interested at least as much in positively gaining truth as in merely escaping dupery) always wait with impunity till the coercive evidence shall have arrived? It seems *a priori* improbable that the truth should be so nicely adjusted to our needs and powers as that. In the great boarding-house of nature, the cakes and the butter and the syrup seldom come out so even and leave the plates so clean. Indeed, we should view them with scientific suspicion if they did.

IX

Moral questions immediately present themselves as questions whose solution cannot wait for sensible proof. A moral question is a question not of what sensibly exists, but of what is good, or would be good if it did exist. Science can tell us what exists; but to compare the *worths,* both of what exists and of what does not exist, we must consult not science, but what Pascal calls our heart. Science herself consults her heart when she lays it down that the infinite ascertainment of fact and correction of false belief are the supreme goods for man. Challenge the statement and science can only repeat it oracularly, or else prove it by showing that such ascertainment and correction bring man all sorts of other goods which man's heart in turn declares. The question of having moral beliefs at all or not having them is decided by our will. Are our moral preferences true or false, or are they only odd biological phenomena, making things good or bad for *us,* but in themselves indifferent? How can your pure intellect decide? If your heart does not *want* a world of moral reality, your head will assuredly never make you believe in one. Mephistophelian scepticism, indeed, will satisfy the head's play-instincts much better than any rigorous idealism can. Some men (even at the student age) are so naturally cool-hearted that the moralistic hypothesis never has for them any pungent life, and in their supercilious presence the hot young moralist always feels strangely ill at ease. The appearance of know-ingness is on their side, of *naiveté* and gullibility on his. Yet, in the inarticulate heart of him, he clings to it that he is not a dupe, and that there is a realm in which (as Emerson says) all their wit and intellectual superiority is no better than the cunning of a fox. Moral scepticism can no more be refuted or proved by logic than intel-lectual scepticism can. When we stick to it that there *is* truth (be it of either kind), we do so with our whole nature, and resolve to stand or fall by the results. The sceptic with his whole nature adopts the doubting attitude; but which of us is the wiser, Omniscience only knows.

Turn now from these wide questions of good to a certain class of questions of fact, questions concerning personal relations, states of mind between one man and another. *Do you like me or not?*—for example. Whether you do or not depends, in countless instances, on whether I meet you half-way, am willing to assume that you must like me, and show you trust and ex-pectation. The previous faith on my part in your liking's existence is in such cases what makes your liking come. But if I stand aloof, and re-fuse to budge an inch until I have objective evi-dence, until you shall have done something apt, as the absolutists say, *ad extorquendum assen-sum meum,* ten to one your liking never comes. How many women's hearts are vanquished by the mere sanguine insistence of some man that they *must* love him! he will not consent to the hypothesis that they cannot. The desire for a certain kind of truth here brings about that spe-cial truth's existence; and so it is in innumerable cases of other sorts. Who gains promotions, boons, appointments, but the man in whose life they are seen to play the part of live hypo-theses, who discounts them, sacrifices other things for their sake before they have come, and takes risks for them in advance? His faith acts on the powers above him as a claim, and creates its own verification.

A social organism of any sort whatever, large or small, is what it is because each mem-ber proceeds to his own duty with a trust that the other members will simultaneously do theirs. Wherever a desired result is achieved by the co-operation of many independent per-sons, its existence as a fact is a pure conse-quence of the precursive faith in one another of those immediately concerned. A govern-ment, an army, a commercial system, a ship, a college, an athletic team, all exist on this con-dition, without which not only is nothing achieved, but nothing is even attempted. A whole train of passengers (individually brave enough) will be looted by a few highwaymen, simply because the latter can count on one another, while each passenger fears that if he makes a movement of resistance, he will be shot before anyone else backs him up. If we believed that the whole car-full would rise at once with us, we should each severally rise, and train-robbing would never even be at-tempted. There are, then, cases where a fact cannot come at all unless a preliminary faith exists in its coming. *And where faith in a fact can help create the fact,* that would be an in-sane logic which should say that faith running ahead of scientific evidence is the "lowest kind of immorality" into which a thinking being can fall. Yet such is the logic by which our scien-tific absolutists pretend to regulate our lives!

X

In truths dependent on our personal action, then, faith based on desire is certainly a lawful and possibly an indispensable thing.

But now, it will be said, these are childish human cases, and have nothing to do with great cosmical matters, like the question of re-ligious faith. Let us then pass on to that. Reli-gions differ so much in their accidents that in discussing the religious question we must make it very generic and broad. What then do we now mean by the religious hypothesis? Science says things are; morality says some things are better than other things; and religion says es-sentially two things.

First, she says that the best things are the more eternal things, the overlapping things, the things in the universe that throw the last stone, so to speak, and say the final word. "Perfection is eternal"—this phrase of Charles Secrétan seems a good way of putting this first affirmation of religion, an affirmation which obviously cannot yet be verified scientifically at all.

The second affirmation of religion is that we are better off even now if we believe her first affirmation to be true.

Now let us consider what the logical ele-ments of this situation are *in case the religious hypothesis in both its branches be really true.* (Of course, we must admit that possibility at the outset. If we are to discuss the question at all, it must involve a living option. If for any of you religion be a hypothesis that cannot, by any living possibility be true, then you need go no farther. I speak to the "saving remnant" alone.) So proceeding, we see, first, that reli-gion offers itself as a *momentous* option. We are supposed to gain, even now, by our belief, and to lose by our non-belief, a certain vital good. Secondly, religion is a *forced* option, so far as that good goes. We cannot escape the issue by remaining sceptical and waiting for more light, because, although we do avoid error in that way *if religion be untrue,* we lose the good, *if it be true,* just as certainly as if we positively chose to disbelieve. It is as if a man should hesitate indefinitely to ask a certain woman to marry him because he was not perfectly sure that she would prove an angel after he brought her home. Would he not cut himself off from that particular angel-possibility as decisively as if he went and married someone else? Scepticism, then, is not avoidance of option; it is option of a certain particular kind of risk. *Better risk loss of truth than chance of error*—that is your faith-vetoer's exact position. He is actively playing his stake as much as the believer is; he is backing the field against the religious hypothesis, just as the believer is backing the religious hypothesis against the field. To preach scepticism to us as a duty until "sufficient evidence" for religion be found, is tantamount therefore to telling us, when in presence of the religious hypothesis, that to yield to our fear of its being error is wiser and better than to yield to our hope that it may be true. It is not intellect against all passions, then; it is only intellect with one passion laying down its law. And by what, forsooth, is the supreme wisdom of this passion warranted? Dupery for dupery, what proof is there that dupery through hope is so much worse than dupery through fear? I, for one, can see no proof; and I simply refuse obedience to the scientist's command to imitate his kind of option, in a case where my own stake is important enough to give me the right to choose my own form of risk. If religion be true and the evidence for it be still insufficient, I do not wish, by putting your extinguisher upon my nature (which feels to me as if it had after all some business in this matter), to forfeit my sole chance in life of getting upon the winning side—that chance depending, of course, on my willingness to run the risk of acting as if my passional need of taking the world religiously might be prophetic and right.

All this is on the supposition that it really may be prophetic and right, and that, even to us who are discussing the matter, religion is a live hypothesis which may be true. Now to most of us religion comes in a still farther way that makes a veto on our active faith even more illogical. The more perfect and more eternal aspect of the universe is represented in our religions as having personal form. The universe is no longer a mere *It* to us, but a *Thou,* if we are religious; and any relation that may be possible from person to person might be possible here. For instance, although in one sense we are passive portions of the universe, in another we show a curious autonomy, as if we were small active centres on our own account. We feel, too, as if the appeal of religion to us were made to our own active good-will, as if evidence might be forever withheld from us unless we met the hypothesis half-way. To take a trivial illustration: just as a man who in a company of gentlemen made no advances, asked a warrant for every concession, and believed no one's word without proof, would cut himself off by such churlishness from all the social rewards that a more trusting spirit would earn—so here, one who should shut himself up in snarling logicality and try to make the gods extort his recognition willy-nilly, or not get it at all, might cut himself off forever from his only opportunity of making the gods' acquaintance. This feeling, forced on us we know not whence, that by obstinately believing that there are gods (although not to do so would be so easy both for our logic and our life) we are doing the universe the deepest service we can, seems part of the living essence of the religious hypothesis. If the hypothesis *were* true in all its parts, including this one, then pure intellectualism, with its veto on our making willing advances, would be an absurdity; and some participation of our sympathetic nature would be logically required. I, therefore, for one, cannot see my way to accepting the agnostic rules for truth-seeking, or wilfully agree to keep my willing nature out of the game. I cannot do so for this plain reason, that *a rule of thinking which would absolutely prevent me from acknowledging certain kinds of truth if those kinds of truth were really there, would be an irrational rule.* That for me is the long and short of the formal logic of the situation, no matter what the kinds of truth might materially be.

I confess I do not see how this logic can be escaped. But sad experience makes me fear that some of you may still shrink from radically saying with me, *in abstracto,* that we have the right to believe at our own risk any hypothesis that is live enough to tempt our will. I suspect, however, that if this is so, it is because you have got away from the abstract logical point of view altogether, and are thinking (perhaps without realizing it) of some particular religious hypothesis which for you is dead. The freedom to "believe what we will" you apply to the case of some patent superstition; and the faith you think of is the faith defined by the schoolboy when he said, "Faith is when you believe something that you know ain't true." I can only repeat that this is misapprehension. *In concreto,* the freedom to believe can only cover living options which the intellect of the individual cannot by itself resolve; and living options never seem absurdities to him who has them to consider. When I look at the religious question as it really puts itself to concrete men, and when I think of all the possibilities which both practically and theoretically it involves, then this command that we shall put a stopper on our heart, instincts and courage, and *wait*—acting of course meanwhile more or less as if religion were *not* true—till doomsday, or till such time as our intellect and sense working together may have raked in evidence enough—this command, I say, seems to me the queerest idol ever manufactured in the philosophic cave. Were we scholastic absolutists, there might be more excuse. If we had an infallible intellect with its objective certitudes, we might feel ourselves disloyal to such a perfect organ of knowledge in not trusting to it exclusively, in not waiting for its releasing word. But if we are empiricists, if we believe that no bell in us tolls to let us know for certain when truth is in our grasp, then it seems a piece of idle fantasticality to preach so solemnly our duty of waiting for the bell. Indeed we *may* wait if we will—I hope you do not think that I am denying that—but if we do so, we do so at our peril as much as if we believed. In either case we *act,* taking our life in our hands. No one of us ought to issue vetoes to the other, nor should we bandy words of

abuse. We ought, on the contrary, delicately and profoundly to respect one another's mental freedom—then only shall we bring about the intellectual republic; then only shall we have that spirit of inner tolerance without which all our outer tolerance is soulless, and which is empiricism's glory; then only shall we live and let live, in speculative as well as in practical things.

I began by a reference to Fitzjames Stephen; let me end by a quotation from him. "What do you think of yourself? What do you think of the world? . . . These are questions with which all must deal as it seems good to them. They are riddles of the Sphinx, and in some way or other we must deal with them. . . . In all important transactions of life we have to take a leap in the dark. . . . If we decide to leave the riddles unanswered, that is a choice. If we waver in our answer, that too is a choice; but whatever choice we make, we make it at our peril. If a man chooses to turn his back altogether on God and the future, no one can prevent him. No one can show beyond reasonable doubt that he is mistaken. If a man thinks otherwise, and acts as he thinks, I do not see how any one can prove that *he* is mistaken. Each must act as he thinks best, and if he is wrong so much the worse for him. We stand on a mountain pass in the midst of whirling snow and blinding mist, through which we get glimpses now and then of paths which may be deceptive. If we stand still, we shall be frozen to death. If we take the wrong road, we shall be dashed to pieces. We do not certainly know whether there is any right one. What must we do? 'Be strong and of a good courage.' Act for the best, hope for the best, and take what comes. . . . If death ends all, we cannot meet death better."

Suggestions for Further Reading

Works by James

The Works of William James. Edited by Frederick Burkhardt. Cambridge: Harvard University Press, 1975—.
   This definitive edition of the writings of James consists of the following:

Pragmatism. Introduction by H. Standish Thayer. 1975.
The Meaning of Truth. Introduction by H. Standish Thayer 1975.
Essays in Radical Empiricism. Introduction by John J. McDermott. 1976.
A Pluralistic Universe. Introduction by Richard J. Bernstein. 1977.
Essays in Philosophy. Introduction by John J. McDermott. 1978.
The Will to Believe. Introduction by Edward H. Madden. 1979.
Some Problems of Philosophy. Introduction by Peter H. Hare. 1979.

The Principles of Psychology. 3 Volumes. Introduction by Gerald E. Myers and Rand B. Evans. 1981.
Essays in Religion and Morality. Introduction by John J. McDermott. 1982.
Talks to Teachers on Psychology. Introduction by Gerald E. Myers. 1983.
Essays in Psychology. Introduction by William R. Woodward. 1983.
Psychology: Briefer Course. Introduction by Michael M. Sokal. 1984.
The Varieties of Religious Experience. Introduction by John E. Smith. 1985.
Essays in Physical Research. Introduction by Robert A. McDermott. 1986.

Further volumes representing James's unpublished papers.

The Letters of William James. 2 Volumes. Edited by Henry James III. Boston: The Atlantic Monthly Press, 1920.

Anthology

The Writings of William James. Edited, with an Introduction and Annotated Bibliography, by John J. McDermott. Chicago: The University of Chicago Press, 1977.

Essential Works on James

Gay Wilson Allen. *William James: A Biography*. New York: The Viking Press, 1967.
Jacques Barzun. *A Stroll with William James*. New York: Harper and Row, 1983.
Patrick Kiaran Dooley. *Pragmatism as Humanism: The Philosophy of William James*. Chicago: Nelson Hall, 1974.
Gerald E. Myers. *William James: His Thought and Life*. New Haven: Yale University Press, 1986.
Ralph Barton Perry. *The Thought and Character of William James*. 2 Volumes. Boston: Little, Brown and Company, 1935.
George Santayana. *Character and Opinion in the United States, with Reminiscences of William James and Josiah Royce and Academic Life in America*. New York: Charles Scribner's Sons, 1920.
Charlene Haddock Seigfried. *Chaos and Context: A Study of William James*. Athens: Ohio University Press, 1978.
Ellen K. Suckiel. *The Pragmatic Philosophy of William James*. Notre Dame, Ind.: University of Notre Dame Press, 1982.
John Wild. *The Radical Empiricism of William James*. New York: Doubleday, 1969.

JOSIAH ROYCE

Introduction by Jacquelyn Ann Kegley

To assess the lifework of Josiah Royce is no small task, for, like others before him, his work was not always appreciated in his time nor even properly labeled and understood by later thinkers. But even more, there were and are those who believe his system of thought to have been refuted by death and his words scattered to the winds of time.[1] But, for Royce, who in *The Problem of Christianity* affirmed a vision of reality as an unfolding process of interpretation, his very own words may be more prophetic and accurate than those estimates of his critics. He writes:

> His [the philosopher's] immediate end may have been unattained, but a thousand years may not be long enough to develop for humanity the full significance of his reflective thought.[2]

Indeed, Royce is an enigmatic figure for many who reflect on American thought and life. He was a flaming-red-headed native Californian who grew up in a rugged mining town during the gold rush and became a Harvard professor who seemed to espouse what many of that time considered an anomaly, at least on the American scene. This puzzle was a philosophical position called idealism, a point of view that had dominated much of Western Europe in the last half of the nineteenth century. The puzzling aspect was its peculiar contrast to the pluralism and open-endedness of the growing, dominant American pragmatism of William James and the later naturalism of John Dewey. Further, it flew in the face of devastating criticisms forthcoming from positivism, logical empiricism, and existentialism. The emphasis was antimetaphysical and thus contrary to any systematic philosophical system such as that of Royce. Further the existentialist; notions of the absolute freedom and highly individualistic risk taking did not seem to fit with an idealism that emphasized the individual's place in the whole. It is thus no accident that Royce was viewed as outdated and outdone by the passage of time. In fact, the fruit of his mature philosophical development, *The Problem of Christianity,* was out of print for over fifty years.

However, as has happened to the view of Wittgenstein and others, the mistake is to believe time makes no difference and to ignore growth and development as an essential part of a thinker's view. It is indeed true that Royce struggles with a notion of a fully self-conscious Absolute Thought or God and, in one of his great works, *The World and the Individual,* presents a fully argued idealistic position on the nature of reality. He also wrote one of the finest interpretative works on idealism, *Lectures on Modern Idealism.*[3] But there is a breadth and depth of Royce's work that is ignored if one merely labels him an idealist. First, as Frank Oppenheim has so clearly established, Royce's work should be seen as evolving through three basic periods: the early period (1883–1895); the middle period (1896–1911); and the mature period (1912–1916).[4] There was definite development in Royce's thought, though there was also continuity. However, too many have narrowly focused on a few aspects of his work, to the neglect of others. Thus, for example, there are those who speak of Royce's religious philosophy, implying this is the totality of the matter, while neglecting the fact that he had a lifelong interest in science and the scientific method. This interest was expressed in early works such as *The Spirit of Modern Philosophy* as well as in many of his later writings on philosophy of science and philosophy of mathematics.[5] In fact, among the students in his graduate seminar in 1913–1914 were people like C. I. Lewis, Norbert Weiner, and T. S. Eliot.[6] Not only that, but there was definite philosophical influence on these thinkers. Thus, C. I. Lewis wrote in his autobiography that the "general tenor" of his thought—conceptual pragmatism—may have "taken shape" under the influence of Josiah Royce.[7]

Further, it is clearly the case that Royce's thought is not out of touch with the American pragmatic tradition, but fully in consonance with it in a number of places. In her book *An Idealistic Pragmatism,* Mary Briody Mahowald concludes not only that there is a genuinely pragmatic element in Royce's thought, but that this element increased as his thought developed.[8] Indeed, in his *Lectures on Modern Idealism,* Royce himself has declared:

> . . . I assert that personally I am both a pragmatist and an absolutist, that I believe each of these doctrines to involve the other and that therefore I regard them not only as reconcilable, but as truth reconciled.[9]

Royce's agreements with the pragmatism of Peirce, James, and Dewey will be evident as we proceed to outline some major themes and areas of his thought.

Josiah Royce, then, we claim, has been misunderstood and misjudged. Further, we believe it especially appropriate to reexamine Royce's thought at this time in the philosophical scene in America. This is true because positions that have been dominant are being abandoned and many are searching for new visions of reality. In Royce's work are themes that are well worth contemplating in our search for new directions in philosophy. Among these themes are (1) his belief that one cannot ignore some sense of the absolute or eternal in dealing with truth and reality; (2) his understanding of science and scientific knowledge as interactive, communal, and socially grounded; (3) his strongly anti-Cartesian, social notions of self and self-knowledge; (4) his understanding of genuine community as an answer to the individualism-collectivism dilemma; and (5) his analysis of religion and religious insight, particularly as developed in *The Problem of Christianity*. It is to these themes that we now turn.

THE ABSOLUTE AND THE ETERNAL

It is in *The World and the Individual*[10] that Royce presents his fully developed argument for idealism, though he has argued many of the central themes in previous works such as *The Religious Aspects of Philosophy* and *The Conception of God*.[11] In addition to this positive approach to idealism he also criticizes other theories of being (reality) that he finds lacking in various ways and thus argues that idealism remains as the only viable option.

Royce's central argument for the Absolute rests on his belief, which he shared with the pragmatists, that thought is purposive and that an idea is an expression of a purpose.[12] Essentially Royce's argument for Absolutist Thought and Will is as follows:

Thought is purposive and the aim of thought is self-possession or self-containment or complete fulfillment of purpose.[13] Thus, a person aims to sing a tune and he sings it. The song itself is the experienced datum and it completely embodies the original purpose.

This self-containment of thought is really the embodiment in some form of what Royce calls the *internal* meanings of ideas. For, what an idea, say, of Mt. Everest, aims to find in its object, that which it is an idea *of,* which Royce calls the *external* meaning of the idea, is nothing whatever but the idea's own conscious purpose of will (internal idea). An idea cannot represent something external either falsely or truly without an intention that brings idea and its representative function into existence.

Further, Royce holds that the final embodiment of the internal meaning of an idea must be individual and determinate. It must be real. In his criticism of critical rationalism in *The World and the Individual,* Royce accepts and reaffirms the basic thesis of this position, namely, that the real is the standard for ideas. "To be," says Royce, "is precisely to fulfill or give warrant to ideas by making possible the experience that the ideas define."[14] Yet Royce felt that one must accept a further implication of this claim about the real, namely, that the real is determinate. Critical rationalism makes reality dependent on what is yet to be, namely, the experiences that would make a claim valid.

But, says Royce, this will not do because a merely possible experience could only answer some of our questions about an object whereas what is needed is the *full* answer. "For you are not put in the wrong by a reality to which you make no reference, and error is possible only concerning objects that we actually mean as our objects."[15] However vague my knowledge of an object may be, if my meaning has any significance, if the realm of validity is really valid, there must be a determinate object of my search such that when I know it or possess it fully I can say, "This is what I meant all along." There must be an identity between our initial purpose and our fulfilled purpose. The real, then, for Royce, is "the *complete embodiment, in individual form, and in final fulfillment, of the internal meaning of finite ideas.*"[16]

Royce held that for truth and error to make sense, the purposes of thought must be fulfilled. This leads directly to Absolute Thought and Will, for this is what gives the final embodiment of internal meanings, which fulfills thought. The Absolute, as Individual, freely chooses its world and by its "idea" (internal meaning) determines the experience (external meaning) in which it finds perfect, rational fulfillment. "The Divine Will is simply *that aspect of the Absolute which is expressed in the concrete and differentiated* individuality of the World."[17]

Thus, we see that Royce agreed with pragmatism on some very fundamental issues, but disagreed at a crucial point. Thus, he was in full agreement with the pragmatists on the purposiveness of thought and also on its practical aspect. For Royce, our ideas counsel our behavior toward objects and they get verification in experience.[18] But Royce believed that pragmatism could not fully account either for the public nature of truth nor for its eternal and absolute aspect. Appeal to verification, argued Royce, is appeal to the consensus of human experience, and this takes one beyond verification. Further, Royce argued, of such a type of experience pragmatism could give no account. Royce writes:

> Pragmatism presupposes a certain unity of meaning and coherence of experience taken as a whole—a unity which can never at any one moment be tested by any human being. Unless the propositions which assert the existence and describe the nature of this presupposed unity are themselves true, Pragmatism has no meaning. But if they are true, Pragmatism presupposes a truth whereof it gives no adequate account.[19]

Royce liked to put the issue another way. Truth, argued Royce, is practical, but it is also decisive; it involves an imperative. It is because of this belief that Royce could not accept the pragmatic notion of "expected working," for in pragmatism, no decision seemed to be involved. Royce writes, *"What is needed for truth is an issue and a decisive counsel.* The word 'expectation' is too deliberately vague . . . truth and falsity are present only in case issues are sharply joined—yes or no."[20]

Royce finds a perfect instance of what he means by absolute truth in an early essay by William James. James describes the situation of the mountain climber who has reached a place where he could not retreat and a chasm that he can possibly jump if he resolutely decides that he can make it. But, asks James, suppose, like Clifford, he is averse to believing without evidence and declines the will to believe. James concludes: He will "leave the matter undecided. I will not believe. . . . Whenever it becomes clear to me that I can leap I will leap. Till then, I decide nothing." But, notes Royce, it is here that James introduces an absolute truth, for "not to decide is itself a decision."[21]

Thus, we have an insight into what Royce called his Absolute Pragmatism. All thought is purposive, all truth is practical. However, Royce thought that the very practical nature of truth demanded its absoluteness. Further, Royce fully agreed with the pragmatists on the public nature of truth, namely, that truth is the ultimately agreed-upon belief, "the ideal limit of endless investigation." What is real establishes itself as the unanimous and "irresistable [sic] effect of inquiry," that is, in the confirmed beliefs of the scientific community. In fact, much is to be learned both about Royce's thought in general and particularly about those aspects of his thought worthy of further consideration when we examine his views on scientific knowledge. Thus, it is to these elements of the Roycean system we now turn.

SCIENTIFIC KNOWLEDGE AS PUBLIC COMMUNAL KNOWLEDGE

As indicated earlier, Royce had a lifelong interest in the nature of our knowledge of the external world, the nature of science and scientific inquiry. Thus, in his early work *The Spirit of Modern Philosophy,* he delineated the World of Description, the world of science, the publicly describable world that manifests reproducibility and permanence and the ability to be categorized and to which such notions as permanence of substance, uniformity, and causation can be applied.[22] However, for Royce all knowledge of external reality, all knowledge of nature, is born out of a social context, a communal foundation, and is utterly dependent upon it.

First of all, says Royce, community experience is that which distinguishes inner from outer, the outer world being the world whose presence can only be indicated to you by your definable communicable experience. Thus, it is social communication that accounts for the importance of spatial definiteness to externality. Royce writes:

> . . . Therefore, as only the definably localizable in space can be independently verified and agreed upon by a number of socially communicating beings, and as only what all can agree upon can stand the social test of externality, the principle that what is for all must, if in space at all, occupy a definite place of size and boundaries, becomes a relatively *a priori* principle for all the things of the verifiable world.[23]

The social grounding of physical knowledge, believed Royce, is also verified in the fact that more reliability is granted to the data of sight and touch than to the data of the other senses. These data and these qualities are those most open to social confirmation. I can see you touching and looking at an object. And if we hold or lift an object together, I can feel your grasp of the object just as surely as I feel the object. But in no similar way can I taste your tasting of the object, nor can I smell your smelling of the object.[24]

For Royce, then, our belief in the reality of nature and our knowledge of nature is inseparably bound up with our belief in the existence of our fellow beings. There is a fundamental relation between our being-with-others and our knowledge of nature. Royce writes:

> Whatever the deeper reality behind Nature may turn out to be—*our* Nature, the realm of matter and of laws with which our science and our popular opinions have to do, is a realm which we conceive as *known* or *knowable to various men* in precisely the general sense in which we regard it as known or knowable to our private selves. Take away the social factor in our present view of Nature, and you would alter the most essential of the characters possessed for us by that physical realm in which we all believe.[25]

With this kind of understanding of external knowledge, it is no surprise that we should find that Royce, fully in the spirit of Thomas Kuhn's *The Structure of Scientific Revolutions,* recognized and pointed to the essentially social and historical nature of science itself. Royce argues that it is social needs of various kinds that guided the development of scientific knowledge, and particularly its drive to mathematize and quantify natural objects. He writes:

> Thus, in all stages of science, the social need of exact and quantitative agreement about commercially important matters has led men to look, amongst natural processes, for phenomena capable of exact description, subject to rigid law, and suitable for meeting the social need for exact description of commercially valuable objects. . . . In terms

of this standard, man henceforth conceives reality, so that in the end, after a long process of this discipline, he at last today believes it *a priori* necessary that real natural objects, in so far as they are real, should be subject to quantitatively exact laws.[26]

Much of Royce's later philosophical concerns were with the nature of scientific methodology. Again and again he affirmed the human and social character of science. Royce was well aware of what today we call the "theory-ladenness" of data, the human constructive aspect of scientific knowledge. Science works with certain leading ideas or guiding principles that are molded, but not predetermined in their details, by experience. We let facts speak, says Royce, but we also "talk back" to facts. We interpret as well as report. The theories of science are human as well as objective. Science is an effort, for Royce, to bring "internal meanings" into harmony with external verifications.[27] Thus, Royce declares, "Science does indeed primarily reveal to us not what the universe is apart from man, but *how man interprets his own experience.*"[28] Thus, Royce is in agreement with the pragmatists' emphasis on the social basis of concepts as well as with their belief that ideas, scientific or otherwise, are tools, instruments for dealing with reality and for predicting consequences of behavior. He is also in harmony with the emphasis in contemporary philosophy of science on the human and relative character of scientific concepts, emphasized by individuals like Kuhn or Feyerabend.

However, he would also be sympathetic to the new realism being defended today among philosophers of science. Science is not purely relative nor a framework of prejudices. There is in scientific knowledge *both* coercive "thereness" and "meanings freely created." There is something of the object both immanent in and transcendental to human consciousness. Royce declared, "Neither God nor man faces any fact that has not something of the immediacy of a sense datum."[29]

However, Royce also attacked any notion of the merely given.[30] It is the function of the given, argued Royce, always to point beyond itself to something not now presented.[31] There is in science both the empirical and the metaempirical.

> . . . Common sense transcends the given blindly; special science transcends the given systematically . . . all alike use the given, depend upon it, and are insofar empirical. And all alike transcend the humanly given, go beyond it, and are insofar relatively meta-empirical.[32]

Once again, Royce wishes to stress the absolute as well as the relative nature of truth, the necessary as well as the contingent elements in knowledge. In fact, the clearest statement of Royce's "Absolute Pragmatism" occurs in his "Principles of Logic." Like Dewey, Royce stresses an instrumentalist approach to logic, namely, thought is constructive of reality, logic is logic of the will. Yet, says Royce, what the "absolute truths" of mathematics and logic reveal to us is the absolute nature of will. Royce's argument is that the "logical constant," namely, the concepts of "relation" and of "class," unite "creation" and "discovery," an element of freedom and arbitrariness and an element of absoluteness. The empirical, or "found," aspect can be seen by observing that it is an empirical fact that a particular physical relation, such as that of father and child, should be present in the world. It is also a matter of experience that there are physical objects to classify, and, insofar as these classifications are arbitrary, they are "creations" or "constructions." The classifications may be suggested to us by physical processes, and if our perceptions followed no other routine, there would be no need for these classifications.

But, says Royce, the concepts of "relation" and "class" and the order system in which they are involved have an absolute nature. Such logical facts as the difference beween *yes* and *no* are not dependent on the contingent aspect of our sensations. The logician's world does have some necessary elements. Their "necessity depends upon the fact that without them no rational activity of any kind is possible."[33]

Thus, Royce is in full agreement with the pragmatic interpretation of the analytic-synthetic distinction, namely, (1) that the term "analytic" is applicable to notions that are ultimate principles of our conceptual schematism and that gain this centrality because of their functional efficacy in unifying our knowledge; (2) that there are subjective, arbitrary elements involved in all theorizing; and (3) that the process of inquiry, the search for truth, is an open one. However, although we can make no premature claims about the "truth" of our scientific theories, nor about what "necessary" truths or principles there are, nevertheless, absolute and necessary truths are to be found. Truth is useful, but it is also *true*. The community consensus is actual and real and the fulfillment of thought's purpose is guaranteed.

Royce thus stands fully in accord with the pragmatic notion of the interactive nature of knowledge, and it is an excellent corrective to the completely passive notion espoused by positivism and logical empiricism. However, with his emphasis on the 'absolute' and 'the necessary,' Royce also provides an interesting alternative to the radical relativism put forth by contemporary philosophers of science such as Feyerabend. Indeed, I would argue that Royce's views on self and community take us beyond all the worn-out dichotomies of absolute-relative, self-world, mind-body, spiritualism-materialism, freedom-determinism, egoism-altruism, to a refreshing new holistic view. It is to these views that I now turn.

ROYCE ON THE SELF

In turning to Royce's view of the self, again like the pragmatists, we find Royce affirming a strongly anti-Cartesian view. The self is not a thing: "Whatever the self is it is not a thing. It is not, in Aristotle's sense, . . . a Substance."[34] Rather, the self is a process, having both a public, physical, and behavioral aspect and a private, inner aspect. First, Royce affirms that one cannot speak of the self as independent of and separate from either body or nature. Genetic and physiological elements are important in the development of a self, and one must see the affinity of conscious human life with all of nature. Thus, in the second volume of *The World and the Individual,* Royce asserts: ". . . we have no right whatever to speak of really unconscious Nature but only of uncommunicative Nature."[35] Royce believes that unconscious and conscious nature share the following four features: "(1) irreversibility; (2) communication; (3) formation of habits; and (4) evolutionary growth."[36] Though there are difficulties with this view of affinities between human beings and nature, it is an insight not only related to the process philosophy of Alfred North Whitehead and the new physics of David Bohm, but also one that has merit for recent discussions of mind-brain-body relations and of animal language, intelligence, and rights.

In addition to stressing the continuity of the human self with nature, Royce equally emphasizes the fully public and empirical character of the self. "The concept of the human self, like the concept of Nature, comes to us, first, as an empirical concept, founded upon a certain class of experiences."[37] The self is a totality of facts, both public and private. Thus, among the public facts that both self and others may observe and comment on are the predominantly corporeal ones such as countenance, body, clothing, and physical actions.[38] And if these facts radically changed, Royce would argue, so would the self. Bodily continuity and the sense of body do function as one criterion, of self-identity, for Royce. "Always the contents which constitute the Ego . . . have been associated with relatively warm and enduring organic sensations viz. sensations coming from within our bodies."[39]

In addition to the public, corporeal facts of self, there is, for Royce, also a set of inner private facts equally important for the notion of an empirical self. There is the "equally empirical and phenomenal Self of the inner life, the series of states of consciousness, the feelings, thoughts, desires, memories, emotions, moods."[40] These, Royce argues, both I and others would acknowledge as belonging to me and going to make up what I am.

Royce, then, unlike some modern behaviorists, sees consciousness and states of consciousness as important aspects of the self. And, like James and Husserl, Royce, as can be seen from our discussion of "internal meanings" of ideas, stresses also the intentionality of consciousness.[41] Mental acts are always directed toward objects and also intend the object as having such-and-such meaning. Objects are also viewed in such-and-such way, that is, from specific perspectives. Thus, like James, Royce discusses the role of selective attention in all acts of consciousness, that is, attention selects only a few of the many impressions impinging on our sensibilities. Many such impressions slip away unretained; attention is thus a modifying, transforming process.[42] We see the world from a particular, often narrow point of view. This, Royce thought, demanded a need for transcendence of self and thus for checking things out with my fellow beings. Objectivity is intersubjectivity. External knowledge, for Royce, as we have already seen, is grounded in social interaction.

However, self-knowledge is equally so grounded. Royce argues that our very self-consciousness arises out of a social contrast between the self and the not-self, between what is mine and what is not mine. Royce writes: "I affirm that our empirical self-consciousness, from moment to moment depends upon a series of contrast effects, whose psychological origin lies in our literal social life. . . ."[43] "Nobody amongst us men comes to self-consciousness, so far as I know except under the persistent influence of his social fellows."[44]

The social process by which self-consciousness develops is seen by Royce as a series of imitative acts. As the child imitates the acts of others, ideas about the meaning of these acts are acquired. Gradually, awareness develops of a basic contrast marking a boundary between two sets of mental contents, perceptions of others' deeds and meanings and perceptions of one's own deeds and meanings. The former appear as uncontrollable and belonging to another, while the latter have connected with them a sense of control. Ego is discovered in the awareness of self-control.

Thus, the self is developed out of a process of social interaction and further self is never known directly but only through interaction and interpretation. The self's continuity is born of community experience and dialogue, dialogue between self and others and dialogue with oneself. Self-reflection, for Royce, is interpretation of self to self. Suppose I remember a former promise. I am then interpreting this bit of my past self to my future self, and I may say to myself, "I am committed to do thus and so." "In brief," says Royce, "my idea of myself is an interpretation of my past—linked also with an interpretation of my hopes and intentions as to my future."[45] The self is a temporal, ongoing process, unified by continual communication. The self continually confers meaning on itself. This is Royce's second criterion of self-identity.

This brings us to the third criterion, namely, ethical value. Self is an expression of purpose. I am an intended future because I set goals and make value judgments about what is worth doing, thinking, seeking. Like Sartre, Royce sees self in terms of moral activity, but, unlike with Sartre, it is not an individualistic, anxiety-filled, forlorn decision maker. A self makes its decisions always in a social context contrasting its plan and ideal with those of others.

> By this meaning of my life plan, by this possession of an ideal, by this Intent always to remain another than my fellows despite my divinely planned unity with them—by this and not by possession of any Soul-Substance, I am defined and created a Self.[46]

In other words, my social and moral self is the result of a dialectic dialogue between self and others. This dialogic process has two important characteristics about it. First, both contact and separateness, similarity and contrast, imitation and creativity, accommodation and nonaccommodation are involved. The "other" allows me to create an external, social self by providing roles I can act out and imitate and by allowing me to internalize the objectified world of culture, to become socialized.

On the other hand, I also must begin to have a distinct sense of my own self and action. I must carve out my own distinctive biography and develop my own individuality. If social conditions prohibit such or I fail to exercise my creativity, I may accommodate myself too much to others and become the "mass person" so dreaded by the existentialists.

Second, the interactive process of self and others is a delicate one and its product, an individual self, is a fragile thing. The formative power of the social situation is immensely strong. This is why we must equally stress the creative role of the individual in making of self *and* the obligation of the community to foster true individuals. Further, the interactive process can develop individuals who are too individualistic, too private, too unsocialized, too rebellious, too unsoftened by social sympathy. In other words, rampant individualism or stifling collectivism are two dangers to be avoided. Royce dealt with these dangers in his *The Problem of Christianity,* where he develops his theory of community. It is to this theory we now turn.

ROYCE'S THEORY OF COMMUNITY

In *The Problem of Christianity* Royce discusses the conditions for the existence of a genuine community. In presenting these, we will be summarizing a number of Roycean ideas previously discussed, thus providing evidence both for the development and continuity of Royce's thought. Thus, the first condition of community is "the power of the individual to extend his life, in ideal fashion, so as to regard it as including past and future events which lie far away in time, and which he does not now personally remember."[47] In other words, the community must have selves with chosen life plans and yet who are also capable of extending the search for meaning beyond their personal plans. And they must be creative, truly individual selves, not mere conformers to the social will.

Communication among selves that involves attentive listening to the ideas and hopes of others is the second condition of true community. Community is, for Royce, a product of interpretation. This is conceived by Royce as a third form of mental activity and knowledge in addition to perception and cognition. It is triadic in nature and involves mediation between two minds. Thus, in interpreting Royce's thought to you, I, (1) the interpreter, who must both understand Royce and know something of my audience, make accessible (2) the object, Royce's thought to (3) a mind, you, to whom the interpretation is addressed. Three items, then, are brought into relationship by this interpretation. Further, the relationship is nonsymmetrical, that is, unevenly arranged with respect to all three of the terms. If the order were reversed, it would change the process.

Further, each of the terms of the relation corresponds to the three dimensions of time: past, present, and future. Thus, Royce's work, written in the past, I interpret to you now for your future interpretation. Thus, interpretation is a temporal process and is irreversible, partial, and ideally infinite. Once I have spoken or written, what has been said cannot be revoked. But neither is it the final word, for, unless arbitrarily stopped, there will be future interpretations of Royce and the process will continue.

Interpretation is also a process that creates community. It involves (1) respect for selves as dynamos of ideas and purposes; (2) the will to interpret, which involves (a) a sense of dissatisfaction with partial meanings and the narrowness of one's own view of things and (b) the aim to unite; and (3) reciprocity and mutuality. Thus, in interpreting Royce to you, I had to be respectful of and loyal to Royce's thought, I had to be somewhat dissatisfied with my own views and ideas, and I had to put my ideas beside those of Royce so that they might interact. In so doing, I risked having my ideas changed and in conveying Royce's thought to you I now risk being told I am wrong and having the community of interpretation rectify my error. By attending to my interpretation of Royce, you chose to enter into the community of interpretation and you may risk having your ideas changed. If the attempt at interpretation is successful, a new meaning will come forth and a new unity of consciousness will be achieved. I will have united my mind and your mind with Royce's in a shared understanding.

Indeed, Royce's third condition for community is that unity actually be achieved. Each of the individuals involved must share a common past and/or a common future, that is, it becomes a community of memory and/or hope. As in the case of the self, community is the bringing forth of an embodied ideal. It involves the commitment of true selves to a higher goal they share. The community, like the self, is both one and many. Royce declares, "A community does not become one . . . by virtue of any reduction or melting of those various selves into a single merely present self or into a mass of passing experience."[48] In true community, there must be shared understanding and cooperation, genuine intersubjective interaction and sharing.

This is quite clear from the six subconditions for community which Royce outlines and Frank M. Oppenheim so clearly paraphrases.[49] These subconditions are: (1) each individual must direct his own deeds of cooperation; (2) each individual must encourage, stimulate, correct, and enjoy the deeds of others, just as do members of a really fine orchestra; (3) each member must appreciate the efforts of every member and understand that only by coordinating efforts can the community achieve its goals; (4) each must be aware of the future hopes of the community; (5) each self should identify his own goals with those of the community; and (6) other selves in the community must concur in accepting each as a fellow member of the community.

These conditions and subconditions are presented by Royce as ideals to be aimed at or achieved. He is fully aware of the realities and dangers of real communal life. As indicated earlier, in *The Problem of Christianity,* Royce provides a careful analysis of how highly cultivated societies train their members both in individualism and collectivism.[50] The individual gains self-consciousness by opposing his will to the social will, while the social will enflames self-will. The socially trained individual is taught not only to value his own will by opposition to the collective will, but also to respect the collective will. Collectivism, by training the individual to pride himself on his own will, at the same time trains this self in collectivism. *"Individualism and collectivism are tendencies, each of which, as our social order grows, intensifies the other.*[51]

Royce further deals with the interactive process of self and other and the difficulty of building community when, in his *War and Insurance,* he analyzes what he calls "essentially dangerous community," namely, any social situation in which only two persons are involved. Royce argues for the need of a third party, an interpreter, to reconcile and mediate the interests of such dangerous pairs as borrower and lender and plaintiff and defendant.[52]

We recall that the work of interpretation asks us to transcend all stopping places, all dyadic relations, all dangerous dualisms that bind us to partial views, for example, materialism versus spiritualism and individualism versus collectivism. However, Royce was very much cognizant of what he identified as an aspect of man that worked against the development of genuine selves and communities, namely, original sin. Original sin expresses itself in the tendency to isolation and the proneness to betray one's ideals. Royce believed that the failure to sound to the depths the original sin of man, the social animal, and of the natural social order he creates leads to many social problems and to a misunderstanding of those conditions that make community possible. Thus, Royce tackled the nature of original sin and its overcoming in *The Problem of Christianity* and other works. It is to this analysis that we now turn.

RELIGION, ORIGINAL SIN, AND THE BELOVED COMMUNITY

To examine Royce's analysis of sin and guilt, I believe, is especially appropriate for this time. This is so for at least three reasons. First, Royce recognizes that sin expresses itself both individually and communally and thus draws our attention to the fact that an individual's sinful attitude and behavior and consequent redemption cannot be analyzed and understood in isolation from the individual's relations with others. Second, Royce's understanding of sin and moral development is quite contemporary. It bears resemblances not only to Freudian and existentialist ideas about guilt but also to the moral development theories of psychologists Kohlberg and Erickson. However, Royce also has insights which go beyond these analyses in important ways. Finally, Royce, I believe, delicately balances stress on the depth of human sin and emphasis on human freedom and responsibility for sinful failings.

In all three of his major works on religion—*The Religious Aspects of Philosophy, The Sources of Religious Insight,* and *The Problem of Christianity*[53]—Royce argues that the essence of any religion is the postulate that man needs to be saved.[54] The need to be saved involves, for Royce, two central ideas, namely, (1) that each individual has an ideal goal or standard in terms of which he estimates the meaning and value of his life and (2) that the conditions of human life work against the achievement of this goal and thus toward rendering one's life a senseless failure because of the falling short of one's true goal.[55]

One condition that works toward the failure to reach one's ideal goal is the very finitude of human consciousness. It rests on our propensity to narrow our focus of attention, to be overly selective. "*Our finitude means, then, an actual inattention—a lack of successful interest, at this conscious instant, in more than a very few details of the Universe.*"[56] Royce is clear that this aspect of consciousness is not itself sinful, but rather provides the condition for sin. It is in human failure to seek to overcome this narrowness of view that sin resides.

Royce believes human sinfulness to involve two aspects. First, there is the sin of irresponsiveness. Because of our tendency toward narrowing our attention, in order fully to develop as human beings, we need deliberately to develop our powers of response to the universe around us. What is required is as much openness as possible. Sin occurs when we deliberately choose to narrow our focus or, more specifically, for Royce, choose to forget what we already know. It is in fact to deliberately disregard a goal of value which we have already identified and established for ourselves. "To sin is *consciously to choose to forget,* through a narrowing of the field of attention, an Ought that one already recognizes."[57]

The second aspect of sin, for Royce, is the sin of pride. Here what is involved is a lack of humility about our limited grasp of truth and reality. We stop the process of inquiry and assume that we have an absolute grasp of reality and truth. What is involved is an absolutizing of the finite. There is inordinate responsiveness to one's own present interests.[58]

In a sense, sin is the failure to recognize that reality and human nature have infinite dimensions. You will recall that, for Royce, the self is to be seen as an ethical category.

That is, one's task is to realize a life plan, to accomplish a unique task so that I am a self and a self who is nobody else. This possibility of aspiring to a goal outside of oneself is the possibility of a demand for self-transcendence.

But self-actualization and self-transcendence are closely related to the finitude of our consciousness. In order to achieve self-actualization, I need to seek self-knowledge. But in this quest I fall prey to my narrowness of view and to sinful, deliberate self-forgetting. Royce writes:

> Nothing is more obvious about the natural course of our lives than is the *narrowness* of view to which we are usually subject. We are not only the victims of conflicting motives, but we are all too narrow to know that this is true. For we see our various interests, so to speak, one at a time. We forget one while living out another. And, so, we are prone to live many lives, seldom noting how ill harmonized they are. . . . We thus come to spend our days thwarting ourselves through the results of our fickleness, yet without knowing who it is that thwarts us. . . . The deeper tragedies of life thus result from this our narrowness of view.[59]

We have already discussed Royce's affirmation of the social grounding of self-consciousness. This belief becomes even more important in this context, for it is obvious to Royce that we need our fellows to help us gain insight into our self and to achieve self-transcendence. Social relations broaden our outlook because they require us to deal with other points of view.

> . . . Our social responsibilities tend to set limits to our fickleness. Social discipline removes some of our inner conflicts by teaching us not to indulge our caprices. Human companionship may calm, may steady our vision, may bring us into intercourse with what is in general much better than a man's subliminal self, namely, his public, his humane, his greater social self, wherein he finds his soul and its interest writ large.[60]

Contact with our fellow human beings thus helps us expand our ideas, broaden our interests, and develop a more social self. Further, our fellow human beings help us judge and refine our behavior and therefore to have a more proper estimation of ourselves. "It is my knowledge of my fellows' doings, and of their behavior toward me—it is this which gives me the basis for the sort of comparison that I use whenever I succeed in more thoughtfully observing myself or estimating myself."[61]

This dependency on others for self-unification, self-knowledge, and self-transcendence, however, as already noted, has negative as well as positive aspects. The very social nature of our existence, in fact, also lays down the second condition for sin. And again, the social order can lead a person to sin in two specific ways. As indicated earlier, Royce saw clearly that in the development of social order, individualism and collectivism are two tendencies that feed on and intensify each other. The more the social will expresses itself, either individuals become more aware of their personal wants, choices, and ideals or individuals accommodate themselves more and more to the collective will.[62] Thus, the social order either constantly fosters that deeply rooted egoism by which man orients everything to himself or it encourages a person to give into the collective will and become a "they," a part of the crowd rather than a unique self.

The social order, then, tempts human beings into the sin of egoism or pride. "The social order, in training individuals, therefore breeds conscious sinners."[63] What is involved is an absolutizing of the self, a withdrawal into a world of self-sufficiency. It also is an attempt to mold the world and others according to one's own self-will. Royce writes: "It is always abstractly possible, therefore, for the Self to conceive its search for self-expression as simply an undertaking not to obey, but to subdue, to its own present purpose, the world which is beyond."[64]

The other sin to which humans are tempted by the social order is that of self-forgetfulness and self-loss. One fails to achieve true self-actualization, to fulfill a life plan that marks one out as uniquely a self different from other selves. One refuses to take responsibility for one's existence. One loses oneself in the crowd. Thus, Royce writes of guilt in terms of self-loss.

> Now, the sense of guilt, if deep and pervasive and passionate, involves at least a dim recognition that there is some central aim of life and that one has come hopelessly short of that aim . . . the true sense of guilt in its greatest manifestation involves a confession that the whole self is somehow tainted, the whole life, for the time being, wrecked.[65]

How, then, can one escape sin and guilt? For Royce the answer is an act of loyalty and an act of grace. The act of loyalty is the individual's decision to love and be loyal to a community and thus to lead a life of devotion to that community. If the community is genuine as well as the loyalty, there will be a union of individual and social will, not a conformity of individual to social will, but a genuine blending. There will be genuine self-fulfillment, for the individual will achieve his or her own unique goal, and yet there will also be self-transcendence in that the individual genuinely chooses and loves the goal of the community. Royce writes:

> . . . even if the individual needs his social world as a means of grace and a gateway to salvation, the social order, in turn, needs individuals that are worth saving and can never be saved itself unless it expresses itself through the deeds and inner lives of souls deeply conscious of the dignity of selfhood, of the infinite worth of unique and intensely conscious personal life.[66]

Thus, while the individual must truly value and love the community and each of its members, equally the community must truly love the individual and value his or her uniqueness.

Here is where, for Royce, an act of grace is required. Such a community can only be created by a potent, loving, and loyal individual, who, acting as a leader, must declare that for him the community is real. In such a leader, and in his spirit, the community will begin its own life—that is, if the leader has the power to create what he loves. Royce believes that for Christianity, for example, there was such a leader in the person of Jesus Christ and that, therefore, the work of Jesus in establishing a genuine community provides the path to Christian salvation. Royce writes:

> We know how Paul conceives the beginning of the new life wherein Christian salvation is to be found. This beginning he refers to the work of Christ. . . . He both knew and loved his community before it existed on earth. . . . On earth he called into this community its first members. He suffered and died that it might have life. Through his death and in his life the community lives. *He is now identical with the spirit of this community.*"[67]

The establishment of the Christian community and of any saving community rests, is achieved, through an act of grace. Grace involves a spiritual bond uniting many individuals into a genuine union, a spiritual bond established by the originating power of the individual creating the community and whose spirit still guides it. It also involves love, love of the community by all its members and love of each member by all other members of the community.[68] In other words, it is a genuine community as described by Royce, a community of shared past and common hope, a community of shared deeds, and a community of communication and interpretation. Royce calls it the beloved community, and human salvation lies in loyalty and love of such a community.

However, Royce realized how deep was the human propensity to sin, and thus that is not all there is to say. There is another and even more tragic type of sin and that is betrayal or treason. After finding his cause, an individual may betray it. The traitor is one who has had an ideal and has loved it with all his heart, soul, mind, and strength, but has been deliberately false to his cause.

Such an act, believed Royce, can only be overcome by an act of atonement. The sinner must be reconciled both to himself and to the community. Love must be restored, but "it will be the love for the member who *has been a traitor,* and the tragedy of the treason will permanently form part in and of this love."[69] How, then, is atonement to be accomplished?

The atonement must be accomplished by the community or, more likely, by an individual acting on behalf of the community as an incarnation, so to speak, of the spirit of the community. It involves a creative act that responds directly to the treasonous act but that also makes the world better than it was before the blow of treason fell on it. *"The world as transformed by this creative deed, is better than it would have been had all else remained the same, but had that deed of treason not been done at all."*[70]

Religion, then, for Royce, addresses the human being's need for salvation. It is to make one aware of the sins of narrowness of vision, pride, and betrayal. It also provides an answer to the overcoming of these sins, namely, love and loyalty and active deeds of atonement. It is now time to assess briefly Royce's analysis of religion, sin, and salvation as well as some of his other claims.

SUMMARY AND ASSESSMENT

Our assessment will begin with his claims about religion and move backward to assess his views of community, self, science and scientific knowledge, and the absolute in truth and reality.

Royce's analysis of religion, and particularly of sin and salvation, I believe, provide us with useful insights. First of all, his view of sin captures the insight of Martin Luther's "*Simul vist us et peccator*," simultaneously justified and sinner. Though I find my cause, my salvation, I can betray it and fall again into sin. In other words, conversion and salvation are ongoing processes, not a single event. Further, the call to loyalty is a call to critical faith and humble awareness that what we take to be worthy of our loyalty may be for this time and place, but not for all times and places and it may even be a mistaken loyalty. It is a continual call to openness and to constant guarding against narrowness of vision. To declare our goal as an absolute is a risk, and we must continually ask, is this providing true self-fulfillment. To have too narrow a vision of the absolute is idolatry, and thus we must follow the Roycean principle of loyalty and ask, Does my allegiance to this goal expand knowledge and community?

Second, Royce's view of sin and salvation as both personal and communal is a needed insight. Sin is sin against self, an act of self-betraying in not achieving one's fullest potential. It has consequences for me. But sin affects others; it has consequences for them. Personally to repent and achieve salvation is not enough. There must be attempts to heal the community. The sinner and others must move out in acts of love and atonement. If a lie is the act of betrayal, an act of truth and openness must occur that increases the sense of trust in the community and makes a sense of individual obligation higher and stronger. Further, it is the sense of community that allows the individual to reach out in love and action. Dietrich Bonhoffer states the issue well in his *Sanctorum Communio*.

> The man living in the fellowship of the I-Thou relationship is given the certainty that he is loved and through his faith in Christ receives the strength to be able to love in return.[71]
>
> . . . It is grace, nothing but grace that we are allowed to live in community with Christian brethren. . . . Communal life is again being recognized by Christians today as the grace that it is, as the extraordinary, the roses and lilies of the Christian life.[72]

Royce is insightful, I believe, in his stress on community as an important part of the religious message. And he calls upon us to be less complacent about the genuineness of community in Christian churches where saved individuals meet only once a week for worship. Indeed, he raises interesting questions for other religions where the emphasis seems much more on individual salvation than upon community and community action— except for Judaism, which has a long history of covenant relationship and consequent moral action.

What, then, about Royce's views on community? Certainly, Royce's views on both self and community provide a healthy corrective to the atomic individualism of the existentialists, who stress self-contained independent existence, the lonely, forlorn, anxiety-stricken self. For someone like Sartre, for example, togetherness with selves is accidental and external and even awful, for others always have "the book," the judgmental attitude, and "Hell is other people." For Royce, it is true that judgment by others plays a key role in self and moral development, but it is also true that it is others who help relieve our moral burden and even carry out acts of atonement for our treacherous deeds.

Further, our world is an ever increasingly interdependent world, and Royce's attempts to deal with dangerous conflicts via mediation and interpretation makes a great deal of sense. Royce's work on the characteristics of genuine community vis-à-vis false communities merits much attention. Neither individualism nor collectivism makes total sense in analyzing social relations, as many sociologists have recognized. Rather, a society is no mere aggregation of properties of its components, but rather involves additional characteristics derived from relationships among these components. The uniqueness of the individuals in relations as well as the uniqueness of their various relations must be recognized.

Before leaving Royce's views on community, however, it must be pointed out that his positive evaluation of community seems to neglect at times, though not always, the sins community can perpetuate on the individual, such as the infringements of freedom and dignity of a totalitarian state or even an overly paternalistic society that commits its mentally ill to institutionalization for "their own good and care."

Royce's holistic anti-Cartesian view of the self, so in concert with that of James and Dewey and other pragmatists, is a wholesome corrective to the current reductionism of behaviorists or identity-state materialists who would reduce self to a repertoire of behavior or collections of brain states. Royce fully recognizes both the role of genetic, physiological, and behavioral components of the self and the inner, conscious, intentional states recognized by humanistic psychology. Further, Royce affirms clearly the value dimension of human experience in his view that the self is essentially an ethical concept. In an age when science and technology are raising tremendous value questions for humankind, questions of rights and goals cannot be ignored. The whys of such technologies as genetic screening and engineering, of psychotechnology and computer-based artificial intelligence are extremely important, and recognition of the human being as a unique life plan worthy of consideration and respect is a valuable emphasis, both for the individual and the community.

This brings us directly to Royce's views on science. Long before Thomas Kuhn and a little before Husserl, Royce recognized that denial of the self-constructive features of human experience leads to a lack of critical reflection on science itself. The scientist-in-action is a creative knower, an interpreter and selector of ideas. Observation is a highly selective process, data collection is always guided by hypothesis and theory. We are well aware of these aspects of science today, and Royce fully recognized them, as did others like Peirce, James, and Dewey. However, Royce also recognized, as did Peirce, that emphasis on the interpretive nature of human consciousness and science as a human endeavor with certain guiding ideas and purposes had to be combined with the very real stubbornness of fact. Royce writes:

> Man is not merely made for science, but science is made for man. It expresses his deepest intellectual needs, as well as his careful observation. It is an effort to bring internal meanings into harmony with external verifications. It attempts to control as well as to submit, to conceive with rational unity as well as to accept data . . . the theories of

science are human, as well as objective, internally rational as well as (when it is possible) subject to external tests.[73]

This, of course, is closely related to the transactional theory of knowledge of the pragmatists. But this leads also to Royce's continual belief in and stress on the absolute in thought, truth, and reality. Today, when an antimetaphysical stance is still part of the philosophical scene and when relativism—all views are equal in importance—is also much defended, Royce's views on the absolute become especially illuminative. One may or may not be persuaded by the logic of the matter. For example, why must thought fulfill itself or why must one be certain that truth is guaranteed? But a philosopher who can argue for both an affirmation of finality and a strong note of future seeking is at least worthy of deep consideration. Thus, Royce affirmed truth as decisive. It was a decision by Absolute Thought to affirm this world and other.

Yet Royce also continually wrote against any false dichotomizing of reality or any absolutizing of the finite, whether in religion or science. Both science and religion, as well as philosophy, are engaged in a common enterprise, namely, the endless task of inquiry, self, and community. Philosophy is, and science and religion should be, for Royce, communities of love for the truth, openness, and responsiveness to experience. "The very existence of science, then, is an illustration of our thesis that the universe is endlessly engaged in the spiritual task of interpreting its own life."[74] As for religion, Royce's message is clear: *"Look forward to the human and visible triumph of no form of the Christian Church."*[75]

NOTES

1. Thus, Morton White writes of Royce: "But, as the saying goes, the bigger they are, the harder they fall; and when the mighty Royce fell, it was as if the temple of American philosophy itself had collapsed." Morton White, *Science and Sentiment: Philosophical Thought from Jonathan Edwards to John Dewey* (New York: Oxford University Press, 1972), p. 239.
2. *The Spirit of Modern Philosophy* (Boston: Houghton Mifflin & Company, 1892), p. 10.
3. *Lectures on Modern Idealism,* ed. J. Loewenberg (New Haven: Yale University Press, 1919).
4. Frank Oppenheim, "Josiah Royce's Intellectual Development: A Hypothesis," *Idealistic Studies* 6 (January 1976): 85–102; and *Royce's Voyage Down Under* (Lexington: University Press of Kentucky, 1980).
5. Daniel Robinson has provided us an excellent anthology of these works: *Royce's Logical Essays* (Dubuque: William C. Brown Company, 1951).
6. For a record of this seminar, see Harry T. Costello, *Josiah Royce's Seminar, 1913–1914,* ed. Grover Smith (New Brunswick, N.J.: Rutgers University Press, 1963).
7. See Fernando R. Molina, "Notes by C. I. Lewis on Royce's Theory of Categories," *Philosophical Research Archives* 1543, p. 183.
8. Mary Briody Mahowald, *An Idealistic Pragmatism* (The Hague: Martinus Nijhoff, 1971), pp. 175–176.
9. *Lectures on Modern Idealism,* p. 258.
10. *The World and the Individual,* 2 vols. (New York: Dover, 1959).
11. *The Religious Aspect of Philosophy* (Boston: Houghton Mifflin & Company, 1885) and *The Conception of God* (New York: The Macmillan Company, 1897).
12. Royce writes: "By the word 'Idea' . . . I shall mean in the end any state of consciousness, whether simple or complex, which, when present, is then and there viewed as at least the partial expression or embodiment of a single conscious purpose." *The World and the Individual,* Vol. I, p. 22.
13. Royce had already argued this in "On Purpose in Thought," in *Fugitive Essays,* ed. J. Loewenberg (Cambridge, Mass.: Harvard University Press, 1920), pp. 216–219.

14. *The World and the Individual,* Vol. I, p. 203.

15. *The Conception of God,* p. 457.

16. *The World and the Individual,* Vol. I, p. 339. Italics are Royce's.

17. *The Conception of God,* p. 202.

18. Royce writes: *A judgement is true if it so guides or counsels our conduct through its interpretation of the object that the deed which it counsels meets our intent, i.e., fulfills as far as it goes the will that we have in mind when following this counsel we choose this.*" "Philadelphia Lectures," Unpublished Papers, Folio 83, No. 2, p. 13. Italics are Royce's.

19. "Error and Truth," in James Hastings, ed., *The Encyclopedia of Religion and Ethics* (New York: Charles Scribner's Sons, 1912), pp. 98–124. This was reprinted in *Royce's Logical Essays* and this quote appears on p. 118 of the reprint.

20. "Philadelphia Lectures," Unpublished Papers, Folio 83, No. 2, p. 13.

21. *Ibid.,* No. 3, p. 4.

22. *The Spirit of Modern Philosophy* (Boston: Houghton Mifflin & Company, 1896), pp. 392ff.

23. "The External World and Social Consciousness," *The Philosophical Review,* 3, 5 (September 1894): 520.

24. *Ibid.,* p. 519.

25. *The World and the Individual,* Vol. II, pp. 165–166. Italics are Royce's.

26. "The Social Factors of the Human Intellect," Unpublished Papers, Folio 68, No. 3 (1897), pp. 18–19.

27. Introduction to H. Poincaré, *The Foundations of Science* (New York: The Science Press, 1913). Reprinted in *Royce's Logical Essays,* pp. 279–280.

28. "Richmond Lectures," Unpublished Papers, Folio 81 (1897), p. 34.

29. "A Critical Study of Reality," Unpublished Papers, Folio 81 (1897), p. 34.

30. "On Definitions and Debates," *The Journal of Philosophy* 9, (January 1912): 85–100.

31. "Columbia Lectures," Unpublished Papers, Folio 74, No. 5 (1910), pp. 52–53.

32. "A Critical Study of Reality," Unpublished Papers, Folio 81, (1897), pp. 34–35, 35a–b.

33. "The Principles of Logic," in *Royce's Logical Essays,* p. 363.

34. *The World and the Individual,* Vol. II, p. 268.

35. *Ibid.,* p. 225.

36. *Ibid.,* pp. 219–224.

37. *Ibid.,* p. 256.

38. *Ibid.,* p. 257.

39. *Ibid.,* p. 264.

40. *Ibid.,* p. 257.

41. For a discussion of some relationships between the thought of Royce and Husserl, see Jacquelyn Ann Kegley, "Royce and Husserl: Some Parallels and Food for Thought," *Transactions of the Charles S. Peirce Society* 14 (Summer 1978): 184–199.

42. *The Religious Aspect of Philosophy* (Boston: Houghton Mifflin & Company, 1885), p. 314. For a summary discussion of James's views on the nature of the consciousness, see Owen J. Flanagan, Jr., *The Science of the Mind* (Cambridge, Mass.: Bradford Books, 1984), pp. 23–53.

43. *The World and the Individual,* Vol. II, p. 200.

44. *Ibid.,* pp. 261–262.

45. *The Problem of Christianity,* Vol. II, p. 42.

46. *The World and the Individual,* Vol. II, p. 276. Italics are Royce's.

47. *The Problem of Christianity,* Vol. II, pp. 60–61.

48. *Ibid.,* p. 67.

49. Frank M. Oppenheim, "A Roycean Road to Community," *International Philosophical Quarterly* 10 (September 1970): 341–377.

50. *The Problem of Christianity,* Vol. I, pp. 127–155.

51. *Ibid.,* p. 152.

52. *War and Insurance* (New York: The Macmillan Company, 1914), pp. 30–35 and passim.

53. *The Religious Aspects of Philosophy* (Boston: Houghton Mifflin & Company, 1885); *The Sources of Religious Insight,* The Brass Lectures, Lake Forest College, 1911 (New York: Charles Scribner's Sons, 1912); and *The Problem of Christianity.*

54. *The Sources of Religious Insight,* pp. 8–9.

55. *Ibid.,* pp. 12, 28–29.

56. *The World and the Individual,* Vol. II, p. 59.

57. *Ibid.,* p. 359.

58. For an excellent analysis of Royce's understanding of sin, see Paul Ramsey, "The Idealistic View of Moral Evil," *Philosophy and Phenomenological Research* (June 1946): 554–589.

59. *The World and the Individual,* Vol. I, pp. 48–49.

60. *Ibid.,* p. 55.

61. *The Problem of Christianity,* pp. 130–131.

62. *Ibid.*, p. 145.

63. *Ibid.*

64. *The World and the Individual,* Vol. II, p. 349.

65. *The Sources of Religious Insight,* p. 66.

66. *Ibid.*, p. 60.

67. *The Problem of Christianity,* Vol. I, pp. 186–187.

68. *Ibid.*, p. 192.

69. *Ibid.*, p. 302.

70. *Ibid.*, p. 308. Italics are Royce's.

71. Dietrich Bonhoffer, *Sanctorum Communio: A Dogmatic Inquiry into the Sociology of the Church,* trans. R. Gregor Smith from the 3rd German ed., 1960 (London: Collins, 1963), p. 119.

72. Dietrich Bonhoffer, *Life Together* (New York: Harper & Row, 1954), p. 21.

73. *Royce's Logical Essays,* pp. 279–280.

74. *The Problem of Christianity,* pp. 429–430.

75. *Ibid.*, p. 430.

The Religious Problems and the Theory of Being

In the literature of Natural Religion at least three different conceptions of the subject are represented. The first of these conceptions regards Natural Religion as a search for what a well-known phrase has called "the way through Nature to God." If we accept this conception, we begin by recognizing both the existence of the physical world and the validity of the ordinary methods and conceptions of the special sciences of nature. We undertake to investigate what light, if any, the broader generalizations of natural science, when once accepted as statements about external reality, throw upon the problems of religion. It belongs, for instance, to this sort of inquiry to ask: What countenance does the present state of science give to the traditional argument from Design?

The second of our three conceptions views Religion less as a doctrine to be proved or disproved through a study of the external world than as a kind of consciousness whose justification lies in its rank amongst the various inner manifestations of our human nature. Man, so this conception holds, is essentially a religious being. He has religion because his own inmost nature craves it. If you wish, then, to justify religion, or even to comprehend it, you must view it, not as a theory to be proved or disproved by an appeal to external reality, but rather as a faith to be estimated through reference to the inner consciousness of those who need, who create, and who enjoy religion. From this point of view the study of Natural Religion concerns itself less with proof than with confession, with a taxing of interior values, and with a description of the religious experience of mankind. A somewhat extended interpretation of this point of view treats the purely historical study of the various religions of mankind as a contribution to our comprehension of Natural Religion.

But a third conception of the study of Natural Religion remains. This third view identifies the doctrine in question with the fundamental Philosophy of Religion. It is the Nature of Things, viewed in the light of the most critical examination of our reason, that is now the object of an inquiry into Natural Religion. The problems at issue are, for this view, those of Aristotle's *Metaphysics,* of Fichte's *Wissenschaftslehre,* of Hegel's *Logik,*—of all the undertakings that, in the history of thought, have most directly attempted the contemplation of Being as Being. For our first conception the student of Natural Religion, having accepted the natural knowledge of his time as valid, and not having attempted to delve beneath the foundations of that knowledge, seeks to interpret external nature in the light of religious interests. For our second conception Natural Religion is viewed simply as the voice of human nature itself, whose faith is to be expressed, whose ideals are to be recorded, whose will and whose needs are to be, above all, consulted and portrayed, since, for this view, the consciousness of those who believe in religious truth is, when once made articulate, its own apology. But, for our third conception, the office of the student of Natural Religion is to deal with the most fundamental metaphysical problems. He is for this view a thoroughgoing critic of the foundations of our faith, and of the means of our insight into the true nature of Reality.

All these three conceptions, however much they may differ, have in common what makes it proper enough to view them as conceptions of the study of Natural Religion. For they are all three concerned with religion; they can all alike be pursued without explicit dependence upon any creed as to a revealed religion; and finally, they are busied about some relation between the natural order of truth and the contents of religious doctrine. They differ in the sort of natural truth that forms their starting-point, or that limits the scope of the invesigation which they propose. I suppose that no one of these various lines of inquiry will ever come to be wholly neglected. But their office is distinct. And I mention them here in order all the more clearly to say, at the outset, that our own business, in these lectures, is with the most neglected and arduous of the methods of studying the relations between religion and the ultimate problems of the Theory of Being. From the first, to be sure, we shall be concerned, in one sense, with human nature, as every philosophy has to be concerned. And in the latter half of this course the Philosophy of Nature will play a part in our investigation. But the

From *The World and the Individual* (New York: Macmillan Company, 1899), pp. 3–43.

central problem of our discussion will be the question: What is Reality?

I

In thus stating, in the opening words, the plan of these lectures, I do so with a full sense of the shadow that such a programme may, at the first glimpse, seem to cast upon the prospects of our whole undertaking. It is true that, in calling the fundamental problems of the Metaphysic of Religion relatively neglected, I do not fail to recognize that they are both ancient and celebrated, and that some of us may think them even hackneyed. It is certainly not uncommon to call them antiquated. But what I have meant by the phrase "relatively neglected" is that, compared with the more easily accessible fashions of dealing with Natural Religion, the strictly metaphysical treatment less frequently involves that sort of ardent hand-to-hand struggle with the genuine issues themselves that goes on when men are hopefully interested in a study for its own sake. It is one thing to expound, or even to assail, the theology of Hegel or of St. Thomas, or to report any of those various quaint opinions of philosophers in which even the popular mind often delights. It is another thing to grapple with the issues of life for one's self. The wiser religions have always told us that we cannot be saved through the piety of our neighbors, but have to work out our own salvation with fear and trembling. Well, just so the theoretical student of Natural Religion has to learn that he cannot comprehend ultimate philosophical truth merely by reading the reports of other people's reasonings, but must do his thinking for himself, not indeed without due instruction, but certainly without depending wholly upon his text-books. And if this be true, then the final issues of religious philosophy may be said to be relatively neglected, so long as students are not constantly afresh grappling with the ancient problems, and giving them renderings due to direct personal contact with their intricacies. It is not a question of any needed originality of opinion, but it is rather a matter of our individual intimacy with these issues.

And now, in recognizing the fact of the comparative neglect of the Theory of Being in the discussions of Natural Religion, I recognize also the motives that tend to make such an inquiry seem, at the first glimpse, unpromising. These motives may be expressed in the forms of three objections, namely, first, that such undertakings are pretentious, by reason of the dignity and the mystery of the topic; secondly, that they are dreary, by reason of the subtle distinctions and the airy abstractions involved in every such research; and thirdly, that they are opposed, in spirit, to the sort of study for which in our day the sciences of experience have given the only worthy model.

Such objections are as inevitable as they are, to lovers of philosophy, harmless. Philosophy necessarily involves a good deal of courage; but so does life in general. It is pretentious to wrestle with angels; but there are some blessings that you cannot win in any other way. Philosophy is an old affair in human history; but that does not make the effort at individuality in one's fashion of thinking a less worthy ideal for every new mind. As to the dreariness of metaphysics, it is always the case, both in religion, and in thinking about religion, that, just as the letter killeth, and the spirit giveth life, so the mere report of tradition is dreary, but the inward life of thinking for one's self the meaning within or behind the tradition constitutes the very coming of the Spirit of Truth himself into our own spirits; and that coming of the Spirit, in so far as it occurs at all, never seems to any of us dreary. As for the fine-drawn distinctions and airy abstractions, no distinction is ever too subtle for you, at the moment when it occurs to you to make that distinction for yourself, and not merely to hear that somebody else has made it. And no abstraction seems to you too airy in the hour when you rise upon your own wings to the region where just the abstraction happens to be an element in the concrete fulness of your thoughtful life. Now it chances to be a truth of metaphysics, as it is an experience of religion, that just when you are most individual, most alone, as it were, in your personal thinking, about ultimate and divine matters, you are most completely one with that universal Spirit of Truth of which we just spoke. It is then your personal process of thinking that both gives interest to the subject and secures your relation to the Reality. Hence not the universality nor yet the ultimate character of the principles of which we think, but rather our own sluggishness in thinking, is responsible for the supposed dreariness of the Theory of Being. As Aristotle observed, that Theory itself is what all men most desire. You may in these regions either think or not think the truth; but you cannot think the truth without loving it; and the dreariness which men often impute to Metaphysics, is merely the dreariness of not understanding the subject,—a sort of dreariness for which indeed there is no help except learning to understand. In fact, nobody can ever regret seeing ultimate truth. That we shall hereafter find to be, so to speak, one of the immediate implications of our very definition of Being. When people complain of philosophy as a dreary enterprise, they are then merely complaining of their own lack of philosophical insight. The lover of philosophy can only offer them his sincerest agreement, and sympathy, so far as concerns the ground of their own complaint. He too shares their complaint, for he is human, and finds his own unwisdom dreary. But he is at least looking lovingly toward yonder shining light, while they walk wearily with their backs to the Celestial City.

As to the supposed opposition between the methods of philosophy and those of the special sciences of experience,—it exists, but it does not mean any real opposition of spirit. Here are two ways of getting insight, not two opposed creeds. The very wealth and the growth of modern empirical research furnish especially strong reasons for supposing that the time is near when the central problems of the Theory of Being shall be ready for restatement. Our life does not grow long and healthily in one region, without being ready for new growth in other regions. The indirect influence of special science upon philosophy is sure, but does not always mean a logical dependence of philosophy upon the empirical results of science. Just so, pure mathematical science has no logical dependence upon physics. Yet we have all heard how largely physical science has influenced the lines of investigation followed by the modern mathematicians. Within the mathematical realm itself, pure Algebra, when once abstractly defined, is not logically dependent upon Geometry for its principles or for its theories, yet some theories of modern Algebra have actually developed largely under the spell, as it were, of ideas of an unquestionable geometrical origin. Now a similar relation, I think, will in future find the development of pure Philosophy, and in particular of Rational Theology, to the progress of the special sciences, both mathematical and empirical. I do not think it right to regard philosophy merely as a compendium of the results of special science. Philosophy has its own field. But on the other hand, to reflect upon the meaning of life and of science (and in such thorough-going Reflection philosophy consists), is a process whose seriousness and wealth must grow as our human life and science progress. And hence every great new advance of science de-

mands a fresh consideration of philosophic issues, and will insure in the end a power to grasp, more critically and more deeply, the central problem of Being itself. Hence the more we possess of special science, the more hope we ought to have for pure Philosophy.

II

. . . My precise undertaking, then, in the following lectures, is to show what we mean by Being in general, and by the special sorts of Reality that we attribute to God, to the World, and to the Human Individual. These I regard as the problems of the ontology of religion. In every step of this undertaking I shall actually be, in a psychological and in an historical sense, dependent, both for my ideas and for their organization, upon this or that philosophical or theological tradition (well known to every student of philosophy); and therefore I must early introduce into my work a sketch of certain philosophical traditions in which we are to be especially interested. Here, of course, you might expect to find, as such an historical introduction to the later critical enterprises, either a summary of the history of the principal religious ideas, or some account of the technical history of the Philosophy of Religion itself. Yet for neither of these two very natural enterprises shall I have time. My very fragmentary historical discussions will be limited to an attempt to depict some of the principal conceptions concerning the ultimate nature of Being, in other words to sketch the history of what one might call the ontological predicate of the expression *to be,* or *to be real,* used as a means of asserting that something exists. I shall dwell upon the nature of Being, because to assert that God is, or that the World is, or even, with Descartes, that I am, implies that one knows what it is to be, or in other words, what the so-called existential predicate itself involves. Now it is true that the existential predicate, the word *is* used to assert the real Being of any object, is often viewed as something of an absolutely simple, ultimate, and indescribable meaning. Yet even if this view were sound, the ultimate and the simple are, in philosophy, as truly and as much topics for reflective study as are the most complex and derived ideas of our minds. Moreover, a great deal of popular religion seems to involve the notion that is both easier and more important to know *that* God is, than to know, with any sort of articulation, *What* God is, so that if you express even a total ignorance of the Divine nature and attribute, there are some very traditionally minded people who will hardly dare to disagree with you, while if you express the least doubt of the assertion that God is, the same people will at once view you with horror as an atheist. Now this preference in much popular religious thinking for the ontological predicate in its purity is not an altogether rational preference. Yet we shall find that it is based upon very deep and even very worthy, if vague, instincts. It is true that if I pretend to know no attributes whatever, characterizing a given object X, I seem to have won very little by believing that X nevertheless exists. Yet the fondness for the Unknowable in theology has been to some extent supported by the dim feeling that even in asserting the bare existence of a being, and especially of God, I am already committed to extremely important attributes, whose definition, even if not yet overt, is already, however darkly, implied in my abstract statement. It is interesting, therefore, to study historically what men have supposed themselves to mean by the ontological predicate.

The basis having been thus laid in the history of the subject, our lectures, at various points in the historical summary, will have at some length to undertake a critical comparison and analysis of the various meanings of the ontological predicate. Such an analysis will constantly show us unexpected connections of these meanings with the concrete interests of religion. We shall find it with ontology, as it certainly is with ethics. People often regard moral philosophy as a topic very abstract and dry. And yet wherever two or three are gathered together indulging in gossip about the doings of their neighbors, their speech, even if it involves out-and-out scandal, is devoted to a more or less critical discussion, to an illustration, and even to a sort of analysis of what are really very deep ethical problems,—problems about what men ought to do, and about the intricate relations between law and passion in human life. Well, as even the most frivolous or scandalous gossip really manifests an intense, if rude concern, for the primal questions of moral philosophy, so our children and all our most simple and devout souls constantly talk ontology, discourse of being, face the central issues of reality, but know it not. Yet once face the true connection of abstract theory and daily life, and then one easily sees that life means theory, and that you deal constantly, and decisively, with the problems of the Theory of Being whenever you utter a serious word. This then is the reason why our ontological studies will bear directly upon the daily concerns of religion.

Our discussion of the general meaning and of the relative value of the various ontological predicates will, moreover, throw light, as we go, upon some of the best known of the special issues of the history of theology. We shall see, for instance, what has been the real motive that has made the doctrine of the speculative Mystics so important a factor in the life of the more complex religious faiths. We shall see too, in the great historical conflicts between the Realistic and the Mystical conceptions of the nature of Reality, the source of some of the most important controversies concerning the being and attributes of God, the existence of the physical world, and the nature of human individuality. Thus we shall gradually approach a position where we shall learn the inevitableness of a certain final conception of the meaning of our ontological predicates; and the result of our critical study will be a light that we may not wholly have anticipated, both upon the conception of God, and upon our notion of the relations between God, the World, and the Human Individual. With the development of these fundamental conceptions, the first of my two series of lectures will close. We shall herewith have stated the bases of religion.

The second series I intend first to devote to the application of our fundamental conceptions to the more special problems of the nature of the human Ego, the meaning of the finite realm called the Physical World, and the interpretation of Evolution. The vast extent of the discussions thus suggested will be limited, in our own case, by the very fact that we shall here be attempting merely the application of a single very general ontological idea to a few problems which we shall view rather as illustrations of our central thesis concerning Reality, than as matters to be exhaustively considered for their own sake. Having thus sketched our Cosmology, if I may call it such, we shall then conclude the whole undertaking by a summary discussion of the problems of Good and Evil, of Freedom, of Immortality and of the destiny of the Individual, still reviewing our problems in the light of our general conception of Being. The title that I shall have given to the whole course of lectures, "The World and the Individual" will thus, I hope, prove to be justified by the scope of our discussion in the two divisions of this course.

III

The plan of the proposed investigation has now been set before you in outline. May I next undertake to indicate a little more precisely not merely what problems we are to attempt, but the sort of positive argument that we are to use, and the kind of result that we may hope to reach? A philosophy must indeed be judged not by its theses, but by its methods; and not upon the basis of mere summaries, but after a consideration of the details of its argument. Yet it helps to make clearer the way through an intricate realm of inquiry if one first surveys, as it were, from above, the country through which, in such an enterprise, the road is to pass. I propose then, to indicate at once, and in the rest of this lecture, where the central problem of the Theory of Being lies, and by what method I think that this problem is, in a general sense, to be solved. To state the proposed solution, however, even in the most abstract and necessarily unconvincing fashion, is to arouse comments as to the meaning of this thesis, as to its consequences, and, above all, in a discussion like the present, as to its bearing upon the more practical interests of religion. I think that we may be helped to an understanding hereafter, if I attempt at once to call out, and, by anticipation, to answer, a few such comments.

I am one of those who hold that when you ask the question: What is an Idea? and: How can Ideas stand in any true relation to Reality? you attack the world-knot in the way that promises most for the untying of its meshes. This way is, of course, very ancient. It is the way of Plato, and, in a sense, already the way of his Master. It is, in a different sense, the way of Kant. If you view philosophy in this fashion, you subordinate the study of the World as Fact to a reflection upon the World as Idea. Begin by accepting, upon faith and tradition, the mere brute Reality of the World as Fact, and there you are, sunk deep in an ocean of mysteries. The further you then proceed in the study of that world, the longer seems the way to God or to clearness, unless you from the start carry with you some sort of faith, perhaps a very blind and immediate faith, that God reigns, or that the facts in themselves are somehow clear. The World as Fact surprises you with all sorts of strange contracts. Now it reveals to you, in the mechanics and physics of the stars or in the processes of living beings, vast realms of marvellous reasonableness; now it bewilders you, in the endless diversities of natural facts, by a chaos of unintelligible fragments and of scattered events; now it lifts up your heart with wondrous glimpses of ineffable goodness; and now it arouses your wrath by frightful signs of cruelty

and baseness. Conceive it as a realm for pure scientific theory; and, so far as your knowledge reaches, it is full at once of the show of a noble order, and of hints of a vain chance. On the other hand, conceive it as a realm of values, attempt to estimate its worth, and it baffles you with caprices, like a charming and yet hopelessly wayward child, or like a bad fairy. That is the world of brute natural fact as you, with your present form of consciousness, are forced to observe it, if you try to get any total impression of its behavior. And so, this World of Fact daily announces itself to you as a defiant mystery—a mystery such as Job faced, and such as the latest agnostic summary of empirical results, in their bearing upon our largest human interests, or such as even the latest pessimistic novel will no doubt any day present afresh to you, in all the ancient unkindliness that belongs to human fortune.

The World as Fact is, then, for all of us, persistently baffling, unless we find somewhere else the key to it. The philosophers of the Platonic type have, however, long ago told us that this defect of our world of fact is due, at bottom, simply to the fault of our human type of consciousness. And hence a whole realm of philosophical inquiry has been devoted, in the best ages of speculative thinking, to a criticism of this human type of consciousness itself. Upon such a criticism, Plato founded his conception of the Ideal World. By such criticism, Plotinus sought to find the way upwards, through Soul to the realm of the Intellect, and beyond the Intellect to his Absolute "One." Through a similar criticism, Scholastic doctrine attempted to purify our human type of consciousness, until it should reach the realm of genuine spirituality, and attain an insight but a little lower than that of the conceived angelic type of intelligence. For all such thinkers, the raising of our type of consciousness to some higher level meant not only the winning of insight into Reality, but also the attainment of an inner and distinctly religious ideal. To a later and less technically pious form of thinking, one sees the transition of Spinoza, who was at once, as we now know, a child of Scholasticism, and a student of the more modern physical conceptions of his day,—at once a mystic, a realist, and a partisan of nature. For Spinoza too, it is our type of finite consciousness that makes our daily world of fact, or, as he prefers to say, of imagination, seem chaotic; and the way to truth still to be found through an inner and reflective purification of experience. A widely different interpretation is given to the same fundamental conceptions, by Kant. But in Kant's case also, remote from his interests is anything savoring of mysticism, the end of philosophical insight is again the vindication of a higher form of consciousness. For Kant, however, this is the consciousness of the Moral Reason, which recognizes no facts as worthy of its form of assurance, except the facts implied by the Good Will, and by the Law of the good will. All these ways then of asserting the primacy of the World as Idea over the World as Fact, agree in dealing with the problem of Reality from the side of the means through which we are supposed to be able to attain reality, that is, from the side of the Ideas.

IV

But if this is to be the general nature of our own inquiry also, then everything for us will depend upon the fundamental questions, already stated, viz., first: What is an Idea? and second: How can an Idea be related to Reality? In the treatment of both these questions, however, various methods and theories at once come into sight. And, to begin with one of the favorite issues, namely the fundamental definition of the word "idea" itself, there is a well-known tendency in a good deal of philosophy, both ancient and modern, either to define an idea, as an Image, destined to picture facts external to the idea, or else, in some other way, to lay stress upon the *externally* cognitive or "representative" value of an idea as its immediately obvious and its most essential aspect. From this point of view, men have conceived that the power of ideas to know a Reality external to themselves, was indeed either something too obvious to excite inquiry, or else an ultimate and inexplicable power. "Ideas exist," says this view, "and they exist as knowing facts external to themselves. And this is their fundamental character." Now I myself shall, in these lectures, regard this power of ideas to cognize facts external to themselves not as a primal fact of existence but as an aspect of ideas which decidedly needs reflective consideration, and a very critical restatement. Hence I cannot here begin by saying: "Ideas are states of mind that image facts external to themselves." That would be useful enough as a definition of ideas in a Psychology of Cognition. For such a Psychology would presuppose what we are here critically to consider, namely, the very possibility of a cognition of Being. But, for the purpose of our present theory, the definition of the term "idea" must be made in such wise as not formally to presuppose the power of ideas to have cognitive relations to outer objects.

Moreover, in attempting a definition of the general term "idea," while I shall not be attempting a psychology of cognition, I shall myself be guided by certain psychological analyses of the mere contents of our consciousness,—analyses which have become prominent in recent discussion. What is often called the active and sometimes also the motor aspect of our mental life, has been much dwelt upon of late. This is no place, and at present we have no need, for a psychological theory of the origin or of the causes of what is called activity, but as a fact, you have in your mental life a sort of consciousness accompanying the processes by which, as the psychologists are accustomed to say, you adjust your organism to its environment; and this sort of consciousness differs, in some notable features, from what takes place in your mind in so far as the mere excitation of your sense organs by the outer world is regarded apart from the experiences that you have when you are said to react upon your impressions. The difference between merely seeing your friend, or hearing his voice, and consciously or actively regarding him as your friend, and behaving towards him in a friendly way, is a difference obvious to consciousness, whatever your theory of the sources of mental activity. Now this difference between outer sense impressions, or images derived from such impressions, and active responses to sense impression, or ideas founded upon such responses, is not merely a difference between what is sometimes called the intellect, and what is called the will. For, as a fact, the intellectual life is as much bound up with our consciousness of our acts as is the will. There is no purely intellectual life, just as there is no purely voluntary life. The difference between knowledge and will, so far as it has a metaphysical meaning, will concern us much later. For the present, it is enough to note that your intelligent ideas of things never consist of mere images of the things, but always involve a consciousness of how you propose to act towards the things of which you have ideas. A sword is an object that you would propose to use, or to regard in one way, while a pen is to be used in another; your idea of the object involves the memory of the appropriate act. Your idea of your friend differs from your idea of your enemy by virtue of your consciousness of your different attitude and intended behaviour towards these objects. Complex scientific ideas, viewed as to their conscious significance, are, as Professor Stout has well said, plans of actions, ways of constructing the objects of your scientific consciousness. Intelligent ideas then, belong, so to speak, to the motor side of your life rather than to the merely sensory. This was what Kant meant by the spontaneity of understanding. To be sure, a true scientific idea is a mental construction supposed to correspond with an outer object, or to imitate that object. But when we try to define the idea in itself, as a conscious fact, our best means is to lay stress upon the sort of will, or active meaning, which any idea involves for the mind that forms the idea.

By the word "Idea," then, as we shall use it when, after having criticized opposing theories, we come to state, in these lectures, our own thesis, I shall mean in the end any state of consciousness, whether simple or complex, which, when present, is then and there viewed as at least the partial expression or embodiment of a single conscious purpose. I shall indeed say nothing for the present as to what causes an idea. But I shall assert that an idea appears in consciousness as having the significance of an act of will. I shall also dwell upon the inner purpose, and not upon the external relations, as the primary and essential feature of an idea. For instance, you sing to yourself a melody, you are then and there conscious that the melody as you hear yourself singing it, partially fulfils and embodies a purpose. Well, in this sense, your melody, at the moment when you sing it, or even when you silently listen to its imagined presence, constitutes a musical idea, and is often so called. You may so regard the melody without yet explicitly dwelling upon the externally cognitive value of the musical idea, as the representative of a melody sung or composed by somebody else. You may even suppose the melody original with yourself, unique, and sung now for the first time. Even so, it would remain just as truly a musical idea, however partial or fragmentary; for it would then and there, when sung, or even when inwardly heard, partly embody your own conscious purpose. In the same sense, any conscious act, at the moment when you perform it, not merely expresses, but is, in my present sense, an idea. To count ten is thus also an idea, if the counting fulfils and embodies, in however incomplete and fragmentary a way, your conscious purpose, and that quite apart from the fact that counting ten may also enable you to cognize the numerical character of facts external to the conscious idea of ten itself. In

brief, an idea, in my present definition may, and, as a fact always does, if you please, appear to be representative of a fact existent beyond itself. But the primary character, which makes it an idea, is not this its representative character, is not its vicarious assumption of the responsibility of standing for a being beyond itself, but is its inner character as relatively fulfilling the purpose (that is, at presenting the partial fulfilment of the purpose), which is in the consciousness of the moment wherein the idea takes place. It is in this sense that we speak of any artistic idea, as present in the creative mind of the artist. I propose, in stating my own view hereafter, to use the word "idea" in this general sense.

Well, this definition of the primary character of an idea, enables me at once to deal with a conception which will play no small part in our later discussions. I refer to the very conception of the Meaning of an idea. One very fair way to define an idea, had we chosen to use that way, might have been to say: An Idea is any state of mind that has a conscious meaning. Thus, according to my present usage of the word "idea," a color, when merely seen, is in so far, for consciousness, no idea. A brute noise, merely heard, is no idea. But a melody, when sung, a picture, when in its wholeness actively appreciated, or the inner memory of your friend now in your mind, is an idea. For each of these latter states means something to you at the instant when you get it present to consciousness. But now, what is this meaning of any idea? What does one mean by a meaning? To this question, I give, for the instant, an intentionally partial answer. I have just said that an idea in any state of mind, or complex of states, that, when present, is consciously viewed as the relatively completed embodiment, and therefore already as the partial fulfilment of a purpose. Now this purpose, just in so far as it gets a present conscious embodiment in the contents and in the form of the complex state called the idea, constitutes what I shall hereafter call the Internal Meaning of the Idea. Or, to repeat, the state or complex of states called the idea, presents to consciousness the expressed although in general the incomplete fulfilment of a purpose. In presence of this fulfilment, one could, as it were, consciously say: "That is what I want, and just in so far I have it. The purpose of singing or of imagining the melody is what I want fulfilled; and, in this musical idea, I have it at least partially fulfilled." Well, this purpose, when viewed as fulfilled through the state called the idea, is the internal meaning of the idea. Or yet once more,—to distinguish our terms a little more sharply,—in advance of the presence of the idea in consciousness, one could abstractly speak of the purpose as somewhat not yet fulfilled. Hereupon let there come the idea as the complex of conscious states, the so-called act wherein this purpose gets, as it were, embodied, and relatively speaking, accomplished. Then, finally, we shall have the internal meaning of the idea, and this internal meaning of the completed idea is the purpose viewed as so far embodied in the idea, the soul, as it were, which the idea gives body. Any idea then, viewed as a collection of states, must have its internal meaning, since, being an idea, it does in some degree embody its purpose. And our two terms, "purpose embodied in the idea," and "internal meaning of the idea," represent the same subject-matter viewed in two aspects. The purpose which the idea, when it comes, is to fulfil, may first be viewed apart from the fulfilment. Then it remains, so far, mere purpose. Or it may be viewed as expressed and so far partially accomplished by means of the complex state called the idea, and then it is termed "the present internal meaning of this state."

V

So now we have defined what we mean by an idea, and what we mean by the internal meaning of an idea. But ideas often seem to have a meaning, yes, as one must add, finite ideas always undertake or appear to have a meaning, that is not exhausted by this conscious internal meaning presented and relatively fulfilled at the moment when the idea is there for our finite view. The melody sung, the artist's idea, the thought of your absent friend—a thought on which you love to dwell: all these not merely have their obvious internal meaning, as meeting a conscious purpose by their very presence, but also they at least appear to have that other sort of meaning, that reference beyond themselves to objects, that cognitive relation to outer facts, that attempted correspondence with outer facts, which many accounts of our ideas regard as their primary, inexplicable, and ultimate character. I call this second, and, for me, still problematic and derived aspect of the nature of ideas, their apparently External Meaning. In this sense it is that I say, "The melody sung by me not only is an idea internally meaning the embodiment of my purpose at the instant when I sing it, but also is an idea that means, and that in this sense externally means, the object called, say, a certain

theme which Beethoven composed." In this same sense, your idea of your absent friend, is, for my definition, an idea primarily, because you now fulfil some of your love for dwelling upon your inner affection for your friend by getting the idea present to mind. But you also regard it as an idea which, in the external sense, is said to mean the real being called your friend, in so far as the idea is said to refer to that real friend, and to resemble him. This external meaning, I say, appears to be very different from the internal meaning, and wholly to transcend the latter.

By thus first distinguishing sharply between the conscious internal meaning of an idea and its apparently external meaning, we get before us an important way of stating the problem of knowledge or, in other words, the problem of the whole relation between Idea and Being. We shall find this not only a very general, but a very fundamental, and, as I believe, despite numerous philosophical discussions, still a comparatively neglected way. And in problems of this kind so much turns upon the statement of the issue, that I must be excused for thus dwelling at length, at this early stage, upon the precise sense in which we are to employ our terms.

Plainly, then, whoever studies either a special science, or a problem of general metaphysics, is indeed concerned with what he then and there views as the external meaning of certain ideas. And an idea, when thus viewed, appears as if it were essentially a sort of imitation or image of a being, and this being, the external object of our thoughtful imitation, appears to be, in so far, quite separate from these our ideas that imitate its characters or that attempt to correspond to them. From such a point of view, our ideas seemed destined to perform a task which is externally set for them by the real world. I count, but I count, in ordinary life, what I take to be real objects, existent quite apart from my counting. Suppose that I count ships seen from the shore. There, says common sense, are the ships, sailing by themselves, and quite indifferent to whether anybody counts them or not. In advance of the counting, the ships, in so far as they are a real collection, have their number. This common sense also presupposes. Let there be seen, yonder, on the sea, nine ships or ten; this number of the real ships is in itself determinate. It does not result from my counting, but is the standard for the latter to follow. The numerical ideas of anybody who counts the ships must either repeat the preëxistent facts, or else fail to report those facts accurately. That alternative seems absolute and final. The question how anybody ever comes to count ships at all, is a question for psychology. But there remains for the seeker after metaphysical truth, just as much for the man of common sense, the apparently sharp alternative: Either actual ships, whose multitude is just what it happens to be, whose number preëxists, in advance of any counting, are correctly represented by the ideas of one who happens to be able to count, or else these ships are incorrectly counted. In the latter case we seem to be forced to say that the counting process misses its external aim. In the former case we say that the ideas expressed by the one who counts are true. But in both cases alike the ideas in question thus appear to be true or false by virtue of their external meaning, by virtue of the fact that they either correspond or do not correspond to facts which are themselves no part of the ideas. This simple instance of the ships and of the ideas of a man who sits watching and counting the ships, is obviously typical of all instances of the familiar relation of ideas to Being, as the metaphysics of common sense views Being, or of the relation of ideas to what we have here called the objects of their external meaning. That ideas have such external meanings, that they do refer to facts existent wholly apart from themselves, that their relation to these facts is one of successful correspondence or of error-producing non-correspondence, that the ideas in so far aim, not merely to embody, like the musical ideas just exemplified, an internal purpose, but also to imitate, in the form of their conscious structure and in the relationship of their own elements, the structure and relationship of a world of independent facts,—what could possibly seem, from such a common-sense point of view, more obvious than all this? And if common sense presupposes that ideas have such external meanings, how much more does not natural science appear to involve the recognition of this essentially imitative function of ideas?

In any special natural science, a scientific description appears as an adjustment, express, conscious, exact, of the internal structure of a system of ideas to the external structure of a world of preëxistent facts; and the business of science has been repeatedly defined, of late years, as simply and wholly taken up with the exact description of the facts of nature. Now the world of Being, when viewed in this light, appears to mean simply the same as the fact world, the external object of our ideas, the object that ideas must imitate, whatever their

internal purpose, unless they want to be false. But for this very reason, no study of the inner structure of ideas, of their conscious conformity to their internal purpose, can so far promise to throw any direct light upon their success in fulfilling their external purpose. Or, as people usually say, you cannot make out the truth about facts by studying your "mere ideas." And so, as people constantly insist, no devotion to the elaboration of the internal meaning of your own ideas can get you in presence of the truth about Being. The world of Being is whatever it happens to be, as the collection of ships is what it is, before you count. Internal purposes cannot predetermine external conformity to truth. You cannot evolve facts out of your inner consciousness. Ideas about Being are not to be justified like melodies, by their internal conformity to the purpose of the moment when they consciously live. They must submit to standards that they themselves in no sense create. Such is the burden of common sense, and of special science, when they tell us about this aspect of the meaning of our ideas.

I state thus explicitly a very familiar view as to the whole externally cognitive function and value of ideas. I mean thus to emphasize the primary appearance of hopeless contrast between the internal purpose and the external validity of ideas. In fact, nothing could seem sharper than the contrast thus indicated between the melody on the one hand, the musical idea, as it comes to mind and is enjoyed for its beauty while it passes before consciousness, and the counting of the ships, on the other hand,—a process whose whole success depends upon its conformity to what seem to be absolutely indifferent and independent outer facts. In the one case we have the embodiment of a conscious inner purpose,—a purpose which is won through the very act of the moment, and by virtue of the mere presence of a certain series of mental contents. In the other case we have a conformity to outer truth,—a conformity that no inner clearness, no well-wrought network of cunning ideal contrivance, can secure, unless the idea first submits to the authority of external existence.

And yet, sharp as is this apparent contrast, every student of philosophy knows how profound are also the motives that have led some philosophers to doubt whether such contrast can really be as ultimate as it seems. After all, the counting of the ships is valid or invalid *not* alone because of the supposed independent being of the ships, but also because of the conscious act whereby just this collection of ships was first consciously selected for counting. After all, then, no idea is true or is false except with reference to the object that this very idea first means to select as its own object. Apart from what the idea itself thus somehow assigns as its own task, even that independent being yonder, if you assume such being, cannot determine the success or failure of the idea. It is the idea that then first says: "I mean this or that object. That is for my object. Of that I am thinking. To that I want to conform." And apart from such conscious selection, apart from such ideal predetermination of the object on the part of the idea, apart from such free voluntary submission of the idea to its self-imposed task, the object itself, the fact world, in its independence, can do nothing either to confirm or refute the idea. Now in this extremely elementary consideration, namely, in the consideration that unless ideas first voluntarily bind themselves to a given task, and so, by their internal purpose, already commit themselves to a certain selection of its object, they are neither true nor false,—in this consideration, I say, there may be hidden consequences that we shall later find momentous for the whole theory of Being and of truth. This consideration, that despite the seemingly hopeless contrast between internal and external meaning, ideas really possess truth or falsity only by virtue of their own selection of their task as ideas, is essentially the same as the consideration that led Kant to regard the understanding as the creator of the phenomenal nature over which science gradually wins conscious control, and that led Hegel to call the world the embodied Idea. This consideration, then, is not novel, but I believe it to be fundamental and of inexhaustible importance. I believe also that some of its aspects are still far too much neglected. And I propose to devote these lectures to its elaboration, and to a study of its relations to the various conceptions of Reality which have determined the scientific and religious life of humanity.

In any case I say, then, at the outset, that the whole problem of the nature of Being will for us, in the end, reduce to the question: How is the internal meaning of ideas consistent with their apparently external meaning? Or again: How is it possible that an idea, which is an idea essentially and primarily because of the inner purpose that it consciously fulfils by its presence, also possesses a meaning that in any sense appears to go beyond this internal pur-

pose? We shall, in dealing with this problem, first find, by a development of the consideration just barely indicated, that the external meaning must itself be interpreted, not primarily in the sense of mere dependence upon the brute facts, but in terms of the inner purpose of the idea itself. We shall, perhaps to our surprise, reach the seemingly paradoxical and essentially idealistic thesis that no being in heaven or in earth, or in the waters under the earth, has power to give to an idea any purpose unless, the idea itself, as idea, as a fragment of life, as a conscious thrill, so to speak, of inner meaning, first somehow truly learns so to develope its internal meaning as to assign to itself just that specific purpose. In other words, we shall find that while, for our purposes, we, the critics, must first sharply distinguish the apparently external purpose that, as it were, from without, we assign to the idea, from the internal meaning of the idea, as present to a passing conscious instant, still, this our assignment of the external purpose, this our assertion that the idea knows or resembles, or imitates, or corresponds to, fact wholly beyond itself, must in the end be justified, if at all, by appeal to the truth, *i.e.* to the adequate expression and development of the internal meaning of the idea itself. In other words, we shall find either that the external meaning is genuinely continuous with the internal meaning, and is inwardly involved in the latter, or else that the idea has no external meaning at all. In brief, our abstract sundering of the apparently external from the consciously internal meaning of the idea must be first made very sharp, as we have just deliberately made it, only in order that later, when we learn the true relations, we may come to see the genuine and final unity of internal and external meaning. Our first definition of the idea seems to make, yes, in its abstract statement deliberately tries to make, as you see, the external meaning something sharply contrasted with the internal meaning. Our final result will simply reabsorb the secondary aspect, the external meaning, into the completed primary aspect,—the completely embodied internal meaning of the idea. We shall assert, in the end, that the final meaning of every complete idea, when fully developed, must be viewed as wholly an internal meaning, and that all apparently external meanings become consistent with internal meanings only by virtue of thus coming to be viewed as aspects of the true internal meaning.

To illustrate this thesis by the cases already used: The melody sung or internally but voluntarily heard, in the moment of memory, is, for the singer's or hearer's consciousness, a musical idea. It has so far its internal meaning. And to say so much first means simply that to the singer, as he sings, or to the silent memory of a musical imagination, the present melody imperfectly and partially fulfils a conscious purpose, the purpose of the flying moment. On the other hand, the melody may be viewed by a critic as an idea corresponding to external facts. The singer or hearer too may himself say as he sings or remembers: "This is the song my beloved sang," or "This is the theme that Beethoven composed in his Fidelio." In such a case, the idea is said to have its apparently external meaning, and this, its reference to facts not now and here given, is the idea's general relation to what we call true Being. And such reference not only seems at first very sharply different from the internal meaning, but must, for our purposes, at first be sundered by definition from that internal meaning even more sharply than common sense distinguishes the two. For abstract sundering is, in us mortals, the necessary preliminary to grasping the unity of truth. The internal meaning is a purpose present in the passing moment, but here imperfectly embodied. Common sense calls it, as such, an expression of transient living intent, an affair of Will. Psychology explains the presence and the partial present efficacy of this purpose by the laws of motor processes, of Habit, or of what is often called association. Ethical doctrine finds in such winning of inner purposes the region where Conscience itself, and the pure moral Intention, are most concerned. On the other hand, the apparently external meaning of the idea is at first said to be an affair of the externally cognitive intellect, and of the hard facts of an independently real world. Not purpose, but the unchangeable laws of the Reality, not the inner life, but the Universe, thus at first seems from without to assign to the idea whatever external meaning it is to obtain. Subject and Object are here supposed to meet,—to meet in this fact that ideas have their external meaning,—but to meet as foreign powers.

Now we are first to recognize, even more clearly, I say, than common sense, the sharpness of this apparent antithesis between the conscious internal and the seemingly external meaning. Here, as I have said, is indeed the world-knot. We are to recognize the problem, but we are, nevertheless, to answer it in the end (when we get behind the appearances, and supplement the abstractions), by the thesis that

at bottom, the external meaning is only apparently external, and, in very truth, is but an aspect of the completely developed internal meaning. We are to assert that just what the internal meaning already imperfectly but consciously is, namely, purpose relatively fulfilled, just that, and nothing else, the apparently external meaning when truly comprehended also proves to be, namely, the entire expression of the very Will that is fragmentarily embodied in the life of the flying conscious idea,—the fulfilment of the very aim that is hinted in the instant. Or, in other words, we are to assert that, in the case mentioned, the artist who composed, the beloved who sang the melody, are in verity present, as truly implied aspects of meaning, and as fulfilling a purpose, in the completely developed internal meaning of the very idea that now, in its finitude, seems to view them merely as absent. I deliberately choose, in this way, a paradoxical illustration. The argument must hereafter justify the thesis. I can here only indicate what we hereafter propose to develop as our theory of the true relation of Idea and Being. It will also be a theory, as you see, of the unity of the whole very World Life itself.

In brief, by considerations of this type, we propose to answer the question: What is to be? by the assertion that: To be means simply to express, to embody the complete internal meaning of a certain absolute system of ideas,—a system, moreover, which is genuinely implied in the true internal meaning or purpose of every finite idea, however fragmentary.

VI

You may observe already, even in this wholly preliminary sketch of the particular form of Idealism to be developed in these lectures, two principal features. First, Our account of the nature of Being, and of the relation between Idea and Being, is to be founded explicitly upon a theory of the way in which ideas possess their own meaning. Secondly, Our theory of the nature of Meaning is to be founded upon a definition in terms of Will and Purpose. We do not indeed say, Our will causes our ideas. But we do say, Our ideas now imperfectly embody our will. And the real world is just our whole will embodied.

I may add, at once, two further remarks concerning the more technical aspects of the argument by which we shall develop our thesis. The first remark is, that the process by which we shall pass from a study of the first or fragmentary internal meaning of finite ideas to that conception of their completed internal meaning in terms of which our theory of Being is to be defined, is a process analogous to that by which modern mathematical speculation has undertaken to deal with its own concepts of the type called by the Germans *Grenzbegriffe,* or Limiting Concepts, or better, Concepts of Limits. As a fact, one of the first things to be noted about our conception of Being is that, as a matter of Logic, it is the concept of a limit, namely of that limit to which the internal meaning or purpose of an idea tends as it grows consciously determinate. Our Being resembles the concept of the so-called irrational numbers. Somewhat as they are related to the various so-called "fundamental series" of rational numbers, somewhat in that way is Being related to the various thinking processes that approach it, as it were, from without, and undertake to define it as at once their external meaning, and their unattainable goal. That which is, is for thought, at once the fulfilment and the limit of the thinking process. The thinking process itself is a process whereby at once meanings tend to become determinate, and external objects tend to become internal meanings. Let my process of determining my own internal meaning simply proceed to its own limit, and then I shall face Being. I shall not only imitate my object as another, and correspond to it from without: I shall become one with it, and so internally possess it. This is a very technical statement of our present thesis, and of our form of Idealism,—a statement which only our later study can justify. But in making that statement here, I merely call attention to the fact that the process of defining limits is one which mathematical science has not only developed, but in large measure, at the present time, prepared for philosophical adaptation, so that to view the concept of Being in this light is to approach it with an interest for which recent research has decidedly smoothed the way. We shall meet both with false ways of defining the limit, and with true ways.

My second remark is closely related to the first, but is somewhat less technical, and involves a return to the practical aspects of our intended theory. I have just said that the development of the conception of an idea whose internal meaning is fully completed, and whose relation to Being is even thereby defined, will involve a discussion of the way in which our internal, our fragmentary finite meanings, as they appear in our flying moments, are to attain a determined character or are to become, as Hegel would say, *bestimmt,* so as to pass from vagueness to precision. Our theory, as you already see, will identify finite ignorance of Reality with finite vagueness of meaning, will assert that the very Absolute, in all its fulness of life, is even now the object that you really mean by your fragmentary passing ideas, and that the defect of your present human form of momentary consciousness lies in the fact that you just now do not know precisely what you mean. Increase of knowledge, therefore, would really involve increase of determination in your present meaning. The universe you have always with you, as your true internal meaning. Only this, your meaning, you now, in view of the defect of your momentary form of consciousness, realize vaguely, abstractly, without determination. And, as we have further asserted, this indetermination of your ideas also involves a hesitant indeterminateness of your momentary will, a vagueness of conscious ideal as well as of idea, a failure not only to possess, but wholly to know what you want. To pass to your real and completed meaning, to the meaning implied in this very moment's vagueness, would be a passage to absolute determinateness. So to pass would therefore be to know with full determination truths of an often desired type, truths such as: What you yourself are; and, who you are, as this individual; what this individual physical fact now before you is. Yes, it would be to know what the whole individual Being called the World is, and who the Individual of Individuals, namely the Absolute, or God himself, is. Just such final determinateness, just such precision, definiteness, finality of meaning, constitutes that limit of your own internal meaning which our theory will hereafter seek to characterize. And so my present remark hereupon is that, in following our enterprise of defining Being, we shall not be looking for mere abstract principles, but we shall be seeking for the most concrete objects in the world, namely for Individual Beings, and for the system that links them in one Individual Whole,—for Individuals viewed as the limits towards which all ideas of universal meanings tend, and for the Absolute as himself simply the highest fulfilment of the very category of Individuality, the Individual of Individuals.

Will, meaning, individuality, these will prove to be the constant accompaniments and the outcome of our whole theory of ideas, of thought, and of being. And in the light of these remarks we may now be able to anticipate more precisely the form of doctrine to which these lectures are to be devoted.

Idealism in some sense is indeed familiar in modern doctrine. And familiar also to readers of idealistic literature is some such assertion, as that the whole of Reality is the expression of a single system of thought, the fulfilment of a single conscious Purpose, or the realm of one internally harmonized Experience. But what the interested learners ask of idealistic teachers to-day is, as you are all aware, a more explicit statement as to just how Thought and Purpose, Idea and Will, and above all finite thought and will, and absolute thought and will, are, by any idealist, to be conceived as related to each other. My definitions in the foregoing have been deliberately intended to prepare the way for our later direct dealing with just these issues. An idea, in the present discussion, is first of all to be defined in terms of the internal purpose, or, if you choose, in terms of the Will, that it expresses consciously, if imperfectly, at the instant when it comes to mind. Its external meaning, its externally cognitive function as a knower of outer Reality, is thus in these lectures to be treated as explicitly secondary to this its internal value, this its character as meaning the conscious fulfilment of an end, the conscious expression of an interest, of a desire, of a volition. To be sure, thus to define, as we shall see, is not to separate knowing from willing, but it is rather to lay stress, from the outset, upon the unity of knowledge and will, first in our finite consciousness, and later, as we shall say, in the Absolute. Our present statement of our doctrine is therefore not to be accused, at any point, of neglecting the aspect of value, the teleological, the volitional aspect, which consciousness everywhere possesses. We shall reach indeed in the end the conception of an Absolute Thought, but this conception will be in explicit unity with the conception of an Absolute Purpose. Furthermore, as we have just asserted, we shall find that the defect of our momentary internal purposes, as they come to our passing consciousness, is that they imply an individuality, both in ourselves and in our facts of experience, which we do not wholly get presented to ourselves at any one instant. Or in other words, we finite beings live in the search for individuality, of life, of will, of experience, in brief, of meaning. The whole meaning, which is the world, the Reality, will prove to be, for this very reason, not a barren Absolute, which de-

vours individuals, not a wilderness such as Meister Eckhart found in God, a *Stille Wüste, da Nieman beime ist,* a place where there is no definite life, nor yet a whole that absorbs definition, but a whole that is just to the finite aspect of every flying moment, and of every transient or permanent form of finite selfhood,—a whole that is an individual system of rationally linked and determinate, but for that very reason not externally determined, ethically free individuals, who are nevertheless One in God. It is just because all meanings, in the end, will prove to be internal meanings, that this which the internal meaning most loves, namely the presence of concrete fulfilment, of life, of pulsating and originative will, of freedom, and of individuality, will prove, for our view, to be of the very essence of the Absolute Meaning of the world. This, I say, will prove to be the sense of our central thesis; and here will be a contrast between our form of Idealism and some other forms.

And thus, in this wholly preliminary statement, I have outlined our task, have indicated its relation to the problems of religion, have suggested its historical affiliations, and have, in a measure, predicted its course. I have defined in general the problem of the relation of the World as Idea to the World as Fact, and have stated our issue as precisely this relation between Ideas and Reality. In order to assist in clarifying our understanding, I have also given a general definition of what an idea is, and have stated the logical contrast between the consciously internal and the apparently external meaning of any finite idea. And finally I have asserted that, in dealing with the problem as to how internal and external meaning can be reduced to a consistent whole, we shall be especially guided to fruitful reflection upon the final relation of the World and the Individual. This, then, is our programme. The rest must be the actual task.

I am not unaware how valueless, in philosophy, are mere promises. All, in this field, must turn upon the method of work. The question in philosophy is not about the interest or the hopefulness of your creed, but about your rational grounds for holding your convictions. I accept the decidedly strict limitations imposed by this consideration, and shall try, when we come to the heart of our critical and constructive task, to be as explicit as the allotted time permits, both in expounding the precise sense of the doctrine now loosely and dogmatically sketched in the foregoing statement, and in explaining the grounds that lead me to prefer it, as a solution both of logical and of empirical problems, to its rivals. But the way of detailed argument is long, and the outlook of the whole enterprise may often seem, as we proceed with our difficulties, dark and perplexing. Introductions also have their rights; and I have meant in these opening words merely to recount the dream of which what follows must furnish both the interpretation and, in a measure, the justification.

The Temporal and the Eternal

The world of the facts that we ought to acknowledge is, in one of its aspects, present (so we have maintained) as the Object of Possible Attention, in every act of finite insight. Finitude means inattention to the wealth and organization of the world's detail.

An obvious objection to this thesis is furnished by the nature of Time. How can Past and Future, which "do not exist," be in any sense "present," in the undistinguished unity of the facts which any finite thinker at any instant acknowledges?

In the Ninth Lecture of the First Series, we briefly considered the topic of temporal Being. We have to return to it here with more detail. There is an ancient distinction of the philosophers between the Temporal and the Eternal. It must be plain at this point, that we ascribe to the true world a certain eternal type of Being. Yet how shall we reconcile this with our equally obvious treatment of the world as existing in time? Plainly we have here a question that is of great importance for any understanding of the categories of experience. It belongs, then, in the context of these earlier discussions of our present series of lectures. Moreover, it is one that will constantly meet us later. The relation of Time to Nature will be of central concern to us. When we come to deal with the individual Self, we shall again have to face the question: In what sense has the Self of the individual a purely Temporal, and in what sense an Eternal type of reality? And before we can answer this question we must be more precise than we have yet been in defining the terms Time and Eternity. The issue here involved has a significance not only theoretical, but also intensely practical. It will need therefore a close and deliberate scrutiny. Time, as we shall soon see, is a concept of fundamentally practical meaning. The definition of the Eternal, on the other hand, has very close relations to the question as to the ultimate significance of all that is practical. Any rational decision as between a pessimistic and an optimistic view of the world, any account of the relations between God and Man, any view of the sense in which the evils and imperfections of the Universe can be comprehended or justified, any account of our ethical consciousness in terms reconcilable with our Idealism,—in brief, any philosophical reconciliation with religion and life, must turn in part upon a distinction between the Temporal and the Eternal, and upon an insight into their unity in the midst of their contrast. The problem at issue is one of the most delicate and, at the same time, one of the simplest of the great issues of philosophy. I shall here have to deal with it at first in a purely theoretical fashion, and shall then proceed to its practical applications. For both aspects of the question we are now fully prepared.

I

Time is known to us, both perceptually, as the psychologists would say, and conceptually. That is, we have a relatively direct experience of time at any moment, and we acknowledge the truth of a relatively indirect conception that we possess of the temporal order of the world. But our conception of time far outstrips in its development and in its organization anything that we are able directly to find in the time that is known to our perceptions. Much of the difficulty that appears in our metaphysical views about time is, however, due to lack of naïveté and directness in viewing the temporal aspects of reality. We first emphasize highly artificial aspects of our conception of time. Then we wonder how these various aspects can be brought into relation with the rest of the real world. Our efforts to solve our problem lead very easily to contradictions. We fail to observe how, in case of our more direct experi-

From *The World and the Individual* (New York: Macmillan Company, 1899), pp. 111–151.

ence of time and of its meaning, various elements are woven into a certain wholeness,—the very elements which, when our artificial conception of time has sundered them, we are prone to view as irreconcilable with one another and with reality.

Our more direct perceptions of time form a complex sort of consciousness, wherein it is not difficult to distinguish several aspects. For the first, some Change is always occurring in our experience. This change may belong to the facts of any sense, or to our emotions, or to our ideas; but for us to be conscious is to be aware of change. Now this changing character of our experience is never the whole story of any of our clearer and more definite kinds of consciousness. The next aspect of the matter lies in the fact that our consciousness of change, wherever it is definite and wherever it accompanies definite successive acts of attention, goes along with the consciousness that for us something comes first, and something next, or that there is what we call a Succession of events. Of such successions, melodies, rhythms, and series of words or of other simple acts form familiar and typical examples. An elementary consciousness of change without such definite successions we can indeed have; but where we observe clearly what a particular change is, it is a change wherein one fact succeeds another.

A succession, as thus more directly experienced by us, involves a certain well-known relation amongst the events that make up the succession. Together these events form a temporal sequence or order. Each one of them is over and past when the next one comes. And this order of the experienced time-series has a determinate direction. The succession passes *from* each event *to* its successor, and not in the reverse direction; so that herein the observed time relations notoriously differ from what we view as space relations. For if in space *b* is next to *a*, we can read the relation equally well as a coexistence of *a* with *b*, and as a coexistence of *b* with *a*. But in case *b* succeeds *a*, as one word succeeds another in a spoken sentence, then the relation is experienced as a passing from *a* to *b*, or as a passing over of *a* into *b*, in such wise that *a* is past, as an event, before *b* comes. This direction of the stream of time forms one of its most notable empirical characters. It is obviously related to that direction of the acts of the will whose logical aspect interested us in connection with the consideration of our discriminating consciousness.

But side by side with this aspect of the tem-

poral order, as we experience this order, stands still another aspect, whose relation to the former has been persistently pointed out by many psychological writers, and as persistently, ignored by many of the metaphysical interpreters of the temporal aspect of the universe. When we more directly experience succession,—as, for instance, when we listen to a musical phrase or to a rhythmic series of drumbeats,—we not only observe that any antecedent member of the series is over and past before the next number comes, but also, and without the least contradiction between these two aspects of our total experience, we observe that this whole succession, with both its former and later members, so far as with relative directness we apprehend the series of drum-beats or of other simple events, is present *at once* to our consciousness, in precisely the sense in which the unity of our knowing mental life always finds present at once many facts. It is, as I must insist, true that for my consciousness *b* is experienced as following *a,* and also that both *a* and *b* are *together* experienced as in this relation of sequence. To say this is no more contradictory than to say that while I experience two parts of a surface as, by virtue of their spatial position, mutually exclusive each of the other, I also may experience the fact that both these mutually exclusive parts go together to form one whole surface. The sense in which they form one surface is, of course, not the sense in which, as parts, they exclude each other, and form different surfaces. Well, just so, the sense in which *b,* as successor of *a,* is such, in the series of events in question, that *a* is over and gone when *b* comes, is not the sense in which *a* and *b* are together elements in the whole experienced succession. But that, in *both* of these senses, the relation of *b* to its predecessor *a* is an experienced fact, is a truth that any one can observe for himself.

If I utter a line of verse, such as

The curfew tolls the knell of parting day,

the sound of the word *day* succeeds the sound of the word *parting,* and I unquestionably experience the fact that, for me, every earlier word of the line is over and past before the succeeding word or the last word, *day,* comes to be uttered or to be heard. Yet this is unquestionably not my whole consciousness about the succession. For I am certainly *also* aware that the *whole* line of poetry, as a succession of uttered sounds (or, at all events, a considerable portion of the line), is present to me at once, and as this one succession, when I speak the line. For only by virtue of experiencing this wholeness do I observe the rhythm, the music, and the meaning of the line. The sense in which the word *parting* is over before the word *day* comes, is like the sense in which one object in space is *where* any other object is *not,* so that the spatial *presence* of one object excludes the presence of another at that same part of space. Precisely so the presence of the word *day* excludes the presence of the word *parting* from its own place in the temporal succession. And, in our experience of succession, each element is *present* in a particular point of the series, in so far as, with reference to that point, other events of the series are either *past,* that is, over and done with, or are *future,* that is, are later in the series, or are *not yet when* this one point of the series is in *this* sense present. Every word of the uttered line of poetry, viewed in its reference to the other words, or to previous and later experiences, is *present* in its own place in the series, is *over and done with* before later events can come, or when they are present, and is *not yet* when the former events of the succession are present. And that all this is true, certainly is a matter of our experience of succession.

But the sense in which, nevertheless, the whole series of the uttered words of the line, or of some considerable portion of the line, is presented to our consciousness *at once,* is precisely the sense in which we apprehend this line as one line, and this succession as one succession. The whole series of words has for us its rhythmic unity, and forms an instance of conscious experience, whose unity we overlook at one glance. And unless we could thus overlook a succession and view at once its serially related and mutually exclusive events, we should never know anything whatever about the existence of succession, and should have no problem about time upon our hands.

This extremely simple and familiar character of our consciousness of succession,—this essentially double aspect of every experience of a present series of events,—this inevitably twofold sense in which the term *present* can be used in regard to our perception of temporal happenings,—this is a matter of the most fundamental importance for our whole conception of Time, and, as I may at once add, for our conception of Eternity. Yet this is also a matter very frequently obscured, in discussion, by various devices often used to express the nature of the facts here in question. Sometimes, for the sake of a laudable attempt to define the term *present* in a wholly unambiguous way, those who are

giving an account of our experience of time are led to assert that, since every part or element of any series of temporal events can be *present* only when all the other elements of the series are temporally non-existent, *i.e.* are either past or future, it must therefore be quite impossible for us to be conscious, *at once,* of a present succession involving a series of such elements. For how, they say, can I be conscious of the presence of all the successive words of the verse of poetry, when only one word is actually and temporally present at any one time? To comprehend how I can become in any sense aware of the series of successive words that constitutes the line of verse, such students of our problem are accustomed to say that when any one word as *passing,* or *day,* is present to my mind, the other words, even of the same line, can be present to consciousness *only* as coexistent memories or images of the former words, or as images of the expected coming words. From this point of view, I never really observe any sequence of conscious events as a sequence at all. I merely apprehend each element by itself; and I directly conclude from the images which in my experience are coexistent with this element, that there have been antecedent, and will be subsequent events in the series.

This interpretation of our consciousness of time is, however, directly counter to our time-experience, as any one may observe it for himself. For we do experience succession, and *at once* we do take note of facts that are in different times. For, I ask you, What word of mine is it that, as this single present word, you just *now* hear me speaking? If I pause a little, you perhaps dwell upon the last word that I utter before pausing, and call that the one present word. Otherwise, however, as I speak to you, you are conscious of series of successive words, of whole phrases, of word groups, of clauses. Within each one of these groups of words, you are indeed more or less clearly aware that every element has its own temporal place; and that, *in so far as* each element is taken by itself as present, the other elements either precede or succeed it, and in *this* sense are not in one time with it. But this very fact itself you know merely in so far as you actually experience series, each of which contains several successive words. These series come to you not merely by virtue of remembered facts, but also as experienced facts.

And in truth, were this not so, you could indeed have no experience of succession at all. You would then experience, at any one moment, merely the single word, or something less than any single word, together with the supposed coexistent and contemporaneous images of actually past or of coming words. But how, in that case, would your experience of time-sequences come to seem to you different from any experience whatever of coexistence? Nor is even this the only difficulty about the doctrine which supposes you to be unable to view a series of successive events as all at once presented to your consciousness. A still deeper difficulty results from such an effort to evade the double sense in which the facts of succession are known in your experience. If you can have present to you only *one* event at a time in a series of successive events, how long, or rather how short, must an event be to contain within itself no succession at all, or no difference between former and latter contents? In vain do you suppose that, at any time, you have directly present to your consciousness only one of the successive words that you hear me speak. Not thus do you escape our difficulty. For a spoken word is itself a series of temporally successive sounds. Can you hear at once the whole spoken word, or can you grasp at once this whole series? If so, my own foregoing account is in principle admitted. For then, in this presence of the facts of succession to your consciousness, there are our two former aspects, both of them, involved. *Each* element of the succession (namely, in this case, the elementary sounds that to your consciousness make up the word) is temporally present just when it occurs, but *not* before or afterwards, in so far as it follows previous elements and succeeds later elements; and also *all* the elements are, in the other sense of the term, *present at once* to consciousness, as constituting this whole succession which you call the word. If, however, you deny that you actually hear, apart from memory or from imagery, any single whole word at once, I shall only the more continue to ask you, What is the least or the simplest element of succession that is such as to constitute a merely present experience, with *no* former or latter contents within it? What apart from any memory or any imagery, and wholly apart from ideas of the past or the future of your experience, is present to you, in an indivisible time instant, just *Now*? The question is obviously unanswerable, just because an absolutely indivisible instant of mathematical time, with no former and latter contained within it, neither constitutes nor contains any temporal event, nor presents to you any fact of temporal experience whatever, just as an indivisible point in space could con-

tain no matter, nor itself ever become, in isolation, an object of spatial experience. On the other hand, an event such that in it you were unable to perceive any succession would help you in no whit to get the idea of time until you experienced it along with other events. What is now before you is a succession, within which are parts; and of these parts each, when and in so far as once your attention fixes it, and takes it in its time relations, is found as a present that in time both precedes and succeeds other facts, while these other facts are also just as truly before you as the observed element called the temporally present one is itself before you. And thus you cannot escape from our twofold interpretation of the experience of temporal succession. You are conscious of a series of successive states presented to you as a whole. You are also aware that each element of the succession excludes the others from its own place in time.

There is, to be sure, another frequent way of describing our consciousness of succession,—and a way that on the whole I find unsatisfactory. According to this view, events come to us in succession in our experience,—let us say the words of a spoken verse,—and *then* something often called the synthetic activity of the mind supervenes, and later binds together into unity, these successive facts, so that when this binding has taken place we *then* recognize the whole fagot of experience as a single succession. This account of the temporal facts, in terms of an activity called a synthesis, helps me, I must confess, no whit. What I find in consciousness is that a succession, such as a rhythm of drumbeats, a musical phrase, a verse of poetry, comes to me as one present whole, present in the sense that I know it all at once. And I also find that this succession is such that it has *within* it a temporal distinction, or order, of earlier and later elements. While these elements are at once known, they are *also* known as such that at the briefer instant *within* the succession when any one of them is to be temporally viewed as a present fact, none of the others are contemporaneous with that fact, but all are either *no longer* or *not yet* when, and in so far as, that element is taken as the present one. And I cannot make this datum of experience any more definite by calling it a synthesis, or the mere result of a synthesis.

I have now characterized the more directly given features in our consciousness of succession. You see, as a result, that we men experience what Professor James, and others, have called our "specious present," as a serial whole, *within* which there are observed temporal differences of former and latter. And this our "specious present" has, when measured by a reference to time-keepers, a length which varies with circumstances, but which appears to be never any very small fraction of a second, and never more than a very few seconds in length. I have earlier referred to this length of our present moments as our characteristic "time-span" of consciousness, and have pointed out how arbitrary a feature and limitation of our consciousness it is. We shall return soon to the question regarding the possible metaphysical significance of this time-span of our own special kind of consciousness.

But it remains here to call closer attention to certain other equally important features of our more direct experience of time-succession. So far, we have spoken, in the main, as if succession were to us a mere matter of given facts, as colors and sounds are given. But all our experience also has relation to the interests whose play and whose success or defeat constitute the life of our will. Every serial succession of which we are conscious therefore has for us some sort of meaning. In it we find our success or our failure. In it our internal meanings are expressed, or hindered, thwarted or furthered. We are interested in life, even if it be, in idle moments, only the dreary interest of wondering what will happen next, or, in distressed moments, the interest in flying from our present fortune, or, in despairing moments, of wishing for the end; still more then if, in strenuous moments, our interest is in pursuing our ideal. And our interest in life means our conscious concern in passing on from any temporal present towards its richer fulfilment, or away from its relative insignificance. Now that Direction of temporal succession of which I before made mention, has the most intimate relations to this our interest in our experience. What is earlier in a given succession is related to what is later as being that *from* which we pass *towards* a desired fulfilment, or in search of a more complete expression of our purpose. We are never content in the temporal present in so far as we view it as temporal, that is, as an event in a series. For such a present has its meaning as a transition from its predecessors towards its successors.

Our temporal form of experience is thus peculiarly the form of the Will as such. Space often seems to spread out before us what we take to be the mere contents of our world; but time gives the form for the expression of all our meanings. Facts, in so far as, with an abstractly false Realism, we sunder them from their meanings, therefore tend to be viewed as merely in relations of coexistence; and the space-world is the favorite region of Realism. But ideas, when conscious, assume the consiously temporal form of inner existence, and appear to us as constructive processes. The visible world, when viewed as at rest, therefore interests us little in comparison with the same world when we take note of its movements, changes, successions. As the kitten ignores the dead leaves until the wind stirs them, but then chases them—so facts in general tend to appear to us all dead and indifferent when we disregard their processes. But in the movements of things lies for us, just as truly as in her small way for the kitten, all the glory and the tragedy, all the life and the meaning of our observed universe. This concern, this interest in the changing, binds us then to the lower animals, as it doubtless also binds us to beings of far higher than human grade. We watch the moving and tend to neglect the apparently changeless objects about us. And that is why narrative is so much more easily effective than description in the poetic arts; and why, if you want to win the attention of the child or of the general public, you must tell the story rather than portray coexistent truths, and must fill time with series of events, rather than merely crowd the space of experience or of imagination with manifold but undramatic details. For space furnishes indeed the stage and the scenery of the universe, but the world's play occurs in time.

Now all these familiar considerations remind us of certain of the most essential characters of our experience of time. Time, whatever else it is, is given to us as that within whose successions, in so far as for us they have a direct interest and meaning, every event, springing from, yet forsaking, its predecessors, aims on, towards its own fulfilment and extinction in the coming of its successors. Our experience of time is thus for us essentially an experience of longing, of pursuit, of restlessness. And this is the aspect which Schopenhauer and the Buddhists have found so intolerable about the very nature of our finite experience. Upon this dissatisfied aspect of finite consciousness we ourselves dwelt when, in the former series of lectures, we were first learning to view the world, for the moment, from the mystic's point of view. As for the higher justification of this aspect of our experience, that indeed belongs elsewhere. But as to the facts, every part of a succession is present in so far as when it is, that which is *no longer* and that which is *not yet* both of them stand in essentially significant, or, if you will, in essentially practical relations to this present. It is true, of course, that when we view relatively indifferent time-series, such as the ticking of a watch or the dropping of rain upon the roof, we can disregard this more significant aspect of succession; and speak of the endless flight of time as an incomprehensible brute fact of experience, and as in so far seemingly meaningless. But no series of experiences upon which attention is fixed is wholly indifferent to us; and the temporal aspect of such series always involves some element of expectancy and some sense of something that no longer is; and both these conscious attitudes color our interest in the presented succession, and give the whole the meaning of life. Time is thus indeed the form of practical activity; and its whole character, and especially that direction of its succession of which we have spoken, are determined accordingly.

II

I have dwelt long upon the time consciousness of our relatively direct experience, because here lies the basis for every deeper comprehension of the metaphysics both of time and of eternity. Our ordinary conception of time as an universal form of existence in the external world, is altogether founded upon a generalization, whose origin is in us men largely and obviously social, but whose materials are derived from our inner experience of the succession of significant events. The conceived relations of Past, Present, and Future in the real world of common-sense metaphysics, appear indeed at first sight, vastly to transcend anything that we ourselves have ever observed in our inner experience. The infinite and irrevocable past that no longer is, the expected infinite future that has as yet no existence, how remote these ideal constructions, supposed to be valid for all gods and men and things, seem at first sight from the brief and significant series of successive events that occur within the brief span of our actual human consciousness. Yet, as we saw in the ninth lecture of our former Series, common sense, as soon as questioned about special cases, actually conceives the Being of both the past and the future as so intimately related to the Being of the present that every definite conception of the real processes of the world, whether these processes are viewed as physical or as historical or explicitly as ethical, depends upon taking the

past, the present, and the future as constituting a single whole, whose parts have no true Being except in their linkage. As a fact, moreover, the term *present*, when applied to characterize a moment or an event in the timestream of the real world, never means, in any significant application, the indivisible present of an ideal mathematical time. The present time, in case of the world at large, has an unity altogether similar to that of the present moment of our inner consciousness. We may speak of the present minute, hour, day, year, century. If we use the term *present* regarding any one of these divisions of time, but regard this time not as the experienced form of the inner succession of our own mental events, but as the time of the real world in which we ourselves form a part, then we indeed conceive that this present is world-embracing, and that suns move, light radiates between stars, that deeds of all men occur, and the minds of all men are conscious, in this same present time of which we thus make mention. Moreover, we usually view the world-time in question in terms of the conceptions of the World of Description, and so we conceive it as infinitely divisible, as measurable by various mathematical and physical devices, and as a continuous stream of occurrence. Yet in whatever sense we speak of the real present time of the world, this present, whether it is the present second, or the present century, or the present geological period, it is, for our conception, as truly a divisible and connected whole region of time, within which a succession of events takes place, as it is a world-embracing and connected time, within whose span the whole universe of present events is comprised. A mathematically indivisible present time, possessing no length, is simply no time at all. Whoever says, "In the universe at large only the present state of things is real, only the present movement of the stars, the present streamings of radiant light, the present deeds and thoughts of men are real; the whole past is dead; the whole future is not yet,"—any such reporter of the temporal existence of the universe may be invited to state how long his real present of the time-world is. If he replies, "The present moment is the absolutely indivisible and ideal boundary between present and future,"—then one may rejoin at once that in a mathematically indivisible instant, having no length, no event happens, nothing endures, no thought or deed takes place,—in brief, nothing whatever temporally exists,—and that, too, whatever conception you may have of Being. But if the real present is a divisible portion of time, then it contains within itself succession, precisely as the "specious present" of psychological time contains such internal succession. But in that case, within the real present of the time-world, there are already contained the distinctions that, in case of the time of experience, we have heretofore observed. If, in what you choose to call the present moment of the world's history, deeds are accomplished, suns actually move from place to place, light waves traverse the ether, and men's lives pass from stage to stage, then *within* what you thus call the present there are distinguishable and more elementary events, arranged in series, such that when any conceived element, or mere elementary portion of any series is taken in relation to its predecessors and successors, it is *not yet* when its antecedents are taken as temporally present, and is *past and gone* when its successors are viewed as present. The world's time is thus in all respects a generalized and extended image and correspondent of the observed time of our inner experience. In the time of our more direct experience, we find a twofold way in which we can significantly call a portion of time a present moment. The present, in our inner experience, means a whole series of events grasped by somebody as having some unity for his consciousness, and as having its own single internal meaning. This was what we meant by the present experience of this musical phrase, this spoken line of verse, this series of rhythmic beats. But, in the other sense of the word, an element within any such whole is present in so far as this element has antecedents and successors, so that they are *no longer* or *not yet* when it is temporally viewed as present, while in turn, in so far as any one of them is viewed as the present element, this element itself is either *not yet* or *no longer.* But precisely so, in the conceptual time of our real world, the Present means any section of the time-stream in so far as, with reference to anybody's consciousness, it is viewed as having relation to this unity of consciousness, and as in a single whole of meaning with this unity. Usually by "our time," or "the real time in which we now live," we mean no very long period of the conceived time-stream of the real world. But we never mean the indivisible *now* of an ideal mathematical time, because, in such an indivisible time-instant, nothing could happen, or endure, or genuinely exist. But within the present, if conceived as a section of the time-stream, there are internal differences of present, past, and future.

For, in a similar fashion, as the actual or supposed length of the "specious present" of our perceptual time is something arbitrary, determined by our peculiar human type of consciousness, so the length of the portion of conceptual time which we call the *present,* in the first sense of that term, namely, in the sense in which we speak of the "present age," is an arbitrary length, determined in this case, however, by our more freely chosen interest in some unity which gives relative wholeness and meaning to this present. If usually the "present age" is no very long time, still, at our pleasure, or in the service of some such unity of meaning as the history of civilization, or the study of geology, may suggest, we may conceive the present as extending over many centuries, or over a hundred thousand years. On the other hand, within the unity of this first present, any distinguishable event or element of an event is *present,* in the second, and more strictly temporal sense in so far as it has predecessors and successors, whereof the first are *no longer,* and the latter *not yet,* when this more elementary event is viewed as happening.

Nor does the parallelism between the perceptual and the conceptual time cease here. The perceptual time was the form in which meaning, and the practically significant aspects of consciousness, get their expression. The same is true of the conceptual time, when viewed in its relations to the real world. Not only is the time of human history, or of any explicitly teleological series of events, obviously the form in which the facts win their particular type of conceived meaning; but even the time of physical science gets its essential characters, as a conception, through considerations that can only be interpreted in terms of the Will, or of our interest in the meaning of the world's happenings.

For the conceived time-series, even when viewed in relation to the World of Description, still differs in constitution from the constitution of a line in space, or from the characters belonging to a mathematically describable physical movement of a body, in ways which can only be expressed in terms of significance. Notoriously, conceptual time has often been described as correspondent in structure to the structure of a line, or as correspondent again, in character, to the character of a uniformly flowing stream, or of some other uniform movement. But a line can be traversed in either direction, while conceptual time is supposed to permit but one way of passing from one instant to another in its course. An uniform flow, or other motion, has, like time, a fixed direction, but might be conceived as returning into itself without detriment to its uniformity. Thus an ideally regular watch "keeps time," as we say, by virtue of the uniformity of its motion; but its hands return ever again to the same places on the face; while the years of conceptual time return not again. And finally, if one supposed an ideally uniform physical flow or streaming in one rectilinear direction only, and in an infinite Euclidean space, the character of this movement might so far be supposed to correspond to that of an ideally conceived mathematical time; except for one thing. The uniformity and unchangeableness of the conceived physical flow would be a merely given character, dependent, perhaps, upon the fact that the physical movement in question was conceived as meeting with no obstacle or external hindrance; but the direction of the flow of time is a character essential to the very conception of time. And this direction of the flow of time can only be expressed in its true necessity by saying that in the case of the world's time, as in the case of the time of our inner experience, we conceive the past as leading towards, as aiming in the direction of the future, in such wise that the future depends for its meaning upon the past, and the past in its turn has its meaning as a process expectant of the future. In brief, only in terms of will, and only by virtue of the significant relations of the stages of a teleological process, has time, whether in our inner experience, or in the conceived world order as a whole, any meaning. Time is the form of the Will; and the real world is a temporal world in so far as, in various regions of that world, seeking differs from attainment, pursuit is external to its own goal, the imperfect tends towards its own perfection, or in brief, the internal meanings of finite life gradually win, in successive stages, their union with their own External Meaning. The general justification for this whole view of the time of the real world is furnished by our idealistic interpretation of Being. The special grounds for regarding the particular Being of time itself as in this special way teleological, are furnished by the foregoing analysis of our own experience of time, and by the fact that the conceptual time in terms of which we interpret the order of the world at large, is fashioned, so to speak, after the model of the time of our own experience.

III

Having thus defined the way in which the conceptual time of the real world of common sense corresponds in its structure to the structure of the time known to our inner perception, we are prepared to sketch our theory both of the sense in which the world of our idealistic doctrine appears to be capable of interpretation as a Temporal order, and of the sense in which, for this same theory, this world is to be viewed as an Eternal order. For, as a fact, in defining time we have already, and inevitably, defined eternity; and a temporal world must needs be, when viewed in its wholeness, an eternal world. We have only to review the structure of Reality in the light of the foregoing analysis in order to bring to our consciousness this result.

And so, first, the real world of our Idealism has to be viewed by us men as a temporal order. For it is a world where purposes are fulfilled, or where finite internal meanings reach their final expression, and attain unity with external meanings. Now in so far as any idea, as a finite Internal Meaning, still seeks its own Other, and consciously pursues that Other, in the way in which, as we have all along seen, every finite idea does pursue its Other, this Other is in part viewed as something beyond, *towards* which the striving is directed. But our human experience of temporal succession is, as we have seen, just such an experience of a pursuit directed towards a goal. And such pursuit demands, as an essential part or aspect of the striving in question, a consciousness that agrees in its most essential respect with our own experience of time. Hence, our only way of expressing the general structure of our idealistic realm of Being is to say that wherever an idea exists as a finite idea, still in pursuit of its goal, there appears to be some essentially temporal aspect belonging to the consciousness in question. To my mind, therefore, time, as the form of the will, is (in so far as we can undertake to define at all the detailed structure of finite reality) to be viewed as the most pervasive form of all finite experience, whether human or extrahuman. In pursuing its goals, the Self lives in time. And, to our view, every real being in the universe, in so far as it has not won union with the ideal, is pursuing that ideal; and, accordingly, so far as we can see, is living in time. Whoever, then, is finite, says, "not yet," and in part seeks his Other as involving what, to the seeker, is still future. For the finite world in general, then, as for us human beings, the distinction of past and future appears to be coextensive with life and meaning.

I have advisedly used, however, the phrase

that the time-consciousness is a "part" or "aspect" of the striving. For from our point of view, the Other, the completion that our finite being seeks, is not *merely* something beyond the present, and is not merely a future experience, but is also inclusive of the very process of the striving itself. For the goal of every finite life is simply the totality whereof this life, in its finitude, is a fragment. When I seek my own goal, I am looking for the whole of myself. In so far as my aim is the absolute completion of my Selfhood, my goal is identical with the whole life of God. But, in so far as, by my whole individual Self, I mean my whole Self in contrast with the Selves of my fellows,—then the completion of my individual expression, in so far as I am this individual and no other,—*i.e.* my goal, as this Self, is still not any one point or experience in my life, nor any one stage of my life, but the totality of my individual life viewed as in contrast with the lives of other individuals. Consequently, while it is quite true that every incomplete being, every finite striving, regards itself as aiming towards a future, because its own goal is not yet attained; we have, nevertheless, to remember that the attainment of the goal involves more than any future moment, taken by itself, could ever furnish. For the Self in its entirety is the whole of a self-representative or recurrent process, and not the mere last moment or stage of that process. As we shall see, there is in fact no last moment. A life seeking its goal is, therefore, indeed, essentially temporal,— but it is so just as music is temporal,—except indeed that music is not only temporal, but temporally finite. For every work of musical art involves significant temporal series, wherein there is progression, and passage from chord to chord, from phrase to phrase, and from movement to movement. But just as any one musical composition has its value not only by virtue of its attainment of its final chord, but also at every stage of the process that leads towards this conclusion; and just as the whole musical composition is, as a whole, an end in itself; so every finite Internal Meaning wins final expression, not merely through the last stage of its life (if it has a last stage), but through its whole embodiment. And, nevertheless, as the music attains wholeness only through succession; so every idea that is to win its complete expression, does so through temporal sequences.

Since, at all events, no other than such a temporal expression of meaning in life is in any wise definable for our consciousness, our Idealism can only express its view of the relation of finite and absolute life by viewing the whole world, and in particular the whole existence of any individual Self, as such a temporal process, wherein there is expressed, by means of a Well-Ordered Series of stages, a meaning that finally belongs to the whole life, but that at every temporal stage of the process in question appears to involve, in part, a beyond,—a something not yet won,—and so a distinction both of the past and the future of this Self from the content of any one stage of the process when that stage is viewed as the present one.

In the sense, therefore, our doctrine is obliged to conceive the entire world-life as including a temporal series of events. When considered with reference to any one of these events, the rest of the events that belong to the series of which any one finite Self takes account, are past and future, that is, they are *no longer* and *not yet;* just as, when viewed with reference to any one chord or phrase in the musical composition, all the other successive elements of the composition are either past or future.

The infinite divisibility of the time of our ordinary scientific conceptions is indeed due to that tendency of our own discriminating attention to an endless interpolation of intermediary stages,—a tendency which we studied in connection with our general account of the World of Description. We have, however, seen reasons, which, applied to time, would lead us to declare that an absolute insight would view the temporal order as a discrete series of facts ordered as any succession of facts expressing one purpose would be ordered, viz. like the whole numbers. On the other hand, we have no reason to suppose that our human consciousness distinctly observes intervals of time that in brevity anywhere nearly approach to the final truth about the temporal order. Within what is for us the least observable happening, a larger insight may indeed discriminate multitudes of events. In dealing with the concept of Nature, we shall see what significant use may be made of the hypothesis that there exists or may exist, finite consciousness for which the series of events that we regard as no longer distinguishable from merely elementary and indivisible happenings, are distinguished so minutely as to furnish content as rich as those which, from our point of view, occupy æons of the world's history. Our right to such hypotheses is incontestable, provided only that they help us to conceive the true unity of experience. Nevertheless, in the last analysis, the Absolute Will must be viewed as expressed in a well-ordered and discrete series of facts, which from our point of view may indeed appear, as we shall still further see, capable of discrimination *ad infinitum*.

But now secondly, and without the least conflict with the foregoing theses, I declare that this same temporal world is, when regarded in its wholeness, an Eternal order. And I mean by this assertion nothing whatever but that the whole real content of this temporal order, whether it is viewed from any one temporal instant as past or as present or as future, is *at once* known, *i.e.* is consciously experienced as a whole, by the Absolute. And I use this expression *at once* in the very sense in which we before used it when we pointd out that to your own consciousness, the whole musical phrase may be and often is known *at once, despite* the fact that each element of the musical succession, when taken as the temporally present one, excludes from its own temporal instant the other members of the sequence, so that they are either *no longer* or *not yet,* at the instant *when* this element is temporally the present one. As we saw before, it is true that, in one sense, each one of the elements or partial events of a sequence excludes the former and the latter elements from being at the time *when* this particular element exists. But that, in another and equally obvious and empirical sense, *all* the members of an actually experienced succession are *at once* to any consciousness which observes the whole succession as a whole, is equally true. The term *present,* as we saw, is naturally used both to name the temporally present when it is opposed to whatever precedes or succeeds this present, and also to name the observed facts of a succession in so far as they are experienced as constituting one whole succession. In so far the term is indeed ambiguous. But even this ambiguity itself is due to the before-mentioned fact that, if you try to find an absolutely simple present temporal fact of consciousness, and still to view it as an event in time, you are still always led, in the World of Description, to observe or to conceive that this temporal fact is a complex event, having a true succession *within* itself. So that the *now* of temporal expression is never a *mere* now, unless indeed it be viewed either as the ideal mathematical instant within which *nothing* takes place, or else as one of the finally simple stages of the discrete series of facts which the absolute insight views as the expression of its Will.

As to the one hypothesis, an absolute instant in the mathematical sense is like a point, an ideal limit, and never appears as any isolated fact of temporal experience. Every *now* within which something happens is therefore *also* a succession; so that every temporal fact, every event, so far as we men can observe it, has to be viewed as present to experience in *both* the senses of the term present; since this fact *when* present may be contrasted with predecessors that are *no longer* and with successors that are *not yet,* while this same fact, when taken as an event occupying time, is viewed as a presented succession with former and latter members contained within it. As to the other hypothesis, it seems clear that we human beings observe no such ultimate and indivisible facts of experience just because, so far as we observe and discriminate facts, we are more or less under the bondage of the categories of the World of Description.

But, in view of the correspondence between the universal time of the world-order, as we conceive it, and the time of our internal experience, as we observe it, the temporal sequences must be viewed as having in the real world, and for the Absolute, the same twofold character that our temporal experiences have for ourselves. *Present,* in what we may call the inclusive sense of the term, is any portion of real time with all its included events, in so far as there is any reason to view it as a whole, and as known in this wholeness by a single experience. *Present,* in what we may by contrast call the exclusive sense, is any one temporal event, in so far as it is contrasted with antecedent and subsequent events, and in so far as it excludes them from coexistence with itself in the same portion of any succession. These two senses of the term *present* do not contradict each other in case of the world-order any more than they do in case of our own inner experience. Both senses express inevitably distinct and yet inseparable connected aspects of the significant life of the conscious will, whether in us, or in the universe at large. Our view declares that all the life of the world, and therefore all temporal sequences, are present at once to the Absolute. Our view also maintains that, without the least conflict with this sense in which the whole temporal order is known at once to the Absolute, there is another sense in which any portion of the temporal sequence of the world may be taken as present, when viewed with reference to the experience of any finite Self whose present it is, and when contrasted with what for this same point of view is the past and the future of the world. Now the events of the temporal order, when viewed in this latter way, are divided, with reference to the point of view of any finite Self, into what *now* is, and what *no longer* is, and what *is to be,* but is *not yet.* These same events, however, in so far as they are viewed at once by the Absolute, are for such view, all equally present. And this their presence is the presence of all time, as a *totum simul,* to the Absolute. And the presence in this sense, of all time at once to the Absolute, constitutes the Eternal order of the world,—eternal, since it is inclusive of all distinctions of temporal past and temporal future,—eternal, since, for this very reason, the totality of temporal events thus present at once to the Absolute has no events that precede, or that follow it, but contains all sequences within it,—eternal, finally, because this view of the world does not, like our partial glimpses of this or of that relative whole of sequence, pass away and give place to some other view, but includes an observation of every passing away, of every sequence, of every event and of whatever in time succeeds and follows that event, and includes all the views that are taken by the various finite Selves.

In order to conceive what, in general, such an eternal view of the temporal order involves, or to conceive in what sense the temporal order of the real world is also an eternal order, we have, therefore, but to remember the sense in which the melody, or other sequence, is known at once to our own consciousness, despite the fact that its elements when viewed merely in their temporal succession are, in so far, *not* at once. As we saw before, the brief span of our consciousness, the small range of succession, that we can grasp at once, constitutes a perfectly arbitrary limitation of our own special type of consciousness. But in principle a time-sequence, however brief, is already viewed in a way that is not *merely* temporal, when, despite its sequence, it is grasped at once, and is thus grasped not through mere memory, but by virtue of actual experience. A consciousness related to the whole of the world's events, and to the whole of time, precisely as our human consciousness is related to a single melody or rhythm, and to the brief but still extended interval of time which this melody or rhythm occupies,—such a consciousness, I say, is an Eternal Consciousness. In principle we already possess and are acquainted with the nature of such a consciousness, whenever we do experience any succession as one whole. The only thing needed to complete our idea of what an actually eternal consciousness

is, is the conceived removal of that arbitrary limitation which permits us men to observe indeed at once a succession, but forbids us to observe a succession at once in case it occupies more than a very few seconds.

IV

This definition of the relations of the Temporal and the Eternal accomplishes all the purposes that are usually in mind when we speak of the divine knowledge as eternal. That eternity is a *totum simul,* the scholastics were well aware; and St. Thomas develops our present concept with a clearness that is only limited by the consequences of his dualistic view of the relation of God and the world. For after he has indeed well defined and beautifully illustrated the inclusive eternity of the divine knowledge, he afterwards conceives the temporal existence of the created world as sundered from the eternal life which belongs to God. And hereby the advantages of an accurate definition of the eternal are sacrificed for the sake of a special dogmatic interest.

Less subtle forms of speculation have led to uses of the word *eternal,* whose meaning is often felt to be far deeper than such usages can render explicit. But as these subtle usages are often stated, they are indeed open to the most obvious objections. An eternal knowledge is often spoken of as if it were one for which there is *no* distinction whatever between past, and present, and future. But such a definition is as absurd as if one should speak of our knowledge of a whole musical phrase or rhythm, when we grasped such a whole at once, as if the *at once* implied that there were for us no temporal distinction between the first and the last beat or note of the succession in question. To observe the succession *at once* is to have present with perfect clearness *all* the time-elements of the rhythm or of the phrase just as they are,— the succession, the tempo, the intervals, the pauses,—and yet, without losing any of their variety, to view them at once as one present musical idea. Now for our theory, that is precisely the way in which the eternal consciousness views the temporal order,—not ignoring one jot or tittle of its sharp distinctions of past or of future, of succession or of duration,—but still viewing the whole time-process as the expression of a single Internal Meaning. What we now call past and future are not merely the *same* for God; and, nevertheless, they are viewed *at once,* precisely as the beginning and the end of the rhythm are not the same for our experience, but are yet at once seen as belonging to one and the same whole succession.

Or again, an eternal knowledge is often supposed to be one that abstracts from time, or that takes no account of time; so that, for an eternal point of view it is as if time were not at all. But to say this is as if one were to speak of observing at once the meaning or character of the whole phrase or rhythm by simply failing to take any note at all of the succession as such. The meaning is the meaning of the succession; and is grasped only by observing this succession as something that involves former and latter elements, while these elements in time exclude one another, and therefore follow, each one *after* its predecessor has temporally ceased, and *before* its successor temporally appears. Just so, we assert that the eternal insight observes the whole of time, and all that happens therein, and is eternal only by virtue of the fact that it does know the whole of time.

Or again, some doctrines often speak of an eternal insight as something wholly and inexplicably *different* from any temporal type of consciousness, so that *how* God views His truth as eternal truth, no man can say. But our theory regards the essential relation of an eternal to a temporal type of consciousness as one of the simplest of the relations that are of primal importance for the definition of the Absolute. Listen to any musical phrase or rhythm, and grasp it as a whole, and you thereupon have present in you the image, so to speak, of the divine knowledge of the temporal order. To view all the course of time just as you then and there view the whole of that sequence,— this is to be possessed of an eternal type of insight.

"But," so many hereupon object,—"it appears impossible to see how this sort of eternal insight is possible, since just now, in time, the infinite past,—including, say, the geological periods and the Persian invasion of Greece, is *no longer,* while the future is *not yet.* How then for God shall this difference of past and future be transcended, and all be seen at once?" I reply, In precisely the same sense all the notes of the melody except this note are not *when* this note sounds, but are either *no longer* or *not yet.* Yet you may know a series of these notes at once. Now precisely so God knows the whole time-sequence of the world at once. The difference is merely one of span. You now exemplify the eternal type of knowledge, even as you listen to any briefest sequence of my words. For you, too, know time even by sharing the image of the Eternal.

Or again, a common wonder appears regarding how the divine knowledge can be in such wise eternal as to suffer no change to occur in it. How God should be unchangeable, yet express His will in a changing world, is an ancient problem. Our doctrine answers the question at a stroke. The knowledge of all change is itself indeed unchangeable, just because any change that occurs or that can occur to any being is already included amongst the objectives known to the eternal point of view. The knowledge of this melody as one whole does not itself consist in an adding of other notes to the melody. The knowledge of all sequences does not itself follow as another sequence. Hence it is indeed not subject to the fate of sequence.

And finally, a mystery is very generally made of the fact that since time appears to us as inevitably infinite, and as therefore not, like the melody or the rhythm, capable of completion, an eternal knowledge, if it involves a knowledge of the whole of time, must be something that has to appear to us self-contradictory and impossible. Any complete answer to this objection involves, of course, a theory of the infinite. Such a theory I have set forth in the Supplementary Essay, published with the First Series of these lectures. The issue involved, that of the positive concept of an infinite whole, is indeed no simple one, and is not capable of any brief presentation. I can here only report that the considerations set forth in that Supplementary Essay have led me to the thesis that a Well-Ordered Infinite Series, under the sole condition that it embodies a single plan, may be rightly viewed as forming a totality, and as an individual whole, precisely as a musical theme or a rhythm is viewed by our experience as such a whole. That the universe itself is such an infinite series, I have endeavored, in that paper, to show in great detail. If you view the temporal order of the world as also forming such an endless whole, expressing a single plan and Will (as I think you have a right to do), then the argument of the Supplementary Essay in question will apply to our present problem. The whole of time will contain a single expression of the divine Will, and therefore, despite its endlessness, the time-world will be present as such a single whole to the Absolute whose Will this is, and whose life all this sequence embodies.

V

In order to refer, as I close, to the practical interest which has guided me through all the abstract considerations even of this present lecture, I may be permitted to anticipate some of our later results about the Self, and, for the sake of illustration, to point out that from our point of view, as we shall later explain it more fully, your life, your Self, your will, your individuality, your deeds, can be and are present at once to the eternal insight of God; while, nevertheless, it is equally true that not only for you, but for God, your life is a genuine temporal sequence of deeds and strivings, whereof, when you view this life at the present temporal instant, the past is just now *no longer,* while the future is *not yet.* This twofold view of your nature, as a temporal process and as an eternal system of fact, is precisely as valid and as obvious as the twofold view of the melody or of the rhythm. Your temporal present looks back, as Will, upon your now irrevocable past. That past is irrevocable because it is the basis of your seeking for the future, and is the so far finished expression of your unique individual Will. Your future is the *not yet* temporally expressed region wherein you, as finite being, seek your own further expression. That future is still, in one aspect, as we shall see, causally undetermined, precisely in so far as therein something unique, that is yours and yours only, is to appear in the form of various individually designed expressions of your life-purpose,—various individual deeds. Therefore, as we shall be able to maintain, despite all your unquestionable causal and moral determinations, there will be an aspect of your future life that will be free, and yours, and such as no causation can predetermine, and such as even God possesses only in so far as your unique individuality furnishes it as a fact in His world.

And nevertheless, your future and your past, your aspect of individuality, and of freedom, and the various aspects wherein you are dependent upon the rest of the world, your whole life of deeds, and your attainment of your individual goal through your deeds,—all these manifold facts that are yours and that constitute you, are present at once to the Absolute,—as facts in the world, as temporal contents eternally viewed,—as a process eternally finished,—but eternally finished precisely by virtue of the temporal sequence of your deeds. And when you wonder how these aspects can be at once the aspects of your one life,—remember what is implied in the consciousness *at once* of the melody or the rhythm as a sequence,—and you will be in possession of the essential principle whereby the whole mystery is explained.

It is this view, once grasped in its various aspects, that will enable us to define in what sense man is one with God, and in what sense he is to be viewd as at present out of harmony with his own relation to God, and in that sense alienated from his true place in the eternal world. And so, in discussing this most elementary category, we are preparing the way for a most significant result as to the whole life of any man.

The temporal man, viewed just now in time, appears, at first, to be sundered even from his own past and future, and still more from God. He is a seeker even for to-morrow's bread,—still more for his salvation. He knows not just at this instant even his own individuality; still less should he immediately observe his relation to the Absolute in his present deed and in his fleeting experience. Only when he laboriously reflects upon his inmost meaning, or by faith anticipates the result of such reflection, does he become aware of how intimately his life is bound up with an Absolute life. This our finite isolation is, however, especially and characteristically a *temporal* isolation. That inattention of which we spoke in the last lecture, is especially an inattention to all but this act, as it now appears to me. I am not one with my own eternal individuality, especially and peculiarly because this passing temporal instant is not the whole of time, and because the rest of time is *no longer* or else *not yet when* this instant passes. Herein lies my peculiarly insurmountable human limitation. This is my present form of consciousness. To be sure, I am not wholly thus bound in the chains of my finitude. Within my present form and span of consciousness there is already exemplified an eternal type of insight, whereby the *totum simul* is in many cases and in brief span won. But beyond this my span of presentation, time escapes me as a past and future that is at once real and still either no longer or else not yet. From the eternal point of view, however, just this my life is *at once* present, in its Individuality and its wholeness. And because of this fact, just in so far as I am the eternal or true Individual, I stand in the presence of God, with all my life open before Him, and its meaning revealed to Him and to me. Yet this my whole meaning, while one with His meaning, remains, in the eternal world, still this unique and individual meaning, which the life of no other individual Self possesses. So that in my eternal expression I lose not my individuality, but rather win my only genuine individual expression, even while I find my oneness with God.

Now, in time, I seek, as if it were far beyond

me, that goal of my Selfhood, that complete expression of my will, which in God, and for God, my whole life at once possesses. I seek this goal as a far-off divine event,—as my future and success. I do well to seek. Seek and ye shall find. Yet the finding,—it does not occur merely as an event in time. It occurs as an eternal experience in this my whole striving. Every struggle, every tear, every misery, every failure, and repentance, and every rising again, every strenuous pursuit, every glimpse of God's truth,—all these are not mere incidents of the search for that which is beyond. They are all events in the life; they too are part of the fulfilment. In eternity all this is seen, and

hereby,—even in and through these temporal failures, I win, in God's presence and by virtue of His fulfilment, the goal of life, which is the whole of life. What no temporal instance ever brings,—what all temporal efforts fail to win, that my true Self in its eternity, and in its oneness with the divine, possesses.

So much it has seemed that I might here venture to anticipate of later results, in order that the true significance of our elementary categories might be, however imperfectly, defined for us from the outset. For all the questions as to our deeper relations to the universe are bound up with this problem of Time and Eternity.

The Body and the Members

We have repeatedly spoken of two levels of human life, the level of the individual and the level of the community. . . . We have also repeatedly emphasized the ethical and religious significance of loyalty; but our definition will help us throw clearer light upon the sources of this worth. And by thus sharpening the outlines of our picture of what a real community is, we shall be made ready to consider whether the concept of the community possesses a more than human significance. . . .

I

Our definition presupposes that there exist many individual selves. Suppose these selves to vary in their present experiences and purposes as widely as you will. Imagine them to be sundered from one another by such chasms of mutual mystery and independence as, in our natural social life, often seem hopelessly to divide and secrete the inner world of each of us from the direct knowledge and estimate of his fellows. But let these selves be able to look beyond their present chaos of fleeting ideas and of warring desires, far away into the past whence they came, and into the future wither their hopes lead them. As they thus look, let each one of them ideally enlarge his own individual life, extending himself into the past and future, so as to say of some far-off event, belonging, perhaps, to other generations of men,

"I view that event as a part of my own life." "That former happening or achievement so predetermined the sense and the destiny which are now mine, that I am moved to regard it as belonging to my own past." Or again: "For that coming event I wait and hope as an event of my own future."

And further, let the various ideal extensions, forwards and backwards, include at least one common event, so that each of these selves regards that event as a part of his own life.

Then, *with reference to the ideal common past and future in question, I say that these selves constitute a community.* This is henceforth to be our definition of a community. The present variety of the selves who are the members of the spiritual body so defined, is not hereby either annulled or slighted. The motives which determine each of them thus ideally to extend his own life, may vary from self to self in the most manifold fashion.

Our definition will enable us, despite all these varieties of the members, to understand in what sense any such community as we have defined exists, and is one.

Into this form, which, when thus summarily described, seems so abstract and empty, life can and does pour the rich contents and ideals which make the communities of our human world so full of dramatic variety and significance.

From *The Problem of Christianity* (Chicago: The University of Chicago Press, 1968), pp. 251–271.

II

The *first* condition upon which the existence of a community, in our sense of the word, depends, is the power of an individual self to extend his life, an ideal fashion, so as to regard it as including past and future events which lie far away in time, and which he does not now personally remember. That this power exists, and that man has a self which is thus ideally extensible in time without any definable limit, we all know.

This power itself rests upon the principle that, however a man may come by his idea of himself, the self is no mere datum, but is in its essence a life which is interpreted, and which interprets itself, and which, apart from some sort of ideal interpretation, is a mere flight of ideas, or a meaningless flow of feelings, or a vision that sees nothing, or else a barren abstract conception. How deep the process of interpretation goes in determining the real nature of the self, we shall only later be able to estimate.

There is no doubt that what we usually call our personal memory does indeed give us assurances regarding our own past, so far as memory extends and is trustworthy. But our trust in our memories is itself an interpretation of their data. All of us regard as belonging, even to our recent past life, much that we cannot just now remember. And the future self shrinks and expands with our hopes and our energies. No one can merely, from without, set for us the limits of the life of the self, and say to us: "Thus far and no farther."

In my ideal extensions of the life of the self, I am indeed subject to some sort of control,—to what control we need not here attempt to formulate. I must be able to give myself some sort of reason, personal, or social, or moral, or religious, or metaphysical, for taking on or throwing off the burden, the joy, the grief, the guilt, the hope, the glory of past and of future deeds and experiences; but I must also myself personally share in this task of determining how much of the past and the future shall ideally enter into my life, and shall contribute to the value of that life.

And if I choose to say, "There is a sense in which *all* the tragedy and the attainment of an endless past and future of deeds and of fortunes enter into my own life," I say only what saints and sages of the most various creeds and experiences have found their several reasons for saying. The fact and the importance of such ideal extensions of the self must therefore be recognized. Here is the first basis for every clear idea of what constitutes a community.

The ideal extensions of the self may also include, as is well known, not only past and future events and deeds, but also physical things, whether now existent or not, and many other sorts of objects which are neither events nor deeds. The knight or the samurai regarded his sword as a part of himself. One's treasures and one's home, one's tools, and the things that one's hands have made, frequently come to be interpreted as part of the self. And any object in heaven or earth may be thus ideally appropriated by a given self. The ideal self of the Stoic or of the Mystic may, in various fashions, identify its will, or its very essence, with the whole universe. The Hindoo seer seeks to realize the words: "I am Brahm;" "That art thou."

In case such ideal extensions of the self are consciously bound up with deeds, or with other events, such as belong to the past or future life which the self regards as its own, our definition of the community warrants us in saying that many selves form one community when all are ideally extended so as to include the same object. But unless the ideal extensions of the self thus consciously involve past and future deeds and events that have to do with the objects in question, we shall not use these extensions to help us to define communities.

For our purposes, the community is a being that attempts to accomplish something in time and through the deeds of its members. These deeds belong to the life which each member regards as, in ideal, his own. It is in this way that both the real and the ideal Church are intended by the members to be communities in our sense. An analogous truth holds for such other communities as we shall need to consider. The concept of the community is thus, for our purposes, a practical conception. It involves the idea of deeds done, and ends sought or attained. Hence I shall define it in terms of members who themselves not only live in time, but conceive their own ideally extended personalities in terms of a time-process. In so far as these personalities possess a life that is for each of them his own, while it is, in some of its events, common to them all, they form a community.

Nothing important is lost, for our conception of the community, by this formal restriction, whereby common objects belong to a community only when these objects are bound up with the deeds of the community. For, when the warrior regards his sword as a part of himself, he does so because his sword is the instrument of his will, and because what he does with his sword belongs to his literal or ideal life. Even the mystic accomplishes his identification of the self and the world only through acts of renunciation or of inward triumph. And these acts are the goal of his life. Until he attains to them, they form part of his ideal future self. Whenever he fully accomplishes these crowning acts of identification, the separate self no longer exists. When knights or mystics form a community, in our sense, they therefore do so because they conceive of deeds done, in common, with their swords, or of mystical attainments that all of them win together.

Thus then, while no authoritative limit can be placed upon the ideal extensions of the self in time, those extensions of the self which need be considered for the purposes of our theory of the community are indeed extensions in time, past or future; or at all events involve such extensions in time.

Memory and hope constantly incite us to the extensions of the self which play so large a part in our daily life. Social motives of endlessly diverse sort move us to consider "far and forgot" as if to us it were near, when we view ourselves in the vaster perspectives of time. It is, in fact, the ideally extended self, and not, in general, the momentary self, whose life is worth living, whose sense outlasts our fleeting days, and whose destiny may be worthy of the interest of beings who are above the level of human individuals. The present self, the fleeting individual of to-day, is a mere gesticulation of the self. The genuine person lives in the far-off past and future as well as in the present. It is, then, the ideally extended self that is worthy to belong to a significant community.

III

The *second* condition upon which the existence of a community depends is the fact that there are in the social world a number of distinct selves capable of social communication, and, in general, engaged in communication.

The distinctness of the selves we have illustrated at length in our previous discussion. We need not here dwell upon the matter further, except to say, expressly, that a community does *not* become one, in the sense of my definition, by virtue of any reduction or melting of these various selves into a single merely present self, or into a mass of passing experience. That mystical phenomena may indeed form part of the life of a community, just as they

may also form part of the life of an individual human being, I fully recognize.

About such mystical or quasi-mystical phenomena, occurring in their own community, the Corinthians consulted Paul. And Paul, whose implied theory of the community is one which my own definition closely follows, assured them in his reply that mystical phenomena are not essential to the existence of the community; and that it is on the whole better for the life of such a community as he was addressing, if the individual member, instead of losing himself "in a mystery," kept his own individuality, in order to contribute his own edifying gift to the common life. Wherein this common life consists we have yet further to see in what follows.

The *third* of the conditions for the existence of the community which my definition emphasizes consists in the fact that the ideally extended past and future selves of the members include at least some events which are, for all these selves, identical. This third condition is the one which furnishes both the most exact, the most widely variable, and the most important of the motives which warrant us in calling a community a real unit. The Pauline metaphor of the body and the members finds, in this third condition, its most significant basis,—a basis capable of exact description.

IV

In addition to the instance which I cited at the last time, when I mentioned the New Zealanders and their legendary canoes, other and much more important illustrations may here serve to remind us how a single common past or future event may be the central means of uniting many selves in one spiritual community. For the Pauline churches the ideal memory of their Lord's death and resurrection, defined in terms of the faith which the missionary apostle delivered to them in his teaching, was, for each believer, an acknowledged occurrence in his own past. For each one was taught the faith, "In that one event my individual salvation was accomplished."

This faith has informed ever since the ideal memory upon which Christian tradition has most of all depended for the establishment and the preservation of its own community. If we speak in terms of social psychology, we are obliged, I think, to regard this belief as the product of the life of the earliest Christian community itself. But once established, and then transmitted from generation to generation, this same belief has been ceaselessly re-creative of the communities of each succeeding age. And the various forms of the Christian Church,—its hierarchical institutions, its schisms, its reformations, its sects, its heresies, have been varied, differentiated, or divided, or otherwise transformed, according as the individual believers who made up any group of followers of Christian tradition have conceived, each his own personal life as including and as determined by that one ideal event thus remembered, namely, his Lord's death and resurrection.

Since the early Church was aware of this dependence of its community upon its memory, it instinctively resisted every effort to deprive that memory of definiteness, to explain it away as the Gnostic heresies did, or to transform it from a memory into any sort of conscious allegory. The idealized memory, the backward looking faith of an individual believer, must relate to events that seem to him living and concrete. Hence the early Church insisted upon the words, "Suffered under Pontius Pilate." The religious instinct which thus insisted was true to its own needs. A very definite event must be viewed by each believer as part of the history of his own personal salvation. Otherwise his community would lose its coherence.

Paul himself, despite his determination to know Christ, not "after the flesh," but "after the Spirit," was unhesitating and uncompromising with regard to so much of the ideal Christian memory as he himself desired each believer to carry clearly in mind. Only by such common memories could the community be constituted. To be sure, the Apostle's Christology, on its more metaphysical side, cared little for such more precise technical formulations as later became historically important for the Church that formulated its creeds. But the events which Paul regarded as essential for salvation must be, as he held, plainly set down.

Since human memory is naturally sustained by commemorative acts, Paul laid the greatest possible stress upon the Lord's Supper, and made the proper ordering thereof an essential part of his ideal as a teacher. In this act of commemoration, wherein each member recalled the origin of his own salvation, the community maintained its united life.

V

The early Church was, moreover, not only a community of memory, but a community of hope. Since, if the community was to exist, and to be vigorously alive, each believer must keep definite his own personal hope, while the event for which all hoped must be, for all, an identical event, something more was needed, in Paul's account of the coming end of the world, than the more dimly conceived common judgment had hitherto been in the minds of the Corinthians to whom Paul wrote. And therefore the great chapter on the resurrection emphasizes equally the common resurrection of all, and the very explicitly individual immortality of each man. Paul uses both the resurrection of Christ, and the doctrine of the spiritual body, to give the sharpest possible outlines to a picture which has ever since dominated not only the traditional Christian religious imagination, but the ideal of the united Church triumphant.

Nowhere better than in this very chapter can one find an example of the precise way in which the fully developed consciousness of a community solves its own problem of the one and the many, by clearly conceiving both the diversity of the members and the unity of the body in terms of the common hope for the same event.

The Apostle had to deal with the doctrine of the immortality of the individual man, and also with the corporate relations of humanity and of the Church to death and to the end of all things. The most pathetic private concerns and superstitions of men, the most conflicting ideas of matter, of spirit, and of human solidarity, had combined, in those days, to confuse the religious ideas which entered into the life of the early Church, when the words "death and resurrection" were in question. The Apostle himself was heir to a seemingly hopeless tangle of ancient and more or less primitive opinions regarding the human self and the cosmos, regarding the soul and the future.

A mystery-religion of Paul's own time might, and often did, assure the individual initiate of his own immortality. The older Messianic hope, or its successor in the early Christian consciousness, might be expressed, and was often expressed, in a picture wherein all mankind were together called before the judgment seat at the end. But minds whose ideas upon such topics came from various and bewildering sources,—minds such as those of Paul's Corinthians, might, and did, inquire: "What will personally happen to me? What will happen to all mankind?" The very contrast between these two questions was, at that time, novel. The growing sense of the significance of the individual self was struggling against various more or less mystical identifications of all mankind with Adam, or with some one divine or demonic power or spirit. Such a struggle still goes on to-day.

But Paul's task it was, in writing this chapter, to clarify his own religious consciousness, and to guide his readers through the mazes of human hope and fear to some precise view, both of human solidarity and individual destiny. His method consisted in a definition of his whole problem in terms of the relations between the individual, the community, and the divine being whom he conceived as the very life of this community. He undertook to emphasize the individual self, and yet to insist upon the unity of the Church and of its Lord. He made perfectly clear in each believer's mind the idea: "I myself, and not another, am to witness and to take part in this last great change." To this end Paul made use of the conception of the individual spiritual body of each man. But Paul also dwelt with equal decisiveness upon the thought, "The last event of the present world is to be, for all of us, *one* event; for we shall all together arise."

These two main thoughts of the great chapter are in the exposition clearly contrasted and united; and against this well-marked background Paul can then place statements about humanity viewed as one corporate entity,— monistic formulations, so to speak,—and can do this without fear of being misunderstood: "The first man Adam became a living soul. The last Adam became a quickening spirit. The first man is of the earth, earthy; the second man is the Lord from heaven." What these more monistic statements about mankind as one corporate entity are to mean, is made clear simply by teaching each believer to say, "I shall myself arise, with my own transformed and incorruptible body;" and also to say, "This event of the resurrection is one for all of us, for we shall arise together."

In such expressions Paul uses traditions whose sources were indeed obscure and whose meaning was, as one might have supposed, hopelessly ambiguous. The interpretations of these traditions on Paul's part might have been such as to lose sight of the destiny of the individual human being through a more or less mystical blending of the whole race. That would have been natural for a mind trained to think of Adam and of mankind as Paul was trained. Or, again, the interpretation might have taken the form of assuring the individual believer that he could win his own immortality, while leaving him no further ground for special interest in the community.

Paul's religious genius aims straight at the central problem of clearing away this ambiguity, and of defining the immortal life, both of the individual and of the community. In the expected resurrection, as Paul pictures it, the individual finds his own life, and the community its common triumph over all the world-old powers of death. And the hope is referred back again to the memory. Was not Christ raised? By this synthesis Paul solves his religious problems, and defines sharply the relation of the individual and the community.

And therefore, whenever, upon the familiar solemn occasions, this chapter is read, not only is individual sorrow bidden to transform itself into an unearthly hope; but even upon earth the living and conscious community of the faithful celebrates the present oneness of spirit in which it triumphs. And the death over which it triumphs is the death of the lonely individual, whom faith beholds raised to the imperishable life in the spirit. This life in the spirit is also the life of the community For the individual is saved, according to Paul, only in and through and with the community and its Lord.

VI

Our present interest in these classic religious illustrations of the idea of the community is not directly due to their historical importance as parts of Christian tradition; but depends upon the help which they give us in seeing how a community, whether it be Christian or not, can really constitute a single entity, despite the multiplicity of its members. Our illustrations have brought before us the fact that hope and memory constitute, in communities, a basis for an unquestionable consciousness of unity, and that this common life in time does not annul the variety of the individual members at any one present moment.

We have still to see, however, the degree to which this consciousness of unity can find expression in an effectively united common life which not only contains common events, but also possesses common deeds and can arouse a common love—a love which passes the love wherewith individuals can love one another.

And here we reach that aspect of the conception of the community which is the most important, and also the most difficult aspect.

VII

A great and essentially dramatic event, such as the imagined resurrection of the bodies of all men,—an event which interests us, and which fixes the attention by its miraculous apparition,—is well adapted to illustrate the union of the one and the many in the process of time. When Paul's genius seized upon this picture,—when, to use the well-known later scholastic phraseology, the spirits of men were thus "individuated by their bodies," even while the event of the resurrection fixed the eye of faith upon one final crisis through which all were to pass "in a moment, in the twinkling of an eye,"—when the Apostle thus instructed the faithful, a great lesson was also taught regarding the means whereby the ideal of a community and the harmonious union of the one and the many can be rendered brilliantly clear to the imagination, and decisively fascinating to the will.

But the lives of communities cannot consist of miraculous crises. A community, like an individual self, must learn to keep the consciousness of its unity through the vicissitudes of an endlessly shifting and often dreary fortune. The monotony of insignificant events, the chaos of lesser conflicts, the friction and the bickerings of the members, the individual failures and the mutual misunderstandings which make the members of a community forget the common past and future,—all these things work against the conscious unity of the life of a community. Memory and hope are alike clouded by multitudes of such passing events. The individual members cannot always recall the sense in which they identify their own lives and selves with what has been, or with what is yet to come.

And—hardest task of all—the members, if they are to conceive clearly of the common life, must somehow learn to bear in mind not merely those grandly simple events which, like great victories, or ancestral feats, or divine interferences, enter into the life of the community from without, and thus make their impression all at once.

No, the true common life of the community consists of deeds which are essentially of the nature of processes of coöperation. That is, the common life consists of deeds which many members perform together, as when the workmen in a factory labor side by side.

Now we all know that coöperation constantly occurs, and is necessary to every form and grade of society. We also know that commerce and industry and art and custom and language consist of vast complexes of coöperations. And in all such cases many men manage in combination to accomplish what no man, and no multitude of men working separately, could conceivably bring to pass. But what we now need to see is the way in which such coöperations can become part, not only of the life, but of the consciousness of a community.

VIII

Every instance of a process of coöperation is an event, or a sequence of events. And our definition of a community requires that, if such coöperative activities are to be regarded as the deeds of a community, there must be individuals, each one of whom says: "That coöperation, in which many distinct individuals take part, and in which I also take part, is, or was, or will be, an event in my life." And many coöperating individuals must agree in saying this of the same process in which they all coöperate.

And all must extend such identifications of the self with these social activities far into the past, or into the future.

But it is notoriously hard—especially in our modern days of the dreary complexity of mechanical labor—for any individual man so to survey, and so to take interest in a vast coöperative activity that he says: "In my own ideally extended past and future that activity, its history, its future, its significance as an event or sequence of events, all have their ideally significant part. That activity, as the coöperation of many in one work, is also my life." To say such things and to think such thoughts grow daily harder for most of the coworkers of a modern social order.

Hence, as is now clear, the existence of a highly organized social life is by no means identical with the existence of what is, in our present and restricted sense, the life of a true community. On the contrary, and for the most obvious reasons, there is a strong mutual opposition between the social tendencies which secure coöperation on a vast scale, and the very conditions which so interest the individual in the common life of his community that it forms part of his own ideally extended life. We met with that opposition between the more or less mechanically coöperative social life,—the life of the social will on the one side, and the life of the true community on the other side,—when we were considering the Pauline doctrine of the law in an earlier lecture. In fact, it is the original sin of any highly developed civilization that it breeds coöperation at the expense of a loss of interest in the community.

The failure to see the reason why this opposition between the tendency to coöperation and the spirit of the community exists; the failure to sound to the depths the original sin of man the social animal, and of the natural social order which he creates;—such failure, I repeat, lies at the basis of countless misinterpretations, both of our modern social problems, and of the nature of a true community, and of the conditions which make possible any wider philosophical generalizations of the idea of the community.

IX

Men do not form a community, in our present restricted sense of that word, merely in so far as the men coöperate. They form a community, in our present limited sense, when they not only coöperate, but accompany this coöperation with that ideal extension of the lives of individuals whereby each coöperating member says: "This activity which we perform together, this work of ours, its past, its future, its sequence, its order, its sense,—all these enter into my life, and are the life of my own self writ large."

Now coöperation results from conditions which a social psychology such as that of Wundt or of Tarde may analyze. Imitation and rivalry, greed and ingenuity, business and pleasure, war and industry, may all combine to make men so coöperate that very large groups of them behave, to an external observer, as if they were units. In the broader sense of the term "community," all social groups that behave as if they were units are regarded as communities. And we ourselves called all such groups communities in our earlier lectures before we came to our new definition.

But we have now been led to a narrower application of the term "community." It is an application to which we have restricted the term simply because of our special purpose in this inquiry. Using this restricted definition of the term "community," we see that groups which coöperate may be very far from constituting communities in our narrower sense. We also see how, in general, a group whose coöperative activities are very highly complex will require a correspondingly long period of time to acquire that sort of tradition and of common expectation which is needed to constitute a community in our sense,—that is, a community conscious of its own life.

Owing to the psychological conditions upon which social coöperation depends, such cooperation can very far outstrip, in the complexity of its processes, the power of any individual

man's wit to understand its intricacies. In modern times, when social cooperation both uses and is so largely dominated by the industrial arts, the physical conditions of coöperative social life have combined with the psychological conditions to make any thorough understanding of the coöperative processes upon which we all depend simply hopeless for the individual, except within some narrow range. Experts become well acquainted with aspects of these forms of coöperation which their own callings involve. Less expert workers understand a less range of the coöperative processes in which they take part. Most individuals, in most of their work, have to coöperate as the cogs coöperate in the wheels of a mechanism. They work together; but few or none of them know how they coöperate, or what they must do.

But the true community, in our present restricted sense of the word, depends for its genuine common life upon such coöperative activities that the individuals who participate in these common activities understand enough to be able, first, to direct their own deeds of coöperation; secondly, to observe the deeds of their individual fellow workers, and thirdly to know that without just this combination, this order, this interaction of the coworking selves, just this deed could not be accomplished by the community. So, for instance, a chorus or an orchestra carries on its coöperative activities. In these cases coöperation is a conscious art. If hereupon these coöperative deeds, thus understood by the individual coworker, are viewed by him as linked, through an extended history with past and future deeds of the community, and if he then identifies his own life with this common life, and if his fellow members agree in this identification, then indeed the community both has a common life, and is aware of the fact. For then the individual coworker not only says: "This past and future fortune of the community belongs to my life;" but also declares: "This past and future deed of coöperation belongs to my life." "This, which none of us could have done alone,—this, which all of us together could not have accomplished unless we were ordered and linked in precisely this way,—this we together accomplished, or shall yet accomplish; and this deed of all of us belongs to my life."

A community thus constituted is essentially a community of those who are artists in some form of coöperation, and whose art constitutes, for each artist, his own ideally extended life. But the life of an artist depends upon his love for his art.

The community is made possible by the fact that each member includes in his own ideally extended life the deeds of coöperation which the members accomplish. When these deeds are hopelessly complex, how shall the individual member be able to regard them as genuinely belonging to his own ideally extended life? He can no longer understand them in any detail. He takes part in them, willingly or unwillingly. He does so because he is social, and because he must. He works in his factory, or has his share, whether greedily or honestly, in the world's commercial activities. And his coöperations may be skilful; and this fact also he may know. But his skill is largely due to external training, not to inner expansion of the ideals of the self. And the more complex the social order grows, the more all this coöperation must tend to appear to the individual as a mere process of nature, and not as his own work,—as a mechanism and not as an ideal extension of himself,— unless indeed love supplies what individual wit can no longer accomplish.

X

If a social order, however complex it may be, actually wins and keeps the love of its members; so that,—however little they are able to understand the details of their present coöperative activities,—they still—with all their whole hearts and their minds and their souls, and their strength—desire, each for himself, that such coöperations should go on; and if each member, looking back to the past, rejoices in the ancestors and the heroes who have made the present life of this social group possible; and if he sees in these deeds of former generations the source and support of his present love; and if each member also looks forward with equal love to the future,—then indeed love furnishes that basis for the consciousness of the community which intelligence, without love, in a highly complex social realm, can no longer furnish. Such love—such loyalty—depends not upon losing sight of the variety of the callings of individuals, but upon seeing in the successful coöperation of all the members precisely that event which the individual member most eagerly loves as his own fulfilment.

When love of the community, nourished by common memories, and common hope, both exists and expresses itself in devoted individual lives, it can constantly tend, despite the complexity of the present social order, to keep the consciousness of the community alive. And when this takes place, the identification of the loyal individual self with the life of the community will tend, both in ideal and in feeling, to identify each self not only with the distant past and future of the community, but with the present activities of the whole social body.

Thus, for instance, when the complexities of business life, and the dreariness of the factory, have, to our minds, deprived our present social coöperations of all or of most of their common significance, the great communal or national festivity, bringing to memory the great events of past and future, not only makes us, for the moment, feel and think as a community with reference to those great past and future events, but in its turn, as a present event, reacts upon next day's ordinary labors. The festivity says to us: "We are one because of our common past and future, because of the national heroes and victories and hopes, and because we love all these common memories and hopes." Our next day's mood, consequent upon the festivity, bids us say: "Since we are thus possessed of this beloved common past and future, let this consciousness lead each of us even to-day to extend his ideal self so as to include the daily work of all his fellows, and to view his fellow members' life as his own."

Thus memory and hope tend to react upon the present self, which finds the brotherhood of present labor more significant, and the ideal identification of the present self with the self of the neighbor easier, because the ideal extension of the self into past and future has preceded.

And so, first, each of us learns to say: "This beloved past and future life, by virtue of the ideal extension, is my own life." Then, finding that our fellows have and love this past and future in common with us, we learn further to say: "In this respect we are all one loving and beloved community." Then we take a further step and say: "Since we are all members of this community, therefore, despite our differences, and our mutual sunderings of inner life, each of us can, and will, ideally extend his present self so as to include the present life and deeds of his fellow."

So it is that, in the ideal church, each member not only looks backwards to the same history of salvation as does his fellow, but is even thereby led to an ideal identification of his present self with that of his fellow member that would not otherwise be possible. Thus, then, common memory and common hope, the central possessions of the community, tend, when enlivened by love, to mould the consciousness of the present, and to link each member to his community by ideal ties which belong to the moment as well as to the stream of past and future life.

XI

Love, when it exists and triumphs over the complexities which obscure and confuse the common life, thus completes the consciousness of the community, in the forms which that consciousness can assume under human conditions. Such love, however, must be one that has the common deeds of the community as its primary object. No one understands either the nature of the loyal life, or the place of love in the constitution of the life of a real community, who conceives such love as merely a longing for the mystical blending of the selves or for their mutual interpenetration, and for that only. Love says to the individual: "So extend yourself, in ideal, that you aim, with all your heart and your soul and your mind and your strength, at *that* life of perfect definite deeds which never can come to pass unless all the members, despite their variety and their natural narrowness, are in perfect coöperation. Let this life be your art and also the art of all your fellow members. Let your community be as a chorus, and not as a company who forget themselves in a common trance."

Nevertheless, as Paul showed in the great chapter, such love of the self for the community can be and will be not without its own mystical element. For since we human beings are as narrow in our individual consciousness as we are, we cannot ideally extend ourselves through clearly understanding the complicated social activities in which the community is to take part. Therefore our ideal extensions of the self, when we love the community, and long to realize its life with intimacy, must needs take the form of *acting as if we could survey,* in some single unity of insight, that wealth and variety and connection which, as a fact, we cannot make present to our momentary view. Since true love is an emotion, and since emotions are present affections of the self, love, in longing for its own increase, and for its own fulfilment, inevitably longs to find what it loves as a fact of experience, and to be in the immediate presence of its beloved. Therefore, the love of a community (a love which, as we now see, is devoted to desiring the realization of an overwhelming vast variety and unity of coöperations), is, as an emotion, discontent with all the present sundering of the selves, and with all the present problems and mysteries of the social order. Such love, then,

restless with the narrowness of our momentary view of our common life, desires this common life to be an immediate presence for all of us. Such an immediate presence of all the community to all the members would be indeed, if it could wholly and simply take place, a mere blending of the selves,—an interpenetration in which the individuals vanished, and in which, for that very reason, the real community would also be lost.

Love,—the love of Paul's great chapter,—the loyalty which stands at the centre of the Christian consciousness,—is, as an emotion, a longing for such a mystical blending of the selves. This longing is present in Paul's account. It is in so far not the whole of charity. It is simply the mystical aspect of the love for the community.

But the Pauline charity is not merely an emotion. It is an interpretation. The ideal extension of the self gets a full and concrete meaning only by being actively expressed in the new deeds of each individual life. Unless each man knows how distinct he is from the whole community and from every member of it, he cannot render to the community what love demands,—namely, the devoted work. Love may be mystical, and work should be directed by clearly outlined intelligence; but the loyal spirit depends upon this union of a longing for unity with a will which needs its own expression in works of loyal art.

XII

The doctrine of the two levels of human existence; the nature of a real community; the sense in which there can be, in individual human beings, despite their narrowness, their variety, and their sundered present lives, a genuine consciousness of the life of a community whereof they are members:—these matters we have now, within our limits, interpreted. The time-process, and the ideal extensions of the self in this time-process, lie at the basis of the whole theory of the community. The union and the contrast of the one and the many in the community, and the relation of the mystical element in our consciousness of the community to the active interpretation of the loyal life, these things have also been reviewed. Incidentally, so to speak, we have suggested further reasons why loyalty, whether in its distinctively Christian forms, or in any others, is a saving principle whenever it appears in an individual human life. For in the love of a community the individual obtains, for his ideally extended self, precisely the unity, the wealth, and the harmony of plan which his sundered natural existence never supplies.

Yet it must be not merely admitted, but emphasized, that all such analyses of the sort of life and of interpretation upon which communities and the loyalty of their members depend, does not and cannot explain the origin of loyalty, the true sources of grace, and the way in which communities of high level come into existence.

On the contrary, all the foregoing account of what a community is shows how the true spirit of loyalty, and the highest level of the consciousness of a human community, is at once so precious, and so difficult to create.

The individual man naturally, but capriciously, loves both himself and his fellow-man, according as passion, pity, memory, and hope move him. Social training tends to sharpen the contrasts between the self and the fellow-man; and higher cultivation, under these conditions of complicated social coöperation which we have just pointed out, indeed makes a man highly conscious that he depends upon his community, but also renders him equally conscious that, as an individual, he is much beset by the complexities of the social will, and does not always love his community, or any community. Neither the origin nor the essence of loyalty is explained by man's tendencies to love his individual fellow-man.

It is true that, within the limits of his power to understand his social order, the conditions which make a man conscious of his community also imply that the man should in some respects identify his life with that. But I may well know that the history, the future, the whole meaning of my community are bound up with my own life; and yet it is not necessary that on that account I should wholeheartedly love my own life. I may be a pessimist. Or I may be simply discontented. I may desire to escape from the life that I have. And I may be aware that my fellows, for the most part, also long to escape.

That the community is above my own individual level I shall readily recognize, since the community is indeed vastly more skilful and incomparably more powerful than I can ever become. But what is thus above me I need not on that account be ready wholly to love. To be sure, that man is indeed a sad victim of a misunderstood life who is himself able to be clearly aware of his community, to identify its history and its future, at least in part, with his own ideally extended life, and who is yet

wholly unable ever to love the life which is thus linked with his own. Yet there remains the fate which Paul so emphasized, and which has determined the whole history of the Christian consciousness: Knowledge of the community is not love of the community. Love, when it comes, comes as from above.

Especially is this true of the love of the ideal community of all mankind. I can be genuinely in love with the community only in case I have somehow fallen in love with the universe. The problem of love is human. The solution of the problem, if it comes at all, will be, in its meaning, superhuman, and divine, if there be anything divine.

What our definition of the community enables us to add to our former views of the meaning of loyalty is simply this: If the universe proves to be, in any sense, of the nature of a community, then love for this community, and for God, will not mean merely love for losing the self, or for losing the many selves, in any interpenetration of selves. If one can find that all humanity, in the sense of our definition, constitutes a real community, or that the world itself is, in any genuine way, of the nature of a community such as we have defined; and *if* hereupon we can come to love this real community,—then the one and the many, the body and the members, our beloved and ourselves, will be joined in a life in which we shall be both preserved as individuals, and yet united to that which we love.

XIII

Plainly a metaphysical study of the question whether the universe is a community will be as powerless as the foregoing analysis of the real nature of human communities to explain the origin of love, or to make any one fall in love with the universe. Yet something has been gained by our analysis of the problem which, from this point onwards, determines our metaphysical inquiry. If our results are in any way positive, they may enable us to view the problem of Christianity, that is, the problem of the religion of loyalty, in a larger perspective than that which human history, when considered alone, determines. The favorite methods of approaching the metaphysical problems of theology end by leaving the individual alone with God, in a realm which seems, to many minds, a realm of merely concepts, of intellectual abstractions, of barren theories. The ways which are just now in favor in the philosophy of religion seem to end in leaving the individual equally alone with his intuitions, his lurid experiences of sudden conversion, or his ineffable mysteries of saintly peace.

May we not hope to gain by a method which follows the plan now outlined? This method, first, encourages a man to interpret his own individual self in terms of the largest ideal extension of that self in time which his reasonable will can acknowledge as worthy of the aims of his life. Secondly, this method bids a man consider what right he has to interpret the life from which he springs, in the midst of which he now lives, as a life that in any universal sense coöperates with his own and ideally expresses its own meaning so as to meet with his own, and to have a history identical with his own. Thirdly, this method directs us to inquire how far, in the social order to which we unquestionably belong, there are features such as warrant in us hoping that, in the world's community, our highest love may yet find its warrant and its fulfilment.

Whatever the fortunes of the quest may be, we have now defined its plan, and have shown its perfectly definite relation to the historical problem of Christianity.

The Will to Interpret

I

. . . The metaphysical inquiry concerning the nature and the reality of the community is still our leading topic. To this topic whatever we shall have to say about interpretation is everywhere subordinate. But, since, if I am right, interpretation is indeed a fundamental cognitive process, we shall need still further to illustrate its nature and its principal forms. Every apparent digression from our main path will quickly lead us back to our central issues. Interpretation is, once for all, the main business of philosophy.

The present lecture will include two stages of movement towards our goal. First, we shall study the elementary psychology of the process of interpretation. Secondly, we shall portray the ideal that guides the truth-loving interpreter. The first of these inquiries will concern topics which are both familiar and neglected. The second part of our lecture will throw light upon the ethical problems with which our study of the Christian ideas has made us acquainted. At the close of the lecture our preparation for an outline of the metaphysics of interpretation will be completed.

II

I have called interpretation an essentially social cognitive process; and such, in fact, it is. Man is an animal that interprets; and therefore man lives in communities, and depends upon them for insight and for salvation.

But the elementary psychological forms in which interpretation appears find a place in our lives whether or no we are in company; just as a child can sing when alone, although singing is, on the whole, a social activity. We shall need to consider how an interpreter conducts his mental processes, even when he is taking no explicit account of other minds than his own.

In looking for the psychological foundations of interpretation, we shall be directed by Charles Peirce's formal definition of the mental functions which are involved. Wherever an interpretation takes place, however little it seems to be an explicit social undertaking, a triadic cognitive process can be observed. Let us look, then, for elementary instances of such triadic processes.

In the earliest of the logical essays to which, at the last time, I referred, Charles Peirce pointed out that every instance of conscious and explicit Comparison involves an elementary form of interpretation. This observation of Peirce's enables us to study interpretation in some of its simplest shapes, relieved of the complications which our social efforts to communicate with other minds usually involve.

Yet, even in this rudimentary form, interpretation involves the motives, which, upon higher levels, make its work so wealthy in results, and so significant in its contrasts with perception and conception.

From *The Problem of Christianity* (Chicago: The University of Chicago Press, 1968), pp. 297–319.

III

The most familiar instances of the mental process known as Comparison seem, at first sight, to consist of a consciousness of certain familiar dyadic relations,—relations of similarity and difference. Red contrasts with green; sound breaks in upon silence; one sensory quality collides, as it were, with another. The "shock of difference" awakens our attention. In other cases, an unexpected similarity of colors and tones attracts our interest. Or perhaps the odors of two flowers, or the flavors of two fruits, resemble one the other. Pairs of perceived objects are, in all these cases, in question. We express our observations in such judgments as: "A resembles B;" "D is unlike E."

Now Peirce's view of the nature of comparison depends upon noticing that familiar as such observations of similarity and dissimilarity may be, no one of them constitutes the whole of any complete act of comparison. Comparison, in the fuller sense of the word, takes place when one asks or answers the question: What constitutes the difference between A and B?" "*Wherein* does A resemble B?" "*Wherein* consists their distinction?" Let me first illustrate such a question in a case wherein the answer is easy.

If you write a word with your own hand, and hold it up before a mirror, your own handwriting becomes more or less unintelligible to you, unless you are already accustomed to read or to write mirror-script. Suppose, however, that instead of writing words yourself, you let someone else show you words already written. And suppose, further, that two words have been written side by side on the same sheet of paper, neither of them by your own hand. Suppose one of them to have been written upright, while the other is the counterpart of the first, except that it is the first turned upside down, or else is the first in mirror-script. If, without knowing how these words have been produced, you look at them, you can directly observe that the two written words differ in appearance, and that they also have a close resemblance. But, unless you were already familiar with the results of inverting a handwriting or of observing it in a mirror, you could not thus directly observe wherein consist the similarities and the differences of the two words which lie before you on the paper.

Since you are actually familiar with mirror-script, and with the results of turning a sheet of paper upside down, you will indeed no doubt be able to name the difference of the two supposed words. But in order to compare the two words thus presented side by side on the same sheet of paper, and to tell wherein they are similar and wherein they differ, you need what Peirce calls a mediating idea, or what he also calls "a third," which, as he phrases the matter, shall "represent" or "interpret" one of the two written words to, or in terms of, the other. You use such a "third" idea when you say, "This word is the mirror-script representative of that word." For now the difference is interpreted.

Thus a complete act of comparison involves such a "third," such a "mediating" image or idea,—such an "interpreter." By means of this "third" you so compare a "first" object with a "second" as to make clear to yourself wherein consists the similarity and the difference between the second and the first. Comparison must be triadic in order to be both explicit and complete. Likenesses and differences are the signs that a comparison is needed. But these signs are not their own interpretation.

. . . Still another familiar instance of comparison will show how needful it is to choose the right "third" in order to complete one's view of the matter. One may long have observed that a friend's face, when seen in a mirror, contrasts with the same face if seen apart from the mirror. . . . The idea of the vertical asymmetries is here the needed "third" which interprets the difference between the man's face when seen in the mirror and when seen out of the mirror.

A lady who had passed part of her life in Australia, and part in England, once told me that, for years, she had never been able to understand the difference which, to her eyes, existed between the full moon as seen in England and as observed by her during her years in Australia. At last she found the right mediating idea, when she came to notice how Orion also gradually became partially inverted during her journeys from English latitudes to those of the far southern seas. For the full moon, as she thus came to know, must be subject to similar apparent inversions; and this was the reason why the "man in the moon" had therefore been undiscoverable when she had heretofore looked for him in Australian skies.

IV

When processes of comparison grow complicated, new "third" terms or "mediators" may be needed at each stage of one's undertaking.

So it is when a literary parallel between two poets or two statesmen is in question. Now one and now another trait or event or fortune or deed may stand out as the mediating idea. But always, in such parallels, it is by means of the use of a "third" that each act of comparison is made possible,—whether the case in question be simple or complex. And the mediator plays each time the part which Peirce first formally defined.

Let there arise the problem of drawing a literary parallel between Shakespeare and Dante. The task appears hopelessly complex and indeterminate until, perhaps, the place which the sonnet occupied in the creative activity of each poet comes to our minds. Then indeed, although the undertaking is still vastly complicated, it is no longer quite so hopeless. If "with this key Shakespeare unlocked his heart," yet held fast its deepest mysteries; while Dante accompanied each of the sonnets of the *Vita Nuova* with a comment and an explanation, yet left unspoken what most fascinates us in the supernatural figure of his beloved,—then "the sonnet," viewed as an idea of a poetical form, mediates between our ideas of the two poets, and represents or interprets each of these ideas to the other.

This last example suggests an endless wealth of complexities. And the interpretation in question is also endlessly inadequate to our demands. But on its highest levels, as in its simplest instances, the process of explicit comparison is thus triadic, and to notice this fact is, for the purpose of our study of comparison, illuminating.

For when we merely set pairs of objects before us, and watch their resemblances and differences, we soon lose ourselves in mazes. Yet even when the mazes are indeed not to be penetrated by any skill, still a triadic comparison is much more readily guided towards the light. "How does A differ from C?" If you can reply to this question by saying that, by means of B, A can be altogether transformed into C, or can, at least, be brought into a close resemblance to C, then the comparison of A to C is made definite.

Let me choose still one more illustration of such a comparison. This time the illustration shall not come from the literary realm; yet it shall be more complex than is the instance of the comparison between a written word and its image in the mirror.

If you cut a strip of paper,—perhaps an inch wide and ten inches long,—you can bring the two ends together and fasten them with glue.

The result will be a ring-strip of paper, whose form is of a type very familiar in the case of belts, finger-rings, and countless other objects. But this form can be varied in an interesting way. Before bringing the ends of the strip together, let one end of the paper be turned 180°. Holding the twisted end of the strip fast, glue it to the other. There now results an endless strip of paper having in it a single twist. Lay side by side an ordinary ring-strip that has no twist, and a ring-strip of paper that has been made in the way just indicated. The latter strip has a single twist in it. Hereupon ask a person who has not seen you make the two ring-strips, to compare them, and to tell you wherein they agree and wherein they differ.

To your question an ordinary observer, to whom this new form of ring-strip is unfamiliar, will readily answer that they obviously differ because one of them has no twist in it, while the other certainly has some kind of twist belonging to its structure. So far the one whom you question indeed makes use of a "third" idea. But this idea probably remains, so far, vague in his mind, and it will take your uninformed observer some time to make his comparison at all complete and explicit.

In order to aid him in his task, you may hereupon call his attention to the further fact that the ring-strip which contains the single twist has two extraordinary properties. It has, namely, but one side; and it also has but one edge. The mention of this fact will at first perplex the uninitiated observer. But when he has taken the trouble to study the new form, he will find that the idea of a "one-sided strip of paper" enables him to compare the new and the old form, and to interpret his idea of the new ring-form to his old idea of an ordinary ring such as has no twist, and possesses two sides.

V

In all the cases of explicit comparison which we have just considered, what takes place has, despite the endless varieties of circumstance, an uniform character.

Whoever compares has before him what we have called two distinct ideas; perhaps his ideas of these two printed or written words; or again, his ideas of these two ring-strips of paper; or, in another instance, his ideas of Dante and of Shakespeare.

And the term "idea" is used, in the present discussion, in the sense which James and other representative pragmatists have made familiar in current discussion. Let us then hold clearly in mind this definition of the term "idea." For we shall even thereby be led to note facts which will lead us beyond what this definition emphasizes.

An idea, in this sense, is a more or less practical and active process, a "leading" as James calls it, whereby some set of conceptions and perceptions tend to be brought into desirable connections. An idea may consist mainly of some effort to characterize the data of perception through the use of fitting conceptions. Or, again, an idea may be a prediction of future perceptions. Or, an idea may be an active seeking for a way to translate conceptual "banknotes" into perceptual cash. In any one idea, either the perceptual or the conceptual elements may, at any one moment, predominate. If the conceptual element is too marked for our purposes, the idea stands in need of perceptual fulfilment. If the perceptual element is too rich for our momentary interests, the idea needs further conceptual clarification. In any case, however, according to this view, the motives of an idea are practical, and the constituents of an idea are either the data of perception, or the conceptual processes whereby we characterize or predict or pursue such data.

But when, in Peirce's sense of the word, we have to make an explicit comparison, we have before us two distinct and contrasting ideas. It is their distinctness, it is their contrast, which determines our task. And these ideas involve, in general, not only different perceptual and different conceptual constituents, but also different and sometimes conflicting "leadings," different and sometimes mutually clashing interests, various and mutually estranged motives, activities, or constructions. These two ideas may contrast as do two forms of art. Or they may stand out the one over against the other as if they were two geometrical structures. They may collide as do two warring passions. They may first meet as simple strangers in our inner world. Their relations may resemble those of plaintiff and defendant in a suit at law. Or they may be as interestingly remote from one another as are the spiritual realms of two great poets. In such endlessly various fashions may the two ideas come before us.

The essential fact for our present study is that, in case of the comparisons which Peirce discusses, the problem, whether you call it a theoretical or a practical problem, is not that of linking percepts to their fitting concepts, nor that of paying the bank bills of conception in the gold of the corresponding perceptions. On the contrary, it is the problem either of arbitrating the conflicts; or of bringing to mutual understanding the estrangements; or of uniting in some community the separated lives of these two distinct ideas,—of ideas which, when left to themselves, decline to coalesce or to coöperate, or to enter into one life.

This problem, in the cases of comparison with which Peirce deals, is solved through a new act. For this act originality and sometimes even genius may be required. This new act consists in the invention or discovery of some third idea, distinct from both the ideas which are to be compared. This third idea, when once found, interprets one of the ideas which are the objects of the comparison, and interprets it to the other, or in the light of the other. What such interpretation means, the instances already considered have in part made clear. But the complexity and the significance of the processes involved require a further study. And this further study may here be centred about the question: What is gained by the sort of comparison which Peirce thus characterizes? And, since we have said that all such comparison involves an activity of interpreting one idea in the light of another, we may otherwise state our question thus: What, in these cases of comparison, is the innermost aim of the Will to Interpret which all these processes of comparison manifest?

VI

The rhythm of the Hegelian dialect, wherein thesis, antithesis, and higher synthesis play their familiar parts, will here come to the minds of some who follow my words; and you may ask wherein Peirce's processes of comparison and interpretation differ from those dialectical movements through division into synthesis, which Hegel long since used as the basis of his philosophy. I reply at once that Peirce's theory of comparison, and of the mediating idea or "third" which interprets, is, historically speaking, a theory not derived from Hegel, by whom at the time when he wrote these early logical papers, Peirce had been in no notable way influenced. I reply, further, that Peirce's concept of interpretation defines an extremely general process, of which the Hegelian dialectical triadic process is a very special case. Hegel's elementary illustrations of his own processes are ethical and historical. Peirce's theory of comparison is quite as well illustrated by purely mathematical as by explic-

itly social instances. There is no essential inconsistency between the logical and psychological motives which lie at the basis of Peirce's
theory of the triad of interpretation, and the
Hegelian interest in the play of thesis, antithesis, and higher synthesis. But Peirce's theory,
with its explicitly empirical origin and its very
exact logical working out, promises new light
upon matters which Hegel left profoundly
problematic.

Returning, however, to those illustrations of
Peirce's theory of comparison which I have already placed before you, let us further consider the motives which make a comparison of
distinct and contrasting ideas significant for the
one who compares.

An idea, as I have said, is, in James's sense,
a practical "leading." An idea, if, in James's
sense, successful, and if successfully employed,
leads through concepts to the desirable or to
the corresponding percepts. But a comparison
of ideas—that, too, is no doubt an active process. To what does it lead? It leads, as we have
seen, to a new, to a third, to an interpreting
idea. And what is this new idea? Is it "cash,"
or has it only "credit-value"? What does it present to our view? What does it bring to our
treasury?

One must for the first answer this question
in a very old-fashioned way. The new, the
third, the interpreting idea, in these elementary cases of comparison, shows us, as far as it
goes, ourselves, and also creates in us a new
grade of clearness regarding what we are and
what we mean. First, I repeat, the new or third
idea shows us ourselves, as we are. Next, it
also enriches our world of self-consciousness.
It at once broadens our outlook and gives our
mental realm definiteness and self-control. It
teaches one of our ideas what another of our
ideas means. It tells us how to know our right
hand from the left; how to connect what comes
to us in fragments; how to live as if life had
some coherent aim. All this is indeed, thus far,
very elementary information about what one
gains by being able to hold three ideas at once
in mind. But, in our own day, such information is important information. For our age,
supposing that the contrast between perception
and conception exhausts the possible types of
cognitive processes, is accustomed to listen to
those who teach us that self-knowledge also
must be either intuitive (and, in that case,
merely fluent and transient) or else conceptual
(and, in that case, abstract and sterile).

But a dual antithesis between perceptual
and conceptual knowledge is once for all in-

adequate to the wealth of the facts of life.
When you accomplish an act of comparison,
the knowledge which you attain is neither
merely conceptual, nor merely perceptual, nor
yet merely a practically active synthesis of perception and conception. It is a third type of
knowledge. It interprets. It surveys from
above. It is an attainment of a larger unity of
consciousness. It is a conspectus. As the tragic
artist looks down upon the many varying lives
of his characters, and sees their various motives not interpenetrating, but coöperating, in
the dramatic action which constitutes his creation,—so any one who compares distinct
ideas, and discovers the third or mediating
idea which interprets the meaning of one in the
light of the other, thereby discovers, or in-
vents, a realm of conscious unity which constitutes the very essence of the life of reason.

Bergson, in his well-known portrayal, has
glorified instinct in its contrast with the intellect. The intellect, as he holds, is a mere user
of tools. Its tools are concepts. It uses them in
its practical daily work to win useful percepts.
It loves to be guided in its daily industries by
rigid law. It is therefore most at home in the
realm of mechanism and of death. Life escapes
its devices. Its concepts are essentially inadequate. Instinct, on the contrary, so far as man
still preserves that filmy cloud of luminous instinct and of intuition which, in Bergson's
opinion, constitutes the most precious resource
of genius, perceives, and sympathizes, and so
comes in touch with reality.

That this account of the cognitive process is
inadequate, both the artist and the prophets
combine with the scientific observers of nature, with the mathematicians, and with the
great constructive statesmen, to show us. Comparison is the instrument of what one may call,
according to one's pleasure, either the observant reason, or the rational intuition whereby
the world's leading minds have always been
guided. And it is comparison, it is interpretation, which teaches us how to deal with the
living, with the significant, and with the genuinely real.

Darwin, for instance, as a naturalist, saw,
compared, and mediated. We all know how
the leading ideas of Malthus furnished the mediating principle, the third, whereby Darwin
first came to conceive how the contrasting
ideas with which his hypotheses had to deal
could be brought into unity. And that such
comparison is peculiarly adapted to deal with
the phenomena of life, let not only the genesis
of Darwin's ideas, but the place of the process

of comparison in the development of all the organic sciences, show.

If we turn to the other extreme of the world of human achievement, in order to learn what is the sovereign cognitive process, we shall find the same answer. For let us ask,—By means of what insight did Amos the prophet meet the religious problems of his own people and of his own day? He faced tragic contrasts, moral, religious, and political. Warring ideas were before him,—ideas, each of which sought its own percepts, through its own concepts of God, of worship, and of success. But Amos introduced into the controversies of his time the still tragic, but inspiring and mediating, idea of the God who, as he declared, delights not in sacrifices but in righteousness. And by this one stroke of religious genius the prophet directed the religious growth of the centuries that were to follow.

Think over the burial psalm, or the Pauline chapters on Charity and the Resurrection, if you would know what part comparison and mediation play in the greatest expressions of the religious consciousness. Remember Lear or the Iliad, if you wish to recall the functions of contrast and of mediation in poetry. Let the Sistine Madonna or Beethoven's Fifth Symphony illustrate the same process in other forms of the artistic consciousness.

If once you have considered a few such instances, then, summing up their familiar lessons, you may note that in none of these cases is it conception, in none of them is it bare perception, least of all is it inarticulate intuition, which has won for us the greatest discoveries, the incomparable treasures in science, in art, or in religion.

The really creative insight has come from those who first compared and then mediated, who could first see two great ideas at once, and then find the new third idea which mediated between them, and illumined.

We often use the word "vision" for this insight which looks down upon ideas as from above, and discovers the "third," thereby uniting what was formerly estranged. If by the word "intuition" one chooses to mean this grade of insight, then one may indeed say that creative mental prowess depends, in general, upon such intuition. But such intuition is no mere perception. It is certainly not conception. And the highest order of genius depends upon reaching the stage of Peirce's "third" type of ideas. Comparison, leading to the discovery of that which mediates and solves, and to the vision of unity, is the psychological basis of poetry, as Shakes-

peare wrote, and of such prophecy as Paul praised when he estimated the spiritual gifts. Comparison, then, and interpretation constitute the cognitive function whereby we deal with life. Instinct and bare perception, left to themselves, can never reach this level.

VII

When we consider the inner life of the individual man, the Will to Interpret appears, then, as the will to be self-possessed. One who compares his own ideas, views them as from above. He aims to pass from blind "leadings" to coherent insight and to resolute self-guidance. What one wins as the special object of one's insight depends, in such cases, upon countless varying psychological conditions, and upon one's success in finding or in inventing suitable mediators for the interpretation of one idea in the light of another. It may therefore appear as if in this realm of interior comparisons, where the objects compared are pairs of ideas, and where results of comparison consist in the invention of a third, there could be no question of attaining fixed or absolute truth. If anywhere pragmatism could be decisively victorious; if anywhere the purely relative and transient would seem in possession of the field,—one might suppose that comparison would constantly furnish us with instances of relative, shifting, and fluent truth.

As a fact, however, this is not the case. Comparison, which is so powerful an instrument in dealing with life, and with the fluent and the personal, is also perfectly capable of bringing us into the presence of the exact and of the necessary. All depends upon what ideas are compared, and upon the purpose for which they are compared, and upon the skill with which the vision of unity is attained.

Let the comparison of the two ring-strips of paper show what I here have in mind. The difference between a ring-strip which contains a single twist, and another which is constructed in the usual way, seems at first sight to be both insignificant and inexact. A closer study shows that the geometry of surfaces that possess but a single side can be developed into as exact a branch of pure mathematics as you can mention. The development in question would depend upon assuming, quite hypothetically, a few simple principles which are suggested, although not indeed capable of being proved, by experience of the type which recent pragmatism has well analyzed. The branch of pure mathematics in question would consist of deductions from these few single principles. The deductions would interpret these principles, viewed in some sort of unity and compared together.

But recent pragmatism has not well analyzed the process whereby, in pure mathematics, the consequences which follow from a set of exactly stated hypotheses are determined. This process, the genuine process of deduction, depends upon a series of ideal experiments. These experiments are performed by means of putting together ideas, two and two, by comparing the ideas that are thus brought together, by discovering mediators, and by reading the results of the combination. This process may lead to perfectly exact results which are absolutely true.

I know of no writer who has better or more exactly analyzed the way in which such ideal experiments can lead to novel and precise results than Peirce has done. His analysis of the deductive process was first made a good while since, and anticipated results which Mr. Bertrand Russell and others have since reached by other modes of procedure.

Peirce has shown that, when you interpret your combinations of ideas through ideal experiments, using, for instance, diagrams and symbols as aids, the outcome may be a truth as exact as the ideas compared are themselves exact. It may also be in your own experience as novel a result as your ideal experiment is novel. It may also be an absolute and immutable truth.

What you discover, in a case of deduction, is not that certain conclusions are, in themselves, considered true, but that they follow from, that they are implied by, certain hypothetically assumed premises. But a discovery that certain premises imply a certain conclusion, is the discovery of a fact. This fact may be found, not by perception, nor by conception, but by interpretation. None the less, it is a fact and it may be momentous.

It is customary to imagine that such a deductive process can get out of given premises nothing novel, but only (as people often say)—only what was already present in the premises. This customary view of deduction is incorrect. As Peirce repeatedly pointed out (long before any other writer had explicitly dealt with the matter), you can write out upon a very few sheets of paper all the principles which are actually used as the fundamental hypotheses that lie at the basis of those branches of pure mathematics which have thus far been developed. Yet the logical consequences which follow from these few mathematical hypotheses

are so numerous that every year a large octavo volume in fine print is needed to contain merely the titles, and very brief abstracts, of the technical papers containing novel results which have been, during that year, published as researches in pure mathematics.

The mathematical papers in question embody, in general, consequences already implied by the few fundamental hypotheses which I have just mentioned. An infinite wealth of still unknown consequences of the same principles remains yet to be explored and stated. All of these consequences can be won, in pure mathematics, by a purely deductive procedure.

Thus endlessly wealthy, thus possessed of an inexhaustible fecundity, is the genuine deductive process. Peirce long ago showed why. And while the mathematical procedure which is in question cannot here be further discussed, it is enough for our present purpose to indicate why this fecundity of deduction exists.

VIII

Deduction, in the real life of the exact sciences, is a process that recent pragmatism has no means of describing, simply because recent pragmatism is the prey of the dual classification of the cognitive processes, and views what it calls the "workings" of ideas merely in terms of the relations between conceptions and perceptions,—between "credit-values" and "cash-values."

Pragmatism, as James defined it, regards an idea as a "leading," whereby one pursues or seeks particulars; and whereby one sometimes obtains, and sometimes fails to obtain, the "cash-values" which one aims to get. Such a doctrine has no place for the understanding of what happens when, looking down as it were from above, one compares two ideas, and looks for a mediating idea. But just this is what happens in all cases of explicit comparison.

Now in the individual case, an interpretation, a mediating idea, may come to mind through almost any play of association, or as the result of almost any degree of skill in invention, or as the outcome either of serious or of playful combinations. In consequence, an interpretation may prove to be, in the single case, of purely relative and momentary truth and value.

But this, on the other hand, need not be the fortune of interpretation. The results of a comparison may express absolute truths,—truths which once seen can never be reversed. This absoluteness itself may be due to either one of two reasons.

In pure mathematics, a deduction, if correct at all, leads to an absolutely correct and irrevocably true discovery of a relation of implication between exactly stated premises and some conclusion. Deduction does this because deduction results from a comparison, and because the ideas compared may be, and in pure mathematics are, exact enough to suggest, at some moment, to the observant reasoner, an interpretation which, if it applies at all, applies universally to every pair of ideas identical in meaning with the pair of ideas here compared.

The act of comparison may be momentary, and may even be as an event, an accident. The inventive watcher of his own ideas may have been led to his deduction by whatever motive you please. But the interpretation, once discovered, may nevertheless represent a truth which is absolute precisely *because* it is hypothetical. For the assertion: "P implies Q," or "If P, then Q," is an assertion about a matter of fact. And this assertion, if true at all, is always and irrevocably true about the same pair of ideas or propositions: P and Q.

Or again, the result of an interpretation may be absolutely true, because, for whatever reason, the interpretation in question counsels the one who makes the interpretation to do some determinate and individual deed. This deed may be such as to accomplish at the moment when it is done, some ideally valuable result. But deeds once done are irrevocable. If, by interpreting your ideas in a certain way, at a certain moment, you have been led to do a worthy deed,—then the interpretation remains as irrevocably true as the good deed remains irrevocably done.

The principle, then, relating to the value and to the truth of one's acts of interior and conscious comparison, is that they express an insight which surveys, as from above, an unity wherein are combined various ideas. These ideas, as they first come, are pragmatic leadings which may be mutually estranged, or mutually hostile, or widely contrasted, or intimately interconnected. But, whatever the ideas may have been before they were compared,—as a result of the comparison of the two ideas, one of them is interpreted in the light of the other. The interpretation may possess all the exactness of mathematics, or all the transiency of a chance observation of the play of one's inner life. It may result in Paul's vision of the charity that never faileth, ruling supreme over the contrasts and the bickerings

of passing passion; or it may solve a problem of comparative natural history or of comparative philology. Whatever the varieties of the cases in question, comparison can occur, and can reach truth, simply because we are wider than any of our ideas, and can win a vision which shall look down upon our own inner warfare, and upon our own former self-estrangements, as well as upon our own inner contrasts of exact definition. This vision observes not data of sense and not mere abstract concepts. Nor does it consist simply in our pragmatic leadings, and in their successes and failures. It observes what may interpret ideas to other ideas; as prophets and poets interpret to us what otherwise would remain, in seeming, hopelessly various and bewilderingly strange. It is not more intuition that we want. It is such interpretation which alone can enlighten and guide and significantly inspire. Upon the comparisons which thus interpret, our spiritual triumphs depend. Such triumphs are not merely the pragmatic successes of single ideas. They are the attainment of mastery over life.

IX

Our lengthy study of comparison and interpretation, as they are present in the inner life of the individual man, has prepared us for a new view of the social meaning of the Will to Interpret. Here I must once more take a temporary leave of Peirce's guidance, and trust to my own resources.

One who compares a pair of his own ideas may attain, if he is successful, that vision of unity, that grade of self-possession, which we have now illustrated. But one who undertakes to interpret his neighbor's ideas is in a different position.

In general as we have seen, an interpreter, in his social relations with other men, deals with two different minds, neither of which he identifies with his own. His interpretation is a "third" or mediating idea. This "third" is aroused in the interpreter's mind through signs which come to him from the mind that he interprets. He addresses this "third" to the mind to which he interprets the first. The psychology of the process of social interpretation, so far as that process goes on in the interpreter's individual mind, is identical with that psychology of comparison which we have now outlined. Nobody can interpret, unless the idea which he interprets has become more or less clearly and explicitly one of his own ideas, and unless he compares it with another idea which is, in some sense, his own.

But, from the point of view of the interpreter, the essential difference between the case where he is interpreting the mind of one of his neighbors to the mind of another neighbor, and the case wherein he is comparing two ideas of his own, is a difference in the clearness of vision which is, under human conditions, attainable.

When I compare two ideas of my own, the luminous self-possession which then, for a time, may come to be mine, forms for me an ideal of success in interpretation. This ideal I can attain only at moments. But these moments set a model for all my interpretations to follow.

When I endeavor to interpret my neighbor's mind, my interpretation has to remain remote from its goal. The luminous vision of the results of comparison comes to me, at best, only partially and with uncertainty. My neighbor's ideas I indeed in a measure grasp, and compare with other ideas, and interpret; but, as I do this, I see through a glass darkly. Only those ideas whose comparisons with other ideas, and whose resulting triadic interpretations I can view face to face, can appear to me to have become in a more intimate and complete sense my own individual ideas. When I possess certain ideas sufficiently to enable me to seek for their interpretation, but so that, try as I will, I can never clearly survey, as from above, the success of any of my attempted interpretations,—then these ideas remain, from my own point of view, ideas that never become wholly my own. Therefore these relatively alien ideas can be interpreted at all only by using the familiar hypothesis that they belong to the self of some one else. Under ordinary social conditions this other mind is viewed as the mind of my neighbor. Neither of my neighbor nor of myself have I any direct intuition. But of my own ideas I can hope to win the knowledge which the most successful comparisons exemplify. Of my neighbor's ideas I can never win, under human conditions, any interpretation but one which remains hypothetical, and which is never observed, under these human conditions, as face to face with its own object, or with the idea of the other neighbors to whom the interpretation is addressed.

The Will to Interpret is, in our social relations, guided by a purpose which we are now ready to bring into close relations with the most significant of all the ethical ideals which, in our foregoing lectures, we have portrayed.

The interpreter, the mind to which he addresses his interpretation, the mind which he undertakes to interpret,—all these appear, in our explicitly human and social world, as three distinct selves,—sundered by chasms which, under human conditions, we never cross, and contrasting in their inner lives in whatever way the motives of men at any moment chance to contrast.

The Will to Interpret undertakes to make of these three selves a Community. In every case of ideally serious and loyal effort truly to interpret this is the simplest, but, in its deepest motives, the most purely spiritual of possible communities. Let us view that simple and ideal community as the intepreter himself views it, precisely in so far as he is sincere and truth-loving in his purpose as interpreter.

X

I, the interpreter, regard you, my neighbor, as a realm of ideas, of "leadings," of meanings, of pursuits, of purposes. This realm is not wholly strange and incomprehensible to me. For at any moment, in my life as interpreter, I am dependent upon the results of countless previous efforts to interpret. The whole past history of civilization has resulted in that form and degree of interpretation of you and of my other fellow-men which I already possess, at any instant when I begin afresh the task of interpreting your life or your ideas. You are to me, then, a realm of ideas which lie outside of the centre which my will to interpret can momentarily illumine with the clearest grade of vision. But I am discontent with my narrowness and with your estrangement. I seek unity with you. And since the same will to interpret you is also expressive of my analogous interests in all my other neighbors, what I here and now specifically aim to do is this: I mean to interpret you to somebody else, to some other neighbor, who is neither yourself nor myself. Three of us, then, I seek to bring into the desired unity of interpretation.

Now if I could succeed in interpreting you to another man as fully as, in my clearest moments, I interpret one of my ideas to another, my process of interpretation would simply reduce to a conscious comparison of ideas. I should then attain, as I succeeded in my interpretation, a luminous vision of your ideas, of my own, and of the ideas of the one to whom I interpret you. This vision would look down, as it were, from above. In the light of it, we, the selves now sundered by the chasms of the social world, should indeed not interpenetrate. For our functions as the mind interpreted, the mind to whom the other is interpreted, and the interpreter, would remain as distinct as now they are. There would be no melting together, no blending, no mystic blur, and no lapse into mere intuition. But for me the vision of the successful interpretation would simply be the attainment of my own goal as interpreter. This attainment would as little confound our persons as it would divide our substance. We should remain, for me, many, even when viewed in this unity.

Yet this vision, if I could win it, would constitute an event wherein your will to be interpreted would also be fulfilled. For if you are indeed ready to accept my service as interpreter, you even now possess this will to be interpreted. And if there exists the one to whom I can interpret you, that other also wills that you should be interpreted to him, and that I should be the interpreter.

If, then, I am worthy to be an interpreter at all, we three,—you, my neighbor, whose mind I would fain interpret,—you, my kindly listener, to whom I am to address my interpretation,— we three constitute a Community. Let us give to this sort of community a technical name. Let us call it a Community of Interpretation.

The form of such a community is determinate.

One goal lies before us all, one event towards which we all direct our efforts when we take part in this interpretation. This ideal event is a goal, unattainable under human social conditions, but definable, as an ideal, in terms of the perfectly familiar experience which every successful comparison of ideas involves. It is a goal towards which we all may work together: you, when you give me the signs that I am to interpret; our neighbor, when he listens to my interpretation; I, when I devote myself to the task.

This goal:—Our individual experience of our successful comparisons of our own ideas shows us wherein it consists, and that it is no goal which an abstract conception can define in terms of credit-values, and that it is also no goal which a possible perception can render to me in the cash of any set of sensory data. Yet it is a goal which each of us can accept as his own. I can at present aim to approach that goal through plans, through hypotheses regarding you which can be inductively tested. I can view that goal as a common future event. We can agree upon that goal. And herewith I interpret not only you as the being whom I am

to interpret, but also myself as in ideal the interpreter who aims to approach the vision of the unity of precisely this community. And you, and my other neighbor to whom I address my interpretation, can also interpret yourselves accordingly.

The conditions of the definition of our community will thus be perfectly satisfied. We shall be many selves with a common ideal future event at which we aim. Without essentially altering the nature of our community, our respective offices can be, at our pleasure, interchanged. You, or my other neighbor, can at any moment assume the function of interpreter; while I can pass to a new position in the new community. And yet, we three shall constitute as clearly as before a Community of Interpretation. The new community will be in a perfectly definite relation to the former one; and may grow out of it by a process as definite as is every form of conscious interpretation.

Thus there can arise, in our community, no problem regarding the one and the many, the quest and the goal, the individual who approaches the goal by one path or by another,— no question to which the definition of the community of interpretation will not at once furnish a perfectly precise answer.

Such an answer will be based upon the perfectly fundamental triadic relation which is essential to every process of interpretation, whether such process takes place within the inner life of an individual human being, or goes on in the world of ordinary social intercourse.

XI

Thus, then, if I assume for the moment the rôle of an interpreter, I can define my office, my Community of Interpretation, and my place in that community.

It will be observed that the sort of truth which, as interpreter, I seek, cannot be stated in terms as simple as those with which the current pragmatism is satisfied. My interpretation, if I offer to our common neighbor any interpretation of your mind, will of course be an idea of my own,—namely, precisely that "third" idea which I contribute to our community as my interpretation of you. And no doubt I shall desire to make as sure as I can that this idea of mine "works." But no data of my individual perception can ever present to me the "workings" which I seek.

For I want my interpretation of you to our neighbor to be such as you would accept and also such as our neighbor would comprehend, were each of us already in the position of the ideal observer from above, whose vision of the luminous unity of my interpretation and its goal I am trying to imitate whenever I try to interpret your mind.

Thus, from the outset, the idea which I offer as my interpretation of your mind, is offered not for the sake of, or in the pursuit of, any individual or private perception of my own, either present or expected or possible. I am not looking for workings that could conceivably be rendered in my perceptual terms. I am ideally aiming at an ideal event,—the spiritual unity of our community. I can define that unity in perfectly empirical terms; because I have compared pairs of ideas which were my own, and have discovered their mediating third idea. But I do not expect to perceive that unity as any occurrence in my own individual life, or as any working of one of my own personal ideas. In brief, I have to define the truth of my interpretation of you in terms of what the ideal observer of all of us would view as the unity which he observed. This truth cannot be defined in merely pragmatic terms.

In a community thus defined, the interpreter obviously assumes, in a highly significant sense, the chief place. For the community is one of interpretation. Its goal is the ideal unity of insight which the interpreter would possess were these who are now his neighbors transformed into ideas of his own which he compared; that is, were they ideas between which his own interpretation successfully mediated. The interpreter appears, then, as the one of the three who is most of all the spirit of the community, dominating the ideal relations of all three members.

But the one who is, in ideal, this chief, is so because he is first of all servant. His office it is to conform to the mind which he interprets, and to the comprehension of the mind to which he addresses his interpretation. And his own ideas can "work" only if his self-surrender, and his conformity to ideas which are not his own, is actually a successful conformity; and only if his approach to a goal which, as a member of a human community of interpretation, he can never reach, is a real approach.

XII

Such are the relationships which constitute a Community of Interpretation. I beg you to observe, as we close, the ethical and religious significance which the structure of such a community makes possible. In case our interpreta-

tions actually approach success, a community of interpretation possesses such ethical and religious significance, with increasing definiteness and beauty as the evolution of such a community passes from simpler to higher stages.

Upon interpretation, as we have already seen, every ideal good that we mortals win together, under our human social conditions, depends. Whatever else men need, they need their communities of interpretation.

It is indeed true that such communities can exist, at any time, in the most various grades of development, of self-consciousness, and of ideality. The communities of interpretation which exist in the market-places of the present social world, or that lie at the basis of the diplomatic intercourse of modern nations, are communities whose ideal goal is seldom present to the minds of their members; and it is not love which often seems to be their consciously ruling motive.

Yet, on the whole, it is not perception, and it is not conception; while it certainly is interpretation which is the great humanizing factor in our cognitive processes and which makes the purest forms of love for communities possible. Loyalty to a community of interpretation enters into all the other forms of true loyalty. No one who loves mankind can find a worthier and more significant way to express his love than by increasing and expressing among men the Will to Interpret. This will inspires every student of the humanities; and is present wherever charity enters into life. When Christianity teaches us to hope for the community of all mankind, we can readily see that the Beloved Community, whatever else it is, will be, when it comes, a Community of Interpretation. When we consider the ideal form and the goal of such a community, we see that in no other form, and with no other ideal, can we better express the constitution of the ideal Church, be that conceived as the Church on earth, or as the Church triumphant in some ideal realm of super-human and all seeing insight, where I shall know even as I am known.

And, if, in ideal, we aim to conceive the divine nature, how better can we conceive it than in the form of the Community of Interpretation, and above all in the form of the Interpreter, who interprets all to all, and each individual to the world, and the world of spirits to each individual.

In such an interpreter, and in his community, the problem of the One and the Many would find its ideally complete expression and solution. The abstract conceptions and the mystical intuitions would be at once transcended, and illumined, and yet retained and kept clear and distinct, in and through the life of one who, as interpreter, was at once servant to all and chief among all, expressing his will through all, yet, in his interpretations, regarding and loving the will of the least of these brethren. In him the Community, the Individual, and the Absolute would be completely expressed, reconciled, and distinguished.

This, to be sure, is, at this point of our discussion, still merely the expression of an ideal, and not the assertion of a metaphysical proposition. But in the Will to Interpret, the divine and the human seem to be in closest touch with each other.

The mere form of interpretation may be indeed momentarily misused for whatever purpose of passing human folly you will. But if the ideal of interpretation is first grasped; and if then the Community of Interpretation is conceived as inclusive of all individuals; and as unified by the common hope of the far-off event of complete mutual understanding; and, finally, if love for this community is awakened,—then indeed this love is able to grasp, in ideal, the meaning of the Church Universal, of the Communion of Saints, and of God the Interpreter.

Merely to define such ideals is not to solve the problems of metaphysics. But it is to remove many obstacles from the path that leads towards insight.

These ideals, however, are grasped and loved whenever one first learns fully to comprehend what Paul meant when he said: "Wherefore let him that speaketh with tongues pray that he may interpret." This word is but a small part of Paul's advice. But in germ it contains the whole meaning of the office, both of philosophy and of religion.

Loyalty to Loyalty, Truth, and Reality

We have deliberately declined, so far, to consider what the causes are to which men ought to be loyal. To turn to this task is the next step in our philosophy of loyalty. . . .

Now, it is obvious that nobody can be equally and directly loyal to all of the countless actual social causes that exist. It is obvious also that many causes which conform to our general definition of a possible cause may appear to any given person to be hateful and evil causes, to which he is justly opposed. A robber band, a family engaged in a murderous feud, a pirate crew, a savage tribe, a Highland robber clan of the old days—these might constitute causes to which somebody has been, or is, profoundly loyal. Men have loved such cases devotedly, have served them for a lifetime. Yet most of us would easily agree in thinking such causes unworthy of anybody's loyalty. Moreover, different loyalties may obviously stand in mutual conflict, whenever their causes are opposed. Family feuds are embittered by the very strength of the loyalty of both sides. My country, if I am the patriot inflamed by the war-spirit, seems an absolutely worthy cause; but my enemy's country usually seems hateful to me just because of my own loyalty; and therefore even my individual enemy may be hated because of the supposed baseness of his cause. War-songs call the individual enemy evil names just because he possesses the very personal qualities that, in our own loyal fellow-countrymen, we most admire. "No refuge could save the hireling and slave." Our enemy, as you see, is a slave, because he serves his cause so obediently. Yet just such service we call, in our own country's heroes, the worthiest devotion.

Meanwhile, in the foregoing account of loyalty as a spiritual good to the loyal man, we have insisted that true loyalty, being a willing devotion of the self to its cause, involves some element of autonomous choice. Tradition has usually held that a man ought to be loyal to just that cause which his social station determines for him. Common sense generally says, that if you were born in your country, and still live there, you ought to be loyal to that country, and to that country only, hating the enemies across the border whenever a declaration of war requires you to hate them. But we have declared that true loyalty includes some

From *The Philosophy of Loyalty* (New York: Macmillan Company, 1908), pp. 107–146, 307–348.

element of free choice. Hence our own account seems still further to have complicated
the theory of loyalty. For in answering in our
last lecture the ethical individualists who objected to loyalty, we have ourselves deliberately given to loyalty an individualistic coloring. And if our view be right, and if tradition
be wrong, so much the more difficult appears
to be the task of defining wherein consists that
which makes a cause worthy of loyalty for a
given man, since tradition alone is for us an
insufficient guide. . . .

. . . If loyalty is a supreme good, the mutually
destructive conflict of loyalties is in general a
supreme evil. If loyalty is a good for all sorts
and conditions of men, the war of man against
man has been especially mischievous, not so
much because it has hurt, maimed, impover-
ished, or slain men, as because it has so often
robbed the defeated of their causes, of their
opportunities to be loyal, and sometimes of
their very spirit of loyalty.

If, then, we look over the field of human life
to see where good and evil have most clus-
tered, we see that the best in human life is its
loyalty; while the worst is whatever has tended
to make loyalty impossible, or to destroy it
when present, or to rob it of its own while it
still survives. And of all things that thus have
warred with loyalty, the bitterest woe of humanity has been that so often it is the loyal
themselves who have thus blindly and eagerly
gone about to wound and to slay the loyalty of
their brethren. The spirit of loyalty has been
misused to make men commit sin against this
very spirit, holy as it is. For such a sin is precisely what any wanton conflict of loyalties
means. Where such a conflict occurs, the best,
namely, loyalty, is used as an instrument in
order to compass the worst, namely, the destruction of loyalty.

It is true, then, that some causes are good,
while some are evil. But the test of good and
evil in the causes to which men are loyal is now
definable in terms which we can greatly simplify in view of the foregoing considerations.

If, namely, I find a cause, and this cause
fascinates me, and I give myself over to its
service, I in so far attain what, for me, if my
loyalty is complete, is a supreme good. But my
cause, by our own definition, is a social cause,
which binds many into the unity of one service.
My cause, therefore, gives me, of necessity,
fellow-servants, who with me share this loyalty, and to whom this loyalty, if complete, is
also a supreme good. So far, then, being loyal

myself, I not only get but give good; for I help
to sustain, in each of my fellow-servants, his
own loyalty, and so I help him to secure his
own supreme good. In so far, then, my loyalty
to my cause is also a loyalty to my fellows'
loyalty. But now suppose that my cause, like
the family in a feud, or like the pirate ship, or
like the aggressively warlike nation, lives by
the destruction of the loyalty of other families,
or of its own community, or of other communities. Then, indeed, I get a good for myself and
for my fellow-servants by our common loyalty;
but I war against this very spirit of loyalty as it
appears in our opponent's loyalty to his own
cause.

And so, a cause is good, not only for me,
but for mankind, in so far as it is essentially a
loyalty to loyalty, that is, is an aid and a furtherance of loyalty in my fellows. It is an evil
cause in so far as, despite the loyalty that it
arouses in me, it is destructive of loyalty in the
world of my fellows. My cause is, indeed, always such as to involve some loyalty to loyalty,
because, if I am loyal to any cause at all, I
have fellow-servants whose loyalty mine supports. But in so far as my cause is a predatory
cause, which lives by overthrowing the loyalties of others, it is an evil cause, because it
involves disloyalty to the very cause of loyalty
itself.

. . . since my loyalty is never my mere fate,
but is always also my choice, I can of course
determine my loyalty, at least to some extent,
by the consideration of the actual good and ill
which my proposed cause does to mankind.
And since I now have the main criterion of the
good and ill of causes before me, I can define a
principle of choice which may so guide me that
my loyalty shall become a good, not merely to
myself, but to mankind.

This principle is now obvious. I may state it
thus: In so far as it lies in your power, so choose
your cause and so serve it, that, by reason of
your choice and of your service, there shall be
more loyalty in the world rather than less. And,
in fact, so choose and so serve your individual
cause as to secure thereby the greatest possible
increase of loyalty among men. More briefly: *In
choosing and in serving the cause to which you
are to be loyal, be, in any case, loyal to loyalty.*

This precept, I say, will express how one
should guide his choice of a cause, in so far as
he considers not merely his own supreme
good, but that of mankind. That such autonomous choice is possible, tends, as we now see,
not to complicate, but to simplify our moral

situation. For if you regard men's loyalty as their fate, if you think that a man must be loyal simply to the cause which tradition sets before him, without any power to direct his own moral attention, then indeed the conflict of loyalties seems an insoluble problem; so that, if men find themselves loyally involved in feuds, there is no way out. But if, indeed, choice plays a part,—a genuine even if limited part, in directing the individual's choice of the cause to which he is to be loyal, then indeed this choice may be so directed that loyalty to the universal loyalty of all mankind shall be furthered by the actual choices which each enlightened loyal person makes when he selects his cause. . . .

. . . Here would be for me not only an unity of inner and outer, but an unity with the unity of all human life. What I sought for myself I should then be explicitly seeking for my whole world. All men would be my fellow-servants of my cause. In principle I should be opposed to no man's loyalty. I should be opposed only to men's blindness in their loyalty, I should contend only against that tragic disloyalty to loyalty which the feuds of humanity now exemplify. I should preach to all others, I should strive to practise myself, that active mutual furtherance of universal loyalty which is what humanity obviously most needs, if indeed loyalty, just as the willing devotion of a self to a cause, is a supreme good.

And since all who are human are as capable of loyalty as they are of reason, since the plainest and the humblest can be as true-hearted as the great, I should nowhere miss the human material for my task. I should know, meanwhile, that if indeed loyalty, unlike the "mercy" of Portia's speech, is not always mightiest in the mightiest, it certainly, like mercy, becomes the throned monarch better than his crown. So that I should be sure of this good of loyalty as something worthy to be carried, so far as I could carry it, to everybody, lofty or humble.

Thus surely it would be humane and reasonable for me to define my cause to myself,—if only I could be assured that there is indeed some practical way of making loyalty to loyalty the actual cause of my life. Our question therefore becomes this: Is there a practical way of serving the universal human cause of loyalty to loyalty? And if there is such a way, what is it? Can we see how personally so to act that we bring loyalty on earth to a fuller fruition, to a wider range of efficacy, to a more effective sovereignty over the lives of men? If so, then indeed we can see how to work for the cause of the genuine kingdom of heaven.

Yet I fear that as you have listened to this sketch of a possible and reasonable cause, such as could be a proper object of our loyalty, you will all the while have objected: This may be a definition of a possible cause, but it is an unpractical definition. For what is there that one can do to further the loyalty of mankind in general? Humanitarian efforts are an old story. They constantly are limited in their effectiveness both by the narrowness of our powers, and by the complexity of the human nature which we try to improve. And if any lesson in philanthropy is well known, it is this, that whoever tries simply to help mankind as a whole, loses his labor, so long as he does not first undertake to help those nearest to him. Loyalty to the cause of universal loyalty—how, then, shall it constitute any practical working scheme of life?

I answer at once that the individual man, with his limited powers can indeed serve the cause of universal loyalty only by limiting his undertakings to some decidedly definite personal range. He must have his own special and personal cause. But this cause of his can indeed be chosen and determined so as to constitute a deliberate effort to further universal loyalty. When I begin to show you how this may be, I shall at once pass from what may have seemed to you a very unpractical scheme of life, to a realm of familiar and commonplace virtuous activities. The only worth of my general scheme will then lie in the fact that, in the light of this scheme, we can, as it were, see the commonplace virtues transfigured and glorified by their relation to the one highest cause of all. My thesis is *that all the commonplace virtues, in so far as they are indeed defensible and effective, are special forms of loyalty to loyalty,* and are to be justified, centralized, inspired, by the one supreme effort to do good, namely, the effort to make loyalty triumphant in the lives of all men.

The first consideration which I shall here insist upon is this: Loyalty, as we have all along seen, depends upon a very characteristic and subtle union of natural interest, and of free choice. Nobody who merely follows his natural impulses as they come is loyal. Yet nobody can be loyal without depending upon and using his natural impulses. If I am to be loyal, my cause must from moment to moment fascinate me, awaken my muscular vigor, stir me with some eagerness for work, even if this be painful work. I cannot be loyal to barren abstractions. I can only be loyal to what my life can interpret in bodily deeds. Loyalty has its elemental appeal to my whole organism. My cause must become one with my human life. Yet all this must occur not without my willing choice. I must control my devotion. It will possess me, but not without my voluntary complicity; for I shall accept the possession. It is, then, with the cause to which you personally are loyal, as it was with divine grace in an older theology. The cause must control you, as divine grace took saving control of the sinner; but only your own will can accept this control, and a grace that merely compels can never save.

Now that such an union of choice with natural interest is possible, is a fact of human nature, which every act of your own, in your daily calling, may be used to exemplify. You cannot do steady work without natural interest; but whoever is the mere prey of this passing interest does no steady work. Loyalty is a perfect synthesis of certain natural desires, of some range of social conformity, and of your own deliberate choice.

In order to be loyal, then, to loyalty, I must indeed first choose forms of loyal conduct which appeal to my own nature. This means that, upon one side of my life, I shall have to behave much as the most unenlightened of the loyal do. I shall serve causes such as my natural temperament and my social opportunities suggest to me. I shall choose friends whom I like. My family, my community, my country, will be served partly because I find it interesting to be loyal to them.

Nevertheless, upon another side, all these my more natural and, so to speak, accidental loyalties, will be controlled and unified by a deliberate use of the principle that, whatever my cause, it ought to be such as to further, so far as in me lies, the cause of universal loyalty. Hence I shall not permit my choice of my special causes to remain a mere chance. My causes must form a system. They must constitute in their entirety a single cause, my life of loyalty. When apparent conflicts arise amongst the causes in which I am interested, I shall deliberately undertake, by devices which we shall hereafter study in these lectures, to reduce the conflict to the greatest possible harmony. Thus, for instance, I may say, to one of the causes in which I am naturally bound up:—

I could not love thee, dear, so much,
Loved I not honour more.

And in this familiar spirit my loyalty will aim to be, even within the limits of my own personal life, an united, harmonious devotion, not to various conflicting causes, but to one system of causes, and so to one cause.

Since this one cause is my choice, the cause of my life, my social station will indeed suggest it to me. My natural powers and preferences will make it fascinating to me, and yet I will never let mere social routine, or mere social tradition, or mere private caprice, impose it upon me. I will be individualistic in my loyalty, carefully insisting, however, that whatever else I am, I shall be in all my practical activity, a loyal individual, and, so far as in me lies, one who chooses his personal causes for the sake of the spread of universal loyalty. Moreover, my loyalty will be a growing loyalty. Without giving up old loyalties I shall annex new ones. There will be evolution in my loyalty.

The choice of my cause will in consequence be such as to avoid unnecessary conflict with the causes of others. So far I shall indeed negatively show loyalty to loyalty. It shall not be my cause to destroy other men's loyalty. Yet since my cause, thus chosen and thus organized, still confines me to my narrow personal range, and since I can do so little directly for mankind, you may still ask whether, by such a control of my natural interests, I am indeed able to do much to serve the cause of universal loyalty.

Well, it is no part of the plan of this discourse to encourage illusions about the range of influence that any one poor mortal can exert. But that by the mere force of my practical and personal loyalty, if I am indeed loyal, I am doing something for the cause of universal loyalty, however narrow my range of deeds, this a very little experience of the lives of other people tends to teach me. For who, after all, most encourages and incites me to loyalty? I answer, any loyal human being, whatever his cause, so long as his cause does not arouse my hatred, and does not directly injure my chance to be loyal. My fellow's special and personal cause need not be directly mine. Indirectly he inspires me by the very contagion of his loyalty. He sets me the example. By his loyalty he shows me the worth of loyalty. Those humble and obscure folk of whom I have before spoken, how precious they are to us all as inspiring examples, because of their loyalty to their own.

From what men, then, have I gained the best aid in discovering how to be myself loyal? From the men whose personal cause is directly and consciously one with my own? That is indeed sometimes the case. But others, whose personal causes were apparently remote in very many ways from mine, have helped me to some of my truest glimpses of loyalty.

. . . Loyalty, then, is contagious. It infects not only the fellow-servant of your own special cause, but also all who know of this act. Loyalty is a good that spreads. Live it and you thereby cultivate it in other men. Be faithful, then, so one may say, to the loyal man; be faithful over your few things, for the spirit of loyalty, secretly passing from you to many to whom you are a stranger, may even thereby make you unconsciously ruler over many things. Loyalty to loyalty is then no unpractical cause. And you serve it not by becoming a mere citizen of the world, but by serving your own personal cause. We set before you, then, no unpractical rule when we repeat our moral formula in this form: Find your own cause, your interesting, fascinating, personally engrossing cause; serve it with all your might and soul and strength; but so choose your cause, and so serve it, that thereby you show forth your loyalty to loyalty, so that because of your choice and service of your cause, there is a maximum of increase of loyalty amongst your fellow-men.

. . . Herewith we approach a thesis which is central in my whole philosophy of loyalty. I announced that thesis in other words in the opening lecture. My thesis is that *all those duties which we have learned to recognize as the fundamental duties of the civilized man, the duties that every man owes to every man, are to be rightly interpreted as special instances of loyalty to loyalty.* In other words, all the recognized virtues can be defined in terms of our concept of loyalty. And this is why I assert that, when rightly interpreted, loyalty is the whole duty of man.

For consider the best-known facts as to the indirect influence of certain forms of loyal conduct. When I speak the truth, my act is directly an act of loyalty to the personal tie which then and there binds me to the man to whom I consent to speak. My special cause is, in such a case, constituted by this tie. My fellow and I are linked in a certain unity,—the unity of some transaction which involves our speech one to another. To be ready to speak the truth to my fellow is to have, just then, no eye to see and no tongue to speak save as this willingly accepted tie demands. In so far, then, speaking the truth is a special instance of loyalty. But whoever speaks the truth, thereby does what

he then can do to help everybody to speak the truth. For he acts so as to further the general confidence of man in man. How far such indirect influence can extend, no man can predict.

Precisely so, in the commercial world, honesty in business is a service, not merely and not mainly to the others who are parties to the single transaction in which at any one time this faithfulness is shown. The single act of business fidelity is an act of loyalty to that general confidence of man in man upon which the whole fabric of business rests. On the contrary, the unfaithful financier whose disloyalty is the final deed that lets loose the avalanche of a panic, has done far more harm to general public confidence than he could possibly do to those whom his act directly assails. Honesty, then, is owed not merely and not even mainly to those with whom we directly deal when we do honest acts; it is owed to mankind at large, and it benefits the community and the general cause of commercial loyalty.

Such a remark is in itself a commonplace; but it serves to make concrete my general thesis that every form of dutiful action is a case of loyalty to loyalty. For what holds thus of truthfulness and of commercial honesty holds, I assert, of every form of dutiful action. Each such form is a special means for being, by a concrete deed, loyal to loyalty.

We have sought for the worthy cause; and we have found it. This simplest possible of considerations serves to turn the chaotic mass of separate precepts of which our ordinary conventional moral code consists into a system unified by the one spirit of universal loyalty. By your individual deed you indeed cannot save the world, but you can at any moment do what in you lies to further the cause which both for you and for the human world constitutes the supreme good, namely, the cause of universal loyalty. Herein consists your entire duty.

Review in the light of this simple consideration, the usually recognized range of human duties. How easily they group themselves about the one principle: *Be loyal to loyalty.*

Have I, for instance, duties to myself? Yes, precisely in so far as I have the duty to be actively loyal at all. For loyalty needs not only a willing, but also an effective servant. My duty to myself is, then, the duty to provide my cause with one who is strong enough and skilful enough to be effective according to my own natural powers. The care of health, self-cultivation, self-control, spiritual power—these are all to be morally estimated with reference to the one principle that, since I have no eyes to see or tongue to speak save as the cause commands, I will be as worthy an instrument of the cause as can be made, by my own efforts, out of the poor material which my scrap of human nature provides. The highest personal cultivation for which I have time is thus required by our principle. But self-cultivation which is not related to loyalty is worthless.

Have I private and personal rights, which I ought to assert? Yes, precisely in so far as my private powers and possessions are held in trust for the cause, and are, upon occasion, to be defended for the sake of the cause. My rights are morally the outcome of my loyalty. It is my right to protect my service, to maintain my office, and to keep my own merely in order that I may use my own as the cause commands. But rights which are not determined by my loyalty are vain pretence.

As to my duties to my neighbors, these are defined by a well-known tradition in terms of two principles, justice and benevolence. These two principles are mere aspects of our one principle. Justice means, in general, fidelity to human ties in so far as they are ties. Justice thus concerns itself with what may be called the mere forms in which loyalty expresses itself. Justice, therefore, is simply one aspect of loyalty—the more formal and abstract side of loyal life. If you are just, you are decisive in your choice of your personal cause, you are faithful to the loyal decision once made, you keep your promise, you speak the truth, you respect the loyal ties of all other men, and you contend with other men only in so far as the defence of your own cause, in the interest of loyalty to the universal cause of loyalty, makes such contest against aggression unavoidable. All these types of activity, within the limits that loyalty determines, are demanded if you are to be loyal to loyalty. Our principle thus at once requires them, and enables us to define their range of application. But justice, without loyalty, is a vicious formalism.

Benevolence, on the other hand, is that aspect of loyalty which directly concerns itself with your influence upon the inner life of human beings who enjoy, who suffer, and whose private good is to be affected by your deeds. Since no personal good that your fellow can possess is superior to his own loyalty, your own loyalty to loyalty is itself a supremely benevolent type of activity. And since your fellow-man is an instrument for the furtherance of the cause of universal loyalty, his welfare also concerns you, in so far as, if you help him to a more efficient life, you make him better

able to be loyal. Thus benevolence is an inevitable attendant of loyalty. And the spirit of loyalty to loyalty enables us to define wherein consists a wise benevolence. Benevolence without loyalty is a dangerous sentimentalism. Thus viewed, then, loyalty to universal loyalty is indeed the fulfilment of the whole law.

What must be true about the universe if even loyalty itself is a genuine good, and not a merely inevitable human illusion?

Well, loyalty is a service of causes. A cause, if it really is what our definition requires, links various human lives to the unity of one life. Therefore, if loyalty has any basis in truth, human lives can be linked in some genuine spiritual unity. Is such unity a fact, or is our belief in our causes a mere point of view, a pathetic fallacy? Surely, if any man, however loyal, discovers that his cause is a dream, and that men remain as a fact sundered beings, not really linked by genuine spiritual ties, how can that man remain loyal? Perhaps his supreme good indeed lies in believing that such unities are real. But if this belief turns out to be an illusion, and if a man detects the illusion, can he any longer get the good out of loyalty?

. . . How paradoxical a world, then, must the real world be, if the faith of the loyal is indeed well founded! A spiritual unity of life, which transcends the individual experience of any man, must be real. For loyalty, as we have seen, is a service of causes that, from the human point of view, appear superpersonal. Loyalty holds these unities to be good. If loyalty is right, the real goodness of these causes is never completely manifested to any one man, or to any mere collection of men. Such goodness, then, if completely experienced at all, must be experienced upon some higher level of consciousness than any one human being ever reaches. If loyalty is right, social causes, social organizations, friendships, families, countries, yes, humanity, as you see, must have the sort of unity of consciousness which individual human persons fragmentarily get, but must have this unity upon a higher level than that of our ordinary human individuality.

Some such view, I say, must be held if we are to regard loyalty as in the end anything more than a convenient illusion. Loyalty has its metaphysical aspect. It is an effort to conceive human life in an essentially superhuman way, to view our social organizations as actual personal unities of consciousness, unities wherein there exists an actual experience of that good which, in our loyalty, we only partially apprehend. If the loyalty of the lovers is indeed well founded in fact, then, they, as separate individuals, do not constitute the whole truth. Their spiritual union also has a personal, a conscious existence, upon a higher than human level. An analogous unity of consciousness, an unity superhuman in grade, but intimately bound up with, and inclusive of, our apparently separate personalities, must exist, if loyalty is well founded, wherever a real cause wins the true devotion of ourselves. Grant such an hypothesis, and then loyalty becomes no pathetic serving of a myth. The good which our causes possess, then, also becomes a concrete fact for an experience of a higher than human level. That union of self-sacrifice with self-assertion which loyalty expresses becomes a consciousness of our genuine relations to a higher social unity of consciousness in which we all have our being. For from this point of view we are, and we have our worth, by virtue of our relation to a consciousness of a type superior to the human type. And meanwhile the good of our loyalty is itself a perfectly concrete good, a good which is present to that higher experience, wherein our cause is viewed in its truth, as a genuine unity of life. And because of this fact we can straightforwardly say: We are loyal not for the sake of the good that we privately get out of loyalty, but for the sake of the good that the cause—this higher unity of experience—gets out of this loyalty. Yet our loyalty gives us what is, after all, our supreme good, for it defines our true position in the world of that social will wherein we live and move and have our being.

I doubt not that such a view of human life,—such an assertion that the social will is a concrete entity, just as real as we are, and of still a higher grade of reality than ourselves,—will seem to many of you mythical enough. Yet thus to view the unity of human life is, after all, a common tendency of the loyal. The fact I have illustrated in every lecture in this course. That such a view need not be mythical, that truth and reality can be conceived only in such terms as these, that our philosophy of loyalty is a rational part of a philosophy which must view the whole world as one unity of consciousness, wherein countless lesser unities are synthesized,—this is a general philosophical thesis which I must next briefly expound to you.

My exposition, as you see, must be, in any case, an attempt to show that the inevitable faith of the loyal—their faith in their causes, and in the real goodness of their causes—has

truth, and since I must thus, in any case, discourse of truth, I propose briefly to show you that whoever talks of any sort of truth whatever, be that truth moral or scientific, the truth of a common sense or the truth of a philosophy, inevitably implies, in all his assertions about truth, that the world of truth of which he speaks is a world possessing a rational and spiritual unity, is a conscious world of experience, whose type of consciousness is higher in its level than is the type of our human minds, but whose life is such that our life belongs as part to this living whole. This world of truth is the one that you must define, so I insist, if you are to regard any proposition whatever as true, and are then to tell, in a reasonable way, what you mean by the truth of that proposition.

The world of truth is therefore essentially a world such as that in whose reality the loyal believe when they believe their cause to be real. Moreover, this truth world has a goodness about it, essentially like that which the loyal attribute to their causes. Truth seeking and loyalty are therefore essentially the same process of life merely viewed in two different aspects. Whoever is loyal serves what he takes to be a truth, namely, his cause. On the other hand, whoever seeks truth for its own sake fails of his own business if he seeks it merely as a barren abstraction, that has no life in it. If a truth seeker knows his business, he is, then, in the sense of our definition, serving a cause which unifies our human life upon some higher level of spiritual being than the present human level. He is therefore essentially loyal. Truth seeking is a moral activity; and on the other hand, morality is wholly inadequate unless the light of eternal truth shines upon it.

This, I say, will be my thesis. Some of you will call it very mystical, or at least a very fantastic thesis. It is not so. It ought to be viewed as a matter of plain sense. It is, I admit, a thesis which many of the most distinguished amongst my colleagues, who are philosophers, nowadays view sometimes with amusement, and sometimes with a notable impatience. This way of regarding the world of truth, which I have just defined as mine, is especially and most vivaciously attacked by my good friends, the pragmatists,—a group of philosophers who have of late been disposed to take truth under their especial protection, as if she were in danger from the tendency of some people who take her too seriously.

When I mention pragmatism, I inevitably bring to your minds the name of one whom we all honor,—the philosopher who last year so persuasively stated, before the audience of this Institute, the pragmatist theory of philosophical method, and of the nature of truth. It is impossible for me to do any justice, within my limits, to the exposition which Professor James gave of his own theory of truth. Yet since the antithesis between his views and those which I have now to indicate to you may be in itself an aid to my own exposition, I beg you to allow me to use, for the moment, some of his assertions about the nature of truth as a means of showing, by contrast, how I find myself obliged to interpret the same problem. The contrast is accompanied, after all, by so much of deeper agreement that I can well hope that my sketch of the current situation in the philosophical controversies about truth may not seem to you merely a dreary report of differences of opinion.

Professor James, in discussing the nature of truth, in his recent book on pragmatism, begins, as some of you will remember, by accepting the classic definition of truth as the agreement of our ideas with reality. Whoever knows or possesses a truth has, then, in his mind, an idea, an opinion, a judgment, or some complex of such states of mind. If his views are true, then these his ideas or opinions are in agreement with something called reality. Thus, for instance, if a loyal man believes his cause, say, his friendship or his club or his nation, to be a reality, and if his belief is true, his loyal opinion is in agreement with the real world. So far, of course, all of you will accept the definition of truth here in question.

Professor James now goes on to point out that, in some cases, our ideas agree with what we call real things by copying those things. So, if, with shut eyes, you think of the clock on the wall, your image of the clock is a copy of its dial. But, as my colleague continues, our power to copy real objects by ideas of our own is obviously a very limited power. You believe that you have at least some true ideas about many objects which are far too complex or too mysterious for you to copy them. Your power to become sure that your ideas do copy the constitution of anything whatever which exists outside of you is also very limited, because, after all, you never get outside of your own experience to see what the real things would be if taken wholly in themselves. Hence, on the whole, one cannot say that the agreement of our ideas with reality which constitutes their truth is essentially such as to demand that our ideas should be copies. For we believe that we have true ideas even when we do not believe them to be copies.

Moreover (and herewith we approach a consideration which is, for my colleague's theory of truth, very essential), not only does truth not consist merely in copying facts; but also truth cannot be defined in terms of any other static or fixed relation between ideas and facts. The only way to conceive that agreement between ideas and facts which constitutes truth is to think of the "practical consequences" which follow from possessing true ideas. "True ideas," in Professor James's words, "lead us, namely, through the acts and other ideas which they instigate, into or up to or towards other parts of experience with which we feel all the while that the original ideas remain in agreement. The connections and transitions come to us, from point to point, as being progressive, harmonious, satisfactory. This function of agreeable leading is what we mean by an idea's verification." So far my colleague's words. He goes on, in his account, to mention many illustrations of the way in which the truth of ideas is tested, both in the world of common sense, and in the world of science, by the usefulness, by the success, which attaches to the following out of true ideas to their actual empirical consequences. The wanderer lost in the woods gets true ideas about his whereabouts whenever he hits upon experiences and ideas which set him following the path which actually leads him home. In science, hypotheses are tested as to their truth, by considering what experiences they lead us to anticipate, and by then seeing whether these anticipations can be fulfilled in a satisfactory way. "True," says Professor James, "is the name for whatever idea starts the verification process." For instance, then, the verifiable scientific hypothesis, if once tested by the success of its results in experience, is in so far declared true. And similarly, the idea of following a given path in the woods in order to get home is declared true, if you follow the path and get home.

In consequence, every true idea is such in so far as it is useful in enabling you to anticipate the sort of experience that you want; and every idea that is useful as a guide of life is in so far true. The personal tests of usefulness, as of truth, are for every one of us personal and empirical. My own direct tests of truth are of course thus limited to my own experience. I find my own ideas true just in so far as I find them guiding me to the experience that I want to get. But of course, as my colleague constantly insists, we give credit, as social beings, to one another's verifications. Hence I regard as true many ideas that I personally have not followed out to any adequately experienced consequences. The "overwhelmingly large" number of the ideas by which we live, "we let pass for true without attempting to verify." We do this, says Professor James, "because it *works* to do so, everything we know conspiring with the belief, and nothing interfering." That is, we regard as true those ideas which we personally find it convenient, successful, expedient to treat as verifiable, even though we never verify them. The warrant of these unverifiable truths is, however, once more, the empirical usefulness of living as if they were verifiable. "Truth lives," says Professor James, "for the most part on a credit system. . . . But this all points to direct face-to-face verification somewhere, without which the fabric of truth collapses like a financial system with no cash basis whatever. You accept my verification of one thing, I yours of another. We trade on each other's truth. But beliefs verified concretely by *somebody* are the posts of the whole superstructure." The indirectly verifiable ideas, that is, the ideas which somebody else verifies, or even those which nobody yet verifies, but which agree sufficiently with verified ideas, we accept because it is advantageous to accept them. It is the same thing, then, to say that an idea is true because it is useful and to say that it is useful because it is true.

Agreement with reality thus turns out, as my colleague insists, "to be an affair of leading,— leading that is useful because it is into quarters that contain objects that are important." And my colleague's account of truth culminates in these notable expressions: " 'The true,' to put it very briefly, is only the expedient in the way of our thinking, just as 'the right' is only the expedient in the way of our behaving." "Pragmatism faces forward towards the future." That is, an idea is true by virtue of its expedient outcome. "It pays for our ideas to be validated, verified. Our obligation to seek truth is part of our general obligation to do what pays. The payment true ideas bring are the sole why of our duty to follow them."

The sum and substance of this theory of truth, as you see, is that the truth of an idea is determined by its "success" in yielding what my colleague frequently calls "the cash values in terms of experience," which appear as consequences of holding this idea. These values may either take the form of direct verifications in terms of sensible facts, as when one finds one's way out of the woods and sees one's home; or else the form of practically satisfying and expedient beliefs, which clash with no sensible experience, and which are personally acceptable to those who hold them. It is "expedient" to connect the latter beliefs with sensible cash values when you can. If you cannot turn them into such cash, you are at liberty to hold them, but with the conviction that, after all, the personally expedient is the true.

In any case, as you see, whatever else truth is, it is nothing static. It changes with the expediencies of your experience. And therefore those who conceive the realm of truth as essentially eternal are the objects of my colleague's most charming philosophical fury.

We have, then, an authoritative exposition of pragmatism before us. You must see that this doctrine, whether it be true doctrine, or whether it be indeed simply for some people an expedient doctrine, is certainly one that concerns our philosophy of loyalty, now that indeed we have reached the place where the relation between loyalty and truth has become, for us, a critically important relation. May we venture to ask ourselves, then: Is this pragmatism a fair expression of what we mean by truth?

In reply let me at once point out the extent to which I personally agree with my colleague, and accept his theory of truth. I fully agree with him that whenever a man asserts a truth, his assertion is a deed,—a practical attitude, an active acknowledgment of some fact. I fully agree that the effort to verify this acknowledgment by one's own personal experience, and the attempt to find truth in the form of a practical congruity between our assertions and our attained empirical results, is an effort which in our individual lives inevitably accompanies and sustains our every undertaking in the cause of truth seeking. Modern pragmatism is not indeed as original as it seems to suppose itself to be in emphasizing such views. The whole history of modern idealism is full of such assertions. I myself, as a teacher of philosophy, have for years insisted upon viewing truth in this practical way. I must joyously confess to you that I was first taught to view the nature of truth in this way when I was a young student of philosophy; and I was taught this by several great masters of modern thought. These masters were Kant, Fichte, Hegel, and Professor James himself, whose lectures, as I heard them in my youth at the Johns Hopkins University, and whose beautiful conversations and letters in later years, inspired me with an insight that helped me, rather against his own advice, to read my German idealists aright, and to see what is, after all, the eternal truth beneath all this pragmatism. For Professor James's pragmatism, despite its entertaining expressions of horror of the eternal, actually does state one aspect of eternal truth. It is, namely, eternally true that all search for truth is a practical activity, with an ethical purpose, and that a purely theoretical truth, such as should guide no significant active process, is a barren absurdity. This, however, is so far precisely what Fichte spent his life in teaching. Professor James taught me, as a student, much the same lesson; and I equally prize and honor all of my masters for that lesson; and I have been trying to live up to it ever since I first began to study the nature of truth.

So far, then, I am a pragmatist. And I also fully agree that, if we ever get truth, the attainment of truth means a living and practical success in those active undertakings in terms of which we have been trying to assert and to verify our truth. I doubt not that to say, "This is true," is the same as to say: "The ideas by means of which I define this truth are the practically and genuinely successful ideas, the ideas such that, when I follow them, I really fulfil my deepest needs." All this I not only admit; but I earnestly insist that truth is an ethical concept; and I thank from my heart the great pragmatist who so fascinated his audience last year in this place; I thank him that he taught them what, in my youth, he helped to teach me, namely, that winning the truth means winning the success which we need, and for which the whole practical nature of our common humanity continually groans and travails together in pain until now.

And yet, and yet all this still leaves open one great question. When we seek truth, we indeed seek successful ideas. But what, in Heaven's name, constitutes success? Truth-seeking is indeed a practical endeavor. But what, in the name of all the loyal, is the goal of human endeavor? Truth is a living thing. We want leading and guidance. "Lead, kindly light,"—thus we address the truth. We are lost in the woods of time. We want the way, the truth, and the life. For nothing else does all our science and our common sense strive. But what is it to have genuine abundance of life? For what do we live?

Here our entire philosophy of loyalty, so far as it has yet been developed, comes to our aid. The loyal, as we have said, are the only human beings who can have any reasonable hope of genuine success. If they do not succeed, then nobody succeeds. And of course the loyal do indeed live with a constant, although not with an exclusive, reference to their own personal experience and to that of other individual men. They feel their present fascination for their cause. It thrills through them. Their loyalty has, even for them, in their individual capacity what Professor James calls a cash value. And of course they like to have their friends share such cash values. Yet I ask you: Are the loyal seeking *only* the mere collection of their private experiences of their personal thrills of fascination? If you hear loyal men say: "We are in this business just for what we as individuals—we and our individual fellows—can get out of it," do you regard that way of speech as an adequate expression of their really loyal spirit? When Arnold von Winkelried rushed on the Austrian spears, did he naturally say: "Look you, my friends, I seek, in experiential terms, the cash value of my devotion; see me draw the cash." My colleague would of course retort that the hero in question, according to the legend, said, as he died: "Make way for liberty." He therefore wanted liberty, as one may insist, to get these cash values. Yes, but liberty was no individual man, and no mere heap of individual men. Liberty was a cause, a certain superhuman unity of the ideal life of a free community. It was indeed expedient that one man should die for the people. But the people also was an *unio mystica* of many in one. For that cause the hero died. And no man has ever yet experienced, in his private and individual life, the whole true cash value of that higher unity. Nor will all the individual Swiss patriots, past, present, or future, viewed as a mere collection of creatures of a day, ever draw the cash in question. If the cause exists, the treasure exists, and is indeed a cash value upon a level higher than that of our passing human life. But loyalty does not live by selling its goods for present cash in the temple of its cause. Such pragmatism it drives out of the temple. It serves, and worships, and says to the cause: "Be thine the glory."

Loyalty, then, seeks success and from moment to moment indeed thrills with a purely fragmentary and temporary joy in its love of its service. But the joy depends on a belief in a distinctly superhuman type of unity of life. And so you indeed cannot express the value of your loyalty by pointing at the mere heap of the joyous thrills of the various loyal individuals. The loyal serve a real whole of life, an experiential value too rich for any expression in merely momentary terms.

Now, is it not very much so with our love of any kind of truth? Of course, we mortals seek for whatever verification of our truths we can get in the form of present success. But can you express our human definition of truth in terms of any collection of our human experiences of personal expediency?

Well, as to our concept of truth, let us consider a test case by way of helping ourselves to answer this question. Let us suppose that a witness appears, upon some witness-stand, and objects to taking the ordinary oath, because he has conscientious scruples, due to the fact that he is a recent pragmatist, who has a fine new definition of truth, in terms of which alone he can be sworn. Let us suppose him, hereupon, to be granted entire liberty to express his oath in his own way. Let him accordingly say, using, with technical scrupulosity, my colleague's definition of truth: "I promise to tell whatever is expedient and nothing but what is expedient, so help me future experience." I ask you: Do you think that this witness has expressed, with adequacy, that view of the nature of truth that you really wish a witness to have in mind? Of course, if he were a typical pragmatist, you would indeed be delighted to hear his testimony on the witness-stand or anywhere else. But would you accept his formula?

But let me be more precise as to the topic of this witness's possible testimony. I will use for the purpose Kant's famous case. Somebody, now dead, let us suppose, has actually left with the witness a sum of money as a wholly secret deposit to be some time returned. No written record was made of the transaction. No evidence exists that can in future be used to refute the witness if he denies the transaction and keeps the money. The questions to be asked the witness relate, amongst other things, to whatever it may be that he believes himself to know about the estate of the deceased. I now ask, not what his duty is, but simply what it is that he rationally means to do in case he really intends to tell the truth about that deposit. Does he take merely the "forward-looking" attitude of my colleague's pragmatism? Does he mean merely to predict, as expedient, certain consequences which he expects to result either to him or to the heirs of the estate? Of course his testimony will have consequences. But is it these which he is trying to predict? Are they his true object? Or does the truth of his statement mean the same as the expediency, either to himself or to the heirs, of any consequence whatever which may follow from his state-

ment? Does the truth of his statement about the deposit even mean the merely present empirical fact that he now feels a belief in this statement or that he finds it just now congruent with the empirical sequences of his present memories? No, for the witness is not trying merely to tell how he feels. He is trying to tell the truth about the deposit. And the witness's belief is not the truth of his belief. Even his memory is not the truth to which he means to be a witness. And the future consequences of his making a true statement are for the witness irrelevant, since they are for the law and the heirs to determine. Yet one means something perfectly definite by the truth of the testimony of that witness. And that truth is simply inexpressible in such terms as those which my colleague employs. Yet the truth here in question is a simple truth about the witness's own personal past experience.

Now, such a case is only one of countless cases where we are trying to tell the truth about something which we all regard as being, in itself, a matter of genuine and concrete experience, while nevertheless we do not mean, "It is expedient just now for me to think this," nor yet, "I predict such and such consequences for my own personal experience, or for the future experience of some individual man; and these predicted consequences constitute the truth of my present assertion." I say there are countless such cases where the truth that we mean is empirical indeed, but transcends all such expediencies and personal consequences. The very assertion, "Human experience, taken as a totality of facts, exists," is a momentous example of just such an assertion. We all believe that assertion. If that assertion is not actually true, then our whole frame of natural science, founded as it is on the common experience of many observers, crumbles into dust, our common sense world is nothing, business and society are alike illusions, loyalty to causes is meaningless. Now that assertion, "Human experience, that is, the totality of the experiences of many men, really exists," is an assertion which you and I regard as perfectly true. Yet no individual man has ever verified, or ever will verify, that assertion. For no man, taken as this individual man, experiences the experience of anybody but himself. Yet we all regard that assertion as true.

My colleague, of course, would say, as in fact he has often said, that his assertion is one of the numerous instances of that process of trading on credit which he so freely illustrates. We do not verify this assertion. But we accept it on credit as verifiable. However, the credit simile is a dangerous one here, so long as one conceives that the verification which would pay the cash would be a payment in the form of such human experience as you and I possess. For the assertion, "The experience of many men exists," is an assertion that is essentially unverifiable by any one man. If the "cash value" of the assertion means, then, its verifiability by any man, then the credit in question is one that simply cannot be turned into such cash by any conceivable process, occurring in our individual lives, since the very idea of the real existence of the experience of many men excludes, by its definition, the direct presence of this experience of various men within the experience of any one of these men. The credit value in question would thus be a *mere* fiat value, so long as the only cash values are those of the experiences of individual men, and the truth of our assertion would mean simply that we find it expedient to treat as verifiable what we know cannot be verified. Hereupon, of course, we should simply be trading upon currency that has no cash value. Whoever does verify the fact that the experience of many men exists, if such a verifier there be, is a superhuman being, an union of the empirical lives of many men in the complex of a single experience. And if our credit of the assertion that many men exist is convertible into cash at all, that cash is not laid up where the moth and rust of our private human experience doth from moment to moment corrupt the very data that we see; but is laid up in a realm where our experiences, past, present, future, are the object of a conspectus that is not merely temporal and transient. Now all the natural sciences make use of the persuasion that the experiences of various men exist, and that there is a unity of such experiences. This thesis, then, is no invention of philosophers.

My colleague, in answer, would of course insist that as a fact you and I are now believing that many men exist, and that human experience in its entirety exists, *merely* because, in the long run, we find that this belief is indeed congruous with our current and purely personal experience, and is therefore an expedient idea of ours. But I, in answer, insist that common sense well feels this belief to be indeed from moment to moment expedient, and yet clearly distinguishes between that expediency and the truth which common sense all the while attributes to the belief. The distinction is precisely the one which my fancied illustration of the pragmatist on the witness-stand has sug-

gested. It is a perfectly universal distinction and a commonplace one. Tell me, "This opinion is true," and whatever you are talking about I may agree or disagree or doubt; yet in any case you have stated a momentous issue. But tell me, "I just now find this belief expedient, it feels to me congruous" and you have explicitly given me just a scrap of your personal biography, and have told me no other truth whatever than a truth about the present state of your feelings.

If, however, you emphasize my colleague's wording to the effect that a truth is such because it proves to be an idea that is expedient "in the long run," I once more ask you: *When* does a man experience the whole of the real facts about the "long run"? At the beginning of the long run, when the end is not yet, or at the end, when, perhaps, he forgets, like many older men, what were once the expediencies of his youth? What decides the truth about the long run? My exalted moments, when anything that I like seems true, or my disappointed moments, when I declare that I have always had bad luck? To appeal to the genuinely real "long run" is only to appeal in still another form to a certain ideally fair conspectus of my own whole life,—a conspectus which I, in my private human experience, never get. Whoever gets the conspectus of my whole life, to see what, in the long run, is indeed for me expedient,—whoever, I say, gets that conspectus, if such a being there indeed is,—is essentially superhuman in his type of consciousness. For he sees what I only get in the form of an idea; namely, the true sense and meaning of my life.

In vain, then, does one try adequately to define the whole of what we mean by truth either in terms of our human feelings of expediency or in terms of our instantaneous thrills of joy in success, or in terms of any other verifications that crumble as the instant flies. All such verifications we use, just as we use whatever perishes. Any such object is a fragment, but we want the whole. Truth is itself a cause, and is largely as one must admit, for us mortals, just now, what we called, in our last lecture, a lost cause—else how should these pragmatists be able thus to imagine a vain thing, and call that truth which is but the crumbling expediency of the moment? Our search for truth is indeed a practical process. The attainment of truth means success. Our verifications, so far as we ever get them, are momentary fragments of that success. But the genuine success that we demand is an ethical success, of precisely the type which all the loyal seek, when they rejoice in giving all for their cause.

But you will now all the more eagerly demand in what sense we can ever get any warrant for saying that we know any truth whatever. In seeking truth we do not seek the mere crumbling successes of the passing instants of human life. We seek a city out of sight. What we get of success within our passing experience is rationally as precious to us as it is, just because we believe that attainment to be a fragment of an essentially superhuman success, which is won in the form of a higher experience than ours,—a conspectus wherein our human experiences are unified. But what warrant have we for this belief?

I will tell you how I view the case. We need unity of life. In recognizing that need my own pragmatism consists. Now, we never find unity present to our human experience in more than a fragmentary shape. We get hints of higher unity. But only the fragmentary unity is won at any moment of our lives. We therefore form ideas—very fallible ideas—of some unity of experience, at unity such as our idea of any science or any art or any united people or of any community or of any other cause, any other union of many human experiences in one, defines. Now, if our ideas are in any case indeed true, then such an unity is as a fact successfully experienced upon some higher level than ours, and is experienced in some conspectus of life which wins what we need, which approves our loyalty, which fulfils our rational will, and which has in its wholeness what we seek. And then we ourselves with all our ideas and strivings are in and of this higher unity of life. Our loyalty to truth is a hint of this unity. Our transient successes are fragments of the true success. But suppose our ideas about the structure of this higher unity to be false in any of their details. Suppose, namely, any of our causes to be wrongly viewed by us. Then there is still real that state of facts, whatever it is, which, if just now known to us, would show us this falsity of our various special ideas. Now, only an experience, a consciousness of some system of contents, could show the falsity of any idea. Hence this real state of facts, this constitution of the genuine universe, whatever it is, must again be a reality precisely in so far as it is also a conspectus of facts of experience.

We therefore already possess at least one true idea, precisely in so far as we say: "The facts of the world are what they are; the real

universe exposes our errors and makes them errors." And when we say this, we once more appeal to a conspectus of experience in which ours is included. For I am in error only in case my present ideas about the true facts of the whole world of experience are out of concord with the very meaning that I myself actively try to assign to these ideas. My ideas are in any detail false, only if the very experience to which I mean to appeal, contains in its conspectus contents which I just now imperfectly conceive. In any case, then, the truth is possessed by precisely that whole of experience which I never get, but to which my colleague also inevitably appeals when he talks of the "long run," or of the experiences of humanity in general.

Whatever the truth, then, or the falsity of any of my special convictions about this or that fact may be, the real world, which refutes my false present ideas in so far as they clash with its wholeness, and which confirms them just in so far as they succeed in having significant relations to its unity,—this real world, I say, is a conspectus of the whole of experience. And this whole of experience is in the closest real relation to my practical life, precisely in so far as, for me, the purpose of my life is to get into unity with the whole universe, and precisely in so far as the universe itself is just that conspectus of experience that we all mean to define and to serve whatever we do, or whatever we say.

But the real whole conspectus of experience, the real view of the totality of life, the real expression of that will to live in and for the whole, which every assertion of truth and every loyal deed expresses—well, it must be a conspectus that includes whatever facts are indeed facts, be they past, present, or future. I call this whole of experience an eternal truth. I do not thereby mean, as my colleague seems to imagine, that the eternal first exists, and that then our life in time comes and copies that eternal order. I mean simply that the whole of experience includes all temporal happenings, contains within itself all changes, and, since it is the one whole that we all want and need, succeeds in so far as it supplements all failures, accepts all, even the blindest of services, and wins what we seek. Thus winning it is practically good and worthy.

But if one insists, How do you know all this? I reply: I know simply that to try to deny the reality of this whole of truth is simply to reaffirm it. Any special idea of mine may be wrong, even as any loyal deed may fail, or as any cause may become, to human vision, a lost cause. But to deny that there is truth, or that there is a real world, is simply to say that the whole truth is that there is no whole truth, and that the real fact is that there is no fact real at all. Such assertions are plain self-contradictions. And on the other hand, by the term "real world," defined as it is for us by our ideal needs, we mean simply that whole of experience in which we live, and in unity with which we alone succeed.

Loyalty, then, has its own metaphysic. This metaphysic is expressed in a view of things which conceives our experience as bound up in a real unity with all experience,—a unity which is essentially good, and in which all our ideas possess their real fulfilment and success. Such a view is true, simply because if you deny its truth you reaffirm that very truth under a new form.

Truth, meanwhile, means, as pragmatism asserts, the fulfilment of a need. But we all need the superhuman, the city out of sight, the union with all life,—the essentially eternal. This need is no invention of the philosophers. It is the need which all the loyal feel, whether they know it or not, and whether they call themselves pragmatists or not. To define this need as pragmatism in its recent forms has done, to reduce truth to expediency, is to go about everything *cash, cash,* in a realm where there is no cash of the sort that loyalty demands, that every scientific inquiry presupposes, and that only the unity of the experiences of many in one furnishes.

If we must, then, conceive recent pragmatism under the figure of a business enterprise,—a metaphor which my colleague's phraseology so insistently invites,—I am constrained therefore to sum up its position thus: First, with a winning clearness, and with a most honorable frankness it confesses bankruptcy, so far as the actually needed cash payments of significant truth are concerned. Secondly, it nevertheless declines to go into the hands of any real receiver, for it is not fond of anything that appears too absolute. And thirdly, it proposes simply and openly to go on doing business under the old style and title of the truth. "After all," it says, "are we not, every one of us, fond of credit values?"

But I cannot conceive the position of the loyal to be, in fact, so hopelessly embarrassed as this. The recent pragmatists themselves are, in fact, practically considered very loyal lovers of genuine truth. They simply have mistaken the true state of their accounts. We all know, indeed, little enough. But the loyal man, I think, whether he imagines himself to be a recent pragmatist or not, has a rational right to say this: My cause partakes of the nature of the only truth and reality that there is. My life is an effort to manifest such eternal truth, as well as I can, in a series of temporal deeds. I may serve my cause ill. I may conceive it erroneously. I may lose it in the thicket of this world of transient experience. My every human deed may involve a blunder. My mortal life may seem one long series of failures. But I know that my cause liveth. My true life is hid with the cause and belongs to the eternal.

Loyalty and Religion

I

. . . We have called this realm of true life, and of genuine and united experience,—this realm which, if our argument at the last time was sound, includes our lives in that very whole which constitutes the real universe,—we have called this realm, I say, an eternal world,—eternal, simply because, according to our theory, it includes all temporal happenings and strivings in the conspectus of a single consciousness and fulfils all our rational purposes together, and is all that we seek to be. For, as we argued, this realm of reality is conscious, is united, is self-possessed, and is perfected through the very wealth of the ideal sacrifices and of the loyal devotion which are united so as to constitute its fulness of being. In view of the philosophy that was thus sketched, I now propose a new definition of loyalty; and I say that this definition results from all of our previous study: *Loyalty is the will to manifest, so far as is possible, the*

From *The Philosophy of Loyalty* (New York: Macmillan Company, 1908), pp. 356–398.

Eternal, that is, the conscious and superhuman unity of life, in the form of the acts of an individual Self. Or, if you prefer to take the point of view of an individual human self, if you persist in looking at the world just as we find it in our ordinary experience, and if you regard the metaphysical doctrine just sketched merely as an ideal theory of life, and *not* as a demonstrable philosophy, I can still hold to my definition of loyalty by borrowing a famous phrase from the dear friend and colleague some of whose views I at the last time opposed. I can, then, simply state my new definition of loyalty in plainer and more directly obvious terms thus: *Loyalty is the Will to Believe in something eternal, and to express that belief in the practical life of a human being.*

This, I say, is my new definition of loyalty, and in its metaphysical form, it is my final definition. Let me expound it further, and let me show a little more in detail how it results from the whole course of our inquiry.

II

. . . Now, whatever may be said of wonders, or of mystical revelations, our philosophy of loyalty is naturally interested in pointing out a road to the spiritual world, if, indeed, there be such a world,—a road, I say, which has a plain relation to our everyday moral life. And it seems to me, both that there is a genuinely spiritual world, and that there is a path of inquiry which can lead from such a practical faith in the higher world as loyalty embodies in its deeds, to a rational insight into the general constitution of this higher realm. I do not offer my opinions upon this subject as having any authority. I can see no farther through stone walls than can my fellow, and I enjoy no special revelations from any super-human realm. But I ask you, as thoughtful people, to consider what your ordinary life, as rational beings, implies as its basis and as its truth.

What I was expounding at the close of my last lecture was a view of things which seems to me to be implied in any attempt to express, in a reasonable way, where we stand in our universe.

We all of us have to admit, I think, that our daily life depends upon believing in realities which are, in any case, just as truly beyond the scope of our ordinary individual experience as any spiritual realm could possibly be. We live by believing in one another's minds as realities. We give credit to countless reports, documents, and other evidences of present and past facts; and we do all this, knowing that such credit cannot be adequately verified by any experience such as an individual man can obtain. Now, the usual traditional account of all these beliefs of ours is that they are forced upon us, by some reality which is, as people say, wholly independent of our knowledge, which exists by itself apart from our experience, and which may be, therefore, entirely alien in its nature to any of our human interests and ideals.

But modern philosophy,—a philosophy in whose historical course of development our recent pragmatism is only a passing incident,—that philosophy which turns upon analyzing the bases of our knowledge, and upon reflectively considering what our human beliefs and ideas are intended to mean and to accomplish, has taught us to see that we can never deal with any wholly independent reality. The recent pragmatists, as I understand them, are here in full and conscious agreement with my own opinion. We can deal with no world which is out of relation to our experience. On the contrary, the real world is known to us in terms of *our* experience, is defined for us by *our* ideas, and is the object of *our* practical endeavors. Meanwhile, to declare anything real is to assert that it has its place in some realm of experience, be this experience human or superhuman. To declare that anything whatever is a fact, is simply to assert that some proposition, which you or I or some other thinking being can express in the form of intelligible ideas, is a true proposition. And the truth of the propositions itself is nothing dead, is nothing independent of ideas and of experience, but is simply the successful fulfilment of some demand,—a demand which you can express in the form of an assertion, and which is fulfilled in so far, and only in so far, as some region of live experience contains what meets that demand. Meanwhile, every proposition, every assertion that anybody can make, is a deed; and every rational deed involves, in effect, an assertion of a fact. If the prodigal son says, "I will arise and go to my father," he even thereby asserts something to be true about himself, his father, and his father's house. If an astronomer or a chemist or a statistician or a man of business reports "this or that is a fact," he even thereby performs a deed,—an act having an ideal meaning, and embodying a live purpose; and he further declares that the constitution of experience is such as to make this deed essentially reasonable, successful, and worthy to be accepted by every man.

The real world is therefore *not* something independent of us. It is a world whose stuff, so to speak,—whose content,—is of the nature of experience, whose structure meets, validates, and gives warrant to our active deeds, and whose whole nature is such that it can be interpreted in terms of ideas, propositions, and conscious meanings, while in turn it gives to our fragmentary ideas and to our conscious life whatever connected meaning they possess. Whenever I have purposes and fail, so far, to carry them out, that is because I have not yet found the true way of expressing my own relation to reality. On the other hand, precisely in so far as I have understood some whole of reality, I have carried out successfully some purpose of mine.

There is, then, no merely theoretical truth, and there is no reality foreign, in its nature, to experience. Whoever actually lives the whole conscious life such as *can* be lived out with a definitely reasonable meaning,—such a being, obviously superhuman in his grade of consciousness, not only knows the real world, but *is* the real world. Whoever is conscious of the whole content of experience possesses all reality. And our search for reality is simply an effort to discover what the whole fabric of experience is into which our human experience is woven, what the system of truth is in which our partial truths have their place, what the ideally significant life is for the sake of which every deed of ours is undertaken. When we try to find out what the real world is, we are simply trying to discover the sense of our own individual lives. And we can define that sense of our lives only in terms of a conscious life in which ours is included, in which our ideas get their full meaning expressed, and in which what we fail to carry out to the full is carried out to the full.

III

Otherwise stated, when I think of the whole world of facts,—the "real world,"—I inevitably think of something that is *my own* world, precisely in so far as that world is an object of any reasonable idea of mine. It is true, of course, that, in forming an idea of my world of facts, I do not thereby give myself, at this instant, the least right to spin out of my inner consciousness any adequate present ideas of the detail of the contents of my real world. In thinking of the real world, I am indeed thinking of the whole of that very system of experience in which my experience is bound up, and in which I, as an individual, have my very limited and narrow place. But just now I am not

in possession of that whole. I have to work for it and wait for it, and faithfully to be true to it. As a creature living along, from moment to moment, in time, I therefore indeed have to wait ignorantly enough for coming experience. I have to use as I can my fallible memory in trying to find out about my own past experience. I have no way of verifying what your experience is, except by using tests—and again the extremely fallible tests—which we all employ in our social life. I need the methods of the sciences of experience to guide me in the study of whatever facts fall within their scope. I use those practical and momentary successes upon which recent pragmatism insists, whenever I try to get a concrete verification of my opinions. And so far I stand, and must rightly stand, exactly where any man of common sense, any student of a science, any plain man, or any learned man stands. I am a fallible mortal, simply trying to find my way as I can in the thickets of experience.

And yet all this my daily life, my poor efforts to remember and to predict, my fragmentary inquiries into this or that matter of science or of business, my practical acknowledgment of your presence as real facts in the real world of experience, my personal definition of the causes to which I devote myself,—these are all undertakings that are overruled, and that are rendered significant, simply in so far as they are reasonable parts of one all-embracing enterprise. This enterprise is my active attempt to find out my true place in the real world. But now I can only define my real world by conceiving it in terms of experience. I can find my place in the world only by discovering where I stand in the whole system of experience. For what I mean by a fact is something that somebody finds. Even a merely possible fact is something only in so far as somebody actually *could* find it. And the sense in which it *is* an actual fact that somebody *could* find in his experience a determinate fact, is a sense which again can only be defined in terms of concrete, living, and not merely possible, and in terms of some will or purpose expressed in a conscious life. Even possible facts, then, are *really* possible only in so far as something is actually experienced, or is found by somebody. Whatever is real, then, be it distant or near, past or future, present to your mind or to mine, a physical fact or a moral fact, a fact of our possible human experience, or a fact of a superhuman type of experience, a purpose, a desire, a natural object or an ideal object, a mechanical system or a value,—whatever, I say, is real, *is real as a content present to some conscious being*. Therefore, when I inquire about the real world, I am simply asking what contents of experience, human or super-human, are actually and consciously found by somebody. My inquiries regarding facts, of whatever grade the facts may be, are therefore inevitably an effort to find out *what the world's experience is*. In all my common sense, then, in all my science, in all my social life, I am trying to discover what the universal conscious life which constitutes the world contains as its contents, and views as its own.

But even this is not the entire story of my place in the real world. For I cannot inquire about facts without forming my own ideas of these facts. In so far as my ideas are true, my own personal ideas are therefore active processes that go on within the conscious life of the world. If my ideas are true, they succeed in agreeing with the very world consciousness that they define. But this agreement, this success, if itself it is a fact at all, is once more a fact of experience,—yet not merely of my private experience, since I myself never personally find, within the limits of my own individual experience, the success that every act of truth seeking demands. If I get the truth, then, at any point of my life, my success is real only in so far as some conscious life, which includes my ideas and my efforts, and which also includes the very facts of the world whereof I am thinking, actually observes my success, in the form of a conspectus of the world's facts, and of my own efforts to find and to define them.

In so far, then, as I get the truth about the world, I myself am a fragmentary conscious life that is included within the conscious conspectus of the world's experience, and that is in one self-conscious unity with that world consciousness. And it is in this unity with the world consciousness that I get my success, and am in concord with the truth.

But of course any particular idea of mine, regarding the world, or regarding any fact in the world, may be false. However, this possibility of my error is itself a real situation of mine, and involves essentially the same relation between the world and myself which obtains in case I have true ideas. For I can be in error about an object only in case I really mean to agree with that object, and to agree with it in a way which only my own purposes, in seeking this agreement, can possibly define. It is only by virtue of my own undertakings that I can fail in my undertakings. It is only because, after all, I am loyal to the world's whole truth that I can so express myself in fal-

lible ideas, and in fragmentary opinions that, as a fact, I may, at any moment, undertake too much for my own momentary success to be assured, so that I can indeed in any one of my assertions fail justly to accord with that world consciousness which I am all the while trying to interpret in my own transient way. But when I thus fail, I momentarily fail *to interpret my place in the very world consciousness whose life I am trying to define*. But my failure, when and in so far as it occurs, is once more a fact,—and therefore a fact for the world's consciousness. If I blunder, but am sincere, if I think myself right, but am not right, then my error is a fact for a consciousness which includes my fallible attempts to be loyal to the truth, but which sees how they just now lose present touch with their true cause. Seeing this my momentary defeat, the world consciousness sees, however, my loyalty, and in its conspectus assigns, even to my fragmentary attempts at truth, their genuine place in the single unity of the world's consciousness. My very failure, then, like every loyal failure, is still a sort of success. It is an effort to define my place in the unity of the world's conspectus of all conscious life. I cannot fall out of that unity. I cannot flee from its presence. And I err only as the loyal may give up their life for their cause. Whether I get truth, then, or whether I err in detail, *my loyal search for truth insures the fact that I am in a significant unity with the world's conscious life*.

The thesis that the world is one whole and a significant whole of conscious life is, for these reasons, a thesis which can only be viewed as an error, by reinstating this very assertion under a new form. For any error of mine concerning the world is possible only in so far as I really mean to assert the truth about the world; and this real meaning of mine can exist only as a fact within the conspectus of consciousness for which the real whole world exists, and within which I myself live.

This, then, in brief, is my own theory of truth. This is why I hold this theory to be no fantastic guess about what may be true, but a logically inevitable conclusion about how every one of us, wise or ignorant, is actually defining his own relation to truth, whether he knows the fact or not. I expressed my theory at the last time in terms of a polemic against the recent pragmatists; but as a fact of their view, in its genuine and deeper meaning, is no more opposed to mine than my young Russian's vehement protest against loyalty, quoted in my second lecture, was, in its true spirit, opposed to my own view. My young Russian, you may remember, hated what he took to be loyalty, just because he was so loyal. And even so my friends, the recent pragmatists, reassert my theory of truth even in their every attempt to deny it. For, amongst other things, they assert that their own theory of truth is actually true. And that assertion implies just such a conspectus of all truth in one view,—just such a conspectus as I too assert.

IV

We first came in sight of this theory of truth, in these discussions, for a purely practical reason. Abstract and coldly intellectual as the doctrine, when stated as I have just stated it, may appear, we had our need to ask what truth is, because we wanted to know whether the loyal are right in supposing, as they inevitably do suppose, that their personal causes, and that their cause of causes, namely, universal loyalty, that any such causes, I say, possess genuine foundation in truth. Loyalty, as we found, is a practical service of superhuman objects. For our causes transcend expression in terms of our single lives. If the cause lives, then all conscious moral life—even our poor human life—is in unity with a superhuman conscious life, in which we ourselves dwell; and in this unity we win, in so far as we are loyal servants of our cause, a success which no transient human experience of ours, no joyous thrill of the flying moment, no bitterness of private defeat and loss, can do more or less than to illustrate, to illumine, or to idealize.

We asked: Is this faith of the loyal in their causes a pathetic fallacy? Our theory of truth has given us a general answer to this intensely practical question. The loyal try to live in the spirit. But, if thereupon they merely open their eyes to the nature of the reasonable truth, they see that it is in the spirit only that they do or can live. They would be living in this truth, as mere passing fragments of conscious life, as mere blind series of mental processes, even if they were not loyal. For all life, however dark and fragmentary, is either a blind striving for conscious unity with the universal life of which it is a fragment, or else, like the life of the loyal, is a deliberate effort to express such a striving in the form of a service of a superhuman cause. *And all lesser loyalties, and all serving of imperfect or of evil causes, are but fragmentary forms of the service of the cause of universal loyalty*. To serve universal loyalty is, however, to view the interests of all conscious life as one; and to do this is to regard

all conscious life as constituting just such an unity as our theory of truth requires. Meanwhile, since truth seeking is indeed itself a practical activity, what we have stated in our theory of truth is itself but an aspect of the very life that the loyal are leading. Whoever seeks any truth is loyal, for he is determining his life by reference to a life which transcends his own. And he is loyal to loyalty; for whatever truth you try to discover is, if true, valid for everybody, and is therefore worthy of everybody's loyal recognition. The loyal, then, are truth seekers; and the truth seekers are loyal. And all of them live for the sake of the unity of all life. And this unity includes us all, but is superhuman.

Our view of truth, therefore, meets at once an ethical and a logical need. The real world is precisely that world in which the loyal are at home. Their loyalty is no pathetic fallacy. Their causes are real facts in the universe. The universe as a whole possesses that unity which loyalty to loyalty seeks to express in its service of the whole of life.

Herewith, however, it occurs to us to ask one final question. Is not this real world, whose true unity the loyal acknowledge by their every deed, and whose conscious unity every process of truth seeking presupposes,—is not this also the world which religion recognizes? If so, what is the relation of loyalty to religion?

The materials for answering this question are now in our hands. We have been so deliberate in preparing them for our present purpose, just for the sake of making our answer the simpler when it comes.

V

We have now defined loyalty as the will to manifest the eternal in and through the deeds of individual selves. As for religion,—in its highest historical forms (which here alone concern us),—religion, as I think, may be defined as follows. Religion (in these its highest forms) *is the interpretation both of the eternal and of the spirit of loyalty through emotion, and through a fitting activity of the imagination*.

Religion, in any form, has always been an effort to interpret and to make use of some superhuman world. The history, the genesis, the earlier and simpler forms of religion, the relations of religion and morality in the primitive life of mankind, do not here concern us. It is enough to say that, in history, there has often been a serious tension between the interests of religion and those of morality. For the higher powers have very generally seemed to man to be either nonmoral or immoral. This very tension, only too frequently, still exists for many people to-day. One of the greatest and hardest discoveries of the human mind has been the discovery of how to reconcile, not religion and science, but religion and morality. Whoever knows even a small portion of the history of the cults of mankind is aware of the difficulties to which I refer. The superhuman has been conceived by men in terms that were often far enough from those which loyalty requires. Whoever will read over the recorded works of a writer nowadays too much neglected, the rugged and magnificently loyal Old Testament prophet Amos, can see for himself how bravely the difficulty of conceiving the superhuman as the righteous, was faced by one of the first who ever viewed the relation of religion and morality as our best teachers have since taught us to view them. And yet such a reader can also see how hard this very task of the prophet was. When we remember also that so great a mind as that of the originator of Buddhism, after all the long previous toil of Hindoo thought upon this great problem, could see no way to reconcile religion and morality, except by bringing them both to the shores of the mysterious and soundless ocean of Nirvana, and sinking them together in its depths (an undertaking which Buddha regarded as the salvation of the world), we get a further view of the nature of the problem. When we remember that St. Paul, after many years of lonely spiritual struggle, attempted in his teaching to reconcile morality and religion by an interpretation of Christianity which has ever since kept the Christian world in a most inspiring ferment of theological controversy and of practical conflict, we are again instructed as to the seriousness of the issue. But as a fact, the experience of the civilized man has gradually led him to see how to reconcile the moral life and the religious spirit. Since this reconciliation is one which our theory of truth, and of the constitution of the real world, substantially justifies, we are now ready for a brief review of the entire situation.

People often say that mere morality is something very remote from true religion. Sometimes people say this in the interests of religion, meaning to point out that mere morality can at best make you a more or less tolerable citizen, while only religion can reconcile you, as such people say, to that superhuman world whose existence and whose support alone make human life worth living. But sometimes almost the same assertion is made in the interest of pure morality, viewed as something independent of religion. Some people tell you, namely, that since, as they say, religion is a collection of doubtful beliefs, of superstitions, and of more or less exalted emotions, morality is all the better for keeping aloof from religion. Suffering man needs your help; your friends need as much happiness as you can give them; conventional morality is, on the whole, a good thing. Learn righteousness, therefore, say they, and leave religion to the fantastic-minded who love to believe. The human is what we need. Let the superhuman alone.

Now, our philosophy of loyalty, aiming at something much larger and richer than the mere sum of human happiness in individual men, has taught us that there is no such sharp dividing line between the human and the superhuman as these attempts to sunder the provinces of religion and morality would imply. The loyal serve something more than individual lives. Even Nietzsche, individualist and ethical naturalist though he was, illustrates our present thesis. He began the later period of his teaching by asserting that "God is dead"; and (lest one might regard this as a mere attack upon monotheism, and might suppose Nietzsche to be an old-fashioned heathen polytheist) he added the famous remark that, in case any gods whatever existed, he could not possibly endure being himself no god. "*Therefore,*" so he reasoned, "*there are no gods.*" All this seems to leave man very much to his own devices. Yet Nietzsche at once set up the cult of the ideal future being called the *Uebermensch* or Superman. And the *Uebermensch* is just as much of a god as anybody who ever throned upon Olympus or dwelt in the sky. And if the doctrine of the "Eternal Recurrence," as Nietzsche defined it, is true, the *Uebermensch* belongs not only to the ideal future, but has existed an endless number of times already.

If our philosophy of loyalty is right, Nietzsche was not wrong in this appeal to the superhuman. The superhuman we indeed have always with us. Life has no sense without it. But the superhuman need not be the magical. It need not be the object of superstition. And if we are desirous of unifying the interests of morality and religion, it is well indeed to begin, as rugged old Amos began, by first appreciating what righteousness is, and then by interpreting righteousness, in a perfectly reasonable and non-superstitious way, in superhuman terms. Then we shall be ready to appreciate what religion, whose roots are indeed by no means wholly in our moral nature, nevertheless has to offer us as a supplement to our morality.

VI

Loyalty is a service of causes. But, as we saw, we do not, we cannot, wait until somebody clearly shows us how good the causes are in themselves, before we set about serving them. We first practically learn of the goodness of our causes through the very act of serving them. Loyalty begins, then, in all of us, in elemental forms. A cause fascinates us—we at first know not clearly why. We give ourselves willingly to that cause. Herewith our true life begins. The cause may indeed be a bad one. But at worst it is our way of interpreting the true cause. If we let our loyalty develop, it tends to turn into the service of the universal cause. Hence I deliberately declined, in this discussion, to *base* my theory of loyalty upon that metaphysical doctrine which I postponed to my latest lectures. It is a very imperfect view of the real world which most youth get before them before they begin to be loyal. Hosts of the loyal actually manifest the eternal in their deeds, and know not that they do so. They only know that they are given over to their cause. The first good of loyalty lies, then, in the fact which we emphasized in our earlier lectures. Reverberating all through you, stirring you to your depths, loyalty first unifies your plan of life, and thereby gives you what nothing else can give,—your self as a life lived in accordance with a plan, your conscience as your plan interpreted for you through your ideal, your cause expressed as your personal purpose in living.

In so far, then, one can indeed be loyal without being consciously and explicitly religious. One's cause, in its first intention, appears to him human, concrete, practical. It is *also* an ideal. It is *also* a superhuman entity. It also really *means* the service of the eternal. But this fact may be, to the hard-working, and especially to the unimaginative, and, in a worldly sense, fairly successful man, a latent fact. He then, to be sure, gradually idealizes his cause as he goes; but this idealizing in so far becomes no very explicitly emphasized process in his life, although, as we have seen, some tendency to deify the cause is inevitable.

Meanwhile, such an imperfectly developed but loyal man may also accept, upon traditional grounds, a religion. This religion will then tell him about a superhuman world. But in so far the religion need not be, to his mind,

an essential factor in his practical loyalty. He may be superstitious; or he may be a religious formalist; or he may accept his creed and his church simply because of their social respectability and usefulness; or, finally, he may even have a rich and genuine religious experience, which still may remain rather a mysticism than a morality, or an æsthetic comfort rather than a love of his cause.

In such cases, loyalty and religion may long keep apart. But the fact remains that loyalty, if sincere, involves at least a latent belief in the superhuman reality of the cause, and means at least an unconscious devotion to the one and eternal cause. But such a belief is also a latent union of morality and religion. Such a service is an unconscious piety. The time may come, then, when the morality will consciously need this union with the religious creed of the individual whose growth we are portraying.

This union must begin to become an explicit union whenever that process which, in our sixth lecture, we called the idealizing of the cause, reaches its higher levels. We saw that those higher levels are reached in the presence of what seems to be, to human vision, a lost cause. If we believe in the lost cause, we become directly aware that we are indeed seeking a city out of sight. If such a cause is real, it belongs to a superhuman world. Now, every cause worthy, as we said, of lifelong service, and capable of unifying our life plans, shows sooner or later that it is a cause *which we cannot successfully express in any set of human experiences of transient joys and of crumbling successes.* Human life taken merely as it flows, viewed merely as it passes by in time and is gone, is indeed a lost river of experience that plunges down the mountains of youth and sinks in the deserts of age. Its significance comes solely through its relations to the air and the ocean and the great deeps of universal experience. For by such poor figures I may, in passing, symbolize that really rational relation of our personal experience to universal conscious experience,—that relation to which I have devoted these last two lectures.

Everybody ought to serve the universal cause in his own individual way. For this, as we have seen, is what loyalty, when it comes to know its own mind, really means. But whoever thus serves inevitably *loses* his cause in our poor world of human sense-experience, because his cause is too good for this present temporal world to express it. And that is, after all, what the old theology meant when it called you and me, as we now naturally are, lost beings. Our deepest loyalty lies in devoting ourselves to causes that are just now lost to our poor human nature. One can express this, of course, by saying that the true cause is indeed real enough, in the higher world, while it is our poor human nature which is lost. Both ways of viewing the case have their truth. Loyalty means a transformation of our nature.

Lost causes, then, we must serve. But as we have seen, in our sixth lecture, loyalty to a lost cause has two companions, grief and imagination. Now, these two are the parents of all the higher forms of genuinely ethical religion. If you doubt the fact, read the scriptures of any of the great ethical faiths. Consult the psalter, the hymns, the devotional books, or the prayers of the church. Such religion interprets the superhuman in forms that our longing, our grief, and our imagination invent, but also in terms that are intended to meet the demands of our highest loyalty. For we are loyal to that unity of life which, as our truer moral consciousness learns to believe, owns the whole real world, and constitutes the cause of causes. In being loyal to universal loyalty, we are serving the unity of life.

This true unity of the world-life, however, is at once very near to us and very far from us. Very near it is; for we have our being in it, and depend upon it for whatever worth we have. Apart from it we are but the gurgling stream soon to be lost in the desert. In union with it we have individual significance in and for the whole. But we are very far from it also, because our human experience throws such fragmentary light upon the details of our relation to its activities. Hence in order to feel our relations to it as vital relations, we have to bring it near to our feelings and to our imaginations. And we long and suffer the loneliness of this life as we do so. But because we know of the details of the world only through our empirical sciences, while these give us rather materials for a rational life than a view of the unity of life, we are indeed left to our imagination to assuage grief and to help in the training of loyalty. For here, that is, precisely as to the *details* of the system of facts whereby our life is linked to the eternal, our science forsakes us. We can know *that* we are thus linked. *How* we are linked, our sciences do not make manifest to us.

Hence the actual content of the higher ethical religions is endlessly rich in legend and in other symbolic portrayal. This portrayal is rich in emotional meaning and in vivid detail. What this portrayal attempts to characterize is, in its general outline, an absolute truth. This truth consists in the following facts: *First, the rational unity and goodness of the world-life; next, its true but invisible nearness to us, despite our ignorance; further, its fulness of meaning despite our barrenness of present experience; and yet more, its interest in our personal destiny as moral beings; and finally, the certainty that, through our actual human loyalty, we come, like Moses, face to face with the true will of the world, as a man speaks to his friend.* In recognizing these facts, we have before us what may be called the creed of the Absolute Religion.

You may well ask, of course, whether our theory of truth, as heretofore expounded, gives any warrant to such religious convictions. I hold that it does give warrant to them. The symbols in which these truths are expressed by one or another religion are indeed due to all sorts of historical accidents, and to the most varied play of the imaginations both of the peoples and of the religious geniuses of our race. But that our relations to the world-life are relations wherein we are consciously met, from the other side, by a superhuman and yet strictly personal conscious life, in which our own personalities are themselves bound up, but which also is not only richer but is more concrete and definitely conscious and real than we are,—this seems to me to be an inevitable corollary of my theory of truth.

VII

And now, finally, to sum up our whole doctrine of loyalty and religion. Two things belonging to the world-life we know—two at least, if my theory is true: *it is defined in terms of our own needs; and it includes and completes our experience.* Hence, in any case, it is precisely as live and elemental and concrete as we are; and there is not a need of ours which is not its own. If you ask why I call it good— well, the very arguments which recent pragmatism has used are, as you remember, here my warrant. A truth cannot be a merely theoretical truth. True is that which successfully fulfils an idea. Whoever, again, is not succeeding, or is facing an evil, or is dissatisfied, is inevitably demanding and defining facts that are far beyond him, and that are not yet consciously his own. A knower of the totality of truth is therefore, of necessity, in possession of the fulfilment of all rational purposes. If, however, you ask why this world-life permits any evil whatever, or any finitude, or any imperfections, I must indeed reply that here is no place for a general discussion of the whole problem of evil, which I have repeatedly and wearisomely considered in other discussions of mine. But this observation does belong here. Our theory of evil is indeed no "shallow optimism," but is founded upon the deepest, the bitterest, and the dearest moral experience of the human race. The *loyal,* and they alone, know the one great good of suffering, of ignorance, of finitude, of loss, of defeat—*and that is just the good of loyalty,* so long as the cause itself can only be viewed as indeed a living whole. Spiritual peace is surely no easy thing. We win that peace only through stress and suffering and loss and labor. But when we find the preciousness of the idealized cause emphasized through grief, we see that, whatever evil is, it at least *may* have its place in an ideal order. What would be the universe without loyalty; and what would loyalty be without trial? And when we remember that, from this point of view, our own griefs are the griefs of the very world consciousness itself, in so far as this world-life is expressed in our lives, it may well occur to us that the life of loyalty with all its griefs and burdens and cares may be the very foundation of the attainment of that spiritual triumph which we must conceive as realized by the world spirit.

Perhaps, however, one weakly says: "If the world will attains in its wholeness what we seek, why need we seek that good at all?" I answer at once that our whole philosophy of loyalty instantly shows the vanity of such speech. Of course, the world-life does *not* obtain the individual good that is involved in my willing loyalty unless indeed *I am loyal.* The cause may in some way triumph without me, but not as *my* cause. We have never defined our theory as meaning that the world-life is *first* eternally complete, but *then* asks us, in an indifferent way, to copy its perfections. Our view is that each of us who is loyal is doing his unique deed in that whole of life which we have called the eternal simply because it is the conspectus of the totality of life, past, present, and future. If my deed were not done, the world-life would miss my deed. Each of us can say that. The very basis of our theory of truth, which we found upon the deeds, the ideas, the practical needs, of each of us, gives every individual his unique place in the world order—his deed that nobody else can do, his will which is his own. "Our wills are ours to make them thine." The unity of the world is *not* an ocean in which we are lost, but a life which is and which needs all our lives in one. Our loyalty defines that unity for us as a living, active

unity. We have come to the unity through the understanding of our loyalty. It is an eternal unity only in so far as it includes all time and change and life and deeds. And therefore, when we reach this view, since the view simply fulfils what loyalty demands, our loyalty remains as precious to us, and as practical, and as genuinely a service of a cause, as it was before. It is no sort of "moral holiday" that this whole world-life suggests to us. It is precisely as a whole life of ideal strivings in which we have our places as individual selves and are such selves only in so far as we strive to do our part in the whole,—it is thus, and thus only, that our philosophy of loyalty regards the universe.

Religion, therefore, precisely in so far as it attempts to conceive the universe as a conscious and personal life of superhuman meaning, and as a life that is in close touch with our own meaning, is eternally true. But now it is just this *general* view of the universe as a rational order that is indeed open to our rational knowledge. No part of such a doctrine gives us, however, the present right as human beings to determine with any certainty the details of the world-life, except in so far as they come within the scope of our scientific and of our social inquiries. Hence, when religion, in the service of loyalty, interprets the world-life to us with symbolic detail, it gives us indeed merely symbols of the eternal truth. That this truth is indeed eternal, that our loyalty brings us into personal relations with a personal world-life, which values our every loyal deed, and needs that deed, all this is true and rational. And just this is what religion rightly illustrates. But the parables, the symbols, the historical incidents that the religious imagination uses in its portrayals,—these are the more or less sacred and transient *accidents* in which the "real presence" of the divine at once shows itself to us, and hides the detail of its inner life from us. These accidents of the religious imagination endure through many ages; but they also vary from place to place and from one nation or race of men to another, and they ought to do so. Whoever sees the living truth of the person and conscious and ethical unity of the world *through* these symbols is possessed of the absolute religion, whatever be his nominal creed or church. Whoever overemphasizes the empirical details of these symbols, and then asks us to accept these details as literally true, commits an error which seems to me simply to invert that error whereof, at the last time, I ventured to accuse my pragmatist friends. Such a literalist, who reads his symbols as revelations of the detailed structure of the divine life, seems to me, namely, to look for the eternal *within* the realm of the mere data of human sense and imagination. To do this, I think, is indeed to seek the risen Lord in the open sepulchre.

Concerning the living truth of the whole conscious universe, one can well say, as one observes the special facts of human sense and imagination: "He is not here; he is arisen." Yet equally from the whole circle of the heaven of that entire self-conscious life which *is* the truth, there comes always, and to all the loyal, the word: "Lo, I am with you always, even unto the end of the world."

Suggestions for Further Reading

Works by Royce

The Hope of the Great Community. New York: Macmillan Company, 1916.
The Philosophy of Loyalty. New York: Macmillan Company, 1908.
The Problem of Christianity. 2 Volumes. New York: Macmillan Company, 1913. Reprinted in a single volume, with an Introduction by John E. Smith; Chicago: The University of Chicago Press, 1968.
The Religious Aspect of Philosophy. Boston: Houghton Mifflin & Company, 1885.
The Sources of Religious Insight. New York: Charles Scribner's Sons, 1912.
The Spirit of Modern Philosophy. Boston: Houghton Mifflin & Company, 1892.
Studies of Good and Evil. New York: D. Appleton, 1898.
The World and the Individual. 2 Volumes. New York: Macmillan Company, 1899. Reprinted, with an Introduction by John E. Smith; New York: Dover, 1959.

Anthology

The Basic Writings of Josiah Royce. 2 Volumes. Edited, with an Introduction, by John J. McDermott. Chicago: The University of Chicago Press, 1969. This includes an "Annotated Bibliography of the Published Works of Josiah Royce," by Ignas K. Skrupskelis.

Essential Works on Royce

John Clendenning. *The Life and Thought of Josiah Royce.* Madison: University of Wisconsin Press, 1985.
James Harry Cotton. *Royce on the Human Self.* Cambridge, Mass.: Harvard University Press, 1954.
Mary Briody Mahowald. *An Idealistic Pragmatist.* The Hague: Martinus Nijhoff, 1972.
Gabriel Marcel. *Royce's Metaphysics.* Chicago: Henry Regnery Company, 1956.
Frank M. Oppenheim. *Royce's Voyage Down Under: A Journey of the Mind.* Lexington: The University Press of Kentucky, 1980.
John E. Smith. *Royce's Social Infinite.* New York: The Liberal Arts Press, 1950.

GEORGE SANTAYANA

Introduction by John Lachs

George Santayana was born in Madrid, Spain, on December 16, 1863. His mother brought him to the United States when he was nine years old and he received his education at Boston Latin School and Harvard University. Although he lived through two world wars, Santayana's life was uneventful. He taught philosophy at Harvard from 1889 to 1912, when he quit his job to devote himself to writing and travel. He went to Europe but established no permanent home anywhere: for forty years he journeyed between Spain, Italy, France, and England. He died in Rome in 1952 and is buried there.

Santayana was a student, and later a colleague, of James and Royce. He read Peirce and profited from his elaborate studies of symbolism. The Library of Living Philosophers volume on Dewey contains an important philosophical exchange between him and Santayana. In it these major American thinkers pay little heed to the similarities in their views and focus on their disagreements. But in spite of significant American influences on his thought, Santayana's great teachers are Plato and especially Aristotle. The categories he uses—such as essence, matter, and substance—are traditional, if not scholastic. His views of morality and of the spiritual life invite comparison with those of Schopenhauer. Santayana's brilliant grasp of the history of philosophy enabled him to draw extensively on a wide variety of sources. His most remarkable achievement is to have forged a unified and novel system out of such disparate elements.

The Sense of Beauty, Santayana's first book, appeared in 1896. He wrote almost without interruption until a few weeks before his death. His literary output includes over twenty volumes of philosophy, literary essays, translations, poetry, even a best-selling novel. Various libraries in the United States still hold unpublished manuscripts by him. A definitive collected edition of his works is in the process of being published by MIT Press.

In spite of a long writing career, Santayana's opinions changed little over the years. The earlier work, especially the five volumes of *The Life of Reason,* attempted to develop a materialist theory of the nature of man by means of an analysis of human thought, institutions, and activities. The humanistic tone of these books made them the admired and influential staple of American liberals for many years after the turn of the century. The later work, especially the four volumes of *The Realms of Being,* repeat many of the same points in more accessible, ontological language. Surprisingly, the clearer books gained little acceptance and it is only now that Santayana's star is on the rise again.

The selections in this volume are all from Santayana's ontological period, which commenced after his resignation from Harvard and reached full maturity with the publication, in 1923, of *Scepticism and Animal Faith.* This book is unquestionably the most important and best of Santayana's philosophical works. It presents a fully developed and original system of thought. The conceptual framework it advances offers a persuasive answer to the modern problem of accommodating the results of science without the loss of the spiritual and moral dimensions of human existence.

The aim of the system is to purify and defend the time-tested beliefs of common sense. But Santayana's sceptical disposition protected him from the naiveté of supposing that we have direct access to common sense through ordinary language or the beliefs that seem natural or intuitively true. Instead, he set as his starting point the primary reality of action. To disentangle the tenets of common sense or "animal faith," we must examine what general beliefs the physical actions necessary for life embody. Eating, for instance, is overt expression of our belief in the independent existence of things and in their power to nourish us. Playing football indicates the conviction that bodies share a common space in which they can, from time to time, touch one another. Waiting for the bus is indication of our tacit commitment that the contents of space are unevenly distributed, while kicking a vicious dog reveals the view that objects in space can have a definite and sustained effect on each other. The philosophy of animal faith consists in the systematic development of all the important general beliefs implicated in action. Its justification is that we affirm these beliefs every time we act; though philosophers can deny them in their private thoughts, they give their denial the lie with each movement and every written word.

Although the system of animal faith could be developed without preliminaries as an inventive approach to the problems of philosophy, Santayana thinks that we must first dispose of traditional views. It would indeed be best if, in accord with the hopes and efforts of many important thinkers, we could find a philosophical method to guarantee the truth and certainty of our opinions. But the power of scepticism makes such search for indubitability futile. It is the possibility of scepticism that destroys traditional epistemology and leaves the field open for animal faith.

The scrutiny to which Santayana subjects our cherished beliefs is unparalleled in the history of scepticism. He begins by questioning our most tenuous opinions, such as those about God, the distant past, and the general structure of the world. It is obvious that these cannot stand up to the rigorous standard of absolute certainty. What about our perceptions? Do they give us incontrovertible information about the world? Santayana notes that sensory consciousness is a combination of some immediately present quality or relation and a collection of beliefs about it and about what it reveals. The quality before the mind is past dispute, but it means nothing and can contribute nothing to knowledge without an account of how it relates to things and other perceptions. Any such account, however, is only a matter of opinion, and opinion is always open to doubt.

The same analysis destroys the sure veracity of memory. When I remember that I had bacon and eggs for breakfast this morning, I might have a picture before me of what the eggs looked like, some sense of how my hands moved, and a pleasant replica of how the bacon tasted. But these data of consciousness do not constitute a memory; I can call them up in anticipation of eating or in idle revery. They become memory only if I (correctly) believe that they match what happened or what I experienced at an earlier time. And this belief is on occasion false and remains ever open to question.

Doubts about memory remove the possibility of knowing persons or selves: such beings have to enjoy self-identity through a period of time and no evidence we could adduce for this amounts to proof. Even mathematics fails to yield certain knowledge because it requires memory: the simple operation of addition itself is impossible unless we remember the first number when we think the second we want to add to it. Finally, Santayana argues that the recognition of an event as a change involves memory of an earlier state and therefore falls short of the dignity of certain information.

We are thus left with nothing but the immediate datum of consciousness. Of this we can be sure when we possess it, but we can know nothing about it and nothing by means of it. The moment we think or say anything concerning it, we lose our assurance. The certainty, therefore, is not that of knowing but of having it, of the simple presence of an unmeaning object before consciousness. The object is neither physical nor mental; it is a changeless, self-identical feature in the contemplation of which we can be absorbed, but which does not characterize anything beyond itself. Certainty can thus be achieved only at the cost of significance. All we can *know,* in the most demanding sense of this term, is the self-identity of whatever may be presented, and this yields no information about either self or world.

The unanswerable force of scepticism yields two important discoveries. The first is the recognition that the sceptic shares with the bulk of the philosophical tradition a single and disastrous criterion of knowledge. According to this standard, knowledge must be unchanging and absolutely certain. The sceptic's success shows not that knowledge is impossible, but only that the rationalist standard by which we measure it is ill conceived. The demand for total assurance is never imposed in science or in daily life; it is a speculative invention of philosophers. For generations, thinkers have established an ideal beyond our reach and, measuring ordinary cognitive attainments by it, have denounced everything everyone has always believed as worthless, uncertified opinion. The result is that by setting unreasonable requirements philosophy distances itself from the concerns of living. In sharp contrast with this, Santayana announces his intention to develop an honest philosophy. By this he means simply the refusal to believe in his reflective moments what he would not or cannot express in his actions. The philosopher is not a detached mind contemplating the world and announcing the standards to which it must aspire. His job is to understand reality, which presupposes the docile acceptance of facts.

The second discovery made possible by the sceptical reduction is of neutral objects, or "essences." These essences are forms or structures that can serve as themes of consciousness. Some of them can be embodied in the material world; as such, they give nature to the things we encounter or eat. Every quality and relation is an essence intrinsically. Each number is an essence or contemplatable form, as is every quality of taste and every human shape from the thin to the obese. Essences are not restricted to what is important or noble or interesting to us. Every conceivable wickedness and ugliness and boredom has its own special form which renders it just what it is. In fact, even events have a characteristic structure or collection of properties: this is the sort of form Santayana calls "tropes." The entirety of *Hamlet* can be seen as a single, immensely complex form, and if we think of it that way, each performance of *Hamlet* becomes but a separate occasion on which a given essence is embodied in an extended event.

The totality of all forms Santayana calls "the realm of essence." It is important not to think of this "realm" as somehow taking up space or as located somewhere in the physical universe or as requiring resources to sustain. For essences are not physical objects and, if the notion of existence is restricted to items that operate in time and space, they do not exist. This does not mean that they lack reality. On the contrary, they are very real indeed, if only we do not mistakenly suppose that reality must mean the possession of physical or causal power. For they are ever ready to be conceived or to be embodied if the requisite organ is available to focus on them or to imprint them on the material world.

Essences are eternal in the sense that time makes no difference to their self-identity. Only the physical world has a history; the number 2 is forever itself without reference to who thinks of it and when. Essences thus do not undergo change. On the contrary, they make alteration possible by providing the features from which and to which existing things can change. But this eternity of forms does not endow them with any moral or metaphysical prerogatives. All essences are on a par in terms of value: none has any intrinsic worth. Whatever good they might be arises from their relation to sentient creatures, and such relations are always external and irrelevant to their nature. This implies that, Plato's views notwithstanding, essences are not intrinsically ideals to which we naturally aspire. Some essence or other may be chosen as a goal by some living being, but even this elevation to a special dignity is alien to their cool and neutral self-identity.

Forms could not, moreover, in and of themselves serve as ideals, because there are too many of them. In fact, Santayana maintains that there is an infinite number of essences, each a little or a lot different from all the rest. It is not difficult to think of this infinity if we begin by noting that there is an infinite number of numbers, each a self-identical essence. Each possible shape is an essence also, as is every possible event. The totality of movements that occur on the court in a basketball game constitutes a complex essence. If we change one of these motions in the minutest way, we have a slightly different whole and thus another essence. By the permutations and combinations of the motions, by changing the identity, shape, and clothes of the players, we can think of an indefinitely large number of basketball-game essences. Is there a perfect game? Yes, if we mean the one in which our team prevails. But clearly no, if we look for the pattern all games approximate but never quite attain. All essences are perfectly what they are and even the most boring contest embodies perfectly one of these perfectly self-identical forms. Which one of the infinite number of them is of concern only to us; the essences themselves are passively available for existence but never seek it.

No essence is dependent for its own reality on embodiment in the material world or envisagement by a mind. If anything, the dependence relation goes the other way: without forms, there could be no specific physical objects and minds would have nothing to think about. Essences, therefore, are absolutely necessary for the existence of anything, even though they themselves do not exist in space and time. Santayana likens them to the garments existence wears or could conceivably wear, and the whole realm of essence to the costumer's gallery which features an inexhaustible supply of garbs.

Much as essences are necessary for there to be a changing material world, they cannot by themselves constitute it. Existence features external, contingent, and shifting relations, none of which can be accounted for by essences alone. The material world is always in flux, is constantly coming into being and passing away; such instability is radically alien to the eternal and placid forms. There must be a force that wrenches some few essences out of the infinity of their realm and endows them with momentary existence. Traditionally, this force used to be thought of as the creative power of God, who selects the best of possible worlds for actualization. But Santayana sees little reason to suppose that the world in which we live is the best in any sense and thinks that attributing intelligence and good will to the ultimate existential force is an expression of excessive optimism.

Accordingly, he names the power that renders essences existent "matter," not in deference to science and its conception of the physical world, but as an expression of his conviction that it is not intelligent and is at best indifferent to human welfare. This means that there is no ultimate reason why matter selects one set of essences for instantiation rather than any other from an infinity of alternatives. The fact that existence falls into habits and tends to repeat the same patterns (tropes) does not remove the arbitrariness of what takes place: the hundredth occurrence of an event is as groundless, though not as surprising, as the first. Matter, therefore, is unintelligible, a surd everywhere present but never reducible to a rational principle.

Santayana calls existence "an insane emphasis" and likens matter to a whirlwind that whips essences, as though they were grains of sand, into the vortex of existence. The total inexplicability of existence is seen best by reflecting on the remarkable fact that even its essence is inadequate to give us an insight into its power. For the essence of existence (or of matter) is but another essence, and no essence can be responsible for calling anything into changing, spatiotemporal being. Matter in its creative role thus has no essence at all; it is the pure other, the natureless counterpart of form. Since our minds can take in only the lucid essences of things, their matter remains to be encountered and dealt with by our bodies.

Following Aristotle, Santayana maintains that all existing things are compounds of matter and form. The entire world of existence is what he calls "substance" or "the field of action." Both of these designations are important to stress. To say that the world is substance amounts to asserting that it exists independently of us and that it is an enduring cosmos rich in potentialities. Adding that it is a field of action cautions us to think of it as a changing, dynamic reality with which we must constantly interact. The stability of substance and the changeability of process are in this way united by Santayana as twin features of a universe to which our primary relation is always that of action.

Change in nature consists of the substitution of one essence for another. This interplay of matter and essence defines Santayana's third realm, the realm of truth. Truth is the permanent fact that some essence did, does, or will at some time characterize a portion of the flux of nature. Ideas, judgments, or propositions are true only because they repeat some element of this truth or, in other words, recapture in mind the essence that was embodied. The truth, therefore, always consists of forms and the realms of truth is simply that segment of the realm of essence which contains all the forms which will have been actualized in the world's history.

This account of truth establishes it as objective and free of any personal, social, or historical influences. It is not, of course, that there are no personal, social, or historical truths. But these truths themselves are objective and unchanging: new perspectives rooted in novel situations and structured by special interests and purposes can make no difference to them. On the contrary, eternally self-identical truths serve as the standard which the historical diversity of views, inquiry itself, must approximate. This is what Santayana means when he says that the truth about anything is the standard comprehensive description of it; he thinks it is an ideal we aim at, it is complete, and it is a permanent record preserved in eternal forms.

Santayana's remarkable affirmation of the objectivity of truth does not compel him to embrace the "eternal verities" of prior philosophical systems. For his objective truths are all humble facts about the world of space and time and about what minds think; they are not grand generalizations or intuitively apprehended principles concerning the nature of reality. Moreover, the presence of truth as a silent witness of whatever occurs neither lessens the labor nor eliminates the tenuousness of human inquiry. We may well capture the truth about some fact without knowing that we did so: the essences constituting the realm of truth are intrinsically no different from those destined never to be embodied. Consequently, truth does not shine by its own light, and to identify an essence as a truth requires the hard work of empirical investigation.

It is excessively unlikely that in our perceptual life we can ever apprehend truth literally or in its immediacy. Our senses, though stimulated by the movements of matter around us, operate on a scale radically different from the subatomic and even the molecular levels of activity that affect us. Accordingly, it is improbable that the essences which characterize nature at those levels could ever be replicated in sensory consciousness. Nor does Santayana think that this matters much: all knowledge is symbolic cognition and, as such, does not require any similarity between the sign in consciousness and what it signifies in the external world. If there were such a resemblance or identity, we could never know it; and if there is none, we shall never miss it so long as appropriate symbolism is available to carry the work of meaning for the mind. Objective truth exerts, therefore, no direct formative influence on the conduct of inquiry: it serves merely as the passive and distant ideal we aim to attain. But our approach to it is gradual at best and, since we must employ the abstract and simplified symbols native to consciousness, it would be a rare and surprising accident if we ever reached it.

Discussion of knowledge brings Santayana's fourth realm of being to the center of attention. The realm of spirit is conditioned in its existence: the lights of consciousness that constitute it are produced by matter when it reaches a very high level of organization. But spirit is not simply matter shaped by complex tropes. It is a novel, irreducibly different, emergent form of being: mind or the cognitive awareness without which knowledge, feeling, and pleasure would be impossible. Values themselves require the work of spirit. If there were no consciousness, creation and destruction within the material world would go on unabated but none of it would be either good or bad.

Santayana's choice of the word "spirit" for awareness reflects his desire to call attention to the spiritual perfection of which the mind is capable. In order to understand spirituality however, we must first get a clear picture of the nature of consciousness. It comes in units called "intuitions," each of which is a moment of cognitive awareness. The intuition is the act of being conscious, which is directed upon an object. The sceptical reduction convinced Santayana that the object directly before the mind is always an essence. Consciousness apprehends the essence, but such immediate grasp does not constitute knowledge in any significant sense. To make it yield information about existing things, it must be related to them. The relating is accomplished by what Santayana calls "intent," the expression in the sphere of mind of the momentum of animal life. Intent takes the presented essence for a sign of the existence and nature of the physical object we confront, and in doing so it converts immediate awareness into knowledge.

Ordinary cognition consists, in this way, of a presentational and a belief element. An essence or group of essences is presented; at the prodding of intent we embrace the conviction that the essence reveals something about existence. The sceptic can suspend this belief, as can the artist when he or she deals with pure forms and shapes and sounds. Mathematicians, in contemplating the relation between theorems or numbers irrespective of what these might tell us about the world, also observe the pure play of essences. And all of us can break the hold of belief over us by simply enjoying the sensory appearances or ideas or daydreams we have without taking an interest in whether they are true or false.

When we banish belief from consciousness, intuition is pure. Given the animal basis of mind, such absorption in the immediate is difficult to sustain. But, for however short a time we can enjoy it, it opens to us a life free from the concerns of daily existence and the partiality of the animal in us. This readiness to behold and to take delight in whatever may be presented is the very essence of mind: although consciousness depends on the human organism—what Santayana calls the "psyche"—for its existence, its nature is to look past the changing world at eternal essences. That mind in its purity should take no interest in the battles of the material world is particularly appropriate because it can gain no satisfaction there. Since it consists only of cognitive acts directed on essences, it can exercise no physical power. The psyche is adequate to deal with the vicissitudes of material life; consciousness neither can nor needs to help. And since it can only look on, its attention to the psyche's work fills its days with frustration and worry.

Pure intuition liberates mind to do what is unique to it. This perfection of consciousness is to be the unattached spectator of all time and existence, the contemplator of every possibility. Such transcendence in thought of the physical is what we normally mean by spirituality; and this is precisely the excellence and fulfillment of which calling consciousness "spirit" reminds us. Absorption in pure intuition, even if temporary, constitutes the spiritual life that, for Santayana, is the only escape from the endless toil and dissatisfaction of animal existence. The spiritual life is free of values and empty of striving: it is the ready contemplation of whatever essence happens our way.

We have, of course, no release from the fate of animals: we are destined to struggle and to die. Nor does Santayana believe that there is a God or a life to come. In a posthumously published fragment he wryly remarks that although he has been called many names, no one has ever called him an optimist. Accordingly, the spiritual life represents only intellectual dominion and ideal escape; physically we continue as vulnerable beasts. Since consciousness is individual, the survival of the community provides no comfort for Santayana. Life has only whatever meaning we find in it before we die: the distant future of mankind is by no means assured, but even if it were, it would be of no significance to those alive today.

If there is no God to distinguish right from wrong and if the world consists of embodied essences that constitute a collection of facts without intrinsic value, there can be no good that is either universal or objective. In fact, Santayana makes a point of disassociating values from any changeless or holy sphere. They are simply expressions of the impulses and interests of needy animals. Nothing, therefore, is good in and of itself, irrespective of our organic strivings and the actual context of the flux of life.

Values arise when organism, environment, and consciousness stand in suitable relations to one another. The specific material constitution of the individual forms the basis of selectivity; to someone with my nature, certain objects in the world are food, others poison. The psyche not only has a definite structure and identifiable needs, it also desires things and pursues its interests relentlessly. Such cravings and seekings are organic, and that means material, facts. In the process of living, my psyche generates an awareness of its efforts, and to this consciousness what I seek appears suffused with goodness. Goodness is an essence that can be intuited but not embodied: its organic equivalent is impulse on the part of the psyche and, when all goes well, satisfactoriness on the part of the objects sought. To call something valuable, therefore, is to say that, as a result of the psyche's interest in it, spirit bathes it in a favorable light or views it as characterized by the essence good.

This remarkable theory escapes the usual objections to naturalistic views of the ground of value. For while it regards the moral life as firmly tied to the desires and predicaments of animals, it refuses to reduce goodness to any one or collection of empirical qualities. It sets, moreover, new standards for pluralism and toleration in moral theory. For it maintains that one's good depends on one's nature, and natures are always individual. The view that our fulfillment is not to be measured by how closely we approximate to some general human ideal is grounded not only in the sympathetic observation of our diversity, but also in Santayana's conception of the realm of essence. The infinity of forms robs them of normative force: instead of all the members of a species having to share a generic essence which prescribes what they ought to be, on this view each can embody in a full and perfect way his or her own form or pattern of existence. With perfection omnimodal, we can display our varied natures with innocent delight. Given the contingencies of society and the physical world, some of these patterns may of course not yield good results. But the judgment passed on them derives not from rigid social standards or the wrath of God, but from their incompatibility with existing facts.

It is from this world of organically based values that the spiritual life gives us reprieve. In pure intuition, æsthetic enjoyment of the immediate takes the place of desire and animal striving. Morality, in the sense of self-realization or of discharging all that is latent in us, constitutes the perfection of the psyche. Spirituality, on the other hand, is the excellence of consciousness or mind. The contrast is reminiscent of Aristotle's distinction between moral and intellectual virtue, but Santayana, characteristically, refuses to accept the blanket Aristotelian claim that contemplation is superior. Values can be compared only in the private imagination, and the validity of the comparison never goes beyond the individual. For some persons it may indeed be true that spirituality is better than action in the world. But there is no legitimate way to generalize this judgment: others, given their different nature, can rightly claim that the peace of contemplating essences is death itself. Since all values are relative to the nature of the persons who hold them, there can be no moral agreement without shared psychic constitution.

Although Santayana's philosophy has been called eclectic, its diverse elements compose a remarkably unified whole. Some commentators maintain that his thought is European, perhaps even scholastic, in character and hence cannot be American in any proper sense. But this judgment presupposes too sharp a contrast between European and American ways of thought, when in fact the continuity between them is obvious and pervasive. Santayana himself had a tendency to resist labeling thoughts by their national origin, and strove to formulate a framework of ideas that would come close to articulating the universal human condition in the world.

In spite of this, however, Santayana's philosophy is undeniably a product of its author's age and social milieu. It shares with the thought of James and Dewey a dogged empiricism and distrust of speculation, a sympathy for varied perfections, and the all-important insistence on the primacy of action. All three great philosophers agree in viewing human beings as natural organisms and nature as an autonomous system. They are at one in their respect for the richness and immediacy of experience, and in grounding the good in the needs and desires of human beings. Although there are significant differences in the details of their ideas, they are in unison on enough fundamental issues to warrant calling Santayana an American philosopher, if James or Dewey is one. In fact, in one respect Santayana is closer to the American grain than most of those native thinkers, such as Peirce, Dewey, and Mead, who are thought to define the tradition. For, remembering Hegel, they tended to stress the formative and nurturing primacy of the community. Santayana, by contrast, celebrates the individual as the fountainhead of all value and the center of the moral world.

Preface to Scepticism and Animal Faith

Here is one more system of philosophy. If the reader is tempted to smile, I can assure him that I smile with him, and that my system—to which this volume is a critical introduction—differs widely in spirit and pretensions from what usually goes by that name. In the first place, *my system is not mine, nor new.* I am merely attempting to express for the reader the principles to which he appeals when he smiles. There are convictions in the depths of his soul, beneath all his overt parrot beliefs, on which I would build our friendship. I have a great respect for orthodoxy; not for those orthodoxies which prevail in particular schools or nations, and which vary from age to age, but for a certain shrewd orthodoxy which the sentiment and practice of laymen maintain everywhere. I think that common sense, in a rough dogged way, is technically sounder than the special schools of philosophy, each of which squints and overlooks half the facts and half the difficulties in its eagerness to find in some detail the key to the whole. I am animated by distrust of all high guesses, and by sympathy with the old prejudices and workaday opinions of mankind: they are ill expressed, but they are well grounded. What novelty my version of things may possess is meant simply to obviate occasions for sophistry by giving to everyday beliefs a more accurate and circumspect form. I do not pretend to place myself at the heart of the universe nor at its origin, nor to draw its periphery. I would lay siege to the truth only as animal exploration and fancy may do so, first from one quarter and then from another, expecting the reality to be not simpler than my experience of it, but far more extensive and complex. I stand in philosophy exactly where I stand in daily life; I should not be honest otherwise. I accept the same miscellaneous witnesses, bow to the same obvious facts, make conjectures no less instinctively, and admit the same encircling ignorance.

My system, accordingly, is *no system of the universe.* The Realms of Being of which I speak are not parts of a cosmos, nor one great cosmos together: they are only kinds or categories of things which I find conspicuously different and worth distinguishing, at least in my own thoughts. I do not know how many things in the universe at large may fall under each of these classes, nor what other Realms of Being may not exist, to which I have no approach or which I have not happened to distinguish in my personal observation of the world. Logic, like language, is partly a free construction and partly a means of symbolising and harnessing in expression the existing diversities of things; and whilst some languages, given a man's constitution and habits, may seem more beautiful and convenient to him than others, it is a foolish heat in a patriot to insist that only his native language is intelligible or right. No language or logic is right in the sense of being identical with the facts it is used to express, but each may be right by being faithful to these facts, as a translation may be faithful. My endeavour is to think straight in such terms as are offered to me, to clear my mind of cant and free it from the cramp of artificial traditions; but I do not ask any one to think in my terms if he prefers others. Let him clean better, if he can, the windows of his soul, that the variety and beauty of the prospect may spread more brightly before him.

Moreover, my system, save in the mocking literary sense of the word, is *not metaphysical.* It contains much criticism of metaphysics, and some refinements in speculation, like the doctrine of essence, which are not familiar to the public; and I do not disclaim being metaphysical because I at all dislike dialectic or disdain immaterial things: indeed, it is of immaterial things, essence, truth, and spirit that I speak chiefly. But logic and mathematics and literary psychology (when frankly literary) are not metaphysical, although their subject-matter is immaterial, and their application to existing things is often questionable. Metaphysics, in the proper sense of the word, is dialectical physics, or an attempt to determine matters of fact by means of logical or moral or rhetorical constructions. It arises by a confusion of those Realms of Being, which it is my special care to distinguish. It is neither physical speculation nor pure logic nor honest literature, but (as in the treatise of Aristotle first called by that name) a hybrid of the three, materialising ideal entities, turning harmonies into forces, and dissolving natural things into terms of discourse. Speculations about the natural world, such as those of the Ionian philosophers, are not metaphysics, but

From *Scepticism and Animal Faith* (New York: Dover, 1955), pp. v–x.

simply cosmology or natural philosophy. Now in natural philosophy I am a decided materialist— apparently the only one living; and I am well aware that idealists are fond of calling materialism, too, metaphysics, in rather an angry tone, so as to cast discredit upon it by assimilating it to their own systems. But my materialism, for all that, is not metaphysical. I do not profess to know what matter is in itself, and feel no confidence in the divination of those *esprits forts* who, leading a life of vice, thought the universe must be composed of nothing but dice and billiard-balls. I wait for the men of science to tell me what matter is, in so far as they can discover it, and am not at all surprised or troubled at the abstractness and vagueness of their ultimate conceptions: how should our notions of things so remote from the scale and scope of our senses be anything but schematic? But whatever matter may be, I call it matter boldly, as I call my acquaintances Smith and Jones without knowing their secrets: whatever it may be, it must present the aspects and undergo the motions of the gross objects that fill the world: and if belief in the existence of hidden parts and movements in nature be metaphysics, then the kitchen-maid is a metaphysician whenever she peels a potato.

My system, finally, though, of course, formed under the fire of contemporary discussions, is *no phase of any current movement*. I cannot take at all seriously the present flutter of the image-lovers against intelligence. I love images as much as they do, but images must be discounted in our waking life, when we come to business. I also appreciate the other reforms and rebellions that have made up the history of philosophy. I prize their sharp criticism of one another and their several discoveries; the trouble is that each in turn has denied or forgotten a much more important truth than it has asserted. The first philosophers, the original observers of life and nature, were the best; and I think only the Indians and the Greek naturalists, together with Spinoza, have been right on the chief issue, the relation of man and of his spirit to the universe. It is not unwillingness to be a disciple that prompts me to look beyond the modern scramble of philosophies: I should gladly learn of them all, if they had learned more of one another. Even as it is, I endeavour to retain the positive insight of each, reducing it to the scale of nature and keeping it in its place; thus I am a Platonist in logic and morals, and a transcendentalist in romantic soliloquy, when I choose to indulge in it. Nor is it necessary, in being teachable by any master, to become eclectic. All these vistas give glimpses of the same wood, and a fair and true map of it must be drawn to a single scale, by one method of projection, and in one style of calligraphy. All known truth can be rendered in any language, although the accent and poetry of each may be incommunicable; and as I am content to write in English, although it was not my mother-tongue, and although in speculative matters I have not much sympathy with the English mind, so I am content to follow the European tradition in philosophy, little as I respect its rhetorical metaphysics, its humanism, and its worldliness.

There is one point, indeed, in which I am truly sorry not to be able to profit by the guidance of my contemporaries. There is now a great ferment in natural and mathematical philosophy and the times seem ripe for a new system of nature, at once ingenuous and comprehensive, such as has not appeared since the earlier days of Greece. We may soon be all believing in an honest cosmology, comparable with that of Heraclitus, Pythagoras, or Democritus. I wish such scientific systems joy, and if I were competent to follow or to forecast their procedure, I should gladly avail myself of their results, which are bound to be no less picturesque than instructive. But what exists to-day is so tentative, obscure, and confused by bad philosophy, that there is no knowing what parts may be sound and what parts merely personal and scatter-brained. If I were a mathematician I should no doubt regale myself, if not the reader, with an electric or logistic system of the universe expressed in algebraic symbols. For good or ill, I am an ignorant man, almost a poet, and I can only spread a feast of what everybody knows. Fortunately exact science and the books of the learned are not necessary to establish my essential doctrine, nor can any of them claim a higher warrant than it has in itself: for it rests on public experience. It needs, to prove it, only the stars, the seasons, the swarm of animals, the spectacle of birth and death, of cities and wars. My philosophy is justified, and has been justified in all ages and countries, by the facts before every man's eyes; and no great wit is requisite to discover it, only (what is rarer than wit) candour and courage. Learning does not liberate men from superstition when their souls are cowed or perplexed; and, without learning, clear eyes and honest reflection can discern the hang of the world, and distinguish the edge of truth from the might of imagination. In the past or in the future, my language and my borrowed knowledge would have been different, but under whatever sky I had been born, since it is the same sky, I should have had the same philosophy.

Ultimate Scepticism

Why should the mystic, in proportion as he dismisses the miscellany of experience as so much illusion, feel that he becomes one with reality and attains to absolute existence? I think that the same survival of vulgar presumptions which leads the romantic solipsist to retain his belief in his personal history and destiny, leads the mystic to retain, and fondly to embrace, the feeling of existence. His speculation is indeed inspired by the love of security: his grand objection to the natural world, and to mortal life, is that they are deceptive, that they cheat the soul that loves them, and prove to be illusions: the assumption apparently being that reality must be permanent, and that he who has hold on reality is safe for ever. In this the mystic, who so hates illusions, is the victim of an illusion himself: for the reality he has hold of is but the burden of a single moment, which in its solipsism thinks itself absolute. What is reality? As I should like to use the term, reality is being of any sort. If it means character or essence, illusions have it as much as substance, and more richly. If it means substance, then sceptical concentration upon inner experience, or ecstatic abstraction, seems to me the last place in which we should look for it. The immediate and the visionary are at the opposite pole from substance; they are on the surface or, if you like, at the top; whereas substance if it is anywhere is at the bottom. The realm of immediate illusion is as real as any other, and very attractive; many would wish it to be the only reality, and hate substance; but if substance exists (which I am not yet ready to assert) they have no reason to hate it, since it is the basis of those immediate feelings which fill them with satisfaction. Finally, if reality means existence, certainly the mystic and his meditation may exist, but not more truly than any other natural fact; and what would exist in them would be a pulse of animal being, kindling that momentary ecstasy, as animal life at certain intensities is wont to do. The theme of that meditation, its visionary object, need not exist at all; it may be incapable of existing if it is essentially timeless and dialectical. The animal mind treats its data as facts, or as signs of facts, but the animal mind is full of the rashest presumptions, positing time, change, a particular station in the midst of events yielding a

particular perspective of those events, and the flux of all nature precipitating that experience at that place. None of these posited objects is a datum in which a sceptic could rest. Indeed, existence or fact, in the sense which I give to these words, cannot be a datum at all, because existence involves external relations and actual (not merely specious) flux: whereas, however complex a datum may be, with no matter what perspectives opening within it, it must be embraced in a single stroke of apperception, and nothing outside it can belong to it at all. The datum is a pure image; it is essentially illusory and unsubstantial, however thunderous its sound or keen its edge, or however normal and significant its presence may be. When the mystic asserts enthusiastically the existence of his immediate, ideal, unutterable object, Absolute Being, he is peculiarly unfortunate in his faith: it would be impossible to choose an image less relevant to the agencies that actually bring that image before him. The burden and glow of existence which he is conscious of come entirely from himself; his object is eminently empty, impotent, non-existent; but the heat and labour of his own soul suffuse that emptiness with light, and the very hum of change within him, accelerated almost beyond endurance and quite beyond discrimination, sounds that piercing note.

The last step in scepticism is now before me. It will lead me to deny existence to any datum, whatever it may be; and as the datum, by hypothesis, is the whole of what solicits my attention at any moment, I shall deny the existence of everything, and abolish that category of thought altogether. If I could not do this, I should be a tyro in scepticism. Belief in the existence of anything, including myself, is something radically incapable of proof, and resting, like all belief, on some irrational persuasion or prompting of life. Certainly, as a matter of fact, when I deny existence I exist; but doubtless many of the other facts I have been denying, because I found no evidence for them, were true also. To bring me evidence of their existence is no duty imposed on facts, nor a habit of theirs: I must employ private detectives. The point is, in this task of criticism, to discard every belief that is a belief merely; and the belief in existence, in the nature of the case, can be a belief only. The datum is an

From *Scepticism and Animal Faith* (New York: Dover, 1955), pp. 33–41.

idea, a description; I may contemplate it without belief; but when I assert that such a thing exists I am hypostatising this datum, placing it in presumptive relations which are not internal to it, and worshipping it as an idol or thing. Neither its existence nor mine nor that of my belief can be given in any datum. These things are incidents involved in that order of nature which I have thrown over; they are no part of what remains before me.

Assurance of existence expresses animal watchfulness: it posits, within me and round me, hidden and imminent events. The sceptic can easily cast a doubt on the remoter objects of this belief; and nothing but a certain obduracy and want of agility prevents him from doubting present existence itself. For what could present existence mean, if the imminent events for which animal sense is watching failed altogether, failed at the very roots, so to speak, of the tree of intuition, and left nothing but its branches flowering *in vacuo?* Expectation is admittedly the most hazardous of beliefs: yet what is watchfulness but expectation? Memory is notoriously full of illusion; yet what would experience of the present be if the veracity of primary memory were denied, and if I no longer believed that anything had just happened, or that I had ever been in the state from which I suppose myself to have passed into this my present condition?

It will not do for the sceptic to take refuge in the confused notion that expectation *possesses* the future, or memory the past. As a matter of fact, expectation is like hunger; it opens its mouth, and something probably drops into it, more or less, very often, the sort of thing it expected; but sometimes a surprise comes, and sometimes nothing. Life involves expectation, but does not prevent death: and expectation is never so thoroughly stultified as when it is not undeceived, but cancelled. The open mouth does not then so much as close upon nothing. It is buried open. Nor is memory in a better case. As the whole world might collapse and cease at any moment, nullifying all expectation, so it might at any moment have sprung out of nothing: for it is thoroughly contingent, and might have begun to-day, with this degree of complexity and illusive memory, as well as long ago, with whatever energy or momentum it was first endowed with. The backward perspective of time is perhaps really an inverted expectation; but for the momentum of life forward, we might not be able to space the elements active in the present so as to assign to them a longer or a shorter history; for we

should not attempt to discriminate amongst these elements such as we could still count on in the immediate future, and such as we might safely ignore: so that our conception of the past implies, perhaps, a distinction between the living and the dead. This distinction is itself practical, and looks to the future. In the absolute present all is specious; and to pure intuition the living are as ghostly as the dead, and the dead as present as the living.

In the sense of existence there is accordingly something more than the obvious character of that which is alleged to exist. What is this complement? It cannot be a feature in the datum, since the datum by definition is the whole of what is found. Nor can it be, in my sense at least of the word existence, the intrinsic construction or specific being of this object, since existence comports external relations, variable, contingent, and not discoverable in a given being when taken alone: for there is nothing that may not lose its existence, or the existence of which might not be conceivably denied. The complement added to the datum when it is alleged to exist seems, then, to be added by *me;* it is the finding, the occurrence, the assault, the impact of that being here and now; it is the experience of it. But what can experience be, if I take away from it the whole of what is experienced? And what meaning can I give to such words as impact, assault, occurrence, or finding, when I have banished and denied my body, my past, my residual present being, and everything except the datum which I find? The sense of existence evidently belongs to the intoxication, to the *Rausch,* of existence itself; it is the strain of life within me, prior to all intuition, that in its precipitation and terror, passing as it continually must from one untenable condition to another, stretches my attention absurdly over what is not given, over the lost and the unattained, the before and after which are wrapped in darkness, and confuses my breathless apprehension of the clear presence of all I can ever truly behold.

Indeed, so much am I a creature of movement, and of the ceaseless metabolism of matter, that I should never catch even these glimpses of the light, if there were not rhythms, pauses, repetitions, and nodes in my physical progress, to absorb and reflect it here and there: as the traveller, hurried in a cloud of smoke and dust through tunnel after tunnel in the Italian Riviera, catches and loses momentary visions of blue sea and sky, which he would like to arrest, but cannot; yet if he had not been rushed and whistled along these particular tunnels, even those snatches, in the form in which they come to him, would have been denied him. So it is the rush of life that, at its open moments, floods me with intuitions, partial and confused, but still revelations; the landscape is wrapped in the smoke of my little engine, and turned into a tantalising incident of my hot journey. What appears (which is an ideal object and not an event) is thus confused with the event of its appearance; the picture is identified with the kindling or distraction of my attention falling by chance upon it; and the strain of my material existence, battling with material accidents, turns the ideal object too into a temporal fact, and makes it seem substantial. But this fugitive existence which I egotistically attach to it, as if its fate was that of my glimpses of it, is no part of its true being, as even my intuition discerns it; it is a practical dignity or potency attributed to it by the irrelevant momentum of my animal life. Animals, being by nature hounded and hungry creatures, spy out and take alarm at any datum of sense or fancy, supposing that there is something substantial there, something that will count and work in the world. The notion of a moving world is brought implicitly with them; they fetch it out of the depths of their vegetating psyche, which is a small dark cosmos, silently revolving within. By being noticed, and treated as a signal for I know not what material opportunity or danger, the given image is taken up into the business world, and puts on the garment of existence. Remove this frame, strip off all suggestion of a time when this image was not yet present, or a time when it shall be past, and the very notion of existence is removed. The datum ceases to be an appearance, in the proper and pregnant sense of this word, since it ceases to imply any substance that appears or any mind to which it appears. It is an appearance only in the sense that its nature is wholly manifest, that it is a specific being, which may be mentioned, thought of, seen, or defined, if any one has the wit to do so. But its own nature says nothing of any hidden circumstances that shall bring it to light, or any adventitious mind that shall discover it. It lies simply in its own category. If a colour, it is just this colour; if a pain, just this pain. Its appearance is not an event: its presence is not an experience; for there is no surrounding world in which it can arise, and no watchful spirit to appropriate it. The sceptic has here withdrawn into the intuition of a surface form, without roots, without origin or environment, without a seat or a locus; a little universe, an immaterial absolute theme, rejoicing merely in its own quality. This theme, being out of all adventitious relations and not in the least threatened with not being the theme it is, has not the contingency nor the fortunes proper to an existence; it is simply that which it inherently, logically, and unchangeably is.

Existence, then, not being included in any immediate datum, is a fact always open to doubt. I call it a fact notwithstanding, because in talking about the sceptic I am positing his existence. If he has any intuition, however little the theme of that intuition may have to do with any actual world, certainly I who think of his intuition, or he himself thinking of it afterwards, see that this intuition of his must have been an event, and his existence at that time a fact; but like all facts and events, this one can be known only by an affirmation which posits it, which may be suspended or reversed, and which is subject to error. Hence all this business of intuition may perfectly well be doubted by the sceptic: the existence of his own doubt (however confidently I may assert it for him) is not given to him then: all that is given is some ambiguity or contradiction in images; and if afterwards he is sure that he has doubted, the sole cogent evidence which that fact can claim lies in the psychological impossibility that, so long as he believes he has doubted, he should not believe it. But he may be wrong in harbouring this belief, and he may rescind it. For all an ultimate scepticism can see, therefore, there may be no facts at all, and perhaps nothing has ever existed.

Scepticism may thus be carried to the point of denying change and memory, and the reality of all facts. Such a sceptical dogma would certainly be false, because this dogma itself would have to be entertained, and that event would be a fact and an existence: and the sceptic in framing that dogma discourses, vacillates, and lives in the act of contrasting one assertion with another—all of which is to exist with a vengeance. Yet this false dogma that nothing exists is tenable intuitively and, while it prevails, is irrefutable. There are certain motives (to be discussed later) which render ultimate scepticism precious to a spiritual mind, as a sanctuary from grosser illusions. For the wayward sceptic, who regards it as no truer than any other view, it also has some utility: it accustoms him to discard the dogma which an introspective critic might be tempted to think self-evident, namely, that he himself lives and thinks. That he does so is true; but to establish that truth he must appeal to animal faith. If he is too proud for that, and simply stares at the datum, the last thing he will see is himself.

The Discovery of Essence

The loss of faith, as I have already observed, has no tendency to banish ideas; on the contrary, since doubt arises on reflection, it tends to keep the imagination on the stretch, and lends to the whole spectacle of things a certain immediacy, suavity, and humour. All that is sordid or tragic falls away, and everything acquires a lyric purity, as if the die had not yet been cast and the ominous choice of creation had not been made. Often the richest philosophies are the most sceptical; the mind is not then tethered in its home paddock, but ranges at will over the wilderness of being. The Indians, who deny the existence of the world, have a keen sense for its infinity and its variegated colours; they play with the monstrous and miraculous in the grand manner, as in the *Arabian Nights*. No critic has had a sharper eye for the outlines of ideas than Hume, who found it impossible seriously to believe that they revealed anything. In the critic, as in the painter, suspension of belief and of practical understanding is favourable to vision; the arrested eye renders every image limpid and unequivocal. And this is not merely an effect of physiological compensation, in that perhaps the nervous energy withdrawn from the preparations for action is allowed to intensify the process of mere sensation. There ensues a logical clarification as well; because so long as belief, interpretation, and significance entered in, the object in hand was ambiguous; in seeking the fact the mind overlooked or confused the datum. Yet each element in this eager investigation—including its very eagerness—is precisely what it is; and if I renounce for the moment all transitive intelligence, and give to each of these elements its due definition, I shall have a much richer as well as clearer collection of terms and relations before me, than when I was clumsily attempting to make up my mind. Living beings dwell in their expectations rather than in their senses. If they are ever to *see* what they see, they must first in a manner stop living; they must suspend the will, as Schopenhauer put it; they must photograph the idea that is flying past, veiled in its very swiftness. This swiftness is not its own fault, but that of my haste and inattention; my hold is loose on it, as in a dream; or else perhaps those veils and that

swiftness are the truth of the picture; and it is they that the true artist should be concerned to catch and to eternalise, restoring to all that the practical intellect calls vague its own specious definition. Nothing is vague in itself, or other than just what it is. Symbols are vague only in respect to their signification, when this remains ambiguous.

It is accordingly an inapt criticism often passed upon Berkeley and Hume that they overlooked vagueness in ideas, although almost every human idea is scandalously vague. No, their intuition of ideas, at least initially, was quite direct and honest. The ambiguity they overlooked lay in the relation of ideas to physical things, which they wished to reduce to groups or series of these pellucid ideas—a chimerical physics. Had they abstained altogether from identifying ideas with objects of natural knowledge (which are events and facts), and from trying to construct material things out of optical and tactile images, they might have much enriched the philosophy of specious reality, and discerned the innocent realm of ideas as directly as Plato did, but more accurately. In this they need not have confused or undermined faith in natural things. Perception *is* faith; more perception may extend this faith or reform it, but can never recant it except by sophistry. These virgin philosophers were like the cubists or futurists in the painting of today. They might have brought to light curious and neglected forms of direct intuition. They could not justly have been charged with absurdity for seeing what they actually saw. But they lapse into absurdity, and that irremediably, if they pretend to be the first and only masters of anatomy and topography.

Far from being vague or abstract the obvious ideas remaining to a complete sceptic may prove too absorbing, too multitudinous, or too sweet. A moral reprobation of them is no less intelligible than is the scientific criticism which rejects them as illusions and as no constituents of the existing world. Conscience no less than business may blame the sceptic for a sort of luxurious idleness; he may call himself a lotus-eater, may heave a sigh of fatigue at doing nothing, and may even feel a touch of the vertigo and wish to close the eyes on all these

From *Scepticism and Animal Faith* (New York: Dover, 1955), pp. 67–76.

images that entertain him to no purpose. But scepticism is an exercise, not a life; it is a discipline fit to purify the mind of prejudice and render it all the more apt, when the time comes, to believe and to act wisely; and meantime the pure sceptic need take no offense at the multiplicity of images that crowd upon him, if he is scrupulous not to trust them and to assert nothing at their prompting. Scepticism is the chastity of the intellect, and it is shameful to surrender it too soon or to the first comer: there is nobility in preserving it coolly and proudly through a long youth, until at last, in the ripeness of instinct and discretion, it can be safely exchanged for fidelity and happiness. But the philosopher, when he is speculative only, is a sort of perpetual celibate; he is bent on not being betrayed, rather than on being annexed or inspired; and although if he is at all wise he must see that the true marriage of the mind is with nature and science and the practical arts, yet in his special theoretic vocation, it will be a boon to him to view all experience simply, in the precision and distinctness which all its parts acquire when not referred to any substance which they might present confusedly, nor to any hypothesis or action which they might suggest.

The sceptic, then, as a consequence of carrying his scepticism to the greatest lengths, finds himself in the presence of more luminous and less equivocal objects than does the working and believing mind; only these objects are without meaning, they are only what they are obviously, all surface. They show him everything thinkable with the greatest clearness and force; but he can no longer imagine that he sees in these objects anything save their instant presence and their face-value. Scepticism therefore suspends all knowledge worthy of the name, all that transitive and presumptive knowledge of facts which is a form of belief; and instead it bestows intuition of ideas, contemplative, æsthetic, dialectical, arbitrary. But whereas transitive knowledge, though important if true, may always be challenged, intuition, on the contrary, which neither has nor professes to have any ulterior object or truth, runs no risks of error, because it claims no jurisdiction over anything alien or eventual.

In this lucidity and calmness of intuition there is something preternatural. Imagine a child accustomed to see clothes only on living persons and hardly distinguishing them from the magical strong bodies that agitate them, and suddenly carry this child into a costumer's shop, where he will see all sorts of garments hung in rows upon manikins, with hollow breasts all of visible wire, and little wooden nobs instead of heads: he might be seriously shocked or even frightened. How should it be possible for clothes standing up like this not to be people? Such abstractions, he might say to himself, are metaphysically impossible. Either these figures must be secretly alive and ready, when he least expects it, to begin to dance, or else they are not real at all, and he can only fancy that he sees them. Just as the spectacle of all these gaunt clothes without bodies might make the child cry, so later might the whole spectacle of nature, if ever he became a sceptic. The little word *is* has its tragedies; it marries and identifies different things with the greatest innocence; and yet no two are ever identical, and if therein lies the charm of wedding them and calling them one, therein too lies the danger. Whenever I use the word *is*, except in sheer tautology, I deeply misuse it; and when I discover my error, the world seems to fall asunder and the members of my family no longer know one another. Existence is the strong body and familiar motion which the young mind expects to find in every dummy. The oldest of us are sometimes no less recalcitrant to the spectacle of the garments of existence—which is all we ever saw of it—when the existence is taken away. Yet it is to these actual and familiar, but now disembowelled objects, that scepticism introduces us, as if to a strange world; a vast costumer's gallery of ideas where all sorts of patterns and models are on exhibition, without bodies to wear them, and where no human habits of motion distract the eye from the curious cut and precise embroideries of every article. This display, so complete in its spectacular reality, not a button nor a feather wanting or unobserved, is not the living crowd that it ought to be, but a mockery of it, like the palace of the Sleeping Beauty. To my conventional mind, clothes without bodies are no less improper than bodies without clothes; yet the conjunction of these things is but human. All nature runs about naked, and quite happy; and I am not so remote from nature as not to revert on occasion to that nakedness—which is unconsciousness—with profound relief. But ideas without things and apparel without wearers seem to me a stranger condition; I think the garments were made to fit the limbs, and should collapse without them. Yet, like the fig leaves of Eden, they are not garments essentially. They become such by accident, when one or another of them is appropriated by the providential buyer—not necessarily human—whose instinct may choose it; or else it is perfectly content to miss its chance, and to lie stacked for ever among its motley neighbours in this great store of neglected finery.

It was the fear of illusion that originally disquieted the honest mind, congenitally dogmatic, and drove it in the direction of scepticism; and it may find three ways, not equally satisfying to its honesty, in which that fear of illusion may be dispelled. One is death, in which illusion vanishes and is forgotten; but although anxiety about error, and even positive error, are thus destroyed, no solution is offered to the previous doubt: no explanation of what could have called forth that illusion or what could have dissipated it. Another way out is by correcting the error, and substituting a new belief for it: but while in animal life this is the satisfying solution, and the old habit of dogmatism may be resumed in consequence without practical inconvenience, speculatively the case is not at all advanced; because no criterion of truth is afforded except custom, comfort, and the accidental absence of doubt; and what is absent by chance may return at any time unbidden. The third way, at which I have now arrived, is to entertain the illusion without succumbing to it, accepting it openly as an illusion, and forbidding it to claim any sort of being but that which it obviously has; and then, whether it profits me or not, it will not deceive me. What will remain of this non-deceptive illusion will then be a truth, and a truth the being of which requires no explanation, since it is utterly impossible that it should have been otherwise. Of course I may still ask why the identity of this particular thing with itself should have occurred to *me;* a question which could only be answered by plunging into a realm of existence and natural history every part and principle of which would be just as contingent, just as uncalled-for, and just as inexplicable, as this accident of my being; but that this particular thing, or any other which might have occurred to me instead, should be constituted as it is raises no problem; for how could *it* have been constituted otherwise? Nor is there any moral offence any longer in the contingency of my view of it, since my view of it involves no error. The error came from a wild belief about it; and the possibility of error came from a wild belief about it; and the possibility of error came from a wild propensity to belief. Relieve now the pressure of that animal haste and that hungry presumption; the error is washed out of the illusion; it is no illusion

now, but an idea. Just as food would cease to be food, and poison poison, if you removed the stomach and the blood that they might nourish or infect; and just as beautiful things would cease to be beautiful if you removed the wonder and the welcome of living souls, so if you eliminate your anxiety, deceit itself becomes entertainment, and every illusion but so much added acquaintance with the realm of form. For the unintelligible accident of existence will cease to appear to lurk in this manifest being, weighting and crowding it, and threatening it with being swallowed up by nondescript neighbours. It will appear dwelling in its own world, and shining by its own light, however brief may be my glimpse of it: for no date will be written on it, no frame of full or of empty time will shut it in; nothing in it will be addressed to me, nor suggestive of any spectator. It will seem an event in no world, an incident in no experience. The quality of it will have ceased to exist: it will be merely the quality which it inherently, logically, and inalienably is. It will be an ESSENCE.

Retrenchment has its rewards. When by a difficult suspension of judgement I have deprived a given image of all adventitious significance, when it is taken neither for the manifestation of a substance nor for an idea in a mind nor for an event in a world, but simply if a colour for that colour and if music for that music, and if a face for that face, then an immense cognitive certitude comes to compensate me for so much cognitive abstention. My scepticism at last has touched bottom, and my doubt has found honourable rest in the absolutely indubitable. Whatever essence I find and note, that essence and no other is established before me. I cannot be mistaken about it, since I now have no object of intent other than the object of intuition. If for some private reason I am dissatisfied, and wish to change my entertainment, nothing prevents; but the change leaves the thing I first saw possessed of all its quality, for the sake of which I perhaps disliked or disowned it. That, while one essence is before me, some one else may be talking of another, which he calls by the same name, is nothing to the purpose; and if I myself change and correct myself, choosing a new essence in place of the old, my life indeed may have shifted its visions and its interests, but the characters they had when I harboured them are theirs without change. Indeed, only because each essence is the essence defined by instant apprehension can I truly be said to have changed my mind; for I can have discarded any one of them only by substituting something different. This new essence could not be different from the former one, if each was not unchangeably itself.

There is, then, a sort of play with the non-existent, or game of thought, which intervenes in all alleged knowledge of matters of fact, and survives that knowledge, if this is ever questioned or disproved. To this mirage of the non-existent, or intuition of essence, the pure sceptic is confined; and confined is hardly the word; because though without faith and risk he can never leave that thin and bodiless plane of being, this plane in its tenuity is infinite; and there is nothing possible elsewhere that, as a shadow and a pattern, is not prefigured there. To consider an essence is, from a spiritual point of view, to enlarge acquaintance with true being; but it is not even to broach knowledge of fact; and the ideal object so defined may have no natural significance, though it has æsthetic immediacy and logical definition. The modest scope of this speculative acquaintance with essence renders it infallible, whilst the logical and æsthetic ideality of its object renders the object eternal. Thus the most radical sceptic may be consoled, without being rebuked nor refuted; he may leap at one bound over the whole human tangle of beliefs and dogmatic claims, elude human incapacity and bias, and take hold of the quite sufficient assurance that any essence or ideal quality of being which he may be intuiting has just the characters he is finding in it, and has them eternally.

This is no idle assurance. After all, the only thing that can ultimately interest me in other men's experience or, apart from animal egotism, in my own, is just this character of the essences which at any time have swum into our ken; not at all the length of time through which we may have beheld them, nor the circumstances that produced their vision; unless these circumstances in turn, when considered, place

before the mind the essences which it delights to entertain. Of course, the choice and the interest of essences come entirely from the bent of the animal that elicits the vision of them from his own soul and its adventures; and nothing but affinity with my animal life lends the essences I am able to discern their moral colour, so that to my mind they are beautiful, horrible, trivial, or vulgar. The good essences are such as accompany and express a good life. In them, whether good or bad, that life has its eternity. Certainly when I cease to exist and to think, I shall lose hold on this assurance; but the theme in which for a moment I found the fulfilment of my expressive impulses will remain, as it always was, a theme fit for consideration, even if no one else should consider it, and I should never consider it again.

Nor is this all. Not only is the character of each essence inalienable, and, so long as it is open to intuition, indubitable, but the realm of essences is infinite. Since any essence I happen to have hit upon is independent of me and would possess its precise character if I had never been born, or had never been led by the circumstances of my life and temperament to apprehend that particular essence, evidently all other essences, which I have not been led to think of, rejoice in the same sort of impalpable being—impalpable, yet the only sort of being that the most rugged experience can ever actually find. Thus a mind enlightened by scepticism and cured of noisy dogma, a mind discounting all reports, and free from all tormenting anxiety about its own fortunes or existence, finds in the wilderness of essence a very sweet and marvellous solitude. The ultimate reaches of doubt and renunciation open out for it, by an easy transition, into fields of endless variety and peace, as if through the gorges of death it had passed into a paradise where all things are crystallised into the image of themselves, and have lost their urgency and their venom.

Knowledge is Faith mediated by Symbols

In the claims of memory I have a typical instance of what is called knowledge. In remembering I believe that I am taking cognisance

not of a given essence by of a remote existence, so that, being myself here and now, I can consider and describe something going on

From *Scepticism and Animal Faith* (New York: Dover, 1955), pp. 164–181.

at another place and time. This leap, which renders knowledge essentially faith, may come to seem paradoxical or impossible like the leap of physical being from place to place or from form to form which is called motion or change, and which some philosophers deny, as they deny knowledge. Is there such a leap in knowing? Am I really here and now when I apprehend some remote thing? Certainly, if by myself I understand the psyche within my body, which directs my outer organs, reacts on external things, and shapes the history and character of the individual animal that bears my name. In this sense I am a physical being in the midst of nature, and my knowledge is a name for the effects which surrounding things have upon me, in so far as I am quickened by them, and readjusted to them. I am certainly confined at each moment to a limited space and time, but may be quickened by the influence of things at any distance, and may be readjusting myself to them. For the naturalist there is accordingly no paradox in the leap of knowledge other than the general marvel of material interaction and animal life.

If by myself, however, I meant pure spirit, or the light of attention by which essences appear and intuitions are rendered actual, it would not be true that I am confined or even situated in a particular place and time, nor that in considering things remote from my body, my thoughts are taking any unnatural leap. The marvel, from the point of view of spirit, is rather than it should need to be planted at all in the sensorium of some living animal, and that, being rooted there, it should take that accidental station for its point of view in surveying all nature, and should dignify one momentary phase of that animal life with the titles of the Here and the Now. It is only spirit, be it observed, that can do this. In themselves all the points of space-time are equally central and palpitating, and every phase of every psyche is a focus for actual readjustments to the whole universe. How then can the spirit, which would seem to be the principle of universality and justice, take up its station in each of these atoms and fight its battles for it, and prostitute its own light in the service of that desperate blindness? Can reason do nothing better than supply the eloquence of prejudice? Such are the puzzles which spirit might find, I will not say in the leap of knowledge, but in the fatality which links the spirit to a material organ so that, in order to reach other things, it is obliged to leap; or rather can never reach other things, because it is tethered to its

starting-point, except by its intent in leaping, and cannot even discover the stepping-stone on which it stands because its whole life is the act of leaping away from it. There is no reason, therefore, in so far as knowledge is an apanage of spirit, why knowledge should not bathe all time and all existence in an equal light, and see everything as it is, with an equal sympathy and immediacy. The problem for the spirit is how it could ever come to pick out one body or another for its cynosure and for its instrument, as if it could not see save through such a little eye-glass, and in such a violent perspective. This problem, I think, has a ready answer, but it is not one that spirit could ever find of itself, without a long and docile apprenticeship in the school of animal faith. This answer is that spirit, with knowledge and all its other prerogatives, is intrinsically and altogether a function of animal life; so that if it were not lodged in some body and expressive of its rhythms and relations, spirit would not exist at all. But this solution, even when spirit is humble enough to accept it, always seems to it a little disappointing and satirical.

Spirit, therefore, has no need to leap in order to know, because in its range as spirit it is omnipresent and omnimodal. Events which are past or future in relation to the phase of the psyche which spirit expresses in a particular instance, or events which are remote from that psyche in space, are not for that reason remote from spirit, or out of its cognitive range: they are merely hidden, or placed in a particular perspective for the moment, like the features of a landscape by the hedges and turns of a road. Just as all essences are equally near to spirit, and equally fit and easy to contemplate, if only a psyche with an affinity to those essences happens to arise; so all existing things, past, future, or infinitely distant, are equally within the range of knowledge, if only a psyche happens to be directed upon them, and to choose terms, however poor or fantastic, in which to describe them. In choosing these terms the psyche creates spirit, for they are essences given in intuition; and in directing her action or endeavour, backward or forward, upon those remote events, she creates intent in the spirit, so that the given essences become descriptions of the things with which the psyche is then busied.

But how, I may ask, can intent distinguish its hidden object, so that an image, distorted or faithful, may be truly or falsely projected *there,* or used to describe *it?* How does the spirit divine that there is such an object, or where it lies? And how can it appeal to a thing which is hidden, the object of mere intent, as to a touchstone or standard for its various descriptions of that object, and say to them, as they suggest themselves in turn: You are too vague, You are absurd, You are better, You are absolutely right?

I answer that it does so by animal presumption, positing whatsoever object instinct is materially predisposed to cope with, as in hunger, love, fighting, or the expectation of a future. But before developing this reply, let me make one observation. Since intuition of essence is not knowledge, knowledge can never lie in an overt comparison of one datum with another datum given at the same time; even in pure dialectic, the comparison is with a datum *believed* to have been given formerly. If both terms were simply given they would compose a complex essence, without the least signification. Only when one of the terms is indicated by intent, without being given exhaustively, can the other term serve to define the first more fully, or be linked with it in an assertion which is not mere tautology. An object of faith—and knowledge is one species of faith—can never, even in the most direct perception, come within the circle of intuition. Intuition of things is a contradiction in terms. If philosophers wish to abstain from faith, and reduce themselves to intuition of the obvious, they are free to do so, but they will thereby renounce all knowledge, and live on passive illusions. No fact, not even the fact that these illusions exist, would ever be, or would ever have been, anything but the false idea that they had existed. There would be nothing but the realm of essence, without any intuition of any part of it, nor of the whole: so that we should be driven back to a nihilism which only silence and death could express consistently; since the least actual assertion of it, by existing, would contradict it.

Even such acquaintance with the realm of essence as constitutes some science or recognisable art—like mathematics or music—lies in intending and positing great stretches of essence not now given, so that the essences now given acquire significance and become pregnant, to my vital feeling, with a thousand things which they do not present actually, but which I know where to look for eventually, and how to await. Suppose a moment ago I heard a clap of thunder, loud and prolonged, but that the physical shock has subsided and I am conscious of repose and silence. I may find some difficulty, although the thing was so recent, in *rehearsing* even now the exact volume, tone, and rumblings of that sound; yet I *know* the theme perfectly, in the sense that when it thunders again, I can say with assurance whether the second crash was longer, louder, or differently modulated. In such a case I have no longer an intuition of the first thunderclap, but a memory of it which is knowledge; and I can define on occasion, up to a certain point and not without some error, the essence given in that particular past intuition. Thus even pure essences can become objects of intent and of tentative knowledge when they are not present in intuition but are approached and posited indirectly, as the essences given on another particular occasion or signified by some particular word. The word or the occasion are natural facts, and my knowledge is focussed upon them in the first instance by ordinary perception or conception of nature: and the essence I hope to recover is elicited gradually, imaginatively, perhaps incorrectly, at the suggestion of those assumed facts, according to my quickness of wit, or my familiarity with the conventions of that art or science. In this way it becomes possible and necessary to learn about essences as if they were things, not initially by a spontaneous and complete intuition, but by coaxing the mind until possibly, at the end, it beholds them clearly. This is the sort of intuition which is mediated by language and by works of fine art; also by logic and mathematics, as they are learned from teachers and out of books. It is not happy intuition of some casual datum: it is laborious recovery, up to a certain point, of the *sort* of essence somebody else may have intuited. Whereas intuition, which reveals an essence directly, is not knowledge, because it has no ulterior object, the designation of some essence by some sign does convey knowledge, to an intelligent pupil, of what that essence was. Obviously such divination of essences present elsewhere, so that they become present here also, in so far as it is knowledge, is trebly faith. Faith first in the document, as a genuine natural fact and not a vapid fancy of my own; for instance, belief that there is a book called the Bible, really handed down from the ancient Jews and the early Christians, and that I have not merely dreamt of such a book. Faith then in the significance of that document, that it means some essence which it is not; in this instance, belief that the sacred writers were not merely speaking with tongues but were signifying some intelligible points in history and philosophy. Faith finally in my success in interpreting that document correctly, so that the essences it suggests to me now are the very essences it expressed originally: in other words, the belief that when I read the Bible I understand it as it was meant, and not fantastically.

I revert now to the question how it is possible to posit an object which is not a datum, and how without knowing positively what this object is I can make it the criterion of truth in my ideas. How can I test the accuracy of descriptions by referring them to a subject-matter which is not only out of view now but which probably has never been more than an object of intent, an event which even while it was occurring was described by me only in terms native to my fancy? If I know a man only by reputation, how should I judge if the reputation is deserved? If I know things only by representations, are not the representations the only things I know?

This challenge is fundamental, and so long as the assumptions which it makes are not challenged in turn, it drives critics of knowledge inexorably to scepticism of a dogmatic sort, I mean to the assertion that the very notion of knowledge is absurd. One assumption is that knowledge should be the intuition: but I have already come to the conclusion that intuition is not knowledge. So long as a knowledge is demanded that shall be intuition, the issue can only be laughter or despair; for if I attain intuition, I have only a phantom object, and if I spurn that and turn to the facts, I have renounced intuition. This assumption alone suffices, therefore, to disprove the possibility of knowledge. But in case the force of this disproof escaped us, another assumption is at hand to despatch the business, namely, the assumption that in a true description—if we grant knowledge by description—the terms should be identical with the constituents of the object, so that the idea should *look like* the thing that it knows. This assumption is derived from the other, or is a timid form of it: for it is supposed that I know by intuiting my idea, and that unless that idea resembled the object I wish to know, I could not even by courtesy be said to have discovered the latter. But the intuition of an idea, let me repeat, is not knowledge; and if a thing resembling that idea happened to exist, my intuition would still not be knowledge of it, but contemplation of the idea only.

Plato and many other philosophers, being in love with intuition (for which alone they were perhaps designed by nature), have identified science with certitude, and consequently entirely condemned what I call knowledge (which is a form of animal faith) or relegated it to an inferior position, as something merely necessary for life. I myself have no passionate attachment to existence, and value this world for the intuitions it can suggest, rather than for the wilderness of facts that compose it. To turn away from it may be the deepest wisdom in the end. What better than to blow out the candle, and to bed! But at noon this pleasure is premature. I can always hold it in reserve, and perhaps nihilism is a system—the simplest of all—on which we shall all agree in the end. But I seem to see very clearly now that in doing so we should all be missing the truth: not indeed by any false assertion, such as may separate us from the truth now, but by dumb ignorance—a dumb ignorance which, when proposed as a solution to actual doubts, is the most radical of errors, since it ignores and virtually denies the pressure of those doubts, and their living presence. Accordingly, so long as I remain awake and the light burning, that total dogmatic scepticism is evidently an impossible attitude. It requires me to deny what I assert, not to mean what I mean, and (in the sense in which seeing is believing) not to believe what I see. If I wish, therefore, to formulate in any way my actual claim to knowledge—a claim which life, and in particular memory, imposes upon me— I must revise the premises of this nihilism. For I have been led to it not by any accidental error, but by the logic of the assumption that knowledge should be intuition of fact. It is this presumption that must be revoked.

Knowledge is no such thing. It is not intramental nor internal to experience. Not only does it not require me to compare two given terms and to find them similar or identical, but it positively excludes any intuitive possession of its object. Intuition subsists beneath knowledge, as vegetative life subsists beneath animal life, and within it. Intuition may also supervene upon knowledge, when all I have learned of the universe, and all my concern for it, turn to a playful or a hypnotising phantom; and any poet or philosopher, like any flower, is free to prefer intuition to knowledge. But in preferring intuition he prefers ignorance. Knowledge is knowledge because it has compulsory objects that pre-exist. It is incidental to the predicaments and labour of life: also to its masterful explorations and satirical moods. It is reflected from events as light is reflected from bodies. It expresses in discourse the modified habits of an active being, plastic to experience, and capable of readjusting its organic attitude to other things on the same material plane of being with itself. The place and the pertinent functions of these several things are indicated by the very attitude of the animal who notices them; this attitude, physical and practical, determines the object of intent, which discourse is about.

When the proverbial child cries for the moon, is the object of his desire doubtful? He points at it unmistakably; yet the psychologist (not to speak of the child himself) would have some difficulty in recovering exactly the sensations and images, the gathering demands and fumbling efforts, that traverse the child's mind while he points. Fortunately all this fluid sentience, even if it could be described, is irrelevant to the question; for the child's sensuous experience is not his object. If it were, he would have attained it. What his object is, his fixed gaze and outstretched arm declare unequivocally. His elders may say that he doesn't know what he wants, which is probably true of them also: that is, he has only a ridiculously false and inconstant idea of what the moon may be in itself. But his attention is arrested in a particular direction, his appetition flows the same way; and if he may be said to know anything, he knows there is something there which he would like to reach, which he would like to know better. He is a little philosopher; and his knowledge, if less diversified and congealed, is exactly like science.

The attitude of his body in pointing to the moon, and his tears, fill full his little mind, which not only reverberates to this physical passion, but probably observes it: and this felt attitude *identifies the object* of his desire and knowledge *in the physical world*. It determines what particular thing, in the same space and time with the child's body, was the object of that particular passion. If the object which the body is after is identified, that which the soul is after is identified too: no one, I suppose, would carry dualism so far as to assert that when the mouth waters at the sight of one particular plum, the soul may be yearning for quite another.

The same bodily attitude of the child *identifies the object in the discourse of an observer*. In perceiving what his senses are excited by, and which way his endeavour is turned, I can see that the object of his desire is the moon, which I too am looking at. That I am looking at the same moon as he can be proved by a little triangulation: our glances converge upon it. If the child has reached the inquisitive age and asks "What is that?" I understand what he means by "that" and am able to reply sapiently "That is the moon," only because our respective bodies, in one common space, are discoverably turned towards one material object, which is stimulating them simultaneously. Knowledge of discourse in other people, or of myself at other times, is what I call literary psychology. It is, or may be, in its texture, the most literal and adequate sort of knowledge of which a mind is capable. If I am a lover of children, and a good psycho-analyst, I may feel for a moment exactly as the child feels in looking at the moon: and I may know that I know his feeling, and very likely he too will know that I know it, and we shall become fast friends. But this rare adequacy of knowledge, attained by dramatic sympathy, goes out to an object which in its existence is known very indirectly: because poets and religious visionaries feel this sort of sympathy with all sorts of imaginary persons, of whose existence and thoughts they have only intuition, not knowledge. If I ask for evidence that such an object exists, and is not an *alter ego* of my private invention, I must appeal to my faith in nature, and to my conventional assumption that this child and I are animals of the same species, in the same habitat, looking at the same moon, and likely to have the same feelings: and finally the psychology of the tribe and the crowd may enable me half to understand how we know that we have the same feelings at once, when we actually share them.

The attitude of the child's body also *identifies the object for him, in his own subsequent discourse*. He is not likely to forget a moon that he cried for. When in stretching his hand towards it he found that he could not touch it, he learned that this bright good was not within his grasp, and he made a beginning in the experience of life. He also made a beginning in science, since he then added the absolutely true predicate "out of reach" to the rather questionable predicates "bright" and "good" (and perhaps "edible") with which his first glimpse had supplied him. That active and mysterious thing, co-ordinate with himself, since it lay in the same world with his body, and affected it—the thing that attracted his hand, was evidently the very thing that eluded it. His failure would have had no meaning and would have taught him nothing—that is, would not have corrected his instinctive reactions—if the object he saw and the object he failed to reach had not been identical; and certainly that object was not brightness nor goodness nor excitements in his brain or psyche, for these are not things he could ever have attempted or expected to touch. It is only things on the scale of the human senses and in the field of those instinctive reactions which sensation calls forth, that can be the primary objects of human knowledge: no other things can be discriminated at first by an animal mind, or can interest it, or can be meant and believed in by it. It is these instinctive reactions that select the objects of attention, designate their locus, and impose faith in their existence. But these reactions may be modified by experience, and the description the mind gives of the objects reacted upon can be revised, or the objects themselves discarded, and others discerned instead. Thus the child's instinct to touch the moon was as spontaneous and as confident at first as his instinct to look at it; and the object of both efforts was the same, because the same external agency aroused them, and with them the very heterogeneous sensations of light and of disappointment. These various terms of sense or of discourse, by which the child described the object under whose attractions and rebuffs he was living, were merely symbols to him, like words. An animal naturally has as many signs for an object as he has sensations or emotions in its presence. These signs are miscellaneous essences—sights, sounds, smells, contacts, tears, provocations—and they are alternative or supplementary to one another, like words in different languages. The most diverse senses, such as smell and sight, if summoned to the same point in the environment, and guiding a single action, will report upon a single object. Even when one sense brings all the news I have, its reports will change from moment to moment with the distance, variation, or suspension of the connection between the object and my body: and this without any relevant change in the object itself. Nay, often the very transformation of the sensation bears witness that the object is unchanged; as music and laughter, overheard as I pass a tavern, are felt and known to continue unabated, and to be no merriment of mine, just because they fade from my ears as I move away.

The object of knowledge being that designated in this way by my bodily attitude, the æsthetic qualities I attribute to it will depend on the particular sense it happens to affect at the moment, or on the sweep and nature of the reaction which it then calls forth on my part. This diversity in signs and descriptions for a single thing is a normal diversity. Diversity, when it is not contradiction, irritates only unreasonably dogmatic people; they are offended

with nature for having a rich vocabulary, and sometimes speaking a language, or employing a syntax, which they never heard at home. It is an innocent prejudice, and it yields easily in a generous mind to pleasure at the wealth of alternatives which animal life affords. Even such contradictions as may arise in the description of things, and may truly demand a solution, reside in the implication of the terms, not in their sensuous or rhetorical diversity: they become contradictory only when they assign to the object contrary movements or contrary effects, not when they merely exhibit its various appearances. Looking at the moon, one man may call it simply a light in the sky; another, prone to dreaming awake, may call it a virgin goddess; a more observant person, remembering that this luminary is given to waxing and waning, may call it the crescent; and a fourth, a full-fledged astronomer, may say (taking the æsthetic essence before him merely for a sign) that it is an extinct and opaque spheroidal satellite of the earth, reflecting the light of the sun from a part of its surface. All these descriptions envisage the same object—otherwise no relevance, conflict, or progress could obtain among them. What that object is in its complete constitution and history will never be known by man; but that this object exists in a known space and time and has traceable physical relations with all other physical objects is a fact posited from the beginning; it was posited by the child when he pointed, and by me when I saw him point. If it did not so exist and (as sometimes happens) he and I were suffering from a hallucination, in thinking we were pointing at the moon we should be discoverably pointing at vacancy: exploration would eventually satisfy us of that fact, and any bystander would vouch for it. But if in pointing at it we were pointing to it, its identity would be fixed without more ado; disputes and discoveries concerning it would be pertinent and soluble, no matter what diversity there might be in the ideal essences—light, crescent, goddess, or satellite—which we used as rival descriptions of it while we pointed.

I find that the discrimination of essence brings a wonderful clearness into this subject. All data and descriptions—light, crescent, goddess, or satellite—are equally essences, terms of human discourse, inexistent in themselves. What exists in any instance, besides the moon and our various reactions upon it, is some intuition, expressing those reactions, evoking that essence, and lending it a specious actuality. The terms of astronomy are essences no less human and visionary than those of mythology; but they are the fruit of a better focussed, more chastened, and more prolonged attention turned upon what actually occurs; that is, they are kept closer to animal faith, and freer from pictorial elements and the infusion of reverie. In myth, on the contrary, intuition wanders idly and uncontrolled; it makes epicycles, as it were, upon the reflex arc of perception; the moonbeams bewitch some sleeping Endymion, and he dreams of a swift huntress in heaven. Myth is nevertheless a relevant fancy, and genuinely expressive; only instead of being guided by a perpetual fresh study of the object posited by animal faith and encountered in action, it runs into marginal comments, personal associations, and rhetorical asides; so that even if based originally on perception, it is built upon principles internal to human discourse, as are grammar, rhyme, music, and morals. It may be admirable as an expression of these principles, and yet be egregiously false if asserted of the object, without discounting the human medium in which it has taken form. Diana is an exquisite symbol for the moon, and for one sort of human loveliness; but she must not be credited with any existence over and above that of the moon, and of sundry short-skirted Dorian maidens. She is not other than they: she is an image of them, the best part of their essence distilled in a poet's mind. So with the description of the moon given by astronomers, which is not less fascinating; this, too, is no added object, but only a new image for the moon known even to the child and me. The space, matter, gravitation, time, and laws of motion conceived by astronomers are essences only, and mere symbols for the use of animal faith, when very enlightened: I mean in so far as they are alleged to constitute knowledge of a world which I must bow to and encounter in action; for if astronomy is content to be a mathematical exercise without any truth, an object of pure intuition, its terms and its laws will, of course, be ultimate realities, apart from what happens to exist: realities in the realm of essence. In the description of the natural world, however, they are mere symbols, mediating animal faith. Science at any moment may recast or correct its conceptions (as it is doing now) giving them a different colour; and the nerve of truth in them will be laid bare and made taut in proportion as the sensuous and rhetorical vesture of these notions is stripped off, and the dynamic relations of events, as found and posited by material exploration, are nakedly recorded.

Knowledge accordingly is belief: belief in a world of events, and especially of those parts of it which are near the self, tempting or threatening it. This belief is native to animals, and precedes all deliberate use of intuitions as signs or descriptions of things; as I turn my head to see who is there, before I see who it is. Furthermore, knowledge is true belief. It is such an enlightening of the self by intuitions arising there, that what the self imagines and asserts of the collateral thing, with which it wrestles in action, is actually true of that thing. Truth in such presumptions or conceptions does not imply adequacy, nor a pictorial identity between the essence in intuition and the constitution of the object. Discourse is a language, not a mirror. The images in sense are parts of discourse, not parts of nature: they are the babble of our innocent organs under the stimulus of things; but these spontaneous images, like the sounds of the voice, may acquire the function of names; they may become signs, if discourse is intelligent and can recapitulate its phases, for the things sought or encountered in the world. The truth which discourse can achieve is truth in its own terms, appropriate description: it is no incorporation or reproduction of the object in the mind. The mind notices and intends; it cannot incorporate or reproduce anything not an intention or an intuition. Its objects are no part of itself even when they are essences, much less when they are things. It thinks the essences, with that sort of immediate and self-forgetful attention which I have been calling intuition; and if it is animated, as it usually is, by some ulterior interest or pursuit, it takes the essences before it for messages, signs, or emanations sent forth to it from those objects of animal faith; and they become its evidences and its description for those objects. Therefore any degree of inadequacy and originality is tolerable in discourse, or even requisite, when the constitution of the objects which the animal encounters is out of scale with his organs, or quite heterogeneous from his possible images. A sensation or a theory, no matter how arbitrary its terms (and all language is perfectly arbitrary), will be true of the object, if it expresses some true relation in which that object stands to the self, so that these terms are not misleading as signs, however poetical they may be as sounds or as pictures.

Finally, knowledge is true belief grounded in experience, I mean, controlled by outer facts. It is not true by accident; it is not shot into the air on the chance that there may be something it may hit. It arises by a movement of the self sympathetic or responsive to surrounding beings, so that these beings become its intended objects, and at the same time an appropriate correspondence tends to be established between these objects and the beliefs generated under their influence.

In regard to the original articles of the animal creed—that there is a world, that there is a future, that things sought can be found, and things seen can be eaten—no guarantee can possibly be offered. I am sure these dogmas are often false; and perhaps the event will some day falsify them all, and they will lapse altogether. But while life lasts, in one form or another this faith must endure. It is the initial expression of animal vitality in the sphere of mind, the first announcement that anything is going on. It is involved in any pang of hunger, of fear, or of love. It launches the adventure of knowledge. The object of this tentative knowledge is things in general, whatsoever may be at work (as I am) to disturb me or awake my attention. The effort of knowledge is to discover what sort of world this disturbing world happens to be. Progress in knowledge lies open in various directions, now in the scope of its survey, now in its accuracy, now in its depth of local penetration. The ideal of knowledge is to become natural science: if it trespasses beyond that, it relapses into intuition, and ceases to be knowledge.

Belief in Substance

All knowledge, being faith in an object posited and partially described, is belief in substance, in the etymological sense of this word; it is belief in a thing or event subsisting in its own plane, and waiting for the light of knowledge to explore it eventually, and perhaps name or define it. In this way my whole past lies waiting for memory to review it, if I have this faculty; and the whole future of the world in the same manner is spread out for prophecy, scientific or visionary, to predict falsely or truly. Yet the future and the past are not ordinarily called substances; probably because the same material substance is assumed to run through both. Nevertheless, from the point of view of knowledge, every event, even if wholly psychological or phenomenal, is a substance. It is a self-existing fact, open to description from the point of view of other events, if in the bosom of these other events there is such plasticity and intent as are requisite for perception, prophecy, or memory.

When modern philosophers deny material substance, they make substances out of the sensations or ideas which they regard as ultimate facts. It is impossible to eliminate belief in substance so long as belief in existence is retained. A mistrust in existence, and therefore in substance, is not unphilosophical; but modern philosophers have not given full expression to this sceptical scruple. They have seldom been disinterested critics, but often advocates of some metaphysic that allured them, and whose rivals they wished to destroy. They deny substance in favour of phenomena, which are hypostatised essences, because phenomena are individually wholly open to intuition; but they forget that no phenomenon can intuit another, and that if it contains knowledge of that other, it must be animated by intent, and besides existing itself substantially must recognise its object as another substance, indifferent in its own being to the cognisance which other substances may take of it. In other words, although each phenomenon in passing is an object of intuition, all absent phenomena, and all their relations, are objects of faith; and this faith must be mediated by some feature in the present phenomenon which faith assumes to be a sign of the existence of other phenomena elsewhere, and of their order. So that in so far as the instinctive claims and transcendent scope of knowledge are concerned, phenomenalism fully retains the belief in substance. In order to get rid of this belief, which is certainly obnoxious to the sceptic, a disinterested critic would need to discard all claims to knowledge, and to deny his own existence and that of all absent phenomena.

For my own part, having admitted discourse (which involves time and existences deployed in time, but synthesised in retrospect), and

From *Scepticism and Animal Faith* (New York: Dover, 1955), pp. 182–191.

having admitted shocks that interrupt discourse and lead it to regard itself as an experience, and having even admitted that such experience involves a self beneath discourse, with an existence and movement of its own—I need not be deterred by any *a priori* objections from believing in substance of any sort. For me it will be simply a question of good sense and circumstantial evidence how many substances I admit, and of what sort.

In the genesis of human knowledge (which I am not attempting to trace here) the substance first posited is doubtless matter, some alluring or threatening or tormenting thing. The ego, as Fichte tells us, unaware of itself, posits a non-ego, and then by reflection posits itself as the agent in that positing, or as the patient which the activity posited in the non-ego posits in its turn. But all this positing would be mere folly, unless it was an intelligent discovery of antecedent facts. Why should a non-existent ego be troubled with the delirious duty of positing anything at all? And, if nothing else exists, what difference could it make what sort of a world the ego posited, or whether it posited a thousand inconsequential worlds, at once or in succession? Fichte, however, was far from sharing that absolute freedom in madness which he attributes to the creative ego; he had a very tight tense mind, and posited a very tense tight world. His myths about the birth of knowledge (or rather of systematic imagination) out of unconscious egos, acts, and positings concealed some modest truths about nature. The actual datum has a background, and Fichte was too wise to ignore so tremendous a fact. Romantic philosophy, like romantic poetry, has its profound ways of recognising its own folly, and so turning it into tragic wisdom. As a matter of fact, the active ego is an animal living in a material world; both the ego and the non-ego exist substantially before acquiring this relation of positing and being posited. The instinct and ability to posit objects, and the occasion for doing so, are incidents in the development of animal life. Positing is a symptom of sensibility in an organism in the presence of other substances in its environment. The sceptic, like the sick man, is intent on the symptom; and positing is his name for felt plasticity in his animal responses. It is not a bad name; because plasticity, though it may seem a passive thing, is really a spontaneous quality. If the substance of the ego were not alive, it would not leap to meet its opportunities, it would not develop new organs to serve its old necessities, and it would not kindle itself to

intuition of essences, nor concern itself to regard those essences as appearances of the substances with which it was wrestling. The whole life of imagination and knowledge comes from within, from the restlessness, eagerness, curiosity, and terror of the animal bent on hunting, feeding, and breeding; and the throb of being which he experiences at any moment is not proper to the datum in his mind's eye—a purely fantastic essence—but to himself. It is out of his organism or its central part, the psyche, that this datum has been bred. The living substance within him being bent, in the first instance, on pursuing or avoiding some agency in its environment, it projects whatever (in consequence of its reactions) reaches its consciousness into the locus whence it feels the stimulus to come, and it thus frames its description or knowledge of objects. In this way the ego really and sagaciously posits the non-ego: not absolutely, as Fichte imagined, nor by a gratuitous fiat, but on occasion and for the best of reasons, when the non-ego in its might shakes the ego out of its primitive somnolence.

Belief in substance is accordingly identical with the claim to knowledge, and so fundamental that no evidence can be adduced for it which does not presuppose it. In recognising any appearance as a witness to substance and in admitting (or even in rejecting) the validity of such testimony, I have already made a substance of the appearance; and if I admit other phenomena as well, I have placed that substance in a world of substances having a substantial unity. It is not to external pressure, through evidence or argument, that faith in substance is due. If the sceptic cannot find it in himself, he will never find it. I for one will honour him in his sincerity and in his solitude. But I will not honour him, nor think him a philosopher, if he is a sceptic only histrionically, in the wretched controversies of the schools, and believes in substance again when off the stage. I am not concerned about make-believe philosophies, but about my actual beliefs. It is only out of his own mouth, or rather out of his own heart, that I should care to convince the sceptic. Scepticism, if it could be sincere, would be the best of philosophies. But I suspect that other sceptics, as well as I, always believe in substance, and that their denial of it is sheer sophistry and the weaving of verbal arguments in which their most familiar and massive convictions are ignored.

It might seem ignominious to believe something on compulsion, because I can't help believing it; when reason awakes in a man it asks for reasons for everything. Yet this demand is unreasonable: there cannot be a reason for everything. It is mere automatic habit in the philosopher to make this demand, as it is in the common man not to make it. When once I have admitted the facts of nature, and taken for granted the character of animal life, and the incarnation of spirit in this animal life, then indeed many excellent reasons for the belief in substance will appear; and not only reasons for using the category of substance, and positing substance of some vague ambient sort, but reasons for believing in a substance rather elaborately defined and scientifically describable in many of its habits and properties. But I am not yet ready for that. Lest that investigation, when undertaken, should ignore its foundations or be impatient of its limits, I must insist here that trust in knowledge, and belief in anything to know, are merely instinctive and, in a manner, pathological. If philosophy were something prior to convention rather than (as it is) only convention made consistent and deliberate, philosophy ought to reject belief in substance and in knowledge, and to entrench itself in the sheer confession and analysis of this belief, as of all others, without assenting to any of them. But I have found that criticism has no first principle, that analysis involves belief in discourse, and that belief in discourse involves belief in substance; so that any pretensions which criticism might set up to being more profound than common sense would be false pretensions. Criticism is only an exercise of reflective fancy, on the plane of literary psychology, an after-image of that faith in nature which it denies; and in dwelling on criticism as if it were more than a subjective perspective or play of logical optics, I should be renouncing all serious philosophy. Philosophy is nothing if not honest; and the critical attitude, when it refuses to rest at some point upon vulgar faith, inhibits all belief, denies all claims to knowledge, and becomes dishonest; because it itself claims to know.

Does the process of experience, now that I trust my memory to report it truly, or does the existence of the self, now that I admit its substantial, dynamic, and obscure life underlying discourse, require me to posit any other substances? Certainly it does. Experience, for animal faith, begins by reporting what is not experience; and the life of the self, if I accept its endeavours as significant, implies an equally substantial, dynamic, ill-reported world around it, in whose movements it is implicated. In

conveying this feeling, as in all else, experience *might* be pure illusion; but if I reject this initial and fundamental suasion of my cognitive life, it will be hard to find anything better to put in its place. I am unwilling to do myself so much useless violence as to deny the validity of primary memory, and assert that I have never, in fact, had any experience at all; and I should be doing myself even greater violence if I denied the validity of perception, and asserted that a thunder-clap, for instance, was only a musical chord, with no formidable event of any sort going on behind the sound. To be startled is to be aware that something sudden and mysterious has occurred not far from me in space. The thunder-clap is felt to be an event in the self and in the not-self, even before its nature as a sound—its æsthetic quality for the self—is recognised at all; I first know I am shaken horribly, and then note how loud and rumbling is the voice of the god that shakes me. That first feeling of something violent and resistless happening in the world at large, is accompanied by a hardly less primitive sense of something gently seething within me, a smouldering life which that alien energy blows upon and causes to start into flame.

If this be not the inmost texture of experience, I do not know what experience is. To me experience has not a string of sensations for its objects; what it brings me is not at all a picture-gallery of clear images, with nothing before, behind, or between them. What such a ridiculous psychology (made apparently by studying the dictionary and not by studying the mind) calls hypotheses, intellectual fictions, or tendencies to feign, is the solid body of experience, on which what it calls sensations or ideas hang like flimsy garments or trinkets, or play like a shifting light and shade. Experience brings belief in substance (as alertness) *before* it brings intuition of essences; it is appetition *before* it is description. Of course sensation would precede idea, if by sensation we understood contact with matter, and by idea pure reverie about ideal things; but if idea means expectation, or consciousness having intent, and if sensation means æsthetic contemplation of data without belief, then idea precedes sensation: because an animal is aware that something is happening long before he can say to himself what that something is, or what it looks like. The ultimate datum to which a sceptic may retreat, when he suspends all life and opinion, some essence, pure and non-existent and out of all relation to minds, bodies, or events—surely that is not the stuff out of which experience is woven: it is but the pattern out of which experience is woven: it is but the pattern or picture, the aesthetic image, which the tapestry may ultimately offer to the gazing eye, incurious of origins, and contemptuous of substance. The radical stuff of experience is much rather breathlessness, or pulsation, or as Locke said (correcting himself) a certain uneasiness; a lingering thrill, the resonance of that much-struck bell which I call my body, the continual assault of some masked enemy, masked perhaps in beauty, or of some strange sympathetic influence, like the cries and motions of other creatures; and also the hastening and rising of some impulse in me in response. Experience, at its very inception, is a revelation of *things;* and these things, before they are otherwise distinguished, are distinguishable into a here and a there, a now and a then, nature and myself in the midst of nature.

It is a mere prejudice of literary psychology, which uses the grammar of adult discourse, like a mythology, in which to render primitive experience—it is a mere prejudice to suppose that experience has only such categories as colour, sound, touch, and smell. These essences are distinguished eventually because the senses that present them can be separated at will, the element each happens to furnish being thus flashed on or cut off, like an electric light: but far more primitive in animal experience are such dichotomies as good and bad, near and far, coming and going, fast and slow, just now and very soon. The first thing experience reports is the existence of something, merely as existence, the weight, strain, danger, and lapse of being. If any one should tell me that this is an abstraction, I should reply that it would seem an abstraction to a parrot, who used human words without having human experience, but it is no abstraction to a man, whose language utters imperfectly, and by a superadded articulation, the life within him. Aristotle, who so often seems merely grammatical, was not merely grammatical when he chose substance to be the first of his categories. He was far more profoundly psychological in this than the British and German psychologists who discard the notion of substance because it is not the datum of any separate sense. None of the separate data of sense, which are only essences, would figure at all in an experience, or would become terms in knowledge, if a prior interest and faith did not apprehend them. Animal watchfulness, lying in wait for the sig-

nals of the special senses, lends them their significance, sets them in their places, and retains them, as descriptions of things, and as symbols in its own ulterior discourse.

This animal watchfulness carries the category of substance with it, asserts existence most vehemently, and in apprehension seizes and throws on the dark screen of substance every essence it may descry. To grope, to blink, to dodge a blow, or to return it, is to have very radical and specific experiences, but probably without one assignable image of the outer senses. Yet a nameless essence, the sense of a moving existence, is there most intensely present; and a man would be a shameless, because an insincere, sceptic, who should maintain that this experience exists *in vacuo,* and does not express, as it feels it does, the operation of a missile flying, and the reaction of a body threatened or hit: motions in substance anterior to the experience, and rich in properties and powers which no experience will ever fathom.

Belief in substance, taken transcendentally, as a critic of knowledge must take it, is the most irrational, animal, and primitive of beliefs: it is the voice of hunger. But when, as I must, I have yielded to this presumption, and proceeded to explore the world, I shall find in its constitution the most beautiful justification for my initial faith, and the proof of its secret rationality. This corroboration will not have any logical force, since it will be only pragmatic, based on begging the question, and perhaps only a bribe offered by fortune to confirm my illusions. The force of the corroboration will be merely moral, showing me how appropriate and harmonious with the nature of things such a blind belief was on my part. How else should the truth have been revealed to me at all? Truth and blindness, in such a case, are correlatives, since I am a sensitive creature surrounded by a universe utterly out of scale with myself: I must, therefore, address it questioningly but trustfully, and it must reply to me in my own terms, in symbols and parables, that only gradually enlarge my childish perceptions. It is as if Substance said to Knowledge: My child, there is a great world for thee to conquer, but it is a vast, an ancient, and a recalcitrant world. It yields wonderful treasures to courage, when courage is guided by art and respects the limits set to it by nature. I should not have been so cruel as to give thee birth, if there had been nothing for thee to master; but having first prepared the field, I set in thy heart the love of adventure.

The Implied Being of Truth

From the beginning of discourse there is a subtle reality posited which is not a thing: I mean the truth. If intuition of essence exists anywhere without discourse, the being of truth need not be posited there, because intuition of itself is intransitive, and having no object other than the datum, can be neither true nor false. Every essence picked up by intuition is equally real in its own sphere; and every degree of articulation reached in intuition defines one of a series of essences, each contained in or containing its neighbour, and each equally central in that infinite progression. The central one, for apprehension, is the one that happens to appear at the moment. Therefore in pure intuition there is no fear of picking up the wrong thing, as if the object were a designated existence in the natural world; and therefore the being of truth is not broached in pure intuition.

Truth is not broached even in pure dialectic, which is only the apprehension of a system of essences so complex and finely articulated, perhaps, as to tax human attention, or outrun it if unaided by some artifice of notation, but essentially only an essence like any other. Truth, therefore, is as irrelevant to dialectic as to merely æsthetic intuition. Logic and mathematics are not true inherently, however cogent or extensive. They are ideal constructions based on ideal axioms; and the question of truth or falsity does not arise in respect to them unless the dialectic is asserted to apply to the natural world, or perhaps when a dispute comes up as to the precise essence signified by some word, such as, for instance, infinity.

When men first invented language and other symbols, or fixed in reflection the master-images of their dreams and thoughts, it seemed to them that they were discovering parts of nature, and that even in those developments they must be either right or wrong. There was a *true* name for every object, a part of its nature. There was a *true* logic, and a *true* ethics, and a *true* religion. Certainly in so far as these mixed disciplines were assertions about alleged facts, they were either right or wrong; but in so far as they were systems of essences, woven together in fancy to express the instincts of the mind, they were only more or less expressive and fortunate and harmonious, but not at all

true or false. Dialectic, though so fine-spun and sustained, is really a more primitive, a more dream-like, exercise of intuition than are animal faith and natural science. It is more spontaneous and less responsible, less controlled by secondary considerations, as poetry is in contrast with prose. If only the animals had a language, or some other fixed symbols to develop in thought, I should be inclined to believe them the greatest of dialecticians and the greatest of poets. But as they seem not to speak, and there is no ground for supposing that they rehearse their feelings reflectively in discourse, I will suppose them to be very empty-headed when they are not very busy; but I may be doing them an injustice. In any case their dreams would not suggest to them the being of truth; and even their external experience may hardly do so.

It might seem, perhaps, that truth must be envisaged even by the animals in action, when things are posited; especially as uncertainty and change of tactics and purpose are often visible in their attitudes. Certainly truth is there, if the thing pursued is such as the animal presumes it to be; and in searching for it in the right quarter and finding it, he enacts a true belief and a true perception, even if he does not realise them spiritually. What he realises spiritually, I suppose, is the pressure of the situation in which he finds himself, and the changes in his object; but that his belief from moment to moment was right or wrong he probably never notices. Truth would then not come within his purview, nor be distinguished amongst his interests. He would want to be successful, not to be right.

So in a man, intent experience, when not reflective, need not disclose the being of truth. Sometimes, in a vivid dream, objects suffer a transformation to which I eagerly adapt myself, changing my feelings and actions with complete confidence in the new facts; and I never ask myself which view was true, and which action appropriate. I live on in perfect faith, never questioning the present circumstances as they appear, nor do I follow my present policy with less assurance than I did the opposite policy a moment before. This happens to me in dreams; but politicians do the same thing in real life, when the lives of

From *Scepticism and Animal Faith* (New York: Dover, 1955), pp. 262–271.

nations are at stake. In general I think that the impulse of action is translated into a belief in changed things long before it reproaches itself with having made any error about them. The recognition of a truth to be discerned may thus be avoided; because although a belief in things must actually be either true or false, it is directed upon the present existence and character of these things, not upon its own truth. The active object posited alone interests the man of action; if he were interested in the rightness of the action, he would not be a man of action but a philosopher. So long as things continue to be perceived in one form or another, and can be posited accordingly, the active impulse is released, and the machine runs on prosperously until some hitch comes, or some catastrophe. It is then always the things that are supposed to have changed, not the forms of folly. Even the most pungent disappointment, as when a man loses a bet, is not regarded otherwise than as a misfortune. It is all the fault of the dice; they might and ought to have turned up differently. This, I say to myself, is an empirical world; all is novelty in it, and it is luck and free will that are to blame. My bet was really right when I made it; there was no error about the future then, for I acted according to the future my fancy painted, which was the only future there was. My act was a creative act of vitality and courage; but afterwards things accountably went wrong, and betrayed their own promise.

I am confirmed in this surmise about the psychology of action by the reasoning of empirical and romantic philosophers, who cling to this instinctive attitude and deny the being of truth. No substance exists, according to their view, but only things as they seem from moment to moment; so that it is idle to contrast opinion with truth, seeing that there is nothing, not even things, except in opinion. They can easily extend this view to the future of opinion or of experience, and maintain that the future does not exist except in expectation; and at a pinch, although the flesh may rebel against such heroic subjectivism, they may say that the past, too, exists only in memory, and that no other past can be thought of or talked about; so that there is no truth, other than current opinion, even about the past. If an opinion about the past, they say, seems problematical when it stands alone, we need but corroborate it by another opinion about the past in order to make it true. In other words, though the word truth is familiar to these philosophers, the idea of it is unintelligible to

them, and absent altogether from their apprehension of the world.

The experience which perhaps makes even the empiricist awake to the being of truth, and brings it home to any energetic man, is the experience of other people lying. When I am falsely accused, or when I am represented as thinking what I do not think, I rebel against that contradiction to my evident self-knowledge; and as the other man asserts that the liar is myself, and a third person might very well entertain that hypothesis and decide against me, I learn that a report may fly in the face of the facts. There is, I then see clearly, a comprehensive standard description for every fact, which those who report it as it happened repeat in part, whereas on the contrary liars contradict it in some particular. And a little further reflection may convince me that even the liar must recognise the fact to some extent, else it would not be *that* fact that he was misrepresenting; and also that honest memory and belief, even when most unimpeachable, are not exhaustive and not themselves the standard for belief or for memory, since they are now clearer and now vaguer, and subject to error and correction. That standard comprehensive description of any fact which neither I nor any man can ever wholly repeat, is the truth about it.

The being of truth thus seems to be first clearly posited in disputation; and a consequence of this accident (for it is an accident from the point of view of the truth itself under what circumstances men most easily acknowledge its authority)—a consequence is that truth is often felt to be somehow inseparable from rival opinions; so that people say that if there was no mind and consequently no error there could be no truth. They mean, I suppose, that nothing can be correct or incorrect except some proposition or judgement regarding some specific fact; and that the same constitution of the fact which renders one description correct, renders any contradictory description erroneous. "Truth" is often used in this abstract sense for correctness, or the quality which all correct judgements have in common; and another word, perhaps "fact" or "reality," would then have to be used for that standard comprehensive description of the object to which correct judgements conform. But a fact is not a description of itself; and as to the word "reality," if it is understood to mean existence, it too cannot designate a description, which is an essence only. Facts are transitory, and any part of existence to which a definite judgement is addressed is transitory too; and when they have lapsed, it is only their essence that subsists and that, being partially recovered and assigned to them in a retrospective judgement, can render this judgement true. Opinions are true or false by repeating or contradicting some part of the truth about the facts which they envisage; and this truth about the facts is the standard comprehensive description of them—something in the realm of essence, but more than the essence of any fact present within the limits of time and space which that fact occupies; for a comprehensive description includes also all the radiations of that fact—I mean, all that perspective of the world of facts and of the realm of essence which is obtained by taking this fact as a centre and viewing everything else only in relation with it. The truth about any fact is therefore infinitely extended, although it grows thinner, so to speak, as you travel from it to further and further facts, or to less and less relevant ideas. It is the splash any fact makes, or the penumbra it spreads, by dropping through the realm of essence. Evidently no opinion can embrace it all, or identify itself with it; nor can it be identified with the facts to which it relates, since they are in flux, and it is eternal.

The word truth ought, I think, to be reserved for what everybody spontaneously means by it: the standard comprehensive description of any fact in all its relations. Truth is not an opinion, even an ideally true one; because besides the limitation in scope which human opinions, at least, can never escape, even the most complete and accurate opinion would give precedence to some terms, and have a direction of survey; and this direction might be changed or reversed without lapsing into error; so that the truth is the field which various true opinions traverse in various directions, and no opinion itself. An even more impressive difference between truth and any true discourse is that discourse is an event; it has a date not that of its subject-matter, even if the subject-matter be existential and roughly contemporary; and in human beings it is conversant almost entirely with the past only, whereas truth is dateless and absolutely identical whether the opinions which seek to reproduce it arise before or after the event which the truth describes.

The eternity of truth is inherent in it: all truths—not a few grand ones—are equally eternal. I am sorry that the word eternal should necessarily have an unction which prejudices dry minds against it, and leads fools to use it without understanding. This unction is not rhetorical, because the nature of truth is really sublime, and its name ought to mark its

sublimity. Truth is one of the realities covered in the eclectic religion of our fathers by the idea of God. Awe very properly hangs about it, since it is the immovable standard and silent witness of all our memories and assertions; and the past and the future, which in our anxious life are so differently interesting and so differently dark, are one seamless garment for the truth, shining like the sun. It is not necessary to offer any evidence for this eternity of truth, because truth is not an existence that asks to be believed in, and that may be denied. It is an essence involved in positing any fact, in remembering, expecting, or asserting anything; and while no truth need be acknowledged if no existence is believed in, and none would obtain if there was no existence in fact, yet on the hypothesis that anything exists, truth has appeared, since this existence must have one character rather than another, so that only one description of it in terms of essence will be complete; and this complete description, covering all its relations, will be the truth about it. No one who understands what is meant by this eternal being of truth can possibly deny it; so that no argument is required to support it, but only enough intensity of attention to express what we already believe.

Inspired people, who are too hot to think, often identify the truth with their own tenets, to signify by a bold hyperbole how certain they feel in their faith; but the effect is rather that they lead foolish people, who may see that this faith may be false, to suppose that therefore the truth may be false also. Eternal truths, in the mouth of both parties, are then tenets which the remotest ancestors of man are reputed to have held, and which his remotest descendants are forbidden to abandon. Of course there are no eternal tenets: neither the opinions of men, nor mankind, nor anything existent can be eternal; eternity is a property of essences only. Even if all the spirits in heaven and earth had been so far unanimous on any point of doctrine, there is no reason, except the monotony and inertia of nature, why their logic or religion or morals should not change to-morrow from top to bottom, if they all suddenly grew wiser or differently foolish.

At the risk of being scholastic I will suggest the uses to which the word eternal and the terms akin to it might be confined if they were made exact.

A thing that occupied but one point of physical time would be *instantaneous*. No essence is instantaneous, because none occupies any part of physical time or space; and I doubt whether any existence is instantaneous either; for if the mathematicians decide that the continuous or extended must be composed of an infinite number of inextended and non-contiguous units, in bowing to their authority I should retain a suspicion that nothing actual is confined to any of these units, but that the smallest event has duration and contains an infinite number of such units; so that one event (though not one instant) can be contiguous to another.

A given essence containing no specious temporal progression or perspective between its parts would be *timeless*. Colour, for instance, or number, is timeless. The timeless often requires to be abstracted from the total datum, because round any essence as actually given there is an atmosphere of duration and persistence, suggesting the existential flux of nature behind the essence. Colour seems to shine, that is, to vibrate. Number seems to mount, and to be built up. The timeless is therefore better illustrated in objects like laws or equations or definitions, which though intent on things in time, select relations amongst them which are not temporal.

A being that should have no external temporal relations and no locus in physical time would be *dateless*. Thus every given essence and every specious present is dateless, internally considered, and taken transcendentally, that is, as a station for viewing other things or a unit framing them in. Though dateless, the specious present is not timeless, and an instant, though timeless, is not dateless.

Whatsoever, having once arisen, never perishes, would be *immortal*. I believe there is nothing immortal.

Whatsoever exists through a time infinite in both directions is *everlasting*. Matter, time, the life of God, souls as Plato conceived them, and the laws of nature are commonly believed to be everlasting. In the nature of the case this can be only a presumption.

That which without existing is contemporary with all times is *eternal*. Truth is dateless and eternal, but not timeless, because, being descriptive of existence, it is a picture of change. It is frozen history. As Plato said that time was a moving image of eternity, we might say that eternity was a synthetic image of time. But it is much more than that, because, besides the description of all temporal things in their temporal relations, it contains everything that is not temporal at all; in other words, the whole realm of essence, as well as the whole realm of truth.

Discernment of Spirit

Is the existence of spirit evident to spirit, and involved in the presence of anything? Is its nature simple and obvious? I think there is something of which this may be said, but not of spirit; for by spirit I understand not only the passive intuition implied in any essences being given, but also the understanding and belief that may greet their presence. Even passive intuition is no datum; there is nothing evident except the given essence itself. Yet, as I have seen above, the mere prolongation of this presence, the recognition of this essence as identical with itself, and the survey of its elements in various orders, very soon impose upon me a distinction between this essence and my intuition of it. This intuition is a fact and an event, as the essence cannot be; so that even if spirit meant nothing but pure consciousness or the activity of a transcendental ego, it would need

to be posited, in view of the felt continuity of discourse, and could not be an element in the given essences. If spirit were defined as the common quality of all appearances, distinguishing them from the rest of the realm of essence which does not appear, spirit would be reduced to an appearance itself. It would be like light, something seen, a luminousness in all objects, not what I understand by it, which is the seeing; not the coloured lights I may observe, but the exercise of sight as distinguished from blindness.

The common quality of all appearances is not spirit but mere Being; that simple and always obvious element to which I referred just now as given in all essences without distinction, and which some philosophers and saints have found so unutterably precious. This is all that is common to all possible appearances,

From *Scepticism and Animal Faith* (New York: Dover, 1955), pp. 272–288.

considered in themselves; but animal tension is not altogether absent even in this abstruse contemplation, and the sense that appearances are assaulting *me* thickens my intuition of their essence into an apprehension of existence, which existence, having no idea of myself, I of course attribute to them, or to the abstract common element in their essences, pure Being, which thus becomes in my eyes absolute existence.

The present stimulus that awakens me out of my material lethargy and keeps my attention more or less taut is not spirit, although, of course, the birth of spirit is involved in my awakening. That stimulus is the strain and rumble of the universal flux, audible in my little sea-shell. It preserves the same groundtone (that of a disturbance or a strain) no matter what image it may bring forth, or even if it brings forth no images but only a pervasive sense of swimming in safety and bliss. This budding sentiment of existence is a recognition not of spirit but of substance, of fact, of force, of an unfathomable mystery.

By spirit I understand the light of discrimination that marks in that pure Being differences of essence, of time, of place, of value; a living light ready to fall upon things, as they are spread out in their weight and motion and variety, ready to be lighted up. Spirit is a fountain of clearness, decidedly wind-blown and spasmodic, and possessing at each moment the natural and historical actuality of an event, not the imputed or specious actuality of a datum. Spirit, in a word, is no phenomenon, not sharing the æsthetic sort of reality proper to essences when given, nor that other sort proper to dynamic and material things; its peculiar sort of reality is to be intelligence in act. Spirit, or the intuitions in which it is realised, accordingly forms a new realm of being, silently implicated in the apparition of essences and in the felt pressure of nature, but requiring the existence of nature to create it, and to call up those essences before it. By spirit essences are transposed into appearances and things into objects of belief; and (as if to compensate them for that derogation from their native status) they are raised to a strange actuality in thought—a moral actuality which in their logical being or their material flux they had never aspired to have: like those rustics and servants at an inn whom a travelling poet may take note of and afterwards, to their astonishment, may put upon the stage with applause.

It is implied in these words, when taken as they are meant, that spirit is not a reality that can be observed; it does not figure among the *dramatis personæ* of the play it witnesses. As the author, nature, and the actors, things, do not emerge from the prompter's box, or remove their make-up so as to exhibit themselves to me in their unvarnished persons, but are satisfied that I should know them only as artists (and I for my part am perfectly willing to stop there in my acquaintance with them); so the spirit in me which their art serves is content not to be put on the stage; that would be far from being a greater honour, or expressing a truer reality, than that which belongs to it as spectator, virtually addressed and consulted and required in everything that the theatre contrives. Spirit can never be observed as an essence is observed, nor encountered as a thing is encountered. It must be enacted; and the essence of it (for of course it has an essence) can be described only circumstantially, and suggested pregnantly. It is actualised in actualising something else, an image or a feeling or an intent or a belief; and it can be discovered only by implication in all discourse, when discourse itself has been posited. The witnesses to the existence of spirit are therefore the same as those to the existence of discourse; but when once discourse is admitted, the existence of spirit in it becomes self-evident; because discourse is a perusal of essence, or its recurring presence to spirit.

Now in discourse there is more than passive intuition; there is intent. This element also implies spirit, and in spirit as man possesses it intent or intelligence is almost always the dominant element. For this reason I shall find it impossible, when I come to consider the realm of spirit, to identify spirit with simple awareness, or with consciousness in the abstract sense of this abused word. Pure awareness or consciousness suffices to exemplify spirit; and there may be cold spirits somewhere that have merely that function; but it is not the only function that only spirits could perform; and the human spirit, having intent, expectation, belief, and eagerness, runs much thicker than that. Spirit is a category, not an individual being: and just as the realm of essence contains an infinite number of essences, each different from the rest, and each nothing but an essence, so the realm of spirit may contain any number of forms of spirit, each nothing but a spiritual fact. Spirit is a fruition, and there are naturally as many qualities of fruition as there are fruits to ripen. Spirit is accordingly qualified by the types of life it actualises, and is individuated by the occasions on which it actualises them. Each occasion generates an intuition numerically distinct, and brings to light an essence qualitatively different. . . .

Thus intelligence in man, being the spiritual transcript of an animal life, is transitional and impassioned. It approaches its objects by a massive attack, groping for them and tentatively spying them before it discovers them unmistakably. It is energetic and creative, in the sense of slowly focussing its object within the field of intuition in the midst of felt currents with a felt direction, themselves the running expression of animal endeavours. All this intuition of turbulence and vitality, which a cold immortal spirit could never know, fills the spirit of man, and renders any contemplation of essences in their own realm only an interlude for him or a sublimation or an incapacity. It also renders him more conscious than a purer spirit would be of his own spirit. For just as I was able to find evidence of intuition in discourse, which in the motionless vision of essence would have eluded me, so in intent, expectation, belief, and emotion, the being of my thoughts rises up and almost hides the vision of my object. Although I myself am a substance in flux, on the same level as the material thing that confronts me, the essences that reveal my own being are dramatic and moral, whereas those that express the thing are sensuous; and these dramatic and moral essences, although their presence involves spirit exactly in the same way, and no more deeply, than the presence of the sensuous essences does, yet seem to suggest its presence more directly and more voluminously.

Hence the popular identification of spirit with the heart, the breath, the blood, or the brain; and the notion that my substantial self and the spirit within me are identical. In fact, they are the opposite poles of my being, and I am neither the one nor the other exclusively. If I am spiritually proud and choose to identify myself with the spirit, I shall be compelled to regard my earthly person and my human thoughts as the most alien and the sorriest of accidents; and my surprise and mortification will never cease at the way in which my body and its world monopolise my attention. If on the contrary I modestly plead guilty to being the biped that I seem, I shall be obliged to take the spirit within me for a divine stranger, in whose heaven it is not given me to live, but who miraculously walks in my garden in the cool of the evening. Yet in reality, incarnation is no anomaly, and the spirit is no intruder. It is as much at home in any animal as in any heaven. In me, it takes my point of view; it is

the voice of my humanity; and what other mansions it may have need not trouble me. Each will provide a suitable shrine for its resident deity and its native oracle. It is a prejudice to suppose that spirit is contaminated by the flesh; it is generated there; and the more varied its instruments and sources are, the more copiously it will be manifested, and the more unmistakably.

. . . Let me turn to the most intellectual powers of spirit—attention, synthesis, perception. These too are voices loudly issuing from the heart of material existence, and proclaiming their origin there not only by their occasions and external connections, but by their inmost moral nature. Why does the spirit stop to collect or to recollect anything? Why not range undisturbed and untrammelled over image after image, without referring one to another or attempting (always in vain) to preserve the design of vanished images, or the order of their appearance, even through the lapse of the sensible elements that filled them in? Because the animal is forming habits. The psyche is plastic; no impression can endure unchanged, as if it had been a substantial little thing in itself, and not a mode, a ripple, in an inherited, transmissible, ever rejuvenated substance. Scarcely is the impression received, but it merges in the general sensitiveness or responsiveness of the organ affected, modifying its previous way of reacting on some natural object, an object reported not by that impression alone, but by many others: so that the synthetic unity of apperception (that most radical of transcendental principles) obeys a compulsion peculiar to animal economy, which no pure spirit would need to share, the compulsion to use things as materials, to drop them and forge ahead, or to eat and to digest them: for the drinking in of light through the eyes, or of currents from other organs, thereby rearranging the habits of the nervous system, is very like the consumption of food, restoring the vegetative functions. Synthesis in thought, correlation, scope, or (as the phrase is) taking things in, is laborious piety on the spirit's part in subservience to the flesh. It is the mental fruit of training, of care: an inner possession rewarding an outer fidelity.

Pure spirit would never need to *apperceive* at all; this is an animal exigency that distracts it from intuition. There is unity in intuition too, of a nebulous sort, as there must be unity in the universe, since it is all there is, however loose its structure or unmarked its limits. Yet in intuition, as in cloud-land, the field is in the act of changing pervasively; every part shifts more or less. Any feature you may distinguish fades and refashions itself irresponsibly; and pure spirit would be perfectly content that it should do so. Perhaps, if it was a young spirit, it would positively whip up the hoop, or blow and distend the bubble, for the fun of seeing it run or burst more gloriously; and it would be happy to think there was no harm done, and nothing left over. The scene would then be cleared for something utterly fresh. The synthetic unity of apperception is something imposed by things on animals, when these things exercise a seductive charm or threaten mischief. Attention cries halt, it reconnoitres, it takes note, it throws a lassoo over the horses of Poseidon, lord of the flux. And why? Because the organs of spirit are structures; they are mechanisms instituted in nature to keep doing certain things, roughly appropriate to the enviroment, itself roughly constant. It is to this approximate fixity of function and habit that spirit owes its distinct ideas, the names it gives to things, and its faith in things, which is a true revelation of their existence—knowledge of them stored for use.

Perception, too, would be a miracle and an impossibility to a spirit conceived as alien to matter. Perception is a stretching forth of intent beyond intuition; it is an exercise of intelligence. Intelligence, the most ideal function of spirit, is precisely its point of closest intimacy with matter, of most evident subservience to material modes of being. The life of matter (at least on the human scale, if not at every depth) is a flux, a passage from this to that, almost forbidding anything to be simply itself, by immediately turning it, in some respect, into something different. If the psyche were a closed round of motions, the spirit it generated (if it generated spirit at all) would certainly not be perceptive or cognitive, but in some way emotional or musical—the music of those spheres. But the round of motions which the psyche is actually wound up to make must be executed in a changeful and precarious environment, not to speak of changes in her own substance. She must hunt, fight, find a mate, protect the offspring, defend the den and the treasure. Perception, intelligence, knowledge accurately transcribe this mode of being, profoundly alien to repose in intuition or to drifting reverie. Perception points to what it does not, save by pointing, know to exist; knowledge is only of the past or the future, both of which are absent; and intelligence talks and talks to an interlocutor—the mind of another

man or god or an eventual self of one's own—whom it can never see and whose replies, conveyed (if at all) through material channels, it is never sure exist morally, or could be understood if they did exist. There is no dilemma in the choice between animal faith and reason, because reason is only a form of animal faith, and utterly unintelligible dialectically, although full of a pleasant alacrity and confidence, like the chirping of birds. The suasion of sanity is physical: if you cut your animal traces, you run mad.

. . . Fact can never be explained, since only another fact could explain it: therefore the existence of a universe rather than no universe, or of one sort of universe rather than another, must be accepted without demur. In this very irrationality or contingency of existence, which is inevitable in any case, I find a clue to the strange presence of spirit in this world. Spirit, the wakefulness of attention, could not have arisen of its own accord; it contains no bias, no principle of choice, but is an impartial readiness to know. It never could have preferred one thing to another, nor preferred existence for itself to non-existence, nor *vice versa*. Attention is not a principle that can select the themes that shall attract attention: to select them it must already have thought of them. As far as its own nature is concerned, attention is equally ready to fall on the just and on the unjust; spirit is equally ready to speak any language, to quicken any body, and to adopt any interest. An instance of spirit cannot be determined by spirit itself either in its occasion, its intensity, or the æsthetic character of the essence presented to it. Chance, matter, fate—some non-spiritual principle or other—must have determined what the spirit in me shall behold, and what it shall endure. Some internal fatality, their own brute existence and wilfulness, must be responsible for the fact that things are as they are, and not otherwise. If any instance of spirit was to arise anywhere, the ground of it (if I speak of grounds at all) must have been irrational. Spirit has the innocence of a child; it pleads not guilty; at most it has become, without knowing how, an accomplice after the fact. It is astonished at everything. It is essentially, wherever it may be found, unsubstantial and expressive; it is essentially secondary. Even if in fact some instance of spirit, some isolated intuition, sprang miraculously into being in an absolute void, and nothing else had ever existed or would exist, yet logically and in its own eyes that intuition would be secondary, since no principle internal to spirit, but only brute chance, would be expressed in the existence of that intuition, and in the arbitrary choice of the essence that happened to appear there. Spirit is therefore of its very nature and by its own confession the voice of something else: it speaks not of itself, but of the Father that sent it. I am accordingly prepared to find some arbitrary world or other in existence; and since this arbitrary world obviously has spirit in it, my problem is reduced to inquiring what features, in this arbitrary existing world, can have called spirit forth and made it their living witness.

. . . The investigation of substance and of the laws of events is the province of physics, and I call everything that science may discover in that direction physical and not spiritual. Even if the substance of things should be sentiency, or a bevy of souls, or a single intense Absolute, it would be nothing but matter to what I call spirit. It would exercise only material functions in kindling the flame of actual intuition, and bearing my light thoughts like bubbles upon its infinite flood. I do not know what matter is in itself: but what metaphysical idealists call spirit, if it is understood to be responsible for what goes on in the world and in myself, and to be the reality of these appearances, is, in respect to my spiritual existence, precisely what I call matter; and I find the description of this matter which the natural sciences supply much more interesting than that given by the idealists, much more beautiful, and much more likely to be true. That there is no spirit in the interstices of matter, where the magicians look for it, nor at the heart of matter, where many metaphysicians would place it, needs no proof to one who understands what spirit is; because spirit is in another realm of being altogether, and needs the being and movement of matter, by its large sweeping harmonies, to generate it, and give it wings. It would be a pity to abandon this consecrated word to those who are grubbing for the atoms of substance, or speculating about a logic in history, or tabulating the capers of ghosts; especially as there is the light of intuition, the principle of actuality in vision and feeling, to call by that name. The popular uses of the word spiritual support this definition of it; because intuition, when it thoroughly dominates animal experience, transmutes it into pure flame, and renders it religious or poetical, which is what is commonly meant by spiritual.

Some Meanings of the Word "Is"

Language is Loose because Significant.—Words, as Bacon said, are wise men's counters, they mark some gain or some wager of thought. If they prejudice philosophy, they contain philosophy. The articulation of language, however, can never be the articulation of things. Language is a by-product of animal life which may eventually serve as a record or as an instrument; it helps to summarize, classify, and analyze man's contact with the world, reducing things to human perspectives on a human scale. Nor can language preserve the scope or movement even of thought, since it marks only certain terms or *termini*—boundary stones like statues at the end of vistas—on which attention is sharply arrested; the approach, the atmosphere, and the setting remain unnamed. A word cannot be adequate if it has a meaning at all; only whistling is adequate. Significant speech is a lasso thrown into the air, lucky if it catches some living thing by a leg or by a horn. It would be idle as well as ungrateful to quarrel with words when one must use them; but in venturing upon a long discourse it may be prudent to notice the degree to which some important term abbreviates the facts it stands for, or puts them under an alien category; and since I am about to distinguish various realms of being, I will begin with some consideration of the word "*is*," for this little word has many meanings.

First meaning of the word "is": Identity.—Of these meanings the most radical and proper is that in which I may say of any thing that it is what it is. This asservation does not commit me to any description of the object nor to any assertion of its existence. I merely note its idiosyncrasy as a particular counter in the pile,

From *Obiter Scripta: Lectures, Essays and Reviews,* eds. Justus Buchler and Benjamin Schwartz (New York: Charles Scribner's Sons, 1936), pp. 189–212.

something which, whatever it may be, is that object and no other. Its qualitative identity enables me to distinguish it, to study it, and to hold it fast in thought, so that I may eventually frame a definition of it, and perhaps assert or deny its existence. The copula properly denotes this singular and exclusive identity of each term with itself; not only in the abstract case of *A is A,* but also when the term (*e.g.,* the triangle) is specifically determined up to a certain degree of articulation (*e.g.,* as a plane enclosed by three straight lines); an articulation which the verb "*to be*" (when I say, Let *a, b, c* be a triangle) registers and posits, so as to permit me to identify the object in question; for if an object had no specific character, it would be meaningless to say that *it* was before me or was the theme of my discourse.

That what I see, I see, or what I am, I am, may seem a vain assertion; practical minds are not interested in any thing except for the sake of something else. They are camp-followers or heralds of the flux of nature, without self-possession. Yet if that which is actual and obvious at the moment never had a satisfying character, no satisfaction would ever be possible, and life would be what a romantic philosophy would make it—a wild-goose chase. In reality, to a simple or to a recollected spirit, the obvious often is enough. Its identity may have a deep charm, like that of a jewel. I may long ruminate upon it, and impress it upon myself by repetitions, as when, fixing my mind's eye on some essence ideally determinate, I say to myself "No, no," or "Business is business." The repetition serves to detach and to render indubitable the essence meant, so that my judgment may recognize it to the exclusion of circumstances, which do not alter essences.

Identity the principle of essence.—This being the most radical intimate meaning of the word "*is,*" I have felt justified in usurping the term "*essence,*" derived from the same root, to designate any ideal or formal nature, any thing always necessarily identical with itself. Essence so understood much more truly *is* than any substance or any experience or any event: for a substance, event, or experience may change its form or may exist only by changing it, so that all sorts of things that are proper to it in one phase will be absent from it in another. It will not be a unit at all, save by external delimitation. Perhaps some abstract constancy in quantity, energy, or continuity may be discovered to run through it, but this constant element will never be the actual experience, event, or substance in its living totality at any moment.

Or perhaps all the phases of such an existence may be viewed together and synthesized into one historical picture; but this picture would again not be the existent substance, experience, or event unrolling itself in act. It would be only a description of that portion of the flux seen under the form of eternity; in other words, it would be an essence and not an existence. Essence is just that character which any existence wears in so far as it remains identical with itself and so long as it does so; the very character which it throws overboard by changing, and loses altogether when it becomes something else. To be able to become something else, to suffer change and yet endure, is the privilege of existence, be it in a substance, an event, or an experience; whereas essences can be exchanged, but not changed. Existence at every step casts off one essence and picks up another: we call it the same existence when we are able to trace its continuity in change, by virtue of its locus and proportions; but often we are constrained to give up the count, and to speak of a new event, a new thing, or a new experience. The essences or forms traversed in mutation render this mutation possible and describable: without their eternal distinctness no part of the flux could differ in any respect from any other part, and the whole world would collapse into a lump without order or quality. So much more profound is the eternal being of the essences traversed in change, than that of the matter or attention or discourse which plays with those essences at touch and go.

Notion of the Realm of Essence.—Nothing, then, more truly *is* than character. Without this wedding garment no guest is admitted to the feast of existence: whereas the unbidden essences do not require that invitation (with which very low characters are sometimes honoured) in order to preserve their proud identity out in the cold. There those few privileged revellers will soon have to rejoin them, not a whit fatter for their brief surfeit of being. After things lose their existence, as before they attain it, although it is true of them that they have existed or will exist, they have no internal being except their essences, quite as if they had never broached Existence at all: yet the identity of each essence with itself and difference from every other essence suffices to distinguish and define them all in eternity, where they form the Realm of Essence. True and false assertions may be made about any one of them, such, for instance, as that it does not exist; or that it includes or excludes some other essence, or is included or excluded by it.

Transition to Looser Meanings: Posited or Problematical Identities.—Nevertheless, the hypnotic charm of identity, or the dialectic pattern of essences, soon wearies a restive animal and seems to him idiotic. Having once observed and established the identity of every essence with itself, I may well turn to something else and put the word "*is*" to more pregnant uses. Identity itself will interest me more when, being that of a thing and not of an essence, it becomes problematical. I shall then be intent, not on some term directly present to intuition, but on some ulterior term signified by one or more different symbols themselves given immediately. The identity of things and persons is regularly masked in this way by their various names or appearances, so that their identity may be denied by the sceptic, and the assertion of it, far from being trivial, may be instructive, surprising or tragic. Thus pointing to a stranger in rags I may say: "This is Odysseus, the King"; or I may discover that XI is eleven, or that 11 is 7×4. Evidently such identifications do not intend to identify the two terms in their immediacy: the present aspect of Odysseus is not that of a king, those two Roman letters are not the English word "eleven," nor is one of those arithmetical symbols actually the other. So when I say "This is John," it would not be a very penetrating criticism of my poor human logic to argue that I was confusing a man with a sound, and pronouncing them identical. The identity is that of John with himself, an intended and existing object. The sound of his name and his image to sight are converging symbols, both signifying the same living person, with his ancestry and continuity in the material world. This term, posited as identical with itself, is removed from immediacy and belongs to a plane of being believed in by me, which if my animal faith misleads me need not exist at all: yet even in that case, I should be setting up a fixed theme of discourse, to which ulterior ideas might also be relevant; as when I point to a picture and say: "This is not Saint George but the Archangel Michael, because he has wings." I am content if the hints of sense, fused in the heat of recognition, lead me to some staunch ideal identity.

Second Meaning: Equivalence.—I may, however, be less concerned with the ulterior essence or thing through which two different symbols are identified than in the diversity of the symbols themselves. It is silly to urge that water is water, but interesting to note that *aqua* is *eau*. Where the native word carries the mind straight to the object, the foreign words interpose their own idiosyncrasy, and I not only notice their presence, but the fact that they have no resemblance whatever to the object they signify. They lead a life of their own, the life of sense or of language, in which touch may be sharpened into smell or sight, and a Latin word may become a French one which retains none of the original sounds, yet has exactly the same meaning. I thus learn that words and sensations may signify the same thing in endlessly different ways; and when some monoglot idiot balks at this wealth of synonyms (like Pierrot willing to touch a "dead man" but not a "corpse"), I can rebuke him by saying, "But it's the same thing!" The thing is indeed the same, but not the æsthetic essences that symbolize it to the fancy. So when Walt Whitman exclaims, "Alabama, Minnesota, Maryland, Vermont!" if his inspiration had not faltered and he had completed the list, the poetic essence of that catalogue would not be identical with the single cry, "The United States!" Attention forms individuals. When the parts are taken separately, each is at the centre of the world, and stops at its own boundary: when they are taken together, no boundaries are visible and many a feature found in one part may form a unit, like a river or a road, with a feature continuing it in another part. Sometimes, too, when two very different expressions are alleged to be equivalent, the identification of their objects seems doubtful or even shocking: as if instead of six square yards of carpet I am offered 7776 square inches of it, or a vote instead of freedom, or the most real of beings instead of God.

Equivalent terms coupled by the word "*is*" are, accordingly, far from identical; and even if the identity of the object meant to be granted, the substitution of one term for the other may make an important difference to the lover of form, thought, or language. Even in matters of business, there is a choice of methods and manners; if you pay a bill in gold or in coppers, by cheque or in bank-notes, the sum may be the same, but the action and the experience are different. The medium in such a transaction may seem irrelevant, but some medium is indispensable, and the interest in the choice of that medium is ineradicable: because the immediate is always with us.

Now in philosophy there is a medium which plays a great part, namely, thought. Thought is an outsider in respect to the things, facts, events, and essences which it considers; for although thought is itself an event and has an essence, it cannot at the time consider that fact. Even that which it considers it cannot exhaust. It identifies, connects, and describes its objects not according to their intrinsic natures but according to their names or images in discourse, and to the dialectical relations of these names or images.

Third Meaning: Definition.—Hence the importance which some philosophers give to definition. They are always asking you to tell them *what* some natural object is—man, matter, time, God—as if any definition whatever which you might offer of such deep-lying realities would be likely to come nearer to the thing as it is than do current names, sundry indications, or even the sum total of your discourse on that subject. Man, they say, *is* a rational animal: a circle *is* a plane figure bounded by a curve every part of which is equally distant from a point within the centre. These definitions may be correct; but if I had no independent knowledge of what a man or a circle was, I could not judge whether they were correct or not. Pure discourse likes to take the bit in its teeth; and a geometer might tell me that he need have no notion whatever of the circle save that which the definition gives him, and that all his deductions would follow just as well from that premise; indeed, it is only from that premise that they must follow if they are to be valid mathematically. The definition of the circle *is* the circle for the geometer. It would therefore be better, and worthier of the purity of deductive science, to drop such terms as circle, which suggests wheels, round eyes, and other vulgar objects, and to invent a symbol or formula to express the definition only, without any images borrowed from sense.

I believe this is the right method of dialectic; and if it is rigorously employed, it keeps discourse revolving about essences alone, and only about such essences as it has explicitly selected. But then, let it be remembered, these essences are not alleged to be the essences of anything existing. What follows from the algebraic formula for the circle is not alleged to hold good of hoops or rose-windows or the course of the planets. So that when any material, visible, or imagined circle is said to *be* a circle in the mathematical sense, the assertion is worse than false: it is irrelevant. Nothing can *be* the definition of it: at best the definition may be true of it. No definition, and no dialectic proceeding from the definition, can vouch for this natural truth. Only animal faith, trust in appearances, or experience in practical arts can justify such a presumption, or can even propose it. Definition is therefore perfectly

useless for natural knowledge; but it is, when strictly adhered to, a fountain of deductions which are unimpeachable in themselves, although their relevance to matters of fact is problematical, and can only be asserted by one who knows those facts independently.

Definitions are complex names and they have the same function as names. They cannot repeat the essence of a thing, because its essence is its whole texture and character. An adequate definition of any existing thing would be as complicated as the thing itself, and true only of that individual, or of such others, if any, as were indistinguishable from it internally. Nevertheless, like names, definitions are sometimes useful. If I asked a man, "Who are you?" he might not unreasonably think the question impertinent, seeing that I was in his presence, and he might reply "I am myself." So when I ask of a thing, "What is that?" if the thing could overhear me, it might justly retort, "I am that I am." If, however, the man I challenged was of a mild and affable temper, and explained that he was Jenkins, that name might not be unmeaning to me. I might instantly conclude that I had not heard of him before, and should probably not hear of him again. So if I learned that the tone before me was a work of poetry, although poetry is proverbially difficult to define, I should know that all further consideration of it on my part was optional. Definitions may inform me of the place in which conventional discourse puts the object before me, and if I trust the wisdom of the definer, I shall have a useful hint concerning the ways of that object. A card may suffice to tell me the sex, rank, and nationality of the person whose name it bears, and may even enable me to guess whether he comes to pay his compliments or to solicit a subscription. Though a name seems to report who a man is, and a definition what a thing is, yet the thing no more is its definition than the man is his name.

Fourth Meaning: Predication.—Most often, perhaps, in common speech, the word "*is*" marks some property in what presumably has other properties as well, as in the formula A is B. Such a formula would be self-contradictory if being always meant identity. Wine is wine, and red is red, but red is not wine nor (in the sense of identity) can wine be red. Yet this is the constant assertion made by the word "*is*" when it attributes qualities to substances or predicates adjectives of nouns.

How an adjective can belong to a substantive is best seen when the adjective is a mere epithet and grammatically redundant, as when Homer speaks of the wine-coloured sea. Predication is supplementary definition, and as definition is never adequate to facts, further definition of them is always possible. The word "sea" and the images it may call up are one complex symbol for that element on which Homer had so often been tossed; the essence "purple," now emerging in the same context, is an added symbol for the same object. Predication is an elaborate naming under pressure of sensation or shifts of thought: it is poetry. Intuition here mixes its pigments and lays them on, stroke by stroke. The whole composition, at each stage, will no doubt be imputed to some substance, as if it formed its essence; but the very multiplication of epithets shows how inexhaustible and external that substance is in its truth; the poet is enduring and celebrating a divine power, and singing its many names. His whole discourse is the modulation of one vast epithet. It does not transgress the sphere of essence, but touches in turn and brings to the focus of attention now one manifestation of the god and now another. In study, whether artistic or scientific, the originality of mind is by no means laid aside; study merely carries out with a greater volume and force the primary poetry of the senses, by which intuition arises in the beginning, when each organ, stimulated by the unimaginable currents of its substance, chooses the essences which shall symbolize that stimulus to consciousness. The essence which any particular organ or any particular poet shall evoke depends, of course, on the material conditions which, in creating intuition at all, create its language, according to the "genius" of that poet or of that organ. Every quality possibly found in any thing, or predicated of it, is a fundamental and separate essence evoked on that occasion. The circumstance that some essences are used as subjects in discourse and some as attributes is itself only rhetorical; but it corresponds to the fact that in nature some formal units are more constant than others; as, for instance, the mass of a body is more constant than its position; therefore, in discourse we call the mass the substance and the position the accident. In the realm of essence, however, all elements are simply juxtaposed, and the trick of predicating one essence of another is only a means of carrying attention from some whole to a feature included in it, or to some larger whole in which it is a feature; in other words a means of analysis or synthesis. The resulting term in both cases is simply an essence, all surface; and

there is no meaning in calling an essence the substance or the attribute of any other. Animal faith, with the intent which expresses it intellectually, may use any or all essences as predicates of a substance posited beyond them; but these predicates are poetic epithets for that substance, not constituents of it. They vary with the senses and genius of the observer. A stained-glass window, after I have studied it for a moment, offers a vastly different essence to my intuition from that contained in my first glimpse of it; and the simplest natural object is far more complicated than any Gothic design.

Fifth Meaning: Existence.—When I assume that there is a substance perhaps without pretending to know what it is, save that I have this local and temporal encounter with it, I am using the word "*is*" in an entirely different sense in which it means existence. This assertion of existence is imposed on me antecedently by the actions or expectations in the midst of which intuition arises, and without which it would never arise; and to this underlying faith is due the habit of predication itself, and the function of giving names. Essences present to intuition would never be predicated of one another, or understood to signify anything but what they obviously are, were they not projected into a common place and time, the seat of a presumed substance, by confusion with which the given essences (in reality only terms for intuition) are reputed to exist too. I do not need to believe in what I actually see; if I could limit myself to seeing, such a belief would be superfluous and unmeaning; but I am compelled to believe in the butt of my actions or the objects of my fears or memories, substances on which my efforts converge, or from which influences radiate upon me. The vague light, without outline or colour, which may first come to me from the church window is certainly not the composition which I afterwards discover there, yet I call them perceptions of the same thing, because I am convinced *a priori*, by the persevering attitude of my body and other converging circumstances, that a common source existed for both images, namely, a single material window fixed in its place, designed by its particular architect and built by his particular masons and glaziers. If no such natural object existed, that vague light and that precise composition would have nothing to do with each other; and unless I surreptitiously assign a natural existence to myself and give dates to those intuitions in my personal history, the light and the composition would have no temporal or spatial relations, and would not belong to one world, or exist at all. For the realm of existence (as I understand the word) is that arena of action, conveniently called nature, of which animals are parts and to which they are addressed before they have intuitions, if they ever have them; and the meaning of intuitions, when they come, is to mark the salient points of this world of nature, in so far as the sensitive animal can cope with it or is affected by it. The terms of intuition, the given essences, come to him as signals; and they are names to him for what exists about him, long before he notices their æsthetic quality. It is a great misfortune, at least for philosophy, that the word "*is*," which denotes the qualitative idiosyncrasy of any essence whatsoever, should also have been used to denote existence, something peculiar to the flux of nature, and only as actually flowing.[1]

Existence means being in external relations.—When the word "*is*" designates existence, it claims for the object of intent a place in this flux; an object of intent (such as I have when on being startled I cry, "what's that?") is sufficiently identified by the external relations through which I approach it. I may completely ignore or mistake its true nature—an error or indifference which would be impossible if that object were not distinguished already as the object I mean to regard. It is whatever is there now, in such a context, creating such a disturbance. Its hidden nature, whatever it may be, is embodied in existence, and turned from an eternal essence into a fact when it is caught somewhere in the net of time, space, evolution, derivation, and association. Lying myself in the same context, I can turn to it by groping; and on coming into material contact with it, I may have rapid and varied intuitions supplying me with various notes, in the terms of my personal senses and emotions, which are my comment on it; perhaps it appears to be something small, black, rapidly moving, and unpleasant. These miscellaneous characteristics, the essences present to my intuition, are its names in my discourse; of course they are not the essence of that object itself, which for all my description reveals might as well be a mouse as a mosquito; nor do I seriously suppose they form its essence, since I remain still curious and apprehensive of what that essence may secretly be; whether, for instance, it may be such as to render the thing poisonous. But since I have only my chance intuitions by which to describe that object, I am tempted to assign existence, for the nonce to this accidental description, as if it were the true essence of the thing; the radical and perpetual occasion of human illusion, dogmatism, and error.

Whether the claim to existence made on behalf of any object is just or not is a question that can never be decided by analyzing the given description of what is said to exist, but only by exploring the flux of nature, by experience or testimony, until the region in which the existing thing is alleged to lie (for if it exists it must lie somewhere) is thoroughly explored, and I can judge whether my original description, granting my terms and my circumstances, was a fair description of what actually lies there. If it was a fair description, I may conclude that what I had in mind really existed; if not, I must admit that I was mistaken, since what really existed was something not fairly describable in that way, nor properly called by that name. A very inadequate designation of the object—for example, in the case of the existence of God—may be perfectly correct and sufficient for human purposes; but the places and times (say the miracles or revelations or eschatological events) in which the existence of such an object would be unmistakably manifested must be definitely fixed; otherwise the *existence* of the object, the very point in question, would not be broached at all; for it is idle to say that a thing exists or does not exist; if I do not say when or where it is to be met with in the world of action.

Sixth Meaning: Actuality.—To this natural sphere the word "existence" may be confined with advantage; for even a living intuition, or bit of actual discourse, is generated at some particular point of space and time and expresses a material predicament of some animal. Had intuition no such root and status in nature, it could not be said to exist. Inwardly considered, each intuition is invisible, being the act of seeing something else; and it cannot run up against itself or find itself in any part of the landscape which it views, and to which it lends a specious unity and actuality. Moreover, if an intuition were not posited from the outside, as the thought of some particular person at some particular time, even its spiritual synthetic function would vanish; for it would be indistinguishable from the unity of the essence discerned—an eternal and non-existential object. A living intuition is, accordingly, a phase of animal life; and apart from such heats of nature the light of thought would never shine and no essence would ever appear. Nevertheless, considered in itself, an intuition is autonomous; it knows nothing of its organs or conditions, but single-mindedly greets whatever essence may appear, or borne onwards by animal faith, idolatrously regards that essence as a whole world, or as a chief part of a world, existing absolutely. Here, surely, is a very vivid and notable event, an existence possessing such unity, scope, and concentration as no other existence possesses; indeed scope, concentration, and unity have no other principle than intuition. Yet in this superlative existence proper to intuition there is something ironical. While it exists so positively that some philosophers admit no other reality, it is indiscoverable in the context of nature where existence must lie. Moreover, a chief characteristic of existence is flux, even conventionally static things, like houses, being composed by external and therefore reversible relations; but intuition (though externally considered it has a date and duration) is a synthesis, and therefore no flux. A flux which was all flux could never appear; in becoming a specious flux, it is caught in a unitary vista. Intuition is not a divisible event, like all events in nature. The separation and temporal order of its terms, like these terms themselves, are specious, an idea of succession and not a succession of facts; and there is no possibility whatever of placing various intuitions, apart from their organs and objects, in any relation of contiguity or succession.

Intuitions are therefore not existences in the same sense as natural things, nor events after the fashion of natural events; and yet we must say of them preeminently that they exist and arise, unless we are willing to banish spirit from nature altogether and to forget, when we do so, that spirit in us is then engaged in discovering nature and in banishing spirit. Why should philosophers wish to impoverish the world in order to describe it more curtly? Its exuberance will make it easier to describe, if they adapt their logic to its constitution. Intuition is an emanation of life, an intellectual response of the animal to his vicissitudes; it is an actualization or hypostasis of formal facts in nature, not an added existence on the same plane as its organ. If either the substance or the intuition were a phenomenon (which neither is), the relation of intuition to substance might be called epiphenomenal; for the two are not collateral, but the intuition is as completely dependent on the body for arising, as the body and nature at large are dependent on intuition for being imagined, loved, or described. This spiritual hypostasis of life into intuition is therefore less and more than natural existence and deserves a different name. I will

call it actuality. *Is,* applied to spirit or to any of its modes, accordingly means is actual; in other words, exists not by virtue of inclusion in the dynamic, incessant, and infinitely divisible flux of nature, but by its intrinsic incandescence, which brings essences to light and creates the world of appearances.

Seventh Meaning: Derivation.—Belief in existence leads to still another use of the word "*is,*" the most misleading of all, by which one thing is said to be another because it is derived from it, or has the same substance. Suppose intuition presents me with a point of light; taking that essence instinctively for the sign of some existence, I may say to myself, "There is a spark." But in the world of nature, to which I am now addressed, a spark is no isolated fact; it has some origin, some substance, some consequences, and these probably interest me much more than my bare intuition of a point of light. But what origin, what substance, what consequences? It is conventionally known to me that a point of light may mean a spark from a horse's hoof, a burning cinder, a rocket, a distant lamp-post, a motor on the road, a revolving light-house, a ship at sea, or a blow in the eye. Nevertheless, ignoring those familiar possibilities, I may say to myself, "This spark is a firefly and not a star." I have thus travelled in search of explanation very far indeed from my datum. Instead of saying, "A point is a point," I first said, "A spark exists"; and then I said, "This spark is an insect." The word "*is*" has become a synonym of "*comes from*"; it attributes to an alleged fact a source in another alleged fact, asserting that the two are continuous genetically, however different they may be in character.

If this license in the use of the word "*is*" be allowed (and it would be pedantic to forbid it), I may still ask which of various suggested things a particular thing is; and I may find myself traversing the whole flux of nature in search for the being of the simplest object. This search becomes more confusing, and at the same time more urgent, when a psychological world is interposed, or substituted for the world of matter; one school of philosophers will then maintain that everything physical is really mental, and another school that everything mental is really physical. A capital instance of this habit is found in the phrase, dear to critical philosophers, that something "is nothing but" something else. Thus we hear that a word is nothing but a *flatus vocis,* that a house is nothing but bricks and mortar, that a mind is nothing but a bundle of perceptions, that God is nothing but a tendency not ourselves that makes for righteousness, or that matter is nothing but a permanent possibility of sensation. The phrase "nothing but" claims adequacy for the definition that follows: but a definition can define adequately an essence only, it cannot pretend to exhaust a fact; therefore, if such assertions are taken strictly, they themselves become "nothing but" definitions of fresh terms, and not discoveries. If on the contrary we take them loosely, as indicating the partial origin of certain facts or ideas, they may be correct; every fact and idea has antecedents which might be discovered if our knowledge of nature and of dreams were sufficiently profound. But in practice this sort of naturalistic analysis is seldom thorough; in none of the five examples given above, for instance, is the origin of the facts or ideas in question assigned correctly. One element in their composition may be specified: but the radical phrase "nothing but," in excluding all other elements (not to speak of the resulting unities of form), turns a shrewd observation into a cheap error. Even if the derivation of any fact could be assigned adequately, that fact would not be identical with what brought it about; and to say that things *are* what they are made of is to use the verb "to be" in a confused and confusing way, although the poverty of language may render such speech inevitable.

Here are seven distinct meanings of the word "*is,*" which it will be well to distinguish if I wish to know what I am saying. In practice

the ambiguities of language are neutralized by looseness and good sense in the interpretation of it; but a philosopher leads himself into foolish difficulties and more foolish dogmas if he assumes that words have fixed meanings to which single facts in nature must correspond. He ought, therefore, to use language more freely than the public rather than more strictly, since he professes to have a clearer view of things. My purpose is not to limit the uses of the word "*is,*" but to become and remain aware that these uses are various, and that no argument in which they figure has the least cogency, even within the sphere of dialectic, until these uses are discriminated.

NOTE

1. The Spanish language is comparatively discriminating in this matter, having three verbs for "to be" which cannot be used interchangeably. "To be or not to be" must be rendered by *existir;* "That is the question" requires *ser;* "There's the rub" demands *estar.* Existence, essence, and condition or position are thus distinguished instinctively; but idiom profits more by this nicety than does philosophy, and I must say despairingly "*Sea lo que Dios quiera,*" "Be it [*i.e.,* let it happen] as God will." Fortunately events have some English verbs to themselves—"occur," "happen," "arise"—and we need not say stupidly that they simply are. The phrase "there is" (like the German *ist da, es giebt, ist vorhanden*) also helps to distinguish existence from pure being.

The Psyche

What our knowledge of the psyche lacks in precision it makes up, after a fashion, in variety and extent. All that is called knowledge of the world, of human nature, of character, and of the passions is a sort of ausculation of the psyche; and the familiarity of our verbal and dramatic conventions often blinds us to their loose application, and to our profound ignorance of the true mechanism of life. Not knowing what we are, we at least can discourse abundantly about our books, our words, and our social actions; and these manifestations of the psyche, though peripheral, are faithful enough

witnesses to her nature. She is that inner moving equilibrium from which these things radiate, and which they help to restore—the equilibrium by which we live, in the sense of not dying; and to keep us alive is her first and essential function. It follows naturally from this biological office that in each of us she is one, vigilant, and predetermined; that she is selfish and devoted, intrepid and vicious, intelligent and mad; for her quick potentialities are solicited and distracted by all sorts of accidents. She slept at first in a seed; there, and from there, as the seed softened, she distributed her organs and put

From *Realms of Being* (New York: Charles Scribner's Sons, 1942), pp. 335–340.

forth her energies, always busier and busier in her growing body, almost losing control of her members, yet reacting from the centre, perhaps only slowly and partially, upon events at her frontiers. If too deeply thwarted her industry becomes distraction; and what we sometimes call her plan, which is only her propensity, may be developed and transformed, if she finds new openings, until it becomes quite a different plan. But against brutal obstacles she will struggle until death; that is, until her central control, her total equilibrium and power of recuperation, are exhausted. Her death may as easily occur by insurrection within her organism—each part of which is a potential centre on its own account—as by hostile action from outside.

I hardly venture to say more. To watch a plant grow, or draw in its leaves, to observe the animals in a zoological garden, is to gain some knowledge of the psyche; to study embryology or the nervous system or insanity or politics, is (or ought to be) to gain more: and every system of science or religion is rich in this sort of instruction for a critic who studies it in order to distinguish whatever may be arbitrary in it, based on human accidents, and without any but a psychic ground. All the errors ever made about other things, if we understand their cause, enlighten us about ourselves; for the psyche is at once the spring of curiosity and the ground of refraction, selection, and distortion in our ideas. Summary reaction, symbolisation, infection with relativity and subjective colouring begins in the senses and is continued in the passions; and if we succeed in removing, by criticism, this personal equation from our science of other things, the part withdrawn, which remains on our hands, is our indirect knowledge of the psyche.

Each man also has direct experience of the psyche within himself, not so much in his verbal thoughts and distinct images—which if they are knowledge at all are knowledge of other things—as in a certain sense of his personal momentum, a pervasive warmth and power in the inner man. As he thinks and acts, intent on external circumstances, he is not unaware of the knot of latent determinate impulses within him which respond to those circumstances. Our thoughts—which we may be said to know well, in that we know we have had them often before—are about anything and everything. We shuffle and iterate them, and live in them a verbal, heated, histrionic life. Yet we little know *why* we have them, or how they arise and change. Nothing

could be more obscure, more physical, than the dynamics of our passions and dreams; yet, especially in moments of suspense or hesitation, nothing could be more intensely felt. There is the coursing of the blood, the waxing and waning of the affections, a thousand starts of smothered eloquence, the coming on of impatience, of invention, of conviction, of sleep. There are laughter and tears, ready to flow quite unbidden, and almost at random. There is our whole past, as it were, knocking at the door; there are our silent hopes; there are our future discourses and decisions working away, like actors rehearsing their parts, at their several fantastic arguments. All this is the psyche's work; and in that sense deeply our own; and our superficial mind is carried by it like a child, cooing or fretting, in his mother's arms. Much of it we feel going on unmistakably within our bodies, and the whole of it in fact goes on there. But the form which belongs to it in its truly physical and psychic character, in its vital bodily tropes, is even less known to us than the mechanism of the heart, or that by which our nerves receive, transmit, and return their signals. The psyche is an object of experience to herself, since what she does at one moment or in one organ she can observe, perhaps, a moment later, or with another organ; yet of her life as a whole she is aware only as we are aware of the engines and the furnaces in a ship in which we travel, half-asleep, or chattering on deck; or as we are aware of a foreign language heard for the first time, perceived in its globular sound and gesticulation and even perhaps in its general issue—that all is probably a dispute about money—yet without distinguishing the words, or the reasons for these precise passionate outbursts. In this way we all endure, without understanding, the existence and the movement of our own psyche: for it is the body that speaks, and the spirit that listens.

The psyche is the self which a man is proud or ashamed of, or probably both at once: not his body in its accidental form, age, and diseases, from which he instinctively distinguishes those initial impulses and thwarted powers which are much more truly himself. And this is the self which, if he lives in a religious age, he may say that he wishes to save, and to find reviving in another world. Yet this self is far from being a stranger to the body; on the contrary, it is more deeply and persistently the essence of the body than is the body itself. It is human, male or female, proper to a particular social and geographical zone; it is still the fountain of youth in old age; it deprecates in a measure the actions and words which circumstances may have drawn from it, and which (it feels) do it enormous injustice; and yet the words and actions which it might have wished to produce instead are all words and actions of the same family, slightly more eloquent in the same human language, slightly more glorious in the same social sphere. The psyche is so much of us, and of our works, as is our own doing.

Conflicts between the flesh and the spirit, between habit and idea, between passion and reason, are real conflicts enough, but they are conflicts between one movement in the psyche and another movement there. Hers is a compound life, moulded by compromise, and compacted of tentative organs, with their several impulses, all initially blind and mechanical. Rarely will any particular psyche impulse or habit more in sympathy with all the rest, or be unquestionably dominant. It follows that what in religion or in moral reflection we call the spirit is a precarious harmony. It is threatened by subject powers always potentially rebellious, and it necessarily regards them as wicked and material in so far as they do not conspire to keep its own flame vivid and pure. And yet the spirit itself has no other fuel. Reason is not a force contrary to the passions, but a harmony possible among them. Except in their interests it could have no ardour, and, except in their world, it could have no point of application, nothing to beautify, nothing to dominate. It is therefore by a complete illusion, though an excusable one, that the spirit denies its material basis, and calls its body a prison or a tomb. The impediments are real, but mutual; and sometimes a second nucleus of passion or fleshiness rises against that nucleus which the spirit expresses, and takes the name of spirit in its turn. Every virtue, and in particular knowledge and thought, have no other root in the world than the co-ordination of their organs with one another and with the material habitat. Certainly such a co-ordination could never arise except in a psyche: the psyche is another name for it: but neither could the psyche have any life to foster and defend, nor any instruments for doing so, if she were not a trope arising in a material flux, and enjoyed a visible dominance there more or less prolonged and extended.

Hypostatic Ethics

Those of us who are what Mr. Russell would call ethical sceptics will be delighted at his way of clearing the ground; it opens before us the prospect of a moral philosophy that should estimate the various values of things known and of things imaginable, showing what combinations of goods are possible in any one rational system, and (if fancy could stretch so far) what different rational systems would be possible in places and times remote enough from one another not to come into physical conflict. Such ethics, since it would express in reflection the dumb but actual interests of men, might have both influence and authority over them; two things which an alien and dogmatic ethics necessarily lacks. The joy of the ethical sceptic in Mr. Russell is destined, however, to be short-lived. Before proceeding to the expression of concrete ideals, he thinks it necessary to ask a preliminary and quite abstract question, to which his essay is chiefly devoted; namely, what is the right definition of the predicate "good," which we hope to apply in the sequel to such a variety of things? And he answers at once: The predicate "good" is indefinable. This answer he shows to be unavoidable, and so evidently unavoidable that we might perhaps have been absolved from asking the question; for, as he says, the so-called definitions of "good"—that it is pleasure, the desired, and so forth—are not definitions of the predicate "good," but designations of the things to which this predicate is applied by different persons. Pleasure, and its rivals, are not synonyms for the abstract quality "good," but names for classes of concrete facts that are supposed to possess that quality. From this correct, if somewhat trifling, observation, however, Mr. Russell, like Mr. Moore before him, evokes a portentous dogma. Not being able to

From *Winds of Doctrine* (Gloucester, Mass.: Peter Smith, 1971), pp. 138–154.

define good, he hypostasises it. "Good and bad," he says, "are qualities which belong to objects independently of our opinions, just as much as round and square do; and when two people differ as to whether a thing is good, only one of them can be right, though it may be very hard to know which is right." "We cannot maintain that for me a thing ought to exist on its own account, while for you it ought not; that would merely mean that one of us is mistaken, since in fact everything either ought to exist, or ought not." Thus we are asked to believe that good attaches to things for no reason or cause, and according to no principles of distribution; that it must be found there by a sort of receptive exploration in each separate case; in other words, that it is an absolute, not a relative thing, a primary and not a secondary quality.

That the quality "good" is indefinable is one assertion, and obvious; but that the presence of this quality is unconditioned is another, and astonishing. My logic, I am well aware, is not very accurate or subtle; and I wish Mr. Russell had not left it to me to discover the connection between these two propositions. Green is an indefinable predicate, and the specific quality of it can be given only in intuition; but it is a quality that things acquire under certain conditions, so much so that the same bit of grass, at the same moment, may have it from one point of view and not from another. Right and left are indefinable; the difference could not be explained without being invoked in the explanation; yet everything that is to the right is not to the right on no condition, but obviously on the condition that some one is looking in a certain direction; and if some one else at the same time is looking in the opposite direction, what is truly to the right will be truly to the left also. If Mr. Russell thinks this is a contradiction, I understand why the universe does not please him. The contradiction would be real, undoubtedly, if we suggested that the *idea* of good was at any time or in any relation the *idea* of evil, or the *intuition* of right that of left, or the *quality* of green that of yellow; these disembodied essences are fixed by the intent that selects them, and in that ideal realm they can never have any relations except the dialectical ones implied in their nature, and these relations they must always retain. But the contradiction disappears when, instead of considering the qualities in themselves, we consider the things of which those qualities are aspects; for the qualities of things are not compacted by implication, but are conjoined irra-

tionally by nature, as she will; and the same thing may be, and is, at once yellow and green, to the left and to the right, good and evil, many and one, large and small; and whatever verbal paradox there may be in this way of speaking (for from the point of view of nature it is natural enough) had been thoroughly explained and talked out by the time of Plato, who complained that people should still raise a difficulty so trite and exploded.[1] Indeed, while square is always square, and round round, a thing that is round may actually be square also, if we allow it to have a little body, and to be a cylinder.

But perhaps what suggests this hypostasis of good is rather the fact that what others find good, or what we ourselves have found good in moods with which we retain no sympathy, is sometimes pronounced by us to be bad; and far from inferring from this diversity of experience that the present good, like the others, corresponds to a particular attitude or interest of ours, and is dependent upon it, Mr. Russell and Mr. Moore infer instead that the presence of the good must be independent of all interests, attitudes, and opinions. They imagine that the truth of a proposition attributing a certain relative quality to an object contradicts the truth of another proposition, attributing to the same object an opposite relative quality. Thus if a man here and another man at the antipodes call opposite directions up, "only one of them can be right, though it may be very hard to know which is right."

To protect the belated innocence of this state of mind, Mr. Russell, so far as I can see, has only one argument, and one analogy. The argument is that "if this were not the case, we could not reason with a man as to what is right." "We do in fact hold that when one man approves of a certain act, while another disapproves, one of them is mistaken, which would not be the case with a mere emotion. If one man likes oysters and another dislikes them, we do not say that either of them is mistaken." In other words, we are to maintain our prejudices, however absurd, lest it should become unnecessary to quarrel about them! Truly the debating society has its idols, no less than the cave and the theatre. The analogy that comes to buttress somewhat this singular argument is the analogy between ethical propriety and physical or logical truth. An ethical proposition may be correct or incorrect, in a sense justifying argument, when it touches what is good as a means, that is, when it is not intrinsically ethical, but deals with causes and effects, or with matters of fact or necessity. But to speak of the truth of an ultimate good would be a false collocation of terms; an ultimate good is chosen, found, or aimed at; it is not opined. The ultimate intuitions on which ethics rests are not debatable, for they are not opinions we hazard but preferences we feel; and it can be neither correct nor incorrect to feel them. We may assert these preferences fiercely or with sweet reasonableness, and we may be more or less incapable of sympathising with the different preferences of others; about oysters we may be tolerant, like Mr. Russell, and about character intolerant; but that is already a great advance in enlightenment, since the majority of mankind have regarded as hateful in the highest degree any one who indulged in pork, or beans, or frogs' legs, or who had a weakness for anything called "unnatural"; for it is the things that offend their animal instincts that intense natures have always found to be, intrinsically and *par excellence,* abominations.

I am not sure whether Mr. Russell thinks he has disposed of this view where he discusses the proposition that the good is the desired and refutes it on the ground that "it is commonly admitted that there are bad desires; and when people speak of bad desires, they seem to mean desires for what is bad." Most people undoubtedly call desires bad when they are generically contrary to their own desires, and call objects that disgust them bad, even when other people covet them. This human weakness is not, however, a very high authority for a logician to appeal to, being too like the attitude of the German lady who said that Englishmen called a certain object *bread,* and Frenchmen called it *pain,* but that it really was *Brod.* Scholastic philosophy is inclined to this way of asserting itself; and Mr. Russell, though he candidly admits that there are ultimate differences of opinion about good and evil, would gladly minimise these differences, and thinks he triumphs when he feels that the prejudices of his readers will agree with his own; as if the constitutional unanimity of all human animals, supposing it existed, could tend to show that the good they agreed to recognise was independent of their constitution.

In a somewhat worthier sense, however, we may admit that there are desires for what is bad, since desire and will, in the proper psychological sense of these words, are incidental phases of consciousness, expressing but not constituting those natural relations that make one thing good for another. At the same time the words desire and will are often used, in a

mythical or transcendental sense, for those material depositions and instincts by which vital and moral units are constituted. It is in reference to such constitutional interests that things are "really" good or bad; interests which may not be fairly represented by any incidental conscious desire. No doubt any desire, however capricious, represents some momentary and partial interest, which lends to its objects a certain real and inalienable value; yet when we consider, as we do in human society, the interests of men, whom reflection and settled purposes have raised more or less to the ideal dignity of individuals then passing fancies and passions may indeed have bad objects, and be bad themselves, in that they thwart the more comprehensive interests of the soul that entertains them. Food and poison are such only relatively, and in view of particular bodies, and the same material thing may be food and poison at once; the child, and even the doctor, may easily mistake one for the other. For the human system whiskey is truly more intoxicating than coffee, and the contrary opinion would be an error; but what a strange way of vindicating this real, though relative, distinction, to insist that whiskey is more intoxicating in itself, without reference to any animal; that it is pervaded, as it were, by an inherent intoxication, and stands dead drunk in its bottle! Yet just in this way Mr. Russell and Mr. Moore conceive things to be dead good and dead bad. It is such a view, rather than the naturalistic one, that renders reasoning and self-criticism impossible in morals; for wrong desires, and false opinions as to value, are conceivable only because a point of reference or criterion is available to prove them such. If no point of reference and no criterion were admitted to be relevant, nothing but physical stress could give to one assertion of value greater force than to another. The shouting moralist no doubt has his place, but not in philosophy.

That good is not an intrinsic or primary quality, but relative and adventitious, is clearly betrayed by Mr. Russell's own way of arguing, whenever he approaches some concrete ethical question. For instance, to show that the good is not pleasure, he can avowedly do nothing but appeal "to ethical judgments with which almost every one would agree." He repeats, in effect, Plato's argument about the life of the oyster, having pleasure with no knowledge. Imagine such mindless pleasure, as intense and prolonged as you please, and would you choose it? Is it your good? Here the British reader, like the blushing Greek youth, is expected to answer instinctively, No! It is an *argumentum ad hominem* (and there can be no other kind of argument in ethics); but the man who gives the required answer does so not because the answer is self-evident, which it is not, but because he is the required sort of man. He is shocked at the idea of resembling an oyster. Yet changeless pleasure, without memory of reflection, without the wearisome intermixture of arbitrary images, is just what the mystic, the voluptuary, and perhaps the oyster find to be good. Ideas, in their origin, are probably signals of alarm; and the distress which they marked in the beginning always clings to them in some measure, and causes many a soul, far more profound than that of the young Protarchus or of the British reader, to long for them to cease altogether. Such a radical hedonism is indeed inhuman; it undermines all conventional ambitions, and is not a possible foundation for political or artistic life. But that is all we can say against it. Our humanity cannot annul the incommensurable sorts of good that may be pursued in the world, though it cannot itself pursue them. The impossibility which people labour under of being satisfied with pure pleasure as a goal is due to their want of imagination, or rather to their being dominated by an imagination which is exclusively human.

The author's estrangement from reality reappears in his treatment of egoism, and most of all in his "Free Man's Religion." Egoism, he thinks, is untenable because, "if I am right in thinking that my good is the only good, then every one else is mistaken unless he admits that my good, not his, is the only good." "Most people . . . would admit that it is better two people's desires should be satisfied than only one person's. . . . Then what is good is not good *for me* or *for you*, but is simply good." "It is, indeed, so evident that it is better to secure a greater good for *A* than a lesser good for *B*, that it is hard to find any still more evident principle by which to prove this. And if *A* happens to be some one else, and *B* to be myself, that cannot affect the question, since it is irrelevant to the general question who *A* and *B* may be." To the question, as the logician states it after transforming men into letters, it is certainly irrelevant; but it is not irrelevant to the case as it arises in nature. If two goods are somehow rightly pronounced to be equally good, no circumstances can render one better than the other. And if the locus in which the good is to arise is somehow pronounced to be indifferent, it will certainly be indifferent whether that good arises in me or in you. But how shall these two pronouncements be made? In practice, values cannot be compared save as represented or enacted in the private imagination of somebody: for we could not conceive that an alien good *was* a good (as Mr. Russell cannot conceive that the life of an ecstatic oyster is a good) unless we could sympathise with it in some way in our own persons; and on the warmth which we felt in so representing the alien good would hang our conviction that it was truly valuable, and had worth in comparison with our own good. The voice of reason, bidding us prefer the greater good, no matter who is to enjoy it, is also nothing but the force of sympathy, bringing a remote existence before us vividly *sub specie boni*. Capacity for such sympathy measures the capacity to recognise duty and therefore, in a moral sense, to have it. Doubtless it is conceivable that all wills should become co-operative, and that nature should be ruled magically by an exact and universal sympathy; but this situation must be actually attained in part, before it can be conceived or judged to be an authoritative ideal. The tigers cannot regard it as such, for it would suppress the tragic good called ferocity, which makes, in their eyes, the chief glory of the universe. Therefore the inertia of nature, the ferocity of beasts, the optimism of mystics, and the selfishness of men and nations must all be accepted as conditions for the peculiar goods, essentially incommensurable, which they can generate severally. It is misplaced vehemence to call them intrinsically detestable, because they do not (as they cannot) generate or recognise the goods we prize.

In the real world, persons are not abstract egos, like *A* and *B*, so that to benefit one is clearly as good as to benefit another. Indeed, abstract egos could not be benefited, for they could not be modified at all, even if somehow they could be distinguished. It would be the qualities or objects distributed among them that would carry, wherever they went, each its inalienable cargo of value, like ships sailing from sea to sea. But it is quite vain and artificial to imagine different goods charged with such absolute and comparable weights; and actual egoism is not the thin and refutable thing that Mr. Russell makes of it. What it really holds is that a given man, oneself, and those akin to him, are qualitatively better than other beings; that the things they prize are intrinsically better than the things prized by others; and that therefore there is no injustice in treating these chosen interests as supreme. The injustice, it is felt, would lie rather in not treat-ing things so unequal unequally. This feeling may, in many cases, amuse the impartial ob-server, or make him indignant; yet it may, in every case, according to Mr. Russell, be abso-lutely just. The refutation he gives of egoism would not dissuade any fanatic from extermi-nating all his enemies with a good conscience; it would merely encourage him to assert that what he was ruthlessly establishing was the ab-solute good. Doubtless such conscientious ty-rants would be wretched themselves, and com-pelled to make sacrifices which would cost them dear; but that would only extend, as it were, the pernicious egoism of that part of their being which they had allowed to usurp a universal empire. The twang of intolerance and of self-mutilation is not absent from the ethics of Mr. Russell and Mr. Moore, even as it stands; and one trembles to think what it may become in the mouths of their disciples. Intolerance itself is a form of egoism, and to condemn egoism intolerantly is to share it.

I cannot help thinking that a consciousness of the relativity of values, if it became preva-lent, would tend to render people more truly social than would a belief that things have in-trinsic and unchangeable values, no matter what the attitude of any one to them may be. If we said that goods, including the right distri-bution of goods, are relative to specific na-tures, moral warfare would continue, but not with poisoned arrows. Our private sense of justice itself would be acknowledged to have but a relative authority, and while we could not have a higher duty than to follow it, we should seek to meet those whose aims were incompatible with it as we meet things physi-cally inconvenient, without insulting them as if they were morally vile or logically contempt-ible. Real unselfishness consists in sharing the interests of others. Beyond the pale of actual unanimity the only possible unselfishness is chivalry—a recognition of the inward right and justification of our enemies fighting against us. This chivalry has long been prac-tised in the battle-field without abolishing the causes of war; and it might conceivably be ex-tended to all the conflicts of men with one another, and of the warring elements within each breast. Policy, hypnotisation, and even surgery may be practised without exorcisms or anathemas. When a man has decided on a course of action, it is a vain indulgence in ex-pletives to declare that he is sure that course is absolutely right. His moral dogma expresses its natural origin all the more clearly the more

hotly it is proclaimed; and ethical absolutism, being a mental grimace of passion, refutes what it says by what it is. Sweeter and more profound, to my sense, is the philosophy of Homer, whose every line seems to breathe the conviction that what is beautiful or precious has not thereby any right to existence; nothing has such a right; nor is it given us to condemn absolutely any force—god or man—that de-stroys what is beautiful or precious, for it has doubtless something beautiful or precious of its own to achieve.

The consequences of a hypostasis of the good are no less interesting than its causes. If the good were independent of nature, it might still be conceived as relevant to nature, by be-ing its creator or mover; but Mr. Russell is not a theist after the manner of Socrates; his good is not a power. Nor would representing it to be such long help his case; for an ideal hyposta-sied into a cause achieves only a mythical inde-pendence. The least criticism discloses that it is natural laws, zoological species, and human ideals, that have been projected into the em-pyrean; and it is no marvel that the good should attract the world where the good, by definition, is whatever the world is aiming at. The hypostasis accomplished by Mr. Russell is more serious, and therefore more paradoxical. If I understand it, it may be expressed as fol-lows: In the realm of eternal essences, before anything exists, there are certain essences that have this remarkable property, that they ought to exist, or at least that, if anything exists, it ought to conform to them. What exists, how-ever, is deaf to this moral emphasis in the eter-nal; nature exists for no reason; and, indeed, why should she have subordinated her own ar-bitrariness to a good that is no less arbitrary? This good, however, is somehow good not-withstanding; so that there is an abysmal wrong in its not being obeyed. The world is, in principle, totally depraved; but as the good is not a power, there is no one to redeem the world. The saints are those who, imitating the impotent dogmatism on high, and despising their sinful natural propensities, keep asserting that certain things are in themselves good and others bad, and declaring to be detestable any other saint who dogmatises differently. In this system the Calvanistic God has lost his creative and punitive functions, but continues to decree groundlessly what is good and what evil, and to love the one and hate the other with an infinite love or hatred. Meanwhile the repro-bate need not fear hell in the next world, but the elect are sure to find it here.

What shall we say of this strangely unreal and strangely personal religion? Is it a ghost of Calvanism, returned with none of its old force but with its old aspect of rigidity? Perhaps: but then, in losing its force, in abandoning its myths, and threats, and rhetoric, this religion has lost its deceptive sanctimony and hypocrisy; and in retaining its rigidity it has kept what made it notable and pathetic; for it is a clear dramatic expression of that human spirit—in this case a most pure and heroic spirit—which it strives so hard to dethrone. After all, the hypostasis of the good is only an unfortunate incident in a great accomplishment, which is the discernment of the good. I have dwelt chiefly on this incident, because in academic circles it is the abuses incidental to true philosophy that create controversy and form schools. Artificial systems, even when they prevail, after a while fatigue their adherents, without ever having convinced or refuted their opponents, and they fade out of existence not by being refuted in their turn, but simply be a tacit agreement to ignore their claims: so that the true insight they were based on is too often buried under them. The hypostasis of philosophical terms is an abuse incidental to the forthright, unchecked use of the intellect; it substitutes for things the limits and distinctions that divide them. So physics is corrupted by logic; but the logic that corrupts physics is perhaps correct, and when it is moral dialectic, it is more important than physics itself. Mr. Russell's ethics *is* ethics. When we mortals have once assumed the moral attitude, it is certain that an indefinable value accrues to some things as opposed to others, that these things are many, that combinations of them have values not belonging to their parts, and that these valuable things are far more specific than abstract pleasure, and far more diffused than one's personal life. What a pity if this pure morality, in detaching itself impetuously from the earth, whose bright satellite it might be, should fly into the abyss at a tangent, and leave us as much in the dark as before!

NOTE

1. Plato, *Philebus,* 14, D. The dialectical element in this dialogue is evidently the basis of Mr. Russell's, as of Mr. Moore's, ethics; but they have not adopted the other elements in it, I mean the political and the theological. As to the political element, Plato everywhere conceives the good as the eligible in life, and refers it to human nature and to the pursuit of happiness—that happiness which Mr. Russell, in a rash moment, says is but a name which some people prefer to give to pleasure. Thus in the *Philebus* (II, D) the good looked for is declared to be "some state and disposition of the soul which has the property of making all men happy"; and later (66, D) the conclusion is that insight is better than pleasure "as an element in human life." As to the theological element, Plato, in hypostasising the good, does not hypostasise it as good, but as cause or power, which is, it seems to me, the sole category that justifies hypostasis, and logically involves it; for if things have a ground at all, that ground must exist before them and beyond them. Hence the whole Platonic and Christian scheme, in making the good independent of private will and opinion, by no means makes it independent of the direction of nature in general and of human nature in particular; for all things have been created with an innate predisposition towards the creative good, and are capable of finding happiness in nothing else. Obligation, in this system, remains internal and vital. Plato attributes a single vital direction and a single moral source to the cosmos. This is what determines and narrows the scope of the true good; for the true good is that relevant to nature. Plato would not have been a dogmatic moralist, had he not been a theist.

The Spiritual Life

The spiritual life, then, is distinguished from worldly morality and intelligence not so much by knowledge as by disillusion: however humble may be its career, it lifts those few and common adventures into the light of eternity. This eternal aspect of things summons spirit out of its initial immersion in sensation and in animal faith and clarifies it into pure spirit. This eternal aspect of things is also their immediate aspect, the dimension in which they are not things but pure essences; for if belief and anxiety be banished from the experience of

From *Platonism and the Spiritual Life* (Gloucester, Mass.: Peter Smith, 1971), pp. 301–304.

any object, only its pure essence remains present to the mind. And this aspect of things, which is immediate psychologically, ontologically is ultimate, since evidently the existence of anything is a temporary accident, while its essence is an indelible variation of necessary Being, an eternal form. The spirit lives in this continual sense of the ultimate in the immediate. Mortal spirits, the spirit in animals, cannot possibly survey pure Being in its infinity; but in so far as they free themselves from false respect for the objects of animal faith and animal passion, they may behold some finite being in its purity. For this reason, established morality and religion, by protecting the eye from too much distraction and fixing it on noble objects, may make a better soil for spirit than does wayward living. Not that spirit may not crop out marvellously in the sinner, as it may in the child or the poet. It notoriously does so; and even in the saint it remains profoundly indifferent to the occasion that may have kindled its flame, be this occasion religious faith or sensuous vision, be it passion, study, or practical dominion over the world. All is grist for the mill, if only there be force of intellect actually to grind that experimental substance and reduce it to some pure essence on which contemplation can feed. But moralities and religions, if they merely extend or exaggerate the pressure of circumstance on the soul, are as dreadful an incubus on the spirit as ever was the animal search for food, love, or safety; indeed, they are but a monstrous and terrifying shadow of these radical compulsions cast needlessly on the screen of heaven.

I ask myself sometimes, is not morality a worse enemy of spirit than immorality? Is it not more hopelessly deceptive and entangling? Those romantic poets, for instance, whose lives were often so irregular—were they not evidently far more spiritual than the good people whom they shocked? Shelley, Leopardi, Alfred de Musset were essentially children of the spirit: they were condemned to flutter on broken wings only for lack of measure and discipline; they were spiritual waifs, untaught to see the relativity and absurdity of their proud passions. The perfect spirit must be a patient hearer, a sober pupil, not an occasional automatic skylark. Yet when spirituality, as in Wordsworth, has to struggle instead against a black coat and a white choker, it seems to be more sadly and decisively stifled, buried alive under a mountain of human alarms and a heavy tombstone of sanctimony. The world, he sighed, is too much with us; but the hills and even the mock Tritons blowing their wreathed horns were not able to banish the world from his conscientious concern. Nothing is able to banish the world except contempt for the world, and this was not in him. It would even have been contrary to his Protestant religion—that so unspiritual determination to wash the world white and clean, adopt it, and set it up for a respectable person. The world is not respectable; it is mortal, tormented, confused, deluded for ever; but it is shot through with beauty, with love, with glints of courage and laughter; and in these the spirit blooms timidly, and struggles to the light among the thorns.

Such is the flitting life of this winged thing, spirit, in this old, sordid, maternal earth. On the one hand, in its innocence, spirit is happy to live in the moment, taking no thought for the morrow; it can enjoy the least gift as gladly as the greatest; it is the fresh, the pure voice of nature, incapable of learned or moral snobbery. It ignores its origin, so buoyant is it; its miraculous light seems to it a matter of course. Its career is everywhere conditioned and oppressed from without, yet it passes through the fire with a serene incredulity, an indomitable independence. On the other hand, the eye of spirit, in its virtual omniscience, sees the visible in its true setting of the invisible; it is fixed instinctively on the countless moments that are not this moment, on the joys that are not this sorrow and the sorrows that are not this joy, on the thousand opinions that are not this opinion and beauties that are not this beauty; understanding too much to be ever imprisoned, loving too much ever to be in love. Spirit chills the flesh and is itself on fire; thought, as Dean Inge says, "becomes passionate, the passions become cold"; or rather they are confronted and controlled by a profound recollection, in which laughter and tears pulse together like the stars in a polar sky, each indelibly bright, and all infinitely distant.

Suggestions for Further Reading

Works by Santayana

Dialogues in Limbo. New York: Charles Scribner's Sons, 1926.
The Life of Reason. New York: Charles Scribner's Sons, 1954.

Obiter Scripta: Lectures, Essays and Reviews. Edited by Justus Buchler and Benjamin Schwartz. New York: Charles Scribner's Sons, 1936.

Physical Order and Moral Liberty. Edited by John and Shirley Lachs. Nashville: Vanderbilt University Press, 1969.

The Realms of Being. New York: Charles Scribner's Sons, 1942.

Scepticism and Animal Faith. New York: Dover, 1955.

The Sense of Beauty. New York: Charles Scribner's Sons, 1896.

Winds of Doctrine and *Platonism and the Spiritual Life*. Gloucester, Mass.: Peter Smith, 1971.

The complete and definitive critical edition of the Collected Works of George Santayana is now in progress. See *The Santayana Edition*. Edited by Herman J. Saatkamp, Jr., and William G. Holzberger. Cambridge, Mass.: MIT Press, forthcoming.

Essential Works on Santayana

John Lachs. *George Santayana*. Boston: Twayne, 1986.

John Lachs, editor. *Animal Faith and Spiritual Life: Previously Unpublished Writings by George Santayana with Critical Essays on His Thought*. New York: Appleton-Century-Crofts, 1967.

Paul A. Schilpp, ed. *The Philosophy of George Santayana. Library of Living Philosophers*. Evanston, Ill.: Northwestern University Press, 1940.

Beth J. Singer. *The Rational Society: A Critical Reading of Santayana's Social Thought*. Cleveland: Case Western Reserve University Press, 1970.

Thimothy L. S. Sprigge. *George Santayana: An Examination of His Philosophy*. London and Boston: Routledge and Kegan Paul, 1974.

JOHN DEWEY
Introduction by John J. Stuhr

DEWEY'S LIFE: CULTURAL CONTEXT AND PHILOSOPHICAL BACKGROUND

. . . it is important, even necessary to appreciate what phases of historical thought—past and present—enter deeply into determination of the thinking of any philosopher.[1]

. . . I seem to be unstable, chameleon-like, yielding one after another to many diverse and even incompatible influences; struggling to assimilate something from each and yet striving to carry it forward in a way that is logically consistent with what has been learned from its predecessors. Upon the whole, the forces that have influenced me have come from persons and from situations more than from books—not that I have not, I hope, learned a great deal from philosophical writings, but that what I have learned from them has been technical in comparison with what I have been forced to think upon and about because of some experience in which I found myself entangled.[2]

. . . I shall never cease to be grateful that I was born at a time and a place where the earlier ideal of liberty and the self-governing community of citizens still sufficiently prevailed so that I unconsciously imbibed a sense of its meaning. In Vermont, perhaps even more than elsewhere, there was embodied in the spirit of the people the conviction that governments were like the houses we live in, made to contribute to our welfare, and that those who lived in them were as free to change and extend the one as they were the other when developing needs of the human family called for such alterations and modifications.[3]

In sketching Dewey's personal and intellectual development, it may be instructive at the outset to recall briefly the context of his extraordinarily vigorous and long life (1859–1952). Dewey's ninety-two years spanned the American Civil War, the Spanish-American War, the Russian Revolution, World War I, the Great Depression, World War II, and Auschwitz. Born in the year in which Darwin's *Origin of Species* appeared, Dewey witnessed the development of relativity theory and quantum mechanics, and the creation and use of the atom bomb. The electric light, telephone, television, automobile, and airplane were invented during his life. In short, Dewey's lifetime was a period of unprecedented and far-reaching change in America and the world.

John Dewey was born in Burlington, Vermont, in 1859, the third of the four sons of Archibald and Lucina Rich Dewey. His parents were third-generation Vermonters, and each had been born and raised on a family farm before moving to Burlington, where John's father became a grocer. With the exception of a winter spent in war-torn northern Virginia, where his father was a quartermaster of a Vermont cavalry regiment, Dewey's childhood was spent in Vermont. There he boated on Lake Champlain and hiked in the Adirondacks, delivered newspapers and tallied lumber, joined the First Congregational

Church at age eleven (at his mother's urging), and did well in public school, though he found it routine and dull. Dewey began high school in 1872, and completed in three years the four-college preparatory course in Latin, Greek, French, English grammar and literature, and mathematics.

At the age of fifteen, Dewey entered the University of Vermont, from which he graduated with seventeen classmates in 1879. In addition to continuing his classical education, Dewey studied evolutionary thought and the philosophies of the German idealists, the Scottish realists, and the intuitionalists. He was also, indeed mainly, stimulated by his extracurricular reading of contemporary English periodicals and their discussions of evolution and the relation of science to traditional values. Following graduation with honors, Dewey taught high school for two years in Oil City, Pennsylvania, developing his lifelong interest in schools and the educational process, and committing himself to further study of philosophy. Dewey spent the following year teaching in a village school near Burlington and studying philosophy on a tutorial basis. At this time he sent an essay, "The Metaphysical Assumptions of Materialism," to W. T. Harris, editor of *Speculative Philosophy*. Harris accepted the article (and, later, two others) and, in response to Dewey's questions, encouraged him to pursue a career in philosophy. Dewey decided on the new graduate school at Johns Hopkins University: he applied for a fellowship, which he did not receive, then applied for a smaller scholarship, which again he did not receive, and, after borrowing $500 from an aunt, finally began the graduate program without aid.

At Johns Hopkins, Dewey studied history and political science (which he found insufficiently philosophical) in addition to philosophy and psychology. He studied logic under Charles Peirce, but had little interest *at this time* in Peirce's important work. He was greatly stimulated, on the other hand, by his work with George S. Morris, whose personality deeply influenced and impressed Dewey, and whose positions Dewey came to adopt at this time. Dewey's early Congregational evangelicalism and undergraduate intuitionalism were rapidly replaced by neo-Hegelian idealism, by a view of reality as an organic unity, and by Morris's mixture of Hegelian and Aristotelian logic (which he called "real" as opposed to "formal" logic). The influence of Morris, according to Dewey, was reenforced both by the general movement of philosophy in this direction (and away from atomistic individualism and sensationalistic empiricism) and by Dewey's own emotional makeup. Terming his earlier study of philosophy a mere "intellectual gymnastic," Dewey described Hegel's synthesis as an "immense release" and a "liberation": ". . . it supplied a demand for unification that was doubtless an intense emotional craving, and yet was a hunger that only an intellectualized subject could easily satisfy."[4] Long after he had abandoned Hegelian idealism for a more naturalistic, experiential view of existence and a more pragmatic, instrumental account of logic and inquiry, Dewey wrote that "acquaintance with Hegel has left a permanent deposit in my thinking."[5] Morris, impressed by Dewey, proved influential in other ways as well: he helped Dewey secure teaching experience and, at last, a fellowship; following Dewey's receipt of the Ph.D. in 1884, Morris was influential in obtaining for Dewey an instructorship at the University of Michigan.

With the exception of a year at the University of Minnesota, Dewey spent the next ten years at the University of Michigan. During this time, Dewey published his *Psychology*, an attempt to combine empirical physiological psychology with philosophical idealism, as well as a study of the philosophy of Leibniz and many articles on idealism, ethics, and education. Here too Dewey began his long friendships and collaboration with James Tufts and George Herbert Mead (whose large influence on his thinking Dewey frequently acknowledged). Dewey married Alice Chipman in 1886; three children were born to them in Michigan, and three more were born following the family move to Chicago.

In 1894, Dewey moved to the University of Chicago to accept a professorship in philosophy and the chairmanship of the Department of Philosophy, Psychology, and Education. Dewey's ten years in Chicago were productive, eventful, and important. The gradual shift begun at Michigan from idealism to pragmatism and instrumentalism became complete during his Chicago years, galvanized by his study of William James's *Principles of Psychology* (which had appeared in 1890). Dewey clearly acknowledged the importance of James's work both in the development of his thinking and in the development of American pragmatism more generally. Referring to James's *Principles* as "the great exception to what was said about no very fundamental vital influence issuing from books," Dewey writes: "The objective biological approach of the Jamesian psychology led straight to the perception of the importance of distinctive social categories, especially communication and participation. It is my conviction that a great deal of our philosophizing needs to be done over again from this point of view, and that there will ultimately result an integrated synthesis in a philosophy congruous with modern science and related to actual needs in education, morals, and religion."[6] Following James, Dewey claims in "The Development of American Pragmatism" that the fundamental categories of perception and conception are sustained by and in their value in application to concrete experiences: "It is therefore not the origin of a concept, it is its application which becomes the criterion of its value; and here we have the whole of pragmatism in embryo."[7]

Dewey's publications during his Chicago years reflect James's influence, make evident his shift from an idealistic psychology to one increasingly behavioristic and social, mark the further development of his pragmatism and instrumentalism, and attest to his continuing interest in educational and social problems. Dewey's work and philosophical orientation dovetailed with that of other important thinkers (including Mead, Tufts, Addison Moore, and Edward Scribner Ames) in a variety of disciplines at Chicago. The publication in 1903 of *Studies in Logical Theory*, with essays by Dewey and others at Chicago, led William James to speak of the "Chicago School" (with Dewey its acknowledged leader) and of the ascendancy of pragmatism in American philosophy.

Dewey's work at Chicago also included his founding of an elementary school, sponsored and supervised by the Department of Philosophy and known as the "laboratory school" or, popularly, the "Dewey school." More than a laboratory for teaching methods, the world-famous school was a vehicle for and focus of cultural inquiry. The theory and aims of the education at this school are generalized in Dewey's *The School and Society* (1900) and *The Child and the Curriculum* (1902). Dewey also worked with supervisors of the Chicago public schools and with Jane Addams at the well-known Hull

House, a settlement house seeking to ameliorate the urban problems facing America's immigrants. Despite his many successes and accomplishments, the Chicago years were not without tragedy for Dewey: his third child died in 1895 at the age of two, and his fourth child died at the age of eight in 1904 (after which the Deweys adopted an orphaned boy in Italy). Furthermore, personal, financial, and political problems within the university culminated in an unpleasant end to the laboratory school and Alice Dewey's work there: it was merged with the Chicago Institute, directed by the University School of Education. Following this, Dewey resigned at once and shortly thereafter accepted a professorship of philosophy at Columbia University in New York City.

Dewey taught at Columbia University and its Teachers College from 1904 until his retirement in 1930, continuing to make New York City his home until his death in 1952. His activities and accomplishments during this time are staggering. His participation in civic, national, and international affairs greatly increased. His work at Teachers College helped spread progressive education throughout the United States, and his writings, lectures, and travels spurred educational changes in many foreign countries, including Japan, China, Turkey, Mexico, and the U.S.S.R. Concerned for academic autonomy and freedom of inquiry, he founded the American Association of University Professors, was involved in the founding of the teacher union movement in New York City, and was a charter member of the New York Teacher's Guild of the American Federation of Teachers. In 1937, at age seventy-eight, Dewey served impressively in Mexico as chairman of the Commission of Inquiry into the Charges Made Against Leon Trotsky in the Moscow Trials. Throughout these years, Dewey wrote voluminously on public affairs and current issues for popular magazines and journals such as *The New Republic*. Despite these activities, Dewey found time for his most important philosophical lecturing and writing during this period. A mere listing of this work[8] demonstrates the depth, scope, and sheer volume of Dewey's philosophical output (which continued past supposed "farewell celebrations" in 1929, 1939, and 1949). Almost all of the selections below are drawn from these writings.

Alice Dewey died in 1927 of arteriosclerosis, having perhaps never fully recovered from the death of her two children and the loss of her involvement and position at the Chicago laboratory school. In 1946, Dewey married Roberta Grant, whose family came from Oil City and had known Dewey for many years. Two children were adopted during John's marriage with Roberta. Dewey enjoyed good health and remained active into his nineties, as his correspondence and publications indicate. He suffered a broken hip while playing with his children in the late autumn of 1951, following his ninety-second birthday; while recovering, he became ill with pneumonia on May 31, 1952, and died the next day.

THE NATURE AND AIMS OF PHILOSOPHY

> . . . philosophy is inherently criticism, having its distinctive position among various modes of criticism in its generality; a criticism of criticism, as it were. Criticism is

discriminating judgment, careful appraisal, and judgment is appropriately termed criticism wherever the subject-matter of discrimination concerns goods or values.

. . . philosophy is and can be nothing but this critical operation and function become aware of itself and its implications, pursued deliberately and systematically. It starts from actual situations of belief, conduct and appreciative perception which are characterized by immediate qualities of good and bad, and from the modes of critical judgment current at any given time in all the regions of value; these are its data, its subject-matter. These values, criticisms, and critical methods, it subjects to further criticism as comprehensive and consistent as possible. The function is to regulate the further appreciation of goods and bads; to give greater freedom and security in those acts of direct selection, appropriation, identification and of rejection, elimination, destruction which enstate and which exclude objects of belief, conduct and contemplation.[9]

The social and moral effects of the separation of theory and practice have been merely hinted at. They are so manifold and so pervasive that an adequate consideration of them would involve nothing less than a survey of the whole field of morals, economics and politics. It cannot be justly stated that these effects are in fact direct consequences of the quest for certainty by thought and knowledge isolated from action. For, as we have seen, this quest was itself a reflex product of actual conditions. But it may be truly asserted that this quest, undertaken in religion and philosophy, has had results which have reinforced the conditions which originally brought it about. Moreover, search for safety and consolation amid the perils of life by means other than intelligent action, by feeling and thought alone, began when actual means of control were lacking, when arts were undeveloped. It had then a relative historic justification that is now lacking. The primary problem for thinking which lays claim to be philosophic in its breadth and depth is to assist in bringing about a reconstruction of all beliefs rooted in a basic separation of knowledge and action; to develop a system of operative ideas congruous with present knowledge and with present facilities of control over natural events and energies.[10]

The sort of thing the philosophers of an earlier period did is now done; in substance it is no longer called for. Persistence in repetition of a work that has little or no significance in the life-conditions (including those of physical science) that now exist is as sure a way as could be found for promoting the remoteness of philosophy from human concerns which is already tending to alienate popular regard and esteem by reducing philosophy to a kind of highly professionalized busy-work. In the meantime, there is a kind of intellectual work to be done which it is of utmost importance to mankind to have done, but which from the general human point of view does not need to be done in the name of philosophy provided only that it be done. From the standpoint of philosophy, that is philosophers, it may not be a matter of life or death but it is a matter of self-respect as well as of popular esteem.[11]

Dewey's work constitutes a sweeping reconstruction of philosophy itself. As a result, any attempt to grasp his thought must include an understanding of his view of the nature of philosophy. What is philosophy, according to Dewey? To begin, Dewey emphasizes that philosophy—like the arts, scientific experimentation, politics, business, sports, and sex—is a human activity: it is an undertaking, a "doing," something that we engage in and undergo. As a reflective activity, moreover, it is purposeful, and thus intrinsically connected to the situation that called forth the reflection. A philosophy thus is situated in experience, and experience in turn supplies the criteria for its evaluation. While this may seem obvious, this view is anything but common in the history of philosophy. As a meaningful, purposeful human activity, philosophy is essentially temporal and spatial: it is historically and culturally located, and this location constitutes and is intrinsic to it. So, the problems, terminology, methods, arguments, and positions of previous philosophers were shaped by and in turn shaped the cultural conditions and problems of the day. Philosophers at present, Dewey insists, also function in intrinsic connection to and through contemporary situations, events, difficulties, and values. These connections, for Dewey, are not bonds that must be broken so as to build a philosophy more true, pure, or eternal. Rather, they define and constitute the context in and through which philosophies as definite historical, cultural occurrences have meaning and mark change.

The implications of this view are profound and far-reaching. Stated negatively, philosophy, for Dewey, is not the achievement of, or even the quest for, certainty. It cannot and does not begin in total doubt or some presuppositionless state and it issues in no absolute knowledge or eternal truths. It does not provide knowledge of supposed final causes or some ultimate, transcendent reality. It concerns no special, self-contained, disciplinary subject matter, problems that are philosophical rather than, for example, psychological, social, economic, biological. It is not a form of disinterested contemplation, a passive mirroring of reality, a spectator sport or form of intellectual voyeurism uninvolved intrinsically with experienced problems and efforts to ameliorate them.

Stated positively, Dewey understands philosophy as follows. First, the ultimate *subject matter* of philosophy is experience and its problems. "Reference to the primacy and ultimacy of the material of ordinary experience protects us," Dewey writes, "from creating artificial problems which deflect the energy and attention of philosophers from the real problems that arise out of actual subject-matter."[12] It is in this spirit that Dewey praises Ralph Waldo Emerson for judging every philosophy by its reference to the immediacies of life[13] and reminds us that philosophy must not be a study of philosophy, but a study, by means of philosophy, of life-experience and our beliefs about and in this experience.[14] This point is made forcefully in *Reconstruction in Philosophy:*

> Instead of the disputes of rivals about the nature of reality, we have the scene of human clash of social purpose and aspirations. Instead of impossible attempts to transcend experience, we have the significant record of the efforts of men to formulate the things of experience to which they are most deeply and passionately attached. Instead of impersonal and purely speculative endeavors to contemplate as remote beholders the nature of absolute things-in-themselves, we have a living picture of the choice of thoughtful men about what they would have life to be, and to what ends they would have men shape their intelligent activities.
>
> . . . When it is acknowledged that under disguise of dealing with ultimate reality, philosophy has been occupied with the precious values embedded in social traditions, that it has sprung from a clash of social ends and from a conflict of inherited institutions with incompatible contemporary tendencies, it will be seen that the task of future philosophy is to clarify men's ideas as to the social and moral strifes of their own day. Its aim is to become so far as is humanly possible an organ for dealing with these conflicts.[15]

Second, the *method* of philosophy, accordingly, is empirical and critical. It is the systematic attempt to intelligently assess experienced values (evident in perception, belief, and action), judgments about these values, and methods of making such judgments. Dewey writes:

> . . . the business of philosophy is *criticism of belief* . . . so widely current socially as to be dominant factors in culture. Methods of critical inquiry mark . . . a philosopher, but the subject-matter with which he deals is not his own. The beliefs themselves are social products, social facts and social forces.[16]

This critical method, for Dewey, is experimental and scientific in the sense in which " 'scientific' means regular methods of controlling the formation of judgments regarding some subject-matter."[17] Dewey contrasts this notion of philosophy as method with the earlier view of philosophy as system: philosophy is primarily method, and system only as method establishes an arragement of problems and ideas as conducive to further inquiry and critical understanding of concrete problems.[18]

Third, the *orientation* of philosophy is thus pragmatic: it is called forth by and in experienced problems, and its consequences in action directed at these problems are the measure of its success and its truth. As such, philosophy is instrumental rather than final:[19]

> The experimental method of modern science, its erection into the ultimate mode of verification, is simply this fact obtaining recognition. Only action can reconcile the old, the general, and the permanent with the changing, the individual, and the new. It is action as progress, as development, making over the wealth of the past into capital with which to do an enlarging and freer business, which alone can find its way out of the cul-de-sac of the theory of knowledge. . . . Then the dominating interest becomes the *use* of knowledge; the conditions under which and ways in which it may be most organically and effectively employed to direct conduct.[20]

> When the practice of knowledge ceased to be dialectical and became experimental, knowing became preoccupied with changes and the test of knowledge became the ability to bring about certain changes. Knowing, for experimental sciences, means a certain kind of intelligently conducted doing; it ceases to be contemplative and becomes in a true sense practical. Now this implies that philosophy, unless it is to undergo a complete break with the authorized spirit of science, must also alter its nature. It must assume a practical nature; it must become operative and experimental.[21]

Action, then, not only yields or establishes truth, but is central to the very meaning of truth:

> Just as to say an idea was true all the time is a way of saying *in retrospect* that it has come out in a certain fashion, so to say that an idea is "eternally true" is to indicate *prospective* modes of application which are indefinitely anticipated. Its meaning, therefore, is strictly pragmatic. It does not indicate a property inherent in the idea as intellec-

tualized existence, but denotes a property of use and employment. Always at hand when needed is a good enough eternal for reasonably minded persons.[22]

Fourth, philosophy, understood as the *result* of this critical method in action, is intrinsically connected to the cultural context in which this method operates. Dewey writes:

> Even in considering the nature of a philsophy we cannot get away from the biological idea of human activity as a response to an environment, in this case a reflective response to a social environment. We cannot understand an act, whether overt or reflective, unless we understand the medium in which it occurs and to which it is a response.[23]

The cultural context of a philosophy—be it an elucidation of meaning, an analysis of concepts, an interpretation of other thinkers, or a recommendation of policies—is an intrinsic aspect of that philosophy. Contexts vary, but some context always exists (even if ignored). Accordingly, the task of philosophy is the critical transformation of the context in which it is called forth, and not the denial of this context in the name of eternal truth, presuppositionless thought, or acultural analysis. It is this spirit that Dewey suggested that *Reconstruction in Philosophy* should be renamed *Reconstruction of Philosophy:* ". . . the distinctive office, problems, and subjectmatter of philosophy grow out of stresses and strains in the community life in which a given form of philosophy arises, and . . . its specific problems vary with the changes in human life that are always going on. . . ."[24]

A PHILOSOPHY OF EXPERIENCE

> Two things have rendered possible a new conception of experience and a new conception of the relation of reason to experience, or, more accurately, of the place of reason *in* experience. The primary factor is the change that has taken place in the actual nature of experience, its contents and methods, as it is actually lived. The other is the development of a psychology based upon biology which makes possible a new scientific formulation of the nature of experience.[25]

> Thus the value of the notion of experience for philosophic reflection is that it denotes both the field, the sun and clouds and rain, seeds, and harvest, and the man who labors, who plans, invents, uses, suffers, and enjoys. Experience denotes what is experienced, the world of events and persons; and it denotes that world caught up into experiencing, the career and destiny of mankind. Nature's place in man is no less significant than man's place in nature. Man in nature is man subjected; nature in man, recognized and used, is intelligence and art.[26]

> In short, the requirement is that we shall think things as they are themselves, not make them into objects constructed by thinking.[27]

Given the above understanding of the nature and tasks of philosophy, perhaps it is not surprising that Dewey's view of experience stands at the center of his philosophy and informs his writings on issues in education, politics, economics, society, morals, art, and religion. At the outset, it is vital to distinguish Dewey's theory of experience and his "empiricism" from the philosophical traditions and theories which he seeks to overcome and abandon. Dewey's major criticisms of traditional empiricism are neatly summarized in "The Need for a Recovery of Philosophy" (included in the selections below). Here Dewey rejects the traditional view of experience as something subjective and psychical, as "particularistic" or composed of discrete sense data assembled by the understanding, as primarily an affair of knowing, as directed primarily at the past, and as something separate from and opposed to thought.

How, then, does Dewey positively characterize experience? In beginning to understand his view, it cannot be overemphasized that Dewey is not using the word "experience" in its conventional sense. For Dewey, experience is not to be understood in terms of the experiencing subject, or as the interaction of a subject and object that exist separate from their interaction. Instead, Dewey's view is radically empirical:[28] experience is an activity in which subject and object are unified and *constituted* as partial features and relations within this ongoing, unanalyzed unity. Dewey warns us not to misconstrue aspects of this unified experience-activity: distinctions made in reflection do not refer to things that exist as separate substances prior to and outside of that reflection. If we do confuse them, we invent the philosophical problem of how to get them together:

> What has been completely divided in philosophical discourse into man *and* world, inner *and* outer, self *and* not-self, subject *and* object, individual *and* social, private *and* public, etc., are in actuality parties in life-transactions. The philosophical 'problem' of trying to get them together is artificial. On the basis of fact, it needs to be replaced by consideration of the conditions under which they occur as *distinctions,* and of the special uses served by the distinctions.[29]

The error of materialist and idealist alike—the error of conferring existential status upon the products of reflection—is the result of neglect of the context of reflection on experience. Philosophers frequently have ignored or overextended this context:

> The trouble is not with analysis, but with the philosopher who ignores the context in which and for the sake of which the analysis occurs. In this sense, a characteristic defect of philosophy *is* connected with analysis. There are a multitude of ways of commiting the analytic fallacy. It is found whenever the distinctions or elements that are discriminated are treated as if they were final and self-sufficient.[30]

> . . . every generalization occurs under limiting conditions set by the contextual situation. When this fact is passed over . . . a principle valid under specifiable conditions is perforce extended without limit. . . . All statements about the universe as a whole, reality as an unconditioned unity, involve the same fallacy. There is genuine meaning in the act of inquiry into the reality of a given situation. . . . Within the limits of context found in any valid inquiry, "reality" thus means the confirmed outcome, actual or

potential, or the inquiry that is undertaken. . . . When "reality" is sought for at large, it is without intellectual import. . . . Results of inquiry are in these philosophers *ipso facto* converted into a sweeping metaphysical doctrine.[31]

The context of reflection on experience includes, for Dewey, at least those aspects he terms "background" and "selective interest." Background constitutes the tacit framework, the setting, the taken-for-granted in any reflection. (Of course, this "given" may become problematic and thus be the subject matter of some other reflection.) Reflection—indeed, all experience—is saturated with the results of past reflection; reflection is never presuppositionless, and experience is always "funded." Selective interest, the concerns or attitude of a subject, is not the subject matter of reflection but rather determines or selects the actual subject matter of reflection. Thus, Dewey writes that the subject, while implicated in all thinking, cannot entirely be made an explicit object of thought, but, since it affects all thought, must be seen as an aspect of context.[32] Selective interest, when acknowledged, does not lead to the impossibility of scientific inquiry or some sort of philosophical subjectivism: "To be objective," Dewey writes, "is to have a certain sort of selective interest operative."[33] Philosophy, then, is not an attempt to transcend or escape all selective interest, but instead to adopt that standpoint which enables us to deal with our problems. Similarly, an account or philosophy of experience arises from within experience itself, from selective interests within a background.

When reflection recognizes this, the primary unity of experience is evident:

> An organism does not live *in* an environment; it lives by means of an environment. . . . The processes of living are enacted by the environment as truly as by the organism; for they *are* an integration.[34]

> . . . natural operations like breathing and digesting, acquired ones like speech and honesty, are functions of the surroundings as truly as of a person. They are the things done by the environment by means of organic structures or acquired dispositions.[35]

> "Environment" is not something around and about human activities in an external sense; it is their *medium,* or *milieu,* in the sense in which a *medium* is *inter*-mediate in the execution or carrying out of human activities, as well as being the channel *through* which they move and the *vehicle by* which they go on.[36]

Dewey stressed this point throughout his work. It is evident in his early writings, such as his famous essay "The Reflex Arc Concept in Psychology:" ". . . the reflex arc idea, as commonly employed, is defective in that is assumes sensory stimulus and motor response as distinct psychical existences, while in reality they are always inside a co-ordination and have their significance purely from the part played in . . . . the co-ordination."[37] It is evident in his last book, *Knowing and the Known,* wherein he terms experience "transactional" rather than "interactional" in an effort to emphasize the unity of subject and object in experience: "Our position is that the traditional language . . . shatters the subject-matter into fragments in advance of inquiry and thus destroys instead of furthering comprehensive observation of it."[38] And it is evident in his 1951 Introduction for a reissue of *Experience and Nature:*

> Were I to write (or rewrite) *Experience and Nature* today I would entitle the book *Culture and Nature* . . . because of my growing realization that the historical obstacles which prevented understanding of my use of "experience" are, for all practical purposes, insurmountable. I would substitute the term "culture" . . . to designate the inclusive subject-matter which characteristically "modern" (post-medieval) philosophy breaks up into dualisms of subject and object, mind and the world, psychological and physical. . . .
>
> It is a prime philosophical consideration that "culture" includes the material and the ideal in their reciprocal interrelationships and (in marked contrast with the prevailing use of "experience") "culture" designates, also in their reciprocal interconnections, that immense diversity of human affairs, interests, concerns, values which compartmentalists pigeonhole under "religion" "aesthetics" "politics" "economics" etc., etc.[39]

In this light, Dewey characterizes experience and its pervasive, generic traits. Dewey develops these points in great detail, and I shall do little more than list them here. First, experience is eventful, active, precarious, and hazardous. Even that which is stable and fixed is merely stable relative to specifiable changes, and is not absolutely stable. Traditional philosophies have denied this in their quests for certainty, their attempts to make stability of meanings and values prevail over the instability of actual experience by converting valued characteristics to be made good in that experience into a metaphysics of an antecedently sure and fixed existence. In longing for a perfect or safe world, that is, philosophers have claimed ultimate reality for their values and have turned the goals of experience into the antecedently existing causal conditions of that experience. Despite this, experience—the unity of experienc*ing* subject and experienc*ed* object—is undeniably precarious, changing, unsettled.

Second, experience is continuous. Experience not only is eventful, it undergoes change itself. That is, experience is not simply a succession of events; rather, these events have a temporal connection and relation. Experience is connected, conjoining and disjoining, resisting and yielding, modifying and being influenced, organized and confused, planned and surprising. Connections, changes, continuities, relations, changing-in-the-direction-of and being-in-transition-toward are pervasive, experienced features of experience. Events interact and transform one another.

Third, experience is not merely changing and continuous; it is historical. Experience, that is, is not an undifferentiated flow; rather, Dewey says, it consists of experiences, affairs with beginnings and endings, initiations and consummations. As such, there are no final ends *for* experience (as traditional teleological philosophies and religions hold), but only ends-in-view (and means to them) *within* experience. Nor is there fate (as mechanists hold), but only orders within historical events—orders that we can control so as to achieve particular ends.

Fourth, experience is qualitative: within each experience there is an immediate, individual, brute quality, a quality that renders an experience *that* particular experience— *that* meal, *that* snowstorm, *that* philosophy lecture, and so on. This qualitative aspect of experience is not an object of knowledge; indeed, Dewey says that qualitative dimension of experience cannot be known or communicated, since the objects of knowledge are mediate rather than immediate, concern the relations among experiences and not the immediate quality of an experience. This qualitative character of experience is not something subjective, for experience is not something subjective: qualities belong as much to the things experienced as to the experiencing subject.[40] So, a particular experience, as it occurs, simply is; that particular experience, as it is connected by reflection to things beyond itself, becomes a sign and refers.

Fifth, this leads to a further characterization of experience: it is experimental and practical. Reflection may make an experience its object, and this attention to the experience as it is related to and indicative of something else makes possible the control of experience. We may, for instance, focus not on the painfulness of a situation as immediate quality, but on the pain as an indication of the presence of certain other conditions, which we may then alter so as to end the pain. It is in this sense that Dewey defines inquiry as the transformation of a situation, identifies the subject matter of inquiry as the conditions upon which the occurrence of (qualitative) experience depends, characterizes knowing as instrumental, and explains that truth is simply the process of verification taken as a product. In this sense, truth is consequential and "made," rather than fixed, and reality (for Dewey as for Peirce) is that which reflective inquiry is forced to reach rather than something given antecedent to it.

Sixth, implicit in the above is the claim that experience is meaningful: communication pervades experience, events become objects with meaning, experience is "funded." The relations and consequences of an object, as determined in inquiry, can become the very meaning (both referential and immanent) of the thing itself. Inquiry may show, for example, that a creaking sound indicates—referentially means—a splitting mast. But this relation may also enter into the nature—the immanent or "had" meaning—of the sound itself, as the sound comes to be heard as the sound of the mast splitting. For Dewey, these transformations are due to language: it is "(1) the agency by which other institutions and acquired habits are *transmitted*," " (2) it *permeates* both the forms and the contents of all other cultural activities," and "(3) it has its own distinctive structure with is capable of abstraction as form."[41] And language, Dewey stresses, operates in and through the behavior or action of a social group or community.

Seventh, in this sense experience is social. Dewey's point here is not simply that one lives with others. In addition, he is claiming that social meanings, conditions, and forms of life enter into and constitute the individual; individual and environment are constituted in and by the inclusive unity of experience or culture. We are creatures of habit, Dewey asserts, and habits, as results of social conditions and demands for certain kinds of activity, constitute the self.[42] Ironically, this fundamental social character of the self is overlooked or denied by much social philosophy:

> The underlying philosophy and psychology of earlier liberalism led to a conception of individuality as something ready-made, already possessed, and needing only the removal of certain legal restrictions to come into full play. It was not conceived as a moving thing, something that is attained only by continuous growth. Because of this failure, the dependence in fact of individuals upon social conditions was made little of . . . social

arrangements and institutions were thought of as things that operate from without, not entering in any significant way into the internal make-up of individuals.[43]

The individual mind, however, is not "individual" but social: its observations, beliefs, meanings, and values are formed by and exist in and through social processes. Thus, Dewey claims that the social is *the* inclusive philosophic idea in *Philosophy and Civilization:* the physical, organic, mental, and individual are distinctions that fall within it and function "only where association is manifested in the form of participation and communication."[44]

THE RECONSTRUCTION OF CULTURE

> American philosophy must be born out of and must repond to the demands of democracy, as democracy strives to voice and to achieve itself on a vaster scale, and in a more thorough and final way than history has previously witnessed. And, democracy is something at once too subtle and too complex and too aspiring to be caught in the meshes of a single philosophical school or sect.
>
> It is, then, to the needs of democracy in America that we turn to find the fundamental problems of philosophy; and to its tendencies, its working forces, that we look for the points of view and the terms in which philosophy will envisage and solve these problems.[45]

> The beginning of a culture stripped of egoistic illusions is the perception that we have as yet no culture; that our culture is something to achieve, to create. . . . To set up as protector of a shrinking classicism requires only the accidents of a learned education, the possession of leisure and a reasonably apt memory for some phrases, and a facile pen for others. To transmute a society built on an industry which is not yet humanized into a society which wields its knowledge and its industrial power in behalf of a democratic culture requires the courage of an inspired imagination.[46]

> We have the physical tools of communication as never before. The thoughts and aspirations congruous with them are not communicated, and hence are not common. Without such communication the public will remain shadowy and formless, seeking spasmodically for itself, but seizing and holding its shadow rather than its substance. Till the Great Society is converted into a Great Community, the Public will remain in eclipse. Communication can alone create a great community. Our Babel is not one of tongues but of the signs and symbols without which shared experience is impossible.[47]

Dewey's important writings on education, ethics, politics, art, and religion are rooted in the view and method of experience outlined above and constitute a *reconstruction,* a reconstruction of both our thinking and our society. Dewey is critically rethinking our dominant beliefs and institutions, arguing that they are founded on faulty conceptions of experience, and are obsolete, irrelevant, and detrimental in light of changes in the actual conditions of contemporary life. These two kinds of arguments run throughout Dewey's work. He constantly faults *theorists* who have invented problems by converting interrelated aspects in experience (and distinguished by reflection) into opposed entitites with separate existence (prior to reflection). Thus, for example, Dewey rejects educational policies that begin with a fixed opposition between child and curriculum, school and society, and education and life. He rejects ethical theories erected on the opposition between means and ends, and criticizes political philosophies and programs rooted in a metaphysical separation of individual and society, and private and public interest. He criticizes the split between aesthetic experience and ordinary life, between art and everyday objects, and between creation and appreciation. And, he rejects the identification of the religious with the supernatural and its underlying dichotomy of natural and divine realms. These dualisms are without basis in actual experience. As such, they give rise to artificial problems that divert our energies; they should be abandoned.

Dewey also constantly faults *institutions* and *practices* that fail to acknowledge and adapt to the changing cultural situation in and through which they exist and operate, and so present themselves as embodying eternal, ahistorical truths. As conditions change—and Dewey thinks they have changed rapidly—these ways of life become outdated, disintegrated with actual life conditions, and detrimental to achievement of shared human purposes. Thus, Dewey rejects and seeks to reconstruct, for example, traditional notions of education, individualism, community, liberalism, the free market, democracy, God, and the religious and aesthetic dimensions of experience.

These general lines of argument are evident in Dewey's writings. These writings are extensive, and I shall simply highlight some of the major instances of these arguments and their conclusions. To begin, Dewey's notion of growth is central to his influential work in education, and his views on education are central to his writings on democracy, community, and the nature of philosophy itself. Dewey defines growth as the cumulative movement of action toward a later result, and stresses that, as such, growth does not *have* an end but rather *is* an end. Accordingly, the educational process is one of continual reconstruction and self-transformation directed at no end beyond itself. (Here it is important to differentiate education in general from the schooling process or formal education.) Since growth, for Dewey, is one with life-experience (and not the end of life), growth is the criterion for assessing cultural practices: Dewey directs us to examine to what extent habits, relationships, practices, associations, institutions, and traditions promote growth and the desire for further growth, renew the meanings of experience, and harmoniously adjust individual and environment. The social environment, Dewey writes, "is truly educative in its effect in the degree in which an individual shares or participates in some conjoint activity" and becomes a "directive guardian" of this shared activity.[48] This makes clear the connection between democracy and education:

> A society which makes provision for participation in its good of all its members on equal terms and which secures flexible readjustment of its institutions through interaction of the different forms of associated life is in so far democratic. Such a society must have a type of education which gives individuals a personal interest in social relationships and control, and the habits of mind which secure social changes without introducing disorder.[49]

Dewey's social and political writings focus on this task of creating a genuinely democratic society, a society in which individualism and community flourish. Individual and community, the private and the public do not stand in necessary opposition; instead, they require one another, and any opposition between them marks not a metaphysical fact but a historical social problem that demands conceptual and political reconstruction. This reconstruction is needed, Dewey argues, because rapid cultural change has submerged the individual by overturning the traditional loyalties and attachments that constitute the basis of real individuality. This reconstructive action has been paralyzed by traditional conceptions of individuality as something "ready-made" and in need only of being unrestricted, and so served by laissez-faire economic policies and traditional political liberalism. These traditional conceptions, blind to their own historical relativity and the developmental character of individuality, once may have served the goals of individuality, liberty, and intelligence, but now, under new conditions, effectively hinder the realization of these goals as they have actual meaning in these new conditions. Thus, Dewey writes:

> Above all, in identifying the extension of liberty in all of its modes with extension of their particular brand of economic liberty, they completely failed to anticipate the bearing of private control of the means of production and distribution upon the effective liberty of the masses in industry as well as in cultural goods.[50]

By contrast, liberty today, Dewey claims, must signify liberation, through the controlled use of science and technology, from material insecurity and economic coercion that prevent many from participating in the resources of our culture, that effectively inhibit genuine growth, and block the transition from a formal democracy to a genuine community.[51] The development of a new individualism, then, requires the creation of a community—what Dewey calls "the Great Community"—and this in turn requires the development and application of critical methods of scientific inquiry for dealing with complex, often technical, social problems.

Efforts to establish a community of and in experience are attempts to liberate experience, to create and extend the shared consummatory values and meanings in our lives. Dewey's writings on the aesthetic and religious dimensions of experience are two particularly rich instances of this. In *Art as Experience*, Dewey identifies art with experience that has a certain purposeful, consummatory, integrated, unified quality. This provides a basis for recovering the continuity between objects of art and everyday objects, and between aesthetic experience and daily living. The philosophic task, then, is pragmatic: it does not consist in efforts to compartmentalize experience or its objects, but in describing the aesthetic and the conditions upon which it depends. Dewey writes:

> A conception of fine art that sets out from its connection with discovered qualities of ordinary experience will be able to indicate the factors and forces that favor the normal development of common human activities into matters of artistic growth. It will also be able to point out those conditions that arrest its normal growth.[52]

In linking aesthetic experience with growth, Dewey connects it with the evaluation of society:

> Esthetic experience is always more than esthetic. In it a body of matters and meanings, not in themselves esthetic, *become* esthetic as they enter into an ordered rhythmic movement toward consummation. . . . The material of esthetic experience in being human—human in connection with the nature of which it is a part—is social. Esthetic experience is a manifestation, a record and celebration of the life of a civilization, a means of promoting its development, and is also the ultimate judgment upon the quality of a civilization.[53]

It is in the same spirit that Dewey carefully distinguishes between religion (as an institutionally organized body of beliefs and practices, often concerned with a supernatural power) and the religious quality of experience (as any "activity pursued in behalf of an ideal end against obstacles and in spite of threats of personal loss because of conviction of its general and enduring value"[54]). Again, this provides a basis for reconstructing continuities between the religious character of experience and everyday life, and for enlarging the latter by means of the former. The religious thus acquires a "human abode" and can be understood in a manner consistent with actual experience and methods of inquiry:

> I have said those things because of a firm belief that the claim on the part of religions to possess a monopoly of ideals and of the supernatural means by which alone, it is alleged, they can be furthered, stands in the way of realization of distinctively religious values inherent in natural experience.[55]

> Ours is the responsibility of conserving, transmitting, rectifying and expanding the heritage of values we have received that those who come after us may receive it more solid and secure, more widely accessible and more generously shared than we received it. Here are all the elements for a religious faith that shall not be confined to sect, class, or race. Such a faith has always been implicitly the common faith of mankind. It remains to make it explicit and militant.[56]

In large part, Dewey's views on cultural reconstruction still wait on our understanding and, above all, our action. Their ultimate and eventual importance, at least in Dewey's own view, must lie in their promotion and justification of this undertaking. Their ultimate value and truth must lie in this practice. The time is ripe, Dewey tells us, for this endeavor.

NOTES

Many of the references below are to the definitive edition of the works of John Dewey, and are abbreviated as follows: *EW* for *John Dewey: The Early Works, 1882–1885*, 5 vols. (Carbondale and Edwardsville: Southern Illinois University Press, 1969–1972); *MW* for *John Dewey: The Middle Works, 1899–1924*, 15 vols. (Carbondale and Edwardsville: Southern Illinois University Press, 1976–1983); *LW* for *John Dewey: The Later Works, 1925–1953*, 10 of 16 projected vols. (Carbondale and Edwardsville: Southern Illinois University Press, 1981—).

1. "Experience, Knowledge and Value: A Rejoinder," in *The Philosophy of John Dewey*, ed. Paul Arthur Schilpp (LaSalle, Ill.: Open Court, 1971), p. 521.

2. "From Absolutism to Experimentalism," *LW*, vol. 5, p. 155.

3. "James Marsh and American Philosophy," *LW,* vol. 5, p. 194.

4. "From Absolutism to Experimentalism," p. 153.

5. Ibid., p. 154. See also the discussion of this period in Dewey's life in George Dykhuizen's *The Life and Mind of John Dewey* (Carbondale and Edwardsville: Southern Illinois University Press, 1973).

6. "From Absolutism to Experimentalism," p. 159.

7. "The Development of American Pragmatism," *LW* vol. 2, p. 16.

8. As a partial list: *How We Think* and *The Influence of Darwin and Other Essays on Contemporary Thought* in 1910; *Essays in Experimental Logic* and *Democracy and Education* in 1916; *Reconstruction in Philosophy* in 1920; *Human Nature and Conduct* in 1922; *Experience and Nature* in 1925, when Dewey was 65; *The Public and its Problems* in 1927; *The Quest for Certainty* in 1929; *Individualism: Old and New* in 1930; *Philosophy and Civilization* in 1931; the revised edition of *Ethics* with James Tufts in 1932; *Art as Experience* and *A Common Faith* in 1934; *Liberalism and Social Action* in 1935; *Logic: The Theory of Inquiry* and *Experience and Education* in 1938; *Freedom and Culture* and *Theory of Valuation* in 1939; *Problems of Men* in 1946; and, with Arthur Bentley, *Knowing and the Known* in 1949.

9. "Existence, Value and Criticism," in *Experience and Nature, LW*, Vol. 1, pp. 298, 302.

10. "The Construction of Good," in *The Quest for Certainty, LW*, Vol. 4, p. 226.

11. Manuscript page in the John Dewey Papers housed in the Special Collections of Morris Library, Southern Illinois University at Carbondale, 102/58/10.

12. "Experience and Philosophic Method," in *Experience and Nature, LW*, Vol. 1, p. 26. Included in the selections below, pp. 350–360.

13. "Emerson—the Philosopher of Democracy," *MW*, Vol. 3, p. 188.

14. "Experience and Philosophic Method," p. 40. Included in the selections below, pp. 350–360.

15. "Changing Conceptions of Philosophy," in *Reconstruction in Philosophy, MW*, Vol. 12, p. 94.

16. "Philosophy," *LW*, Vol. 5, p. 164.

17. "Logical Conditions of a Scientific Treatment of Morality," *MW*, Vol. 3, p. 3.

18. "Philosophy and American National Life," *MW*, Vol. 3, pp. 76–77. See also "The Significance of the Problem of Knowledge, *EW*, Vol. 5, p. 22; and "The Pragmatism of Peirce," *MW*, Vol. 10, p. 77.

19. "Philosophy and American National Life," *MW*, Vol. 3, pp. 76–77.

20. "The Significance of the Problem of Knowledge," pp. 21–22.

21. "Changed Conceptions of the Ideal and the Real," in *Reconstruction in Philosophy*, p. 149.

22. "The Intellectual Criterion for Truth," *MW*, Vol. 4, p. 71. See also "What Pragmatism Means by Practical," *MW*, Vol. 4, p. 109.

23. "Philosophy," p. 163.

24. "Introduction: Reconstruction as Seen Twenty-Five Years Later," *MW*, Vol. 12, p. 256. See also the discussion in "Philosophy and American National Life": ". . . a philosophy has to be conceived and stated in terms of conditions and factors that are moving generally in non-philosophic life" (p. 73).

25. "Changed Conceptions of Experience and Reason," in *Reconstruction in Philosophy, MW*, Vol. 12, pp. 127–128. See also Dewey's discussion of Whitehead's substitution of the idea of organism for the idea of mechanism: "The Changing Intellectual Climate," *LW*, Vol. 2, p. 223.

26. "Appendix 2: Experience and Philosophic Method," *LW*, Vol. 1, p. 384.

27. Introduction to *Essays in Experimental Logic, MW*, Vol. 10, p. 337.

28. See the discussions of radical empiricism above, pp. 7, 99, 125, and 180.

29. *Knowing and the Known* (Boston: Beacon Press, 1949), p. 276.

30. "Context and Thought," *LW*, Vol. 6, pp. 6–7.

31. Ibid., pp. 8–9.

32. Ibid., p. 14ff.

33. Ibid.

34. "The Existential Matrix of Inquiry: Biological," in *Logic: The Theory of Inquiry, LW*, Vol. 12, forthcoming.

35. "Habits as Social Functions," in *Human Nature and Conduct, MW.*, Vol. 14, p. 15.

36. *Knowing and the Known*, p. 169.

37. "The Reflex Arc Concept in Psychology," *EW*, Vol. 5, p. 99.

38. *Knowing and the Known*, pp. 110–111.

39. "Appendix 1: The Unfinished Introduction" to *Experience and Nature*, pp. 361–363.

40. "Nature, Life and Body-Mind," in *Experience and Nature*, pp. 198ff.

41. "The Existential Matrix of Inquiry: Cultural," in *Logic: The Theory of Inquiry*, forthcoming. See also the discussion of communication in *Democracy and Education, MW*, Vol. 9. Dewey writes: "Society not only

continues to exist *by* transmission, *by* communication, but it may fairly be said to exist *in* transmission, *in* communication" (p. 7).

42. See "The Place of Habit in Conduct," in *Human Nature and Conduct.*

43. *Liberalism and Social Action* (New York: Capricorn Books/G. P. Putnam's, 1935, 1963), p. 39.

44. See "The Inclusive Philosophic Idea," *LW,* Vol. 3, pp. 41–54.

45. "Philosophy and American National Life," pp. 73–74.

46. "American Education and Culture," *MW,* Vol. 10, p. 198.

47. "The Eclipse of the Public," in *The Public and its Problems, LW,* Vol. 2, pp. 323–324.

48. *Democracy and Education,* pp. 26, 332.

49. Ibid., p. 105.

50. *Liberalism and Social Action,* pp. 35–36.

51. Ibid., p. 48. See also "Towards a New Individualism," in *Individualism: Old and New, LW,* Vol. 5, pp. 85–86.

52. *Art as Experience* (New York: Capricorn/G. P. Putnam's, 1934, 1958), p. 11.

53. Ibid., p. 326.

54. *A Common Faith* (New Haven: Yale University Press, 1934), p. 27.

55. Ibid., pp. 27–28.

56. Ibid., p. 87.

The Need for a Recovery of Philosophy

Intellectual advance occurs in two ways. At times increase of knowledge is organized about old conceptions, while these are expanded, elaborated and refined, but not seriously revised, much less abandoned. At other times, the increase of knowledge demands qualitative rather than quantitative change; alteration, not addition. Men's minds grow cold to their former intellectual concerns; ideas that were burning fade; interests that were urgent seem remote. Men face in another direction; their older perplexities are unreal; considerations passed over as negligible loom up. Former problems may not have been solved, but they no longer press for solution.

Philosophy is no exception to the rule. But it is unusually conservative—not, necessarily, in proffering solutions, but in clinging to problems. It has been so allied with theology and theological morals as representatives of men's chief interests, that radical alteration has been shocking. Men's activities took a decidedly new turn, for example, in the seventeenth century, and it seemed as if philosophy, under the lead of thinkers like Bacon and Descartes, was to execute an about-face. But, in spite of the ferment, it turned out that many of the older problems were but translated from Latin into the vernacular or into the new terminology furnished by science.

The association of philosophy with academic teaching has reinforced this intrinsic conservatism. Scholastic philosophy persisted in universities after men's thoughts outside of the walls of colleges had moved in other directions. In the last hundred years intellectual advances of science and politics have in like fashion been crystallized into material of instruction and now resist further change. I would not say that the spirit of teaching is hostile to that of liberal inquiry, but a philosophy which exists largely as something to be taught rather than wholly as something to be reflected upon is conducive to discussion of views held by others rather than to immediate response. Philosophy when taught inevitably magnifies the history of past thought, and leads professional philosophers to approach their subject-matter through its formulation in received systems. It tends, also, to emphasize points upon which men have divided into schools, for these lend themselves to retrospective definition and elaboration. Consequently, philosophical discussion is likely to be a dressing out of antithetical traditions, where criticism of one view is thought to afford proof of the truth of its opposite (as if formulation of views guaranteed logical exclusives). Direct preoccupation with contemporary difficulties is left to literature and politics.

If changing conduct and expanding knowledge ever required a willingness to surrender not merely old solutions but old problems it is now. I do not mean that we can turn abruptly away from all traditional issues. This is impossible; it would be the undoing of the one who attempted it. Irrespective of the professionalizing of philosophy, the ideas philosophers discuss are still those in which Western civilization has been bred. They are in the backs of the heads of educated people. But what serious-minded men not engaged in the professional business of philosophy most want to know is what modifications and abandonments of intellectual inheritance are required by the newer industrial, political, and scientific movements. They want to know what these newer movements mean when translated into general ideas. Unless professional philosophy can mobilize itself sufficiently to assist in this clarification and redirection of men's thoughts, it is likely to get more and more sidetracked from the main currents of contemporary life.

This essay may, then, be looked upon as an attempt to forward the emancipation of philosophy from too intimate and exclusive attachment to traditional problems. It is not in intent a criticism of various solutions that have been offered, but raises a question *as to the genuineness, under the present conditions of science and social life, of the problems.*

The limited object of my discussion will, doubtless, give an exaggerated impression of my conviction as to the artificiality of much recent philosophizing. Not that I have wilfully exaggerated in what I have said, but that the limitations of my purpose have led me not to say many things pertinent to a broader purpose. A discussion less restricted would strive

From "The Need for a Recovery of Philosophy" in *John Dewey: The Middle Works, 1899–1924*, Vol. 10, Ed. Jo Ann Boydston (Carbondale and Edwardsville: Southern Illinois University, 1980), pp. 3–11, 22–24, 37–48.

to enforce the genuineness, in their own context, of questions now discussed mainly because they have been discussed rather than because contemporary conditions of life suggest them. It would also be a grateful task to dwell upon the precious contributions made by philosophic systems which as a whole are impossible. In the course of the development of unreal premises and the discussion of artificial problems, points of view have emerged which are indispensable possessions of culture. The horizon has been widened; ideas of great fecundity struck out; imagination quickened; a sense of the meaning of things created. It may even be asked whether these accompaniments of classic systems have not often been treated as a kind of guarantee of the systems themselves. But while it is a sign of an illiberal mind to throw away the fertile and ample ideas of a Spinoza, a Kant, or a Hegel, because their setting is not logically adequate, it is surely a sign of an undisciplined one to treat their contributions to culture as confirmations of premises with which they have no necessary connection.

I

A criticism of current philosophizing from the standpoint of the traditional quality of its problems must begin somewhere, and the choice of a beginning is arbitrary. It has appeared to me that the notion of experience implied in the questions most actively discussed gives a natural point of departure. For, if I mistake not, it is just the inherited view of experience common to the empirical school and its opponents which keeps alive many discussions even of matters that on their face are quite remote from it, while it is also this view which is most untenable in the light of existing science and social practice. Accordingly I set out with a brief statement of some of the chief contrasts between the orthodox description of experience and that congenial to present conditions.

(i) In the orthodox view, experience is regarded primarily as a knowledge-affair. But to eyes not looking through ancient spectacles, it assuredly appears as an affair of the intercourse of a living being with its physical and social environment. (ii) According to tradition experience is (at least primarily) a psychical thing, infected throughout by "subjectivity." What experience suggests about itself is a genuinely objective world which enters into the actions and sufferings of men and undergoes modifications through their responses. (iii) So far as anything beyond a bare present is

recognized by the established doctrine, the past exclusively counts. Registration of what has taken place, reference to precedent, is believed to be the essence of experience. Empiricism is conceived of as tied up to what has been, or is, "given." But experience in its vital form is experimental, an effort to change the given; it is characterized by projection, by reaching forward into the unknown; connexion with a future is its salient trait. (iv) The empirical tradition is committed to particularism. Connexions and continuities are supposed to be foreign to experience, to be by-products of dubious validity. An experience that is an undergoing of an environment and a striving for its control in new directions is pregnant with connexions. (v) In the traditional notion experience and thought are antithetical terms. Inference, so far as it is other than a revival of what has been given in the past, goes beyond experience; hence it is either invalid, or else a measure of desperation by which, using experience as a springboard, we jump out to a world of stable things and other selves. But experience, taken free of the restrictions imposed by the older concept, is full of inference. There is, apparently, no conscious experience without inference; reflection is native and constant.

These contrasts, with a consideration of the effect of substituting the account of experience relevant to modern life for the inherited account, afford the subject-matter of the following discussion.

Suppose we take seriously the contribution made to our idea of experience by biology,—not that recent biological science discovered the facts, but that it has so emphasized them that there is no longer an excuse for ignoring them or treating them as negligible. Any account of experience must now fit into the consideration that experiencing means living; and that living goes on in and because of an environing medium, not in a vacuum. Where there is experience, there is a living being. Where there is life, there is a double connexion maintained with the environment. In part, environmental energies constitute organic functions; they enter into them. Life is not possible without such direct support by the environment. But while all organic changes depend upon the natural energies of the environment for their origination and occurrence, the natural energies sometimes carry the organic functions prosperously forward, and sometimes act counter to their continuance. Growth and decay, health and disease, are alike continuous with activities of the natural surroundings. The difference lies in the bearing of what happens upon future life-activity. From the standpoint of this future reference environmental incidents fall into groups: those favorable to life-activities, and those hostile.

The successful activities of the organism, those within which environmental assistance is incorporated, react upon the environment to bring about modifications favorable to their own future. The human being has upon his hands the problem of responding to what is going on around him so that these changes will take one turn rather than another, namely, that required by its own further functioning. While backed in part by the environment, its life is anything but a peaceful exhalation of environment. It is obliged to struggle—that is to say, to employ the direct support given by the environment in order indirectly to effect changes that would not otherwise occur. In this sense, life goes on by means of controlling the environment. Its activities must change the changes going on around it; they must neutralize hostile occurrences; they must transform neutral events into cooperative factors or into an efflorescence of new features.

Dialectic developments of the notion of self-preservation, of the *conatus essendi,* often ignore all the important facts of the actual process. They argue as if self-control, self-development, went on directly as a sort of unrolling push from within. But life endures only in virtue of the support of the environment. And since the environment is only incompletely enlisted in our behalf, self-preservation—or self-realization or whatever—is always indirect—always an affair of the way in which our present activities affect the direction taken by independent changes in the surroundings. Hindrances must be turned into means.

We are also given to playing loose with the conception of adjustment, as if that meant something fixed—a kind of accommodation once for all (ideally at least) of the organism *to* an environment. But as life requires the fitness of the environment to the organic functions, adjustment to the environment means not passive acceptance of the latter, but acting so that the environing changes take a certain turn. The "higher" the type of live, the more adjustment takes the form of an adjusting of the factors of the environment to one another in the interest of life; the less the significance of living, the more it becomes an adjustment to a given environment till at the lower end of the scale the differences between living and the non-living disappear.

These statements are of an external kind. They are about the conditions of experience, rather than about experiencing itself. But assuredly experience as it concretely takes place bears out the statements. Experience is primarily a process of undergoing: a process of standing something; of suffering and passion, of affection, in the literal sense of these words. The organism has to endure, to undergo, the consequences of its own actions. Experience is no slipping along in a path fixed by inner consciousness. Private consciousness is an incidental outcome of experience of a vital objective sort; it is not its source. Undergoing, however, is never mere passivity. The most patient patient is more than a receptor. He is also an agent—a reactor, one trying experiments, one concerned with undergoing in a way which may influence what is still to happen. Sheer endurance, side-steeping evasions, are, after all, ways of treating the environment with a view to what treatment will accomplish. Even if we shut ourselves up in the most clam-like fashion, we are doing something; our passivity is an active attitude, not an extinction of response. Just as there is no assertive action, no aggressive attack upon things as they are, which is all action, so there is no undergoing which is not on our part also a going on and a going through.

Experience, in other words, is a matter of *simultaneous* doings and sufferings. Our undergoings are experiments in varying the course of events; our active tryings are trials and tests of ourselves. This duplicity of experience shows itself in our happiness and misery, our successes and failures. Triumphs are dangerous when dwelt upon or lived off from; successes use themselves up. Any achieved equilibrium of adjustment with the environment is precarious because we cannot evenly keep pace with changes in the environment. These are so opposed in direction that we must choose. We must take the risk of casting in our lot with one movement or the other. Nothing can eliminate all risk, all adventure; the one thing doomed to failure is to try to keep even with the whole environment at once—that is to say, to maintain the happy moment when all things go our way.

The obstacles which confront us are stimuli to variation, to novel response, and hence are occasions of progress. If a favor done us by the environment conceals a threat, so its disfavor is a potential means of hitherto unexperienced modes of success. To treat misery as anything but misery, as for example a blessing in disguise or a necessary factor in good, is disingenuous apologetics. But to say that the progress of the race has been stimulated by ills undergone, and that men have been moved by what they suffer to search out new and better courses of action is to speak veraciously.

The preoccupation of experience with things which are coming (are now coming, not just to come) is obvious to any one whose interest in experience is empirical. Since we live forward; since we live in a world where changes are going on whose issue means our weal or woe; since every act of ours modifies these changes and hence is fraught with promise, or charged with hostile energies—what should experience be but a future implicated in a present! Adjustment is no timeless state; it is a continuing process. To say that a change takes time may be to say something about the event which is external and uninstructive. But adjustment of organism to environment takes time in the pregnant sense; every step in the process is conditioned by reference to further changes which it effects. What is going on in the environment is the concern of the organism; not what is already "there" in accomplished and finished form. In so far as the issue of what is going on may be affected by intervention of the organism, the moving event is a challenge which stretches the agent-patient to meet what is coming. Experiencing exhibits things in their unterminated aspect moving toward determinate conclusions. The finished and done with is of import as affecting the future, not on its own account: in short, because it is not, really, done with.

Anticipation is therefore more primary than recollection; projection than summoning of the past; the prospective than the retrospective. Given a world like that in which we live, a world in which environing changes are partly favorable and partly callously indifferent, and experience is bound to be prospective in import; for any control attainable by the living creature depends upon what is done to alter the state of things. Success and failure are the primary "categories" of life; achieving of good and averting of ill are its supreme interests; hope and anxiety (which are not self-enclosed states of feeling, but active attitudes of welcome and wariness) are dominant qualities of experience. Imaginative forecast of the future is this forerunning quality of behavior rendered available for guidance in the present. Day-dreaming and castle-building and esthetic realization of what is not practically achieved are offshoots of this paractical trait, or else practical intelligence is a chastened fantasy. It

makes little difference. Imaginative recovery of the bygone is indispensable to successful invasion of the future, but its status is that of an instrument. To ignore its import is the sign of an undisciplined agent; but to isolate the past, dwelling upon it for its own sake and giving it to the eulogistic name of knowledge, is to substitute the reminiscence of old-age for effective intelligence. The movement of the agent-patient to meet the future is partial and passionate; yet detached and impartial study of the past is the only alternative to luck in assuring success to passion.

II

This description of experience would be but a rhapsodic celebration of the commonplace were it not in marked contrast to orthodox philosophical accounts. The contrast indicates that traditional accounts have not beem empirical, but have been deductions, from unnamed premises, of what experience *must* be. Historic empiricism has been empirical in a technical and controversial sense. It has said, Lord, Lord, Experience, Experience; but in practice it has served ideas *forced into* experience, not *gathered from* it. . . .

. . . The description of experience has been forced into conformity with this prior conception; it has been primarily a deduction from it, actual empirical facts being poured into the molds of the deductions. The characteristic feature of this prior notion is the assumption that experience centres in, or gathers about, or proceeds from a centre or subject which is outside the course of natural existence, and set over against it:—it being of no importance, for present purposes, whether this antithetical subject is termed soul, or spirit, or mind, or ego, or consciousness, or just knower or knowing subject. . . .

The problem of knowledge as conceived in the industry of epistemology is the problem of knowlede *in general*—of the possibility, extent, and validity of knowledge in general. What does this "in general" mean? In ordinary life there are problems a-plenty of knowledge in particular; every conclusion we try to reach, theoretical or practical, affords such a problem. But there is no problem of knowledge in general. I do not mean, of course, that general statements cannot be made about knowledge, or that the problem of attaining these general statements is not a genuine one. On the contrary, specific instances of success and failure in inquiry exist, and are of such a character that one can discover the conditions conducing to success and failure. Statement of these conditions constitutes logic, and is capable of being an important aid in proper guidance of further attempts at knowing. But this logical problem of knowledge is at the opposite pole from the epistemological. Specific problems are about right conclusions to be reached—which means, in effect, right ways of going about the business of inquiry. They imply a difference between knowledge and error consequent upon right and wrong methods of inquiry and testing; not a difference between experience and the world. The problem of knowledge *überhaupt* exits because it is assumed that there is a knower in general, who is outside of the world to be known, and who is defined in terms antithetical to the traits of the world. With analogous assumptions, we could invent and discuss a problem of digestion in general. All that would be required would be to conceive the stomach and food-material as inhabiting different worlds. Such an assumption would leave on our hands the question of the possibility, extent, nature, and genuineness of any transaction between stomach and food. . . .

V

What are the bearings of our discussion upon the conception of the present scope and office of philosophy? What do our conclusions indicate and demand with reference to philosophy itself? For the philosophy which reaches such conclusions regarding knowledge and mind must apply them, sincerely and whole-heartedly, to its idea of its own nature. For philosophy claims to be one form or mode of knowing. If, then, the conclusion is reached that knowing is a way of employing empirical occurrences with respect to increasing power to direct the consequences which flow from things, the application of the conclusion must be made to philosophy itself. It, too, becomes not a contemplative survey of existence nor an analysis of what is past and done with, but an outlook upon future possibilities with reference to attaining the better and averting the worse. Philosophy must take, with good grace, its own medicine.

It is easier to state the negative results of the changed idea of philosophy than the positive ones. The point that occurs to mind most readily is that philosophy will have to surrender all pretension to be peculiarly concerned with ultimate reality, or with reality as a complete (i.e., completed) whole: with *the* real object.

The surrender is not easy of achievement. The philosophic tradition that comes to us from classic Greek thought and that was reinforced by Christian philosophy in the Middle Ages discriminates philosophical knowing from other modes of knowing by means of an alleged peculiarly intimate concern with supreme, ultimate, true reality. To deny his trait to philosophy seems to many to be the suicide of philosophy; to be a systematic adoption of skepticism or agnostic positivism. . . .

It is often said that pragmatism, unless it is content to be a contribution to mere methodology, must develop a theory of Reality. But the chief characteristic trait of the pragmatic notion of reality is precisely that no theory of Reality in general, *überhaupt,* is possible or needed. It occupies the position of an emancipated empiricism or a thoroughgoing naïve realism. It finds that "reality" is a *denotative* term, a word used to designate indifferently everything that happens. Lies, dreams, insanities, deceptions, myths, theories are all of them just the events which they specifically are. Pragmatism is content to take its stand with science; for science finds all such events to be subject-matter of description and inquiry—just like stars and fossils, mosquitoes and malaria, circulation and vision. It also takes its stand with daily life, which finds that such things really have to be reckoned with as they occur interwoven in the texture of events.

The only way in which the term reality can ever become more than a blanket denotative term is through recourse to specific events in all their diversity and thatness. Speaking summarily, I find that the retention by philosophy of the notion of a Reality fedually superior to the events of everyday occurrence is the chief source of the increasing isolation of philosophy from common sense and science. For the latter do not operate in any such region. As with them of old, philosophy in dealing with real difficulties finds itself still hampered by reference to realities more real, more ultimate, than those which directly happen.

I have said that identifying the cause of philosophy with the notion of superior reality is the cause of an *increasing* isolation from science and practical life. The phrase reminds us that there was a time when the enterprise of science and the moral interests of men both moved in a universe invidiously distinguished from that of ordinary occurrence. While all that happens is equally real—since it really happens—happenings are not of equal worth. Their respective consequences, their import, varies tremendously.

Counterfeit money, although real (or rather *because* real), is really different from valid circulatory medium, just as disease is really different from health; different in specific structure and so different in consequences. In occidental thought, the Greeks were the first to draw the distinction between the genuine and the spurious in a generalized fashion and to formulate and enforce its tremendous significance for the conduct of life. But since they had at command no technique of experiemental analysis and no adequate technique of mathematical analysis, they were compelled to treat the difference of the true and the false, the dependable and the deceptive, as signifying two kinds of existence, the truly real and the apparently real.

Two points can hardly be asserted with too much emphasis. The Greeks were wholly right in the feeling that questions of good and ill, as far as they fall within human control, are bound up with discrimination of the genuine from the spurious, of "being" from what only pretends to be. But because they lacked adequate instrumentalies for coping with this difference in specific situations, they were forced to treat the difference as a wholesale and rigid one. Science was concerned with vision of ultimate and true reality; opinion was concerned with getting along with apparent realities. Each had its appropriate region permanently marked off. Matters of opinion could never become matters of science; their intrinsic nature forbade. When the practice of science went on under such conditions, science and philosophy were one and the same thing. Both had to do with ultimate reality in its rigid and insuperable difference from ordinary occurrences.

We have only to refer to the way in which medieval life wrought the philosophy of an ultimate and supreme reality into the context of practical life to realize that for centuries political and moral interests were bound up with the distinction between the absolutely real and the relatively real. The difference was no matter of a remote technical philosophy, but one which controlled life from the cradle to the grave, from the grave to the endless life after death. By means of a vast institution, which in effect was state as well as church, the claims of ultimate reality were enforced; means of access to it were provided. Acknowledgment of The Reality brought security in this world and salvation in the next. It is not necessary to report the story of the change which has since taken place. It is enough for our purposes to note that none of the modern philosophies of a superior reality, or *the* real object, idealistic or realistic, holds that its insight makes a difference like that between sin and holiness, eternal condemnation and eternal bliss. While in its own context the philosophy of ultimate reality entered into the vital concerns of men, it now tends to be an ingenious dialectic exercised in professorial corners by a few who have retained ancient premises while rejecting their application to the conduct of life.

The increased isolation from science of any philosophy identified with the problem of *the* real is equally marked. For the growth of science has consisted precisely in the invention of an equipment, a technique of appliances and procedures, which, accepting all occurrences as homogeneously real, proceeds to distinguish the authenticated from the spurious, the true from the false, by specific modes of treatment in specific situations. The procedures of the trained engineer, of the competent physician, of the laboratory expert, have turned out to be the only ways of discriminating the counterfeit from the valid. And they have revealed that the difference is not one of antecedent fixity of existence, but one of mode of treatment and of the consequences thereon attendant. After mankind has learned to put its trust in specific procedures in order to make its discriminations between the false and the true, philosophy arrogates to itself the enforcement of the distinction at its own cost.

More than once, this essay has intimated that the counterpart of the idea of invidiously real reality is the spectator notion of knowledge. If the knower, however defined, is set over against the world to be known, knowing consists in possessing a transcript, more or less accurate but otiose, of real things. Whether this transcript is presentative in character (as realists say) or whether it is by means of states of consciousness which represent things (as subjectivists say), is a matter of great importance in its own context. But, in another regard, this difference is negligible in comparison with the point in which both agree. Knowing is viewing from outside. But it it be true that the self or subject of experience is part and parcel of the course of events, it follows that the self *becomes* a knower. It becomes a mind in virtue of a distinctive way of partaking in the course of events. The significant distinction is no longer between the knower *and* the world; it is between different ways of being in and of the movement of things; between a brute physical way and a purposive, intelligent way.

There is no call to repeat in detail the statements which have been advanced. Their net purport is that the directive presence of future possibilities in dealing with existent conditions is what is meant by knowing; that the self becomes a knower or mind when anticipation of future consequences operates as its stimulus. What we are now concerned with is the effect of this conception upon the nature of philosophic knowing.

As far as I can judge, popular response to pragmatic philosophy was moved by two quite different considerations. By some it was thought to provide a new species of sanctions, a new mode of apologetics, for certain religious ideas whose standing had been threatened. By others, it was welcomed because it was taken as a sign that philosophy was about to surrender its otiose and speculative remoteness; that philosophers were beginning to recognize that philosophy is of account only if, like everyday knowing and like science, it affords guidance to action and thereby makes a difference in the event. It was welcomed as a sign that philosophers were willing to have the worth of their philosophizing measured by responsible tests.

I have not seen this point of view emphasized, or hardly recognized, by professional critics. The difference of attitude can probably be easily explained. The epistemological universe of discourse is so highly technical that only those who have been trained in the history of thought think in terms of it. It did not occur, accordingly, to non-technical readers to interpret the doctrine that the meaning and validity of thought are fixed by differences made in consequences and in satisfactoriness to mean consequences in personal feelings. Those who were professionally trained, however, took the statement to mean that consciousness or mind in the mere act of looking at things modifies them. It understood the doctrine of test of validity by consequences to mean that apprehensions and conceptions are true if the modifications effected by them were of an emotionally desirable tone.

Prior discussion should have made it reasonably clear that the source of this misunderstanding lies in the neglect of temporal considerations. The change made in things by the self in knowing is not immediate and, so to say, cross-sectional. It is longitudinal—in the redirection given to changes already going on. Its analogue is found in the changes which take place in the development of, say, iron ore into a watch-spring, not in those of the miracle of transubstantiation. For the static, cross-sectional, non-temporal relation of subject and object, the pragmatic hypothesis substitutes apprehension of a thing in terms of the results in other things which it is tending to effect. For the unique epistemological relation, it substitutes a practical relation of a familiar type:—responsive behavior which changes in time the subject-matter to which it applies. The unique thing about the responsive behavior which constitutes knowing is the specific difference which marks it off from other modes of response, namely, the part played in it by anticipation and prediction. Knowing is the act, stimulated by this foresight, of securing and averting consequences. The success of the achievement measures the standing of the foresight by which response is directed. The popular impression that pragmatic philosophy means that philosophy shall develop ideas relevant to the actual crisis of life, ideas influential in dealing with them and tested by the assistance they afford, is correct.

Reference to practical response suggests, however, another misapprehension. Many critics have jumped at the obvious association of the word pragmatic with practical. They have assumed that the intent is to limit all knowledge, philosophic included, to promoting "action," understanding by action either just any bodily movement, or those bodily movements which conduce to the preservation and grosser well-being of the body. James's statement that general conceptions must "cash in" has been taken (especially by European critics) to mean that the end and measure of intelligence lies in the narrow and coarse utilities which it produces. Even an acute American thinker, after first criticizing pragmatism as a kind of idealistic epistemology, goes on to treat it as a doctrine which regards intelligence as a lubricating oil facilitating the workings of the body.

One source of the misunderstanding is suggested by the fact that "cashing in" to James meant that a general idea must always be capable of verification in specific existential cases. The notion of "cashing in" says nothing about the breadth or depth of the specific consequences. As an empirical doctrine, it could not say anything about them in general; the specific cases must speak for themselves. If one conception is verified in terms of eating beefsteak, and another in terms of a favorable credit balance in the bank, that is not because of anything in the theory, but because of the specific nature of the conceptions in question, and because there exist particular events like hunger and trade. If there are also existences in which the most liberal esthetic ideas and the most generous moral conceptions can be verified by specific embodiment, assuredly so much the better. The fact that a strictly empirical philosophy was taken by so many critics to imply an *a priori* dogma about the kind of consequences capable of existence is evidence. I think, of the inability of many philosophers to think in concretely empirical terms. Since the critics were themselves accustomed to get results by manipulating the concepts of "consequences" and of "practice," they assumed that even a would-be empiricist must be doing the same sort of thing. It will, I suppose, remain for a long time incredible to some that a philosopher should really intend to go to specific experiences to determine of what scope and depth practice admits, and what sort of consequences the world permits to come into being. Concepts are so clear; it takes so little time to develop their implications; experiences are so confused, and it requires so much time and energy to lay hold of them. And yet these same critics charge pragmatism with adopting subjective and emotional standards!

As a matter of fact, the pragmatic theory of intelligence means that the function of mind is to project new and more complex ends—to free experience from routine and from caprice. Not the use of thought to accomplish purposes already given either in the mechanism of the body or in that of the existent state of society, but the use of intelligence to liberate and liberalize action, is the pragmatic lesson. Action restricted to given and fixed ends may attain great technical efficiency; but efficiency is the only quality to which it can lay claim. Such action is mechanical (or becomes so), no matter what the scope of the pre-formed end, be it the Will of God or *Kultur*. But the doctrine that intelligence develops within the sphere of action for the sake of possibilities not yet given is the opposite of a doctrine of mechanical efficiency. Intelligence *as* intelligence is inherently forward-looking; only by ignoring its primary function does it become a mere means for an end already given. The latter *is* servile, even when the end is labeled moral, religious, or esthetic. But action directed to ends to which the agent has not previously been attached inevitably carries with it a quickened and enlarged spirit. A pragmatic intelligence is a creative intelligence, not a routine mechanic.

All this may read like a defense of pragmatism by one concerned to make out for it the best case possible. Such is not, however, the intention. The purpose is to indicate the extent to which intelligence frees action from a mechanically instrumental character. Intelligence is, indeed, instrumental *through* action to the determination of the qualities of future experience. But the very fact that the concern of intelligence is with the future, with the as-yet-unrealized (and with the given and the established only as conditions of the realization of possibilities), makes the action in which it takes effect generous and liberal; free of spirit. Just that action which extends and approves intelligence has an intrinsic value of its own in being instrumental:—the intrinsic value of being informed with intelligence in behalf of the enrichment of life. By the same stroke, intelligence becomes truly liberal: knowing is a human undertaking, not an esthetic appreciation carried on by a refined class or a capitalistic possession of a few learned specialists, whether men of science or of philosophy.

More emphasis has been put upon what philosophy is not than upon what it may become. But it is not necessary, it is not even desirable, to set forth philosophy as a scheduled program. There are human difficulties of an urgent, deep-seated kind which may be clarified by trained reflection, and whose solution may be forwarded by the careful development of hypotheses. When it is understood that philosophic thinking is caught up in the actual course of events, having the office of guiding them towards a prosperous issue, problems will abundantly present themselves. Philosophy will not solve these problems; philosophy is vision, imagination, reflection—and these functions, apart from action, modify nothing and hence resolve nothing. But in a complicated and perverse world, action which is not informed with vision, imagination, and reflection, is more likely to increase confusion and conflict than to straighten things out. It is not easy for generous and sustained reflection to become a guiding and illuminating method in action. Until it frees itself from identification with problems which are supposed to depend upon Reality as such, or its distinction from a world of Appearance, or its relation to a Knower as such, the hands of philosophy are tied. Having no chance to link its fortunes with a responsible career by suggesting things to be tried, it cannot identify itself with questions which actually arise in the vicissitudes of life. Philosophy recovers itself when it ceases to be a device for dealing with the problems of philosophers and becomes a method, cultivated by philosophers, for dealing with the problems of men.

Emphasis must vary with the stress and special impact of the troubles which perplex men. Each age knows its own ills, and seeks its own remedies. One does not have to forecast a particular program to note that the central need of any program at the present day is an adequate conception of the nature of intelligence and its place in action. Philosophy cannot disavow responsibility for many misconceptions of the nature of intelligence which now hamper its efficacious operation. It has at least a negative task imposed upon it. It must take away the burdens which it has laid upon the intelligence of the common man in struggling with his difficulties. It must deny and eject that intelligence which is naught but a distant eye, registering in a remote and alien medium the spectacle of nature and life. To enforce the fact that the emergence of imagination and thought is relative to the connexion of the sufferings of men with their doings is of itself to illuminate those sufferings and to instruct those doings. To catch mind in its connexion with the entrance of the novel into the course of the world is to be on the road to see that intelligence is itself the most promising of all novelties, the revelation of the meaning of that transformation of past into future which is the reality of every present. To reveal intelligence as the organ for the guidance of this transformation, the sole director of its quality, is to make a declaration of present untold significance for action. To elaborate these convictions of the connexion of intelligence with what men undergo because of their doings and with the emergence and direction of the creative, the novel, in the world is of itself a program which will keep philosophers busy until something more worth while is forced upon them. For the elaboration has to be made through application to all the disciplines which have an intimate connexion with human conduct:—to logic, ethics, esthetics, economics, and the procedure of the sciences formal and natural.

I also believe that there is a genuine sense in which the enforcement of the pivotal position of intelligence in the world and thereby in control of human fortunes (so far as they are manageable) is the peculiar problem in the problems of life which come home most closely to ourselves—to ourselves living not merely in the early twentieth century but in the United States. It is easy to be foolish about the connexion of thought with national life. But I do not see how any one can question the distinctively national color of English, or French, or German philosophies. And if of late the history of thought has come under the domination of the German dogma of an inner evolution of ideas, it requires but a little inquiry to convince oneself that the dogma itself testifies to a particularly nationalistic need and origin. I believe that philosophy in America will be lost between chewing a historic cud long since reduced to woody fibre, or an apologetics for lost causes (lost to natural science), or a scholastic, schematic formalism, unless it can somehow bring to consciousness America's own needs and its own implicit principle of successful action.

This need and principle, I am convinced, is the necessity of a deliberate control of policies by the method of intelligence, an intelligence which is not the faculty of intellect honored in text-books and neglected elsewhere, but which is the sum-total of impulses, habits, emotions, records and discoveries which forecast what is desirable and undesirable in future possibilities, and which contrive ingeniously in behalf of imagined good. Our life has no background of sanctified categories upon which we may fall back; we rely upon precedent as authority only to our own undoing—for with us there is such a continuously novel situation that final reliance upon precedent entails some class interest guiding us by the nose whither it will. British empiricism, with its appeal to what has been in the past, is, after all, only a kind of *a priorism*. For it lays down a fixed rule for future intelligence to follow; and only the immersion of philosophy in technical learning prevents our seeing that this is the essence of *a priorism*.

We pride ourselves upon being realistic, desiring a hard-headed cognizance of facts, and devoted to mastering the means of life. We pride ourselves upon a practical idealism, a lively and easily moved faith in possibilities as yet unrealized, in willingness to make sacrifice for their realization. Idealism easily becomes a sanction of waste and carelessness, and realism a sanction of legal formalism in behalf of things as they are—the rights of the possessor. We thus tend to combine a loose and ineffective optimism with assent to the doctrine of take who take can: a deification of power. All peoples at all times have been narrowly realistic in practice and have then employed idealization to cover up in sentiment and theory their brutalities. But never, perhaps, has the tendency been so dangerous and so tempting as with ourselves. Faith in the power of intelligence to imagine a future which is the projection of the desirable in the present, and to invent the instrumentalities of its realization, is our salvation. And it is a faith which must be nurtured and made articulate: surely a sufficiently large task for our philosophy.

The Postulate of Immediate Empricism

Immediate empiricism postulates that things—anything, everything, in the ordinary or non-technical use of the term "thing"—are what they are experienced as. Hence, if one wishes to describe anything truly, his task is to tell what it is experienced as being. If it is a horse that is to be described, or the *equus* that is to be defined, then must the horse-trader, or the jockey, or the timid family man who wants a "safe driver," or the zoologist or the paleontologist tell us what the horse is which is experienced. If these accounts turn out different in some respects, as well as congruous in others, this is not reason for assuming the content of one to be exclusively "real," and that of others to be "phenomenal"; for each account of what is experienced will manifest that it is the account *of* the horse-dealer, or *of* the zoologist, and hence will give the conditions requisite for understanding the differences as well as the agreements of the various accounts. And the principle varies not a whit if we bring in the psychologist's horse, the logician's horse or the metaphysician's horse.

In each case, the nub of the question is, *what sort of experience* is denoted or indicated: a concrete and determinate experience, varying, when it varies, in specific real elements, and agreeing, when it agrees, in specific real elements, so that we have a contrast, not between *a* Reality, and various approximations to, or phenomenal representations of Reality, but between different reals of experience. And the reader is begged to bear in mind that from this standpoint, when "an experience" or "some sort of experience" is referred to, "some thing" or "some sort of thing" is always meant.

Now, this statement that things are what they are experienced to be is usually translated into the statement that things (or, ultimately, Reality, Being) *are* only and just what they are *known* to be or that things are, or Reality *is*, what it is for a conscious knower—whether the knower be conceived primarily as a perceiver or as a thinker being a further and secondary question. This is the root-paralogism of all idealisms, whether subjective or objective, pyschological or epistemological. By our postulate, things are what they are experienced to be; and, unless knowing is the sole and only genuine mode of experiencing, it is fallacious to say that Reality is just and exclusively what it is or would be to an all-competent all-knower; or even that it *is*, relatively and piecemeal, what it is to a finite and partial knower. Or, put more positively, knowing is one mode of experiencing, and the primary philosophic demand (from the standpoint of immediatism) is to find out *what* sort of an experience knowing is—or, concretely how things are experienced when they are experienced *as* known things.[1] By concretely is meant, obviously enough (among other things), such an account of the experience of things as known that will bring out the characteristic traits and distinctions they possess as things of a knowing experience, as compared with things experienced aesthetically, or morally, or economically, or technologically. To assume that, because from the *standpoint of the knowledge experience* things *are* what they are known to be, therefore, metaphysically, absolutely, without qualification, everything in its reality (as distinct from its "appearance," or phenomenol occurrence) is what a knower would find it to be, is, from the immediatist's standpoint, if not the root of all philosophic evil, at least one of its main roots. For this leaves out of account what the knowledge standpoint is itself *experienced as*.

I start and am flustered by a noise heard. Empirically, that noise *is* fearsome; it *really* is, not merely phenomenally or subjectively so. That *is* what it is experienced as being. But, when I experience the noise as a *known* thing, I find it to be innocent of harm. It is the tapping of a shade against the window, owing to movements of the wind. The experience has changed; that is, the thing experienced has changed—not that an unreality has given place to a reality, nor that some transcendental (unexperienced) Reality has changed,[2] not that truth has changed, but just and only the concrete reality experienced has changed. I now feel ashamed of my fright; and the noise as

From, with very slight change, the *Journal of Philosophy, Psychology and Scientific Methods*, Vol. II, No. 15, July, 1905. "The Postulate of Immediate Empiricism" in *John Dewey: The Middle Works, 1899–1924*, Vol. 3, Ed. Jo Ann Boydston (Carbondale and Edwardsville: Southern Illinois University Press, 1977), pp. 158–166.

fearsome is changed to noise as a wind-curtain fact, and hence practically indifferent to my welfare. This is a change of experienced, existence effected through the medium of cognition. The content of the latter experience cognitively regarded is doubtless *truer* than the content of the earlier; but it is in no sense more real. To call it truer, moreover must, from the empirical standpoint, mean a concrete *difference* in actual things experienced.[3] Again, in many cases, only in retrospect is the prior experience cognitionally regarded at all. In such cases, it is only in regard to contrasted content *in* a subsequent experience that the determination "truer" has force.

Perhaps some reader may now object that as matter of fact the entire experience *is* cognitive, but that the earlier parts of it are only imperfectly so, resulting in a phenomenon that is not real; while the latter part, being a more complete cognition, results in what is relatively, at least, more real.[4] In short, a critic may say that, when I was frightened by the noise, I *knew* I was frightened; otherwise there would have been no experience at all. At this point, it is necessary to make a distinction so simple and yet so all-fundamental that I am afraid the reader will be inclined to pooh-pooh it away as a mere verbal distinction. But to see that to the empiricist this distinction is not verbal, but genuine, is the precondition of any understanding of him. The immediatist must, by his postulate, ask what is the fright experienced *as*. Is what is actually experienced, I-know-I-am-frightened, or I-*am*-frightened? I see absolutely no reason for claiming that the experience *must* be described by the former phrase. In all probability (and all the empiricist logically needs is just one case of this sort) the experience is simply and just of fright-at-the-noise. Later one may (or may not) have an experience describable *as* I-know-I-am- (or-was) and improperly or properly, frightened. But this is a different experience—that is, a different *thing*. And if the critic goes on to urge that the person "*really*" must have known that he was frightened, I can only point out that the critic is shifting the venue. He may be right, but, if so, it is only because the "really" is something not concretely experienced (whose nature accordingly is the critic's business); and this is to depart from the empiricist's point of view, to attribute to him a postulate he expressly repudiates.

The material point may come out more clearly if I say that we must make a distinction between a thing as *cognitive,* and one as *cognized.*[5] I should define a cognitive experi-

ence as one that has certain bearings or implications which induce and fulfill themselves in a subsequent experience in which the relevant thing is experienced *as* cognized, *as* a known object, and is thereby transformed, or reorganized. The fright-at-the-noise in the case cited is obviously *cognitive,* in this sense. By description, it induces an investigation or inquiry in which both noise and fright are objectively stated or presented—the noise as a shade-wind fact, the fright as an organic reaction to a sudden acoustic stimulus, a reaction that under the given circumstances was useless or even detrimental, a maladaptation. Now, pretty much all of experience is of this sort (the "is" meaning, of course, is experienced *as*), and the empiricist is false to his principle if he does not duly note this fact.[6] But he is equally false to his principle if he permits himself to be confused as to the concrete differences in the two things experienced.

There are two little words through explication of which the empiricist's position may be brought out—"*as*" and "*that.*" We may express his presupposition by saying that things are what they are experienced *as* being; or that to give a just account of anything is to tell what *that* thing is experienced to be. By these words I want to indicate the absolute, final, irreducible and inexpugnable concrete *quale* which everything experienced not so much *has* as *is*. To grasp this aspect of empiricism is to see what the empiricist means by objectivity, by the element of control. Suppose we take, as a crucial case for the empiricist, an out and out illusion, say of Zöllner's lines. These are experienced as convergent; they are "truly" parallel. If things are what the are experienced as being, how can the distinction be drawn between illusion and the true state of the case? There is no answer to this question except by sticking to the fact that the experience of the lines as divergent is a concrete qualitative thing or *that*. It is *that* experience which it is, and no other. And if the reader rebels at the iteration of such obvious tautology, I can only reiterate that the realization of the *meaning* of this tautology is the key to the whole question of the objectivity of experience, as that stands to the empiricist. The lines of *that* experience *are* divergent: not merely *seem* so. The question of truth is not as to whether Being or Non-Being, Reality or mere Appearance, is experienced, but as to the *worth* of a certain concretely experienced thing. The only way of passing upon this question is by sticking in the most uncompromising fashion to *that* experience as real.

That experience is that two lines with certain cross-hatchings are apprehended as convergent; only by taking that experience as real and as fully real, is there any basis for or way of going to an experienced knowledge that the lines are parallel. It is in the concrete thing *as experienced* that all the grounds and clues to its own intellectual or logical rectification are contained. It is because this thing, afterwards adjudged false, is a concrete *that,* that it develops into a corrected experience (that is, experience of a corrected thing—we reform things just as we reform ourselves or a bad boy) whose full content is not a whit more real, but which is true or truer.[7]

If *any* experience, then a *determinate* experience; and this determinateness is the only, and is the adequate, principle of control, or "objectivity." The experience may be of the vaguest sort. I may not see any thing which I can identify as a familiar object——a table, a chair, etc. It may be dark; I may have only the vaguest impression that there is something which looks like a table. Or I may be completely befogged and confused, as when one rises quickly from sleep in a pitch-dark room. But this vagueness, this doubtfulness, this confusion is the thing experienced and, *qua* real, is as "good" a reality as the self-luminous vision of an Absolute. It is not just vagueness, doubtfulness, confusion, at large or in general. It is *this* vagueness, and no other; absolutely unique, absolutely what *it* is.[8] Whatever gain in clearness, in fullness, in trueness of content is experienced must grow out of some element in the experience of *this* experienced *as* what it is. To return to the illusion: If the experience of the lines as convergent is illusory, it is because of some elements in the thing as experienced, not because of something defined in terms of externality to this particular experience. If the illusoriness can be detected, it is because the thing experienced is real, having within its experienced reality elements whose *own mutual* tension effects its reconstruction. Taken concretely, the experience of convergent lines contains within itself the elements of the transformation of its own content. It is *this* thing, and not some separate truth, that clamors for its own reform. There is, then, from the empiricist's point of view, no need to search for some aboriginal *that* to which all successive experiences are attached, and which is somehow thereby undergoing continuous change. Experience is always of *thats;* and the most comprehensive and inclusive experience of the universe that the philosopher himself can obtain is the experience of a characteristic *that.* From the empiricist's point of view, this is as true of the exhaustive and complete insight of a hypothetical all-knower as of the vague, blind experience of the awakened sleeper. As reals, they stand on the same level. As trues, the latter has by definition the better of it; but if this insight is in any way the truth of the blind awakening, it is because the latter has, in its *own* determinate *quale,* elements of real continuity with the former; it is, *ex hypothesi,* transformable through a series of experienced reals without break of continuity, into the absolute thought-experience. There is no need of logical manipulation to effect the transformation, nor *could* any logical consideration effect it. If effected at all it is just by immediate experiences, each of which is just as real (no more, no less) as either of the terms between which they lie. Such, at least, is the meaning of the empiricist's contention. So, when he talks of experience, he does not mean some grandiose, remote affair that is cast like a net around a succession of fleeting experiences; he does not mean an indefinite total, comprehensive experience which somehow engirdles an endless flux, he means that *things* are what they are experienced to be, and that every experience is *some* thing.

From the postulate of empiricism, then (or, what is the same thing, from a *general* consideration of the concept of experience), nothing can be deduced, not a single philosophical proposition.[9] The reader may hence conclude that all this just comes to the truism that experience is experience, or is what it is. If one attempts to draw conclusions from the bare concept of experience, the reader is quite right. But the real significance of the principle is that of a method of philosophical analysis—a method identical in kind (but differing in problem and hence in operation) with that of the scientist. If you wish to find out what subjective, objective, physical, mental, cosmic, psychic, cause, substance, purpose, activity, evil, being, quality—any philosophic term, in short—means, go to experience and see what the thing is experienced *as.*

Such a method is not spectacular; it permits of no off-hand demonstrations of God, freedom, immortality, nor of the exclusive reality of matter, or ideas, or consciousness, etc. But it supplies a way of telling what all these terms mean. It may seem insignificant, or chillingly disappointing, but only upon condition that it be not worked. Philosophic conceptions have, I believe, outlived their usefulness considered as stimulants to emotion, or as a species of sanctions; and a larger, more fruitful and more valuable career awaits them considered as specifically experienced meanings. . . .

NOTES

1. I hope the reader will not therefore assume that from the empiricist's standpoint knowledge is of small worth or import. On the contrary, from the empiricist's standpoint it has *all* the worth which it is concretely experienced as possessing—which is simply tremendous. But the exact *nature* of this worth is a thing to be found out in describing what we mean by experiencing objects as known—the actual differences made or found in experience.

2. Since the non-empiricist believes in things-in-themselves (which he may term "atoms," sensations," transcendental unities, a priori concepts, an absolute experience, or whatever), and since he finds that the empiricist makes much of change (as he must, since change is continuously experienced) he assumes that the empiricist means *his own* non-empirical Realities are in continual flux, and he naturally shudders at having his divinities so violently treated. But, once recognize that the empiricist doesn't have any such Realities at all, and the entire problem of the relation of change to reality takes a very different aspect.

3. It would lead us aside from the point to try to tell just what is the nature of the experienced difference we call truth. Professor James's recent articles may well be consulted. The point to bear in mind here is just what sort of a thing the empiricist must mean by true, or truer (the noun Truth is, of course, a generic name for all cases of "Trues"). The adequacy of any particular account is not a matter to be settled by general reasoning, but by finding out what sort of an experience the truth-experience actually is.

4. I say "relatively," because the transcendalist still holds that finally the cognition is imperfect, giving us only some symbol or phenomenon of Reality (which *is* only in the Absolute or in some Thing-in-Itself)—otherwise the curtain-wind fact would have as much ontological reality as the existence of the Absolute itself: a conclusion at which the non-empiricist perhorresces, for no reason obvious to me—save that it would put an end to his transcendentalism.

5. In general, I think the distinction between -*ive* and -*ed* one of the most fundamental of philosophic distinctions, and one of the most neglected. The same holds of -*tion* and -*ing*.

6. What is criticized, now as "geneticism" (if I may coin the word) and now as "pragmatism" is, in its truth, just the fact that the empiricist does take account of the experienced "drift, occasion and contexture" of things experienced—to use Hobbes's phrase.

7. Perhaps the point would be clearer if expressed in this way: Except as subsequent estimates of *worth* are introduced, "real" means only existent. The eulogistic connotation that makes the term Reality equivalent to *true* or *genuine* being has great pragmatic significance, but its confusion with reality as existence is the point aimed at in the above paragraph.

8. One does not so easily escape medieval Realism as one thinks. Either every experienced thing has its own determinateness, its own unsubstitutable, unredeemable reality, or else "generals" *are* separate existences after all.

9. Excepting, of course, some negative ones. One could say that certain views are certainly *not* true, because, by hypothesis, they refer to nonentities, *i.e.,* non-empiricals. But even here the empricist must go slowly. From his own standpoint, even the most professedly transcendental statements are, after all, real as experiences, and hence negotiate some transaction with facts. For this reason, he cannot, in theory, reject them *in toto,* but has to show concretely how they arose and how they are to be corrected. In a word, his logical relationship to statements that profess to relate to things-in-themselves, unknowables, inexperienced substances, etc., is precisely that of the psychologist to the Zöllner lines.

Experience and Philosophic Method

The title of this volume, Experience and Nature, is intended to signify that the philosophy here presented may be termed either empirical naturalism or naturalistic empiricism, or, taking "experience" in its usual signification, naturalistic humanism.

To many the associating of the two words will seem like talking of a round square, so engrained

From "Experience and Philosophic Method," in *Experience and Nature, John Dewey: The Later Works, 1925–1953,* Vol. 1, Ed. Jo Ann Boydston (Carbondale and Edwardsville: Southern Illinois University Press, 1981, pp. 10–14, 16–21, 26–28, 30–31, 33–41.

is the notion of the separation of man and experience from nature. Experience, they say, is important for those beings who have it, but is too causal and sporadic in its occurrence to carry with it any important implications regarding the nature of Nature. Nature, on the other hand, is said to be complete apart from experience. Indeed, according to some thinkers the case is even in worse plight: Experience to them is not only something extraneous which is occasionally superimposed upon nature, but it forms a veil or screen which shuts us off from nature, unless in some way it can be "transcended." So something non-natural by way of reason or intuition is introduced, something supra-empirical. According to an opposite school experience fares as badly, nature being thought to signify something wholly material and mechanistic; to frame a theory of experience in naturalistic terms is, accordingly, to degrade and deny the noble and ideal values that characterize experience.

I know of no route by which dialectical argument can answer such objections. They arise from associations with words and cannot be dealt with argumentatively. One can only hope in the course of the whole discussion to disclose the meanings which are attached to "experience" and "nature," and thus insensibly produce, if one is fortunate, a change in the significations previously attached to them. This process of change may be hastened by calling attention to another context in which nature and experience get on harmoniously together—wherein experience presents itself as the method, and the only method, for getting at nature, penetrating its secrets, and wherein nature empirically disclosed (by the use of empirical method in natural science) deepens, enriches and directs the further development of experience.

In the natural sciences there is a union of experience and nature which is not greeted as a monstrosity; on the contrary, the inquirer must use empirical method if his findings are to be treated as genuinely scientific. The investigator assumes as a matter of course that experience, controlled in specifiable ways, is the avenue that leads to the facts and laws of nature. He uses reason and calculation freely; he could not get along without them. But he sees to it that ventures of this theoretical sort start from and terminate in directly experienced subject-matter. Theory may intervene in a long course of reasoning, many portions of which are remote from what is directly experienced. But the vine of pendant theory is attached at both ends to the pillars of observed subject-matter. And this experienced material is the same for the scientific man and the man in the street. The latter cannot follow the intervening reasoning without special preparation. But stars, rocks, trees, and creeping things are the same material of experience for both.

These commonplaces take on sigificance when the relation of experience to the formation of a philosophic theory of nature is in question. They indicate that experience, if scientific inquiry is justified, is no infinitesimally thin layer or foreground of nature, but that it penetrates into it, reaching down into its depths, and in such a way that its grasp is capable of expansion; it tunnels in all directions and in so doing brings to the surface things at first hidden—as miners pile high on the surface of the earth treasures brought from below. Unless we are prepared to deny all validity to scientific inquiry, these facts have a value that cannot be ignored for the general theory of the relation of nature and experience.

It is sometimes contended, for example, that since experience is a late comer in the history of our solar system and plant, and since these occupy a trivial place in the wide areas of celestial space, experience is at most a slight and insignificant incident in nature. No one with an honest respect for scientific conclusions can deny that experience as an existence is something that occurs only under highly specialized conditions, such as are found in a highly organized creature which in turn requires a specialized environment. There is no evidence that experience occurs everywhere and everywhen. But candid regard for scientific inquiry also compels the recognition that when experience does occur, no matter at what limited portion of time and space, it enters into possession of some portion of nature and in such a manner as to render other of its precincts accessible.

A geologist living in 1928 tells us about events that happened not only before he was born but millions of years before any human being came into existence on this earth. He does so by starting from things that are now the material of experience. Lyell revolutionized geology by perceiving that the sort of thing that can be experienced now in the operations of fire, water, pressure, is the sort of thing by which the earth took on its present structural forms. Visiting a natural history museum, one beholds a mass of rock and, reading a label, finds that it comes from a tree that grew, so it is affirmed, five million years ago. The geologist did not leap from the thing he can see and touch to some event in by-gone ages; he collated this observed thing with many others, of different kinds, found all over the globe; the results of his comparisons he than compared with data of other experiences, say, the astronomer's. He translates, that is, observed coexistences into non-observed, inferred sequences. Finally he dates his object, placing it in an order of events. By the same sort of method he predicts that at certain places some things not yet experienced will be observed, and then he takes pains to bring them within the scope of experience. The scientific conscience is, moreover, so sensitive with respect to the necessity of experience that when it reconstructs the past it is not fully satisfied with inferences drawn from even a large and cumulative mass of uncontradicted evidence; it sets to work to institute conditions of heat and pressure and moisture, etc., so as actually to reproduce in experiment that which he has inferred.

These commonplaces prove that experience is *of* as well as *in* nature. It is not experience which is experienced, but nature—stones, plants, animals, diseases, health, temperature, electricity, and so on. Things interacting in certain ways *are* experience; they are what is experienced. Linked in certain other ways with another natural object—the human organism—they are *how* things are experienced as well. Experience thus reaches down into nature; it has depth. It also has breadth and to an indefinitely elastic extent. It stretches. That stretch constitutes inference.

Dialectical difficulties, perplexities due to definitions given to the concepts that enter into the discussion, may be raised. It is said to be absurd that what is only a tiny part of nature should be competent to incorporate vast reaches of nature within itself. But even were it logically absurd one would be bound to cleave to it as a fact. Logic, however, is not put under a strain. The fact that something is an occurrence does not decide what kind of an occurrence it is; that can be found out only by examination. To argue from an experience "being an experience" to what it is of and about is warranted by no logic, even though modern thought has attempted it a thousand times. A bare event is no event at all; *something* happens. What that something is, is found out by actual study. This applies to seeing a flash of lightning and holds of the longer event called experience. The very existence of science is evidence that experience is such an occurrence that it penetrates into nature and expands without limit through it.

These remarks are not supposed to prove anything about experience and nature for philosophical doctrine; they are not supposed to settle anything about the worth of empirical naturalism. But they do show that in the case of natural science we habitually treat experience as starting point, and as method for dealing with nature, and as the goal in which nature is disclosed for what it is. To realize this fact is at least to weaken those verbal associations which stand in the way of apprehending the force of empirical method in philosophy.

The same considerations apply to the other objection that was suggested: namely, that to view experience naturalistically is to reduce it to something materialistic, depriving it of all ideal significance. If experience actually presents esthetic and moral traits, then these traits may also be supposed to reach down into nature, and to testify to something that belongs to nature as truly as does the mechanical structure attributed to it in physical science. To rule out that possibility by some general reasoning is to forget that the very meaning and purport of empirical method is that things are to be studied on their own account, so as to find out what is revealed when they are experienced. The traits possessed by the subject-matters of experience are as genuine as the characteristics of sun and electron. They are *found,* experienced, and are not to be shoved out of being by some trick of logic. When found, their ideal qualities are as relevant to the philosophic theory of nature as are the traits found by physical inquiry.

To discover some of these general features of experienced things and to interpret their significance for a philosophic theory of the universe in which we live is the aim of this volume. From the point of view adopted, the theory of empirical method in philosophy does for experienced subject-matter on a liberal scale what it does for special sciences on a technical scale. It is this aspect of method with which we are especially concerned in the present chapter. . . .

This empirical method I shall call the *denotative* method. That philosophy is a mode of reflection, often of a subtle and penetrating sort, goes without saying. The charge that is brought against the non-empirical method of philosophizing is not that it depends upon theorizing, but that it fails to use refined, secondary products as a path pointing and leading back to something in primary experience. The resulting failure is three-fold.

First, there is no verification, no effort even to test and check. What is even worse, secondly, is that the things of ordinary experience do not get enlargement and enrichment of meaning as they do when approached through the medium of scientific principles and reasonings. This lack of function reacts, in the third place, back upon the philosophic subject-matter in itself. Not tested by being employed to see what it leads to in ordinary experience and what new meanings it contributes, this subject-matter becomes arbitrary, aloof—what is called "abstract" when that word is used in a bad sense to designate something which exclusively occupies a realm of its own without contact with the things of ordinary experience.

As the net outcome of these three evils, we find that extraordinary phenomenon which accounts for the revulsion of many cultivated persons from any form of philosophy. The objects of reflection in philosophy, being reached by methods that seem to those who employ them rationally mandatory, are taken to be "real" in and of themselves—and supremely real. Then it becomes an insoluble problem why the things of gross, primary experience, should be what they are, or indeed why they should be at all. The refined objects of reflection in the natural sciences, however, never end by rendering the subject-matter from which they are derived a problem; rather, when used to describe a path by which some goal in primary experience is designated or denoted, they solve perplexities to which that crude material gives rise but which it cannot resolve of itself. They become means of control, of enlarged use and enjoyment of ordinary things. They may generate new problems, but these are problems of the same sort, to be dealt with by further use of the same methods of inquiry and experimentation. The problems to which empirical method gives rise afford, in a word, opportunities for more investigations yielding fruit in new and enriched experiences. But the problems to which non-empirical method gives rise in philosophy are blocks to inquiry, blind alleys; they are puzzles rather than problems, solved only by calling the original material of primary experience, "phenomenal," mere appearance, mere impressions, or by some other disparaging name.

Thus there is here supplied, I think, a first-rate test of the value of any philosophy which is offered us: Does it end in conclusions which, when they are referred back to ordinary life-experiences and their predicaments, render them more significant, more luminous to us, and make our dealings with them more fruitful? Or does it terminate in rendering the things of ordinary experience more opaque than they were before, and in depriving them of having in "reality" even the significance they had previously seemed to have? Does it yield the enrichment and increase of power of orindary things which the results of physical science afford when applied in every-day affairs? Or does it become a mystery that these ordinary things should be what they are; and are philosophic concepts left to dwell in separation in some technical realm of their own? It is the fact, I repeat, that so many philosophies terminate in conclusions that make it necessary to disparge and condemn primary experience, leading those who hold them to measure the sublimity of their "realities" as philosophically defined by remoteness from the concerns of daily life, which leads cultivated common sense to look askance at philosophy.

These general statements must be made more definite. We must illustrate the meaning of empirical method by seeing some of its results in contrast with those to which non-empirical philosophies conduct us. We begin by noting that "experience" is what James called a double-barrelled word.[1] Like its congeners, life and history, it includes *what* men do and suffer, *what* they strive for, love believe and endure, and also *how* men act and are acted upon, the ways in which they do and suffer, desire and enjoy, see, believe, imagine—in short, processes of *experiencing*. "Experience" denotes the planted field, the sowed seeds, the reaped harvests, the changes of night and day, spring and autumn, wet and dry, heat and cold, that are observed, feared, longed for; it also denotes the one who plants and reaps, who works and rejoices, hopes, fears, plans, invokes magic or chemistry to aid him, who is downcast or triumphant. It is "double-barrelled" in that it recognizes in its primary integrity no division between act and material, subject and object, but contains them both in an unanalyzed totality. "Thing" and "thought," as James says in the same connection, are single-barrelled; they refer to products discriminated by reflection-out of primary experience.[2]

It is significant that "life" and "history" have the same fullness of undivided meaning. Life denotes a function, a comprehensive activity, in which organism and environment are included. Only upon reflective analysis does it break up into external conditions—air breathed, food taken, ground walked upon—and internal structures—lungs respiring, stomach digesting, legs walking. The scope of "history" is notorious: it is the deeds enacted, the tragedies undergone; and it is the human comment, record, and interpretation that inevitable follow. Objectively, history takes in rivers, mountains, fields and forests, laws and institutions; subjectively it includes the purposes and plans, the desires and emotions, through which these things are administered and transformed.

Now empirical method is the only method which can do justice to this inclusive integrity of "experience." It alone takes this integrated unity as the starting point for philosophic thought. Other methods begin with results of a reflection that has already torn in two the subject-matter experienced and the operations and states of experiencing. The problem is then to get together again what has been sundered— which is as if the king's men started with the fragments of the egg and tried to construct the whole egg out of them. For empirical method the problem is nothing so impossible of solution. Its problem is to note how and why the whole is distinguished into subject and object, nature and mental operations. Having done this, it is in a position to see *to what effect* the distinction is made: how the distinguished factors function in the further control and enrichment of the subject-matters of crude but total experience. Non-empirical method starts with a reflective product as if it were primary, as if it were the originally "given." To non-empirical method, therefore, object and subject, mind and matter (or whatever words an ideas are used) are separate and independent. Therefore it has upon its hands the problem of how it is possible to know at all; how an outer world can affect an inner mind; how the acts of mind can reach out and lay hold of ojbects defined in antithesis to them. Naturally it is at a loss for an answer, since its premises make the fact of knowledge both unnatural and unempirical. One thinker turns metaphysical materialist and denies reality to the mental; another turns psychological idealist, and holds that matter and force are merely disguised psychical events. Solutions are given up as a hopeless task, or else different schools pile one intellectual complication on another only to arrive by a long and tortuous course at that which naïve experience already has in its own possession.

The first and perhaps the greatest difference made in philosophy by adoption respectively of empirical or non-empirical method is, thus, the difference made in what is selected as original material. To a truly naturalistic empiricism, the moot problem of the relation of subject and object is the problem of what consequences follow in and for primary experience from the distinction of the physical and the psychological or mental from each other. The answer is not far to seek. To distinguish in reflection the physical and to hold it in temporary detachment is to be set upon the road that conducts to tools and technologies, to construction of mechanisms, to the arts that ensue in the wake of the sciences. That these constructions make possible a better regulation of the affairs of primary experience is evident. Engineering and medicine, all the utilities that make for expansion of life, are the answer. There is better administration of old familiar things, and there is invention of new objects and satisfactions. Along with this added ability in regulation goes enriched meaning and value in things, clarification, increased depth and continuity—a result even more precious than is the added power of control.

The history of the development of the physical sciences is the story of the enlarging possession by mankind of more efficacious instrumentalities for dealing with the conditions of life and action. But when one neglects the connection of these scientific objects with the affairs of primary experience, the result is a picture of a world of things indifferent to human interests because it is wholly apart from experience. It is more than merely isolated, for it is set in opposition. Hence when it is viewed as fixed and final in itself it is a source of oppression to the heart and paralysis to imagination. Since this picture of the physical universe and philosophy of the character of physical objects is contradicted by every engineering project and every intelligent measure of public hygiene, it would seem to be time to examine the foundations upon which it rests, and find out how and why such conclusions are come to.

When objects are isolated from the experience through which they are reached and in which they function, experience itself becomes reduced to the mere process of experiencing, and experiencing is therefore treated as if it were also complete in itself. We get the absurdity of an experiencing which experiences only itself, states and processes of consciousness, instead of the things of nature. Since the seventeenth century this conception of experience as the equivalent of subjective private consciousness set over against nature, which consists wholly of physical objects, has wrought havoc in philosophy. It is responsible for the feeling mentioned at the outset that "nature" and "experience" are names for things which have nothing to do with each other.

Let us inquire how the matter stands when

these mental and physical objects are looked at in their connection with experience in its primary and vital modes. As has been suggested, these objects are not original, isolated and self-sufficient. They represent the discriminated analysis of the process of experiencing from subject-matter experienced. Although breathing is in fact a function that includes both air and the operations of the lungs, we may detach the latter for study, even though we cannot separate it in fact. So while we always know, love, act for and against *things,* instead of experiencing ideas, emotions and mental intents, the attitudes themselves may be made a special object of attention, and thus come to form a distinctive subject-matter of reflective, although not of primary, experience.

We primarily observe things, not observations. But the *act* of observation may be inquired into and form a subject of study and become thereby a refined object; so many the acts of thinking, desire, purposing, the state of affection, reverie, etc. Now just as long as these attitudes are not distinguished and abstracted, they are incorporated into subject-matter. It is a notorious fact that the one who hates finds the one hated an obnoxious and despicable character; to the lover his adored one is full of intrinsically delightful and wonderful qualities. The connection between such facts and the fact of animism is direct. . . .

There is another important result for philosophy of the use of empirical method which, when it is developed, introduces our next topic. Philosophy, like all forms of reflective analysis, takes us away, for the time being, from the things had in primary experience as they directly act and are acted upon, used and enjoyed. Now the standing temptation of philosophy, as its course abundantly demonstrates, is to regard the results of reflection as having, in and of themselves, a reality superior to that of the material of any other mode of experience. The commonest assumption of philosophies, common even to philosophies very different from one another, is the assumption of the identity of objects of knowledge and ultimately real objects. The assumption is so deep that it is usually not expressed; it is taken for granted as something so fundamental that it does not need to be stated. A technical example of the view is found in the contention of the Cartesian school—including Spinoza— that emotion as well as sense is but confused thought which when it becomes clear and definite or reaches its goal is *cognition.* That esthetic and moral experience reveal traits of real things as truly as does intellectual experience, that poetry may have a metaphysical import as well as science, is rarely affirmed, and when it is asserted, the statement is likely to be meant in some mystical or esoteric sense rather than in a straightforward everyday sense.

Suppose however that we start with no presuppositions save that what is experienced, since it is a manifestation of nature, may, and indeed, must be used as testimony of the characterstics of natural events. Upon this basis, reverie and desire are pertitnent for a philosophic theory of the true nature of things; the possibilities present in imagination that are not found in observation, are something to be taken into account. The features of objects reached by scientific or reflective experiencing are important, but so are all the phenomena of magic, myth, politics, painting and penitentiaries. The phenomena of social life are as relevant to the problem of the relation of the individual and universal as are those of logic; the existence in political organization of boundaries and barriers, of centralization, of interaction across boundaries, of expansion and absorption, will be quite as important for metaphysical theories of the discrete and the continuous as is anything derived from chemical analysis. The existence of ignorance as well as of wisdom, of error and even insanity as well as of truth will be taken into account.

That is to say, nature is construed in such a way that all these things, since they are actual, are naturally possible; they are not explained away into mere "appearance" in contrast with reality. Illusions are illusions, but the occurrence of illusions is not an illusion, but a genuine reality. What is really "in" experience extends much further than that which at any time is *known.* From the standpoint of knowledge, objects must be distinct; their traits must be explicit; the vague and unrevealed is a limitation. Hence whenever the habit of identifying reality with the object of knowledge as such prevails, the obscure and vague are explained away. It is important for philosophic theory to be aware that the distinct and evident are prized and why they are. But it is equally important to note that the dark and twilight abound. For in any object of primary experience there are always potentialities which are not explicit; any object that is overt is charged with possible consequences that are hidden; the most overt act has factors which are not explicit. Strain thought as far as we may and not all consequences can be foreseen or made an express or known part of reflection and decision. In the face of such empirical facts, the assumption that nature in itself is all of the same kind, all distinct, explicit and evident, having no hidden possibilities, no novelties or obscurities, is possible only on the basis of a philosophy which at some point draws an arbitrary line between nature and experience.

In the assertion (implied here) that the great vice of philosophy is an arbitrary "intellectualism," there is no slight cast upon intelligence and reason. By "intellectualism" as an indictment is meant the theory that all experiencing is a mode of knowing, and that all subject-matter, all nature, is, in principle, to be reduced and transformed till it is defined in terms identical with the characteristics presented by refined objects of science as such. The assumption of "intellectualism" goes contrary to the facts of what is primarily experienced. For things are objects to be treated, used, acted upon and with, enjoyed and endured, even more than things to be known. They are things *had* before they are things cognized.

The isolation of traits characteristic of objects known, and then defined as the sole ultimate realities, accounts for the denial to nature of the characters which make things lovable and contemptible, beautiful and ugly, adorable and awful. It accounts for the belief that nature is an indifferent, dead mechanism; it explains why characteristics that are the valuable and valued traits of objects in actual experience are thought to create a fundamentally troublesome philosophical problem. Recognition of their genuine and primary reality does not signify that no thought and knowledge enter in when things are loved, desired and striven for; it signifies that the former are subordinate, so that the genuine problem is how and why, to what effect, things thus experienced are transformed into objects in which cognized traits are supreme and affectional and volitional traits incidental and subsidiary. . . .

We have spoken of the difference which acceptance of empirical method in philosophy makes in the problem of subject-object and in that of the alleged all-inclusiveness of cognitive experience.[3] There is an intimate connection between these two problems. When real objects are identified, point for point, with knowledge-objects, all affectional and volitional objects are inevitably excluded from the "real" world, and are compelled to find refuge in the privacy of an experiencing subject or mind. Thus the notion of the ubiquity of all comprehensive cognitive experience results by a necessary logic in setting up a hard and fast wall between the experienc-

ing subject and that nature which is experienced. The self becomes not merely a pilgrim but an unnaturalized and unnaturalizable alien in the world. The only way to avoid a sharp separation between the mind which is the centre of the processes of experiencing and the natural world which is experienced is to acknowledge that all modes of experiencing are ways in which some genuine traits of nature come to manifest realization.

The favoring of cognitive objects and their characteristics at the expense of traits that excite desire, command action and produce passion, is a special instance of a principle of selective emphasis which introduces partiality and partisanship into philosophy. Selective emphasis, with accompanying omission and rejection, is the heart-beat of mental life. To object to the operation is to discard all thinking. But in ordinary matters and in scientific inquiries, we always retain the sense that the material chosen is selected for a purpose; there is no idea of denying what is left out, for what is omitted is merely that which is not relevant to the particular problem and purpose in hand.

But in philosophies, this limiting condition is often wholly ignored. It is not noted and remembered that the favored subject-matter is chosen for a purpose and that what is left out is just as real and important in its own characteristic context. It tends to be assumed that because qualities that figure in poetical discourse and those that are central in friendship do not figure in scientific inquiry, they have no reality, at least not the kind of unquestionable reality attributed to the mathematical, mechanical or magneto-electric properties that constitute matter. It is natural to men to take that which is of chief value to them at the time as *the* real. Reality and superior value are equated. In ordinary experience this fact does no particular harm; it is at once compensated for by turning to other things which since they also present value are equally real. But philosophy often exhibits a cataleptic rigidity in attachment to that phase of the total objects of experience which has become especially dear to a philosopher. *It* is real at all hazards and only it; other things are real only in some secondary and Pickwickian sense. . . .

This bias toward treating objects selected because of their value in some special context as the "real," in a superior and invidious sense, testifies to an empirical fact of importance. Philosophical simplifications are due to choice, and choice marks an interest *moral* in the broad sense of concern for what is good.

Our constant and unescapable concern is with prosperity and adversity, success and failure, achievement and frustration, good and bad. Since we are creatures with lives to live, and find ourselves within an uncertain environment, we are constructed to note and judge in terms of bearing upon weal and woe—upon value. Acknowledgment of this fact is a very different thing, however, from the transformation effected by philosophers of the traits they find good (simplicity, certainty, nobility, permanence, etc.) into fixed traits of real Being. The former presents something *to be accomplished,* to be brought about by the *actions* in which choice is manifested and made genuine. The latter ignores the need of action to effect the better and to prove the honesty of choice; it converts what is desired into antecedent and final features of a reality which is supposed to need only logical warrant in order to be contemplatively enjoyed as true Being.

For reflection the eventual is always better or worse than the given. But since it would also be better if the eventual good were now given, the philosopher, belonging by status to a leisure class relieved from the urgent necessity of dealing with conditions, converts the eventual into some kind of Being, something which *is,* even if it does not *exist.* Permanence, real essence, totality, order, unity, rationality, the *unum, verum et bonum* of the classic tradition, are eulogistic predicates. When we find such terms used to describe the foundations and proper conclusions of a philosophic system, there is ground for suspecting that an artificial simplification of existence has been performed. Reflection determining preference for an eventual good has dialectically wrought a miracle of transubstantiation. . . .

Honest empirical method will state when and where and why the act of selection took place, and thus enable others to repeat it and test its worth. Selective choice, denoted as an empirical event, reveals the basis and bearing of intellectual simplifications; they then cease to be of such a self-enclosed nature as to be affairs only of opinion and argument, admitting no alternatives save complete acceptance or rejection. Choice that is disguised or denied is the source of those astounding differences of philosophic belief that startle the beginner and that become the plaything of the expert. Choice that is avowed is an experiment to be tried on its merits and tested by its results. Under all the captions that are called immediate knowledge, or self-sufficient certitude of belief, whether logical, esthetic or epistemo-

logical, there is something selected for a purpose, and hence not simple, not self-evident and not intrinsically eulogizable. State the purpose so that it may be re-experienced, and its value and the pertinency of selection undertaken in its behalf may be tested. The purport of thinking, scientific and philosophic, is not to eliminate choice but to render it less arbitrary and more significant. It loses its arbitrary character when its quality and consequences are such as to commend themselves to the reflection of others after they have betaken themselves to the situations indicated; it becomes significant when reason for the choice is found to be weighty and its consequences momentous. When choice is avowed, others can repeat the course of the experience; it is an experiment to be tried, not an automatic safety device. . . .

This discussion of empirical method has had a double content. On one hand, it has tried to make clear, from the analogy of empirical method in scientific inquiry, what the method signifies (and does *not* signify) for philosophy. Such a discussion would, however, have little definite import unless the *difference* that is made in philosophy by the adoption of empirical method is pointed out. For that reason, we have considered some typical ways and important places in which traditional philosophies have gone astray through failure to connect their reflective results with the affairs of everyday primary experience. Three sources of large fallacies have been mentioned, each containing within itself many more sub-varieties than have been hinted at. The three are the complete separation of subject and object, (of *what* is experienced from *how* it is experienced); the exaggeration of the features of known objects at the expense of the qualities of objects of enjoyment and trouble, friendship and human association, art and industry; and the exclusive isolation of the results of various types of selective simplification which are undertaken for diverse unavowed purposes.

It does not follow that the products of these philosophies which have taken the wrong, because non-empirical, method are of no value or little worth for a philosophy that pursues a strictly empirical method. The contrary is the case, for no philosopher can get away from experience even it he wants to. The most fantastic views ever entertained by superstitious people had some basis in experienced fact; they can be explained by one who knows enough about them and about the conditions under which they were formed. And philoso-

phers have been not more but less superstitious than their fellows; they have been, as a
class, unusually reflective and inquiring. If
some of their products have been fantasies, it
was not because they did not, even unwit-
tingly, start from empirical method; it was not
wholly because they substituted unchecked
imagination for thought. No, the trouble has
been that they have failed to note the empirical needs that generate their problems, and
have failed to return the refined products back
to the context of actual experience, there to
receive their check, inherit their full content of
meaning, and give illumination and guidance
in the immediate perplexities which originally
occasioned reflection.

The chapters which follow make no pretence, accordingly, of starting to philosophize
afresh as if there were no philosophies already
in existence, or as if their conclusions were empirically worthless. Rather the subsequent discussions rely, perhaps excessively so, upon the
main results of great philosophic systems, endeavoring to point out their elements of
strength and of weakness when their conclusions are employed (as the refined objects of
all reflection must be employed) as guides
back to the subject-matter of crude, everyday
experience.

Our primary experience as it comes is of
little value for purposes of analysis and control, crammed as it is with things that need
analysis and control. The very existence of reflection is proof of its deficiencies. Just as ancient astronomy and physics were of little scientific worth, because, owing to the lack of
apparatus and techniques of experimental
analysis, they had to take the things of primary
observation at their face value, so "common-
sense" philosophy usually repeats current conventionalities. What is averred to be implicit
reliance upon what is given in common experience is likely to be merely an appeal to prejudice to gain support for some fanaticism or defence for some relic of conservative tradition
which is beginning to be questioned.

The trouble, then, with the conclusions of
philosophy is not in the least that they are results of reflection and theorizing. It is rather
that philosophers have borrowed from various
sources the conclusions of special analyses,
particularly of some ruling science of the day,
and imported them direct into philosophy,
with no check by either the empirical objects
from which they arose or those to which the
conclusions in question point. Thus Plato traf-
ficked with the Pythagoreans and imported

mathematical concepts; Descartes and Spinoza
took over the presuppositions of geometrical
reasoning; Locke imported into the theory of
mind the Newtonian physical corpuscles, converting them into given "simple ideas"; Hegel
borrowed and generalized without limit the rising historical method of his day; contemporary
English philosophy has imported from mathematics the notion of primitive indefinable
propositions, and given them a content from
Locke's simple ideas, which had in the meantime become part of the stock in trade of psychological science.

Well, why not, as long as what is borrowed has
a sound scientific status? Because in scientific
inquiry, refined methods justify themselves by
opening up new fields of subject-matter for
exploration; they create new techniques of observation and experimentation. Thus when the
Michelson-Morley experiment disclosed, as a
matter of gross experience, facts which did not
agree with the results of accepted physical laws,
physicists did not think for a moment of denying
the validity of what was found in that experience, even though it rendered questionable an
elaborate intellectual appartus and system. The
coincidence of the bands of the interferometer
was accepted as its face value in spite of its incompatibility with Newtonian physics. Because
scientific inquirers accepted it at its face value
they at once set to work to reconstruct their theories; they questioned their reflective premises,
not the full "reality" of what they saw. This task
of re-adjustment compelled not only new reasonings and calculations in the development of a
more comprehensive theory, but opened up new
ways of inquiry into experienced subject-matter.
Not for a moment did they think of explaining
away the features of an object in gross experience because it was not in logical harmony with
theory—as philosophers have so often done.
Had they done so, they would have stultified
science and shut themselves off from new problems and new findings in subject-matter. In
short, the material of refined scientific method is
continuous with that of the actual world as it is
concretely experienced.

But when philosophers transfer into their
theories bodily and as finalities the refined
conclusions they borrow from the sciences,
whether logic, mathematics or physics, these
results are not employed to reveal new subject-
matters and illuminate old ones of gross experience; they are employed to cast discredit on
the latter and to generate new and artificial
problems regarding the reality and validity of
the things of gross experience. Thus the dis-

coveries of psychologists taken out of their own empirical context are in philosophy employed to cast doubt upon the reality of things external to mind and to selves, things and properties that are perhaps the most salient characteristics of ordinary experience. Similarly, the discoveries and methods of physical science, the concepts of mass, space, motion, have been adopted wholesale in isolation by philosophers in such a way as to make dubious and even incredible the reality of the affections, purposes and enjoyments of concrete experience. The objects of mathematics, symbols of relations having no explicit reference to actual existence, efficacious in the territory to which mathematical technique applies, have been employed in philosophy to determine the priority of essences to existence, and to create the insoluble problem of why pure essence ever descends into the tangles and tortuosities of existence.

What empirical method exacts of philosophy is two things: First, that refined methods and products be traced back to their origin in primary experience, in all its heterogeneity and fullness; so that the needs and problems out of which they arise and which they have to satisfy be acknowledged. Secondly, that the secondary schools methods and conclusions be brought back to the things of ordinary experience, in all their coarseness and crudity, for verification. In this way, the methods of analytic reflection yield material which form the ingredients of a method of designation, denotation, in philosophy. A scientific work in physics or astronomy gives a record of calculations and deductions that were derived from past observations and experiments. But it is more than a record; it is also an indication, an assignment, of further observations and experiments to be performed. No scientific report would get a hearing if it did not describe the apparatus by means of which experiments were carried on and results obtained; not that apparatus is worshipped, but because this procedure tells other inquirers how they are to go to work to get results which will agree or disagree in their experience with those previously arrived at, and thus confirm, modify and rectify the latter. The recorded scientific result is in effect a *designation* of a method to be followed and a *prediction* of what will be found when specified observations are set on foot. That is all a philosophy can be or do. In the chapters that follow I have undertaken a revision and reconstruction of the conclusions, the reports, a number of historic philosophic systems, in

order that they may be usable methods by which one may go to his own experience, and, discerning what is found by use of the method, come to understand better what is already within the common experience of mankind.

There is a special service which the study of philosophy may render. Empirically pursued it will not be a study of philosophy but a study, by means of philosophy, of life-experience. But this experience is already overlaid and saturated with the products of the reflection of past generations and by-gone ages. It is filled with interpretations, classifications, due to sophisticated thought, which have become incorporated into what seems to be fresh naïve empirical material. It would take more wisdom than is possessed by the wisest historic scholar to track all of these absorbed borrowings to their original sources. If we may for the moment call these materials prejudices (even if they are true, as long as their source and authority is unknown), then philosophy is a critique of prejudices. These incorporated results of past reflection, welded into the genuine materials of first-hand experience, may become organs of enrichment if they are detected and reflected upon. If they are not detected, they often obfuscate and distort. Clarification and emancipation follow when they are detected and cast out; and one great object of philosophy is to accomplish this task.

An empirical philosophy is in any case a kind of intellectual disrobing. We cannot permanently divest ourselves of the intellectual habits we take on and wear when we assimilate the culture of our own time and place. But intelligent furthering of culture demands that we take some of them off, that we inspect them critically to see what they are made of and what wearing them does to us. We cannot achieve recovery of primitive naïveté. But there is attainable a cultivated naïveté of eye, ear and thought, one that can be acquired only through the discipline of severe thought. If the chapters which follow contribute to an artful innocence and simplicity they will have served their purpose.

I am loath to conclude without reference to the larger liberal humane value of philosophy when pursued with empirical method. The most serious indictment to be brought against non-empirical philosophies is that they have cast a cloud over the things of ordinary experience. They have not been content to rectify them. They have discredited them at large. In casting aspersion upon the things of everyday experience, the things of action and affection and social intercourse, they have done something worse than fail to give these affairs the intelligent direction they so much need. It would not matter much if philosophy had been reserved as a luxury of only a few thinkers. We endure many luxuries. The serious matter is that philosophies have denied that common experience is capable of developing from within itself methods which will secure direction for itself and will create inherent standards of judgment and value. No one knows how many of the evils and deficiencies that are pointed to as reasons for flight from experience are themselves due to the disregard of experience shown by those peculiarly reflective. To waste of time and energy, to disillusionment with life that attends every deviation from concrete experience must be added the tragic failure to realize the value that intelligent search could reveal and mature among the things of ordinary experience. I cannot calculate how much of current cynicism, indifference and pessimism is due to these causes in the deflection of intelligence they have brought about. It has even become in many circles a sign of lack of sophistication to imagine that life is or can be a fountain of cheer and happiness. Philosophies no more than religions can be acquitted of responsibility for bringing this result to pass. The

transcendental philosopher has probably done more than the professed sensualist and materialist to obscure the potentialities of daily experience for joy and for self-regulation. If what is written in these pages has no other result than creating and promoting a respect for concrete human experience and its potentialities, I shall be content.

NOTES

1. *Essays in Radical Empiricism*, p. 10.
2. It is not intended, however, to attribute to James precisely the interpretation given in the text.
3. To avoid misapprehension, it may be well to add a statement on the latter point. It is not denied that any experienced subject-matter whatever may *become* an object of reflection and cognitive inspection. But the emphasis is upon "become"; the cognitive never *is* all-inclusive: that is, when the material of a prior non-cognitive experience is the object of knowledge, it and the act of knowing are themselves included within a new and wider non-cognitive experience—and *this* situation can never be transcended. It is only when the temporal character of experienced things is forgotten that the idea of the total "transcendence" of knowledge is asserted.

Existence as Precarious and Stable

We have substituted sophistication for superstition, at least measurably so. But the sophistication is often as irrational and as much at the mercy of words as the superstition it replaces. Our magical safeguard against the uncertain character of the world is to deny the existence of chance, to mumble universal and necessary law, the ubiquity of cause and effect, the uniformity of nature, universal progress, and the inherent rationality of the universe. These magic formulae borrow their potency from conditions that are not magical. Through science we have secured a degree of power of prediction and of control; through tools, machinery and an accompanying technique we have made the world more conformable to our needs, a more secure abode. We have heaped

up riches and means of comfort between ourselves and the risks of the world. We have professionalized amusement as an agency of escape and forgetfulness. But when all is said and done, the fundamentally hazardous character of the world is not seriously modified, much less eliminated. Such an incident as the last war and preparations for a future war remind us that it is easy to overlook the extent to which, after all, our attainments are only devices for blurring the disagreeable recognition of a fact, instead of means of altering the fact itself.

What has been said sounds pessimistic. But the concern is not with morals but with metaphysics, with, that is to say, the nature of the existential world in which we live. It would

From "Existence as Precarious and Stable," in *Experience and Nature, John Dewey: The Later Works, 1925–1953,* Vol. 1, Ed. Jo Ann Boydston, (Carbondale and Edwardsville: Southern Illinois University, 1981, pp. 45–47, 51–52, 57–58, 61–63.

have been as easy and more comfortable to emphasize good luck, grace, unexpected and unwon joys, those unsought for happenings which we so significantly call happiness. We might have appealed to good fortune as evidence of this important trait of hazard in nature. Comedy is as genuine as tragedy. But it is traditional that comedy strikes a more superficial note than tragedy. And there is an even better reason for appealing to misfortunes and mistakes as evidence of the precarious nature of the world. The problem of evil is a well-recognized problem, while we rarely or never hear of a problem of good. Goods we take for granted; they are as they should be; they are natural and proper. The good is a recognition of our deserts. When we pull out a plum we treat it as evidence of the *real* order of cause and effect in the world. For this reason it is difficult for the goods of existence to furnish as convincing evidence of the uncertain character of nature as do evils. It is the latter we term accidents, not the former, even when their adventitious character is as certain.

What of it all, it may be asked? In the sense in which an assertion is true that uncontolled distribution of good and evil is evidence of the precarious, uncertain nature of existence, it is a truism, and no problem is forwarded by its reiteration. But it is submitted that just this predicament of the inextricable mixture of stability and uncertainty gives rise to philosophy, and that it is reflected all its recurrent problems and issues. If classic philosophy says so much about unity and so little about unreconciled diversity, so much about the eternal and permanent, and so little about change (save as something to be resolved into combinations of the permanent), so much about necessity and so little about contingency, so much about the comprehending universal and so little about the recalcitrant particular, it may well be because the ambiguousness and ambivalence of reality are actually so pervasive. Since these things form the problem, solution is more apparent (although not more actual), in the degree in which whatever of stability and assurance the world presents is fastened upon and asserted.

Upon their surface, the reports of the world which form our different philosophies are various to the point of stark contrariness. They range from spiritualism to materialism, from absolutism to relativistic phenomenalism, from transcendentalism to positivism, from rationalism to sensationalism, from idealism to realism, from subjectivism to bald objectivism, from Platonic realism to nominalism. The array of contradictions is so imposing as to suggest to sceptics that the mind of man had tackled an impossible job, or that philosophers have abandoned themselves to vagary. These radical oppositions in philosophers suggest however another consideration. They suggest that all their different philosophies have a common premise, and that their diversity is due to acceptance of a common premise. Variant philosophies may be looked at as different ways of supplying recipes for denying to the universe the character of contingency which it possesses so integrally that its denial leaves the reflecting mind without a clew, and puts subsequent philosophising at the mercy of temperament, interest and local surroundings.

Quarrels among conflicting types of philosophy are thus family quarrels. They go on within the limits of a too domestic circle, and can be settled only by venturing further afield, and out of doors. Concerned with imputing complete, finished and sure character to the world of real existence, even if things have to be broken into two disconnected pieces in order to accomplish the result, the character desiderated can plausibly be found in reason or in mechanism; in rational conceptions like those of mathematics, or brute things like sensory data; in atoms or in essences; in consciousness or in a physical externality which forces and overrides consciousness.

As against this common identification of reality with what is sure, regular and finished, experience in unsophisticated forms gives evidence of a different world and points to a different metaphysics. We live in a world which is an impressive and irresistible mixture of sufficiencies, tight completenesses, order, recurrences which make possible prediction and control, and singularities, ambiguities, uncertain possibilities, processes going on to consequences as yet indeterminate. They are mixed not mechanically but vitally like the wheat and tares of the parable. We may recognize them separately but we cannot divide them, for unlike wheat and tares they grow from the same root. Qualities have defects as necessary conditions of their excellencies; the instrumentalities of truth are the causes of error; change gives meaning to permanence and recurrence makes novelty possible. A world that was wholly risky would be a world in which adventure is impossible, and only a living world can include death. Such facts have been celebrated by thinkers like Heracleitus and Lao-tze; they have been greeted by theologians as furnishing occasions for exercise of divine grace; they have been elaborately formulated by various schools under a principle of relativity, so defined as to become itself final and absolute. They have rarely been frankly recognized as fundamentally significant for the formation of a naturalistic metaphysics. . . .

Since thinkers claim to be concerned with knowledge of existence, rather than with imagination, they have to make good the pretention to knowledge. Hence they transmute the imaginative perception of the stably good object into a definition and description of true reality in contrast with lower and specious existence, which, being precarious and incomplete, along involves us in the necessity of choice and active struggle. Thus they remove from actual existence the very traits which generate philosophic reflection and which give point and bearing to its conclusions. In briefest formula, "reality" becomes what we wish existence to be, after we have analyzed its defects and decided upon what would remove them; "reality" is what existence would be if our reasonably justified preferences were so completely established in nature as to exhaust and define its entire being and thereby render search and struggle unnecessary. What is left over, (and since trouble, struggle, conflict, and error still empirically exist, something *is* left over) being excluded by definition from full reality is assigned to a grade or order of being which is asserted to be metaphysically inferior; an order variously called appearance, illusion, mortal mind, or the merely empirical, against what really and truly is. Then the problem of metaphysics alters: instead of being a detection and description of the generic traits of existence, it becomes an endeavor to adjust or reconcile to each other two separate realms of being. Empirically we have just what we started with: the mixture of the precarious and problematic with the assured and complete. But a classificatory device, based on desire and elaborated in reflective imagination, has been introduced by which the two traits are torn apart, one of them being labelled reality and the other appearance. The genuinely moral problem of mitigating and regulating the troublesome factor by active employment of the stable factor then drops out of sight. The dialectic problem of logical reconciliation of two notions has taken its place. . . .

The union of the hazardous and the stable, of the incomplete and the recurrent, is the condition of all experienced satisfaction as truly as of our predicaments and problems. While it is the source of ignorance, error and failure of expectation, it is the source of the delight which fulfillments bring. For if there were nothing in the way, if there were no deviations and resistances, fulfillment would be at once, and in so being would fulfill nothing, but merely be. It would not be in connection with desire or satisfaction. Moreover when a fulfillment comes and is pronounced good, it is *judged* good, distinguished and asserted, simply because it is in jeopardy, because it occurs amid indifferent and divergent things. Because of this mixture of the regular and that which cuts across stability, a good object once experienced acquires ideal quality and attracts demand and effort to itself. A particular ideal may be an illusion, but having ideals is no illusion. It embodies features of existence. Although imagination is often fantastic it is also an organ of nature; for it is the appropriate phase of indeterminate events moving toward eventualities that are now but possibilities. A purely stable world permits of no illusions, but neither is it clothed with ideals. It just exists. To be good is to be better than; and there can be no better except where there is shock and discord combined with enough assured order to make attainment of harmony possible. Better objects when brought into existence are existent not ideal; they retain ideal quality only retrospectively as commemorative of issue from prior conflict and prospectively, in contrast with forces which make for their destruction. Water that slakes thirst, or a conclusion that solves a problem have ideal character as long as thirst or problem persists in a way which qualifies the result. But water that is not a satisfaction of need has no more ideal quality than water running through pipes into a reservoir; a solution ceases to be a solution and becomes a bare incident of existence when its antecedent generating conditions of doubt, ambiguity and search are lost from its context. While the precarious nature of existence is indeed the source of all trouble, it is also an indispensable condition of ideality, becoming a sufficient condition when conjoined with the regular and assured.

We long, amid a troubled world, for perfect being. We forget that what gives meaning to the notion of perfection is the events that create longing, and that, apart from them, a "perfect" world would mean just an unchanging brute existential thing. The ideal significance of esthetic objects is no exception to this principle. Their satisfying quality, their power to compose while they arouse, is not dependent upon definite prior desire and effort as is the case with the ideally satisfying quality of practical and scientific objects. It is part of their peculiar satisfying quality to be gratuitous, not purchased by endeavor. The contrast to other things of this detachment from toil and labor in a world where most realizations have to be bought, as well as the contrast to trouble and uncertainty, give esthetic objects their peculiar traits. If all things came to us in the way our esthetic objects do, none of them would be a source of esthetic delight. . . .

A philosophy which accepts the denotative or empirical method accepts at full value the fact that reflective thinking transforms confusion, ambiguity and discrepancy into illumination, definiteness and consistency. But it also points to the contextual situation in which thinking occurs. It notes that the starting point is the actually *problematic,* and that the problematic phase resides in some actual and specifiable situation.

It notes that the means of converting the dubious into the assured, and the incomplete into the determinate, is use of assured and established things, which are just as empirical and as indicative of the nature of experienced things as is the uncertain. It thus notes that thinking is no different in kind from the use of natural materials and energies, say fire and tools, to refine, reorder, and shape other natural materials, say ore. In both cases, there are matters which as they stand are unsatisfactory and there are also adequate agencies for dealing with them and connecting them. At no point of place is there any jump outside empirical, natural objects and their relations. Thought and reason are not specific powers. They consist of the procedures intentionally employed in the application to each other of the unsatisfactorily confused and indeterminate on one side and the regular and stable on the other. Generalizing from such observations, empirical philosophy perceives that thinking is a continuous process of temporal reorganization within one and the same world of experienced things, not a jump from the latter world into one of objects constituted once for all by thought. It discovers thereby the empirical basis of rational idealism, and the point at which it empirically goes astray. Idealism fails to take into account the specified or concrete character of the uncertain situation in which thought occurs; it fails to note the empirically concrete nature of the subject-matter, acts, and tools by which determination and consistency are reached; it fails to note that the conclusive eventual objects having the latter properties are themsevles as many as the situations dealt with. The conversion of the logic of reflection into an ontology of rational being is thus due to arbitrary conversion of an eventual natural function of unification into a causal antecedent reality; this in turn is due to the tendency of the imagination working under the influence of emotion to carry unification from an actual, objective and experimental enterprise, limited to particular situations where it is needed, into an unrestricted, wholesale movement which ends in an all-absorbing dream.

The occurrence of reflection is crucial for dualistic metaphysics as well as for idealistic ontologies. Reflection occurs only in situations qualified by uncertainty, alternatives, questioning, search, hypotheses, tentative trials or experiments which test the worth of thinking. A naturalistic metaphysics is bound to consider reflection as itself a natural event occurring *within* nature because of traits of the latter. It is bound to inference from the empirical traits of thinking in precisely the same way as the sciences make inferences from the happening of suns, radioactivity, thunder-storms or any other natural event. Traits of reflection are as truly indicative or evidential of the traits of *other* things as are the traits of these events. A theory of the nature of the occurrence and career of a sun reached by denial of the obvious traits of the sun, or by denial that these traits are so connected with the traits of other natural events that they can be used as evidence concerning the nature of these other things, would hardly possess scientific standing. Yet philosophers, and strangely enough philosophers who call themselves realists, have constantly held that the traits which are characteristic of thinking, namely, uncertainty, ambiguity, alternatives, inquiring, search, selection, experimental reshaping of external conditions, do not possess the same existential character as do the objects of valid knowledge. They have denied that these traits are evidential of the character of the world within which thinking occurs. They have not, as realists, asserted that these traits are mere appearances; but they have often asserted and implied that such things are only personal or psychological in contrast with a world of objective nature. But the interests of empirical and denotative method and of naturalistic metaphysics wholly coincide. The world must actually be such as to generate ignorance and inquiry; doubt and hypothesis, trial and temporal conclusions; the latter being such that they develop out of existences which while wholly "real" are not as satisfactory, as good, or as significant, as those into which they are eventually re-organized. The ultimate evidence of genuine hazard, contingency, irregularity and indeterminateness in nature is thus found in the occurrence of thinking. The traits of natural existence which generate the fears and adorations of superstitious barbarians generate the scientific procedures of disciplined civilization. The superiority of the latter does not consist in the fact that they are based on "real" existence, while the former depend wholly upon a human nature different from nature in general. It consists in the fact that scientific inquiries reach *objects* which are better, because reached by method which controls them and which adds greater control to life itself, method which mitigates accident, turns contingency to account, and releases thought and other forms of endeavor.

The conjunction of problematic and determinate characters in nature renders every existence, as well as every idea and human act, an experiment in fact, even though not in design. To be intelligently experimental is but to be conscious of this intersection of natural conditions so as to profit by it instead of being at its mercy. The Christian idea of this world and this life as a probation is a kind of distorted recognition of the situation; distorted because

it applied wholesale to one stretch of existence in contrast with another, regarded as original and final. But in truth anything which can exist at any place and at any time occurs subject to tests imposed upon it by surroundings, which are only in part compatible and reinforcing. These surroundings test its strength and measure its endurance. As we can discourse of change only in terms of velocity and acceleration which involve relations to other things, so assertion of the permanent and enduring is comparative. The stablest thing we can speak of is not free from conditions set to it by other things. That even the solid earth mountains, the emblems of constancy, appear and disappear like the clouds is an old theme of moralists and poets. The fixed and unchanged being of the Democritean atom is now reported by inquirers to possess some of the traits of his nonbeing, and to embody a temporary equilibrium in the economy of nature's compromises and adjustments. A thing may endure *secula seculorum* and yet not be everlasting; it will crumble before the gnawing tooth of time, as it exceeds a certain measure. Every existence is an event. . . .

Nature, Communication and Meaning

Of all affairs, communication is the most wonderful. That things should be able to pass from the plane of external pushing and pulling to that of revealing themselves to man, and thereby to themselves; and that the fruit of communication should be participation, sharing, is a wonder by the side of which transubstantiation pales. When communication occurs, all natural events are subject to reconsideration and revision; they are re-adapted to meet the requirements of conversation, whether it be public discourse or that preliminary discourse termed thinking. Events turn into objects, things with a meaning. They may be referred to when they do not exist, and thus be operative among things distant in space and time, through vicarious presence in a new medium. Brute efficiencies and inarticulate consummations as soon as they can be spoken

of are liberated from local and accidental contexts, and are eager for naturalization in any non-insulated, communicating, part of the world. Events when once they are named lead an independent and double life. In addition to their original existence, they are subject to ideal experimentation: their meanings may be infinitely combined and re-arranged in imagination, and the outcome of this inner experimentation—which is thought—may issue forth in interaction with crude or raw events. Meanings having been deflected from the rapid and roaring stream of events into a calm and traversable canal, rejoin the main stream, and color, temper and compose its course. Where communication exists, things in acquiring meaning, thereby acquire representatives, surrogates, signs and implicates, which are infinitely more

From "Nature, Communication and Meaning," in *Experience and Nature, John Dewey: The Later Works, 1925–1953,* Vol. 1, Ed. Jo Ann Boydston (Carbondale and Edwardsville: Southern Illinois University Press, 1981), pp. 132–133, 138, 141–142, 145–151, 158–161.

amenable to management, more permanent and more accommodating, than events in their first estate.

By this fashion, qualitative immediacies cease to be dumbly rapturous, a possession that is obsessive and an incorporation that involves submergence: conditions found in sensations and passions. They become capable of survey, contemplation, and ideal or logical elaboration; when something can be said of qualities they are purveyors of instruction. Learning and teaching come into being, and there is no event which may not yield information. A directly enjoyed thing adds to itself meaning, and enjoyment is thereby idealized. Even the dumb pang of an ache achieves a significant existence which it can be designated and descanted upon; it ceases to be merely oppressive and becomes important; it gains importance, because it becomes representative; it has the dignity of an office.

In view of these increments and transformations, it is not suprising that meanings, under the name of forms and essences, have often been hailed as modes of Being beyond and above spatial and temporal existence, invulnerable to vicissitude; nor that thought as their possession has been treated as a non-natural spiritual energy, disjoined from all that is empirical. Yet there is a natural bridge that joins the gap between existence and essence; namely communication, language, discourse. Failure to acknowledge the presence and operation of natural interaction in the form of communication creates the gulf between existence and essence, and that gulf is factitious and gratuitous. . . .

When events have communicable meaning, they have marks, notations, and are capable of con-notation and de-notation. They are more than mere occurrences; they have implications. Hence inference and reasoning are possible; these operations are reading the message of things, which things utter because they are involved in human associations. When Aristotle drew a distinction between sensible things that are more noted—known—to us and rational things that are more noted—known—in themselves, he was actually drawing a distinction between things that operate in a local, restricted universe of discourse, and things whose marks are such that they readily enter into indefinitely extensive and varied discourse.

The interaction of human beings, namely, association, is not different in origin from other modes of interaction. There is a peculiar absurdity in the question of how individuals become social, if the question is taken literally. Human beings illustrate the same traits of both immediate uniqueness and connection, relationship, as do other things. No more in their case than in that of atoms and physical masses is immediacy the whole of existence and therefore an obstacle to being acted upon by and affecting other things. Everything that exists in as far as it is known and knowable is in interaction with other things. It is associated, as well as solitary, single. The catching up of human individuals into association is thus no new and unprecedented fact; it is a manifestation of a commonplace of existence. Significance resides not in the bare fact of association, therefore, but in the consequences that flow from the distinctive patterns of human association. There is, again, nothing new or unprecedented in the fact that assemblage of things confers upon the assembly and its constituents, new properties by means of unlocking energies hitherto pent in. The significant consideration is that assemblage of organic human beings transforms sequence and coexistence into participation. . . .

The heart of language is not "expression" of something antecedent, much less expression of antecedent thought. It is communication; the establishment of cooperation in an activity in which there are partners, and in which the activity of each is modified and regulated by partnership. To fail to understand is to fail to come into agreement in action; to misunderstand is to set up action at cross purposes. Take speech as behavioristically as you will, including the elimination of all private mental states, and it remains true that it is markedly distinguished from the signaling acts of animals. Meaning is not indeed a psychic existence; it is primarily a property of behavior, and secondarily a property of objects. But the behavior of which it is a quality is a distinctive behavior; cooperative, in that response to another's act involves contemporaneous response to a thing as entering into the other's behavior, and this upon both sides. It is difficult to state the exact physiological mechanism which is involved. But about the fact there is no doubt. It constitutes the intelligibility of acts and things. Possession of the capacity to engage in such activity is intelligence. Intelligence and meaning are natural consequences of the peculiar form which interaction sometimes assumes in the case of human beings. . . .

Language is specifically a mode of interaction of at least two beings, a speaker and a hearer; it presupposes an organized group to which these creatures belong, and from whom they have acquired their habits of speech. It is therefore a relationship, not a particularity. This consideration alone condemns traditional nominalism. The meaning of signs moreover always includes something common as between persons and an object. When we attribute meaning to the speaker as *his* intent, we take for granted another person who is to share in the execution of the intent, and also something, independent of the persons concerned, through which the intent is to be realized. Persons and thing must alike serve as means in a common, shared consequence. This community of partaking is meaning.

The invention and use of tools have played a large part in consolidating meanings, because a tool is a thing used as means to consequences, instead of being taken directly and physically. It is intrinsically relational, anticipatory, predictive. Without reference to the absent, or "transcendence," nothing is a tool. The most convincing evidence that animals do not "think" is found in the fact that they have no tools, but depend upon their own relatively-fixed bodily structures to effect results. Because of such dependence they have no way of distinguishing the immediate existence of anything from its potential efficiencies; no way of projecting its consequences to define a nature or essence. Anything whatever used as a tool exhibits distinction and identification. Fire existentially burns; while fire which is employed in order to cook and keep warm, especially after other things, like rubbing sticks together, are used as means to generate it, is an existence having meaning and potential essence. The presence of inflammation and terror or discomfort is no longer the whole story; an occurrence is now an object; and while it is absurd to hold (as idealism virtually does) that the meaning of an existence is the real substance of the existence, it is equally absurd not to recognize the full transformative import of what has happened.

As to be a tool, or to be used as means for consequences, is to have and to endow with meaning, language, being the tool of tools, is the cherishing mother of all significance. For other instrumentalities and agencies, the things usually thought of as appliances, agencies and furnishings, can originate and develop only in social groups made possible by language. Things become tools ceremonially and institutionally. The notoriously conventionalized and traditional character of primitive utensils and their attendant symbolizations demonstrate this fact. Moreover,

tools and artifices of agency are always found in connection with some division of labor which depends upon some device of communication. The statement can be proved in a more theoretical way. Immediacy as such is transient to the point of evanescence, and its flux has to be fixed by some easily recoverable and recurrent act within control of the organism, like gesture and spoken sounds, before things can be intentionally utilized. A creature might accidentally warm itself by a fire or use a stick to stir the ground in a way which furthered the growth of food-plants. But the effect of comfort ceases with the fire, existentially; a stick even though once used as a lever would revert to the status of being just a stick, unless the *relationship* between it and its consequence were distinguished and retained. Only language, or some form of artificial signs, serves to register the relationship and make it fruitful in other contexts of particular existence. Spears, urns, baskets, snares may have originated accidentally in some consummatory consequence of natural events. But only repetition through concerted action accounts for their becoming institutionalized as tools, and this concert of action depends upon the use of memoranda and communication. To make another aware of the possibility of a use or objective relationship is to perpetuate what is otherwise an incident as an agency; communication is a condition of consciousness.

Thus every meaning is generic or universal. It is something common between speaker, hearer and the things to which speech refers. It is universal also as a means of generalization. For a meaning is a method of action, a way of using things as means to a shared consummation, and method is general, though the things to which it is applied are peculiar. The meaning, for example, or portability is something in which two persons and an object share. But portability after it is once apprehended becomes a way of treating other things; it is extended widely. Whenever there is a chance, it is applied; application ceases only when a thing refuses to be treated in this way. And even then refusal may be only a challenge to develop the meaning of portability until the thing can be transported. Meanings are rules for using and interpreting things; interpretation being always an imputation of potentiality for some consequence.

It would be difficult to imagine any doctrine more absurd than the theory that general ideas or meanings arise by the comparison of a number of particulars, eventuating in the recognition of something common to them all. Such a comparison may be employed to check a suggested widened application of a rule. But generalization is carried spontaneously as far as it will plausibly go; usually much further than it will actually go. A newly acquired meaning is forced upon everything that does not obviously resist its application, as a child uses a new word whenever he gets a chance or as he plays with a new toy. Meanings are self-moving to new cases. In the end, conditions force a chastening of this spontaneous tendency. The scope and limits of application are ascertained experimentally in the process of application. The history of science, to say nothing of popular beliefs, is sufficient indication of the difficulty found in submitting this irrational generalizing tendency to the discipline of experience. To call it *a priori* is to express a fact; but to impute the *a priori* character of the generalizing force of meanings to *reason* is to invert the facts. Rationality is acquired when the tendency becomes circumspect, based upon observation and tested by deliberate experiment.

Meaning is objective as well as universal. Originating as a concerted or combined method of using or enjoying things, it indicates a possible interaction, not a thing in separate singleness. A meaning may not of course have the particular objectivity which is imputed to it, as whistling does not actually portend wind, nor the ceremonial sprinkling of water indicate rain. But such magical imputations of external reference testify to the objectivity of meaning as such. Meanings are naturally the meaning of something or other; difficulty lies in discriminating the right thing. It requires the discipline of ordered and deliberate experimentation to teach us that some meanings delightful or horrendous as they are, are meanings communally developed in the process of communal festivity and control, and do not represent the polities, and ways and means of nature apart from social arts. Scientific meanings were superadded to esthetic and affectional meanings when objects instead of being defined in terms of their consequences in social interactions and discussion were defined in terms of their consequences with respect to one another. This discrimination permitted esthetic and affective objects to be freed from magical imputations, which were due to attributing to them *in rerum natura* the consequences they had in the transmitted culture of the group.

Yet the truth of classic philosophy in assigning objectivity to meanings, essences, ideas remains unassailable. It is heresy to conceive meanings to be private, a property of ghostly psychic existences. Berkeley with all his nominalism, saw that "ideas," though particular in existence, are general in function and office. His attribution of the ideas which are efficacious in conduct to an order established by God, while evincing lack of perception of their naturalistic origin in communication or communal interaction, manifests a sounder sense of the objectivity of meanings than has been shown by those who eliminated his theology while retaining his psychology. The inconsistency of the sensationalists who, stopping short of extreme scepticism, postulate that some associations of ideas correspond to conjunctions among things is also reluctantly extorted evidence of how intimation of the objectivity of ideas haunts the mind in spite of theory to the contrary.

Meanings are objective because they are modes of natural interaction; such an interaction, although primarily between organic beings, as includes things and energies external to living creatures. The regulative force of legal meanings affords a convenient illustration. A traffic policeman holds up his hand or blows a whistle. His act operates as a signal to direct movements. But it is more than an episodic stimulus. It embodies a rule of social action. Its proximate meaning is its near-by consequences in coordination of movements of persons and vehicles; its ulterior and permanent meaning—essence—is its consequence in the way of security of social movements. Failure to observe the signal subjects a person to arrest, fine or imprisonment. The essence embodied in the policeman's whistle is not an occult reality superimposed upon a sensuous or physical flux and imparting form to it; a mysterious subsistence somehow housed within a psychical event. Its essence is the rule, comprehensive and persisting, the standardized habit, of social interaction, and for the sake of which the whistle is used. The pattern, archetype, that forms the essence of the whistle as a particular noise is an orderly arrangement of the movements of persons and vehicles established by social agreement as its consequence. This meaning is independent of the psychical landscape, the sensations and imagery, of the policeman and others concerned. But it is not on that account a timeless spiritual ghost nor pale logical subsistence divorced from events.

The case is the same with the essence of any non-human event, like gravity, or virtue, or vertebrate. Some consequences of the interaction of things concern us; the consequences are not *merely* physical; they enter finally into human action and destiny. Fire burns and the burning is of moment. It enters experience; it is fascinating to watch swirling flames; it is important to avoid its dangers and to utilize its beneficial potencies. When we name an event, calling it fire, we speak proleptically; we do not name an immediate event; that is impossible. We employ a term of discourse; we invoke a meaning, namely, the potential consequences of the existence. The ultimate meaning of the noise made by the traffic officer is the total consequent system of social behavior, in which individuals are subjected, by means of noise, to social coordination; its proximate meaning is a coordination of the movements of persons and vehicles in the neighborhood and directly affected. Similarly the ultimate meaning, or essence, denominated fire, is the consequences of certain natural events within the scheme of human activities, in the experience of social intercourse, the hearth and domestic altar, shared comfort, working of metals, rapid transit, and other such affairs. "Scientifically," we ignore these ulterior meanings. And quite properly; for when a sequential order of changes is determined, the final meaning in immediate enjoyments and appreciations is capable of control.

While classic thought, and its survival in later idealisms, assumed that the ulterior human meanings, meanings of direct association in discourse, are forms of nature apart from their place in discourse, modern thought is given to making a sharp separation between meanings determined in terms of the causal relationship of things and meanings in terms of human association. Consequently, it treats the latter as negligible or as purely private, not the meanings of natural events at all. It identifies the proximate meanings with the only valid meanings, and abstract relations become an idol. To pass over in science the human meanings of the consequences of natural interactions is legitimate; indeed it is indispensable. To ascertin and state meanings in abstraction from social or shared situations is the only way in which the latter can be intelligently modified, extended and varied. Mathematical symbols have least connection with distinctively human situations and consequences; and the finding of such terms, free from esthetic and moral significance, is a necessary part of the technique. Indeed, such elimination of ulterior meanings supplies perhaps the best possible empirical definition of mathemtical relations. They are meanings without direct reference to human behavior. Thus an essence becomes wholly "intel-

lectual" or scientific, devoid of consummatory implication; it expresses the purely instrumental without reference to the objects to which the events in question are instrumental. It then becomes the starting point of reflection that may terminate in ends or consequences in human suffering and enjoyment not previously experienced. Abstraction from any particular consequence (which is the same thing as taking instrumentality generally), opens the way to new uses and consequences. . . .

If scientific discourse is instrumental in function, it also is capable of becoming an enjoyed object to those concerned in it. Upon the whole, human history shows that thinking in being abstract, remote and technical has been laborious; or at least that the process of attaining such thinking has been rendered painful to most by social circumstances. In view of the importance of such activity and its objects, it is a priceless gain when it becomes an intrinsic delight. Few would philosophize if philosophic discourse did not have its own inhering fascination. Yet it is not the satisfactoriness of the activity which defines science or philosophy; the definition comes from the structure and function of subject-matter. To say that knowledge as the fruit of intellectual discourse is an end in itself is to say what is esthetically and morally true for some persons, but it conveys nothing about the structure of knowledge; and it does not even hint that its objects are not instrumental. These are questions that can be decided only by an examination of the things in question. Impartial and disinterested thinking, discourse in terms of scrutinized, tested, and related meanings, is a fine art. But it is an art as yet open to comparatively few. Letters, poetry, song, the drama, fiction, history, biography, engaging in rites and ceremonies hallowed by time and rich with the sense of the countless multitudes that share in them, are also modes of discourse that, detached from immediate instrumental consequences of assistance and cooperative action, are ends for most persons. In them discourse is both instrumental and final. No person remains unchanged and has the same future efficiencies, who shares in situations made possible by communication. Subsequent consequences may be good or bad, but they are there. The part of wisdom is not to deny the causal fact because of the intrinsic value of the immediate experience. It is to make the immediately satisfactory object the object which will also be most fertile.

The saying of Matthew Arnold that poetry is

a criticism of life sounds harsh to the ears of some persons of strong esthetic bent; it seems to give poetry a moral and instrumental function. But while poetry is not a criticism of life in intent, it is in effect, and so is all art. For art fixes those standards of enjoyment and appreciation with which other things are compared; it selects the objects of future desires; it stimulates effort. This is true of the objects in which a particular person finds his immediate or esthetic values, and it is true of collective man. The level and style of the arts of literature, poetry, ceremony, amusement, and recreation which obtain in a community, furnishing the staple objects of enjoyment in that community, do more than all else to determine the current direction of ideas and endeavors in the community. They supply the meanings in terms of which life is judged, esteemed, and criticized. For an outside spectator, they supply material for a critical evaluation of the life led by that community.

Communication is uniquely instrumental and uniquely final. It is instrumental as liberating us from the otherwise overwhelming pressure of events and enabling us to live in a world of things that have meaning. It is final as a sharing in the objects and arts precious to a community, a sharing whereby meanings are enhanced, deepened and solidified in the sense of communion. Because of its characteristic agency and finality, communication and its congenial objects are objects ultimately worthy of awe, admiration, and loyal appreciation. They are worthy as means, because they are the only means that make life rich and varied in meanings. They are worthy as ends, because in such ends man is lifted from his immediate isolation and shares in a communion of meanings. Here, as in so many other things, the great evil lies in separating instrumental and final functions. Intelligence is partial and specialized, because communication and participation are limited, sectarian, provincial, confined to class, party, professional group. By the same token, our enjoyment of ends is luxurious and corrupting for some; brutal, trivial, harsh for others; exclusion from the life of free and full communication excluding both alike from full possession of meanings of the things that enter experience. When the instrumental and final functions of communication live together in experience, there exists an intelligence which is the method and reward of the common life, and a society worthy to command affection, admiration, and loyalty.

The Pattern of Inquiry

The existence of inquiries is not a matter of doubt. They enter into every area of life and into every aspect of every area. In everyday living, men examine; they turn things over intellectually; they infer and judge as "naturally" as they reap and sow, produce and exchange commodities. As a mode of conduct, inquiry is as accessible to objective study as are these other modes of behavior. Because of the intimate and decisive way in which inquiry and its conclusions enter into the management of all affairs of life, no study of the latter is adequate save as it is noted how they are affected by the methods and instruments of inquiry that currently obtain. Quite apart, then, from the particular hypothesis about logical forms that is put forth, study of the objective facts of inquiry is a matter of tremendous import, practically and intellectually. These materials provide the theory of logical forms with a subject-matter that is not only objective but is objective in a fashion that enables logic to avoid the three mistakes most characteristic of its history.

1. In virtue of its concern with objectively observable subject-matter by reference to which reflective conclusions can be tried and tested, dependence upon subjective and "mentalistic" states and processes is eliminated.

2. The distinctive existence and nature of forms is acknowledged. Logic is not compelled, as historic "empirical" logic felt compelled to do, to reduce logical forms to mere transcripts of the empirical materials that antecede the existence of the former. Just as art-forms and legal forms are capable of independent discussion

From "The Pattern of Inquiry," in *Logic: The Theory of Inquiry, John Dewey: The Later Works, 1925–1953,* Vol. 12, Ed. Jo Ann Boydston (Carbondale and Edwardsville: Southern Illinois University Press, 1986), pp. 106–122.

and development, so are logical forms, even though the "independence" in question is intermediate, not final and complete. As in the case of these other forms, they originate *out of* experiential material, and when constituted introduce new ways of operating with prior materials, which ways modify the material out of which they develop.

3. Logical theory is liberated from the unobservable, transcendental and "intuitional."

When methods and results of inquiry are studied as objective data, the distinction that has often been drawn between noting and reporting the ways in which men *do* think, and prescribing the ways in which they *ought* to think, takes on a very different interpretation from that usually given. The usual interpretation is in terms of the difference between the psychological and the logical, the latter consisting of "norms" provided from some source wholly outside of and independent of "experience."

The way in which men *do* "think" denotes, as it is *here* interpreted, simply the ways in which men at a given time carry on their inquiries. So far as it is used to register a difference from the ways in which they *ought* to think, it denotes a difference like that between good and bad farming or good and bad medical practice. Men think in ways they should not when they follow methods of inquiry that experience of past inquiries shows are not competent to reach the intended end of the inquiries in question.

Everybody knows that today there are in vogue methods of farming generally followed in the past which compare very unfavorably in their results with those obtained by practices that have already been introduced and tested. When an expert tells a farmer he *should* do thus and so, he is not setting up for a bad farmer an ideal drawn from the blue. He is instructing him in methods that have been tried and that have proved successful in procuring results. In a similar way we are able to contrast various kinds of inquiry that are in use or that have been used in respect to their economy and efficiency in reaching warranted conclusions. We know that some methods of inquiry are better than others in just the same way in which we know that some methods of surgery, farming, road-making, navigating or what-not are better than others. It does not follow in any of these cases that the "better" methods are ideally perfect, or that they are regulative or "normative" because of conformity to some absolute form. They are the

methods which experience up to the present time shows to be the best methods available for achieving certain results, while abstraction of these methods does supply a (relative) norm or standard for further undertakings.

The search for the pattern of inquiry is, accordingly, not one instituted in the dark or at large. It is checked and controlled by knowledge of the kinds of inquiry that have and that have not worked; methods which, as was pointed out earlier, can be so compared as to yield reasoned or rational conclusions. For, through comparison-contrast, we ascertain *how* and *why* certain means and agencies have provided warrantably assertible conclusions, while others have not and *cannot* do so in the sense in which "cannot" expresses an intrinsic incompatibility between means used and consequences attained.

We may now ask: What is the *definition* of Inquiry? That is, what is the most highly generalized conception of inquiry which can be justifiably formulated? The definition that will be expanded, directly in the present chapter and indirectly in the following chapters, is as follows: *Inquiry is the controlled or directed transformation of an indeterminate situation into one that is so determinate in its constituent distinctions and relations as to convert the elements of the original situation into a unified whole.*

The original indeterminate situation is not only "open" to inquiry, but it is open in the sense that its constituents do not hang together. The determinate situation on the other hand, *qua* outcome of inquiry, is a closed and, as it were, finished situation or "universe of experience." "Controlled or directed" in the above formula refers to the fact that inquiry is competent in any given case in the degree in which the operations involved in it actually do terminate in the establishment of an objectively unified existential situation. In the intermediate course of transition and transformation of the indeterminate situation, *dis*course through use of symbols is employed as means. In received logical terminology, propositions, or terms and the relations between them, are intrinsically involved.

I. *The Antecedent Conditions of Inquiry: The Indeterminate Situation.* Inquiry and questioning, up to a certain point, are synonymous terms. We inquire when we question; and we inquire when we seek for whatever will provide an answer to a question asked. Thus it is of the very nature of the indeterminate situation which evokes inquiry to be *questionable;*

or, in terms of actuality instead of potentiality, to be uncertain, unsettled, disturbed. The peculiar quality of what pervades the given materials, constituting them a situation, is not just uncertainty at large; it is a unique doubtfulness which makes that situation to be just and only the situation it is. It is this unique quality that not only evokes the particular inquiry engaged in but that exercises control over its special procedures. Otherwise, one procedure in inquiry would be as likely to occur and to be effective as any other. Unless a situation is uniquely qualified in its very indeterminateness, there is a condition of complete panic; response to it takes the form of blind and wild overt activities. Stating the matter from the personal side, we have "lost our heads." A variety of names serves to characterize indeterminate situations. They are disturbed, troubled, ambiguous, confused, full of conflicting tendencies, obscure, etc.

It is the *situation* that has these traits. We are doubtful because the situation is inherently doubtful. Personal states of doubt that are not evoked by and are not relative to some existential situation are pathological; when they are extreme they constitute the mania of doubting. Consequently, situations that are disturbed and troubled, confused or obscure, cannot be straightened out, cleared up and put in order, by manipulation of our personal states of mind. The attempt to settle them by such manipulations involves what psychiatrists call "withdrawal from reality." Such an attempt is pathological as far as it goes, and when it goes far it is the source of some form of actual insanity. The habit of disposing of the doubtful as if it belonged only to *us* rather than to the existential situation in which we are caught and implicated is an inheritance from subjectivistic psychology. The biological antecedent conditions of an unsettled situation are involved in that state of imbalance in organic-environmental interactions which has already been described. Restoration of integration can be effected, in one case as in the other, only by operations which actually modify existing conditions, not by merely "mental" processes.

It is, accordingly, a mistake to suppose that a situation is doubtful only in a "subjective" sense. The notion that in actual existence everything is completely determinate has been rendered questionable by the progress of physical science itself. Even if it had not been, complete determination would not hold of existences as an *environment*. For Nature is an environment only as it is involved in interac-

tion with an organism, or self, or whatever name be used.[1]

Every such interaction is a temporal process, not a momentary cross-sectional occurrence. The situation in which it occurs is indeterminate, therefore, with respect to its *issue*. If we call it *confused*, then it is meant that its outcome cannot be anticipated. It is called *obscure* when its course of movement permits of final consequences that cannot be clearly made out. It is called *conflicting* when it tends to evoke discordant responses. Even were existential conditions unqualifiedly determinate in and of themselves, they are indeterminate in *significance:* that is, in what they import and portend in their interaction with the organism. The organic responses that enter into the production of the state of affairs that is temporally later and sequential are just as existential as are environing conditions.

The immediate *locus* of the problem concerns, then, what kind of responses the organism shall make. It concerns the interaction of organic responses and environing conditions in their movement toward an existential issue. It is a commonplace that in any troubled state of affair *things* will come out differently according to what is done. The farmer won't get grain unless he plants and tills; the general will win or lose the battle according to the way he conducts it, and so on. Neither the grain nor the tilling, neither the outcome of the battle nor the conduct of it, are "mental" events. Organic interaction becomes inquiry when existential consequences are anticipated; when environing conditions are examined with reference to their potentialities; and when responsive activities are selected and ordered with reference to actualization of some of the potentialities, rather than others, in a final existential situation. Resolution of the indeterminate situation is active and operational. If the inquiry is adequately directed, the final issue is the unified situation that has been mentioned.

II. *Institution of a Problem.* The unsettled or indeterminate situation might have been called a *problematic* situation. This name would have been, however, proleptic and anticipatory. The indeterminate situation becomes problematic in the very process of being subjected to inquiry. The indeterminate situation comes into existence from existential causes, just as does, say, the organic imbalance of hunger. There is nothing intellectual or cognitive in the existence of such situations, although they are the necessary condition of cognitive operations or inquiry. In themselves they are precognitive. The first result of evocation of inquiry is that the situation is taken, adjudged, to be problematic. To see what a situation requires inquiry is the initial step in inquiry.[2]

Qualification of a situation as problematic does not, however, carry inquiry far. It is but an initial step in institution of a problem. A problem is not a task to be performed which a person puts upon himself or that is placed upon him by others—like a so-called arithmetical "problem" in school work. A problem represents the partial transformation by inquiry of a problematic situation into a determinate situation. It is a familiar and significant saying that a problem well put is half-solved. To find out *what* the problem and problems are which a problematic situation presents to be inquired into, is to be well along in inquiry. To mis-take the problem involved is to cause subsequent inquiry to be irrelevant or to go astray. Without a problem, there is blind groping in the dark. The way in which the problem is conceived decides what specific suggestions are entertained and which are dismissed; what data are selected and which rejected; it is the criterion for relevancy and irrelevancy of hypotheses and conceptual structures. On the other hand, to set up a problem that does not grow out of an actual situation is to start on a course of dead work, nonetheless dead because the work is "busy work." Problems that are self-set are mere excuses for seeming to do something intellectual, something that has the semblance but not the substance of scientific activity.

III. *The Determination of a Problem-Solution.* Statement of a problematic situation in terms of a problem has no meaning save as the problem instituted has, in the very terms of its statement, reference to a possible solution. Just because a problem well stated is on its way to solution, the determining of a genuine problem is a *progressive* inquiry; the cases in which a problem and its probable solution flash upon an inquirer are cases where much prior ingestion and digestion have occurred. If we assume, prematurely, that the problem involved is definite and clear, subsequent inquiry proceeds on the wrong track. Hence the question arises: How is the formation of a genuine problem so controlled that further inquiries will move toward a solution?

The first step in answering this question is to recognize that no situation which is *completely* indeterminate can possibly be converted into a problem having definite constituents. The first step then is to search out the *constituents* of a given situation which, as constituents, are settled. When an alarm of fire is sounded in a crowded assembly hall, there is much that is indeterminate as regards the activities that may produce a favorable issue. One may get out safely or one may be trampled and burned. The fire is characterized, however, by some settled traits. It is, for example, located *somewhere.* Then the aisles and exits are at fixed places. Since they are settled or determinate in *existence,* the first step in institution of a problem is to settle them in *observation.* There are other factors which, while they are not as temporally and spatially fixed, are yet observable constituents; for example, the behavior and movements of other members of the audience. All of these observed conditions taken together constitute "the facts of the case." They constitute the terms of the problem, because they are conditions that must be reckoned with or taken account of in any relevant solution that is proposed.

A *possible* relevant solution is then suggested by the determination of factual conditions which are secured by observation. The possible solution presents itself, therefore, as an *idea,* just as the terms of the problem (which are facts) are instituted by observation. Ideas are anticipated consequences (forecasts) of what will happen when certain operations are executed under and with respect to observed conditions.[3] Observation of facts and suggested meanings or ideas arise and develop in correspondence with each other. The more the facts of the case come to light in consequence of being subjected to observation, the clearer and more pertinent become the conceptions of the way the problem constituted by these facts is to be dealt with. On the other side, the clearer the idea, the more definite, as a truism, become the operations of observation and of execution that must be performed in order to resolve the situation.

An idea is first of all an anticipation of something that may happen; it marks a *possibility.* When it is said, as it sometimes is, that science is *prediction,* the anticipation that constitutes every idea an idea is grounded in a set of controlled observations and of regulated conceptual ways of interpreting them. Because inquiry is a progressive determination of a problem and its possible solution, ideas differ in grade according to the stage of inquiry reached. At first, save in highly familiar matters, they are vague. They occur at first simply as suggestions; suggestions just spring up, flash upon us, occur to us. They may then become stimuli to direct an overt activity but they have as yet no logical status. Every idea originates as a suggestion, but not every suggestion is an idea. The suggestion becomes an idea when it is examined with reference to its functional fitness; its capacity as a means of resolving the given situation.

This examination takes the form of reasoning, as a result of which we are able to appraise better than we were at the outset, the pertinency and weight of the meaning now entertained with respect to its functional capacity. But the final test of its possession of these properties is determined when it actually functions—that is, when it is put into operation so as to institute by means of observation facts not previously observed, and is then used to organize them with other facts into a coherent whole.

Because suggestions and ideas are of that which is not present in given existence, the meanings which they involve must be embodied in some symbol. Without some kind of symbol no idea; a meaning that is completely disembodied can not be entertained or used. Since an existence (which *is* an existence) is the support and vehicle of a meaning and is a symbol instead of a merely physical existence only in this respect, embodied meanings or ideas are capable of objective survey and development. To "look at an idea" is not a mere literary figure of speech.

"Suggestions" have received scant courtesy in logical theory. It is true that when they just "pop into our heads," because of the workings of the psycho-physical organism, they are not logical. But they are both the conditions and the primary stuff of logical ideas. The traditional empiristic theory reduced them, as has already been pointed out, to mental copies of physical things and assumed that they were *per se* identical with ideas. Consequently it ignored the function of ideas in directing observation and in ascertaining relevant facts. The rationalistic school, on the other hand, saw clearly that "facts" apart from ideas are trivial, that they acquire import and significance only in relation to ideas. But at the same time it failed to attend to the operative and functional nature of the latter. Hence, it treated ideas as equivalent to the ultimate structure of "Reality." The Kantian formula that apart from each other "perceptions are blind and conceptions empty"

marks a profound logical insight. The insight, however, was radically distorted because perceptual and conceptual contents were supposed to originate from different sources and thus required a third activity, that of synthetic understanding, to bring them together. In logical fact, perceptual and conceptual materials are instituted in functional correlativity with each other, in such a manner that the former locates and describes the problem while the latter represents a possible method of solution. Both are determinations in and by inquiry of the original problematic situation whose pervasive quality controls their institution and their contents. Both are finally checked by their capacity to work together to introduce a resolved unified situation. As distinctions they represent logical divisions of labor.

IV. *Reasoning.* The necessity of developing the meaning-contents of ideas in their relations to one another has been incidentally noted. This process, operating with symbols (constituting propositions) is reasoning in the sense of ratiocination or rational discourse.[4] When a suggested meaning is immediately accepted, inquiry is cut short. Hence the conclusion reached is not grounded, even if it happens to be correct. The check upon immediate acceptance is the examination of the meaning as a meaning. This examination consists in noting what the meaning in question implies in relation to other meanings in the system of which it is a member, the formulated relation constituting a proposition. If such and such a relation of meanings is accepted, then we are committed to such and such other relations of meanings because of their membership in the same system. Through a series of intermediate meanings, a meaning is finally reached which is more clearly *relevant* to the problem in hand than the originally suggested idea. It indicates operations which can be performed to test its applicability, whereas the original idea is usually too vague to determine crucial operations. In other words, the idea or meaning when developed in discourse directs the activities which, when executed, provide needed evidential material.

The point made can be most readily appreciated in connection with scientific reasoning. An hypothesis, once suggested and entertained, is developed in relation to other conceptual structures until it receives a form in which it can instigate and direct an experiment that will disclose precisely those conditions which have the maximum possible force in determining whether the hypothesis should be accepted or rejected. Or it may be that the experiment will indicate what modifications are required in the hypothesis so that it may be applicable, i.e., suited to interpret and organize the facts of the case. In many familiar situations, the meaning that is most relevant has been settled because of the eventuations of experiments in prior cases so that it is applicable almost immediately upon its occurrence. But, indirectly, if not directly, an idea or suggestion that is not developed in terms of the constellation of meanings to which it belongs can lead only to overt response. Since the latter terminates inquiry, there is then no adequate inquiry into the meaning that is used to settle the given situation, and the conclusion is in so far logically ungrounded.

V. *The Operational Character of Facts-Meanings.* It was stated that the observed facts of the case and the ideational contents expressed in ideas are related to each other, as, respectively, a clarification of the problem involved and the proposal of some possible solution; that they are, accordingly, functional divisions in the work of inquiry. Observed facts in their office of locating and describing the problem are existential; ideational subject-matter is non-existential. How, then, do they cooperate with each other in the resolution of an existential situation? The problem is insoluble save as it is recognized that both observed facts and entertained ideas are operational. Ideas are operational in that they instigate and direct further operations of observation; they are proposals and plans for acting upon existing conditions to bring new facts to light and to organize all the selected facts into a coherent whole.

What is meant by calling facts operational? Upon the negative side what is meant is that they are not self-sufficient and complete in themselves. They are selected and described, as we have seen, for a purpose, namely statement of the problem involved in such a way that its material both indicates a meaning relevant to resolution of the difficulty and serves to test its worth and validity. In regulated inquiry facts are selected and arranged with the express intent of fulfilling this office. They are not merely *results* of operations of observation which are executed with the aid of bodily organs and auxiliary instruments of art, but they are the particular facts and kinds of facts that will link up with one another in the definite ways that are required to produce a definite end. Those not found to connect

with others in furtherance of this end are dropped and others are sought for. Being functional, they are necessarily operational. Their function is to serve as evidence and their evidential quality is judged on the basis of their capacity to form an ordered whole in response to operations prescribed by the ideas they occasion and support. If "the facts of the case" were final and complete in themselves, if they did not have a special operative force in resolution of the problematic situation, they could not serve as evidence.

The operative force of facts is apparent when we consider that no fact in isolation has evidential potency. Facts are evidential and are tests of an idea in so far as they are capable of being organized with one another. The organization can be achieved only as they *interact* with one another. When the problematic situation is such as to require extensive inquiries to effect its resolution, a series of interactions intervenes. Some observed facts point to an idea that stands for a possible solution. This idea evokes more observations. Some of the newly observed facts link up with those previously observed and are such as to rule out other observed things with respect to their evidential function. The new order of facts suggests a modified idea (or hypothesis) which occasions new observations whose result again determines a new order of facts, and so on until the existing order is both unified and complete. In the course of this serial process, the ideas that represent possible solutions are tested or "proved."

Meantime, the order of facts, which present themselves in consequence of the experimental observations the ideas call out and direct, are *trial* facts. They are provisional. They are "facts" if they are observed by sound organs and techniques. But they are not on that account the *facts of the case*. They are tested or "proved" with respect to their evidential function just as much as ideas (hypotheses) are tested with reference to their power to exercise the function of resolution. The operative force of both ideas and facts is thus practically recognized in the degree in which they are connected with *experiment*. Naming them "operational" is but a theoretical recognition of what is involved when inquiry satisfies the conditions imposed by the necessity for experiment.

I recur, in this connection, to what has been said about the necessity for symbols in inquiry. It is obvious, on the face of matters, that a possible mode of solution must be carried in symbolic form since it is a possibility, not an assured present existence. Observed facts, on the other hand, are existentially present. It might seem therefore, that symbols are not required for referring to them. But if they are not carried and treated by means of symbols, they lose their provisional character, and in losing this character they are categorically asserted and inquiry comes to an end. The carrying on of inquiry requires that the facts be taken as *representative* and not just as *presented*. This demand is met by formulating them in propositions—that is, by means of symbols. Unless they are so represented they relapse into the total qualitative situation.

VI. *Common Sense and Scientific Inquiry.* The discussion up to this point has proceeded in general terms which recognized no distinction between common sense and scientific inquiry. We have now reached a point where the community of pattern in these two distinctive modes of inquiry should receive explicit attention. It was said in earlier chapters that the difference between them resides in their respective subject-matters, not in their basic logical forms and relations; that the difference in subject-matters is due to the difference in the problems respectively involved; and, finally, that this difference sets up a difference in the ends or objective consequences they are concerned to achieve. Because common sense problems and inquiries have to do with the interactions into which living creatures enter in connection with environing conditions in order to establish objects of use and enjoyment, the symbols employed are those which have been determined in the habitual culture of a group. They form a system but the system is practical rather than intellectual. It is constituted by the traditions, occupations, techniques, interests, and established institutions of the group. The meanings that compose it are carried in the common everyday language of communication between members of the group. The meanings involved in this common language system determine what individuals of the group may and may not do in relation to physical objects and in relations to one another. They regulate *what* can be used and enjoyed and *how* use and enjoyment shall occur.

Because the symbol-meaning systems involved are connected directly with cultural life-activities and are related to each other in virtue of this connection, the specific meanings which are present have reference to the specific and limited environing conditions under which the group lives. Only those things of the environment that are taken, according to custom and tradition, as having connection with and bearing upon this life, enter into the meaning system. There is no such thing as disinterested intellectual concern with either physical or social matters. For, until the rise of science, there were no problems of common sense that called for such inquiry. Disinterestedness existed practically in the demand that group interests and concerns be put above private needs and interests. But there was no intellectual disinterestedness beyond the activities, interests and concerns of the group. In other words, there was no science as such, although, as was earlier pointed out, there did exist information and techniques which were available for the purposes of scientific inquiry and out of which the latter subsequently grew.

In scientific inquiry, then, meanings are related to one another on the ground of their character *as* meanings, freed from direct reference to the concerns of a limited group. Their intellectual abstractness is a product of this liberation, just as the "concrete" is practically identified by directness of connection with environmental interactions. Consequently a new language, a new system of symbols related together on a new basis, comes into existence, and in this new language semantic coherence, as such, is the controlling consideration. To repeat what has already been said, connection with problems of use and enjoyment is the source of the dominant role of qualities, sensible and moral, and of ends in common sense.

In science, since meanings are determined on the ground of their relation as meanings to one another, *relations* become the objects of inquiry and qualities are relegated to a secondary status, playing a part only as far as they assist in institution of relations. They are subordinate because they have an instrumental office, instead of being themselves, as in prescientific common sense, the matters of final importance. The enduring hold of common sense is testified to historically by the long time it took before it was seen that scientific objects are strictly relational. First tertiary qualities were eliminated; it was recognized that moral qualities are not agencies in determining the structure of nature. Then secondary qualities, the wet-dry, hot-cold, light-heavy, which were the explanatory principles of physical phenomena in Greek science, were ejected. But so-called primary qualities took their place, as with Newton and the Lockeian formulation of Newtonian existential postulates. It was not until the threshold of our time was reached that scientific inquirers perceived that their own problems and methods required an interpretation of "primary qualities" in terms of relations, such as position, motion and temporal span. In the structure of distinctively scientific objects these relations are indifferent to qualities.

The foregoing is intended to indicate that the different objectives of common sense and of scientific inquiry demand different subject-matters and that this difference in subject-matters is not incompatible with the existence of a common pattern in both types. There are, of course, secondary logical forms which reflect the distinction of properties involved in the change from qualitative and teleological subject-matter to non-qualitative and non-teleological relations. But they occur and operate within the described community of pattern. They are explicable, and explicable only, on the ground of the distinctive problems generated by scientific subject-matter. The independence of scientific objects from limited and fairly direct reference to the environment as a factor in activities of use and enjoyment, is equivalent, as has already been intimated, to their *abstract* character. It is also equivalent to their *general* character in the sense in which the generalizations of science are different from the generalizations with which common sense is familiar. The generality of *all* scientific subject-matter as such means that it is freed from restriction to conditions which present themselves at particular times and places. Their reference is to *any* set of time and place conditions—a statement which is not to be confused with the doctrine that they have no reference to actual existential occasions. Reference to time-place of existence is necessarily involved, but it is reference to whatever set of existences fulfills the general relations laid down in and by the constitution of the scientific object.[5]

Summary. Since a number of points have been discussed, it will be well to round up conclusions reached about them in a summary statement of the structure of the common pattern of inquiry. Inquiry is the directed or controlled transformation of an indeterminate situation into a determinately unified one. The transition is achieved by means of operations of two kinds which are in functional correspondence with each other. One kind of operations deals with ideational or conceptual subject-matter. This subject-matter stands for possible ways and ends of resolution. It anticipates a

solution, and is marked off from fancy because, or, in so far as, it becomes operative in instigation and direction of new observations yielding new factual material. The other kind of operations is made up of activities involving the techniques and organs of observation. Since these operations are existential they modify the prior existential situation, bring into high relief conditions previously obscure, and relegate to the background other aspects that were at the outset conspicuous. The ground and criterion of the execution of this work of emphasis, selection and arrangement is to delimit the problem in such a way that existential material may be provided with which to test the ideas that represent possible modes of solution. Symbols, defining terms and propositions, are necessarily required in order to retain and carry forward both ideational and existential subject-matters in order that they may serve their proper functions in the control of inquiry. Otherwise the problem is taken to be closed and inquiry ceases.

One fundamentally important phase of the transformation of the situation which constitutes inquiry is central in the treatment of judgment and its functions. The transformation is existential and hence temporal. The pre-cognitive unsettled situation can be settled only by modification of its constituents. Experimental operations change existing conditions. Reasoning, as such, can provide means for effecting the change of conditions but by itself cannot effect it. Only execution of existential operations directed by an idea in which ratiocination terminates can bring about the re-ordering of environing conditions required to produce a settled and unified situation. Since this principles also applies to the meanings that are elaborated in science, the experimental production and re-arrangement of physical conditions involved in natural science is further evidence of the unity of the pattern of inquiry. The temporal quality of inquiry means, then, something quite other than the process of inquiry takes time. It means that the objective subject-matter of inquiry undergoes temporal modification. . . .

NOTES

1. Except of course a purely mentalistic name, like *consciousness*. The alleged problem of "interactionism" versus automatism, parallelism, etc., is a

problem (and an insoluble one) because of the assumption involved in its statement—the assumption, namely, that the interaction in question is with something mental instead of with biological-cultural human beings.

2. If by "two-valued logic" is meant a logic that regards "true and false" as the sole logical values, then such a logic is necessarily so truncated that clearness and consistency in logical doctrine are impossible. Being the matter of a problem is a primary logical property.

3. The theory of *ideas* that has been held in psychology and epistemology since the time of Locke's successors is completely irrelevant and obstructive in logical theory. For in treating them as copies of perceptions or "impressions," it ignores the prospective and anticipatory character that defines *being* an idea. Failure to define ideas functionally, in the reference they have to a solution of a problem, is one reason

they have been treated as merely "mental." The notion, on the other hand, that ideas are fantasies is a derivative. Fantasies arise when the function an idea performs is ruled out when it is entertained and developed.

4. "Reasoning" is sometimes used to designate *inference* as well as ratiocination. When so used in logic the tendency is to identify inference and implication and thereby seriously to confuse logical theory.

5. The consequences that follow are directly related to the statement . . .that the elimination of qualities and ends is intermediate; that, in fact, the construction of purely relational objects has enormously liberated and expanded common sense uses and enjoyments by conferring control over production of qualities, by enabling new ends to be realistically instituted, and by providing competent means for achieving them.

Education as Growth

1. *The Conditions of Growth*—In directing the activities of the young, society determines its own future in determining that of the young. Since the young at a given time will at some later date compose the society of that period, the latter's nature will largely turn upon the direction children's activities were given at an earlier period. This cumulative movement of action toward a later result is what is meant by growth.

The primary condition of growth is immaturity. This may seem to be a mere truism—saying that a being can develop only in some point in which he is undeveloped. But the prefix "im" of the word immaturity means something positive, not a mere void or lack. It is noteworthy that the terms "capacity" and "potentiality" have a double meaning, one sense being negative, the other positive. Capacity may denote mere receptivity, like the capacity of a quart measure. We may mean by potentiality a merely dormant or quiescent state—a capacity to become something different under external influences. But we also mean by capacity an ability, a power; and by potentiality potency, force. Now when we say that immaturity means the possibility of

growth, we are not referring to absence of powers which may exist at a later time; we express a force positively present—the *ability* to develop.

Our tendency to take immaturity as mere lack, and growth as something which fills up the gap between the immature and the mature is due to regarding childhood *comparatively,* instead of intrinsically. We treat it simply as a privation because we are measuring it by adulthood as a fixed standard. This fixes attention upon what the child has not, and will not have till he becomes a man. This comparative standpoint is legitimate enough for some purposes, but if we make it final, the question arises whether we are not guilty of an overweening presumption. Children, if they could express themselves articulately and sincerely, would tell a different tale; and there is excellent adult authority for the conviction that for certain moral and intellectual purposes adults must become as little children.

The seriousness of the assumption of the negative quality of the possibilities of immaturity is apparent when we reflect that it sets up as an ideal and standard a static end. The fulfillment of growing is taken to mean an *accom-*

From "Education as Growth," in *Democracy and Education, John Dewey: The Middle Works, 1899–1924,* Vol. 9, Ed. Jo Ann Boydston, (Carbondale and Edwardsville: Southern Illinois University Press, 1980), pp. 46–58.

plished growth: that is to say, an Ungrowth, something which is no longer growing. The futility of the assumption is seen in the fact that every adult resents the imputation of having no further possibilities of growth; and so far as he finds that they are closed to him mourns the fact as evidence of loss, instead of falling back on the achieved as adequate manifestation of power. Why an unequal measure for child and man?

Taken absolutely, instead of comparatively, immaturity designates a positive force or ability,—the *power* to grow. We do not have to draw out or educe positive activities from a child, as some educational doctrines would have it. Where there is life, there are already eager and impassioned activities. Growth is not something done to them; it is something they do. The positive and constructive aspect of possibility gives the key to understanding the two chief traits of immaturity, dependence and plasticity. (1) It sounds absurd to hear dependence spoken of as something positive, still more absurd as a power. Yet if helplessness were all there were in dependence, no development could ever take place. A merely impotent being has to be carried, forever, by others. The fact that dependence is accompanied by growth in ability, not by an ever increasing lapse into parasitism, suggests that it is already something constructive. Being merely sheltered by others would not promote growth. For (2) it would only build a wall around impotence. With reference to the physical world, the child is helpless. He lacks at birth and for a long time thereafter power to make his way physically, to make his own living. If he had to do that by himself, he would hardly survive an hour. On this side his helplessness is almost complete. The young of the brutes are immeasurably his superiors. He is physically weak and not able to turn the strength which he possesses to coping with the physical environment.

1. The thoroughgoing character of this helplessness suggests, however, some compensating power. The relative ability of the young of brute animals to adapt themselves fairly well to physical conditions from an early period suggests the fact that their life is not intimately bound up with the life of those about them. They are compelled, so to speak, to have physical gifts because they are lacking in social gifts. Human infants, on the other hand, can get along with physical incapacity just because of their social capacity. We sometimes talk and think as if they simply happend to be *physi-* *cally* in a social environment; as if social forces exclusively existed in the adults who take care of them, they being passive recipients. If it were said that children are themselves marvelously endowed with *power* to enlist the co-operative attention of others, this would be thought to be a backhanded way of saying that others are marvelously attentive to the needs of children. But observation shows that children are gifted with an equipment of the first order for social intercourse. Few grown-up persons retain all of the flexible and sensitive ability of children to vibrate sympathetically with the attitudes and doings of those about them. Inattention to physical things (going with incapacity to control them) is accompanied by a corresponding intensification of interest and attention as to the doings of people. The native mechanism of the child and his impulses all tend to facile social responsiveness. The statement that children, before adolescence, are egotistically self-centered, even if it were true, would not contradict the truth of this statement. It would simply indicate that their social responsiveness is employed on their own behalf, not that it does not exist. But the statement is not true as matter of fact. The facts which are cited in support of the alleged pure egoism of children really show the intensity and directness with which they go to their mark. If the ends which form the mark seem narrow and selfish to adults, it is only because adults (by means of a similar engrossment in their day) have mastered these ends, which have consequently ceased to interest them. Most of the remainder of children's alleged native egoism is simply an egoism which runs counter to an adult's egoism. To a grown-up person who is too absorbed in his own affairs to take an interest in children's affairs, children doubtless seem unreasonably engrossed in *their* own affairs.

From a social standpoint, dependence denotes a power rather than a weakness; it involves interdependence. There is always a danger that increased personal independence will decrease the social capacity of an individual. In making him more self-reliant, it may make him more self-sufficient; it may lead to aloofness and indifference. It often makes an individual so insensitive in his relations to others as to develop an illusion of being really able to stand and act alone—an unnamed form of insanity which is responsible for a large part of the remediable suffering of the world.

2. The specific adaptability of an immature creature for growth constitutes his *plasticity*.

This is something quite different from the plasticity of putty or wax. It is not a capacity to take on change of form in accord with external pressure. It lies near the pliable elasticity by which some persons take on the color of their surroundings while retaining their own bent. But it is something deeper than this. It is essentially the ability to learn from experience; the power to retain from one experience something which is of avail in coping with the difficulties of a later situation. This means power to modify actions on the basis of the results of prior experiences, the power to *develop dispositions*. Without it, the acquisition of habits is impossible.

It is a familiar fact that the young of the higher animals, and especially the human young, have to *learn* to utilize their instinctive reactions. The human being is born with a greater number of instinctive tendencies than other animals. But the instincts of the lower animals perfect themselves for appropriate action at an early period after birth, while most of those of the human infant are of little account just as they stand. An original specialized power of adjustment secures immediate efficiency but, like a railway ticket, it is good for one route only. A being who, in order to use his eyes, ears, hands, and legs, has to experiment in making varied combinations of their reactions, achieves a control that is flexible and varied. A chick, for example, pecks accurately at a bit of food in a few hours after hatching. This means that definite coordinations of activities of the eyes in seeing and of the body and head in striking are perfected in a few trials. An infant requires about six months to be able to gauge with approximate accuracy the action in reaching which will coordinate with his visual activities; to be able, that is, to tell whether he can reach a seen object and just how to execute the reaching. As a result, the chick is limited by the relative perfection of its original endowment. The infant has the advantage of the *multitude* of instinctive tentative reactions and of the experiences that accompany them, even though he is at a temporary disadvantage because they cross one another. In learning an action, instead of having it given ready-made, one of necessity learns to vary its factors, to make varied combinations of them, according to change of circumstances. A possibility of continuing progress is opened up by the fact that in learning one act, methods are developed good for use in other situations. Still more important is the fact that the human being

acquires a habit of learning. He learns to learn.

The importance for human life of the two facts of dependence and variable control has been summed up in the doctrine of the significance of prolonged infancy.[1] This prolongation is significant from the standpoint of the adult members of the group as well as from that of the young. The presence of dependent and learning beings is a stimulus to nurture and affection. The need for constant continued care was probably a chief means in transforming temporary cohabitations into permanent unions. It certainly was a chief influence in forming habits of affectionate and sympathetic watchfulness; that constructive interest in the well-being of others which is essential to associated life. Intellectually, this moral development meant the introduction of many new objects of attention; it stimulated foresight and planning for the future. Thus there is a reciprocal influence. Increasing complexity of social life requires a longer period of infancy in which to acquire the needed powers; this prolongation of dependence means prolongation of plasticity, or power of acquiring variable and novel modes of control. Hence it provides a further push to social progress.

2. *Habits as Expressions of Growth*—We have already noted that plasticity is the capacity to retain and carry over from prior experience factors which modify subsequent activities. This signifies the capacity to acquire habits, or develop definite dispositions. We have now to consider the salient features of habits. In the first place, a habit is a form of executive skill, of efficiency in doing. A habit means an ability to use natural conditions as means to ends. It is an active control of the environment through control of the organs of action. We are perhaps apt to emphasize the control of the body at the expense of control of the environment. We think of walking, talking, playing the piano, the specialized skills chracteristic of the etcher, the surgeon, the bridge-builder, as if they were simply ease, deftness, and accuracy on the part of the organism. They are that, of course; but the measure of the value of these qualities lies in the economical and effective control of the environment which they secure. To be able to walk is to have certain properties of nature at our disposal—and so with all other habits.

Education is not infrequently defined as consisting in the acquisition of those habits that effect an adjustment of an individual and his environment. The definition expresses an essential phase of growth. But it is essential that adjustment be understood in its active sense of *control* of means for achieving ends. If we think of a habit simply as a change wrought in the organism, ignoring the fact that this change consists in ability to effect subsequent changes in the environment, we shall be led to think of "adjustment" as a conformity to environment as wax conforms to the seal which impresses it. The environment is thought of as something fixed, providing in its fixity the end and standard of changes taking place in the organism; adjustment is just fitting ourselves to this fixity of external conditions.[2] Habit as *habituation* is indeed something *relatively* passive; we get used to our surroundings—to our clothing, our shoes, and gloves; to the atmosphere as long as it is fairly equable; to our daily associates, etc. Conformity to the environment, a change wrought in the organism without reference to ability to modify surroundings, is a marked trait of such habituations. Aside from the fact that we are not entitled to carry over the traits of such adjustments (which might well be called *accommodations,* to mark them off from active adjustments) into habits of active use of our surroundings, two features of habituations are worth notice. In the first place, we get used to things by *first* using them.

Consider getting used to a strange city. At first, there is excessive stimulation and excessive and ill-adapted response. Gradually certain stimuli are selected because of the relevancy, and others are degraded. We can say either that we do not respond to them any longer, or more truly that we have effected a persistent response to them—an equilibrium of adjustment. This means, in the second place, that this enduring adjustment supplies the background upon which are made specific adjustments, as occasion arises. We are never interested in changing the *whole* environment; there is much that we take for granted and accept just as it already is. Upon this background our activities focus at certain points in an endeavor to introduce needed changes. Habituation is thus our adjustment to an environment which at the time we are not concerned with modifying, and which supplies a leverage to our active habits.

Adaptation, in fine, is quite as much adaptation *of* the environment to our own activities as of our activities *to* the environment. A savage tribe manages to live on a desert plain. It adapts itself. But its adapation involves a maximum of accepting, tolerating, putting up with things as they are, a maximum of passive acquiescence, and a minimum of active control, of subjection to use. A civilized people enters upon the scene. It also adapts itself. It introduces irrigation; it searches the world for plants and animals that will flourish under such conditions; it improves, by careful selection, those which are growing there. As a consequence, the wilderness blossoms as a rose. The savage is merely habituated; the civilized man has habits which transform the environment.

The significance of habit is not exhausted, however, in its executive and motor phase. It means formation of intellectual and emotional disposition as well as an increase in ease, economy, and efficiency of action. Any habit marks an *inclination*—an active preference and choice for the conditions involved in its exercise. A habit does not wait, Micawberlike, for a stimulus to turn up so that it may get busy; it actively seeks for occasions to pass into full operation. If its expression is unduly blocked, inclination shows itself in uneasiness and intense craving. A habit also marks an intellectual disposition. Where there is a habit, there is acquaintance with the materials and equipment to which action is applied. There is a definite way of understanding the situations in which the habit operates. Modes of thought, of observation and reflection, enter as forms of skill and of desire into the habits that make a man an engineer, an architect, a physician, or a merchant. In unskilled forms of labor, the intellectual factors are at minumum precisely because the habits involved are not of a high grade. But there are habits of judging and reasoning as truly as of handling a tool, painting a picture, or conducting an experiment.

Such statements are, however, understatements. The habits of mind involved in habits of the eye and hand supply the latter with their significance. Above all, the intellectual element in a habit fixes the relation of the habit to varied and elastic use, and hence to continued growth. We speak of *fixed* habits. Well, the phrase may mean powers so well established that their possessor always has them as resources when needed. But the phrase is also used to mean ruts, routine ways, with loss of freshness, open-mindedness, and originality. Fixity of habit may mean that something has a fixed hold upon us, instead of our having a free hold upon things. This fact explains two points in a common notion about habits: their identification with mechanical and external modes of action to the neglect of mental and moral attitudes, and the tendency to give them a bad meaning, an identification with "bad habits." Many a person would feel surprised to have his aptitude in his chosen profession called a habit, and would naturally think of his use of tobacco, liquor, or profane language as typical of the meaning of habit. A habit is to him something which has a hold on him, something not easily thrown off even though judgment condemn it.

Habits reduce themselves to routine ways of acting, or degenerate into ways of action to which we are enslaved just in the degree in which intelligence is disconnected from them. Routine habits are unthinking habits; "bad" habits are habits so severed from reason that they are opposed to the conclusions of conscious deliberation and decision. As we have seen, the acquiring of habits is due to an original plasticity of our natures: to our ability to vary responses till we find an appropriate and efficient way of acting. Routine habits, and habits that possess us instead of our possessing them, are habits which put an end to plasticity. They mark the close of power to vary. There can be no doubt of the tendency of organic plasticity, of the physiological basis, to lessen with growing years. The instinctively mobile and eagerly varying action of childhood, the love of new stimuli and new developments, too easily passes into a "settling down," which means aversion to change and a resting on past achievements. Only an environment which secures the full use of intelligence in the process of forming habits can counteract this tendency. Of course, the same hardening of the organic conditions affects the physiological structures which are involved in thinking. But this fact only indicates the need of persistent care to see to it that the function of intelligence is invoked to its maximum possibility. The short-sighted method which falls back on mechanical routine and repetition to secure external efficiency of habit, motor skill without accompanying thought, marks a deliberate closing in of surroundings upon growth.

3. *The Educational Bearings of the Conception of Development*—We have had so far but little to say in this chapter about education. We have been occupied with the conditions and implications of growth. If our conclusions are justified, they carry with them, however, definite educational consequences. When it is said that education is development, everything depends upon *how* development is conceived. Our net conclusion is that life is development,

and that developing, growing, is life. Translated into its educational equivalents, this means (*i*) that the educational process has no end beyond itself; it is its own end; and that (*ii*) the educational process in one of continual reorganizing, reconstructing, transforming.

1. Development when it is interpeted in *comparative* terms, that is, with respect to the special traits of child and adult life, means the direction of power into special channels: the formation of habits involving executive skill, definiteness of interest, and specific objects of observation and thought. But the comparative view is not final. The child has specific powers; to ignore that fact is to stunt or distort the organs upon which his growth depends. The adult uses his powers to transform his environment, thereby occasioning new stimuli which redirect his powers and keep them developing. Ignoring this fact means arrested development, a passive accommodation. Normal child and normal adult alike, in other words, are engaged in growing. The difference between them is not the difference between growth and no growth, but between the modes of growth appropriate to different conditions. With respect to the development of powers devoted to coping with specific scientific and economic problems we may say the child should be growing in manhood. With respect to sympathetic curiosity, unbiased responsiveness, and openness of mind, we may say that the adult should be growing in childlikeness. One statement is as true as the other.

Three ideas which have been criticized, namely, the merely privative nature of immaturity, static adjustment to a fixed environment, and rigidity of habit, are all connected with a false idea of growth or development,— that it is a movement toward a fixed goal. Growth is regarded as *having* an end, instead of *being* an end. The educational counterparts of the three fallacious ideas are first, failure to take account of the instinctive or native powers of the young; secondly, failure to develop initiative in coping with novel situations; thirdly, an undue emphasis upon drill and other devices which secure automatic skill at the expense of personal perception. In all cases, the adult environment is accepted as a standard for the child. He is to be brought up *to* it.

Natural instincts are either disregarded or treated as nuisances—as obnoxious traits to be suppressed, or at all events to be brought into conformity with external standards. Since conformity is the aim, what is distinctively individual in a young person is brushed aside, or regarded as a source of mischief or anarchy. Conformity is made equivalent to uniformity. Consequently, there are induced lack of interest in the novel, aversion to progress, and dread of the uncertain and the unknown. Since the end of growth is outside of and beyond the process of growing, external agents have to be resorted to to induce movements towards it. Whenever a method of education is stigmatized as mechanical, we may be sure that external pressure is brough to bear to reach an external end.

2. Since in reality there is nothing to which growth is relative save more growth, there is nothing to which education is subordinate save more education. It is a commonplace to say that education should not cease when one leaves school. The point of this commonplace is that the purpose of school education is to insure the continuance of education by organizing the powers that insure growth. The inclination to learn from life itself and to make the conditions of life such that all will learn in the process of living is the finest product of schooling.

When we abandon the attempt to define immaturity by means of fixed comparison with adult accomplishments, we are compelled to give up thinking of it as denoting lack of desired traits. Abandoning this notion, we are also forced to surrender our habit of thinking of instruction as a method of supplying this lack by pouring knowledge into a mental and moral hole which awaits filling. Since life means growth, a living creature lives as truly and positively at one stage as at another, with the same intrinsic fullness and the same absolute claims. Hence education means the enterprise of supplying the conditions which insure growth, or adequacy of life, irrespective of age. We first look with impatience upon immaturity, regarding it as something to be got over as rapidly as possible. Then the adult formed by such educative methods looks back with impatient regret upon childhood and youth as a scene of lost opportunities and wasted powers. This ironical situation will endure till it is recognized that living has its own intrinsic quality and that the business of education is with that quality.

Realization that life is growth protects us from that so-called idealizing of childhood which in effect is nothing but lazy indulgence. Life is not to be identified with every superficial act and interest. Even though it is not always easy to tell whether what appears to be mere surface fooling is a sign of some nascent as yet untrained power, we must remember that mani-

festations are not to be accepted as ends in themselves. They are signs of possible growth. They are to be turned into means of development, of carrying power forward, not indulged or cultivated for their own sake. Excessive attention to surface phenomena (even in the way of rebuke as well as of encouragement) may lead to their fixation and thus to arrested development. What impulses are moving toward, not what they have been, is the important thing for parent and teacher. The true principle of respect for immaturity cannot be better put than in the words of Emerson: "Respect the child. Be not too much his parent. Trespass not on his solitude. But I hear the outcry which replies to this suggestion: Would you verily throw up the reins of public and private discipline; would you leave the young child to the mad career of his own passions and whimsies, and call this anarchy a respect for the child's nature? I answer,— Respect the child, respect him to the end, but also respect yourself. . . . The two points in a boy's training are, to keep his *naturel* and train off all but that; to keep his *naturel,* but stop off his uproar, fooling, and horse-play; keep his nature *and arm it with knowledge in the very direction in which it points.*" And as Emerson goes on to show this reverence for childhood and youth instead of opening up an easy and easy-going path to the instructors, "involves at once immense claims on the time, the thought, on the life of the teacher. It requires time, use, insight, event, all the great lessons and assistances of God; and only to think of using it implies character and profoundness."

Summary—Power to grow depends upon needs for others and plasticity. Both of these conditions are at their height in childhood and youth. Plasticity or the power to learn from experience means the formation of habits. Habits give control over the environment, power to utilize it for human purposes. Habits take the form both of habituation, or a general and persistent balance of organic activities with the surroundings, and of active capacities to readjust activity to meet new conditions. The former furnishes the background of growth; the latter constitute growing. Active habits involve thought, invention, and initiative in applying capacities to new aims. They are opposed to routine which marks an arrest of growth. Since growth is the characteristic of life, education is all one with growing; it has no end beyond itself. The criterion of the value of school education is the extent in which it creates a desire for continued growth and supplies means for making the desire effective in fact.

NOTES

1. Intimations of its significance are found in a number of writers, but John Fiske, in his *Excursions of an Evolutionist,* is accredited with its first systematic exposition.

2. This conception is, of course, a logical correlate of the conceptions of the external relation of stimulus and response, considered in the last chapter, and of the negative conceptions of immaturity and plasticity noted in this chapter.

The Lost Individual

The development of a civilization that is outwardly corporate—or rapidly becoming so— has been accompanied by a submergence of the individual. Just how far this is true of the individual's opportunities in action, how far initiative and choice in what an individual does are restricted by the economic forces that make for consolidation, I shall not attempt to say. It is arguable that there has been a diminution of the range of decision and activity for the many along with exaggeration of opportunity of personal expression for the few. It may be contended that no one class in the past has the power now possessed by an industrial oligarchy. On the other hand, it may be held that this power of the few is, with respect to genuine individuality, specious; that those outwardly in control are in reality as much carried by forces external to themselves as are the many; that in fact these forces impel them into a common mold to such an extent that individuality is suppressed.

What is here meant by "the lost individual" is, however, so irrelevant to this question that it is not necessary to decide between the two views. For by it is meant a moral and intellectual fact which is independent of any manifestation of power in action. The significant thing is that the loyalties which once held individuals, which gave them support, direction and unity of outlook on life, have well-nigh disappeared. In consequence, individuals are confused and bewildered. It would be difficult to find in history an epoch as lacking in solid and assured objects of belief and approved ends of action as is the present. Stability of individuality is dependent upon stable objects to which allegiance firmly attaches itself. There are, of course, those who are still militantly fundamentalist in religious and social creed. But

their very clamor is evidence that the tide is set against them. For the others, traditional objects of loyalty have become hollow or are openly repudiated, and they drift without sure anchorage. Individuals vibrate between a past that is intellectually too empty to give stability and a present that is too diversely crowded and chaotic to afford balance or direction to ideas and emotion.

Assured and integrated individuality is the product of definite social relationships and publicly acknowledged functions. Judged by this standard, even those who seem to be in control, and to carry the expression of their special individual abilities to a high pitch, are submerged. They may be captains of finance and industry, but until there is some consensus of belief as to the meaning of finance and industry in civilization as a whole, they cannot be captains of their own souls—their beliefs and aims. They exercise leadership surreptitiously and, as it were, absent-mindedly. They lead, but it is under cover of impersonal and socially undirected economic forces. Their reward is found not in what they do, in their social office and function, but in a deflection of social consequences to private gain. They receive the acclaim and command the envy and admiration of the crowd, but the crowd is also composed of private individuals who are equally lost to a sense of social bearings and uses.

The explanation is found in the fact that while the actions promote corporate and collective results, these results are outside their intent and irrelevant to that reward of satisfaction which comes from a sense of social fulfillment. To themselves and to others, their business is private and its outcome is private profit. No complete satisfaction is possible where such

From "The Lost Individual," in *Individualism, Old and New, John Dewey: The Later Works, 1925–1953,* Vol. 5, Ed. Jo Ann Boydston (Carbondale and Edwardsville: Southern Illinois University Press, 1984), pp. 66–76.

a split exists. Hence the absence of a sense of social value is made up for by an exacerbated acceleration of the activities that increase private advantage and power. One cannot look into the inner consciousness of his fellows, but if there is any general degree of inner contentment on the part of those who form our pecuniary oligarchy, the evidence is sadly lacking. As for the many, they are impelled hither and yon by forces beyond their control.

The most marked trait of present life, economically speaking, is insecurity. It is tragic that millions of men desirous of working should be recurrently out of employment; aside from cyclical depressions there is a standing army at all times who have no regular work. We have not any adequate information as to the number of these persons. But the ignorance even as to the numbers is slight compared with our inability to grasp the psychological and moral consequences of the precarious condition in which vast multitudes live. Insecurity cuts deeper and extends more widely than bare unemployment. Fear of loss of work, dread of the oncoming of old age, create anxiety and eat into self-respect in a way that impairs personal dignity. Where fears abound, courageous and robust individuality is undermined. The vast development of technological resources that might bring security in its train has actually brought a new mode of insecurity, as mechanization displaces labor. The mergers and consolidations that mark a corporate age are beginning to bring uncertainty into the economic lives of the higher salaried class, and that tendency is only just in its early stage. Realization that honest and industrious pursuit of a calling or business will not guarantee any stable level of life lessens respect for work and stirs large numbers to take a chance of some adventitious way of getting the wealth that will make security possible: witness the orgies of the stock-market in recent days.

The unrest, impatience, irritation and hurry that are so marked in American life are inevitable accompaniments of a situation in which individuals do not find support and contentment in the fact that they are sustaining and sustained members of a social whole. They are evidence, psychologically, of abnormality, and it is as idle to seek for their explanation within the deliberate intent of individuals as it is futile to think that they can be got rid of by hortatory moral appeal. Only an acute maladjustment between individuals and the social conditions under which they live can account for such widespread pathological phenomena. Feverish love of anything as long as it is a change which is distracting, impatience, unsettlement, nervous discontentment, and desire for excitement, are not native to human nature. They are so abnormal as to demand explanation in some deep-seated cause.

I should explain a seeming hypocrisy on the same ground. We are not consciously insincere in our professions of devotion to ideals of "service"; they mean something. Neither the Rotarian nor the big business enterprise uses the term merely as a cloak for "putting something over" which makes for pecuniary gain. But the lady doth protest too much. The wide currency of such professions testifies to a sense of a social function of business which is expressed in words because it is so lacking in fact, and yet which is felt to be rightfully there. If our external combinations in industrial activity were reflected in organic integrations of the desires, purposes and satisfactions of individuals, the verbal protestations would disappear, because social utility would be a matter of course.

Some persons hold that a genuine mental counterpart of the outward social scheme is actually forming. Our prevailing mentality, our "ideology," is said to be that of the "business mind" which has become so deplorably pervasive. Are not the prevailing standards of value those derived from pecuniary success and economic prosperity? Were the answer unqualifiedly in the affirmative, we should have to admit that our outer civilization is attaining an inner culture which corresponds to it, however much we might disesteem the quality of that culture. The objection that such a condition is impossible, since man cannot live by bread, by material prosperity alone, is tempting, but it may be said to beg the question. The conclusive answer is that the business mind is not itself unified. It is divided within itself and must remain so as long as the results of industry as the determining force in life are corporate and collective while its animating motives and compensations are so unmitigatedly private. A unified mind, even of the business type, can come into being only when conscious intent and consummation are in harmony with consequences actually effected. This statement expresses conditions so psychologically assured that it may be termed a law of mental integrity. Proof of the existence of the split is found in the fact that while there is much planning of future development with a view to dividends within large business corporations, there is no corresponding coordinated planning of social development.

The growth of corporateness is arbitrarily restricted. Hence it operates to limit individuality, to put burdens on it, to confuse and submerge it. It crowds more out than it incorporates in an ordered and secure life. It has made rural districts stagnant while bringing excess and restless movement to the city. The restriction of corporateness lies in the fact that it remains on the cash level. Men are brought together on the one side by investment in the same joint stock company, and on the other hand by the fact that the machine compels mass production in order that investors may get their profits. The results affect all society in all its phases. But they are as inorganic as the ultimate human motives that operate are private and egoistic. An economic individualism of motives and aims underlies our present corporate mechanisms, and undoes the individual.

The loss of individuality is conspicuous in the economic region because our civilization is so predominantly a business civilization. But the fact is even more obvious when we turn to the political scene. It would be a waste of words to expatiate on the meaninglessness of present political platforms, parties and issues. The old-time slogans are still reiterated, and to a few these words still seem to have a real meaning. But it is too evident to need argument that on the whole our politics, as far as they are not covertly manipulated in behalf of the pecuniary advantage of groups, are in a state of confusion; issues are improvised from week to week with a constant shift of allegiance. It is impossible for individuals to find themselves politically with surety and efficiency under such conditions. Political apathy broken by recurrent sensations and spasms is the natural outcome.

The lack of secure objects of allegiance, without which individuals are lost, is especially striking in the case of the liberal. The liberalism of the past was characterized by the possession of a definite intellectual creed and program; that was its distinction from conservative parties which needed no formulated outlook beyond defense of things as they were. In contrast, liberals operated on the basis of a thought-out social philosophy, a theory of politics sufficiently definite and coherent to be easily translated into a program of policies to be pursued. Liberalism today is hardly more than a temper of mind, vaguely called forward-looking, but quite uncertain as to where to look and what to look forward to. For many individuals, as well as in its social results, this fact is hardly less than a tragedy. The tragedy

may be unconscious for the mass, but they show its reality in their aimless drift, while the more thoughtful are consciously disturbed. For human nature is self-possessed only as it has objects to which it can attach itself.

I do not think it is fantastic to connect our excited and rapacious nationalism with the situation in which corporateness has gone so far as to detach individuals from their old local ties and allegiances but not far enough to give them a new centre and order of life. The most militaristic of nations secures the loyalty of its subjects not by physical force but through the power of ideas and emotions. It cultivates ideals of loyalty, of solidarity, and common devotion to a common cause. Modern industry, technology and commerce have created modern nations in their external form. Armies and navies exist to protect commerce, to make secure the control of raw materials, and to command markets. Men would not sacrifice their lives for the purpose of securing economic gain for a few if the conditions presented themselves to their minds in this bald fashion. But the balked demand for genuine cooperativeness and reciprocal solidarity in daily life finds an outlet in nationalistic sentiment. Men have a pathetic instinct toward the adventure of living and struggling together; if the daily community does not feed this impulse, the romantic imagination pictures a grandiose nation in which all are one. If the simple duties of peace do not establish a common life, the emotions are mobilized in the service of a war that will supply its temporary stimulation.

I have thus far made no reference to what many persons would consider the most serious and the most overtly evident of all the modes of loss of secure objects of loyalty—religion. It is probably easy to exaggerate the extent of the decadence of religion in an outward sense, church membership, church-going and so on. But it is hardly possible to overstate its decline as a vitally integrative and directive force in men's thought and sentiments. Whether even in the ages of the past that are called religious, religion was itself the actively central force that it is sometimes said to have been may be doubted. But it cannot be doubted that it was the symbol of the existence of conditions and forces that gave unity and a centre to men's views of life. It at least gathered together in weighty and shared symbols a sense of the objects to which men were so attached as to have support and stay in their outlook on life.

Religion does not now effect this result. The divorce of church and state has been followed by that of religion and society. Wherever religion has not become a merely private indulgence, it has become at best a matter of sects and denominations divided from one another by doctrinal differences, and united internally by tenets that have a merely historical origin, and a purely metaphysical or else ritualistic meaning. There is no such bond of social unity as once united Greeks, Romans, Hebrews, and Catholic medieval Europe. There are those who realize what is portended by the loss of religion as an integrating bond. Many of them despair of its recovery through the development of social values to which the imagination and sentiments of individuals can attach themselves with intensity. They wish to reverse the operation and to form the social bond of unity and of allegiance by regeneration of the isolated individual soul.

Aside from the fact that there is no consensus as to what a new religious attitude is to centre itself about, the injunction puts the cart before the horse. Religion is not so much a root of unity as it is its flower or fruit. The very attempt to secure integration for the individual, and through him for society, by means of a deliberate and conscious cultivation of religion, is itself proof of how far the individual has become lost through detachment from acknowledged social values. It is no wonder that when the appeal does not take the form of dogmatic fundamentalism, it tends to terminate in either some form of esoteric occultism or private estheticism. The sense of wholeness which is urged as the essence of religion can be built up and sustained only through membership in a society which has attained a degree of unity. The attempt to cultivate it first in individuals and then extend it to form an organically unified society is fantasy. Indulgence in this fantasy infects such interpretations of American life as are found, to take one signal example, in Waldo Frank's *The Rediscovery of America*.[1] It marks a manner of yearning and not a principle of construction.

For the idea that the outward scene is chaotic because of the machine, which is a principle of chaos, and that it will remain so until individuals reinstitute wholeness within themselves, simply reverses the true state of things. The outward scene, if not fully organized, is relatively so in the corporateness which the machine and its technology have produced; the inner man is the jungle which can be subdued to order only as the forces of organization at work in externals are reflected in corresponding patterns of thought, imagination and emotion. The sick cannot heal themselves by means of their disease, and disintegrated individuals can achieve unity only as the dominant energies of community life are incorporated to form their minds. If these energies were, in reality, mere strivings for private pecuniary gain, the case would indeed be hopeless. But they are constituted by a collective art of technology, which individuals merely deflect to their private ends. There are the beginnings of an objective order through which individuals may get their bearings.

Conspicuous signs of the disintegration of individuality due to failure to reconstruct the self so as to meet the realities of present social life have not been mentioned. In a census that was taken among leaders of opinion concerning the urgency of present social problems, the state of law, the courts, lawlessness and criminality stood at the head of the list, and by a considerable distance. We are even more emphatically than when Kipling wrote the words, the people that make "the laws they flout, and flout the laws they make." We combine an ardor unparalleled in history for "passing" laws with a casual and deliberate disregard for them when they are on the statute books. We believe—to judge by our legislative actions—that we can create morals by law (witness the prohibition amendment for an instance on a large scale) and neglect the fact that all laws except those which regulate technical procedures are registrations of existing social customs and their attendant moral habits and purposes. I can, however, only think of this phenomenon as a symptom, not as a cause. It is a natural expression of a period in which changes in the structure of society have dissolved old bonds and allegiances. We attempt to make good this social relaxation and dissolution by legal enactments, while the actual disintegration discloses itself in the lawlessness which reveals the artificial character of this method of securing social integrity.

Volumes could be formed by collecting articles and editorials written about relaxation of traditional moral codes. A movement has caught public attention, which, having for some obscure reason assumed the name "humanism," proposes restraint and moderation, exercised in and by the higher volition of individuals, as the solution of our ills. It finds that naturalism as practiced by artists and mechanism as taught by philosophers who take their clew from natural science, have broken down the inner laws and imperatives which can alone bring order and loyalty. I should be glad to be able to believe that artists and intellectuals have any power in their hands; if they had, after using it to bring evil to society, they might change face and bring healing to it. But a sense of fact, together with a sense of humor, forbids the acceptance of any such belief. Literary persons and academic thinkers are now, more than ever, effects, not causes. They reflect and voice the disintegration which new modes of living, produced by new forms of industry and commerce, have introduced. They give witness to the unreality that has overtaken traditional codes in the face of the impact of new forces; indirectly, they proclaim the need of some new synthesis. But this synthesis can be humanistic only as the new conditions are themselves taken into account and are converted into the instrumentalities of a free and humane life. I see no way to "restrain" or turn back the industrial revolution and its consequences. In the absence of such a restraint (which would be efficacious if only it could occur), the urging of some inner restraint through the exercise of the higher personal will, whatever that may be, is itself only a futile echo of just the old individualism that has so completely broken down.

There are many phases of life which illustrate to anyone who chooses to think in terms of realities instead of words the utter irrelevance of the proposed remedy to actual conditions. One might take the present estate of amusements, of the movies, the radio, and organized vicarious sport, and ask just how this powerful eruption in which the resources of technology are employed for economic profit is to be met by the application of the inner *frein* or brake. Perhaps the most striking instance is found in the disintegration due to changes in family life and sex morale. It was not deliberate human intention that undermined the traditional household as the centre of industry and education and as the focus of moral training; that sapped the older institution of enduring marriage. To ask the individuals who suffer the consequences of the general undermining and sapping to put an end to the consequences by acts of personal volition is merely to profess faith in moral magic. Recovery of individuals capable of stable and effective self-control can be had only as there is first a humbler exercise of will to observe existing social realities and to direct them according to their own potentialities.

Instances of the flux in which individuals are loosened from the ties that once gave order and support to their lives are glaring. They are indeed so glaring that they blind our eyes to the causes which produce them. Individuals are groping their way through situations which they do not direct and which do not give them direction. The beliefs and ideals that are uppermost in their consciousness are not relevant to the society in which they outwardly act and which constantly reacts upon them. Their conscious ideas and standards are inherited from an age that has passed away; their minds, as far as consciously entertained principles and methods of interpretation are concerned, are at odds with actual conditions. This profound split is the cause of distraction and bewilderment.

Individuals will refind themselves only as their ideas and ideals are brought into harmony with the realities of the age in which they act. The task of attaining this harmony is not an easy one. But it is more negative than it seems. If we could inhibit the principles and standards that are merely traditional, if we could slough off the opinions that have no living relationship to the situations in which we live, the unavowed forces that now work upon us unconsciously but unremittingly would have a chance to build minds after their own pattern, and individuals might, in consequence, find themselves in possession of objects to which imagination and emotion would stably attach themselves.

I do not mean, however, that the process of rebuilding can go on automatically. Discrimination is required in order to detect the beliefs and institutions that dominate merely because of custom and inertia, and in order to discover the moving realities of the present. Intelligence must distinguish, for example, the tendencies of the technology which produce the new corporateness from those inheritances proceeding out of the individualism of an earlier epoch which arrest and divide the operation of the new dynamics. It is difficult for us to conceive of individualism except in terms of stereotypes derived from former centuries. Individualism has been identified with ideas of initiative and invention that are bound up with private and exclusive economic gain. As long as this conception possesses our minds, the ideal of harmonizing our thought and desire with the realities of present social conditions will be interpreted to mean accommodation and surrender. It will even be understood to signify rationalization of the evils of existing society. A stable recovery of individuality waits upon an elimination of the older economic and political individualism, an elimination which will liberate imagination and endeavor for the task of making corporate society contribute to the free culture of its members. Only by economic revision can the sound element in the older individualism—equality of opportunity—be made a reality.

It is the part of wisdom to note the double meaning of such ideas as "acceptance." There is an acceptance that is of the intellect; it signifies facing facts for what they are. There is another acceptance that is of the emotions and will; that involves commitment of desire and effort. So far are the two from being identical that acceptance in the first sense is the precondition of all intelligent refusal of acceptance in the second sense. There is a prophetic aspect to all observation; we can perceive the meaning of what exists only as we forecast the consequences it entails. When a situation is as confused and divided within itself as is the present social estate, choice is implicated in observation. As one perceives different tendencies and different possible consequences, preference inevitably goes out to one or the other. Because acknowledgment in thought brings

with it intelligent discrimination and choice, it is the first step out of confusion, the first step in forming those objects of significant allegiance out of which stable and efficacious individuality may grow. It might even perform the miracle of rendering conservatism relevant and thoughtful. It certainly is the prerequisite of an anchored liberalism.

NOTE

1. After a brilliant exposition of the dissolution of the European synthesis, he goes on to say "man's need of order and his making of order are his science, his art, his religion; and these are all to be referred to the initial sense of order called the self," quite oblivious of the fact that this doctrine of the primacy of the self is precisely a reaction of the romantic and subjective age to the dissolution he has depicted, having its meaning only in that dissolution.

Search for The Great Community

. . . That government exists to serve its community, and that this purpose cannot be achieved unless the community itself shares in selecting its governors and determining their policies, are a deposit of fact left, as far as we can see, permanently in the wake of doctrines and forms, however transitory the latter. They are not the whole of the democratic idea, but they express it in its political phase. Belief in this political aspect is not a mystic faith as if in some overruling providence that cares for children, drunkards and others unable to help themselves. It marks a well-attested conclusion from historic facts. We have every reason to think that whatever changes may take place in existing democratic machinery, they will be of a sort to make the interest of the public a more supreme guide and criterion of governmental activity, and to enable the public to form and manifest its purposes still more authoritatively. In this sense the cure for the ailments of democracy is more democracy. The prime difficulty, as we have seen, is that of discovering the means by which a scattered, mobile and manifold public may so recognize itself as to define

and express its interests. This discovery is necessarily precedent to any fundamental change in the machinery. We are not concerned therefore to set forth counsels as to advisable improvements in the political forms of democracy. Many have been suggested. It is no derogation of their relative worth to say that consideration of these changes is not at present an affair of primary importance. The problem lies deeper; it is in the first instance an intellectual problem: the search for conditions under which the Great Society may become the Great Community. When these conditions are brought into being they will make their own forms. Until they have come about, it is somewhat futile to consider what political machinery will suit them.

In a search for the conditions under which the inchoate public now extant may function democratically, we may proceed from a statement of the nature of the democratic idea in its generic social sense.[1] From the standpoint of the individual, it consists in having a responsible share according to capacity in forming and directing the activities of the groups to which one belongs and in participating ac-

From "Search for The Great Community," in *The Public and Its Problems, John Dewey: The Later Works, 1925–1953.* Vol. 2, Ed. Jo Ann Boydston (Carbondale and Edwardsville: Southern Illinois University Press, 1984), pp. 327–350.

cording to need in the values which the groups sustain. From the standpoint of the groups, it demands liberation of the potentialities of members of a group in harmony with the interests and goods which are common. Since every individual is a member of many groups, this specification cannot be fulfilled except when different groups interact flexibly and fully in connection with other groups. A member of a robber band may express his powers in a way consonant with belonging to that group and be directed by the interest common to its members. But he does so only at the cost of repression of those of his potentialities which can be realized only through membership in other groups. The robber band cannot interact flexibly with other groups; it can act only through isolating itself. It must prevent the operation of all interests save those which circumscribe it in its separateness. But a good citizen finds his conduct as a member of a political group enriching and enriched by his participation in family life, industry, scientific and artistic associations. There is a free give-and-take: fullness of integrated personality is therefore possible of achievement, since the pulls and responses of different groups reenforce one another and their values accord.

Regarded as an idea, democracy is not an alternative to other principles of associated life. It is the idea of community life itself. It is an ideal in the only intelligible sense of an ideal: namely, the tendency and movement of some thing which exists carried to its final limit, viewed as completed, perfected. Since things do not attain such fulfillment but are in actuality distracted and interfered with, democracy in this sense is not a fact and never will be. But neither in this sense is there or has there ever been anything which is a community in its full measure, a community unalloyed by alien elements. The idea or ideal of a community presents, however, actual phases of associated life as they are freed from restrictive and disturbing elements, and are contemplated as having attained their limit of development. Wherever there is conjoint activity whose consequences are appreciated as good by all singular persons who take part in it, and where the realization of the good is such as to effect an energetic desire and effort to sustain it in being just because it is a good shared by all, there is in so far a community. The clear consciousness of a communal life, in all its implications, constitutes the idea of democracy.

Only when we start from a community as a fact, grasp the fact in thought so as to clarify and enhance its constituent elements, can we reach an idea of democracy which is not utopian. The conceptions and shibboleths which are traditionally associated with the idea of democracy take on a veridical and directive meaning only when they are construed as marks and traits of an association which realizes the defining characteristics of a community. Fraternity, liberty and equality isolated from communal life are hopeless abstractions. Their separate assertion leads to mushy sentimentalism or else to extravagant and fanatical violence which in the end defeats its own aims. Equality then becomes a creed of mechanical identity which is false to facts and impossible of realization. Effort to attain it is divisive of the vital bonds which hold men together; as far as it puts forth issue, the outcome is a mediocrity in which good is common only in the sense of being average and vulgar. Liberty is then thought of as independence of social ties, and ends in dissolution and anarchy. It is more difficult to sever the idea of brotherhood from that of a community, and hence it is either practically ignored in the movements which identify democracy with Individualism, or else it is a sentimentally appended tag. In its just connection with communal experience, fraternity is another name for the consciously appreciated goods which accrue from an association in which all share, and which give direction to the conduct of each. Liberty is that secure release and fulfillment of personal potentialities which take place only in rich and manifold association with others: the power to be an individualized self making a distinctive contribution and enjoying in its own way the fruits of association. Equality denotes the unhampered share which each individual member of the community has in the consequences of associated action. It is equitable because it is measured only be need and capacity to utilize, not by extraneous factors which deprive one in order that another may take and have. A baby in the family is equal with others, not because of some antecedent and structural quality which is the same as that of others, but in so far as his needs for care and development are attended to without being sacrificed to the superior strength, possessions and matured abilities of others. Equality does not signify that kind of mathematical or physical equivalence in virtue of which any one element may be substituted for another. It denotes effective regard for whatever is distinctive and unique in each, irrespective of physical and psychological inequalities. It is not a natural possession but is a fruit of the community when its action is directed by its character as a community.

Associated or joint activity is a condition of the creation of a community. But association itself is physical and organic, while community life is moral, that is emotionally, intellectually, consciously sustained. Human beings combine in behavior as directly and unconsciously as do atoms, stellar masses and cells; as directly and unknowingly as they divide and repel. They do so in virtue of their own structure, as man and woman unite, as the baby seeks the breast and the breast is there to supply its need. They do so from external circumstances, pressure from without, as atoms combine or separate in presence of an electric charge, or as sheep huddle together from the cold. Associated activity needs no explanation; things are made that way. But no amount of aggregated collective action of itself constitutes a community. For beings who observe and think, and whose ideas are absorbed by impulses and become sentiments and interests, "we" is as inevitable as "I." But "we" and "our" exist only when the consequences of combined action are perceived and become an object of desire and effort, just as "I" and "mine" appear on the scene only when a distinctive share in mutual action is consciously asserted or claimed. Human associations may be ever so organic in origin and firm in operation, but they develop into societies in a human sense only as their consequences, being known, are esteemed and sought for. Even if "society" were as much an organism as some writers have held, it would not on that account be society. Interactions, transactions, occur *de facto* and the results of interdependence follow. But participation in activities and sharing in results are additive concerns. They demand *communication* as a prerequisite.

Combined activity happens among human beings; but when nothing else happens it passes as inevitably into some other mode of interconnected activity as does the interplay of iron and the oxygen of water. What takes place is wholly describable in terms of energy, or, as we say in the case of human interactions, of force. Only when there exist *signs* or *symbols* of activities and of their outcome can the flux be viewed as from without, be arrested for consideration and esteem, and be regulated. Lightning strikes and rives a tree or rock, and the resulting fragments take up and continue the process of interaction, and so on and on. But when phases of the process are repre-

sented by signs, a new medium is interposed. As symbols are related to one another, the important relations of a course of events are recorded and are preserved as meanings. Recollection and foresight are possible; the new medium facilitates calculation, planning, and a new kind of action which intervenes in what happens to direct its course in the interest of what is foreseen and desired.

Symbols in turn depend upon and promote communication. The results of conjoint experience are considered and transmitted. Events cannot be passed from one to another, but meanings may be shared by means of signs. Wants and impulses are then attached to common meanings. They are thereby transformed into desires and purposes, which, since they implicate a common or mutually understood meaning, present new ties, converting a conjoint activity into a community of interest and endeavor. Thus there is generated what, metaphorically, may be termed a general will and social consciousness: desire and choice on the part of individuals in behalf of activities that, by means of symbols, are communicable and shared by all concerned. A community thus presents an order of energies transmuted into one of meanings which are appreciated and mutually referred by each to every other on the part of those engaged in combined action. "Force" is not eliminated but is transformed in use and direction by ideas and sentiments made possible by means of symbols.

The work of conversion of the physical and organic phase of associated behavior into a community of action saturated and regulated by mutual interest in shared meanings, consequences which are translated into ideas and desired objects by means of symbols, does not occur all at once nor completely. At any given time, it sets a problem rather than marks a settled achievement. We are born organic beings associated with others, but we are not born members of a community. The young have to be brought within the traditions, outlook and interests which characterize a community by means of education: by unremitting instruction and by learning in connection with the phenomena of overt association. Everything which is distinctively human is learned, not native, even though it could not be learned without native structures which mark man off from other animals. To learn in a human way and to human effect is not just to acquire added skill through refinement of original capacities.

To learn to be human is to develop through the give-and-take of communication an effective sense of being an individually distinctive member of a community; one who understands and appreciates its beliefs, desires and methods, and who contributes to a further conversion of organic powers into human resources and values. But this translation is never finished. The old Adam, the unregenerate element in human nature, persists. It shows itself wherever the method obtains of attaining results by use of force instead of by the method of communication and enlightenment. It manifests itself more subtly, pervasively and effectually when knowledge and the instrumentalities of skill which are the product of communal life are employed in the service of wants and impulses which have not themselves been modified by reference to a shared interest. To the doctrine of "natural" economy which held that commercial exchange would bring about such an interdependence that harmony would automatically result, Rousseau gave an adequate answer in advance. He pointed out that interdependence provides just the situation which makes it possible and worth while for the stronger and abler to exploit others for their own ends, to keep others in a state of subjection where they can be utilized as animated tools. The remedy he suggested, a return to a condition of independence based on isolation, was hardly seriously meant. But its desperateness is evidence of the urgency of the problem. Its negative character was equivalent to surrender of any hope of solution. By contrast it indicates the nature of the only possible solution: the perfecting of the means and ways of communication of meanings so that genuinely shared interest in the consequences of interdependent activities may inform desire and effort and thereby direct action.

This is the meaning of the statement that the problem is a moral one dependent upon intelligence and education. We have in our prior account sufficiently emphasized the role of technological and industrial factors in creating the Great Society. What was said may even have seemed to imply acceptance of the deterministic version of an economic interpretation of history and institutions. It is silly and futile to ignore and deny economic facts. They do not cease to operate because we refuse to note them, or because we smear them over with sentimental idealizations. As we have also noted, they generate as their result overt and external conditions of action and these are known with various degrees of adequacy. What actually happens in consequence of industrial forces is dependent upon the presence or absence of perception and communication of consequences, upon foresight and its effect upon desire and endeavor. Economic agencies produce one result when they are left to work themselves out on the merely physical level, or on that level modified only as the knowledge, skill and technique which the community has accumulated are transmitted to its members unequally and by chance. They have a different outcome in the degree in which knowledge of consequences is equitably distributed, and action is animated by an informed and lively sense of a shared interest. The doctrine of economic interpretation as usually stated ignores the transformation which meanings may effect; it passes over the new medium which communication may interpose between industry and its eventual consequences. It is obsessed by the illusion which vitiated the "natural economy": an illusion due to failure to note the difference made in action by perception and publication of its consequences, actual and possible. It thinks in terms of antecedents, not of the eventual; of origins, not fruits.

We have returned, through this apparent excursion, to the question in which our earlier discussion culminated: What are the conditions under which it is possible for the Great Society to approach more closely and vitally the status of a Great Community, and thus take form in genuinely democratic societies and state? What are the conditions under which we may reasonably picture the Public emerging from its eclipse?

The study will be an intellectual or hypothetical one. There will be no attempt to state how the required conditions might come into existence, nor to prophesy that they will occur. The object of the analysis will be to show that *unless* ascertained specifications are realized, the Community cannot be organized as a democratically effective Public. It is not claimed that the conditions which will be noted will suffice, but only that at least they are indispensable. In other words, we shall endeavor to frame a hypothesis regarding the democratic state to stand in contrast with the earlier doctrine which has been nullified by the course of events.

Two essential constituents in that older theory, as will be recalled, were the notions that each individual is of himself equipped with the intelligence needed, under the operation of self-interest, to engage in political affairs; and that general suffrage, frequent elections of officials and majority rule are sufficient to ensure the responsibility of elected rulers to the desires and interests of the public. As we shall see, the second conception is logically bound up with the first and stands or falls with it. At the basis of the scheme lies what Lippmann has well called the idea of the "omnicompetent" individual: competent to frame policies, to judge their results; competent to know in all situations demanding political action what is for his own good, and competent to enforce his idea of good and the will to effect it against contrary forces. Subsequent history has proved that the assumption involved illusion. Had it not been for the misleading influence of a false psychology, the illusion might have been detected in advance. But current philosophy held that ideas and knowledge were functions of a mind or consciousness which originated in individuals by means of isolated contact with objects. But in fact, knowledge is a function of association and communication; it depends upon tradition, upon tools and methods socially transmitted, developed and sanctioned. Faculties of effectual observation, reflection and desire are habits acquired under the influence of the culture and institutions of society, not readymade inherent powers. The fact that man acts from crudely intelligized emotion and from habit rather than from rational consideration, is now so familiar that it is not easy to appreciate that the other idea was taken seriously as the basis of economic and political philosophy. The measure of truth which it contains was derived from observation of a relatively small group of shrewd business men who regulated their enterprises by calculation and accounting, and of citizens of small and stable local communities who were so intimately acquainted with the persons and affairs of their locality that they could pass competent judgment upon the bearing of proposed measures upon their own concerns.

Habit is the mainspring of human action, and habits are formed for the most part under the influence of the customs of a group. The organic structure of man entails the formation of habit, for, whether we wish it or not, whether we are aware of it or not, every act effects a modification of attitude and set which directs future behavior. The dependence of habit-forming upon those habits of a group which constitute customs and institutions is a natural consequence of the helplessness of infancy. The social consequences of habit have been stated once for all by James: "Habit is the enormous fly-wheel of society, its most precious conservative influence. It alone is what keeps us within the bounds of ordinance, and saves the children of fortune from the up-

risings of the poor. It alone prevents the hardest and most repulsive walks of life from being deserted by those brought up to tread therein. It keeps the fisherman and the deck-hand at sea through the winter; it holds the miner in his darkness, and nails the countryman to his log-cabin and his lonely farm through all the months of snow; it protects us from invasion by the natives of the desert and the frozen zone. It dooms us all to fight out the battle of life upon the lines of our nurture or our early choice, and to make the best of a pursuit that disagrees, because there is no other for which we are fitted and it is too late to begin again. It keeps different social strata from mixing."

The influence of habit is decisive because all distinctively human action has to be learned, and the very heart, blood and sinews of learning is creation of habitudes. Habits bind us to orderly and established ways of action because they generate ease, skill and interest in things to which we have grown used and because they instigate fear to walk in different ways, and because they leave us incapacitated for the trial of them. Habit does not preclude the use of thought, but it determines the channels within which it operates. Thinking is secreted in the interstices of habits. The sailor, miner, fisherman and farmer think, but their thoughts fall within the framework of accustomed occupations and relationships. We dream beyond the limits of use and wont, but only rarely does revery become a source of acts which break bounds; so rarely that we name those in whom it happens demonic geniuses and marvel at the spectacle. Thinking itself becomes habitual along certain lines; a specialized occupation. Scientific men, philosophers, literary persons, are not men and women who have so broken the bonds of habits that pure reason and emotion undefiled by use and wont speak through them. They are persons of a specialized infrequent habit. Hence the idea that men are moved by an intelligent and calculated regard for their own good is pure mythology. Even if the principle of self-love actuated behavior, it would still be true that the *objects* in which men find their love manifested, the objects which they take as constituting their peculiar interests, are set by habits reflecting social customs.

These facts explain why the social doctrinaires of the new industrial movement had so little prescience of what was to follow in consequence of it. These facts explain why the more things changed, the more they were the same; they account, that is, for the fact that instead of the sweeping revolution which was expected to result from democratic political machinery, there was in the main but a transfer of vested power from one class to another. A few men, whether or not they were good judges of their own true interest and good, were competent judges of the conduct of business for pecuniary profit, and of how the new governmental machinery could be made to serve their ends. It would have taken a new race of human beings to escape, in the use made of political forms, from the influence of deeply engrained habits, of old institutions and customary social status, with their inwrought limitations of expectation, desire and demand. And such a race, unless of disembodied angelic constitution, would simply have taken up the task where human beings assumed it upon emergence from the condition of anthropoid apes. It spite of sudden and catastrophic revolutions, the essential continuity of history is doubly guaranteed. Not only are personal desire and belief functions of habit and custom, but the objective conditions which provide the resources and tools of actions, together with its limitations, obstructions and traps, are precipitates of the past, perpetuating, willy-nilly, its hold and power. The creation of a *tabula rasa* in order to permit the creation of a new order is so impossible as to set at naught both the hope of buoyant revolutionaries and the timidity of scared conservatives.

Nevertheless, changes take place and are cumulative in character. Observation of them in the light of their recognized consequences arouses reflection, discovery, invention, experimentation. When a certain state of accumulated knowledge, of techniques and instrumentalities is attained, the process of change is so accelerated, that, as to-day, it appears externally to be the dominant trait. But there is a marked lag in any corresponding change of ideas and desires. Habits of opinion are the toughest of all habits; when they have become second nature, and are supposedly thrown out of the door, they creep in again as stealthily and surely as does first nature. And as they are modified, the alteration first shows itself negatively, in the disintegration of old beliefs, to be replaced by floating, volatile and accidentally snatched up opinions. Of course there has been an enormous increase in the amount of knowledge possessed by mankind, but it does not equal, probably, the increase in the amount of errors and half-truths which have got into circulation. In social and human matters, especially, the development of a critical sense and methods of discriminating judg-

ment has not kept pace with the growth of careless reports and of motives for positive misrepresentation.

What is more important, however, is that so much of knowledge is not knowledge in the ordinary sense of the word, but is "science." The quotation marks are not used disrespectfully, but to suggest the technical character of scientific material. The layman takes certain conclusions which get into circulation to be science. But the scientific inquirer knows that they constitute science only in connection with the methods by which they are reached. Even when true, they are not science in virtue of their correctness, but by reason of the apparatus which is employed in reaching them. This apparatus is so highly specialized that it requires more labor to acquire ability to use and understand it than to get skill in any other instrumentalities possessed by man. Science, in other words, is a highly specialized language, more difficult to learn than any natural language. It is an artificial language, not in the sense of being factitious, but in that of being a work of intricate art, devoted to a particular purpose and not capable of being acquired nor understood in the way in which the mother tongue is learned. It is, indeed, conceivable that sometime methods of instruction will be devised which will enable laymen to read and hear scientific material with comprehension, even when they do not themselves use the apparatus which is science. The latter may then become for large numbers what students of language call a passive, if not an active, vocabulary. But that time is in the future.

For most men, save the scientific workers, science is a mystery in the hands of initiates, who have becomes adepts in virtue of following ritualistic ceremonies from which the profane herd is excluded. They are fortunate who get as far as a sympathetic appreciation of the methods which give pattern to the complicated apparatus: methods of analytic, experimental observation, mathematical formulation and deduction, constant and elaborate check and test. For most persons, the reality of the apparatus is found only in its embodiments in practical affairs, in mechanical devices and in techniques which touch life as it is lived. For them, electricity is *known* by means of the telephones, bells and lights they use, by the generators and magnetos in the automobiles they drive, by the trolley cars in which they ride. The physiology and biology they are acquainted with is that they have learned in taking precautions against germs and from the physicians they depend upon for health. The science of what might be supposed to be closest to them, of human nature, was for them an esoteric mystery until it was applied in advertising, salesmanship and personnel selection and management, and until, through psychiatry, it spilled over into life and popular consciousness, through its bearings upon "nerves," the morbidities and common forms of crankiness which make it difficult for persons to get along with one another and with themselves. Even now, popular psychology is a mass of cant, of slush and of superstition worthy of the most flourishing days of the medicine man.

Meanwhile the technological application of the complex apparatus which is science has revolutionized the conditions under which associated life goes on. This may be known as a fact which is stated in a proposition and assented to. But it is not known in the sense that men understand it. They do not know it as they know some machine which they operate, or as they know electric light and steam locomotives. They do not understand *how* the change has gone on nor *how* it affects their conduct. Not understanding its "how," they cannot use and control its manifestations. They undergo the consequences, they are affected by them. They cannot manage them, though some are fortunate enough—what is commonly called good fortune—to be able to exploit some phase of the process for their own personal profit. But even the most shrewd and successful man does not in any analytic and systematic way—in a way worthy to compare with the knowledge which he has won in lesser affairs by means of the stress of experience—know the system within which he operates. Skill and ability work within a framework which we have not created and do not comprehend. Some occupy strategic positions which give them advance information of forces that affect the market; and by training and an innate turn that way they have acquired a special technique which enables them to use the vast impersonal tide to turn their own wheels. They can dam the current here and release it there. The current itself is as much beyond them as was ever the river by the side of which some ingenious mechanic, exploying a knowledge which was transmitted to him, erected his sawmill to make boards of trees which he had not grown. That within limits those successful in affairs have knowledge and skill is not to be doubted. But such knowledge goes relatively but little further than that of the competent skilled operator who manages a machine. It

suffices to employ the conditions which are before him. Skill enables him to turn the flux of events this way or that in his own neighborhood. It gives him no control of the flux.

Why should the public and its officers, even if the latter are termed statesmen, be wiser and more effective? The prime condition of a democratically organized public is a kind of knowledge and insight which does not yet exist. In its absence, it would be the height of absurdity to try to tell what it would be like if it existed. But some of the conditions which must be fulfilled if it is to exist can be indicated. We can borrow that much from the spirit and method of science even if we are ignorant of it as a specialized apparatus. An obvious requirement is freedom of social inquiry and of distribution of its conclusions. The notion that men may be free in their thought even when they are not in its expression and dissemination has been sedulously propagated. It had its origin in the idea of a mind complete in itself, apart from action and from objects. Such a consciousness presents in fact the spectacle of mind deprived of its normal functioning, because it is baffled by the actualities in connection with which alone it is truly mind, and is driven back into secluded and impotent revery.

There can be no public without full publicity in respect to all consequences which concern it. Whatever obstructs and restricts publicity, limits and distorts public opinion and checks and distorts thinking on social affairs. Without freedom of expression, not even methods of social inquiry can be developed. For tools can be evolved and perfected only in operation; in application to observing, reporting and organizing actual subject-matter; and this application cannot occur save through free and systematic communication. The early history of physical knowledge, of Greek conceptions of natural phenomena, proves how inept become the conceptions of the best endowed minds when those ideas are elaborated apart from the closest contact with the events which they purport to state and explain. The ruling ideas and methods of the human sciences are in much the same condition to-day. They are also evolved on the basis of past gross observation, remote from constant use in regulation of the material of new observations.

The belief that thought and its communication are now free simply because legal restrictions which once obtained have been done away with is absurd. Its currency perpetuates the infantile state of social knowledge. For it blurs recognition of our central need to possess conceptions which are used as tools of directed inquiry and which are tested, rectified and caused to grow in actual use. No man and no mind was ever emancipated merely by being left alone. Removal of formal limitations is but a negative condition; positive freedom is not a state but an act which involves methods and instrumentalities for control of conditions. Experience shows that sometimes the sense of external oppression, as by censorship, acts as a challenge and arouses intellectual energy and excites courage. But a belief in intellectual freedom where it does not exist contributes only to complacency in virtual enslavement, to sloppiness, superficiality and recourse to sensations as a substitute for ideas: marked traits of our present estate with respect to social knowledge. On one hand, thinking deprived of its normal course takes refuge in academic specialism, comparable in its way to what is called scholasticism. On the other hand, the physical agencies of publicity which exist in such abundance are utilized in ways which constitute a large part of the present meaning of publicity: advertising, propaganda, invasion of private life, the "featuring" of passing incidents in a way which violates all the moving logic of continuity, and which leaves us with those isolated intrusions and shocks which are the essence of "sensations."

It would be a mistake to identify the conditions which limit free communication and circulation of facts and ideas, and which thereby arrest and pervert social thought or inquiry, merely with overt forces which are obstructive. It is true that those who have ability to manipulate social relations for their own advantage have to be reckoned with. They have an uncanny instinct for detecting whatever intellectual tendencies even remotely threaten to encroach upon their control. They have developed an extraordinary facility in enlisting upon their side the inertia, prejudices and emotional partisanship of the masses by use of a technique which impedes free inquiry and expression. We seem to be approaching a state of government by hired promoters of opinion called publicity agents. But the more serious enemy is deeply concealed in hidden entrenchments.

Emotional habituations and intellectual habitudes on the part of the mass of men create the conditions of which the exploiters of sentiment and opinion only take advantage. Men have got used to an experimental method in physical and technical matters. They are still afraid of it in human concerns. The fear is the more efficacious because like all deep-lying fears it is covered up and disguised by all kinds of rationalizations. One of its commonest forms is a truly religious idealization of, and reverence for, established institutions; for example in our own politics, the Constitution, the Supreme Court, private property, free contract and so on. The words "sacred" and "sanctity" come readily to our lips when such things come under discussion. They testify to the religious aureole which protects the institutions. If "holy" means that which is not to be approached nor touched, save with ceremonial precautions and by specially anointed officials, then such things are holy in contemporary political life. As supernatural matters have progressively been left high and dry upon a secluded beach, the actuality of religious taboos has more and more gathered about secular institutions, especially those connected with the nationalistic state.[2] Psychiatrists have discovered that one of the commonest causes of mental disturbance is an underlying fear of which the subject is not aware, but which leads to withdrawal from reality and to unwillingness to think things through. There is a social pathology which works powerfully against effective inquiry into social institutions and conditions. It manifests itself in a thousand ways; in querulousness, in impotent drifting, in uneasy snatching at distractions, in idealization of the long established, in a facile optimism assumed as a cloak, in riotous glorification of things "as they are," in intimidation of all dissenters—ways which depress and dissipate thought all the more effectually because they operate with subtle and unconscious pervasiveness.

The backwardness of social knowledge is marked in its division into independent and insulated branches of learning. Anthropology, history, sociology, morals, economics, political science, go their own ways without constant and systematized fruitful interaction. Only in appearance is there a similar division in physical knowledge. There is continuous cross-fertilization between astronomy, physics, chemistry and the biological sciences. Discoveries and improved methods are so recorded and organized that constant exchange and intercommunication take place. The isolation of the humane subjects from one another is connected with their aloofness from physical knowledge. The mind still draws a sharp separation between the world in which man lives and the life of man in and by that world, a cleft reflected in the separation of man himself into a body and a mind, which, it is currently supposed, can be known and dealt with apart. That for the past three centuries energy should have gone chiefly into physical inquiry, beginning with the things most remote from man such as heavenly bodies, was to have been expected. The history of the physical sciences reveals a certain order in which they developed. Mathematical tools had to be employed before a new astronomy could be constructed. Physics advanced when ideas worked out in connection with the solar system were used to describe happenings on the earth. Chemistry waited on the advance of physics; the sciences of living things required the material and methods of physics and chemistry in order to make headway. Human psychology ceased to be chiefly speculative opinion only when biological and physiological conclusions were available. All this is natural and seemingly inevitable. Things which had the most outlying and indirect connection with human interests had to be mastered in some degree before inquiries could competently converge upon man himself.

Nevertheless the course of development has left us of this age in a plight. When we say that a subject of science is technically specialized, or that it is highly "abstract," what we practically mean is that it is not conceived in terms of its bearing upon human life. All *merely* physical knowledge is technical, couched in a technical vocabulary communicable only to the few. Even physical knowledge which does affect human conduct, which does modify what we do and undergo, is also technical and remote in the degree in which its bearings are not understood and used. The sunlight, rain, air and soil have always entered in visible ways into human experience; atoms and molecules and cells and most other things with which the sciences are occupied affect us, but not visibly. Because they enter life and modify experience in imperceptible ways, and their consequences are not realized, speech about them is technical; communication is by means of peculiar symbols. One would think, then, that a fundamental and ever-operating aim would be to translate knowledge of the subject-matter of physical conditions into terms which are generally understood, into signs denoting human consequences of services and disservices rendered. For ultimately all consequences which enter human life depend upon physical conditions; they can be understood and mastered only as the latter are taken into account. One would think, then, that any state of affairs which

tends to render the things of the environment unknown and incommunicable by human beings in terms of their own activities and sufferings would be deplored as a disaster; that it would be felt to be intolerable, and to be put up with only as far as it is, at any given time, inevitable.

But the facts are to the contrary. Matter and the material are words which in the minds of many convey a note of disparagement. They are taken to be foes of whatever is of ideal value in life, instead of as conditions of its manifestation and sustained being. In consequence of this division, they do become in fact enemies, for whatever is consistently kept apart from human values depresses thought and renders values sparse and precarious in fact. There are even some who regard the materialism and dominance of commercialism of modern life as fruits of undue devotion to physical science, not seeing that the split between man and nature, artifically made by a tradition which originated before there was understanding of the physical conditions that are the medium of human activities, is the benumbing factor. The most influential form of the divorce is separation between pure and applied science. Since "application" signifies recognized bearing upon human experience and well-being, honor of what is "pure" and contempt for what is "applied" has for its outcome a science which is remote and technical, communicable only to specialists, and a conduct of human affairs which is haphazard, biased, unfair in distribution of values. What is applied and employed as the alternative to knowledge in regulation of society is ignorance, prejudice, class-interest and accident. Science is converted into knowledge in its honorable and emphatic sense *only* in application. Otherwise it is truncated, blind, distorted. When it is then applied, it is in ways which explain the unfavorable sense so often attached to "application" and the "utilitarian": namely, use for pecuniary ends to the profit of a few.

At present, the application of physical science is rather *to* human concerns than *in* them. That is, it is external, made in the interests of its consequences for a possessing and acquisitive class. Application *in* life would signify that science was absorbed and distributed; that it was the instrumentality of that common understanding and thorough communication which is the precondition of the existence of a genuine and effective public. The use of science to regulate industry and trade has gone on steadily. The scientific revolution of the seventeenth century was the precursor of the industrial revolution of the eighteenth and nineteenth. In consequence, man has suffered the impact of an enormously enlarged control of physical energies without any corresponding ability to control himself and his own affairs. Knowledge divided against itself, a science to whose incompleteness is added in artificial split, has played its part in generating enslavement of men, women and children in factories in which they are animated machines to tend inanimate machines. It has maintained sordid slums, flurried and discontented careers, grinding povery and luxurious wealth, brutal exploitation of nature and man in times of peace and high explosives and noxious gases in time of war. Man, a child in understanding of himself, has placed in his hands physical tools of incalculable power. He plays with them like a child, and whether they work harm or good is largely a matter of accident. The instrumentality becomes a master and works fatally as if possessed of a will of its own—not because it has a will but because man has not.

The glorification of "pure" science under such conditions is a rationalization of an escape; it marks a construction of an asylum of refuge, a shirking of responsibility. The true purity of knowledge exists not when it is uncontaminated by contact with use and service. It is wholly a moral matter, an affair of honesty, impartiality and generous breadth of intent in search and communication. The adulteration of knowledge is due not to its use, but to vested bias and prejudice, to one-sidedness of outlook, to vanity, to conceit of possession and authority, to contempt or disregard of human concern in its use. Humanity is not, as was once thought, the end for which all things were formed; it is but a slight and feeble thing, perhaps an episodic one, in the vast stretch of the universe. But for man, man is the centre of interest and the measure of importance. The magnifying of the physical realm at the cost of man is but an abdication and a flight. To make physical science a rival of human interests is bad enough, for it forms a diversion of energy which can ill be afforded. But the evil does not stop there. The ultimate harm is that the understanding by man of his own affairs and his ability to direct them are sapped at their root when knowledge of nature is disconnected from its human function.

It has been implied throughout that knowledge is communication as well as understanding. I well remember the saying of a man, uneducated from the standpoint of the schools, in speaking of certain matters: "Sometime they will be found out and not only found out, but they will be known." The schools may suppose that a thing is known when it is found out. My old friend was aware that a thing is fully known only when it is published, shared, socially accessible. Record and communication are indispensable to knowledge. Knowledge cooped up in a private consciousness is a myth, and knowledge of social phenomena is peculiarly dependent upon dissemination, for only by distribution can such knowledge be either obtained or tested. A fact of community life which is not spread abroad so as to be a common possession is a contradiction in terms. Dissemination is something other than scattering at large. Seeds are sown, not by virtue of being thrown out at random, but by being so distributed as to take root and have a chance of growth. Communication of the results of social inquiry is the same thing as the formation of public opinion. This marks one of the first ideas framed in the growth of political democracy as it will be one of the last to be fulfilled. For public opinion is judgment which is formed and entertained by those who constitute the public and is about public affairs. Each of the two phases imposes for its realization conditions hard to meet.

Opinions and beliefs concerning the public presuppose effective and organized inquiry. Unless there are methods for detecting the energies which are at work and tracing them through an intricate network of interactions to their consequences, what passes as public opinion will be "opinion" in its derogatory sense rather than truly public, no matter how widespread the opinion is. The number who share error as to fact and who partake of a false belief measures power for harm. Opinion casually formed and formed under the direction of those who have something at stake in having a lie believed can be *public* opinion only in name. Calling it by this name, acceptance of the name as a kind of warrant, magnifies its capacity to lead action estray. The more who share it, the more injurious its influence. Public opinion, even if it happens to be correct, is intermittent when it is not the product of methods of investigation and reporting constantly at work. It appears only in crises. Hence its "rightness" concerns only an immediate emergency. Its lack of continuity makes it wrong from the standpoint of the course of events. It is as if a physician were able to deal for the moment with an emergency in disease but could not adapt his treatment of it to the underlying conditions which brought it about. He may then "cure" the disease—that is, cause its present alarming symptoms to subside—but he does not modify its causes; his treatment may even effect them for the worse. Only continuous inquiry, continuous in the sense of being connected as well as persistent, can provide the material of enduring opinion about public matters.

There is a sense in which "opinion" rather than knowledge, even under the most favorable circumstances, is the proper term to use—namely, in the sense of judgment, estimate. For in its strict sense, knowledge can refer only to what *has* happened and been done. What is still *to be* done involves a forecast of a future still contingent, and cannot escape the liability to error in judgment involved in all anticipation of probabilities. There may well be honest divergence as to policies to be pursued, even when plans spring from knowledge of the same facts. But genuinely public policy cannot be generated unless it be informed by knowledge, and this knowledge does not exist except when there is systematic, thorough, and well-equipped search and record.

Moreover, inquiry must be as nearly contemporaneous as possible; otherwise it is only of antiquarian interest. Knowledge of history is evidently necessary for connectedness of knowledge. But history which is not brought down close to the actual scene of events leaves a gap and exercises influence upon the formation of judgments about the public interest only by guess-work about intervening events. Here, only too conspicuously, is a limitation of the existing social sciences. Their material comes too late, too far after the event, to enter effectively into the formation of public opinion about the immediate public concern and what is to be done about it.

A glance at the situation shows that the physical and external means of collecting information in regard to what is happening in the world have far outrun the intellectual phase of inquiry and organization of its results. Telegraph, telephone, and now the radio, cheap and quick mails, the printing press, capable of swift reduplication of material at low cost, have attained a remarkable development. But when we ask what sort of material is recorded and how it is organized, when we ask about the intellectual form in which the material is presented, the tale to be told is very different. "News" signifies something which has just happened, and which is new just because it deviates from the old and regular. But its *meaning* depends upon relation to what it im-

ports, to what its social consequences are. This important cannot be determined unless the new is placed in relation to the old, to what has happened and been integrated into the course of events. Without coordination and consecutiveness, events are not events, but mere occurrences, intrusions; an event implies that out of which a happening proceeds. Hence even if we discount the influence of private interests in procuring suppression, secrecy and misrepresentation, we have here an explanation of the triviality and "sensational" quality of so much of what passes as news. The catastrophic, namely, crime, accident, family rows, personal clashes and conflicts, are the most obvious forms of breaches of continuity; they supply the element of shock which is the strictest meaning of sensation; they are the *new* par excellence, even though only the date of the newspaper could inform us whether they happened last year or this, so completely are they isolated from their connections.

So accustomed are we to this method of collecting, recording and presenting social changes, that it may well sound ridiculous to say that a genuine social science would manifest its reality in the daily press, while learned books and articles supply and polish tools of inquiry. But the inquiry which alone can furnish knowledge as a precondition of public judgments must be contemporary and quotidian. Even if social sciences as a specialized apparatus of inquiry were more advanced than they are, they would be comparatively impotent in the office of directing opinion on matters of concern to the public as long as they are remote from application in the daily and unremitting assembly and interpretation of "news." On the other hand, the tools of social inquiry will be clumsy as long as they are forged in places and under conditions remote from contemporary events.

What has been said about the formation of ideas and judgments concerning the public apply as well to the distribution of the knowledge which makes it an effective possession of the members of the public. Any separation between the two sides of the problem is artificial. The discussion of propaganda and propagandism would alone, however, demand a volume, and could be written only by one much more experienced than the present writer. Propaganda can accordingly only be mentioned, with the remark that the present situation is one unprecedented in history. The political forms of democracy and quasi-democratic habits of thought on social matters have compelled a certain amount of public discussion and at least the simulation of general consultation in arriving at political decisions. Representative government must at least seem to be founded on public interests as they are revealed to public belief. The days are past when government can be carried on without any pretense of ascertaining the wishes of the governed. In theory, their assent must be secured. Under the older forms, there was no need to muddy the sources of opinion on political matters. No current of energy flowed from them. To-day the judgments popularly formed on political matters are so important, in spite of all factors to the contrary, that there is an enormous premium upon all methods which affect their formation.

The smoothest road to control of political conduct is by control of opinion. As long as interests of pecuniary profit are powerful, and a public has not located and identified itself, those who have this interest will have an unresisted motive for tampering with the springs of political action in all that affects them. Just as in the conduct of industry and exchange generally the technological factor is obscured, deflected and defeated by "business," so specifically in the management of publicity. The gathering and sale of subject-matter having a public import is part of the existing pecuniary system. Just as industry conducted by engineers on a factual technological basis would be a very different thing from what it actually is, so the assembling and reporting of news would be a very different thing if the genuine interests of reporters were permitted to work freely.

One aspect of the matter concerns particularly the side of dissemination. It is often said, and with a great appearance of truth, that the freeing and perfecting of inquiry would not have any especial effect. For, it is argued, the mass of the reading public is not interested in learning and assimilating the results of accurate investigation. Unless these are read, they cannot seriously affect the thought and action of members of the public; they remain in secluded library alcoves, and are studied and understood only by a few intellectuals. The objection is well taken save as the potency of art is taken into account. A technical high-brow presentation would appeal only to those technically high-brow; it would not be news to the masses. Presentation is fundamentally important, and presentation is a question of art. A newspaper which was only a daily edition of a quarterly journal of sociology or political science would undoubtedly possess a limited circulation and a narrow influence. Even at that, however, the mere existence and accessibility of such material would have some regulative effect. But we can look much further than that. The material would have such an enormous and widespread human bearing that its bare existence would be an irresistible invitation to a presentation of it which would have a direct popular appeal. The freeing of the artist in literary presentation, in other words, is as much a precondition of the desirable creation of adequate opinion on public matters as is the freeing of social inquiry. Men's conscious life of opinion and judgment often proceeds on a superficial and trivial plane. But their lives reach a deeper level. The function of art has always been to break through the crust of conventionalized and routine consciousness. Common things, a flower, a gleam of moonlight, the song of a bird, not things rare and remote, are means with which the deeper levels of life are touched so that they spring up as desire and thought. This process is art. Poetry, the drama, the novel, are proofs that the problem of presentation is not insoluble. Artists have always been the real purveyors of news, for it is not the outward happening in itself which is new, but the kindling by it of emotion, perception and appreciation.

We have but touched lightly and in passing upon the conditions which must be fulfilled if the Great Society is to become a Great Community; a society in which the ever-expanding and intricately ramifying consequences of associated activities shall be known in the full sense of that word, so that an organized, articulate Public comes into being. The highest and most difficult kind of inquiry and a subtle, delicate, vivid and responsive art of communication must take possession of the physical machinery of transmission and circulation and breathe life into it. When the machine age has thus perfected its machinery it will be a means of life and not its despotic master. Democracy will come into its own, for democracy is a name for a life of free and enriching communion. It had its seer in Walt Whitman. It will have its consummation when free social inquiry is indissolubly wedded to the art of full and moving communication.

NOTES

1. The most adequate discussion of this ideal with which I am acquainted is T. V. Smith's *The Democratic Way of Life.*

2. The religious character of nationalism has been forcibly brought out by Carlton Hayes, in his *Essays on Nationalism,* especially Chap. 4.

The Live Creature and Aesthetic Experience

THE LIVE CREATURE

By one of the ironic perversities that often attend the course of affairs, the existence of the works of art upon which formation of an esthetic theory depends has become an obstruction to theory about them. For one reason, these works are products that exist externally and physically. In common conception, the work of art is often identified with the building, book, painting, or statue in its existence apart from human experience. Since the actual work of art is what the product does with and in experience, the result is not favorable to understanding. In addition, the very perfection of some of these products, the prestige they possess because of a long history of unquestioned admiration, creates conventions that get in the way of fresh insight. When an art product once attains classic status, it somehow becomes isolated from the human conditions under which it was brought into being and from the human consequences it engenders in actual life-experience.

When artistic objects are separated from both conditions of origin and operation in experience, a wall is built around them that renders almost opaque their general significance, with which esthetic theory deals. Art is remitted to a separate realm, where it is cut off from that association with the materials and aims of every other form of human effort, undergoing, and achievement. A primary task is thus imposed upon one who undertakes to write upon the philosophy of the fine arts. This task is to restore continuity between the refined and intensified forms of experience that are works of art and the everyday events, doings, and sufferings that are universally recognized to constitute experience. Mountain peaks do not float unsupported; they do not even just rest upon the earth. They *are* the earth in one of its manifest operations. It is the business of those who are concerned with the theory of the earth, geographers and geologists, to make this fact evident in its various implications. The theorist who would deal philosophically with fine art has a like task to accomplish. . . .

In order to *understand* the esthetic in its ultimate and approved forms, one must begin with it in the raw; in the events and scenes that hold the attentive eye and ear of man, arousing his interest and affording him enjoyment as he looks and listens: the sights that hold the crowd—the fire-engine rushing by; the machines excavating enormous holes in the earth; the human-fly climbing the steeple-side; the men perched high in air on girders, throwing and catching red-hot bolts. The sources of art in human experience will be learned by him who sees how the tense grace of the ball-player infects the onlooking crowd; who notes the delight of the housewife in tending her plants, and the intent interest of her goodman in tending the patch of green in front of the house; the zest of the spectator in poking the wood burning on the hearth and in watching the darting flames and crumbling coals. These people, if questioned as to the reason for their actions, would doubtless return reasonable answers. The man who poked the sticks of burning wood would say he did it to make the fire burn better; but he is none the less fascinated by the colorful drama of change enacted before his eyes and imaginatively partakes in it. He does not remain a cold spectator. What Coleridge said of the reader of poetry is true in its way of all who are happily absorbed in their activities of mind and body: "The reader should be carried forward, not merely or chiefly by the mechanical impulse of curiosity, not by a restless desire to arrive at the final solution, but by the pleasurable activity of the journey itself."

The intelligent mechanic engaged in his job, interested in doing well and finding satisfaction in his handiwork, caring for his materials and tools with genuine affection, is artistically engaged. The difference between such a worker and the inept and careless bungler is as great in the shop as it is in the studio. Often-times the product may not appeal to the esthetic sense of those who use the product. The fault, however, is oftentimes not so much the worker as with the conditions of the market for which his product is designed. Were conditions and op-

From "The Live Creature" and "Having an Experience," in *Art as Experience* (New York: The Putnam Publishing Group, 1958), pp. 3–6, 35–57.

portunities different, things as significant to the eye as those produced by earlier craftsmen would be made.

So extensive and subtly pervasive are the ideas that set Art upon a remote pedestal, that many a person would be repelled rather than pleased if told that he enjoyed his casual recreations, in part at least, because of their esthetic quality. The arts which today have most vitality for the average person are things he does not take to be arts: for instance, the movie, jazzed music, the comic strip, and, too frequently, newspaper accounts of love-nests, murders, and exploits of bandits. For, when what he knows as art is relegated to the museum and gallery, the unconquerable impulse towards experiences enjoyable in themselves finds such outlet as the daily environment provides. Many a person who protests against the museum conception of art, still shares the fallacy from which that conception springs. For the popular notion comes from a separation of art from the objects and scenes of ordinary experience that many theorists and critics pride themselves upon holding and even elaborating. The time when select and distinguished objects are closely connected with the products of usual vocations are the times when appreciation of the former is most rife and most keen. When, because of their remoteness, the objects acknowledged by the cultivated to be works of fine art seem anemic to the mass of people, esthetic hunger is likely to seek the cheap and the vulgar. . . .

HAVING AN EXPERIENCE

Experience occurs continuously, because the interaction of live creature and environing conditions is involved in the very process of living. Under conditions of resistance and conflict, aspects and elements of the self and the world that are implicated in this interaction qualify experience with emotions and ideas so that conscious intent emerges. Oftentimes, however, the experience had is inchoate. Things are experienced but not in such a way that they are composed into *an* experience. There is distraction and dispersion; what we observe and what we think, what we desire and what we get, are at odds with each other. We put our hands to the plow and turn back; we start and then we stop, not because the experience has reached the end for the sake of which it was initiated but because of extraneous interruptions or of inner lethargy.

In contrast with such experience, we have

an experience when the material experienced runs its course to fulfillment. Then and then only is it integrated within and demarcated in the general stream of experience from other experiences. A piece of work is finished in a way that is satisfactory; a problem receives its solution; a game is played through; a situation, whether that of eating a meal, playing a game of chess, carrying on a conversation, writing a book, or taking part in a political campaign, is so rounded out that its close is a consummation and not a cessation. Such an experience is a whole and carries with it its own individualizing quality and self-sufficiency. It is *an* experience.

Philosophers, even empirical philosophers, have spoken for the most part of experience at large. Idiomatic speech, however, refers to experiences each of which is singular, having its own beginning and end. For life is no uniform uninterrupted march or flow. It is a thing of histories, each with its own plot, its own inception and movement toward its close, each having its own particular rhythmic movement; each with its own unrepeated quality pervading it throughout. A flight of stairs, mechanical as it is, proceeds by individualized steps, not by undifferentiated progression, and an inclined plane is at least marked off from other things by abrupt discreteness.

Experience in this vital sense is defined by those situations and episodes that we spontaneously refer to as being "real experiences"; those things of which we say in recalling them, "that *was* an experience." It may have been something of tremendous importance—a quarrel with one who was once an intimate, a catastrophe finally averted by a hair's breadth. Or it may have been something that in comparison was slight—and which perhaps because of its very slightness illustrates all the better what is to be an experience. There is that meal in a Paris restaurant of which one says "that *was* an experience." It stands out as an enduring memorial of what food may be. Then there is that storm one went through in crossing the Atlantic—the storm that seemed in its fury, as it was experienced, to sum up in itself all that a storm can be, complete in itself, standing out because marked out from what went before and what came after.

In such experiences, every successive part flows freely without seam and without unfilled blanks, into what ensues. At the same time there is no sacrifice of the self-identity of the parts. A river, as distinct from a pond, flows. But its flow gives a definiteness and interest to its successive portions greater than exist in the homogenous portions of a pond. In an experience, flow is from something to something. As one part leads into another and as one part carries on what went before, each gains distinctness in itself. The enduring whole is diversified by successive phases that are emphases of its varied colors.

Because of continuous merging, there are no holes, mechanical junctions, and dead centers when we have *an* experience. There are pauses, places of rest, but they punctuate and define the quality of movement. They sum up what has been undergone and prevent its dissipation and idle evaporation. Continued acceleration is breathless and prevents parts from gaining distinction. In a work of art, different acts, episodes, occurrences melt and fuse into unity, and yet do not disappear and lose their own character as they do so—just as in a genial conversation there is a continuous interchange and blending, and yet each speaker not only retains his own character but manifests it more clearly than in his wont.

An experience has a unity that gives it its name, *that* meal, that storm, that rupture of friendship. The existence of this unity is constituted by a single *quality* that pervades the entire experience in spite of the variation of its constituent parts. This unity is neither emotional, practical, nor intellectual, for these terms name distinctions that reflection can make within it. In discourse *about* an experience, we must make use of these adjectives of interpretation. In going over an experience in mind *after* its occurence, we may find that one property rather than another was sufficiently dominant so that it characterizes the experience as a whole. There are absorbing inquiries and speculations which a scientific man and philosopher will recall as "experiences" in the emphatic sense. In final import they are intellectual. But in their actual occurrence they were emotional as well; they were purposive and volitional. Yet the experience was not a sum of these different characters; they were lost in it as distinctive traits. No thinker can ply his occupation save as he is lured and rewarded by total integral experiences that are intrinsically worth while. Without them he would never know what it is really to think and would be completely at a loss in distinguishing real thought from the spurious article. Thinking goes on in trains of ideas, but the ideas form a train only because they are much more than what an analytic psychology calls ideas. They are phases, emotionally and practically distinguished, of a developing underlying quality; they are its moving variations, not separate and independent like Locke's and Hume's so-called ideas and impressions, but are subtle shadings of a pervading and developing hue.

We say of an experience of thinking that we reach or draw a conclusion. Theoretical formulation of the process is often made in such terms as to conceal effectually the similarity of "conclusion" to the consummating phase of every developing integral experience. These formulations apparently take their cue from the separate propositions that are premisses and the proposition that is the conclusion as they appear on the printed page. The impression is derived that there are first two independent and ready-made entities that are then manipulated so as to give rise to a third. In fact, in an experience of thinking, premisses emerge only as a conclusion becomes manifest. The experience, like that of watching a storm reach its height and gradually subside, is one of continuous movement of subject-matters. Like the ocean in the storm, there are a series of waves; suggestions reaching out and being broken in a clash, or being carried onwards by a coöperative wave. If a conclusion is reached, it is that of a movement of anticipation and cumulation, one that finally comes to completion. A "conclusion" is no separate and independent thing; it is the consummation of a movement.

Hence *an* experience of thinking has its own esthetic quality. It differs from those experiences that are acknowledged to be esthetic, but only in its materials. The material of the fine arts consists of qualities; that of experience having intellectual conclusion are signs or symbols having no intrinsic quality of their own, but standing for things that may in another experience be qualitatively experienced. The difference is enormous. It is one reason why the strictly intellectual art will never be popular as music is popular. Nevertheless, the experience itself has a satisfying emotional quality because it possesses internal integration and fulfillment reached through ordered and organized movement. This artistic structure may be immediately felt. In so far, it is esthetic. What is even more important is that not only is this quality a significant motive in undertaking intellectual inquiry and in keeping it honest, but that no intellectual activity is an integral event (is *an* experience), unless it is rounded out with this quality. Without it, thinking is inconclusive. In short, esthetic cannot be sharply marked off from intellectual experience since the latter must bear an esthetic stamp to be itself complete.

The same statement holds good of a course of

action that is dominantly practical, that is, one that consists of overt doings. It is possible to be efficient in action and yet not have a conscious experience. The activity is too automatic to permit of a sense of what it is about and where it is going. It comes to an end but not to a close or consummation in consciousness. Obstacles are overcome by shrewd skill, but they do not feed experience . . . For in much of our experience we are not concerned with the connection of one incident with what went before and what comes after. There is no interest that controls attentive rejection or selection of what shall be organized into the developing experience. Things happen, but they are neither definitely included nor decisively excluded; we drift. We yield according to external pressure, or evade and compromise. There are beginnings and cessations, but no genuine initiations and concludings. One thing replaces another, but does not absorb it and carry it on. There is experience, but so slack and discursive that it is not *an* experience. Needless to say, such experiences are anesthetic.

Thus the non-esthetic lies within two limits. At one pole is the loose succession that does not begin at any particular place and that ends—in the sense of ceasing—at no particular place. At the other pole is arrest, constriction, proceeding from parts having only a mechanical connection with one another. There exists so much of one and the other of these two kinds of experience that unconsciously they come to be taken as norms of all experience. Then, when the esthetic appears, it so sharply contrasts with the picture that has been formed of experience, that it is impossible to combine its special qualities with the features of the picture and the esthetic is given an outside place and status. The account that has been given of experience dominantly intellectual and practical is intended to show that there is no such contrast involved in having an experience; that, on the contrary, no experience of whatever sort is a unity unless it has esthetic quality.

The enemies of the esthetic are neither the practical nor the intellectual. They are the humdrum; slackness of loose ends; submission to convention in practice and intellectual procedure. Rigid abstinence, coerced submission, tightness on one side and dissipation, incoherence and aimless indulgence on the other, are deviations in opposite directions from the unity of an experience. Some such considerations perhaps induced Aristotle to invoke the "mean proportional" as the proper designation of what is distinctive of both virtue and the esthetic. He was formally correct. "Mean" and "proportion" are, however, not self-explanatory, nor to be taken over in a prior mathematical sense, but are properties belonging to an experience that has a developing movement toward its own consummation.

I have emphasized the fact that every integral experience moves toward a close, an ending, since it ceases only when the energies active in it have done their proper work. This closure of a circuit of energy is the opposite of arrest, of *stasis*. Maturation and fixation are polar opposite. Struggle and conflict may be themselves enjoyed, although they are painful, when they are experienced as means of developing an experience; members in that they carry it forward, not just because they are there. There is, as will appear later, an element of undergoing, of suffering in its large sense, in every experience. Otherwise there would be no taking in of what preceded. For "taking in" in any vital experience is something more than placing something on the top of consciousness over what was previously known. It involves reconstruction which may be painful. Whether the necessary undergoing phase is by itself pleasurable or painful is a matter of particular conditions. It is indifferent to the total esthetic quality, save that there are few intense esthetic experiences that are wholly gleeful. They are certainly not to be characterized as amusing, and as they bear down upon us they involve a suffering that is none the less consistent with, indeed a part of, the complete perception that is enjoyed.

I have spoken of the esthetic quality that rounds out an experience into completeness and unity as emotional. The reference may cause difficulty. We are given to thinking of emotions as things as simple and compact as are the words by which we name them. Joy, sorrow, hope, fear, anger, curiosity, are treated as if each in itself were a sort of entity that enters full-made upon the scene, an entity that may last a long time or a short time, but whose duration, whose growth and career, is irrelevant to its nature. In fact emotions are qualities, when they are significant, of a complex experience that moves and changes. I say, when they are *significant,* for otherwise they are but the outbreaks and eruptions of a disturbed infant. All emotions are qualifications of a drama and they change as the drama develops. Persons are sometimes said to fall in love at first sight. But what they fall into is not a thing of that instant. What would love be were it compressed into a moment in which there is no room for cherishing and for solicitude? The intimate nature of emotion is manifested in the experience of one watching a play on the stage or reading a novel. It attends the development of a plot; and a plot requires a stage, a space, wherein to develop and time in which to unfold. Experience is emotional but there are not separate things called emotions in it.

By the same token, emotions are attached to events and objects in their movement. They are not, save in pathological instances, private. And even an "objectless" emotion demands something beyond itself to which to attach itself, and thus it soon generates a delusion in lack of something real. Emotion belongs of a certainty to the self. But it belongs to the self that is concerned in the movement of events toward an issue that is desired or disliked. We jump instantaneously when we are scared, as we blush on the instant when we are ashamed. But fright and shamed modesty are not in this case emotional states. Of themselves they are but automatic reflexes. In order to become emotional they must become parts of an inclusive and enduring situation that involves concern for objects and their issues. The jump of fright becomes emotional fear when there is found or thought to exist a threatening object that must be dealt with or escaped from. The blush becomes the emotion of shame when a person connects, in thought, an action he has performed with an unfavorable reaction to himself of some other person.

Physical things from far ends of the earth are physically transported and physically caused to act and react upon one another in the construction of a new object. The miracle of mind is that something similar takes place in experience without physical transport and assembling. Emotion is the moving and cementing force. It selects what is congruous and dyes what is selected with its color, thereby giving qualitative unity to materials externally disparate and dissimilar. It thus provides unity in and through the varied parts of an experience. When the unity is of the sort already described, the experience has esthetic character even though it is not, dominantly, an esthetic experience. . . .

There are, therefore, common patterns in various experiences, no matter how unlike they are to one another in the details of their subject matter. There are conditions to be met without which an experience cannot come to be. The outline of the common pattern is set by the fact that every experience is the result of interaction between a live creature and some aspect of the world in which he lives. A man does something; he lifts, let us say, a stone. In consequence he undergoes, suffers, something: the weight, strain, texture of the surface of the thing lifted. The properties thus undergone determine further doing. The stone is too heavy or too angular, not solid enough; or else the properties undergone show it is fit for the use for which it is intended. The process continues until a mutual adaptation of the self and the object emerges and that particular experience comes to a close. What is true of this simple instance is true, as to form, of every experience. The creature operating may be a thinker in his study and the environment with which he interacts may consist of ideas instead of a stone. But interaction of the two constitutes the total experience that is had, and the close which completes it is the institution of a felt harmony.

An experience has pattern and structure, because it is not just doing and undergoing in alternation, but consists of them in relationship. To put one's hand in the fire that consumes it is not necessarily to have an experience. The action and its consequence must be joined in perception. This relationship is what gives meaning; to grasp it is the objective of all intelligence. The scope and content of the relations measure the significant content of an experience. A child's experience may be intense, but, because of lack of background from past experience, relations between undergoing and doing are slightly grasped, and the experience does not have great depth or breadth. No one ever arrives at such maturity that he perceives all the connections that are involved. There was once written (by Mr. Hinton) a romance called "The Unlearner." It portrayed the whole endless duration of life after death as a living over of the incidents that happened in a short life on earth, in continued discovery of the relationships involved among them.

Experience is limited by all the causes which interfere with perception of the relations between undergoing and doing. There may be interference because of excess on the side of doing or of excess on the side of receptivity, of undergoing. Unbalance on either side blurs the perception of relations and leaves the experience partial and distorted, with scant or false meaning. Zeal for doing, lust for action, leaves many a person, especially in this hurried and impatient human environment in which we live, with experience of an almost incredible paucity, all on the surface. No one experience has a chance to complete itself because something else is entered upon so speedily. What is called experience becomes so dispersed and miscellaneous as hardly to deserve the name. Resistance is treated as an obstruction to be beaten down, not as an invitation to reflection. An individual comes to seek, unconsciously even more than by deliberate choice, situations in which he can do the most things in the shortest time.

Experiences are also cut short from maturing by excess of receptivity. What is prized is then the mere undergoing of this and that, irrespective of perception of any meaning. The crowding together of as many impressions as possible is thought to be "life," even though no one of them is more than a flitting and a sipping. The sentimentalist and the daydreamer may have more fancies and impressions pass through their consciousness than has the man who is animated by lust for action. But his experience is equally distorted, because nothing takes root in mind when there is no balance between doing and receiving. Some decisive action is needed to order to establish contact with the realities of the world and in order that impressions may be so related to facts that their value is tested and organized.

Because perception of relationship between what is done and what is undergone constitutes the work of intelligence, and because the artist is controlled in the process of his work by his grasp of the connection between what he has already done and what he is to do next, the idea that the artist does not think as intently and penetratingly as a scientific inquirer is absurd. A painter must consciously undergo the effect of his every brush stroke or he will not be aware of what he is doing and where his work is going. Moreover, he has to see each particular connection of doing and undergoing in relation to the whole that he desires to produce. To apprehend such relations is to think, and is one of the most exacting modes of thought. The difference between the picture of different painters is due quite as much to differences of capacity to carry on this thought as it is to differences of sensitivity to bare color and to differences in dexterity of execution. As respects the basic quality of pictures, difference depends, indeed, more upon the quality of intelligence brought to bear upon perception of relations than upon anything else— though of course intelligence cannot be separated from direct sensitivity and is connected, though in a more external manner, with skill.

Any idea that ignores the necessary rôle of intelligence in production of works of art is based upon identification of thinking with use of one special kind of material, verbal signs and words. To think effectively in terms of relations of qualities is as severe a demand upon thought as to think in terms of symbols, verbal and mathematical. Indeed, since words are easily manipulated in mechanical ways, the production of a work of genuine art probably demands more intelligence than does most of the so-called thinking that goes on among those who pride themselves on being "intellectuals." . . .

Art denotes a process of doing or making. This is as true of fine as of technological art. Art involves molding of clay, chipping of marble, casting of bronze, laying on of pigments, construction of buildings, singing of songs, playing of instruments, enacting rôles on the stage, going through rhythmic movements in the dance. Every art does something with some physical material, the body or something outside the body, with or without the use of intervening tools, and with a view to production of something visible, audible, or tangible. So marked is the active or "doing" phase of art, that the dictionaries usually define it in terms of skilled action, ability in execution. The Oxford Dictionary illustrates by a quotation from John Stuart Mill: "Art is an endeavor after perfection in execution" while Matthew Arnold calls it "pure and flawless workmanship."

The word "esthetic" refers, as we have already noted, to experience as appreciative, perceiving, and enjoying. It denotes the consumer's rather than the producer's standpoint. It is Gusto, taste; and, as with cooking, overt skillful action is on the side of the cook who prepares, while taste is on the side of the consumer, as in gardening there is a distinction between the gardener who plants and tills and the householder who enjoys the finished product.

These very illustrations, however, as well as the relation that exists in having an experience between doing and undergoing, indicate that the distinction between esthetic and artistic cannot be pressed so far as to become a separation. Perfection in execution cannot be measured or defined in terms of execution; it implies those who perceive and enjoy the product that is executed. The cook prepares food for the consumer and the measure of the value of what is prepared is found in consumption. Mere perfection in execution, judged in its own terms in isolation, can probably be attained better by a machine than by human art. By itself, it is at most technique, and there are great artists who are not in the first ranks as technicians (witness Cézanne), just as there are great performers on the piano who are not great esthetically, and as Sargent is not a great painter.

Craftsmanship to be artistic in the final sense must be "loving"; it must care deeply for the subject matter upon which skill is exercised. A sculptor comes to mind whose busts are marvelously exact. It might be difficult to tell in the presence of a photograph of one of them and of a photograph of the original which was of the person himself. For virtuosity they are remarkable. But one doubts whether the maker of the busts had an experience of his own that he was concerned to have those share who look at his products. To be truly artistic, a work must also be esthetic—that is, framed for enjoyed receptive perception. Constant observation is, of course, necessary for the maker while he is producing. But if his perception is not also esthetic in nature, it is a colorless and cold recognition of what has been done, used as a stimulus to the next step in a process that is essentially mechanical.

In short, art, in its form, unites the very same relation of doing and undergoing, outgoing and incoming energy, that makes an experience to be an experience. Because of elimination of all that does not contribute to mutual organization of the factors of both action and reception into one another, and because of selection of just the aspects and traits that contribute to their interpenetration of each other, the product is a work of esthetic art. Man whittles, carves, sings, dances, gestures, molds, draws and paints. The doing or making is artistic when the perceived result is of such a nature that *its* qualities *as perceived* have controlled the question of production. The act of producing that is directed by intent to produce something that is enjoyed in the immediate experience of perceiving his qualities that a spontaneous or uncontrolled activity does not have. The artist embodies in himself the attitude of the perceiver while he works.

Suppose, for the sake of illustration, that a finely wrought object, one whose texture and proportions are highly pleasing in perception, has been believed to be a product of some primitive people. Then there is discovered evidence that proves it to be an accidental natural product. As an external thing, it is now precisely what it was before. Yet at once it ceases to be a work of art and becomes a natural "curiosity." It now belongs in a museum of natural history, not in a museum of art. And the extraordinary thing is that the difference that is thus made is not one of just intellectual classification. A difference is made in appre-

ciative perception and in a direct way. The esthetic experience—in its limited sense—is thus seen to be inherently connected with the experience of making.

The sensory satisfaction of eye and ear, when esthetic, is so because it does not stand by itself but is linked to the activity of which it is the consequence. Even the pleasures of the palate are different in quality to an epicure than in one who merely "likes" his food as he eats it. The difference is not of mere intensity. The epicure is conscious of much more than the taste of the food. Rather, there enter into the taste, as directly experienced, qualities that depend upon reference to its source and its manner of production in connection with criteria of excellence. As production must absorb into itself qualities of the product as perceived and be regulated by them, so, on the other side, seeing, hearing, tasting, become esthetic when relation to a distinct manner of activity qualifies what is perceived.

There is an element of passion in all esthetic perception. Yet when we are overwhelmed by passion, as in extreme rage, fear, jealousy, the experience is definitely non-esthetic. There is no relationship felt to the qualities of the activity that has generated the passion. Consequently, the material of the experience lacks elements of balance and proportion. For these can be present only when, as in the conduct that has grace or dignity, the act is controlled by an exquisite sense of the relations which the act sustains—its fitness to the occasion and to the situation.

The process of art in production is related to the esthetic in perception organically—as the Lord God in creation surveyed his work and found it good. Until the artist is satisfied in perception with what he is doing, he continues shaping and reshaping. The making comes to an end when its result is experienced as good—and that experience comes not by mere intellectual and outside judgment but in direct perception. An artist, in comparison with his fellows, is one who is not only especially gifted in powers of execution but in unusual sensitivity to the qualities of things. This sensitivity also directs his doing and makings.

As we manipulate, we touch and feel, as we look, we see; as we listen, we hear. The hand moves with etching needle or with brush. The eye attends and reports the consequence of what is done. Because of this intimate connection, subsequent doing is cumulative and not a matter of caprice nor yet of routine. In an emphatic artistic-esthetic experience, the relation is so close that it controls simultaneously both the doing and the perception. Such vital intimacy of connection cannot be had if only hand and eye are engaged. When they do not, both of them, act as organs of the whole being, there is but a mechanical sequence of sense and movement, as in walking that is automatic. Hand and eye, when the experience is esthetic, are but instruments through which the entire live creature, moved and active throughout, operates. Hence the expression is emotional and guided by purpose.

Because of the relation between what is done and what is undergone, there is an immediate sense of things in perception as belonging together or as jarring; as reeinforcing or as interfering. The consequences of the act of making as reported in sense show whether what is done carries forward the idea being executed or marks a deviation and break. In as far as the development of an experience is *controlled* through reference to these immediately felt relations of order and fulfillment, that experience becomes dominantly esthetic in nature. The urge to action becomes an urge to that kind of action which will result in an object satisfying in direct perception. The potter shapes his clay to make a bowl useful for holding grain; but he makes it in a way so regulated by the series of perceptions that sum up the serial acts of making, that the bowl is marked by enduring grace and charm. The general situation remains the same in painting a picture or molding a bust. Moreover, at each stage there is anticipation of what is to come. This anticipation is the connecting link between the next doing and its outcome for sense. What is done and what is undergone are thus reciprocally, cumulatively, and continuously instrumental to each other.

The doing may be energetic, and the undergoing may be acute and intense. But unless they are related to each other to form a whole in perception, the thing done is not fully esthetic. The making for example may be a display of technical virtuosity, and the undergoing a gush of sentiment or a revery. If the artist does not perfect a new vision in his process of doing, he acts mechanically and repeats some old model fixed like a blue print in his mind. An incredible amount of observation and of the kind of intelligence that is exercised in perception of qualitative relations characterizes creative work in art. The relations must be noted not only with respect to one another, two by two, but in connection with the whole under construction; they are exercised in imagination as well as in observation. Irrelevancies arise that are tempting distractions; digressions suggest themselves in the guise of enrichments. There are occasions when the grasp of the dominant idea grows faint, and then the artist is moved unconsciously to fill in until his thought grows strong again. The real work of an artist is to build up an experience that is coherent in perception while moving with constant change in its development.

When an author puts on paper ideas that are already clearly conceived and consistently ordered, the real work has been previously done. Or, he may depend upon the greater perceptibility induced by the activity and its sensible report to direct his completion of the work. The mere act of transcription is esthetically irrelevant save as it enters integrally into the formation of an experience moving to completeness. Even the composition conceived in the head and, therefore, physically private, is public in its significant content, since it is conceived with reference to execution in a product that is perceptible and hence belongs to the common world. Otherwise it would be an aberration or a passing dream. The urge to express through painting the perceived qualities of a landscape is continuous with demand for pencil or brush. Without external embodiment, an experience remains incomplete; physiologically and functionally, sense organs are motor organs and are connected, by means of distribution of energies in the human body and not merely anatomically, with other motor organs. It is no linguistic accident that "building," "construction," "work," designate both a process and its finished product. Without the meaning of the verb that of the noun remains blank.

Writer, composer of music, sculptor, or painter can retrace, during the process of production, what they have previously done. When it is not satisfactory in the undergoing or perceptual phase of experience, they can to some degree start afresh. This retracing is not readily accomplished in the case of architecture—which is perhaps one reason why there are so many ugly buildings. Architects are obliged to complete their idea before its translation into a complete object of perception takes place. Inability to build up simultaneously the idea and its objective embodiment imposes a handicap. Nevertheless, they too are obliged to think out their ideas in terms of the medium of embodiment and the object of ultimate perception unless they work mechanically and by rote. Probably the esthetic quality of medieval cathedrals is due in some measure to the fact that their constructions were not so much controlled by plans and specifications made in advance as is now the case. Plans grew as the building grew. But even a Minerva-like product, if it is artistic, presupposes a prior period of gestation in which doings and perceptions projected in imagination interact and mutually modify one another. Every work of art follows the plan of, and pattern of, a complete experience, rendering it more intensely and concentratedly felt.

It is not so easy in the case of the perceiver and appreciator to understand the intimate union of doing and undergoing as it is in the case of the maker. We are given to supposing that the former merely takes in what is there in finished form, instead of realizing that this taking in involves activities that are comparable to those of the creator. But receptivity is not passivity. It, too, is a process consisting of a series of responsive acts that accumulate toward objective fulfillment. Otherwise, there is not perception but recognition. The difference between the two is immense. Recognition is perception arrested before it has a chance to develop freely. In recognition there is a beginning of an act of perception. But this beginning is not allowed to serve the development of a full perception of the thing recognized. It is arrested at the point where it will serve some *other* purpose, as we recognize a man on the street in order to greet or to avoid him, not so as to see him for the sake of seeing what is there.

In recognition we fall back, as upon a stereotype, upon some previously formed scheme. Some detail or arrangement of details serves as cue for bare identification. It suffices in recognition to apply this bare outline as a stencil to the present object. Sometimes in contact with a human being we are struck with traits, perhaps of only physical characteristics, of which we were not previously aware. We realize that we never knew the person before; we had not seen him in any pregnant sense. We now begin to study and to "take in." Perception replaces bare recognition. There is an act of reconstructive doing, and consciousness becomes fresh and alive. *This* act of seeing involves the coöperation of motor elements even though they remain implicit and do not become overt, as well as coöperation of all funded ideas that may serve to complete the new picture that is forming. Recognition is too easy to arouse vivid consciousness. There is not enough resistance between new and old to secure consciousness of the experience that is had. Even a dog that barks and wags his tail joyously on seeing his

master return is more fully alive in his reception of his friend than is a human being who is content with mere recognition.

Bare recognition is satisfied when a proper tag or label is attached, "proper" signifying one that serves a purpose outside the act of recognition—as a salesman identifies wares by a sample. It involves no stir of the organism, no inner commotion. But an act of perception proceeds by waves that extend serially throughout the entire organism. There is, therefore, no such thing in perception as seeing or hearing *plus* emotion. The perceived object or scene is emotionally pervaded throughout. When an aroused emotion does not permeate the material that is perceived or thought of, it is either preliminary or pathological.

The esthetic or undergoing phase of experience is receptive. It involves surrender. But adequate yielding of the self is possible only through a controlled activity that may well be intense. In much of our intercourse with our surroundings we withdraw; sometimes from fear, if only of expending unduly our store of energy; sometimes from preoccupation with other matters, as in the case of recognition. Perception is an act of the going-out of energy in order to receive, not a withholding of energy. To steep ourselves in a subject-matter we have first to plunge into it. When we are only passive to a scene, it overwhelm us and, for lack of answering activity, we do not perceive that which bears us down. We must summon energy and pitch it at a responsive key in order to *take* in.

Every one knows that it requires apprenticeship to see through a microscope or telescope, and to see a landscape as the geologist sees it. The idea that esthetic perception is an affair for odd moments is one reason for the backwardness of the arts among us. The eye and the visual apparatus may be intact; the object may be physically there, the cathedral of Notre Dame, or Rembrandt's portrait of Hendrik Stoeffel. In some bald sense, the latter may be "seen." They may be looked at, possibly recognized, and have their correct names attached. But for lack of continuous interaction between the total organism and the objects, they are not perceived, certainly not esthetically. A crowd of visitors steered through a picture-gallery by a guide, with attention called here and there to some high point, does not perceive; only by accident is there even interest in seeing a picture for the sake of subject matter vividly realized.

For to perceive, a beholder must *create* his

own experience. And his creation must include relations comparable to those which the original producer underwent. They are not the same in any literal sense. But with the perceiver, as with the artist, there must be an ordering of the elements of the whole that is in form, although not in details, the same as the process of organization the creator of the work consciously experienced. Without an act of recreation the object is not perceived as a work of art. The artist selected, simplified, clarified, abridged and condensed according to his interest. The beholder must go through these operations according to his point of view and interest. In both, an act of abstraction, that is of extraction of what is significant, takes place. In both, there is comprehension in its literal signification—that is, a gathering together of details and particulars physically scattered into an experienced whole. There is work done on the part of the percipient as there is on the part of the artist. The one who is too lazy, idle, or indurated in convention to perform this work will not see or hear. His "appreciation" will be a mixture of scraps of learning with conformity to norms of conventional admiration and with a confused, even if genuine, emotional excitation.

The considerations that have been presented imply both the community and the unlikeness, because of specific emphasis, of *an* experience, in its pregnant sense, and esthetic experience. The former has esthetic quality; otherwise its materials would not be rounded out into a single coherent experience. It is not possible to divide in a vital experience the practical, emotional, and intellectual from one another and to set the properties of one over against the characteristics of the others. The emotional phase binds parts together into a single whole; "intellectual" simply names the fact that the experience has meaning; "practical" indicates that the organism is interacting with events and objects which surround it. The most elaborate philosophic or scientific inquiry and the most ambitious industrial or political enterprise has, when its different ingredients constitute an integral experience, esthetic quality. For then its varied parts are linked to one another, and do not merely succeed one another. And the parts through their experienced linkage move toward a consummation and close, not merely to cessation in time. This consummation, moreover, does not wait in consciousness for the whole undertaking to be finished. It is anticipated throughout and is recurrently savored with special intensity.

Nevertheless, the experiences in question are dominantly intellectual or practical, rather than *distinctively* esthetic, because of the interest and purpose that initiate and control them. In an intellectual experience, the conclusion has value on its own account. It can be extracted as a formula or as a "truth," and can be used in its independent entirety as factor and guide in other inquiries. In a work of art there is no such single self-sufficient deposit. The end, the terminus, is significant not by itself but as the integration of the parts. It has no other existence. A drama or novel is not the final sentence, even if the characters are disposed of as living happily ever after. In a distinctively esthetic experience, characteristics that are subdued in other experiences are dominant; those that are subordinate are controlling—namely, the characteristics in virtue of which the experience is an integrated complete experience on its own account.

In every integral experience there is form because there is dynamic organization. I call the organization dynamic because it takes time to complete it, because it is a growth. There is inception, development, fulfillment. Material is ingested and digested through interaction with that vital organization of the results of prior experience that constitutes the mind of the worker. Incubation goes on until what is conceived is brought forth and is rendered perceptible as part of the common world. An esthetic experience can be crowded into a moment only in the sense that a climax of prior long enduring processes may arrive in an outstanding movement which so sweeps everything else into it that all else is forgotten. That which distinguishes an experience as esthetic is conversion of resistance and tensions, of excitations that in themselves are temptations to diversion, into a movement toward an inclusive and fulfilling close.

Experiencing like breathing is a rhythm of intakings and outgivings. Their succession is punctuated and made a rhythm by the existence of intervals, periods in which one phase is ceasing and the other is inchoate and preparing. William James aptly compared the course of a conscious experience to the alternate flights and perchings of a bird. The flights and perchings are intimately connected with one another; they are not so many unrelated lightings succeeded by a number of equally unrelated hoppings. Each resting place in experience is an undergoing in which is absorbed and taken home the consequences of prior doing, and, unless the doing is that of utter caprice or sheer routine, each doing carries in itself meaning that has been extracted and conserved. As with the advance of an army, all gains from what has been already effected are periodically consolidated, and always with a view to what is to be done next. If we move too rapidly, we get away from the base of supplies—of accrued meanings—and the experience is flustered, thin, and confused. If we dawdle too long after having extracted a net value, experience perishes of inanition.

The *form* of the whole is therefore present in every member. Fulfilling, consummating, are continuous functions, not mere ends, located at one place only. An engraver, painter, or writer is in process of completing at every stage of his work. He must at each point retain and sum up what has gone before as a whole and with reference to a whole to come. Otherwise there is no consistency and no security in his successive acts. The series of doings in the rhythm of experience give variety and movement; they save the work from monotony and useless repetitions. The undergoings are the corresponding elements in the rhythm, and they supply unity; they save the work from the aimlessness of a mere succession of excitations. An object is peculiarly and dominantly esthetic, yielding the enjoyment characteristic of esthetic perception, when the factors that determine anything which can be called an experience are lifted high above the threshold of perception and are made manifest for their own sake.

Faith and Its Object

All religions, as I pointed out in the preceding chapter, involve specific intellectual beliefs, and they attach—some greater, some less—importance to assent to these doctrines as true, true in the intellectual sense. They have literatures held especially sacred, containing historical material with which the validity of the religions is connected. They have developed a doctrinal apparatus it is incumbent upon "believers" (with varying degrees of strictness in different religions) to accept. They also insist that there is some special and isolated channel of access to the truths they hold.

No one will deny, I suppose, that the present crisis in religion is intimately bound up with these claims. The skepticism and agnosticism that are rife and that from the standpoint of the religionist are fatal to the religious spirit are directly bound up with the intellectual contents, historical, cosmological, ethical, and theological, asserted to be indispensable in everything religious. There is no need for me here to go with any minuteness into the causes that have generated doubt and disbelief, uncertainty and rejection, as to these contents. It is enough to point out that all the beliefs and ideas in question, whether having to do with historical and literary matters, or with astronomy, geology and biology, or with the creation and structure of the world and man, are connected with the supernatural, and that this connection is the factor that has brought doubt upon them; the factor that from the standpoint of historic and institutional religions is sapping the religious life itself.

The obvious and simple facts of the case are that some views about the origin and constitution of the world and man, some views about the course of human history and personages and incidents in that history, have become so interwoven with religion as to be identified with it. On the other hand, the growth of knowledge and of its methods and tests has been such as to make acceptance of these beliefs increasingly onerous and even impossible for large numbers of cultivated men and women. With such persons, the result is that the more these ideas are used as the basis and justification of a religion, the more dubious that religion becomes. . .

The significant bearing for my purpose of all this is that new methods of inquiry and reflection have become for the educated man today the final arbiter of all questions of fact, existence, and intellectual assent. Nothing less than a revolution in the "seat of intellectual authority" has taken place. This revolution, rather than any particular aspect of its impact upon this and that religious belief, is the cen-

---

From "Faith and Its Object," in *A Common Faith* (New Haven: Yale University Press, 1934), pp. 29–35, 37–54, 56–57.

tral thing. In this revolution, every defeat is a stimulus to renewed inquiry; every victory won is the open door to more discoveries, and every discovery is a new seed planted in the soil of intelligence, from which grow fresh plants with new fruits. The mind of man is being habituated to a new method and ideal: There is but one sure road of access to truth— the road of patient, cooperative inquiry operating by means of observation, experiment, record and controlled reflection. . . .

The positive lesson is that religious qualities and values if they are real at all are not bound up with any single item of intellectual assent, not even that of the existence of the God of theism; and that, under existing conditions, the religious function in experience can be emancipated only through surrender of the whole notion of special truths that are religious by their own nature, together with the idea of peculiar avenues of access to such truths. For were we to admit that there is but one method for ascertaining fact and truth—that conveyed by the word "scientific" in its most general and generous sense—no discovery in any branch of knowledge and inquiry could then disturb the faith that is religious. I should describe this faith as the unification of the self through allegiance to inclusive ideal ends, which imagination presents to us and to which the human will responds as worthy of controlling our desires and choices.

It is probably impossible to imagine the amount of intellectual energy that has been diverted from normal processes of arriving at intellectual conclusions because it has gone into rationalization of the doctrines entertained by historic religions. The set that has thus been given the general mind is much more harmful, to my mind, than are the consequences of any one particular item of belief, serious as have been those flowing from acceptance of some of them. The modern liberal version of the intellectual content of Christianity seems to the modern mind to be more rational than some of the earlier doctrines that have been reated against. Such is not the case in fact. The theological philosophers of the Middle Ages had no greater difficulty in giving rational form to all the doctrines of the Roman church than has the liberal theologian of today in formulating and justifying intellectually the doctrines he entertains. This statement is as applicable to the doctrine of continuing miracles, penance, indulgences, saints and angels, etc., as to the trinity, incarnation, atonement, and the sacraments. The fundamental question, I repeat, is not of this and that article of intellectual belief but of intellectual habit, method and criterion.

One method of swerving aside the impact of changed knowledge and method upon the intellectual content of religion is the method of division of territory and jurisdiction into two parts. Formerly these were called the realm of nature and the realm of grace. They are now often known as those of revelation and natural knowledge. Modern religious liberalism has no definite names for them, save, perhaps, the division, referred to in the last chapter, between scientific and religious experience. The implication is that in one territory the supremacy of scientific knowledge must be acknowledged, while there is another region, not very precisely defined, of intimate personal experience wherein other methods and criteria hold sway.

This method of justifying the peculiar and legitimate claim of certain elements of belief is always open to the objection that a positive conclusion is drawn from a negative fact. Existing ignorance or backwardness is employed to assert the existence of a division in the nature of the subject-matter dealt with. Yet the gap may only reflect, at most, a limitation now existing but in the future to be done away with. The argument that because some province or aspect of experience has not yet been "invaded" by scientific methods, it is not subject to them, is as old as it is dangerous. Time and time again, in some particular reserved field, it has been invalidated. Psychology is still in its infancy. He is bold to the point of rashness who asserts that intimate personal experience will never come within the ken of natural knowledge.

It is more to the present point, however, to consider the region that is claimed by religionists as a special reserve. It is mystical experience. The difference, however, between mystic experience and the theory about it that is offered to us must be noted. The experience is a fact to be inquired into. The theory, like any theory, is an interpretation of the fact. The idea that by its very nature the experience is a veridical realization of the direct presence of God does not rest so much upon examination of the facts as it does upon importing into their interpretation a conception that is formed outside them. In its dependence upon a prior conception of the supernatural, which is the thing to be proved, it begs the question. . . .

There is no reason for denying the existence of experiences that are called mystical. On the contrary, there is every reason to suppose that, in some degree of intensity, they occur so frequently that they may be regarded as normal manifestations that take place at certain rhythmic points in the movement of experience. The assumption that denial of a particular interpretation of their objective content proves that those who make the denial do not have the experience in question, so that if they had it they would be equally persuaded of its objective source in the presence of God, has no foundation in fact. As with every empirical phenomenon, the occurrence of the state called mystical is simply an occasion for inquiry into its mode of causation. There is no more reason for converting the experience itself into an immediate knowledge of its cause than in the case of an experience of lightning or any other natural occurrence.

My purpose, then, in this brief reference to mysticism is not to throw doubt upon the existence of particular experiences called mystical. Nor is it to propound any theory to account for them. I have referred to the matter merely as an illustration of the general tendency to mark off two distinct realms in one of which science has jurisdiction, while in the other, special modes of immediate knowledge of religious objects have authority. This dualism as it operates in contemporary interpretation of mystic experience in order to validate certain beliefs is but a reinstatement of the old dualism between the natural and the supernatural, in terms better adapted to the cultural conditions of the present time. Since it is the conception of the supernatural that science calls in question, the circular nature of this type of reasoning is obvious.

Apologists for a religion often point to the shift that goes on in scientific ideas and materials as evidence of the unreliability of science as a mode of knowledge. They often seem peculiarly elated by the great, almost revolutionary, change in fundamental physical conceptions that has taken place in science during the present generation. Even if the alleged unreliability were as great as they assume (or even greater), the question would remain: Have we any other recourse for knowledge? But in fact they miss the point. Science is not constituted by any particular body of subject-matter. It is constituted by a method, a method of changing beliefs by means of tested inquiry as well as of arriving at them. It is its glory, not its condemnation, that its subject-matter develops as the method is improved. There is no special subject-matter of belief that is sacrosanct. The identification of science with a particular set of beliefs and ideas

is itself a hold-over of ancient and still current dogmatic habits of thought which are opposed to science in its actuality and which science is undermining.

For scientific method is adverse not only to dogma but to doctrine as well, provided we take "doctrine" in its usual meaning—a body of definite beliefs that need only to be taught and learned as true. This negative attitude of science to doctrine does not indicate indifference to truth. It signifies supreme loyalty to the method by which truth is attained. The scientific-religious conflict ultimately is a conflict between allegiance to this method and allegiance to even an irreducible minimum of belief so fixed in advance that it can never be modified.

The method of intelligence is open and public. The doctrinal method is limited and private. This limitation persists even when knowledge of the truth that is religious is said to be arrived at by a special mode of experience, that termed "religious." For the latter is assumed to be a very special kind of experience. To be sure it is asserted to be open to all who obey certain conditions. Yet the mystic experience yields, as we have seen, various results in the way of belief to different persons, depending upon the surrounding culture of those who undergo it. As a method, it lacks the public character belonging to the method of intelligence. Moreover, when the experience in question does not yield consciousness of the presence of God, in the sense that is alleged to exist, the retort is always at hand that it is not a genuine religious experience. For by definition, only that experience *is* religious which arrives at this particular result. The argument is circular. The traditional position is that some hardness or corruption of heart prevents one from having the experience. Liberal religionists are now more humane. But their logic does not differ.

It is sometimes held that beliefs about religious matters are symbolic, like rites and ceremonies. This view may be an advance upon that which holds to their literal objective validity. But as usually put forward it suffers from an ambiguity. Of what are the beliefs symbols? Are they symbols of things experienced in other modes than those set apart as religious, so that the things symbolized have an independent standing? Or are they symbols in the sense of standing for some transcendental reality—transcendental because not being the subject-matter of experience generally? Even the fundamentalist admits a certain quality and degree of symbolism in the latter sense in objects of religious belief. For he holds that the objects of these beliefs are so far beyond finite human capacity that our beliefs must be couched in more or less metaphorical terms. The conception that faith is the best available substitute for knowledge in our present estate still attaches to the notion of the symbolic character of the materials of faith; unless by ascribing to them a symbolic nature we mean that these materials stand for something that is verifiable in general and public experience.

Were we to adopt the latter point of view, it would be evident not only that the intellectual articles of a creed must be understood to be symbolic of moral and other ideal values, but the facts taken to be historic and used as concrete evidence of the intellectual articles are themselves symbolic. These articles of a creed present events and persons that have been made over by the idealizing imagination in the interest, at their best, of moral ideals. Historic personages in their divine attributes are materializations of the ends that enlist devotion and inspire endeavor. They are symbolic of the reality of ends moving us in many forms of experience. The ideal values that are thus symbolized also marked human experience in science and art and the various modes of human association: they mark almost everything in life that rises from the level of manipulation of conditions as they exist. It is admitted that the objects of religion are ideal in contrast with our present state. What would be lost if it were also admitted that they have authoritative claim upon conduct just because they are ideal? The assumption that these objects of religion exist already in some realm of Being seems to add nothing to their force, while it weakens their claim over us as ideals, in so far as it bases that claim upon matters that are intellectually dubious. The question narrows itself to this: Are the ideals that move us genuinely ideal or are they ideal only in contrast with our present estate?

The import of the question extends far. It determines the meaning given to the word "God." On one score, the word can mean only a particular Being. On the other score, it denotes the unity of all ideal ends arousing us to desire and actions. Does the unification have a claim upon our attitude and conduct because it is already, apart from us, in realized existence, or because of its own inherent meaning and value? Suppose for the moment that the word "God" means the ideal ends that at a given time and place one ac-

knowledges as having authority over his volition and emotion, the values to which one is supremely devoted, as far as these ends, through imagination, take on unity. If we make this supposition, the issue will stand out clearly in contrast with the doctrine of religions that "God" designates some kind of Being having prior and therefore non-ideal existence.

The word "non-ideal" is to be taken literally in regard to some religions that have historically existed, to all of them as far as they are neglectful of moral qualities in their divine beings. It does not apply in the same *literal* way to Judaism and Christianity. For they have asserted that the Supreme Being has moral and spiritual attributes. But it applies to them none the less in that these moral and spiritual characters are thought of as properties of a particular existence and are thought to be of religious value for us because of this embodiment in such an existence. Here, as far as I can see, is the ultimate issue as to the difference between a religion and the religious as a function of experience.

The idea that "God" represents a unification of ideal values that is essentially imaginative in origin when the imagination supervenes in conduct is attended with verbal difficulties owing to our frequent use of the word "imagination" to denote fantasy and doubtful reality. But the reality of ideal ends as ideals is vouched for by their undeniable power in action. An ideal is not at illusion because imagination is the organ through which it is apprehended. For *all* possibilities reach us through the imagination. In a definite sense the only meaning that can be assigned the term "imagination" is that things unrealized in fact come home to use and have power to stir us. The unification effected through imagination is not fanciful, for it is the reflex of the unification of practical and emotional attitudes. The unity signifies not a single Being, but the unity of loyalty and effort evoked by the fact that many ends are one in the power of their ideal, or imaginative, quality to stir and hold us.

We may well ask whether the power and significance in life of the traditional conceptions of God are not due to the ideal qualities referred to by them, the hypostatization of them into an existence being due to a conflux of tendencies in human nature that converts the object of desire into an antecedent reality (as was mentioned in the previous chapter) with beliefs that have prevailed in the cultures of the past. For in the older cultures the idea of the supernatural was "natural," in the sense in which "natural" signifies something customary and familiar. It seems more credible that religious persons have been supported and consoled by the reality with which ideal values appeal to them than that they have been upborne by sheer matter of fact existence. That, when once men are inured to the idea of the union of the ideal and the physical, the two should be so bound together in emotion that it is difficult to institute a separation, agrees with all we know of human psychology.

The benefits that will accrue, however, from making the separation are evident. The dislocation frees the religious values of experience once for all from matters that are continually becoming more dubious. With that release there comes emancipation from the necessity of resort to apologetics. The reality of ideal ends and values in their authority over us is an undoubted fact. The validity of justice, affection, and that intellectual correspondence of our ideas with realities that we call truth, is so assured in its hold upon humanity that it is unnecessary for the religious attitude to encumber itself with the apparatus of dogma and doctrine. Any other conception of the religious attitude, when it is adequately analyzed, means that those who hold it care more for force than for ideal values—since all that an Existence can add is force to establish, to punish, and to reward. There are, indeed, some persons who frankly say that their own faith does not require any guarantee that moral values are backed up by physical force, but who hold that the masses are so backward that ideal values will not affect their conduct unless in the popular belief these values have the sanction of a power that can enforce them and can execute justice upon those who fail to comply.

There are some persons, deserving of more respect, who say: "We agree that the beginning must be made with the primacy of the ideal. But why stop at this point? Why not search with the utmost eagerness and vigor for all the evidence we can find, such as is supplied by history, by presence of design in nature, which may lead on to the belief that the ideal is already extant in a Personality having objective existence?"

One answer to the question is that we are involved by this search in all the problems of the existence of evil that have haunted theology in the past and that the most ingenious apologists have not faced, much less met. If these apologists had not identified the existence of ideal goods with that of a Person supposed to originate and support them—a

Being, moreover, to whom omnipotent power is attributed—the problem of the occurrence of evil would be gratuitous. The significance of ideal ends and meanings is, indeed, closely connected with the fact that there are in life all sorts of things that are evil to us because we would have them otherwise. Were existing conditions wholly good, the notion of possibilities to be realized would never emerge.

But the more basic answer is that while if the search is conducted upon a strictly empirical basis there is no reason why it should not take place, as a matter of fact it is always undertaken in the interest of the supernatural. Thus it diverts attention and energy from ideal values and from the exploration of actual conditions by means of which they may be promoted. History is testimony to this fact. Men have never fully used the powers they possess to advance the good in life, because they have waited upon some power external to themselves and to nature to do the work they are responsible for doing. Dependence upon an external power is the counterpart of surrender of human endeavor. Nor is emphasis on exercising our own powers for good an egoistical or a sentimentally optimistic recourse. It is not the first, for it does not isolate man, either individually or collectively, from nature. It is not the second, because it makes no assumption beyond that of the need and responsibility for human endeavor, and beyond the conviction that, if human desire and endeavor were enlisted in behalf of natural ends, conditions would be bettered. It involves no expectation of a millennium of good.

Belief in the supernatural as a necessary power for apprehension of the ideal and for practical attachment to it has for its counterpart a pessimistic belief in the corruption and impotency of natural means. That is axiomatic in Christian dogma. But this apparent pessimism has a way of suddenly changing into an exaggerated optimism. For according to the terms of the doctrine, if the faith in the supernatural is of the required order, regeneration at once takes place. Goodness, in all essentials, is thereby established; if not, there is proof that the established relation to the supernatural has been vitiated. This romantic optimism is one cause for the excessive attention to individual salvation characteristic of traditional Christianity. Belief in a sudden and complete transmutation through conversion and in the objective efficacy of prayer, is too easy a way out of difficulties. It leaves matters in general just about as they were before; that is, sufficiently bad so that there is additional support for the idea that only supernatural aid can better them. The position of natural intelligence is that there exists a *mixture* of good and evil, and that reconstruction in the direction of the good which is indicated by ideal ends, must take place, if at all, through continued co-operative effort. There is at least enough impulse toward justice, kindliness, and order so that if it were mobilized for action, not expecting abrupt and complete transformation to occur, the disorder, cruelty, and oppression that exist would be reduced.

The discussion has arrived at a point where a more fundamental objection to the position I am taking needs consideration. The misunderstanding upon which this objection rests should be pointed out. The view I have advanced is sometimes treated as if the identification of the divine with ideal ends left the ideal wholly without roots in existence and without support from existence. The objection implies that my view commits one to such a separation of the ideal and the existent that the ideal has no chance to find lodgment even as a seed that might grow and bear fruit. On the contrary, what I have been criticizing is the *identification* of the ideal with a particular Being, especially when that identification makes necessary the conclusion that this Being is outside of nature, and what I have tried to show is that the ideal itself has its roots in natural conditions; it emerges when the imagination idealizes existence by laying hold of the possibilities offered to thought and action. There are values, goods, actually realized upon a natural basis—the goods of human association, of art and knowledge. The idealizing imagination seizes upon the most precious things found in the climacteric moments of experience and projects them. We need no external criterion and guarantee for their goodness. They are had, they exist as good, and out of them we frame our ideal ends.

Moreover, the ends that result from our projection of experienced goods into objects of thought, desire and effort exist, only they exist *as* ends. Ends, purposes, exercise determining power in human conduct. The aims of philanthropists, of Florence Nightingale, of Howard, of Wilberforce, of Peabody, have not been idle dreams. They have modified institutions. Aims, ideals, do not exist simply in "mind"; they exist in character, in personality and action. One might call the roll of artists, intellectual inquirers, parents, friends, citizens who are neighbors, to show that purposes exist in an *operative* way. What I have been objecting to, I repeat, is

not the idea that ideals are linked with existence and that they themselves exist, through human embodiment, as forces, but the idea that their authority and value depend upon some prior complete embodiment—as if the efforts of human beings in behalf of justice, or knowledge or beauty, depended for their effectiveness and validity upon assurance that there already existed in some supernal region a place where criminals are humanely treated, where there is no serfdom or slavery, where all facts and truths are already discovered and possessed, and all beauty is eternally displayed in actualized form.

The aims and ideals that move us are generated through imagination. But they are not made out of imaginary stuff. They are made out of the hard stuff of the world of physical and social experience. The locomotive did not exist before Stevenson, nor the telegraph before the time of Morse. But the conditions for their existence were there in physical material and energies and in human capacity. Imagination seized hold upon the idea of a rearrangement of existing things that would evolve new objects. The same thing is true of a painter, a musician, a poet, a philanthropist, a moral prophet. The new vision does not arise out of nothing, but emerges through seeing, in terms of possibilities, that is, of imagination, old things in new relations serving a new end which the new end aids in creating.

Moreover the process of creation is experimental and continuous. The artist, scientific man, or good citizen, depends upon what others have done before him and are doing around him. The sense of new values that become ends to be realized arises first in dim and uncertain form. As the values are dwelt upon and carried forward in action they grow in definiteness and coherence. Interaction between aim and existent conditions improves and tests the ideal; and conditions are at the same time modified. Ideals change as they are applied in existent conditions. The process endures and advances with the life of humanity. What one person and one group accomplish becomes the standing ground and starting point of those who succeed them. When the vital factors in this natural process are generally acknowledged in emotion, thought and action, the process will be both accelerated and purified through elimination of that irrelevant element that culminates in the idea of the supernatural. When the vital factors attain the religious force that has been drafted into supernatural religions, the resulting reinforcement will be incalculable.

These considerations may be applied to the idea of God, or, to avoid misleading conceptions, to the idea of the divine. This idea is, as I have said, one of ideal possibilities unified through imaginative realization and projection. But this idea of God, or of the divine, is also connected with all the natural forces and conditions—including man and human association—that promote the growth of the ideal and that further its realization. We are in the presence neither of ideals completely embodied in existence nor yet of ideals that are mere rootless ideals, fantasies, utopias. For there are forces in nature and society that generate and support the ideals. They are further unified by the action that gives them coherence and solidity. It is this *active* relation between ideal and actual to which I would give the name "God." I would not insist that the name *must* be given. There are those who hold that the associations of the term with the supernatural are so numerous and close that any use of the word "God" is sure to give rise to misconception and be taken as a concession to traditional ideas.

They may be correct in this view. But the facts to which I have referred are there, and they need to be brought out with all possible clearness and force. There exist concretely and experimentally goods—the values of art in all its forms, of knowledge, of effort and of rest after striving, of education and fellowship, of friendship and love, of growth in mind and body. These goods are there and yet they are relatively embryonic. Many persons are shut out from generous participation in them; there are forces at work that threaten and sap existent goods as well as prevent their expansion. A clear and intense conception of a union of ideal ends with actual conditions is capable of arousing steady emotion. It may be fed by every experience, no matter what its material.

In a distracted age, the need for such an idea is urgent. It can unify interests and energies now dispersed; it can direct action and generate the heat of emotion and the light of intelligence. Whether one gives the name "God" to this union, operative in thought and action, is a matter for individual decision. But the *function* of such a working union of the ideal and actual seems to me to be identical with the force that has in fact been attached to the conception of God in all the religions that have a spiritual content; and a clear idea of that function seems to me urgently needed at the present time.

The sense of this union may, with some persons, be furthered by mystical experiences, using the term "mystical" in its broadest sense. That result depends largely upon temperament. But there is a marked difference between the union associated with mysticism and the union which I had in mind. There is nothing mystical about the latter; it is natural and moral. Nor is there anything mystical about the perception or consciousness of such union. Imagination of ideal ends pertinent to actual conditions represents the fruition of a disciplined mind. There is, indeed, even danger that resort to mystical experiences will be an escape, and that its result will be the passive feeling that the union of actual and ideal is already accomplished. But in fact this union is active and practical; it is a *uniting,* not something given.

One reason why personally I think it fitting to use the word "God" to denote that uniting of the ideal and actual which has been spoken of, lies in the fact that aggressive atheism seems to me to have something in common with traditional supernaturalism. I do not mean merely that the former is mainly so negative that it fails to give positive direction to thought, though that fact is pertinent. What I have in mind especially is the exclusive preoccupation of both militant atheism and supernaturalism with man in isolation. For in spite of supernaturalism's reference to something beyond nature, it conceives of this earth as the moral center of the universe and of man as the apex of the whole scheme of things. It regards the drama of sin and redemption enacted within the isolated and lonely soul of man as the one thing of ultimate importance. Apart from man, nature is held either accursed or negligible. Militant atheism is also affected by lack of natural piety. The ties binding man to nature that poets have always celebrated are passed over lightly. The attitude taken is often that of man living in an indifferent and hostile world and issuing blasts of defiance. A religious attitude, however, needs the sense of a connection of man, in the way of both dependence and support, with the enveloping world that the imagination feels is a universe. Use of the words "God" or "divine" to convey the union of actual with ideal may protect man from a sense of isolation and from consequent despair or defiance.

In any case, whatever the name, the meaning is selective. For it involves no miscellaneous worship of everything in general. It selects those factors in existence that generate and support our idea of good as an end to be striven for. It excludes a multitude of forces that at any given time are irrelevant to this function. Nature produces whatever gives reinforcement and direction but also what occasions discord and confusion. The "divine" is thus a term of human choice and aspiration. A humanistic religion, if it excludes our relation to nature, is pale and thin, as it is presumptuous, when it takes humanity as an object of worship. . . .

For, I would remind readers in conclusion, it is the intellectual side of the religious attitude that I have been considering. I have suggested that the religious element in life has been hampered by conceptions of the supernatural that were imbedded in those cultures wherein man had little control over outer nature and little in the way of sure method of inquiry and test. The crisis today as to the intellectual content of religious belief has been caused by the change in the intellectual climate due to the increase of our knowledge and our means of understanding. I have tried to show that this change is not fatal to the religious values in our common experience, however adverse its impact may be upon historic religions. Rather, provided that the methods and results of intelligence at work are frankly adopted, the change is liberating.

It clarifies our ideals, rendering them less subject to illusion and fantasy. It relieves us of the incubus of thinking of them as fixed, as without power of growth. It discloses that they develop in coherence and pertinency with increase of natural intelligence. The change gives aspiration for natural knowledge a definitely religious character, since growth in understanding of nature is seen to be organically related to the formation of ideal ends. The same change enables man to select those elements in natural conditions that may be organized to support and extend the sway of ideals. All purpose is selective, and all intelligent action includes deliberate choice. In the degree in which we cease to depend upon belief in the supernatural, selection is enlightened and choice can be made in behalf of ideals whose inherent relations to conditions and consequences are understood. Were the naturalistic foundations and bearings of religion grasped, the religious element in life would emerge from the throes of the crisis in religion. Religion would then be found to have its natural place in every aspect of human experience that is concerned with estimate of possibilities, with emotional stir by possibilities as yet unrealized, and with all action in behalf of their realization. All that is significant in human experience falls within this frame.

Suggestions for Further Reading

Works by Dewey

John Dewey: The Early Works, 1882–1898. 5 Vols. Edited by Jo Ann Boydston. Carbondale and Edwardsville: Southern Illinois University Press, 1969–1972.

John Dewey: The Middle Works, 1899–1924. 15 Vols. Edited by Jo Ann Boydston. Carbondale and Edwardsville: Southern Illinois University Press, 1976–1983.

John Dewey: The Later Works, 1925–1953. 10 (of 16 projected) Vols. Edited by Jo Ann Boydston. Carbondale and Edwardsville: Southern Illinois University Press, 1981–.

In addition to the above definitive edition of Dewey's complete writings, other editions of a few of his books are still in print—e.g., *A Common Faith, Art as Experience, Democracy and Education, Experience and Nature, The Public and its Problems,* and *The Quest for Certainty.*

Anthologies

Intelligence in the Modern World. Edited, with an Introduction, by Joseph Ratner. New York: Random House, 1939.

The Philosophy of John Dewey. Edited, with an Introduction and Commentary, by John J. McDermott. Chicago: The University of Chicago Press, 1981.

Essential Works on Dewey

Richard J. Bernstein. *John Dewey.* New York: Washington Square Press, 1967. (Reprinted, Reseda, Calif.: Ridgeview, 1981.)

Jo Ann Boydston and Kathleen Poulos, editors. *Checklist of Writings About John Dewey.* Carbondale and
     Edwardsville: Southern Illinois University Press, 1978. (Also see Boydston's *Guide to the Works of John
     Dewey.* Carbondale and Edwardsville: Southern Illinois University Press, 1970.)
James Campbell. *Pragmatism and Reform: Social Reconstruction in the Thought of John Dewey and George
     Herbert Mead.* Ann Arbor: University Microfilms International, 1979.
George Dicker. *Dewey's Theory of Knowledge.* Philadelphia: Philosophical Monographs, 1976.
George Dykhuizen. *The Life and Mind of John Dewey.* Carbondale and Edwardsville: Southern Illinois
     University Press, 1973.
James Gouinlock. *John Dewey's Philosophy of Value.* New York: Humanities Press, 1972.
Arthur S. Lothstein. *From Privacy to Praxis: The Case for John Dewey as a Radical Social Philosopher.* Ann
     Arbor: University Microfilms International, 1980.
Paul A. Schilpp, editor. *The Philosophy of John Dewey.* LaSalle, Ill.: Open Court, 1939.
Ralph Sleeper. *The Necessity of Pragmatism: John Dewey's Conception of Philosophy.* New Haven: Yale
     University Press, 1986.
John J. Stuhr. *Experience as Activity: Dewey's Metaphysics.* Ann Arbor: University Microfilms International,
     1976.

GEORGE HERBERT MEAD

Introduction by David L. Miller

George Herbert Mead was born in South Hadley, Massachusetts, in 1863 and died in Chicago, Illinois, in 1931. Some of his most influential colleagues at the University of Michigan (1891–1894) were John Dewey, Alfred Lloyd, and Charles H. Cooley, and at the University of Chicago (1894–1931), John Dewey, James Hayden Tufts, Edward Scribner Ames, James Rowland Angell, C. Judson Herrick, Albert A. Michaelson, and W. I. Thomas. In Germany, during his graduate studies (1890–1891), he was infuenced mainly by Wilhelm Wundt, from whom he learned much about the function of gestures. While in Germany, he also studied with Friedrich Paulson, Hermann Ebbinghaus, and Wilhelm Dilthey, who had a direct influence on Mead's social theory of the self. There were three other factors of a general nature that influenced Mead and constituted for him the chief-perspective that conditioned all of his thinking, namely, Darwinian evolution, the scientific method, and the theory of democracy.

In the following I hope to indicate Mead's most salient ideas and bring out what I believe are their significant implications. These are not limited to social psychology. They include also epistemology, philosophy of science, individual creativity, the freedom of the individual, and the chief function of reflective intelligence.

MEAD'S MOST SIGNIFICANT INSIGHT

Mead's most important insight can be stated briefly, as follows: if an organism, by its gesture, calls out in itself the same response that it evokes in another participant in the social process, then that gesture is a significant symbol—which is to say, that gesture is a linguistic gesture and its meaning is shared by both the one who makes it and by the other, to whom it is addressed. The implications of this insight are momentous, but first let us understand precisely what it means to evoke in oneself, by one's gesture, the same response that one evokes in another.

If we consider the gestures of lower animals, we see that the growl of a dog A, say, may evoke the response of running away by another dog, B. We can ask, What does the growl by A mean to B? The answer, it means running away. In brief, the meaning of the growl, the stimulus, is the response it evokes in the other. Here we see that it would not make sense to say A evokes in itself the same response that it evokes in B; A does not run away. Also, the response by B is an overt observable response. But, as we will see, in the case of a linguistic gesture it evokes the *same* response in the one who makes it and in the other, and we must clarify the meaning of "the same response."

If A says to B, "Close the door," and if B does so, A does not make the same overt response as does B. B's overt response is made by B, not by A. A cannot possibly do what B does. No one can possibly perform overtly the role performed by another. Why did Mead say, then, that by a linguistic gesture (significant symbol) A can evoke in himself the *same* response that he evokes in B? The answer is that these are not overt responses; they are covert responses. This kind of response gives us the *form* of the overt response. It is a mental response, it is a concept, or, as some would say, it is an idea. The concept or form of an overt act is a universal; it is also social in that it is shared by all who understand it, and it is the meaning of the linguistic gesture. Thus, when A evokes in himself and *same* response that he evokes in B, A and B have the same concept, the same meaning. There is only one concept and it is shared by both. The response by A and B are functionally identical.[1]

As stated above, a concept is a universal. In Peirce's terms, it comes under the category of Thirdness; it is analogous to habit, law, and, since it is the form of an overt response, it has in it the temporal element; and this makes Mead a process philosopher. (This will be discussed later.)

MINDS AND SELVES

Mead is the first to give us a clear conception of the linguistic gesture and, consequently, an unambiguous definition of language. Lower animals may communicate with each other by use of gestures, but they do not use significant symbols (linguistic gestures); consequently, they do not have a language.[2] Rather, an animal, A, may make a gesture that is sensed by another animal, B, and this gesture may evoke a direct response from B, but neither A nor B has a concept. They do not have (in mind) the general form of the response made by B. A does not anticipate the response made by B, just as a worker bee does not anticipate the response its "dance" will evoke in other bees that sense it, nor does the dancing bee intend anything by its gesture. Briefly, lower animals respond immediately and directly to gestures without the intervention of concepts (meanings) between the stimulus (gesture) and the response evoked by it. The mental process, or what might well be called symbolic interaction or the symbolic process, occurs between the linguistic gesture (the stimulus) and the overt response evoked by it. Accordingly, the person who makes a linguistic gesture and the one to whom it is addressed and who understands it both share the meaning of the gesture prior to the overt response that one intends to evoke by it. Hence, in contrast with the responses to gestures made by lower animals, responses evoked by linguistic gestures are not direct, but indirect. They are responses evoked by the meaning of the gesture, by concepts. Inasmuch as the symbolic process lies between the linguistic gesture and the final overt response evoked by it, there is room for choice, evaluation, and freedom. If lower animals can be said to have freedom, it is not the kind of freedom made possible by linguistic gestures.

Without linguistic gestures (significant symbols) there can be no shared meanings, and shared meanings are an essential component of every mind. They constitute the social component of mind. Lower animals have intelligence, that is, they can learn and they form habits, but they do not have minds as the term is used by Mead. They cannot bring the form (the concept) of a habit to the level of awareness or consciousness. The social component of mind is what Mead calls the perspective of the community or the voice of the community, sometimes called the generalized other. Before a child can have a private perspective and a mind, it must first have the perspective of the community. It is a "we" before it is an "I." It does not differentiate clearly between itself and the other, the group. At first it does not address itself as "I" but rather as "John" or as "baby." As W. I. Thomas explains in "The Definition of the Situation,"[3] many of the responses to objects and situations made by children are prescribed or stipulated by their parents and by others around them. It is when the child realizes that its desires, inclinations, and actual responses to a situation are contrary to those prescribed by others, that is, contrary to the attitude of members of the significant other, that it becomes aware of itself. At that time the self emerges, and the child then has both an "I" and a "me." The "me" component includes one's habits and ways of responding to situations, as well as one's ways of thinking about situations, that are shared with other members of the group. Also included in the "me" are one's skills and everything that has been incorporated into the self that can be brought to bear on the solution of problems that one might encounter. The "I" is the evaluator, the appraiser, the decider, the initiator of action, and the actor or role performer. The "I" distinguishes every individual from every other member of the group. Also included in the "I" is that indefinable something called personality as well as "a private perspective" that is the result of the creative capacity of the individual.

When the individual can respond to his own gesture and his own behavior from the perspective of the other, that response includes an awareness of one's self, and one is, ipso facto, self-conscious. At this juncture one has a self and at the same time one has developed the capacity to reflect intelligently, that is, to use a significant symbols or linguistic gestures. One's mind consists of a process, a symbolic process, whereby one reflects back on oneself (on one's actual or proposed conduct) from the standpoint of the other, usually the generalized other.

ROLE TAKING AND REFLECTIVE INTELLIGENCE

Reflective intelligence is a dialectic process. It is a conversation between the "I" and the "me," the "I" and the "other," by means of linguistic gestures. This dialectic process arises when there is a conflict between the community perspective and the private perspective of the individual. When the individual is confronted with a situation that cannot be satisfactorily responded to in a customary or traditional manner, that is, by the contents of the "me," then the individual, through the creative capacity of the "I," may propose a new kind of response to the situation. This amounts to a new (private) perspective in that it offers a new interpretation with a corresponding new response as a solution to the problem at hand.

This private perspective can exist only in relation to the old public perspective, the perspective of the generalized other, which is also contained in the "me" of the creative individual who proposes a new way of responding. Symbolic interaction, the dialectic process, is an attempt to reconcile a private perspective with the major part of the public perspective or with the generalized other. When a reconciliation has been made, the private perspective, the new idea created by the "I," is incorporated into the public perspective and the generalized other has been modified. It has been enriched, and a part of it may have been deleted.

Here we see that Mead does not draw a rigid line between the individual and other members of his community. A new idea had by an individual does, for a time, belong to that individual alone, and it is part of his biography. But if it is accepted by the group, it is no longer private or subjective. It is then incorporated into the public perspective and is objective. No normal individual is content to believe that he alone has an idea that is not acceptable to any other person. No matter the extent to which a person may at first, because of his idea, be isolated and even ridiculed, he always wants to gain respect in a community, even if he has to form a new community. If we make clear Mead's understanding of how new ideas, had by so-called dissidents, are essential to the solution of problems that confront us when we encounter new situations, we will be much more tolerant of dissident voices. We will see, also, what is meant by individualism. It does not entail, as some have said, antisociality. Nor does it mean isolationism, as if a person, to be a "true individual," must segregate himself from the group and be content with his own purely private perspective. Finally, an understanding of Mead's theory of the functional relationship between the individual and society, between a private perspective and the public perspective (the generalized other), will enable us to see that Mead conceived of democracy, the theory of evolution and emergence, and the experimental method in science as all having the same general pattern in their operation. Each is a process, and each proceeds from a conflict leading to the dialectic process by which conflicts are resolved because of a reconciliation between (1) a new idea (had by an individual) and the group (2) a mutation and the species, (3) a new hypothesis by a scientist and the relatively stable body of scientific knowledge accepted by the scientific community. In each, particular individuals are the source of changes resulting in the resolution of conflicts.

THE PLACE OF THE INDIVIDUAL IN SCIENCE, DEMOCRACY, AND EVOLUTION

For Mead the locus of worth and dignity is in individuals, not in the species, nor is it in a transcendent community or in institutions. That is to say, the social component of the self, the "me," is servant to the "I." Ends and values are within the "I," and the means of achievement is the "me." Institutions and laws exist for the sake of individuals. Furthermore, the source of creativity and of all advancements made in solving our social and scientific problems is particular individuals freely expressing newly proposed hypotheses for the solution of problems of concern to their various communities. Mead is not a social determinist. In deliberating, the individual uses the voice of the community, the generalized other. It conditions one's deliberation and gives one a sound basis for reflective intelligence, but deliberation is a conversation between the "I" and the generalized other due to a conflict in attitudes within the self. When an individual experiences a phenomenon or has an idea that does not seem to fit traditional responses, this is a conflict between the "I" and the "me." A resolution of the conflict is achieved through the dialectic process, through a conversation of the "I" and the "me." This resolution is a reconciliation of the new idea with the generalized other, but it requires a modification of the generalized other in some respect. The entire generalized other cannot be completely changed all at once. Rather, there must be change with continuity between a present new idea and the great historical body of knowledge. Mead's account of the functional relationship between the "I" and the "me," the "I" and the other, lays the basis for a clear understanding of the meaning of human freedom.

In traditional societies and, for the most part, in totalitarian societies, as in dogmatic religious sects, it is assumed that the ways of living and making a living are relatively fixed and that the function of governing officials is to administer. Such societies are relatively closed societies, making no room in their theory of government for major changes. If major changes are made, they are made through revolution or dissension, resulting quite often in substituting one rigid constitution or dogmatic creed for another. In such cases, there is disruption and the absence of the kind of continuity found in the democratic process of the solution of political and social problems. In a democracy the form of revolution has been changed from brute force and war to discussion, conversation, and arbitration. Thus, peaceful change, leading to social adjustments, has been institutionalized and provided for in constitutions themselves. Mead says, "We may fairly say that . . . we find in representative government and growing democracy, revolutions incorporated in the institution of government itself."[4] Again, Mead says:

> Wherein lies the creative activity of the reconstructive activity of an individual in a democratic society? The individual cannot oppose himself to the whole social order and attempt to set up his own will. Wherein, then, lies the reconstructiveness? It lies, first of all in the statement of the problem. . . . The step which can be taken under these circumstances is some project which can meet that particular problem. . . . The individual puts his program in universal form. The thing he presents is essentially a social affair which arises through his thinking, his idea. I think there is a complete parallel between the social situation and that of the scientist. The scientist has his own hypothesis, and the question is, Is it the one on which the community as a whole can act or work? The individual is trying to restate his community in such a way that what he does can be a natural function in the community.[5]

> . . . this relation between the individual and the world which may arise through the realization of his idea is the basis of the most profound distinction between the ancient world and the modern.[6]

In Mead's class lectures and elsewhere he emphasized that one of the most important consequences of the Renaissance was the recognition of the place of the individual in experimental science and in democracy. New kinds of experiences that are exceptional to accepted laws and theories constitute the basis for reconstructions in all areas. These experiences are had first by particular individuals, and they constitute the data of science. Mead would agree with Popper and others that one duty of the scientist is to try to falsify existing accepted beliefs and generalized statements about the world of fact.

As is well known, the individualism of the Renaissance led, in some instances, to the extreme position of subjective idealism and solipsism and was interpreted by some as antisocial. However, Mead's social-behavioristic theory of self and mind explains fully that neither could exist apart from the social component, the "me" or the generalized other, which is in fact a constituent part of self and mind. A person is not all "I," not all subjective, and one cannot have an "I" without the "me." It is the functional relation between the "I" and the "me," the self and society, the individual and the other, that Mead wants to explain, as progress is made in science and in the solution of social problems. For Mead it is impossible for individualism to be antisocial, as solipsism and a private language are impossible; but in every instance of the expression of individualism the "me" is servant to the "I," as stated above. This means that in reflective intelligence the "I" uses the "me," the generalized other, as a means for advances in the solution of problems that concern the community. We use old habits as a means of getting rid of undesirable ones and establishing new ones, even as "Rousseau had to find both sovereign and subject in the citizen, and Kant had to find both the giver of the moral law and the subject of the law in the rational being."[7]

For Mead, evolution, emergence of the novel, the democratic process, and the application of the scientific method are all processes of adjustment in which the individual has a central role. The individual is the mediator between the old and the new, the old system with reference to which a new kind of experience is an exception and the new system after adjustment is made and after there is a reconciliation between the exceptional experience and a new hypothesis that accounts for it. Again, in reflective intelligence, the dialectic process, carried on by individuals, lies between a statement of the problem and its solution, which is a new adjustment. Mead subsumes each of these different kinds of adjustment under the general name, "the principle of sociality."

> When the new form has established its citizenship the botanist can exhibit the mutual adjustments that have taken place. . . . but to identify sociality with the result is to identify it with system merely. It is rather the stage betwixt and between the old system and the new that I am referring to. If emergence is a feature of reality, this phase of adjustment, which comes between the ordered universe before the emergent has arisen and after it has come to terms with the newcomer, must be a feature also of reality.[8]

Finally:

> I wish to emphasize the fact that the appearance of mind is only the culmination of that sociality which is found throughout the universe, its culmination lying in the fact that the organism, by occupying the attitudes of others, can occupy its own attitude in the role of the other.[9]

INDIVIDUAL FREEDOM

The use of linguistic gestures enables humans to break out of a present, to anticipate future events, to have a calendar by which they can distinguish clearly between past, present, and future. Lower animals without a language live only in a sensuous present; they have no calendar and cannot bring the concept of things to the level of consciousness. Nor can they indicate to *themselves* things that are absent. Having no calendar, they cannot remember in the sense in which humans remember. Having no significant symbols, they have no concepts.

Breaking out of the present requires the symbolic process, that symbolic interaction by means of which the individual can internalize the social process of adjustment. By this means, the individual can evaluate, plan, and choose; and therein lies human freedom. Individual freedom means, first of all, allowing concepts of ends (to be reached later) to control one's behavior in attaining those ends.

The symbolic process is a phase of adjustment lying between the problem at hand and its solution or between doubt and a satisfactory resolution of doubt when a planned overt act is satisfactorily completed. And although neither the symbolic process nor mind is reducible to overt action, it is related to it, and is carried on only by individuals. Symbolic interaction, the symbolic process, is a conversation between the "I" and the other. Without the use of the attitude of the community, the "I" could not function, and this is why the "me" is servant to the "I." In reflective intelligence, the "I" is responding to the responses of the "me" and to its own later responses.[10]

MEAD AND PROCESS PHILOSOPHY

All process philosophers hold that it takes time for any actual entity to be. William James says, "What really *exists* is not things made but things in the making."[11] The real is process. Mead says, "The act is the unit of existence." And whenever there is action, something is interacting with something else. This is Peirce's *Secondness,* interaction. Also, entities interact with each other in a lawful way, just as hydrogen and oxygen interact in a specifiable, lawful manner. This is Peirce's *Thirdness,* habit, rule, law, the universal way in which entities interact.[12]

Here I want to make explicit what I believe is implicit in the pragmatic tradition but what has not been sufficiently clarified, namely, that the locus of universality (similarity, form, the universal) is in the process. Universals do not, as Plato held, have an ontological status apart from existing particulars, nor do they consist of some common static property that resides in separate individuals.[13] We find universals in Thirdness, in habit and law. Two or more things can be said to be similar, or to belong to the same class, if they function in the same manner—that is, if, in their behavior, they conform to the same law, but not because there is a common property that resides in each. Two similar entities are existentially different but functionally identical if, in interaction, they function alike. (We are not required here to define functional identity, since it resides in Thirdness, which is a category.) 'Habit' and 'law' themselves imply a possible repetition of instances of the "same" kind, instances that conform to the law.

All pragmatists are concerned with habits in conjunction with learning and behavior, and with the results of reflective intelligence. Peirce, James, and Mead hold that thinking, if successful, leads finally to the formation of habits, and that by reflective intelligence individuals can condition themselves to respond in a rulelike manner, resulting in habit. James (and Peirce) held that "The laws of nature are nothing but the immutable habits which the different elementary sorts of matter follow in their actions and reactions on each other."[14] James commends Hume for his treatment of habit in connection with the association of ideas.

It is interesting to note that Hume denied that there are abstract general ideas (following Berkeley). Hume argued that we think in terms of particular ideas only, and by custom, habit, or the association of ideas, one particular leads us to think of another that is similar. Thus, in effect, for Hume, the association of ideas and habit functions as did universals for rationalists and realists. Had Hume been a process philosopher he might have located universals in habit, in law, in Peirce's *Thirdness*, where, it seems to me, it properly belongs—though no pragmatist nor other process philosopher has explicitly stated this view. This means that universality is in the process itself.

When particulars have meaning for us, it is in terms of the lawful way in which they interact with other things. The meaning an object has for us is the way in which we interact with it and it interacts with other things, and meanings are always stated in universal terms. Mead defines meanings in terms of reactions. The meaning of a gesture, for example, is the response it evokes; and the meaning of a significant gesture is a universal response, evoked by all who understand its meaning, or by a habitual response shared by the group.

James says we know objects in terms of our habitual responses to them, and Piaget believes resemblance in objects is due to the identity of our reactions to these objects. Mead says: "When we feel that we have adjusted ourselves to a comprehensive set of reactions toward an object, we feel that the meaning of the object is ours."[15] Also: "The response becomes a meaning, when it is indicated by the general [universal] attitude both to the self and to others."[16] By "meaning," Mead means a conceptual understanding of an object. We have an understanding of objects in terms of concepts that are communicable from the self to the other, by use of significant symbols. Concepts are general, universal, sharable. They are implicit responses to one's later possible overt responses. In this sense they are inhibited responses of which one is aware. Thus, the locus of meaning is in universal, sharable responses, and they are constitutive of the social component of individual minds.

Accordingly, we think of and understand all events, objects, and phenomena in terms of concepts of the habitual, rulelike, or lawful manner in which they interact with each other—in terms of Peirce's Thirdness. Berkeley and Hume were correct in claiming that we cannot have abstract general ideas, that is, we cannot have an idea or a conception of a triangle that is at once obtuse, acute, right angular, etc., and yet none of these. But we can have a conception that each of these particular triangles will fit or answer to, namely a plane figure enclosed by three straight lines. In this sense all triangles are functionally identical. Just so, we can have a conception of the law of gravitational attraction to which all particular bodies conform. Also, just as we have a conception of laws, so we can have a conception of, say, the habit of smoking cigarettes to which each particular instance of smoking conforms. I am defending the view that we understand particular objects, events, transactions in terms of the universal, even as did Plato and Aristotle, but the universal is the lawful manner in which particulars interact, in Thirdness. It is that of which we can have a conception. A particular as such, without relation to other particulars, has no meaning to anyone, and universals cannot reside in them, that is, in Firstness. Thus, pragmatists are not realists in the traditional sense of the word, nor of course are they nominalists or conceptualists. They are process philosophers, and this requires that universals be the uniform manner in which particulars of a class transact. Peirce is often called a realist, and so he was, but not in the traditional sense. He held, rather, that anyone who accepts Thirdness is a realist, anyone who denies it is not.

We should not be misled into believing that we know that particulars belong to the same class before we know the lawful manner in which they interact with other particulars. The fact is, we locate two or more particulars in the same class *because* they function in the same way. This is why they can be said to be identical in some respect. They are not existentially identical, nor is there an identical property that each possesses. They are functionally identical. If two or more particulars function in the same way (Thirdness), they can be said to be similar in that respect, and, therefore, they belong to the same class. Had Hume been a process philosopher, he might well have defined similarity in this manner, and the problems of both traditional realism and nominalism, as well as abstract general ideas, would have disappeared. (This, of course, would have been impossible without Hume's granting that there are interactions and transactions between and among things. This was contrary to his theory of causal relations.)

But, someone may ask, what about the color red—can we define it in terms of how it interacts? From a purely physical point of view, it is clear that we can—in terms of how light interacts with physical objects upon which it impinges and from which it is reflected, that is, in terms of the length of light waves. From a psychological point of view, we can define it in terms of our *response* to it. In animal psychology, we determine whether an animal can distinguish between, say, red and yellow in terms of their responses. Recall that Mead said that the meaning of a stimulus is the response it evokes.

Some philosophers and psychologists have asked, When two people, x and y, upon looking at an object, both say it is red, how can we possibly know that their visual experience is the same? (What x calls red, y might call yellow if he had the same sensation.) Put in this form the question is unanswerable and meaningless. But if x asks y to bring him a red ball, and y does so, then the meaning of their sense experiences is the same and functionally identical. Our common world is not in our individual sense perceptions, but in the meanings they have for us, and this is determined in terms of reactions and responses in Thirdness. We cannot communicate sensations, pains, or pleasures from one person to another, but we can and do communicate meanings. Mead contends that neither meanings nor minds can be separated from behavior.

Apparently all philosophers, epistemologists, and scientists since the time of Socrates,

Plato, and Aristotle hold that we know particulars in terms of universals. And, thus, when we know the universal that can be predicated of a particular, we know its "essence," and consequently we know the *what* a particular is. So far pragmatists, although they are process philosophers, will agree. But a basic difference between the ancient philosophers, who were substance philosophers, and the pragmatists concerns both the locus of the universal and its nature. For the ancients, say, Plato and Aristotle, the universal or the essence of particulars is (1) static, immutable, nontemporal and (2) after Aristotle its locus is in particulars in isolation from other particulars or apart from all relations to other particulars.

As a pragmatist, I am defending the claim that the locus of universals is in Thirdness, law, habit. And since we know in terms of universals, Thirdness, we cannot know particulars in isolation, but only insofar as they interact with others; and what we know is, again, the lawful or habitual way in which they interact. It may be possible to experience an entity without bringing it to the level of cognition. This would amount to an experience of the bare "given," as C. I. Lewis and Dewey call it, without an interpretation of it. Be that as it may, we cannot know the given in isolation from other givens, without a knowledge of how it functions in a system, that is, without systematizing it. Thirdness has no ontological status apart from Secondness, nor Secondness apart from Firstness. Each by itself is an abstraction from the actual, from process involving all three.

Mead does not discuss universals extensively, but what he says is illuminating and to the point:

> . . . one has a nail to drive, he reaches for the hammer and finds it gone, and he does not stop to look for it, but reaches for something else he can use, a brick or a stone, anything having the necessary weight to give momentum to the blow. Anything that he can get hold of that will serve the purpose will be a hammer. That sort of response which involves the grasping of a heavy object is a universal.[17]

I believe Mead would agree that a brick, a stone, or a hammer can be said to belong to the same class because they function in the same manner; they are functionally identical, though essentially different. Also:

> Language makes it possible to hold on to these mental objects [concepts]. Abstractions exist for lower animals, but they cannot hold them.[18]

Mead was concerned with defining and understanding mind, meanings, and universals in terms of responses. If a linguistic gesture elicits a functionally identical response by the one who makes it as it does in the other, then the meaning of it is the same for both. I have expanded the notion of response to include reactions. If two particulars, x and y, react in the same (lawful) way with z, they belong to the same class and, in that respect, have the same meaning to us.

One may ask, What difference does it make whether we think of universality as do realists, nominalists, conceptualists, or pragmatists? Briefly, the pragmatists clarify for epistemologists and scientists what is meant by knowledge. Just as Galileo stated knowledge in terms of motion and mathematical equations and thereby introduced kinematics and dynamics, by means of which he got inside change and was able to measure acceleration, the rate of change of velocity, so the pragmatists emphasize that knowing consists in getting inside processes and controlling them by means of efficient causes, not formal or final causes. For Mead, to know in practical terms is to be able, by efficient causes, to control processes directed toward ends of our own choosing. To control a response we must have control over the stimulus.

NOTES

1. For further elucidation, see *The Individual and the Social Self: Unpublished Works of George Herbert Mead,* David L. Miller (Chicago: The University of Chicago Press, 1982). See especially "Functional Identity of Response" and "Functional Identity of Stimulus," pp. 197–217.

2. In *The Language of Bees,* Karl von Frisch provides no evidence that the worker bee that makes a dance on the honeycomb after depositing nectar is, by its dance, using a significant symbol or making a linguistic gesture. To be a linguistic gesture, the one who makes it must have a concept shared with the other. In this regard, see David L. Miller, "The Meaning of Role-Taking," *Symbolic Interaction* 4, 7 (Fall 1981): 167–175.

3. W. I. Thomas, "The Definition of the Situation," in *Symbolic Interaction* (Rockleigh, N.J.: Allyn and Bacon, 1978).

4. *Selected Writings of George Herbert Mead,* ed. Andrew Reck (Chicago: The University of Chicago Press, 1982), p. 150.

5. *The Philosophy of the Act,* ed. Charles W. Morris, in collaboration with John M. Brewster, Albert M. Dunham, and David L. Miller (Chicago: The University of Chicago Press, 1938), pp. 662–663.

6. *Selected Writings of George Herbert Mead,* p. 185.

7. *The Philosophy of the Present,* ed Arthur E. Murphy (Chicago: Open Court, 1932), p. 52. (Also included in the selections in this volume; see below, p. 470.)

8. Ibid., p. 47. (Also included in the selections in this volume; see below, p. 468.)

9. Ibid., p. 86.

10. For further development of this point, see David L. Miller, "The Meaning of Freedom from the Perspective of G. H. Mead's Theory of the Self," *The Southern Journal of Philosophy* 4 (1982). pp. 453–464.

11. William James, *The Works of William James: A Pluralistic Universe* (Cambridge, Mass.: Harvard University Press, 1977), p. 117.

12. On this point, see David L. Miller, "The Meaning of Sameness or Family Resemblance in the Pragmatic Tradition," *Tulane Studies in Philosophy* (1972): 51–62.

13. See John J. Stuhr, "Socratic Questions and Radical Empiricist Ethics," *Transactions of The Charles S. Peirce Society* 20, 1 (1984): 38–49.

14. William James, *The Works of William James: The Principles of Psychology,* Vol. I (Cambridge, Mass.: Harvard University Press, 1981), p. 109.

15. *Selected Writings of George Herbert Mead,* p. 244.

16. Ibid., p. 247.

17. *Mind, Self, and Society: From The Standpoint of a Social Behaviorist,* ed. Charles W. Morris (Chicago: The University of Chicago Press, 1936), p. 83. (Also included in the selections in this volume; see below, p. 440.)

18. Ibid.

Social Psychology, Behaviorism, and the Concept of the Gesture

Social psychology studies the activity or behavior of the individual as it lies within the social process; the behavior of an individual can be understood only in terms of the behavior of the whole social group of which he is a member, since his individual acts are involved in larger, social acts which go beyond himself and which implicate the other members of that group.

We are not, in social psychology, building up the behavior of the social group in terms of the behavior of the separate individuals composing it; rather, we are starting out with a given social whole of complex group activity, into which we analyze (as elements) the behavior of each of the separate individuals composing it. We attempt, that is, to explain the conduct of the individual in terms of the organized conduct of the social group, rather than to account for the organized conduct of the social group in terms of the conduct of the separate individuals belonging to it. For social psychology, the whole (society) is prior to the part (the individual), not the part to the whole; and the part is explained in terms of the whole, not the whole in terms of the part or parts. The social act[1] is not explained by building it up out-of stimulus plus response; it must be taken as a dynamic whole—as something going on—no part of which can be considered or understood by itself—a complex organic process implied by each individual stimulus and response involved in it.

In social psychology we get at the social process from the inside as well as from the outside. Social psychology is behavioristic in the sense of starting off with an observable activity—the dynamic, on-going social process, and the social acts which are its component elements—to be studied and analyzed scientifically. But it is not behavioristic in the sense of ignoring the inner experience of the individual—the inner phase of that process or activity. On the contrary, it is particularly concerned with the rise of such experience within the process as a whole. It simply works from the outside to the inside instead of from the inside to the outside, so to speak, in its endeavor to determine how such experience does arise within the process. The act, then, and not the tract, is the fundamental datum in both social and individual psychology when behavioristically conceived, and it has both an inner and an outer phase, an internal and an external aspect.

These general remarks have had to do with our point of approach. It is behavioristic, but unlike Watsonian behaviorism it recognizes the parts of the act which do not come to external observation, and it emphasizes the act of the human individual in its natural social situation.

. . . If we take Wundt's parallelistic statement we get a point of view from which we can approach the problem of social experience. Wundt undertook to show the parallelism between what goes on in the body as represented by processes of the central nervous system, and what goes on in those experiences which the individual recognizes as his own. He had to find that which was common to these two fields—what in the psychical experience could be referred to in physical terms.[2]

Wundt isolated a very valuable conception of the gesture as that which becomes later a symbol, but which is to be found in its earlier stages as a part of a social act.[3] It is that part of the social act which serves as a stimulus to other forms involved in the same social act. I have given the illustration of the dog-fight as a method of presenting the gesture. The act of each dog becomes the stimulus to the other dog for his response. There is then a relationship between these two; and as the act is responded to by the other dog, it, in turn, undergoes change. The very fact that the dog is ready to attack another becomes a stimulus to the other dog to change his own position or his own attitude. He has no sooner done this than the change of attitude in the second dog in turn causes the first dog to change his attitude. We have here a conversation of gestures. They are not, however, gestures in the sense that they are significant. We do not assume that the dog says to himself, "If the animal comes from this direction he is going to spring at my throat and I will turn in such a way." What does take place is an actual change in his own position due to the direction of the approach of the other dog.

From *Mind, Self, and Society: From the Standpoint of a Social Behaviorist,* Ed. Charles M. Morris (Chicago: The University of Chicago Press, 1934). pp. 6–8, 42–43, 63, 65–68.

. . . In such a process there would be no mechanism for imitation. One dog does not imitate the other. The second dog assumes a different attitude to avoid the spring of the first dog. The stimulus in the attitude of one dog is not to call out the response in itself that it calls out in the other. The first dog is influenced by its own attitude, but it is simply carrying out the process of a prepared spring, so that the influence on the dog is simply in reinforcing the process which is going on. It is not a stimulus to the dog to take the attitude of the other dog.

When, however, one is making use of the vocal gesture, if we assume that one vocal element is a stimulus to a certain reply, then when the animal that makes use of that vocal gesture hears the resulting sound he will have aroused in himself at least a tendency to respond in the same way as the other animal responds. . . . There is here a selective process by which is picked out what is common. "Imitation" depends upon the individual influencing himself as others influence him, so that he is under the influence not only of the other but also of himself in so far as he uses the same vocal gesture.

The vocal gesture, then, has an importance which no other gesture has. We cannot see ourselves when our face assumes a certain expression. If we hear ourselves speak we are more apt to pay attention. One hears himself when he is irritated using a tone that is of an irritable quality, and so catches himself. But in the facial expression of irritation the stimulus is not one that calls out an expression in the individual which it calls out in the other. One is more apt to catch himself up and control himself in the vocal gesture than in the expression of the countenance.

It is only the actor who uses bodily expressions as a means of looking as he wants others to feel. He gets a response which reveals to him how he looks by continually using a mirror. He registers anger, he registers love, he registers this, that, or the other attitude, and he examines himself in a glass to see how he does so. When he later makes use of the gesture it is present as a mental image. He realizes that that particular expression does call out fright. If we exclude vocal gestures, it is only by the use of the mirror that one could reach the position where he responds to his own gestures as other people respond. But the vocal gesture is one which does give on this capacity for answering to one's own stimulus as another would answer.

If there is any truth in the old axiom that the bully is always the coward, it will be found to rest on the fact that one arouses in himself that attitude of fear which his bullying attitude arouses in another, so that when put into a particular situation which calls his bluff, his own attitude is found to be that of the others. If one's own attitude of giving way to the bullying attitude of others is one that arouses the bullying attitude, he has in that degree aroused the attitude of bullying in himself. There is a certain amount of truth in this when we come back to the effect upon one's self of the gesture of which he makes use. In so far as one calls out the attitude in himself that one calls out in others, the response is picked out and strengthened. That is the only basis for what we call imitation. It is not imitation in the sense of simply doing what one sees another person doing. The mechanism is that of an individual calling out in himself the response which he calls out in another, consequently giving greater weight to those responses than to the other responses, and gradually building up those sets of responses into a dominant whole. That may be done, as we say, unconsciously. It is just a gradual picking up of the notes which are common to both of them. And that is true wherever there is imitation.

So far as exclamatory sounds are concerned (and they would answer in our own vocal gestures to what is found in those of animals), the response to these does not enter into immediate conversation, and the influence of these responses on the individual are comparatively slight. It seems to be difficult to bring them into relationship with significant speech. We are not consciously frightened when we speak angrily to someone else, but the meaning of what we say is always present to us when we speak. The response in the individual to an exclamatory cry which is of the same sort as that in the other does not play any important part in the conduct of the form. The response of the lion to its roar is of very little importance in the response of the form itself, but our response to the meaning of what we say is constantly attached to our conversation. We must be constantly responding to the gesture we make if we are to carry on successful vocal conversation. The meaning of what we are saying is the tendency to respond to it. You ask somebody to bring a visitor a chair. You arouse the tendency to get the chair in the other, but if he is slow to act you get the chair yourself. The response to the vocal gesture is the doing of a certain thing, and you arouse that same tendency in yourself. You are always replying to yourself, just as other people reply. You assume that in some degree there must be identity in the reply. It is action on a common basis.

I have contrasted two situations to show what a long road speech or communication has to travel from the situation where there is nothing but vocal cries over to the situation in which significant symbols are utilized. What is peculiar to the latter is that the individual responds to his own stimulus in the same way as other people respond. Then the stimulus becomes significant; then one is saying something. As far as a parrot is concerned, its "speech" means nothing, but where one significantly says something with his own vocal process he is saying it to himself as well as to everybody else within reach of his voice. It is only the vocal gesture that is fitted for this sort of communication, because it is only the vocal gesture to which one responds or tends to respond as another person tends to respond to it. It is true that the language of the hands is of the same character. One sees one's self using the gestures which those who are deaf make use of. They influence one the same way as they influence others. Of course, the same is true of any form of script. But such symbols have all been developed out of the specific vocal gesture, for that is the basic gesture which does influence the individual as it influences others.

NOTES

1. "A social act may be defined as one in which the occasion or stimulus which sets free an impulse is found in the character or conduct of a living form that belongs to the proper environment of the living form whose impulse it is. I wish, however, to restrict the social act to the class of acts which involve the co-operation of more than one individual, and whose object as defined by the act, in the sense of Bergson, is a social object. I mean by a social object one that answers to all the parts of the complex act, though these parts are found in the conduct of different individuals. The objective of the acts is then found in the life-process of the group, not in those of the separate individuals alone." [From "The Genesis of the Self and Social Control," *International Journal of Ethics,* XXXV (1925), 263–64].

2. [Cf. *Grundzüge der physiologischen Psychologie.*] The fundamental defect of Wundt's psychophysical parallelism is the fundamental defect of all psychological parallelism: the required parallelism is not in fact complete on the psychical side, since only the sensory and not the motor phase of the physiological process of experience has a psychic correlate; hence the psychical aspect of the required parallelism can be completed only physiologically, thus breaking it down. And this fundamental, defect of his psychophysical parallelism vitiates the analysis of social experiences—and especially of communication—which he bases upon the assumption of that parallelism.

3. [*Völkerpsychologie,* Vol. I. For Mead's treatment of Wundt compare "The Relations of Psychology and Philology," *Psychological Bulletin,* I (1904), 375 ff., with the more critical "The Imagination in Wundt's Treatment of Myth and Religion," *ibid.,* III (1906), 393 ff.]

Thought, Communication, and the Significant Symbol

We have contended that there is no particular faculty of imitation in the sense that the sound or the sight of another's response is itself a stimulus to carry out the same reaction, but rather that if there is already present in the individual an action like the action of another, then there is a situation which makes imitation possible. What is necessary now to carry through that imitation is that the conduct and the gesture of the individual which calls out a response in the other should also tend to call out the same response in himself. In the dog-

fight this is not present: the attitude in the one dog does not tend to call out the same attitude in the other. In some respects that actually may occur in the case of two boxers. The man who makes a feint is calling out a certain blow from his opponent, and that act of his own does have that meaning to him, that is, he has in some sense initiated the same act in himself. It does not go clear through, but he has stirred up the centers in his central nervous system which would lead to his making the same blow that his opponent is led to make, so that he

From *Mind, Self, and Society: From the Standpoint of a Social Behaviorist,* Ed. Charles W. Morris (Chicago: The University of Chicago Press, 1934), pp. 68–75.

calls out in himself, or tends to call out, the same response which he calls out in the other. There you have the basis for so-called imitation. Such is the process which is so widely recognized at present in manners of speech, of dress, and of attitudes.

We are more or less unconsciously seeing ourselves as others see us. We are unconsciously addressing ourselves as others address us; in the same way as the sparrow takes up the note of the canary we pick up the dialects about us. Of course, there must be these particular responses in our own mechanism. We are calling out in the other person something we are calling out in ourselves, so that unconsciously we take over these attitudes. We are unconsciously putting ourselves in the place of others and acting as others act. I want simply to isolate the general mechanism here, because it is of very fundamental importance in the development of what we call self-consciousness and the appearance of the self. We are, especially through the use of the vocal gestures, continually arousing in ourselves those responses which we call out in other persons, so that we are taking the attitudes of the other persons into our own conduct. The critical importance of language in the development of human experience lies in this fact that the stimulus is one that can react upon the speaking individual as it reacts upon the other.

A behaviorist, such as Watson, holds that all of our thinking is vocalization. In thinking we are simply starting to use certain words. That is in a sense true. However, Watson does not take into account all that is involved here, namely, that these stimuli are the essential elements in elaborate social processes and carry with them the value of those social processes. The vocal process as such has this great importance, and it is fair to assume that the vocal process, together with the intelligence and thought that go with it, is not simply a playing of particular vocal elements against each other. Such a view neglects the social context of language.[1]

The importance, then, of the vocal stimulus lies in this fact that the individual can hear what he says and in hearing what he says is tending to respond as the other person responds. When we speak now of this response on the part of the individual to the others we come back to the situation of asking some person to do something. We ordinarily express that by saying that one knows what he is asking you to do. Take the illustration of asking someone to do something, and then doing it

one's self. Perhaps the person addressed does not hear you or acts slowly, and then you carry the action out yourself. You find in yourself, in this way, the same tendency which you are asking the other individual to carry out. Your request stirred up in you that same response which you stirred up in the other individual. How difficult it is to show someone else how to do something which you know how to do yourself! The slowness of the response makes it hard to restrain yourself from doing what you are teaching. You have aroused the same response in yourself as you arouse in the other individual.

In seeking for an explanation of this, we ordinarily assume a certain group of centers in the nervous system which are connected with each other, and which express themselves in the action. If we try to find in a central nervous system something that answers to our word "chair," what we should find would be presumably simply an organization of a whole group of possible reactions so connected that if one starts in one direction one will carry out one process, if in another direction one will carry out another process. The chair is primarily what one sits down in. It is a physical object at a distance. One may move toward an object at a distance and then enter upon the process of sitting down when one reaches it. There is a stimulus which excites certain paths which cause the individual to go toward that object and to sit down. Those centers are in some degree physical. There is, it is to be noted, an influence of the later act on the earlier act. The later process which is to go on has already been initiated and that later process has its influence on the earlier process (the one that takes place before this process, already initiated, can be completed). Now, such an organization of a great group of nervous elements as will lead to conduct with reference to the objects about us is what one would find in the central nervous system answering to what we call an object. The complications are very great, but the central nervous system has an almost infinite number of elements in it, and they can be organized not only in spatial connection with each other, but also from a temporal standpoint. In virtue of this last fact, our conduct is made up of a series of steps which follow each other, and the later steps may be already started and influence the earlier ones. The thing we are going to do is playing back on what we are doing now. That organization in the neural elements in reference to what we call a physical object would be what we call a conceptual object stated in terms of the central nervous system.

In rough fashion it is the initiation of such a set of organized sets of responses that answers to what we call the idea or concept of a thing. If one asked what the idea of a dog is, and tried to find that idea in the central nervous system, one would find a whole group of responses which are more or less connected together by definite paths so that when one uses the term "dog" he does tend to call out this group of responses. A dog is a possible playmate, a possible enemy, one's own property or somebody else's. There is a whole series of possible responses. There are certain types of these responses which are in all of us, and there are others which vary with the individuals, but there is always an organization of the responses which can be called out by the term "dog." So if one is speaking of a dog to another person he is arousing in himself this set of responses which he is arousing in the other individual.

It is, of course, the relationship of this symbol, this vocal gesture, to such a set of responses in the individual himself as well as in the other that makes of that vocal gesture what I call a significant symbol. A symbol does tend to call out in the individual a group of reactions such as it calls out in the other, but there is something further that is involved in its being a significant symbol: this response within one's self to such a word as "chair," or "dog," is one which is a stimulus to the individual as well as a response. This is what, of course, is involved in what we term the meaning of a thing, or its significance.[2] We often act with reference to objects in what we call an intelligent fashion, although we can act without the meaning of the object being present in our experience. One can start to dress for dinner, as they tell of the absent-minded college professor, and find himself in his pajamas in bed. A certain process of undressing was started and carried out mechanically; he did not recognize the meaning of what he was doing. He intended to go to dinner and found he had gone to bed. The meaning involved in his action was not present. The steps in this case were all intelligent steps which controlled his conduct with reference to later action, but he did not think about what he was doing. The later action was not a stimulus to his response, but just carried itself out when it was once started.

When we speak of the meaning of what we are doing we are making the response itself that we are on the point of carrying out a stimulus to our action. It becomes a stimulus to a later stage of action which is to take place from the point of view of this particular response. In the case of the boxer the blow that he is starting to direct toward his opponent is to call out a certain response which will open up the guard of his opponent so that he can strike. The meaning is a stimulus for the preparation of the real blow he expects to deliver. The response which he calls out in himself (the guarding reaction) is the stimulus to him to strike where an opening is given. This action which he has initiated already in himself thus becomes a stimulus thus becomes a stimulus for his later response. He knows what his opponent is going to do, since the guarding movement is one which is already aroused, and becomes a stimulus to strike where the opening is given. The meaning would not have been present in his conduct unless it became a stimulus to strike where the favorable opening appears.

Such is the difference between intelligent conduct on the part of animals and what we call a reflective individual.[3] We say the animal does not think. He does not put himself in a position for which he is responsible; he does not put himself in the place of the other person and say, in effect, "He will act in such a way and I will act in this way." If the individual can act in this way, and the attitude which he calls out in himself can become a stimulus to him for another act, we have meaningful conduct. Where the response of the other person is called out and becomes a stimulus to control his action, then he has the meaning of the other person's act in his own experience. That is the general mechanism of what we term "thought," for in order that thought may exist there must be symbols, vocal gestures generally, which arouse in the individual himself the response which he is calling out in the other, and such that from the point of view of that response he is able to direct his later conduct. It involves not only communication in the sense in which birds and animals communicate with each other, but also an arousal in the individual himself of the response which he is calling out in the other individual, a taking of the rôle of the other, a tendency to act as the other person acts. One participates in the same process the other person is carrying out and controls his action with reference to that participation. It is that which constitutes the meaning of an object, namely, the common response in one's self as in the other person, which becomes, in turn, a stimulus to one's self.

If you conceive of the mind as just a sort of conscious substance in which there are certain impressions and states, and hold that one of those states is a universal, then a word becomes purely arbitrary—it is just a symbol.[4] You can then take words and pronounce them backwards, as children do; there seems to be absolute freedom of arrangement and language seems to be an entirely mechanical thing that lies outside of the process of intelligence. If you recognize that language is, however, just a part of a co-operative process, that part which does lead to an adjustment to the response of the other so that the whole activity can go on, then language has only a limited range of arbitrariness. If you are talking to another person you are, perhaps, able to scent the change in his attitude by something that would not strike a third person at all. You may know his mannerism, and that becomes a gesture to you, a part of the response of the individual. There is a certain range possible within the gesture as to what is to serve as the symbol. We may say that a whole set of separate symbols with one meaning are acceptable; but they always are gestures, that is, they are always parts of the act of the individual which reveal what he is going to do to the other person so that when the person utilizes the clue he calls out in himself the attitude of the other. Language is not ever arbitrary in the sense of simply denoting a bare state of consciousness by a word. What particular part of one's act will serve to direct co-operative activity is more or less arbitrary. Different phases of the act may do it. What seems unimportant in itself may be highly important in revealing what the attitude is. In that sense one can speak of the gesture itself as unimportant, but it is of great importance as to what the gesture is going to reveal. This is seen in the difference between the purely intellectual character of the symbol and its emotional character. A poet depends upon the latter; for him language is rich and full of values which we, perhaps, utterly ignore. In trying to express a message in something less than ten words, we merely want to convey a certain meaning, while the poet is dealing with what is really living tissue, the emotional throb in the expression itself. There is, then, a great range in our use of language; but whatever phase of this range is used is a part of a social process, and it is always that part by means of which we affect ourselves as we affect others and mediate the social situation through this understanding of what we are saying. That is fundamental for any language; if it is going to be language one has to understand what he is saying, has to affect himself as he affects others.

NOTES

1. Gestures, if carried back to the matrix from which they spring, are always found to inhere in or involve a larger social act of which they are phases. In dealing with communication we have first to recognize its earliest origins in the unconscious conversation of gestures. Conscious communication—conscious conversation of gestures—arises when gestures become signs, that is, when they come to carry for the individuals making them and the individuals responding to them, definite meanings or significations in terms of the subsequent behavior of the individuals making them; so that, by serving as prior indications, to the individuals responding to them, of the subsequent behavior of the individuals making them, they make possible the mutual adjustment of the various individual components of the social act to one another, and also, by calling forth in the individuals making them the same responses implicitly that they call forth explicitly in the individuals to whom they are made, they render possible the rise of self-consciousness in connection with this mutual adjustment.

2. The inclusions of the matrix or complex of attitudes and responses constituting any given social situation or act, within the experience of any one of the individuals implicated in that situation or act (the inclusion within his experience of his attitudes toward other individuals, of their responses to his attitudes toward them, of their attitudes toward him, and of his response to these attitudes) is all that an *idea* amounts to; or at any rate is the only basis for its occurrence or existence "in the mind" of the given individual.

In the case of the unconscious conversation of gestures, or in the case of the process of communication carried on by means of it, none of the individuals participating in it is conscious of the meaning of the conversation—that meaning does not appear in the experience of any one of the separate individuals involved in the conversation or carrying it on; whereas, in the case of the conscious conversation of gestures, or in the case of the process of communication carried on by means of it, each of the individuals participating in it is conscious of the meaning of the conversation, precisely because that meaning does appear in his experience, and because such appearance is what consciousness of that meaning implies.

3. For the nature of animal conduct see "Concerning Animal Perception," *Psychological Review,* XIV (1907), 383 ff.

4. Müller attempts to put the values of thought into language; but this attempt is fallacious, because language has those values only as the most effective mechanism of thought merely because it carries the conscious or significant conversation of gestures to its highest and most perfect development. There

must be some sort of an implicit attitude (that is, a response which is initiated without being fully carried out) in the organism making the gesture—an attitude which answers to the overt response to the gesture on the part of another individual, and which corresponds to the attitude called forth or aroused in this other organism by the gesture—if thought is to develop in the organism making the gesture. And it is the central nervous system which provides the mechanism for such implicit attitudes or responses.

The identification of language with reason is in one sense an absurdity, but in another sense it is valid. It is valid, namely, in the sense that the process of language brings the total social act into the experience of the given individual as himself involved in the act, and thus makes the process of reason possible. But though the process of reason is and must be carried on in terms of the process of language—in terms, that is, of words—it is not simply constituted by the latter.

Meaning

We are particularly concerned with intelligence on the human level, that is, with the adjustment to one another of the acts of different human individuals within the human social process; an adjustment which takes place through communication: by gestures on the lower planes of human evolution, and by significant symbols (gestures which possess meanings and are hence more than mere substitute stimuli) on the higher planes of human evolution.[1]

The central factor in such adjustment is "meaning." Meaning arises and lies within the field of the relation between the gesture of a given human organism and the subsequent behavior of this organism as indicated to another human organism by that gesture. If that gesture does so indicate to another organism the subsequent (or resultant) behavior of the given organism, then it has meaning. In other words, the relationship between a given stimulus—as a gesture—and the later phases of the social act of which it is an early (if not the initial) phase constitutes the field within which meaning originates and exists. Meaning is thus a development of something objectively there as a relation between certain phases of the social act; it is not a psychical addition to that act and it is not an "idea" as traditionally conceived. A gesture by one organism, the resultant of the social act in which the gesture is an early phase, and the response of another organism to the gesture, are the relata in a triple or threefold relationship of gesture to first organism, of gesture to second organism, and of gesture to subsequent phases of the given social act; and this threefold relationship constitutes the matrix within which meaning arises, or

which develops into the field of meaning. The gesture stands for a certain resultant of the social act, a resultant to which there is a definite response on the part of the individuals involved therein; so that meaning is given or stated in terms of response. Meaning is implicit—if not always explicit—in the relationship among the various phases of the social act to which it refers, and out of which it develops. And its development takes place in terms of symbolization at the human evolutionary level.

We have been concerning ourselves, in general, with the social process of experience and behavior as it appears in the calling out by the act of one organism of an adjustment to that act in the responsive act of another organism. We have seen that the nature of meaning is intimately associated with the social process as it thus appears, that meaning involves this three-fold relation among phases of the social act as the context in which it arises and develops: this relation of the gesture of one organism to the adjustive response of another organism (also implicated in the given act), and to the completion of the given act—a relation such that the second organism responds to the gesture of the first as indicating or referring to the completion of the given act. For example, the chick's response to the cluck of the mother hen is a response to the meaning of the cluck; the cluck refers to danger or to food, as the case may be, and has this meaning or connotation for the chick.

The social process, as involving communication, is in a sense responsible for the appearance of new objects in the field of experience

From *Mind, Self, and Society: From the Standpoint of a Social Behaviorist,* Ed. Charles W. Morris (Chicago: The University of Chicago Press, 1934), pp. 75–82.

of the individual organisms implicated in that process. Organic processes or responses in a sense constitute the objects to which they are responses; that is to say, any given biological organism is in a way responsible for the existence (in the sense of the meanings they have for it) of the objects to which it physiologically and chemically responds. There would, for example, be no food—no edible objects—if there were no organisms which could digest it. And similarly, the social process in a sense constitutes the objects to which it responds, or to which it is an adjustment. That is to say, objects are constituted in terms of meanings within the social process of experience and behavior through the mutual adjustment to one another of the responses or actions of the various individual organisms involved in that process, an adjustment made possible by means of a communication which takes the form of a conversation of gestures in the earlier evolutionary stages of that process, and of language in its later stages.

Awareness or consciousness is not necessary to the presence of meaning in the process of social experience. A gesture on the part of one organism in any given social act calls out a response on the part of another organism and its outcome; and a gesture is a symbol of the result of the given social act of one organism (the organism making it) in so far as it is responded to by another organism (thereby also involved in that act) as indicating that result. The mechanism of meaning is thus present in the social act before the emergence of consciousness or awareness of meaning occurs. The act or adjustive response of the second organism gives to the gesture of the first organism the meaning which it has.

Symbolization constitutes objects not constituted before, objects which would not exist except for the context of social relationships wherein symbolization occurs. Language does not simply symbolize a situation or object which is already there in advance; it makes possible the existence or the appearance of that situation or object, for it is a part of the mechanism whereby that situation or object is created. The social process relates the responses of one individual to the gestures of another, as the meanings of the latter, and is thus responsible for the rise and existence of new objects in the social situation, objects dependent upon or constituted by these meanings. Meaning is thus not to be conceived, fundamentally, as a state of consciousness, or as a set of organized relations existing or subsisting

mentally outside the field of experience into which they enter; on the contrary, it should be conceived objectively, as having its existence entirely within this field.[2] The response of one organism to the gesture of another in any given social act is the meaning of that gesture, and also is in a sense responsible for the appearance or coming into being of the new object— or new content of an old object—to which that gesture refers through the outcome of the given social act in which it is an early phase. For, to repeat, objects are in a genuine sense constituted within the social process of experience, by the communication and mutual adjustment of behavior among the individual organisms which are involved in that process and which carry it on. Just as in fencing the parry is an interpretation of the thrust, so, in the social act, the adjustive response of one organism to the gesture of another is the interpretation of that gesture by that organism—it is the meaning of that gesture.

At the level of self-consciousness such a gesture becomes a symbol, a significant symbol. But the interpretation of gestures is not, basically, a process going on in a mind as such, or one necessarily involving a mind; it is an external, overt, physical, or physiological process going on in the actual field of social experience. Meaning can be described, accounted for, or stated in terms of symbols or language at its highest and most complex stage of development (the stage it reaches in human experience), but language simply lifts out of the social process a situation which is logically or implicitly there already. The language symbol is simply a significant or conscious gesture.

Two main points are being made here: (1) that the social process, through the communication which it makes possible among the individuals implicated in it, is responsible for the appearance of a whole set of new objects in nature, which exist in relation to it (objects, namely, of "common sense"); and (2) that the gesture of one organism and the adjustive response of another organism to that gesture within any given social act bring out the relationship that exists between the gesture as the beginning of the given act and the completion or resultant of the given act, to which the gesture refers. These are the two basic and complementary logical aspects of the social process.

The result of any given social act is definitely separated from the gesture indicating it by the response of another organism to that gesture, a response which points to the result of that act as indicated by that gesture. This situation is all there—is completely given—on the non-mental, non-conscious level, before the analysis of it on the mental or conscious level. Dewey says that meaning arises through communication.[3] It is to the content to which the social process gives rise that this statement refers; not to bare ideas or printed words as such, but to the social process which has been so largely responsible for the objects constituting the daily environment in which we live: a process in which communication plays the main part. That process can give rise to these new objects in nature only in so far as it makes possible communication among the individual organisms involved in it. And the sense in which it is responsible for their existence—indeed for the existence of the whole world of common-sense objects—is the sense in which it determines, conditions, and makes possible their abstraction from the total structure of events, as identities which are relevant for everyday social behavior; and in that sense, or as having that meaning, they are existent only relative to that behavior. In the same way, at a later, more advanced stage of its development, communication is responsible for the existence of the whole realm of scientific objects as well as identities abstracted from the total structure of events by virtue of their relevance for scientific purposes.

The logical structure of meaning, we have seen, is to be found in the threefold relationship of gesture to adjustive response and to the resultant of the given social act. Response on the part of the second organism to the the gesture of the first is the interpretation—and brings out the meaning—of that gesture, as indicating the resultant of the social act which it initiates, and in which both organisms are thus involved. This threefold or triadic relation between gesture, adjustive response, and resultant of the social act which the gesture initiates is the basis of meaning; for the existence of meaning depends upon the fact that the adjustive response of the second organism is directed toward the resultant of the given social act as initiated and indicated by the gesture of the first organism. The basis of meaning is thus objectively there in social conduct, or in nature in its relation to such conduct. Meaning is a content of an object which is dependent upon the relation of an organism or group of organisms to it. It is not essentially or primarily a psychical content (a content of mind or consciousness), for it need not

be conscious at all, and is not in fact until significant symbols are evolved in the process of human social experience. Only when it becomes identified with such symbols does meaning become conscious. The meaning of a gesture on the part of one organism is the adjustive response of another organism to it, as indicating the resultant of the social act it initiates, the adjustive response of the second organism being itself directed toward or related to the completion of that act. In other words, meaning involves a reference of the gesture of one organism to the resultant of the social act it indicates or initiates, as adjustively responded to in this reference by another organism; and the adjustive response of the other organism is the meaning of the gesture.

Gestures may be either conscious (significant) or unconscious (non-significant). The conversation of gestures is not significant below the human level, because it is not conscious, that is, not *self*-conscious (though it is conscious in the sense of involving feelings or sensations). An animal as opposed to a human form, in indicating something to, or bringing out a meaning for, another form, is not at the same time indicating or bringing out the same thing or meaning to or for himself; for he has no mind, no thought, and hence there is no meaning here in the significant or self-conscious sense. A gesture is not significant when the response of another organism to it does not indicate to the organism making it what the other organism is responding to.[4]

Much subtlety has been wasted on the problem of the meaning of meaning. It is not necessary, in attempting to solve this problem, to have recourse to psychical states, for the nature of meaning, as we have seen, is found to be implicit in the structure of the social act, implicit in the relations among its three basic individual components: namely, in the triadic relation of a gesture of one individual, a response to that gesture by a second individual, and completion of the given social act initiated by the gesture of the first individual. And the fact that the nature of meaning is thus found to be implicit in the structure of the social act provides additional emphasis upon the necessity, in social psychology, of starting off with the initial assumption of an ongoing social process of experience and behavior in which any given group of human individuals is involved, and upon which the existence and development of their minds, selves, and self-consciousness depend.

NOTES

1. [See also "Social Consciousness and the Consciousness of Meaning," *Psychological Bulletin,* VII (1910), 397 ff.; "The Mechanism of Social Consciousness," *Journal of Philosophy,* IX (1912), 401 ff.]

2. Nature has meaning and implication but not indication by symbols. The symbol is distinguishable from the meaning it refers to. Meanings are in nature, but symbols are the heritage of man (1924).

3. See *Experience and Nature,* chap. v.

4. There are two characters which belong to that which we term "meanings," one is participation and the other is communicability. Meaning can arise only in so far as some phase of the act which the individual is arousing in the other can be aroused in himself. There is always to this extent participation. And the result of this participation is communicability, i.e., the individual can indicate to himself what he indicates to others. There is communication without significance where the gesture of the individual calls out the response in the other without calling out or tending to call out the same response in the individual himself. Significance from the standpoint of the observer may be said to be present in the gesture which calls out the appropriate response in the other or others within a co-operative act, but it does not become signficant to the individuals who are involved in the act unless the tendency to the act is aroused within the individual who makes it, and unless the individual who is directly affected by the gesture puts himself in the attitude of the individual who makes the gesture.

Universality

Our experience does recognize or find that which is typical, and this is as essential for an adequate theory of meaning as is the element of particularity. There are not only facts of red, for example, but there is in the experience a red which is identical so far as experience has been concerned with some other red. One can isolate the red just as a sensation, and as such it is passing; but in addition to that passing character there is something that we call universal, something that gives a meaning to it. The event is a color, it is red, it is a certain kind of red—and that is something which does not have a passing character in the statement of color itself. If we go over from particular contents of this sort to other objects, such as a chair, a tree, a dog, we find there something that is distinguishable from the particular object, plant, or animal that we have about us. What we recognize in a dog is not the group of sensuous elements, but rather the character of being a dog, and unless we have some reason for interest in this particular dog, some problem as to its ownership or its likelihood to bite us, our relationship to the animal is to a universal—it is just a dog. If a person asks you what you saw you reply that it was a dog. You would not know the color of the dog; it was just a dog in general that you saw.

There is a meaning here that is given in the experience itself, and it is this meaning or universal character with which a behavioristic psychology is supposed to have difficulty in dealing. When there is a response to such an animal as a dog there is a response of recognition as well as a response toward an object in the landscape; and this response of recognition is something that is universal and not particular. Can this factor be stated in behavioristic terms? We are not, of course, interested in philosophical implications; we are not interested in the metaphysics of the dog; but we are interested in the recognition which would belong to any other animal of the same sort. Now, is there a response of such a universal character in our nature that it can be said to answer to this recognition of what we term the universal? It is the possibility of such a behavioristic statement that I endeavor to sketch.

What the central nervous system presents is not simply a set of automatisms, that is, certain inevitable reactions to certain specific stimuli, such as taking our hand away from a radiator that is touched, or jumping when a loud sound occurs behind us. The nervous system provides not only the mechanism for that sort of conduct but also for recognizing an object to which we are going to respond; and that recog-

From *Mind, Self, and Society: From the Standpoint of a Social Behaviorist,* Ed. Charles W. Morris (Chicago: The University of Chicago Press, 1934), pp. 82–90.

nition can be stated in terms of a response that may answer to any one of a certain group of stimuli. That is, one has a nail to drive, he reaches for the hammer and finds it gone, and he does not stop to look for it, but reaches for something else he can use, a brick or a stone, anything having the necessary weight to give mementum to the blow. Anything that he can get hold of that will serve the purpose will be a hammer. That sort of response which involves the grasping of a heavy object is a universal.[1] If the object does call out that response, no matter what its particular character may be, one can say that it has a universal character. It is something that can be recognized because of this character, notwithstanding the variations that are involved in the individual instances.

Now, can there be in the central nervous system a mechanism which can be aroused so that it will give rise to this response, however varied the conditions are otherwise? Can there be a mechanism of a sufficiently complicated character to represent the objects with which we deal—objects that have not only spatial dimensions, but also temporal dimensions? An object such as a melody, a tune, is a unitary affair. We hear the first notes and we respond to it as a whole. There is such a unity in the lives presented by biographies which follow a man from his birth to his death, showing all that belongs to the growth of the individual and the changes that take place in his career. Now, is there something in the central nervous system that can answer to such characters of the object, so that we can give a behavioristic account of an object so complicated as a melody or a life? The mere complication does not present serious difficulty, because the central nervous system has an almost infinite number of elements and possible combinations, but can one find a structure there in the central nervous system that would answer to a certain type of response which represents for us the character of the object which we recognize, as distinct from the mere sensations?

Recognition always implies a something that can be discovered in an indefinite number of objects. One can only sense a color once, in so far as "color" means an immediate relationship of the light waves to the retina of a normal nervous system. That experience happens and is gone, and cannot be repeated. But something is recognized, there is a universal character given in the experience itself which is at least capable of an indefinite number of repetitions. It is this which has been supposed to be beyond the behavioristic explanation or

statement. What a behavioristic psychology does is to state that character of the experience in terms of the response. It may be said that there cannot be a universal response, but only a response to a particular object. On the contrary, in so far as the response is one that can take place with reference to the brick, a stone, a hammer, there is a universal in the form of the response that answers to a whole set of particulars, and the particulars may be indefinite in number, provided only they have certain characters in relation to the response. The relationship of this response to an indefinite number of stimuli is just the relationship that is represented in what we call "recognition." When we use the term "recognition" we may mean no more than that we pick up an object that serves this particular purpose; what we generally mean is that the character of the object that is a stimulus to its recognition is present in our experience. We can have, in this way, something that is universal as over against various particulars. I think we can recognize in any habit that which answers to different stimuli; the response is universal and the stimulus is particular. As long as this element serves as a stimulus, calls out this response, one can say the particular comes under this universal. That is the statement of the behavioristic psychology of the universal form as over against the particular instance.

The next point is rather a matter of degree, illustrated by the more complex objects such as a symphony, or a life, with all their variations and harmonious contrasts. When a music critic discusses such a complex object as a symphony can we say that there is something in the central nervous system that answers to the object which the critic has before him? Or take the biography of a great man, a Lincoln or a Gladstone, where the historian, say Morley, has before him that entire life with all its indefinite number of elements. Can he be said to have in his central nervous system an object that answers to that attitude of recognizing Gladstone in all his changes as the same Gladstone? Could one, if he had the mechanism to do so, pick out in the historian's brain what answers to Gladstone? What would it be, supposing that it could be done? It would certainly not be just a single response to the name Gladstone. In some way it must represent all of the connections which took place in his experience, all those connections which were involved in his conduct in so far as their analogues took place in Gladstone's life. It must be some sort of a unity, such a unity that if this whole is touched at any point it may bring out any other element in the historian's experience of Gladstone. It may throw light on any phase of his character; it may bring out any of the situations in which Gladstone figures. All of this must be potentially present in such a mapping of Gladstone in Morley's central nervous system. It is indefinitely complex, but the central nervous system is also indefinitely complex. It does not represent merely spatial dimensions but temporal dimensions also. It can represent an action which is delayed, which is dependent upon an earlier reaction; and this later reaction can, in its inception, but before it takes place overtly, influence the earlier reaction.

We can conceive, then, in the structure of the central nervous system such a temporal dimension as that of the melody, or recognition of the notes and their distance from each other in the scale, and our appreciation of these as actually affected by the beginning of our response to the later notes, as when we are expecting a certain sort of an ending. If we ask how that expectation shows itself in our experience we should have difficulty in detailing it in terms of behavior, but we realize that this experience is determined by our readiness to respond to later notes and that such readiness can be there without the notes being themselves present. The way in which we are going to respond to a major or minor ending does determine the way in which we appreciate the notes that are occurring. It is that attitude that gives the character of our appreciation of all extended musical compositions. What is given at the outset is determined by the attitude to what is to come later. That is a phase of our experience which James has illustrated by his discussion of the sensory character of such conjunctions as "and," "but," "though." If you assert a proposition and add, "but," you determine the attitude of the hearer toward it. He does not know what you are going to introduce, but he does know there is some sort of an exception to it. His knowledge is not stated in reflective form, but is rather an attitude. There is a "but" attitude, an "if" attitude, a "though" attitude. It is such attitudes which we assume toward the beginning of a melody, toward the rhythm involved in poetry; it is these attitudes that give the import to the structure of what we are dealing with.

There are certain attitudes which we assume toward a rising column or toward its supports, and we only have to have suggestions of the object to call out those attitudes. The artist and the sculptor play upon these attitudes just as the musician does. Through the indication of the stimuli each is able to bring in the reflection of the complexities of a response. Now, if one can bring in a number of these and get a multiform reflection of all of these attitudes into harmony, he calls out an aesthetic response which we consider beautiful. It is the harmonizing of these complexities of response that constitutes the beauty of the object. There are different stimuli calling out an indefinite number of responses and the natures of these are reflected back into our immediate experience, and brought into harmonious relationship with each other. The later stages of the experience itself can be present in the immediate experience which influences them. Given a sufficiently complicated central nervous system, we can then find an indefinite number of responses, and these responses can be not ony immediate but delayed, and as delayed can be already influencing present conduct.

We can thus find, in some sense, in the central nervous system what would answer to complex objects, with their somewhat vague and indefinite meaning, as they lie in our actual experience—objects complex not only spatially but also temporally. When we respond to any phase of these objects all the other values are there ready to play into it, and give it its intellectual and emotional content. I see no reason why one should not find, then, in the organization of the attitude as presented in the central nervous system, what it is we refer to as the meaning of the object, that which is universal. The answering of the response to an indefinite number of stimuli which vary from each other is something that gives us the relation of the universal to the particular, and the complexity of the object may be as indefinitely great as are the elements in the central nervous system that represent possible temporal and spatial combinations of our own conduct. We can speak, then, legitimately of a certain sort of response which a Morley has to a Gladstone, a response that can find its expression in the central nervous system, taking into account all of its complexities.

[So far we have stressed the universality or generality of the response as standing over against the particularity of the stimulus which evokes it. I now wish to call attention to the social dimension of universality.]

Thinking takes place in terms of universals, and a unversal is an entity that is distinguishable from the object by means of which we think it. When we think of a spade we are not confined in our thought to any particular spade. Now if we think of the universal spade there must be something that we think about, and that is confessedly not given in the particular occurrence which is the occasion of the thought. The thought transcends all the occurrences. Must we assume a realm of such entities, essences or subsistents, to account for our thinking? That is generally assumed by modern realists. Dewey's answer seems to be that we have isolated by our abstracting attention certain features of spades which are irrelevant to the particular different spades, though they have their existence or being in these particular spades. These characters which will occur in any spade that is a spade are therefore irrelevant to any one of them. We may go farther and say that these characters are irrelevant to the occurrence of the spades that arise and are worn out. In other words, they are irrelevant to time, and may be called eternal objects or entities. But, says Dewey, this irrelevancy of these characters to time in our thought does not abstract their being from the particular spades. . . . Dewey quite agrees with the realists aforesaid that the meaning is not lodged in the word itself, that is, he is not a nominalist. He insists, however, that the meaning resides in the spade as a character which has arisen through the social nature of thinking. I suppose we can say in current terminology that meanings have emerged in social experience, just as colors emerged in the experience of organisms with the apparatus of vision.[2]

Meaning as such, i.e., the object of thought, arises in experience through the individual stimulating himself to take the attitude of the other in his reaction toward the object. Meaning is that which can be indicated to others while it is by the same process indicated to the indicating individual. In so far as the individual indicates it to himself in the rôle of the other, he is occupying his perspective, and as he is indicating it to the other from his own perspective, and as that which is so indicated is identical, it must be that which can be in different perspectives. It must therefore be a universal, at least in the identity which belongs to the different perspectives which are organized in the single perspective, and in so far as the principle of organization is one which admits of other perspectives than those actually present, the universality may be logically indefinitely extended. Its universality in conduct, however, amounts only to the irrelevance of the differences of the different perspectives to the characters which are indicated by the significant

symbols in use, i.e., the gestures which indicate to the individual who uses them what they indicate to the others, for whom they serve as appropriate stimuli in the co-operative process.

The significant gesture or symbol always presupposes for its significance the social process of experience and behavior in which it arises; or, as the logicians say, a universe of discourse is always implied as the context in terms of which, or as the field within which, significant gestures or symbols do in fact have significance. This universe of discourse is constituted by a group of individuals carrying on and participating in a common social process of experience[3] and behavior, within which these gestures or symbols have the same or common meanings for all members of that group, whether they make them or address them to other individuals, or whether they overtly respond to them as made or addressed to them by other individuals. A universe of discourse is simply a system of common or social meanings.[4]

The very universality and impersonality of thought and reason is from the behavioristic standpoint the result of the given individual taking the attitudes of others toward himself, and of his finally crystallizing all these particular attitudes into a single attitude or standpoint which may be called that of the "generalized other."

Alternative ways of acting under an indefinite number of different particular conditions or in an indefinite number of different particular situations—ways which are more or less identical for an indefinite number of normal individuals—are all that universals (however treated in logic or metaphysics) really amount to; they are meaningless apart from the social acts in which they are implicated and from which they derive their significance.[5]

NOTES

1. Abstraction and universals are due to conflict and inhibition: a wall is something to be avoided and something to be jumped, and while both it is mental, a concept. Language makes it possible to hold on to these mental objects. Abstractions exist for lower animals but they cannot hold them (1924).

2. This paragraph is selected from a manuscript, "The Philosophy of John Dewey." To be published in the 1936 *International Journal of Ethics.*

3. A common world exists . . . only in so far as there is a common (group) experience (MS.)

4. Our so-called laws of thought are the abstrac-

tions of social intercourse. Our whole process of abstract thought, technique and method is essentially social (1912).

The organization of the social act answers to what we call the universal. Functionally it is the universal (1930).

5. All the enduring relations have been subject to revision. There remain the logical constants, and the deductions from logical implications. To the same category belong the so-called universals or concepts. They are the elements and structure of a universe of discourse. In so far as in social conduct with others and with ourselves we indicate the characters that endure in the perspective of the group to which we belong and out of which we arise, we are indicating

that which relative to our conduct is unchanged, to which, in other words, passage is irrelevant. A metaphysics which lifts these logical elements out of their experiential habitat and endows them with a subsistential being overlooks the fact that the irrelevance to passage is strictly relative to the situation in conduct within which the reflection arises, that while we can find in different situations a method of conversation and so of thought which proves irrelevant to the differences in the situations, and so provides a method of translation from one perspective to another, this irrelevance belongs only to the wider character which the problem in reflection assumes, and never transcends the social conduct within which the method arises (MS).

The Nature of Reflective Intelligence

In the type of temporary inhibition of action which signifies thinking, or in which reflection arises, we have presented in the experience of the individual, tentatively and in advance and for his selection among them, the different possibilities or alternatives of future action open to him within the given social situation—the different or alternative ways of completing the given social act wherein he is implicated, or which he has already initiated. Reflection or reflective behavior arises only under the conditions of self-consciousness, and makes possible the purposive control and organization by the individual organism of its conduct, with reference to its social and physical environment, i.e., with reference to the various social and physical situations in which it becomes involved and to which it reacts. The organization of the self is simply the organization, by the individual organism, of the set of attitudes toward its social environment—and toward itself from the standpoint of that environment, or as a functioning element in the process of social experience and behavior constituting that environment—which it is able to take. It is essential that such reflective intelligence be dealt with from the point of view of social behaviorism.

I said a moment ago that there is something involved in our statement of the meaning of an object which is more than the mere response, however complex that may be. We may respond to a musical phrase and there

may be nothing in the experience beyond the response; we may not be able to say why we respond or what it is we respond to. Our attitude may simply be that we like some music and do not like other music. Most of our recognitions are of this sort. We pick out the book we want but could not say what the character of the book is. We probably could give a more detailed account of the countenance of a man we meet for the first time than of our most intimate friends. With our friends we are ready to start our conversation the moment they are there; we do not have to make sure who they are. But if we try to pick out a man who has been described to us we narrowly examine the person to make sure he answers to the account that is given to us. With a person with whom we are familiar we carry on our conversation without thinking of these things. Most of our processes of recognition do not involve this identification of the characters which enable us to identify the objects. We may have to describe a person and we find we cannot do it—we know him too well. We may have to pick those details out, and then if we are taking a critical attitude we have to find out what it is in the object that calls out this complex response. When we are doing that we are getting a statement of what the nature of the object is, or if you like, its meaning. We have to indicate to ourselves what it is that calls out this particular re-

From *Mind, Self, and Society: From the Standpoint of a Social Behaviorist,* Ed. Charles W. Morris (Chicago: The University of Chicago Press, 1934), pp. 90–100.

sponse. We recognize a person, say, because of the character of his physique. If one should come into the room greatly changed by a long attack of sickness, or by exposure to the tropical sun, one's friends would not be able to recognize him immediately. There are certain elements which enable us to recognize a friend. We may have to pick out the characters which make recognition successful, to indicate those characters to somebody or to ourselves. We may have to determine what the stimuli are that call out a response of this complex character. That is often a very difficult thing to do, as is evidenced by musical criticism. A whole audience may be swept away by a composition and perhaps not a person there will be able to state what it is in the production that calls out this particular response, or to tell what the various reactions are in these individuals. It is an unusual gift which can analyze that sort of an object and pick out what the stimulus is for so complex an action.

What I want to call attention to is the process by which there is an indication of those characters which do call out the response. Animals of a type lower than man respond to certain characters with a nicety that is beyond human capacity, such as odor in the case of a dog. But it would be beyond the capacity of a dog to indicate to another dog what the odor was. Another dog could not be sent out by the first dog to pick out this odor. A man may tell how to identifty another man. He can indicate what the characters are that will bring about a certain response. That ability absolutely distinguishes the intelligence of such a reflective being as man from that of the lower animals, however intelligent they may be. We generally say that man is a rational animal and lower animals are not. What I wanted to show, at least in terms of behavioristic psychology, is that what we have in mind in this distinction is the indication of those characters which lead to the sort of response which we give to an object. Pointing out the characters which lead to the response is precisely that which distinguishes a detective office that sends out a man, from a bloodhound which runs down a man. Here are two types of intelligence, each one specialized; the detective could not do what the bloodhound does and the bloodhound could not do what the detective does. Now, the intelligence of the detective over against the intelligence of the bloodhound lies in this capacity to indicate what the particular characters are which will call out his response of taking the man.[1]

Such would be a behaviorist's account of what is involved in reason. When you are reasoning you are indicating to yourself the characters that call our certain responses—and that is all you are doing. If you have the angle and a side you can determine the area of a triangle; given certain characters there are certain responses indicated. There are other processes, not exactly rational, out of which you can build up new responses from old ones. You may pick out responses which are there in other reactions and put them together. A book of directions may provide a set of stimuli which lead to a certain set of responses, and you pick them out of your other complex responses, perhaps as they have not been picked out before. When you write on a typewriter you may be instructed as to the way in which to use it. You can build up a fairly good technique to start with, but even that is a process which still involves the indication of the stimuli to call out the various responses. You unite stimuli which have not been united in the past, and then these stimuli take with them the compound responses. It may be a crude response at first, and must be freed from the responses had in the past. The way in which you react toward the doubling of letters when you write is different from the way you react in writing the letters on a typewriter. You make mistakes because the responses you utilize have been different, have been connected with a whole set of other responses. A drawing teacher will sometimes have pupils draw with the left hand rather than the right hand, because the habits of the right hand are very difficult to get rid of. This is what you are doing when you act in a rational fashion: you are indicating to yourself what the stimuli are that will call out a complex response, and by the order of the stimuli you are determining what the whole of the response will be. Now, to be able to indicate those stimuli to other persons or to yourself is what we call rational conduct as distinct from the unreasoning intelligence of the lower animals, and from a good deal of our own conduct.

Man is distinguished by that power of analysis of the field of stimulation which enables him to pick out one stimulus rather than another and so to hold on to the response that belongs to that stimulus, picking it out from others, and recombining it with others. You cannot get a lock to work. You notice certain elements, each of which brings out a certain sort of response; and what you are doing is holding on to these processes of response by giving attention to the stimuli. Man can combine not only the responses already there, which is the thing an animal lower than man can do, but the human individual can get into his activities and break them up, giving attention to specific elements, holding the responses that answer to these particular stimuli, and then combining them to build up another act. That is what we mean by learning or by teaching a person to do a thing. You indicate to him certain specific phases or characters of the object which call out certain sorts of responses. We state that generally by saying consciousness accompanies only the sensory process and not the motor process. We can directly control the sensory but not the motor processes; we can give our attention to a particular element in the field and by giving such attention and so holding on to the stimulus we can get control of the response. That is the way we get control of our action; we do not directly control our response through the motor paths themselves.

There is no capacity in the lower forms to give attention to some analyzed element in the field of stimulation which would enable them to control the response. But one can say to a person "Look at this, just see this thing" and he can fasten his attention on the specific object. He can direct attention and so isolate the particular response that answers to it. That is the way in which we break up our complex activities and thereby make learning possible. What takes place is an analysis of the process by giving attention to the specific stimuli that call out a particular act, and this analysis makes possible a reconstruction of the act. An animal makes combinations, as we say, only by trial and error, and the combination that is successful simply maintains itself.

The gesture as worked out in the conduct of the human group serves definitely to indicate just these elements and thus to bring them within the field of voluntary attention. There is, of course, a fundamental likeness between voluntary attention and involuntary attention. A bright light, a peculiar odor, may be something which takes complete control of the organism and in so far inhibits other activity. A voluntary action, however, is dependent upon the indication of a certain character, pointing it out, holding on to it, and so holding on to the response that belongs to it. That sort of an analysis is essential to what we call human intelligence, and it is made possible by language.

The psychology of attention ousted the psychology of association. An indefinite number of associations were found which lie in our experience with reference to anything that comes before us, but associational psychology never explained why one association rather than another was the dominant one. It laid down rules that if a certain association had been intense, recent, and frequent it would be dominant, but often there are in fact situations in which what seems to be the weakest element in the situation occupies the mind. It was not until the psychologist took up the analysis of attention that he was able to deal with such situations, and to realize that voluntary attention is dependent upon indication of some character in the field of stimulation. Such indication makes possible the isolation and recombination of responses.

In the case of the vocal gesture there is a tendency to call out the response in one form that is called out in the other, so that the child plays the part of parent, or teacher, or preacher. The gesture under those conditions calls out certain responses in the individual which it calls out in the other person, and carrying it out in the individual isolates that particular character of the stimulus. The response of the other is there in the individual isolating the stimulus. If one calls out quickly to a person in danger, he himself is in the attitude of jumping away, though the act is not performed. He is not in danger, but he has those particular elements of the response in himself, and we speak of them as meanings. Stated in terms of the central nervous system, this means that he has stirred up its upper tracts which would lead to the actual jumping away. A person picks out the different responses involved in escape when he enters the theater and notices the signs on the program cautioning him to choose the nearest exit in case of fire. He has all the different responses, so to speak, listed before him, and he prepares what he is going to do by picking out the different elements and putting them together in the way required. The efficiency engineer comes in to pick out this, that, or the other thing, and chooses the order in which they should be carried out. One is doing the same himself in so far as he is self-conscious. Where we have to determine what will be the order of a set of responses, we are putting them together in a certain fashion, and we can do this because we can indicate the order of the stimuli which are going to act upon us. That is what is involved in the human intelligence as distinguished from the intelligence type of the lower forms. We cannot tell an elephant that he is to take hold of the other elephant's tail; the stimulus will not indicate the same thing to the elephant as to ourselves. We can create a situation which is a stimulus to the elephant but we cannot get the elephant to indicate to itself what this stimulus is so that he has the response to it in his own system.

The gesture provides a process by means of which one does arouse in himself the reaction that might be aroused in another, and this is not a part of his immediate reaction in so far as his immediate physical environment is concerned. When we tell a person to do something the response we have is not the doing of the actual thing, but the beginning of it. Communication gives to us those elements of response which can be held in the mental field. We do not carry them out, but they are there constituting the meanings of these objects which we indicate. Language is a process of indicating certain stimuli and changing the response to them in the system of behavior. Language as a social process has made it possible for us to pick out responses and hold them in the organism of the individual, so that they are there in relation to that which we indicate. The actual gesture is, within limits, arbitrary. Whether one points out with his finger, or points with the glance of the eye, or motion of the head, or the attitude of the body, or by means of a vocal gesture in one language of another, is indifferent, provided it does call out the response that belongs to that thing which is indicated. That is the essential part of language. The gesture must be one that calls out the response in the individual, or tends to call out the response in the individual, which its utilization will bring out in another's response. Such is the material with which the mind works. However slight, there must be some sort of gesture. To have the response isolated without an indication of a stimulus is almost a contradiction in terms. I have been trying to point out what this process of communication does in the way of providing us with the material that exists in our mind. It does this by furnishing those gestures which in affecting us as they affect others call out the attitude which the other takes, and that we take in so far as we assume his rôle. We get the attitude, the meaning, within the field of our own control, and that control consists in combining all these various possible responses to furnish the newly constructed act demanded by the problem. In such a way we can state rational conduct in terms of a behavioristic psychology.

I wish to add one further factor to our account: the relation of the temporal character of the nervous system to foresight and choice.

The central nervous system makes possible the implicit initiation of a number of possible alternative responses with reference to any given object or objects for the completion of any already initiated act, in advance of the actual completion of that act; and thus makes possible the exercise of intelligent or reflective choice in the acceptance of that one among these possible alternative responses which is to be carried into overt effect.[2]

Human intelligence, by means of the physiological mechanism of the human central nervous system, deliberately selects one from among the several alternative responses which are possible in the given problematic environmental situation; and if the given response which it selects is complex—i.e., is a set or chain or group or succession of simple responses—it can organize this set or chain of simple responses in such a way as to make possible the most adequate and harmonious solution by the individual of the given environmental problem.

It is the entrance of the alternative possibilities of future response into the determination of present conduct in any given environmental situation, and their operation, through the mechanism of the central nervous system, as part of the factors or conditions determining present behavior, which decisively contrasts intelligent conduct or behavior with reflex, instinctive, and habitual conduct or behavior—delayed reaction with immediate reaction. That which takes place in present organic behavior is always in some sense an emergent from the past, and never could have been precisely predicted in advance—never could have been predicted on the basis of a knowledge, however complete, of the past, and of the conditions in the past which are relevant to its emergence; and in the case of organic behavior which is intelligently controlled, this element of spontaneity is especially prominent by virtue of the present influence exercised over such behavior by the possible future results or consequences which it may have. Our ideas of or about future conduct are our tendencies to act in several alternative ways in the presence of a given environmental situation—tendencies or attitudes which can appear, or be implicitly aroused, in the structure of the central nervous system in advance of the overt response or reaction to that situation, and which thus can enter as determining factors into the control or selection of this overt response. Ideas, as distinct from acts, or as failing to issue in overt behavior, are simply what we do not do; they are possibilities of overt responses which we test out implicitly in the central nervous system and then reject in favor of those which we do in fact act upon or carry into effect. The process of intelligent conduct is essentially a process of selection from among various alternatives; intelligence is largely a matter of selectivity.

Delayed reaction is necessary to intelligent conduct. The organization, implicit testing, and final selection by the individual of his overt responses or reactions to the social situations which confront him and which present him with problems of adjustment, would be impossible if his overt responses or reactions could not in such situations be delayed until this process of organizing, implicitly testing, and finally selecting is carried out; that is, would be impossible if some overt response or other to the given environmental stimuli had to be immediate. Without delayed reaction, or except in terms of it, no conscious or intelligent control over behavior could be exercised; for it is through this process of selective reaction—which can be selective only because it is delayed—that intelligence operates in the determination of behavior. Indeed, it is this process which constitutes intelligence. The central nervous system provides not only the necessary physiological mechanism for this process, but also the necessary physiological condition of delayed reaction which this process presupposes. Intelligence is essentially the ability to solve problems of present behavior in terms of its possible future consequences as implicated on the basis of past experience—the ability, that is, to solve the problems of present behavior in the light of, or by reference to, both the past and the future; it involves both memory and foresight. And the process of exercising intelligence is the process of delaying, organizing, and selecting a response or reaction to the stimuli of the given environmental situation. The process is made possible by the mechanism of the central nervous system, which permits the individual's taking of the attitude of the other toward himself, and thus becoming an object

to himself. This is the most effective means of adjustment to the social environment, and indeed to the environment in general, that the individual has at his disposal.

An attitude of any sort represents the beginning, or potential initiation, of some composite act or other, a social act in which, along with other individuals, the individual taking the given attitude is involved or implicated. The traditional supposition has been that the purposive element in behavior must ultimately be an idea, a conscious motive, and hence must imply or depend upon the presence of a mind. But the study of the nature of the central nervous sytem shows that in the form of physiological attitudes (expressed in specific physiological sets) different possible completions to the given act are there in advance of its actual completion, and that through them the earlier parts of the given act are affected or influenced (in present conduct) by its later phases; so that the purposive element in behavior has a physiological seat, a behavioristic basis, and is not fundamentally nor necessarily conscious or psychical.

NOTES

1. Intelligence and knowledge are inside the process of conduct. Thinking is an elaborate process of . . . . presenting the world so that it will be favorable for conduct, so that the ends of life of the form may be reached (MS).

Thinking is pointing out—to think about a thing is to point it out before acting (1924).

2. It is an advantage to have these responses ready before we get to the object. If our world were right on top of us, in contact with us, we would have no time for deliberation. There would be only one way of responding to that world.

Through his distance organs and his capacity for delayed responses the individual lives in the future with the possibility of planning his life with reference to that future (1931).

The Self and the Organism

We can distinguish very definitely between the self and the body. The body can be there and can operate in a very intelligent fashion without there being a self involved in the experience. The self has the characteristic that it is an object to itself, and that characteristic dis-

---

From *Mind, Self, and Society: From the Standpoint of a Social Behaviorist,* Ed. Charles W. Morris (Chicago: The University of Chicago Press, 1934), pp. 136–141.

tinguishes it from other objects and from the body. It is perfectly true that the eye can see the foot, but it does not see the body as a whole. We cannot see our backs; we can feel certain portions of them, if we are agile, but we cannot get an experience of our whole body. There are, of course, experiences which are somewhat vague and difficult of location, but the bodily experiences are for us organized about a self. The foot and hand belong to the self. We can see our feet, especially if we look at them from the wrong end of an opera glass, as strange things which we have difficulty in recognizing as our own. The parts of the body are quite distinguishable from the self. We can lose parts of the body without any serious invasion of the self. The mere ability to experience different parts of the body is not different from the experience of a table. The table presents a different feel from what the hand does when one hand feels another, but it is an experience of something with which we come definitely into contact. The body does not experience itself as a whole, in the sense in which the self in some way enters into the experience of the self.

It is the characteristic of the self as an object to itself that I want to bring out. This characteristic is represented in the word "self," which is a reflexive, and indicates that which can be both subject and object. This type of object is essentially different from other objects, and in the past it has been distinguished as conscious, a term which indicates an experience with, an experience of, one's self. It was assumed that consciousness in some way carried this capacity of being an object to itself. In giving a behavioristic statement of consciousness we have to look for some sort of experience in which the physical organism can become an object to itself.[1]

When one is running to get away from someone who is chasing him, he is entirely occupied in this action, and his experience may be swallowed up in the objects about him, so that he has, at the time being, no consciousness of self at all. We must be, of course, very completely occupied to have that take place, but we can, I think, recognize that sort of a possible experience in which the self does not enter. We can, perhaps, get some light on that situation through those experiences in which in very intense action there appear in the experience of the individual, back of this intense action, memories and anticipations. Tolstoi as an officer in the war gives an account of having pictures of his past experience in the midst of

his most intense action. There are also the pictures that flash into a person's mind when he is drowning. In such instances there is a contrast between an experience that is absolutely wound up in outside activity in which the self as an object does not enter, and an activity of memory and imagination in which the self is the principal object. The self is then entirely distinguishable from an organism that is surrounded by things and acts with reference to things, including parts of its own body. These latter may be objects like other objects, but they are just objects out there in the field, and they do not involve a self that is an object to the organism. This is, I think, frequently overlooked. It is that fact which makes our anthropomorphic reconstructions of animal life so fallacious. How can an individual get outside himself (experientially) in such a way as to become an object to himself? This is the essential psychological problem of selfhood or of self-consciousness; and its solution is to be found by referring to the process of social conduct or activity in which the given person or individual is implicated. The apparatus of reason would not be complete unless it swept itself into its own analysis of the field of experience; or unless the individual brought himself into the same experiental field as that of the other individual selves in relation to whom he acts in any given social situation. Reason cannot become impersonal unless it takes an objective, non-affective attitude toward itself; otherwise we have just consciousness, not *self*-consciousness. And it is necessary to rational conduct that the individual should thus take an objective, impersonal attitude toward himself, that he should become an object to himself. For the individual organism is obviously an essential and important fact or constituent element of the empirical situation in which it acts; and without taking objective account of itself as such, it cannot act intelligently, or rationally.

The individual experiences himself as such, not directly, but only indirectly, from the particular standpoints of other individual members of the same social group, or from the generalized standpoint of the social group as a whole to which he belongs. For he enters his own experience as a self or individual, not directly or immediately, not by becoming a subject to himself, but only in so far as he first becomes an object to himself just as other individuals are objects to him or in his experience; and he becomes an object to himself only by taking the attitudes of other individuals toward himself within a social environment or context of experience and behavior in which both he and they are involved.

The importance of what we term "communication" lies in the fact that it provides a form of behavior in which the organism or the individual may become an object to himself. It is that sort of communication which we have been discussing—not communication in the sense of the cluck of the hen to the chickens, or the bark of a wolf to the pack, or the lowing of a cow, but communication in the sense of significant symbols, communication which is directed not only to others but also to the individual himself. So far as that type of communication is a part of behavior it at least introduces a self. Of course, one may hear without listening; one may see things that he does not realize; do things that he is not really aware of. But it is where one does respond to that which he addresses to another and where that response of his own becomes a part of his conduct, where he not only hears himself but responds to himself, talks and replies to himself as truly as the other person replies to him, that we have behavior in which the individuals become objects to themselves.

Such a self is not, I would say, primarily the physiological organism. The physiological organism is essential to it,[2] but we are at least able to think of a self without it. Persons who believe in immortality, or believe in ghosts, or in the possibility of the self leaving the body, assume a self which is quite distinguishable from the body. How successfully they can hold these conceptions is an open question, but we do, as a fact, separate the self and the organism. It is fair to say that the beginning of the self as an object, so far as we can see, is to be found in the experiences of people that lead to the conception of a "double." Primitive people assume that there is a double, located presumably in the diaphragm, that leaves the body temporarily in sleep and completely in death. It can be enticed out of the body of one's enemy and perhaps killed. It is represented in infancy by the imaginary playmates which children set up, and through which they come to control their experiences in their play.

The self, as that which can be an object to itself, is essentially a social structure, and it arises in social experience. After a self has arisen, it in a certain sense provides for itself its social experiences, and so we can conceive of an absolutely solitary self. But it is impossible to conceive of a self arising outside of social experience. When it has arisen we can think of a person in solitary confinement for the rest of his life, but who still has himself as a companion, and is able to think and to converse with himself as he had communicated with others. That process to which I have just referred, of responding to one's self as another responds to it, taking part in one's own conversation with others, being aware of what one is saying and using that awareness of what one is saying to determine what one is going to say thereafter—that is a process with which we are all familiar. We are continually following up our own address to other persons by an understanding of what we are saying, and using that understanding in the direction of our continued speech. We are finding out what we are going to say, what we are going to do, by saying and doing, and in the process we are continually controlling the process itself. In the conversation of gestures what we say calls out a certain response in another and that in turn changes our own action, so that we shift from what we started to do because of the reply the other makes. The conversation of gestures is the beginning of communication. The individual comes to carry on a conversation of gestures with himself. He says something, and that calls out a certain reply in himself which makes him change what he was going to say. One starts to say something, we will presume an unpleasant something, but when he starts to say it he realizes it is cruel. The effect on himself of what he is saying checks him; there is here a conversation of gestures between the individual and himself. We mean by significant speech that the action is one that affects the individual himself, and that the effect upon the individual himself is part of the intelligent carrying-out of the conversation with others. Now we, so to speak, amputate that social phase and dispense with it for the time being, so that one is talking to one's self as one would talk to another person.[3]

NOTES

1. Man's behavior is such in his social group that he is able to become an object to himself, a fact which constitutes him a more advanced product of evolutionary development than are the lower animals. Fundamentally it is this social fact—and not his alleged possession of a soul or mind with which he, as an individual, has been mysteriously and supernaturally endowed, and with which the lower animals have not been endowed—that differentiates him from them.

2. *a*) All social interrelations and interactions are rooted in a certain common sociophysiological endowment of every individual involved in them. These physiological bases of social behavior—which have their ultimate seat or locus in the lower part of the individual's central nervous system—are the bases of such behavior, precisely because they in themselves are also social; that is, because they consist in drives or instincts or behavior tendencies, on the part of the given individual, which he cannot carry out or give overt expression and satisfaction to without the cooperative aid of one or more other individuals. The physiological processes of behavior of which they are the mechanisms are processes which necessarily involve more than one individual, processes in which other individuals besides the given individual are perforce implicated. Examples of the fundamental social relations to which these physiological bases of social behavior give rise are those between the sexes (expressing the reproductive instinct), between parent and child (expressing the parental instinct), and between neighbors (expressing the gregarious instinct). These relatively simple and rudimentary physiological mechanisms or tendencies of individual human behavior, besides constituting the physiological bases of all human social behavior, are also the fundamental biological materials of human nature; so that when we refer to human nature, we are referring to something which is essentially social.

b) Sexually and parentally, as well as in its attacks and defenses, the activities of the physiological organism are social in that the acts begun within the organism require their completion in the actions of others . . . . But while the pattern of the individual act may be said to be in these cases social, it is only so in so far as the organism seeks for the stimuli in the attitudes and characters of other forms for the completion of its own responses, and by its behavior tends to maintain the other as a part of its own environment. The actual behavior of the other or the others is not initiated in the individual form as a part of its own pattern of behavior (MS).

3. It is generally recognized that the specifically social expressions of intelligence, or the exercise of what is often called "social intelligence," depend upon the given individual's ability to take the roles of, or "put himself in the place of," the other individuals implicated with him in given social situations; and upon his consequent sensitivity to their attitudes toward himself and toward one another. These specifically social expressions of intelligence, of course, acquire unique significance in terms of our view that the whole nature of intelligence is social to the very core—that this putting of one's self in the places of others, this taking by one's self of their rôles or attitudes, is not merely one of the various aspects or expressions of intelligence or of intelligent behavior, but is the very essence of its character. Spearman's "X factor" in intelligence—the unknown factor which, according to him, intelligence contains—is simply (if our social theory of intelligence is correct) this ability of the intelligent individual to take the attitude of the other, or the attitudes of others, thus realizing the significations or grasping the meanings of the symbols or gestures in terms of which thinking proceeds; and thus being able to carry on with himself the internal conversation with these symbols or gestures which thinking involves.

The Self, the Generalized Other, "I," and "Me"

We were speaking of the social conditions under which the self arises as an object. In addition to language we found two illustrations, one in play and the other in the game, and I wish to summarize and expand my account on these points. I have spoken of these from the point of view of children. We can, of course, refer also to the attitudes of more primitive people out of which our civilization has arisen. A striking illustration of play as distinct from the game is found in the myths and various of the plays which primitive people carry out, especially in religious pageants. The pure play attitude which we find in the cases of little children may not be found here, since the participants are adults, and undoubtedly the relationship of these play processes to that which they interpret is more or less in the minds of even the most primitive people. In the process of interpretation of such rituals, there is an organization of play which perhaps might be compared to that which is taking place in the kindergarten in dealing with the plays of little children, where these are made into a set that will have a definite structure or relationship. At least something of the same sort is found in the play of primitive people. This type of activity belongs, of course, not to the everyday life of the people in their dealing with the objects

From *Mind, Self, and Society: From the Standpoint of a Social Behaviorist*, Ed. Charles W. Morris (Chicago: The University of Chicago Press, 1934), pp. 152–154, 164–165, 173–175.

about them—there we have a more or less definitely developed self-consciousness—but in their attitudes toward the forces about them, the nature upon which they depend; in their attitude toward this nature which is vague and uncertain, there we have a much more primitive response; and that response finds its expression in taking the rôle of the other, playing at the expression of their gods and their heroes, going through certain rites which are the representation of what these individuals are supposed to be doing. The process is one which develops, to be sure, into a more or less definite technique and is controlled; and yet we can say that it has arisen out of situations similar to those in which little children play at being a parent, at being a teacher—vague personalities that are about them and which affect them and on which they depend. These are personalities which they take, rôles they play, and in so far control the development of their own personality. This outcome is just what the kindergarten works toward. It takes the characters of these various vague beings and gets them into such an organized social relationship to each other that they build up the character of the little child.[1] The very introduction of organization from outside supposes a lack of organization at this period in the child's experience. Over against such a situation of the little child and primitive people, we have the game as such.

The fundamental difference between the game and play is that in the latter the child must have the attitude of all the others involved in that game. The attitudes of the other players which the participant assumes organize into a sort of unit, and it is that organization which controls the response of the individual. The illustration used was of a person playing baseball. Each one of his own acts is determined by his assumption of the action of the others who are playing the game. What he does is controlled by his being everyone else on that team, at least in so far as those attitudes affect his own particular response. We get then an "other" which is an organization of the attitudes of those involved in the same process.

The organized community or social group which gives to the individual his unity of self may be called "the generalized other." The attitude of the generalized other is the attitude of the whole community.[2]

. . . It has been the tendency of psychology to deal with the self as a more or less isolated and independent element, a sort of entity that could conceivably exist by itself. It is possible that there might be a single self in the universe if we start off by identifying the self with a certain feeling-consciousness. If we speak of this feeling as objective, then we can think of that self as existing by itself. We can think of a separate physical body existing by itself, we can assume that it has these feelings or conscious states in question, and so we can set up that sort of a self in thought as existing simply by itself.

Then there is another use of "consciousness" with which we have been particularly occupied, denoting that which we term thinking or reflective intelligence, a use of consciousness which always has, implicitly at least, the reference to an "I" in it. This use of consciousness has no necessary connection with the other; it is an entirely different conception. One usage has to do with a certain mechanism, a certain way in which an organism acts. If an organism is endowed with sense organs then there are objects in its environment, and among those objects will be parts of its own body.[3] It is true that if the organism did not have a retina and a central nervous system there would not be any objects of vision. For such objects to exist there have to be certain physiological conditions, but these objects are not in themselves necessarily related to a self. When we reach a self we reach a certain sort of conduct, a certain type of social process which involves the interaction of different individuals and yet implies individuals engaged in some sort of co-operative activity. In that process a self, as such, can arise.

. . . We have discussed at length the social foundations of the self, and hinted that the self does not consist simply in the bare organization of social attitudes. We may now explicitly raise the question as to the nature of the "I" which is aware of the social "me." I do not mean to raise the metaphysical question of how a person can be both "I" and "me," but to ask for the significance of this distinction from the point of view of conduct itself. Where in conduct does the "I" come in as over against the "me"? If one determines what his position is in society and feels himself as having a certain function and privilege, these are all defined with reference to an "I," but the "I" is not a "me" and cannot become a "me." We may have a better self and a worse self, but that again is not the "I" as over against the "me," because they are both selves. We approve of one and disapprove of the other, but when we bring up one or the other they are there for such approval as "me's." The "I" does not get into the limelight; we talk to ourselves, but do not see ourselves. The "I" reacts to the self which arises through the taking of the attitudes of others. Through taking those attitudes we have introduced the "me" and we react to it as an "I."

. . . The "I" is the response of the organism to the attitudes of the others; the "me" is the organized set of attitudes of others which one himself assumes. The attitudes of the others constitute the organized "me," and then one reacts toward that as an "I."

NOTES

1. "The Relation of Play to Education," *University of Chicago Record,* I (1896–97), 140 ff.
2. It is possible for inanimate objects, no less than for other human organisms, to form parts of the generalized and organized—the completely socialized—other for any given human individual, in so far as he responds to such objects socially or in a social fashion (by means of the mechanism of thought, the internalized conversation of gestures). Any thing—any object or set of objects, whether animate or inanimate, human or animal, or merely physical—toward which he acts, or to which he responds, socially, is an element in what for him is the generalized other; by taking the attitudes of which toward himself he becomes conscious of himself as an object or individual, and thus develops a self or personality. Thus, for example, the cult, in its primitive form, is merely the social embodiment of the relation between the given social group or community and its physical environment—an organized social means, adopted by the individual members of that group or community, of entering into social relations with that environment, or (in a sense) of carrying on conversations with it; and in this way that environment becomes part of the total generalized other for each of the individual members of the given social group or community.
3. Our constructive selection of our environment is what we term "consciousness," in the first sense of the term. The organism does not project sensuous qualities—colors, for example—into the environment to which it responds; but it endows this environment with such qualities, in a sense similar to that in which an ox endows grass with the quality of being food, or in which—speaking more generally—the relation between biological organisms and certain environmental contents give rise to food objects. If there were no organisms with particular sense organs there would be no environment, in the proper or usual sense of the term. An organism constructs (in the selective sense) its environment; and consciousness often refers to the character of the environment in so far as it is determined or constructively selected by our human organisms, and depends upon the relationship between the former (as thus selected or constructed) and the latter.

The Social Foundations and Functions of Thought and Communication

In the same socio-physiological way that the human individual becomes conscious of himself he also becomes conscious of other individuals; and his consciousness both of himself and of other individuals is equally important for his own self-development and for the development of the organized society or social group to which he belongs.

The principle which I have suggested as basic to human social organization is that of communication involving participation in the other. This requires the appearance of the other in the self, the identification of the other with the self, the reaching of self-consciousness through the other. This participation is made possible through the type of communication which the human animal is able to carry out—a type of communication distinguished from that which takes place among other forms which have not this principle in their societies. I discussed the sentinel, so-called, that may be said to communicate his discovery of the danger to the other members, as the clucking of the hen may be said to communicate to the chick. There are conditions under which the gesture of one form serves to place the other forms in the proper attitude toward external conditions. In one sense we may say the one form communicates with the other, but the difference between that and self-conscious communication is evident. One form does not know that communication is taking place with the other. We

From *Mind, Self, and Society: From the Standpoint of a Social Behaviorist,* Ed. Charles W. Morris, (Chicago: The University of Chicago Press, 1934), pp. 253–256, 260.

get illustrations of that in what we term mob-consciousness, the attitude which an audience will take when under the influence of a great speaker. One is influenced by the attitudes of those about him, which are reflected back into the different members of the audience so that they come to respond as a whole. One feels the general attitude of the whole audience. There is then communication in a real sense, that is, one form communicates to the other an attitude which the other assumes toward a certain part of the environment that is of importance to them both. That level of communication is found in forms of society which are of lower type than the social organization of the human group.

In the human group, on the other hand, there is not only this kind of communication but also that in which the person who uses this gesture and so communicates assumes the attitude of the other individual as well as calling it out in the other. He himself is in the rôle of the other person whom he is so exciting and influencing. It is through taking this rôle of the other that he is able to come back on himself and so direct his own process of communication. This taking the rôle of the other, an expression I have so often used, is not simply of passing importance. It is not something that just happens as an incidental result of the gesture, but it is of importance in the development of cooperative activity. The immediate effect of such rôle-taking lies in the control which the individual is able to exercise over his own response.[1] The control of the action of the individual in a co-operative process can take place in the conduct of the individual himself if he can take the rôle of the other. It is this control of the response of the individual himself through taking the rôle of the other that leads to the value of this type of communication from the point of view of the organization of the conduct in the group. It carries the process of co-operative activity farther than it can be carried in the herd as such, or in the insect society.

And thus it is that social control, as operating in terms of self-criticism, exerts itself so intimately and extensively over individual behavior or conduct, serving to integrate the individual and his actions with reference to the organized social process of experience and behavior in which he is implicated. The physiological mechanism of the human individual's central nervous system makes it possible for him to take the attitudes of other individuals, and the attitudes of the organized social group of which he and they are members, toward himself, in terms of his integrated social relations to them and to the group as a whole; so that the general social process of experience and behavior which the group is carrying on is directly presented to him in his own experience, and so that he is thereby able to govern and direct his conduct consciously and critically, with reference to his relations both to the social group as a whole and to its other individual members, in terms of this social process. Thus he becomes not only self-conscious but also self-critical; and thus, through self-criticism, social control over individual behavior or conduct operates by virtue of the social origin and basis of such criticism. That is to say, self-criticism is essentially social criticism, and behavior controlled by self-criticism is essentially behavior controlled socially.[3] Hence social control, so far from tending to crush out the human individual or to obliterate his self-conscious individuality, is, on the contrary, actually constitutive of and inextricably associated with that individuality; for the individual is what he is, as a conscious and individual personality, just in as far as he is a member of society, involved in the social process of experience and activity, and thereby socially controlled in his conduct.

The very organization of the self-conscious community is dependent upon individuals taking the attitude of the other individuals. The development of this process, as I have indicated, is dependent upon getting the attitude of the group as distinct from that of a separate individual—getting what I have termed a "generalized other." I have illustrated this by the ball game, in which the attitudes of a set of individuals are involved in a co-operative response in which the different rôles involve each other. In so far as a man takes the attitude of one individual in the group, he must take it in its relationship to the action of the other members of the group; and if he is fully to adjust himself, he would have to take the attitudes of all involved in the process. The degree, of course, to which he can do that is restrained by his capacity, but still in all intelligent processes we are able sufficiently to take the rôles of those involved in the activity to make our own action intelligent. The degree to which the life of the whole community can get into the self-conscious life of the separate individuals varies enormously. History is largely occupied in tracing out the development which could not have been present in the actual experience of the members of the community at the time the historian is writing about. Such an account explains the importance of history. One can look back over that which took place, and bring out changes, forces, and interests which nobody at the time was conscious of. We have to wait for the historian to give the picture because the actual process was one which transcended the experience of the separate individuals.

. . . It is necessary to emphasize this because philosophy and the dogmas that have gone with it have set up a process of thought and a thinking substance that is the antecedent of these very processes within which thinking goes on. Thinking, however, is nothing but the response of the individual to the attitude of the other in the wide social process in which both are involved, and the directing of one's anticipatory action by these attitudes of the others that one does assume. Since that is what the process of thinking consists in, it cannot simply run by itself.

I have been looking at language as a principle of social organization which has made the distinctively human society possible. Of course, if there are inhabitants in Mars, it is possible for us to enter into communication with them in as far as we can enter into social relations with them. If we can isolate the logical constants which are essential for any process of thinking, presumably those logical constants would put us into a position to carry on communication with the other community. They would constitute a common social process so that one could possibly enter into a social process with any other being in any historical period or spatial position. By means of thought one can project a society into the future or past, but we are always presupposing a social relationship within which this process of communication takes place. The process of communication cannot be set up as something that exists by itself, or as a presupposition of the social process. On the contrary, the social process is presupposed in

order to render thought and communication possible.

NOTES

1. From the standpoint of social evolution, it is this bringing of any given social act, or of the total social process in which that act is a constituent, directly and as an organized whole into the experience of each of the individual organisms implicated in that act, with reference to which he may consequently regulate and govern his individual conduct, that constitutes the peculiar value and significance of self-consciousness in these individual organisms.

We have seen that the process or activity of thinking is a conversation carried on by the individual between himself and the generalized other; and that the general form and subject matter of this conversation is given and determined by the appearance in experience of some sort of problem to be solved. Human intelligence, which expresses itself in thought, is recognized to have this character of facing and dealing with any problem of environmental adjustment which confronts an organism possessing it. And thus, as we have also seen, the essential characteristic of intelligent behavior is delayed responses—a halt in behavior while thinking is going on; this delayed response and the thinking for the purposes of which it is delayed (including the final selection, as the result of the thinking, of the best or most expedient among the several responses possible in the given environmental situation) being made possible physiologically through the mechanism of the central nervous system, and socially through the mechanism of language.

2. Freud's conception of the psychological "censor" represents a partial recognition of this operation of social control in terms of self-criticism, a recognition, namely, of its operation with reference to sexual experience and conduct. But this same sort of censorship or criticism of himself by the individual is reflected also in all other aspects of his social experience, behavior, and relations—a fact which follows naturally and inevitably from our social theory of the self.

Science Raises Problems for Philosophy—Realism and Pragmatism

The point that needs particularly to be recognized in an approach to the pragmatic doctrine is the relationship of thinking to conduct. The undertaking of the Romantic idealists and the rationalists was to present thought as that

which discovered the world. It had the distinct business of finding out what the nature of things is. That is, cognition is a process which arose, so to speak, for its own sake. One is curious, one wants to know the world; and

From *Movements of Thought in the Nineteenth Century,* Ed. Meritt A. Moore, (Chicago: The University of Chicago Press, 1938), pp. 344–352.

knowledge is a simple getting of the nature of the world. Its tests lie, from that standpoint, in the product or in the nature of what is known. This is a copy theory of knowledge; one has in his mind the impression of that which exists outside; or one may have a coherence theory such as that to which I have referred above, that which fits into a structure which lies outside. The function of knowledge in either case is to give as close a resemblance as possible to something which lies outside the mind.

If we approach the world from the standpoint of the sort of experience with which the psychology we have been presuming deals, we can see that intelligence in its simplest phase, and also in a later phase, really lies inside of a process of conduct. The animal, even the plant, has to seek out what is essential to its life. It has to avoid that which is dangerous for it in its life-process. A plant shows its intelligence by driving down its roots, in its adjustment to the climate. When you get into the animal kingdom, you find much more adjustment and an environment which involves more dangers, in which the getting of food, the avoiding of enemies, the carrying-on of the process of reproduction, take on the form of an adventure. Intelligence consists in the stimulation of those elements which are of importance to the form itself, the selection of both positive and negative elements, getting what is desirable, avoiding what is dangerous. These are the ways in which intelligence shows itself.

For example, the intelligence of the human form is one which has arisen through its ability to analyze this world by discrimination, and, through significant symbols, to indicate to other forms with which it works and to the form itself what the elements are that are of importance to it. It is able to set up such a structure of symbols, images, which stand for the object that it needs. Thinking is an elaborate process of selecting, an elaborate process of presenting the world so that it will be favorable for conduct. Whatever is its later function—it has one of knowledge, which is for its own sake—in its earlier phases we have intelligence, and then thought, as lying inside of conduct. That is, the test of intelligence is found in action. The test of the object is found in conduct itself. What the animal needs is its food, freedom from its enemy. If it responds to the right stimuli, it reaches that food, that safety. The animal has no other test as to whether it has made such a proper selection except in the result attained. You can test your stimulus only by the result of

your conduct which is in answer to it. You see, that takes the research method over into life. The animal, for example, faces a problem. It has to adjust itself to a new situation. The way in which it is going brings danger or offers some unexpected possibility of getting food. It acts upon this and thus gets a new object; and if its response to that object is successful, it may be said to be the true object for that stimulus. It is true in the sense that it brings about a result which the conduct of the animal calls for. If we look upon the conduct of the animal form as a continual meeting and solving of problems, we can find in this intelligence, even in its lowest expression, an instance of what we call "scientific method" when this has been developed into the technique of the most elaborate science. The animal is doing the same thing the scientist is doing. It is facing a problem, selecting some element in the situation which may enable it to carry its act through to completion. There is inhibition there. It tends to go in one direction, then another direction; it tends to seek this thing and avoid that. These different tendencies are in conflict; and until they can be reconstructed, the action cannot go on. The only test the animal can bring to such a reconstruction of its habits is the ongoing of its activity. This is the experimental test; can it continue in action? And that is exactly the situation found also in science.

Take such a problem, for example, as that of the radiation of the sun or of the stars. It is assumed that the radiation is due to the compression which comes with attraction. Then, knowing what the mass of the star is, what the direction of attraction is, and the compression that follows from it, one can figure out how much heat the star can radiate. On that basis it was figured out some forty years ago that the sun has not been in its present condition for a period of more than twenty million years and that it might be perhaps seventeen million years before it became dark and cold, so far as the earth is concerned. Geologists, on the other hand, were turning back the pages of the history of the earth and working out its history. In this process they got various tests as to what the time periods had been. And all these tests called for far longer periods than the astro-physicist was willing to grant. The former dealt in terms of a hundred million years. In recent research we have discovered a new test which is perhaps the most accurate of all; that is the radiation of radioactive bodies. We know, for example, that bodies of this type are continually breaking down. We can see them doing it. In the dark we can see the sparkling which represents a continual discharge of energy, the breaking-down of higher atomic structures into lower. At first this process seemed to be indefinite; but when it was worked out, it was found that such a process in radium might last for several hundred years. The rate of disintegration could be figured out. We know something about the elements, the parts of the earth, that are radioactive; and in that way we can determine what the rate is at which certain minerals which result from such a disintegration as this could have formed, how long a time would be necessary to build them up. Taking this and all the other tests, the scientists set up their theory of the history of the world—the geologist writing his history on one time schedule, and the physicist writing his on the basis of another. We get a clash here. One calls for a period of several hundred million years; the other denies any period longer than twenty million years. There you get a typical scientific problem.

What I want to point out is that it stops the scientist in his process of reconstructing the past. You are reconstructing it on one doctrine or the other. You cannot use both of them. And yet there are facts which lie behind each of them. What is the source of the energy of the sun? It is not burning up coal. It undoubtedly produces heat by the very compression that follows from attraction. That is the only source of heat which can be found. On that basis the age of the earth is twenty million years. And yet, here we have a history which the geologist and the archeological zoölogist and the botanist have been writing on the basis of other data. And the two stop each other. The process of writing the history of the earth cannot be continued, because the two theories are in conflict with each other. You have these exceptional situations arising over against each other. What is taking place is the recognition that there is another source of energy which has not been attacked, so to speak, in the doctrine of the scientists themselves. This very energy, which is found in the process of radiation which we make use of in our radium watches and clocks, represents a source of energy which the suns may themselves be drawing upon. In its process of radiation, the sun is actually turning out more than four million tons of energy per square yard every few minutes. It is using itself up. Its mass is passing over into the form of radiation. We know that light has weight. Of course, that weight represents just so much mass. Mass must come from the radiation of the sun. The sun is breaking down its own atoms and getting the energy that is in them. We do not know just what the exact process is by which this takes place, whether it is due simply to the immense crushing power of such a great mass as that at the center; but we know that there is much energy in an atom. If you could explode an atom, I think it is said that you could carry the S.S. Leviathan across the ocean on the amount of atomic energy found in a drop of oil—perhaps it is two or three drops if you like, I have forgotten the figures—but there is an enormous amount of energy shut up in the structure of the atoms themselves.

Given such a problem as that, what does the scientist do? He proceeds to start to write his history of the stars as he finds them, the giant and the dwarf stars, the white and blue and red stars, in their different stages of evolution. He starts to write of them on the basis of the hypothesis that these suns have been continually expending the energy involved in their atomic structure in the form of radiation. And that is brought, of course, into its relationship with the geological and biological history of the earth. Could one go on writing the history of the stars and of the surface of the earth so that they do not come into conflict with each other? It was found that there is plenty of time provided under the now recognized form of expenditure of the energy of the sun—a hundred million years or so, instead of twenty million years. So the process of interpreting the world, working out the scientific statement by means of the new hypothesis, could be continued.

Now, what constitutes the test of the hypothesis? The test of it is that you can continue the sort of conduct that was going on. It is the same sort of test which the animal finds. If it finds itself in a difficult situation and sees escape, it rushes off in that direction and gets away. That is a fair test, for it, of what we call a hypothesis. It did not present ideas to itself in terms of significant symbols, but it was a good working hypothesis. It could continue its action of living that way, where it could not have continued it otherwise.

Well, in the same fashion, from a logical standpoint, the scientist is engaged in stating the past history of the world, and he comes up against this blank wall of insufficient time. Now, when he collates the history of the surface and the history of the radiation of the sun, he gets a clue—a hole, so to speak—which will let him escape from that difficulty. That constitutes the test of the truth of the hypothesis. It means that he can continue the process of stating the history of the world within which he is living. And, of course, the process of stating the world, stating our past, is a process of getting control over that world, getting its meaning for future conduct.

That is the importance of the pragmatic doctrine. It finds its test of the so-called "true" in hypotheses and in the working of these hypotheses. And when you ask what is meant by the "working of the hypotheses," we mean that a process which has been inhibited by a problem can, from this standpoint, start working again and going on. Just as the animal no longer stands there, dodging this way and that to avoid its enemy, but can shoot away and get out of danger, so the scientist does not simply have to stand before a history which allows him only twenty million years and a history of two or three hundred million years. He can now continue the process of giving the history of the world, having this conception of the source of energy which had not been recognized before. Putting it into behavioristic terms, what we mean by the test of the truth is the ability to continue a process which had been inhibited.

A certain statement of the pragmatic doctrine implied that a thing was true if it satisfied desire. And the critics of the doctrine thought that this satisfaction meant the pleasure one could get out of it. That is, if a hypothesis was pleasing to an individual, then it was true. What I have just stated is, however, what is implied in this doctrine—that the test of truth lies in the continued working of the very processes that have been checked in the problem. It is a pleasant thing to get going again after we have been caught and shut in. It is a pleasant thing to have a new planet swim into our ken. But it is not pleasure which constitutes the test, but the ability to keep going, to keep on doing things which we have been trying to do but which we had to stop. That is one phase of the pragmatic doctrine—the testing of a hypothesis by its working.

The other phase I have touched on earlier. You see the attitude of which I have been speaking brings the process of knowing inside of conduct. Here, again, you have a relationship between pragmatic doctrine and the behavioristic type of psychology. Knowing is a process of adjustment; it lies within this process. Cognition is simply a development of the selective attitude of an organism toward its environment and the readjustment that follows upon such a selection. This selection we ordinarily connect with what we call "discrimination," the pointing-out of things and the analysis in this pointing. This is a process of labeling the elements so that you can refer to each under its proper tag, whether that tag is a pointing of the finger, a vocal gesture, or a written word. The thinking process is to enable you to reconstruct your environment so that you can act in a different fashion, so that your knowledge lies inside of the process and is not a separate affair. It does not belong to a world of spirit by itself. Knowledge is power; it is a part of conduct that brings out the other phase that is connected with pragmatism, especially in Dewey's statement.

This phase is its instrumentalism. What selection, and its development into reflective thought, gives us is the tools we need, the instruments we need to keep up our process of living in the largest sense. Knowledge is a process of getting the tools, the instruments. Go back to the illustration I have used above of the atoms as a source of energy. This concept becomes a tool by means of which the length of the life of the stars can be estimated. And when you have that, you can relate it to the age of life on the surface of the earth.

Perhaps the best statement to bring out the importance of this instrumentalism is the term "scientific apparatus." We think of that generally as the actual tools of the scientist; but we know that the term "apparatus" is also used for the ideas, the units, the relations, the equations. When we speak of a scientist's apparatus we are thinking of the very ideas of which he can make use, just as he can use the things which he has in his laboratory. An idea of a certain type, such as that of the energy of an atom, becomes a tool by means of which one is able to construct the picture of a star as a source of energy. There, you see, the object as such is a means which enables one to carry on a process of reconstruction such as is given in scientific doctrine.

Well then, the sources of the pragmatic doctrine are these: one is behavioristic psychology, which enables one to put intelligence in its proper place within the conduct of the form, and to state that intelligence in terms of the activity of the form itself; the other is the research process, the scientific technique, which comes back to the testing of a hypothesis by its working. Now, if we connect these two by recognizing that the testing in its working-out means the setting-free of inhibited acts and processes, we can see that both of them lead up to such a doctrine as the one

I have just indicated, and that perhaps the most important phase of it is this: that the process of knowing lies inside of the process of conduct. For this reason pragmatism has been spoken of as a practical sort of philosophy, a sort of bread-and-butter philosophy. It brings the process of thought, of knowledge, inside of conduct.

Mind Approached Through Behavior—Can Its Study Be Made Scientific?

The older psychology was structural. That is, it took experience as we find it to pieces and found certain relations between the various elements of it. These it explained through association. The latter psychology is functional rather than structural. It recognizes certain functions of conduct. We get experiences of distant objects, and their import for us lies in what we are going to do about them. We are hungry, and we set about getting food. We have become stifled with the air in the room, and we get out-of-doors. We are acting, and in our actions we determine what the relations are going to be between the various elements in experience. The structure of the act is the important character of conduct. This psychology also is called motor psychology, as over against the older psychology of sensation; voluntary psychology, as over against the mere association of ideas with each other. Finally, the development of these different phases got expression in behavioristic psychology, which gives itself to the study of this conduct to which I have referred. It undertakes to approach the mind from the point of view of the action of the individual. As a psychology, behaviorism has turned away, then, from the category of consciousness as such. Accounts of consciousness had been largely static in character. There were certain states of consciousness, certain impressions—the imagery men had in a spiritual substance that was impressed from without by certain experiences. The senses were the organs through which impressions were made on a substantial entity called "consciousness," and they were made in a certain way, in a spatial, temporal order. Consciousness was dealt with as a sort of substance which received impressions. Following upon this came the fruitful statement of Professor James.

For James, consciousness is not to be regarded as a static substance receiving impressions from without. It is rather a stream that flows on. And this stream has various characteristics, those that we express by its substantive and transitive character. It gathers about a certain experience and then passes on from that to another. Another analogy that James used was of the bird that alights on one branch and then flies to another, continually moving from one point to another point. The transitive phases of experience are those answering to relations; the substantives are those that answer to what we call the "things we perceive." If one is speaking, relating something, and says "and" and then stops at that point, we have the feeling of being ready to go on to something else. The feeling is just as definite an experience as that of yellow or red, of hot or cold; it is an experience of "and," one that is transitive, that is moving on. And these experiences are qualitatively different from each other. If, instead of saying "and," the speaker said "but," we should have an entirely different attitude toward what is to follow. In fact, our whole grasp of what we are hearing or reading depends upon the feelings we have for these different relating articles. If we come upon a thought with a "though" in it, we have one attitude toward what is to come; if "also," a different attitude. We are ready for a certain sort of content. We have a definite sort of experience answering to these relations which appear immediately in experience.

There is also another very important phase of experience which Professor James emphasizes, that which is represented by the spotlight of our attention as over against the fringe of the experience. If one gives his attention to something immediately before him, there lies about this experience a fringe which is very important in the recognition, in the value of that to which one gives attention. For ex-

From *Movements of Thought in the Nineteenth Century,* Ed. Merritt A. Moore (Chicago: The University of Chicago Press), pp. 386–390, 396–397, 403–404.

ample, when we are reading, we often have the experience of a world which is not immediately before us. The eye in moving over the page has caught a word several lines below. We have to hunt for it to find out what it was. It lies there in the fringe of our immediate experience, and we are ready for it when it appears. But still more, these different attitudes which are connected with the different particles, the "and," "but," "though," "also," also represent the fringe. We are immediately considering something, but we are already going on to something else. And the beginnings of that something else to which we are going on are already forming in the realization of our experience. They are taking place, and they represent the fringe of experience which comes in to interpret that to which we are giving attention.

These conceptions of James's which were so fruitful for the psychological consideration of experience do represent definitely a process which gets its whole statement in our conduct. We are going on to something besides that which is before us. And the structure of the experience itself depends on what we are going on to do. If we see something, we have at least aroused in the organism a tendency to meet it, or to avoid it. And it is this experience of what the contact will be that comes in to give the meaning to that which we actually see. We are continually interpreting what we see by the something that is represented by possible future conduct. So, to understand what is appearing in experience, we must take into account not only the immediate stimulus as such but also the response. The response is there partly in the actual tendency toward the object and also in our memory images, the experiences that we have had in the past. And this relationship of the response to the stimulus is one of very great importance in the analysis of our perception.

Professor Dewey brought out that fact in a memorable article on the stimulus-response concept. He pointed out that the very attitude of being acted upon by a stimulus is continually affected by the response. We start to do something, and the process of doing it is continually affecting the very stimulus we have received. A familiar illustration is that of the carpenter who is sawing on a line. The response of the organism to the stimulation of the line is there to determine what he will look for. He will keep his eye on the line because he is continually sawing. The process of listening is a process in which we turn the head in such a way that we will be able to catch what we are hearing—the listening is essential to the hearing. The process of responding is always present, determining the way in which we shall receive our so-called "impressions." That is, the organism is not simply a something that is receiving impressions and then answering to them. It is not a sensitive protoplasm that is simply receiving these stimuli from without and then responding to them. The organism is doing something. It is primarily seeking for certain stimuli. When we are hungry, we are sensitive to the odors of food. When we are looking for a book, we have a memory image of the back of the book. Whatever we are doing determines the sort of a stimulus which will set free certain responses which are there ready for expression, and it is the attitude of action which determines for us what the stimulus will be. Then, in the process of acting we are continually selecting just what elements in the field of stimulation will set the response successfully free. We have to carry out our act so that the response as it goes on is continually acting back upon the organism, selecting for us just those stimuli which will enable us to do what we started to do.

. . . What is further involved here, that which James did not bring out which Dewey does, is that there is always some inhibition of these actions. If one could actually run away before the terrifying object, if one could keep ahead of it, so to speak, give full expression to the tendency to run, one would not be terrified. If one could actually strike the very moment one had the impulse to strike, he would not be angry. It is the checking of the response that is responsible for the emotion, or is essential at least to the emotion. Even in the case of joy, if there were no hesitancy about the way in which one expressed his happiness, there would not be that emotion.

We can approach the emotion, then, from the point of view of our own responses to the attitudes of the organism. Here the James-Lange theory recognizes the visceral, as well as the motor, responses involved in the act. We spoke of the emotion as our effective experience of these attitudes. The impulse is something that can be stated at least in terms of the response of the organism itself. It is, of course, out of the impulse that desires, intentions, arise. What is added to the impulse and desire is the image of what we intend. And here we seem to find ourselves in what might be regarded in an unassailable field of consciousness as such. By its very definition imagery would be not the object, but some copy of the object; not the past event, but some memory of the past event; not future conduct, but a picture of future conduct. If you ask, now, where this image is, you would be at a loss to locate it. The easiest thing is to say that it is in consciousness, whether you put that consciousness in your head or say that you cannot locate it spatially. In any case, it is a relationship to something in your head. At least, the assumption of our physiological psychology is that an image answers to the excitement of certain nerve elements which have been excited in past experience. A cruder form of physiological psychology assumed that pictures of what had happened, were lodged, so to speak, in nerve cells, and, if the organism pressed a button, these pictures would come out. But further study revealed the fact that the nerve cells were no more than paths and junctions of paths. They should not be regarded as cubbyholes in which memory images or any other images are stored away. Just where the image is, is, I say, questionable. But you cannot say that the image is not in the objective world, for many of them are.

. . . Well, that is the way in which behavioristic psychology, if carried out consistently enough, can cover the field of psychology without bringing in the dubious conception of consciousness. There are matters which are accessible only to the individual, but even these cannot be identified with conspiciousness as such because we find we are continually utilizing them as making up our world. What you can do is to get at the organism as something that you can study. Now it is true that you cannot tell what a man is thinking about unless he chooses to tell. If he tells, you have access to that as well as he has; and you know what he is going to do, and it can enter into your own conduct. You can get at your own conduct and at the conduct of other people by considering that conduct in an objective sort of fashion. That is what behavioristic psychology is trying to do, trying to avoid the ambiguity of the term "consciousness." And what is of importance about this psychology is that it carries us back, as I have said, to the act as such. It considers the organism as active. It is out of the interest in the act itself and the relationship of thought to the act itself that the last phase of more recent philosophy dealt with above, that is, pragmatism, arises. Out of the type of psychology which you may call "behavioristic" came a large part of the stimulus for a pragmatic philosophy. There were several sources, of course; but that is one of the principal ones.

The Nature of Scientific Knowledge

We have reached certain points in the implications of the method of experimental science which may be summarily restated. In the first place, the scientist's knowing is a search for the unknown, a discovery, but it is a search for what has disappeared in the conflicts of conduct, that is, for objects which will remove the antagonism—it is a search for the solution of a problem. This dissipates the Platonic puzzle of how we can seek to know what is unknown. It is interesting to note that Plato's solution of the puzzle is found in the form of ignorance as a problem, that of recollecting what has been forgotten. Unfortunately this theory could not apply to the discovery of new types of objects which were foreign to the world of past experience.

In the second place, experimental science implies a real world uninfected by the problem, which can be used to test the discoveries which science makes. If knowledge is discovery of the unknown, this world is not known—it is simply there.

In the third place, as the world that is there is not known and may not therefore as non-known have ascribed to it the sort of logical necessity that does obtain in the logical structure of hypotheses, experimental science finds nothing contradictory in the later appearance of a problem in any portion of the world which has been used to test the solution of a former problem. That a contradiction should appear in the hypothesis is proof of its faulty and, in that sense, unreal, character, but that the sun

From *The Philosophy of the Act,* Ed. Charles W. Morris, John M. Brewster, Albert M. Dunham, and David L. Miller (Chicago: The University of Chicago Press, 1938), pp. 45–62.

ceases to be an object revolving about the earth in no way invalidates the world by which we test the hypothesis of the revolution of the earth on its axis by the shifting of the path of the pendulum's swing. Logical necessity obtains in the field of reflective thinking. To transfer it to the world that is there, and within which thought is occupied in the solution of problems, would be to dismiss experimental science as a meaningless and pernicious discipline and to return to the science of dogma.

In the fourth place, in observation and in experiment, science finds a field that belongs both to the world that is there and to the reflective thought of discovery, that is, of knowledge. The problem does not exist *in vacuo*. It is in the world that is there, but a certain portion of the world that is there has disappeared. The disease that is conveyed by contact disappears in the evidence of sporadic cases, notwithstanding its epidemic character. But the scourge is all the more tragically there. The instances of the disease are now observed and recorded by physicians and health officers who are seeking to discover the mechanism of the spread of the infection. These data embodied in various hypotheses exist in the minds of the investigators. As the observations of competent investigators of the actual epidemic, they are there as parts of the experiences of these individuals, and the records of them are parts of their biographies. The test case of the heroic scientist, who has remained immune to the fever after wearing the clothes of those who were sick of it and sleeping in their beds, and who succumbs to it when stung by the mosquito, begins in the field of scientific data and personal biographies and ends in the impersonal world to which belongs the two-chaptered history of the yellow-fever parasite. In so far as these data are imbedded in the lives of these individuals, they are personal but hard facts. So long as they are tentatively suggestive of objects that would harmonize conflicting ways of cataloguing and treating the disease, they are in the minds of men as part of the structure of their ideas.

We must distinguish here between what belongs to the experience of the individual qua individual and what is in his mind and may be termed "subjective." In the former sense the observation may be called private because the investigator alone observes it. Indeed it may be such an instance that he alone can observe it, if, for example, it is his own ache or pain, or if no one else has seen it, and it is an instance that is not repeated. This circum-

stance does not abstract it from the world that is there, since these men are there in that world together with the events that take place in their lives. But, in so far as the experience suggests what is known of the relation of the mosquito to malaria and a possible parasitic organism that may be the cause of yellow fever, we are in the presence of an idea and of what we will call "subjective." Such an object is not as yet there and may never be there. It is an ideal object. Such objects, as before remarked, have the same locus as erroneous objects after the error has been detected and are not to be confused, because they are placed in individuals' minds, with individuals' experiences, which are peculiar to them, but are objects in the world that is there. I am not, of course, ignoring the problems involved in this distinction. I am for the time being merely insisting that experimental science never takes the position so common in philosophy, which confuses the two. To the experimental scientist the data of observation and experiment never lose the actuality of the unquestioned world because they can happen for the time being only in the lives of particular individuals, or because they are fitted to serve in the mental processes of discovery. They are solid realities that can bridge the gaps between discredited theories and the discoveries of science.

It is the position of the positivist that what is observed is, as a fact of experience, there in a sense in which it never can be false. He recognizes that there may be false inferences drawn from the observation or the experiment, but as a fact of immediate experience it simply is and therefore is not open to possible question. This assumption does not answer to the procedure of science, for whatever may be the theory of sensation, the scientist's observation always carries a content or character in what is observed that may conceivably be shown under other conditions to be erroneous, though the probability of this be very slight. In psychological terms, an observation is never a mere determination of a sensation (if there is any such thing in adult experience) but is a perception, and, whether all perceptions involve judgments or not, they are frequently illusory, as, for example, in the perceptions of mirrored objects, and can never be free from the possibility of analogous errors.

What gives to the observation or experiment its validity is its position in the world that is there, that is not questioned. It is indeed carefully isolated from what has fallen into question, and this meticulous cleansing from all implications of the abandoned doctrine, and all as yet hypothetical interpretations, creates the impression of an experience which may not be subjected to any further question; but, as we know, there is no part or portion of the world that may not conceivably be the field of a scientific problem.

In the so-called exact sciences we seem to approach an object which is nearly free from all possibility of contingency—the physical particles. These particles are approximations to that which is unextended in space and time, but they carry a character—that of mass or of electrical energy—which does not approach zero, however minute it may become, and it is a character which is reached from numberless observations and not a little speculative theory. Furthermore, the procedures in our laboratories and observatories by which these characters are reached involve perceptual objects of the most complex nature, subject under other conditions to all sorts of conceivable questions. In other words, while the methods of mathematical analysis and extensive abstraction constitute a body of doctrines which in themselves are necessary, as long as the terms carry the same references, their applications are dependent upon their functioning within the problematic situations which arise in research science and appeal for their validity in practice to the court of observation and experiment.

The scientist's attitude is that of a man in a going concern which requires at various points readjustments and reconstructions. The success of the readjustments and reconstructions is found in the triumph over the difficulty, as evidenced by the fact that the concern continues to operate. He finds his tests in the parts of the whole which still operate. This does not imply that readjustments may not be called for later at these very points to which he now appeals for confirmation of the success of his solutions of the immediate problems before him. Surrounding the most profound analysis of the structure of the matter, and the widest survey of the galaxies of the heavens, lies the field of things within which experiment and observation take place without question, and which gives its validity to cosmologies and electronic theories of matter. It may seem a misnomer to speak of the world within which lie the observation and experiment as surrounding such hypothetical constructions as the electrical theory of matter, or the galactic form of the universe, since these hypothetical constructions so far transcend, in the subatomic world or in the indefinite stretches of the heavens, all the world of objects which includes our observations and experiments. We seem rather to be islanded at a very minute region occupied by perceptual objects that are in their constitution vague, indeterminate, and incurably contingent, surrounded from within and from without by a universe, which science presents, that is occupied by objects that approximate exactness of definition and necessity in their forms and changes. And yet the scientist, when he times microscopic oil drops as they move toward or away from charged plates, or when he measures the distances of photographed stars from one another before and during an eclipse, has not at all the attitude of a man perched insecurely upon obscure and adventitious data. The world that is there has taken up into itself all the order, definition, and necessity of earlier scientific advance. It is not there as hypothesis, in so far as the hypotheses have justified themselves in experiment, nor is it there as analyzed relations, events, and particles. These characters have passed into things, and for the time being at any rate, they are there unanalyzed, with the same authority as that of the so-called sensible experience. It is only necessary to emphasize again the distinction of the data as parts of the mental process of anticipating hypothetical objects, and as imbedded in the world of unquestioned reality in the experience of the individuals to whom the problem has come and who are trying to solve it, as well as in the impersonal world within which these individuals exist.

What renders such a statement of the world (not as known but as there) somewhat bizarre is that we enter the world of the scientist by the process of learning. In schools and institutions of higher learning we are taught the doctrines of modern science. Most of us take no part in the work of discovering what is there found out, but we acquire it by a process of learning, in which we may retrace some of the steps which research has followed, while in the main we accept it largely on faith in the men and their methods, especially faith in the checking-up of the results of certain individuals by all the others in the field. Scientific journalism as well as the daily press keeps us informed of the latest advances, and, having learned these facts, we say that we now know them. The world that stretches so far beyond our experience seems in this sense a world of knowledge.

It is true that all acquirement of information, in so far as it is more than a mere parrot-like facility in repeating what is read or heard, is a reflective process in which a problematic situation is met with discovery, though the hypotheses and their tests are those of others. Our own hypotheses and tests have to do largely with the competence of the sources upon which we draw. Admitting, however, all the criticism the layman can bring to his education, this world of knowledge is evidently of quite a different character from the world that is there, the world that is seen and felt, whose reality is the touchstone of our discoveries and inventions, and very different from the discoveries and inventions themselves, which are the knowledge par excellence of research science.

It is in the acquirement of information that the copy theory finds its explanation. There, what is known must answer feature for feature to its prototype. This field of so-called knowledge is that of the assimilation of the experience of others to one's own experience. There may be involved in it the discovery of these experiences by the individual, and it is in so far knowledge, but the content of that which is said to be learned is not discovered in the sense in which the other has discovered it.

In its simplest form what takes place here is the indication to one individual by another of an object which is of moment in their cooperative activity. This gesture becomes symbolic when it arouses in the individuals the attitudes which reaction to the objects involves, together, generally, with some imagery of the result of that action. It becomes communication when the individual indicating the object takes also the attitude of the individual to whom he is indicating it plus that of his response, while the individual to whom the object is indicated takes the attitude of him who is indicating it. We call this taking of one anothers' attitudes consciousness of what we are doing and of what the other is doing, and we incorrectly apply the term "knowledge" to this. The mechanism and import of this social procedure will be discussed later. What I wish to point out at present is that this process in itself does not involve discovery, any more than does that of perception. When doubt and discrepancies arise in the process of communication, as they continually do arise, the necessity of establishing agreement between the symbols mutually used, and that which they symbolize and the results of the conduct they imply, calls for a one to one correspondence between the symbols and those things and characters symbolized in the experiences of the different individuals, and this gives rise to the theory of knowledge as an agreement between the state of mind and that which is known. Such a determination of mutual agreement in co-operative conduct is indeed essential not only to this conduct but to what is called "thinking" in the individual, but it is not a discovery of that which needs to be known. It is at most a part of the technique by which the discovery is made. When the discrepancy arises, we must discover what the import of the symbols is, and here real knowledge takes place. We find out what the other person is referring to—in common parlance, what he means—but the process can go on without discrepancies. The other indicates to us what is there, and our so-called consciousness of this need not introduce any reflective attitude in our conduct. To call the correspondence between the attitudes involved in pointing out a savage dog and the conduct which takes place "knowledge," whether one points it out to one's self or to another, is to give to "knowledge" an entirely different value from that involved in discovery.

In any education that is worthy of the name, what is acquired does go toward the solution of the problems that we all carry with us, and is the subject of reflection, and leads to the fashioning of new hypotheses and the appearance of new objects; but this takes place after the communication which is the mutual indication of objects and characters by the use of gestures which are common symbols, that is, symbols with identical references. The correspondence theory of knowledge has grown up around the recognition of the relation between that which the symbol refers to in the object and the attitudes of response in others and in ourselves. There is here a one to one correspondence, but the relation of these objects and their characters to what we can infer from them in the discovery of the novel element which meets our problematic situations is of an entirely different sort.

In this "meeting of minds" which takes place in conversation, learning, reading, and thinking, there are generally present problematic situations and discovery, though this is by no means always the case. If someone informs us that an expected acquaintance has arrived, there is no more of a problem, or discovery in the sense of a solution, than would be involved in the friend's appearing around the corner. The varied landscape and hurry of events that sweep us along in books of travel and adventure embrace no more of reflection than the travel and adventure in which we are involved. A great deal of learning is a direct following of indications, or a gradual taking-over of the form and technique of others that goes on without inference. A good deal of thinking even, notably much of reverie and also straight-away ordering of conduct in an unquestioned situation, may be free from dubitation and ratiocination. A field of concentrated inferential thought does include the common reference of symbols in conversation, writing, and thinking—in other words, that part of logic which has to do with the technique of communication either with others or with one's self—together with the epistemologies and metaphysics which have sprung from this and obscured it with their tangled and forest growth. Here lie the problems of successful reference to identical objects and characters through identical symbols mutually employed by different selves, and these problems are of peculiar interest and importance to those involved in the exact and mathematical sciences. These problems demand theories of definition and implication, in so far as this does not depend upon the concrete content of that to which reference is made.

The environment of living organisms is constantly changing, is constantly invaded with other and different things. The assimilation of what occurs and that which recurs with what is elapsing and what has elapsed is called "experience." Without anticipating a later discussion of the social nature of the self and of thinking, I shall claim that the analysis of experimental science, including experimental psychology, never operates in a mind or an experience that is not social, and by the term 'social" I imply that in the thought of the scientist the supposition of his mind and his self always involves other minds and selves as presuppositions and as standing upon the same level of existence and evidence. It may be that the scientist, in a self-centered moment, might think away all else but his self and its thinking, but even if in imagination he succeeded in annihilating all save the dot on the *i*, its having any thoughts at all would depend entirely upon its preserving its previous habits of conversing with others and so with himself; and, as this precious hoard of past experience wore away under incessant use and decay, the dot would follow the *i* into nonentity. The dividend that I wish to see declared on this social nature of mind and the self is the equal immediacy that may attach to the assimilation of others' experience with that of our own. We so inevitably utilize the attitude of the other, which is involved in addressing ourselves and in attending to him,

that we give the same logical validity to what he relates of his experience as that which we give to what we relate to ourselves of our own past experience, unless on other grounds we are occupying the seat of the critic. It has, of course, only the validity that attaches to a relation, and is one remove from the assurance that attaches to the so-called memory image. But this validity at this remove is all that we can claim for most of our memory. Memory images constitute but a minute part of the past that stretches out behind us. For most of it we depend upon records, which come back to one form or another of language, and we refresh our memory as really in inquiring of a companion what took place on a certain occasion as in questioning ourselves. His testimony may not be as trustworthy as our own because of difference of interest and possible prejudice, but on other occasions for the same reason his testimony may outrank our own in reliability. While the actual image of the event has an evidential character that is peculiar, not infrequently it may be shown by the testimony of others to have been the product of imagination or to have been shifted from its proper place in the record. But still more fundamentally, the building-up of a memory record involves, in the first place, a social world as definitely as the physical world, within which the events took place, and involves, in the second place, experience which was actually or potentially social in its nature to the extent that whatever happens or has happened to us has its character over against actual or possible audiences or observers whose selves are essential to the existence of our own selves, the mechanism of whose conversation is not only as immediate as our replies but, when imported into the inner forum, constitutes the mechanism of our own thought.

I am anticipating the detailed presentation of this doctrine of mind to make clear my distinction between information and knowledge as discovery through inference. Information is the experience arising from the direction of attention through the gestures of others to objects and their characters, and cannot be called "knowledge" if that term is denied to perception as immediate experience under the direction of the attention springing from the organic interest of the individual. Perception is not itself to be distinguished from information, in so far as one uses a social mechanism in pointing out objects and characters to himself as another. The perceptions of a self may be already in the form of information. Logically stated they exist in a universe of discourse. Knowledge, on the other hand, deliberately fashions hypothetical objects whose reality it tests by observation and experiment. The justification for this is found in the actual disappearance of objects and their characters in the problems that arise in conduct.

Actually so much both of perception and of information is shot through with reflective construction and reconstruction that it is difficult to disentangle them from each other. It is, however, a part of scientific technique to accomplish this disentanglement. Observations and experiments are always in the form of information, even while they are being made, but they are scrupulously teased out from the web of inference and hypothesis. From this purity depart in varying degrees our perceptions as well as our information. It is a commonplace that one may be very well informed and do very little thinking, indeed be quite helpless over against a situation in which the information must be used to suggest or test hypotheses. The reliability itself of the observation or information, however, does call for a certain sort of verification, that of its repetition, either in the experience of the individual or in the mouths of other witnesses, and here, as above remarked, we find the source of the copy or correspondence theories of knowledge. Indeed, if information is knowledge, the copy theory of knowledge is entirely legitimate.

In presenting the world that is there as in some sense surrounding what is problematic, it was stated that what had in the past been approved by experiment and observation was taken up into this world and resided there as organized objects, things behaving toward one another in expected manners. Over against these unquestioned things lie the elements and relations of the working hypotheses of science. These are in a peculiar degree the objects of our knowledge. They are still lacking in complete verification. They are received only provisionally, and the objects which we constitute by means of them are complex hypotheses anticipating further tests in the use which we make of them. While they work, they pass as objects, but always with a proviso attached, which keeps the scientist's attention alive to possible departures from the result which the hypothesis implies. He is looking for such departures and eager to find them. In such far-reaching speculations as those regarding the structure of matter this field of knowledge is enormously extended, though it does not actually include the world within which the observation and experiment themselves take place, though the analysis which the investigation involves extends into the world of unquestioned things. For the purposes of our calculations we state the apparatus of our laboratories, for example, in the same terms which we use in our hypothetical constructions and thus seem to bring them within the scope of the investigation. But the scientist is in no doubt in regard to the distinction between the finding of fact and the hypothetical form in which he has stated things which are there, irrespective of the validity of the expressions into which they have been translated. Such translations may be perhaps called "objects of knowledge," though with the recognition that the success or failure of the hypothesis, into the terms of which we have translated these unquestioned things and their processes, does not affect their reality in the observation or experiment. In this sense there is no limit to the field of knowledge, for we may state the whole universe in terms of such working hypotheses, if we only remember the limits of this formulation. But it is also necessary to recognize that the *raison d'être* for translation is found in the function of the apparatus of experimental science and not in the revelation of reality. What reveals this latter fact is the ineradicable difference between the immediate concrete event to which appeal is made in experiment and observation, and any formulation of this in terms of a current working hypothesis. The actual position of the spectral line, or of the photographic image on the plate, is the brute fact by which the hypothesis is tested, and there is no methodological relation between the exactly determined position of these and a resolution of them into, say, electrons. It is conceivable that this should be done. It would vastly confuse and delay the attainment of any knowledge from the measurement and would have no conceivable connection with getting that knowledge. To call such a translation "knowledge" is to depart from the significance which the term "knowledge" has in an experimental science.

The world, then, in which science operates has, at its core and in a certain sense surrounding its findings and speculations, the environment of immediate experience. At the point of its problems the immediate things are so analyzed that they may pass into the formulations of the scientist's hypothesis, while the finding of observation and experiment remains immediate experience, that is, is located in the surrounding borderland. It is these two aspects of the world of immediate experience that call for especial attention. From the standpoint of the discovery of the new, from the standpoint of research, the world of immediate experience is a core and seems to be reduced to the island of vague, indeterminate, and contingent data that are contrasted with the clear-cut, sharply defined, and necessary elements and events of scientific theory; an apparently incongruous situation, for the acceptance of the clear-cut, sharply defined, and necessary world is dependent upon the findings in the island of vague, indeterminate, and contingent data, the field of observation and experiment. It is an apparent incongruity that has given birth to much philosophic speculation.

That the incongruity is only apparent is fairly evident, since the scientist, out of whose method and its achievements it has arisen, is not aware of it. If it were presented to him in the terms just used, he would presumably reply that one cannot both have his cake and eat it; that, if one is in search of definition and certainty at a point in experience at which they have disappeared, it is but natural that the definition of the problem should exhibit this fact of their disappearance and that the very data which will serve in the verification of a hypothetical order of defined and necessary things must be themselves infected with indeterminateness and contingency; that the home of experimental medicine is in the hospital; that the gospel of science summons not the logically righteous but sinners to repentance. He would likely add, however, that because, before the discovery of the germ of yellow fever, the clinical picture of the disease was indeterminate and its incidence contingent, there would have been no justification in ascribing the same indeterminateness and contingency to the clinical picture of diphtheria—in other words, that the form in which the data appear in any one problem is pertinent to that problem alone.

But while the statement of the problem, together with the observation and experiment that are involved in verification, constitutes a core of immediate experience whose analyzed elements are indeterminate and contingent as compared with defined elements and necessary relations in a hypothetical scientific theory, these data do belong to objects in an immediate world that is a going concern, and such is unquestioned. Such a world may be said to contain the problem within itself, and so to surround the problem. It has taken up into itself the solutions of past problems successfully solved. There is involved in it also a considera-

ble apparatus of working hypothesis, which is not always distinguished from the world that is there. The distinction lies in the fact that back of the working hypothesis there is always a question mark, and in the back of the scientist's mind in using the working hypothesis lies the problem implied in its being only a working hypothesis. The world that is there is the common world within which the intelligent community lives and moves and has its being. In physical diameter it may be a small world as compared with the scope of physical hypotheses which in a logical sense it surrounds. Its logical compass of the hypothesis is shown in the data of observation and experiment that must be brought to bear upon the hypothesis before it can be established.

This compass of the problem, and the hypothetical solution of it, is logical in so far as the analysis involved in the problem, the inference involved in the formation of the hypothesis, and the sufficiency of evidence involved in observation and experiment all rest upon a world of things that is there, not as known but as containing conditions of knowledge. But the world that is there includes and surrounds the problem in the sense that the problem is also there within the field of conduct, for, as has been indicated, the problem arises in the conduct of individuals and out of the conflict of acts which inhibit one another because the same object calls out mutually antagonistic responses. When these problems pass into the field of reflection, they are so formulated that they would occur in any experience, that is, they take on a universal form. Such a formulation is essential to the reflective process of their solution. Their actual occurrence, however, in the world that is there awaits the advent of the conflict of responses in the experience of some individual; and the solution as well, inasmuch as it departs from the common or universal habits of the community, must be an individual achievement before it can become the attitude of all and be thus universalized. So located in its historical setting, the problem is evidently as completely surrounded by the world that is there as the hole left by a name that has been forgotten in surrounded by all the other names and things and happenings by which one attempts its recall. But while occurrence of the problem and of its solution must be in the field of conduct of some one individual, the things and events that constitute its border are matters of common and undisputed validity. The problem must happen to an individual, it can have no other locus than in his biography, but the terms in which he defines it and seeks its solution must be universal, that is, have common import.

This location of the problem in the experience of the individual in its historical setting dates not only the problem but also the world within which that problem arises. For a world within which an essential scientific problem has arisen is a different world from that within which this problem does not exist, that is, different from the world that is there when this problem has been solved. The world of Daltonian atoms and electricity (which was considered a form of motion), within which appeared the problem of the ion in electrolysis and the breakup of the atom in radioactive substances, is a different world from that whose ultimate elements are particles of electricity. Such worlds dated by the problems upon whose solutions they have appeared are social in the sense that they belong to the history of the human community, since reflective thought is a social undertaking, and since the individual in whose experience both the problem and its solution must arise presupposes the community out of which he springs.

It is the double aspect of these worlds that has been the occasion of so much philosophic speculation. On the one hand, they have provided the tests of reality for experimental science, and, on the other, they have successively lost their validity and have passed away into the realm of ideas. I have already indicated the scientist's rejoinder to this apparent assault upon his method. His method implies not that there has been, is, or will be any one authentic world that constitutes the core and envelope of his problems, but that there always have been, and are, and will be facts, or data, which, stated in terms of these different worlds by the individuals in whose experience they have appeared, can be recognized as identical; and that every world in which problems appear and are attacked by the experimental method is in such a sense a going concern that it can test hypothetical solutions. I have further insisted that as a scientist his goal in the pursuit of knowledge is not a final world but the solution of his problem in the world that is there.

There have existed two different attitudes toward these so-called facts or data. Because it has been assumed that the observations of the old watchers of the heavens in the valley of Mesopotamia, and of Hipparchus, and of Tycho Brahe, and present astronomers possessed a certain identity, there has arisen a picture of the world made up of that which can be regarded as common to all, a picture made of abstractions. It is a picture through which we can look before and after, and determine the date of Thales when he predicted an eclipse, and what eclipses will take place a thousand years hence. If we assign a metaphysical reality to these facts, we reach a universe which has been the subject matter of popular and technical philosophies. If, on the other hand, we restrict ourselves to the determinations of experimental science, we have nothing but the common indication of things and characters in a world that is there, an indication that abstracts from all but that which is there when a problematic situation has robbed it of some object and concentrates attention upon those characters and things which are the stimuli to mutually inhibiting responses. As I have already insisted, it is only in the experience of the individual, at some moment in that experience, that such a conflict can take place. Nonproblematic things are there for everyone. But while these observations took place in individual experiences, in the experiences of those individuals for whom these problems arose, it is the assumption of experimental science that a like experience would have arisen for any other individual whose experience had been infected with the same problem and that, in so far as successive problems have involved identical problematic elements, it is possible to identify the same observation in the experience of different individuals.

The Mesopotamian soothsayer who had hit upon the succession of the eclipses and enshrined it in the Great Saros, and the Greek astronomer who by a scientific explanation of the eclipses had worked out the same succession, and the modern Copernican astronomer who substitutes the motion of the earth in its orbit for that of the sun about the earth and dates these eclipses still more accurately, were all observing the same phenomenon. For each there was a different world that was there, but in these worlds there were actual or identical observations of individuals which connect these worlds with one another and enable the later thinker to take up into his own the worlds that have preceded his. The common content of these observations, by means of which different worlds are strung together in human history, depends upon the assumption that different individuals have had or would have the same experiences. So far as there is any universality in these contents, it goes back to an actual or implied indication of the same things and characters by different individuals, in the same or like situations, that is, it goes back to implications in regard to social behavior in inferential processes, especially to the social nature of the knowledge or evidential import of observation.

However, the experimental scientist, apart from some philosophic bias, is not a positivist. He has no inclination to build up a universe out of such scientific data, which in their abstraction can be identified as parts of many different worlds. The reference of his data is always to the solution of problems in the world that is there about him, the world that tests the validity of his hypothetical reconstructions. Nothing would more completely squeeze the interest out of his world than the resolution of it into the data of observation.

The Social Nature of the Present

The social nature of the present arises out of its emergence. I am referring to the process of readjustment that emergence involves. Nature takes on new characters, for example with the appearance of life, or the stellar system takes on new characters with the loss of mass by the collapse of atoms through the processes that go on within a star. There is an adjustment to this new situation. The new objects enter into relationship with the old. The determining conditions of passage set the conditions under which they survive, and the old objects enter into new relations with what has arisen. I am here using the term "social" with reference not to the new system, but to the process of readjustment. An outstanding illustration is found in ecology. There is an answer in the community in the meadow or the forest to the entrance of any new form, if that form can survive. When the new form has established its citizenship the botanist can exhibit the mutual adjustments that have taken place. The world has become a different world because of the advent, but to identify sociality with this result is to identify it with system merely. It is rather the stage betwixt and between the old system and the new that I am referring to. If emergence is a feature of reality this phase of adjustment, which comes between the ordered universe before the emergent has arisen and that after it has come to terms with the newcomer, must be a feature also of reality. It can be illustrated in the appearance of a planet upon the hypothetical approach of the stellar visitor that occasioned at the origin of our planetary system. There was a period at which the substance of our own earth was part of the sun's revolving outer sheath. Now it is a body separated from the stellar mass, still revolving, but in its own orbit. The fact that the planet is exhibiting the same momentum in its distant orbit as that which carried it about the star before its advent as a planet, does not do away with the fact that there is now a planetary system where here was formerly only a single stellar body, nor with that stage in which the substance of the planet was to be was in both systems. Now what we are accustomed to call social is only a so-called consciousness of such a process, but the process is not identical with the consciousness of it, for that is an awareness of the situation. The social situation must be there if there is to be consciousness of it.

Now it is clear that such a social character can belong only to the moment at which emergence takes place, that is to a present. We may in ideation recall the process, but such a past is not a reintegration of the affair as it went on, for it is undertaken from the standpoint of the present emergence, and is frankly hypothetical. It is the past that our present calls for, and it is tested by its fitting into that situation. If, *per impossible,* we were to reach that past event as it took place we should have to be in that event, and then compare it with what we now present as its history. This is not only a contradiction in terms, but it also belies the function of the past in experience. This function is a continual reconstruction as a chronicle to serve the purposes of present interpretation. We seem to approach this complete recall, if I may use this expression, in identifying the fundamental laws of nature, such as those of motion, which we say must have been and must always be what they are now; and it is here that relativity is most illuminating. It frankly

From *The Philosophy of the Present,* Ed. Arthur E. Murphy (Chicago: The University of Chicago Press, 1932), pp. 47–67.

reduces the sort of reality that could be the identical content of past, present and future to an ordered arrangement of events in a space-time that, by definition, could be as little in any past of scientific imagination as it could be found in our perceptual world. The geometry of space-time denies emergence unless it is brought in by way of Whitehead's metaphysics; and if I am not mistaken such a view must surrender the ordered geometry of space-time that Whitehead retains. Without emergence there are no distinguishable events thanks to which time emerges. The events and intervals to which the relativist refers are the constants that shake out of the elaborate mathematics which the realization of the social character of the universe has shown to be necessary.

The social character of the universe we find in the situation in which the novel event is in both the old order and the new which its advent heralds. Sociality is the capacity of being several things at once. The animal traverses the ground in pursuit of his prey, and is at once a part of the system of distribution of energies which makes his locomotion possible and a part of the jungle system which is a part of the life system on the surface of the inanimate globe. Now we recognize that if we are to estimate the energy of locomotion that he is going to expend we must take into account his ferocity, his state of hunger, and the attraction or fear that his prey excites within him, and equally we recognize that if we are to estimate these characteristics of the form we must be able to measure the energy-expressions in his organism and in the environment. There is as genuine a sociality in his relation to his environment as in his relation to the prey or to his mate or to his pack, and the mark of it is that we habitually estimate characteristics that belong to the object as a member of one system by those which belong to it in another. So we measure motion by the distances covered in the consistent set at rest, or the dimensions of that set by the motions involved in measurement. The relativist discovered that this mutual estimation involved a change in the units of measurement, and that a transformation must be made if ideal exactness is to be attained. We seem to be in the same situation in biology. Accurately to estimate the living process in energy-distributions we should be able to transform inorganic physico-chemical process into organic process, which unfortunately we have not been able to do.

If we examine the bases of this estimation from one system to another we find two char-

acteristics, one is the emergence of the event from the conditions under which it has appeared—that which, as we have seen, gives rise to its history and may be brought under the general term of evolution. The second is the carrying on of identical conditions from the past into the present. The appearances of the planets, when related to the laws of mass and motion, fall into an ordered series, and from this standpoint the object is looked at as arising out of the old. From the standpoint of its emergence it is considered as in both systems, but only in so far common laws obtain in each. The substance of the arising planet is a piece of the sun, moving with the momentum which belongs to it in that capacity, and it is also an object in a system within which the sun has a definite mass that follows from the mass and motion of the planet with reference to the sun. In a similar fashion in Galilean dynamics accelerations and decelerations were emergents in a field of motion of masses in an absolute space.

It remained for relativity to set up motion itself as an entity which arises under certain conditions—those of frames of reference—out of logically antecedent conditions of events at intervals from each other within space-time. But these conditions no longer lie within the range of possible experience. It remains true however that what is motion from one standpoint within experience is rest from another. The relativity of motion had long been recognized. With the surrender of absolute space and the successful development of Einstein's general relativity, the emergence of motion and rest out of the more abstract situation that expresses what is common to both frames of reference or perspectives and appears in one as motion and in the other as rest, seems to be logically demanded. And yet, as I have just indicated, such a formulation takes us outside the scheme of development I have sketched above. It involves the relation of appearance and reality, of the subjective and the objectively real, not the relation of an emergent object arising out of the past to that which conditions it. We appear to have left an evolutionary philosophy of science and to be passing into a rationalistic phase in which reality is offered to us only in patterns of logic and mathematics. I suspect however that we are much too close to the great changes which have taken place within the last fifty years to be able to get them into their proper perspective.

I wish to suggest that the social character of the present offers another standpoint from which to regard this situation. I have spoken of the social implications of the emergent present as offered in the occupation by the new object of the old system and the new, sociality as given in immediate relation of the past and present. There is another aspect of sociality, that which is exhibited in the systematic character of the passing present. As we have seen, in the passage from the past into the future the present object is both the old and the new, and this holds for its relations to all other members of the system to which it belongs. Before the approach to our sun of the stellar visitor, the portion of the sun which became the earth was determined in its character by its relationships to those portions of the sun's substance which became the other planets. As it is drawn out into its planetary position it retains this character which arises from the former configuration and assumes the new character which is expressed in the perturbations of its orbit through the influences of its neighbors. The point is that a body belonging to a system, and having its nature determined by its relations to members of that system, when it passes into a new systematic order will carry over into its process of readjustment in the new system something of the nature of all members of the old. So in the history of a community, the members carry over from an old order their characters as determined by social relations into the readjustments of social change. The old system is found in each member and in a revolution becomes the structure upon which the new order is established. So Rousseau had to find both sovereign and subject in the citizen, and Kant had to find both the giver of the moral law and subject of the law in the rational being. To revert to the evolution of the planetary system, the earth's orbit still maps out the central sun of which it was a part, and its relative motions with reference to other members of the planetary system reflect their positions in the sun before the stellar visitor arrived.

I have referred to the increase in mass of a moving object as an extreme example of sociality. That is, if we keep this increase in mass within the field of possible experience, we have to treat the moving body as in two different systems, for the moving object has its own time and space and mass due to its motion, which time, space and mass are different from those of the system relative to which it is moving. The paradoxes arising out of this occupation of a different system on the part of a moving body are familiar. What I wish to point out is that we reach here the extreme limit of this

sociality, for every body, thanks to its velocity, has a certain space-time and energy system. This velocity is, however, relative to the system within which the body is moving, and the body would have another velocity relative to another system moving with reference to the first. The body would then have an indefinite number of measurements of mass in the indefinite number of systems with reference to which it can be conceived of as moving. It is occupying all these different systems.

Now we may set up a metaphysical space-time, with its coincidences of events and its intervals, as the reality to which these frames of reference refer, or we may keep within the field of experience and use the transformation formulae which have been shown to be necessary for exact measurement. The question arises as to just what is involved in the use of the transformation formulae. In the immediate situations within which the relativity of motion is present in experience, such as the possibility of one's own train being in motion while the neighboring train is at rest, no transformation is required. In such cases we cover up the difference in time systems by saying that the differences in spatial and temporal dimensions are so impossibly small that they cannot be brought into application, that it is only when we reach velocities which approach that of light that appreciable differences arise and call for recognition. This is covering up a matter of fundamental importance. When a train is passing us it is in our own world of space and time. If we should take the relativistic standpoint and regard the train as at rest and the earth as rushing by it, we should indeed be passing from one perspective to another, but then the train would not be moving, and in the present case the train is moving. When we calculate the change in spatial, temporal and mass characters of an alpha particle which is shot out of an atom, we are treating it, of course, as in another space-time than our own, for we are giving to it the dimensions that belong to its space-time including the change in mass character. Now from the standpoint of Newtonian relativity two space-time systems are alternatives, they cannot both be applied to the same situation, except alternatively. But when we use the Lorentz transformation formula, we are giving the body the characteristics which belong to another space-time system and using the result in our own. This is confessed when the statement is simply made that a body increases its mass with its velocity, and we fail to add that the units of spatial and temporal measurement change also, that is, that we are in another frame of reference which is alternative to our own and cannot be simultaneously applied. We are told, however, that if an aeroplane were passing us at 161,000 miles a second we should see the foreshortening and the slowing down of the temporal extension of processes, that is, we should see in our own space-time system the effects of being in the other space-time system.[1] That is, the two frames of reference cease to be alternatives. In the case of the Fitzgerald foreshortening, there was no such assumption of being in both systems at once, but in this case there was no reference to difference in simultaneities.

Now Einstein undertakes to give the procedure by means of which we can be thus in one space-time system and record in it the effects of the differences due to the alternative space-time system. This procedure assumes first of all the uniform velocity of light as a fact in nature. In the second place on the basis of this uniform velocity of light a signal system is set up by which we can establish in our system that the same events are not simultaneous in the system that is moving with reference to ours as are simultaneous in our own. Furthermore, the effect of this difference can be made evident, as in the case of the passing aeroplane, through vision, that is, through light. What this amounts to is that as spatial perspectives arise for us in our static landscape, so there are discovered to be temporal perspectives over against moving objects in the landscape. This perspective character of a temporal sort is discoverable only over against motions of very great velocities, but the principle of them is as definitely given as in the case of the spatial perspectives. That principle is that dimensions as revealed by measurement must be foreshortened in the direction of the motion, provided this takes place in a visual field. If the velocity of light were infinite there would be no foreshortening, for then the light wave that left one end of an object would reach us at the same moment as the light wave from the other end, no matter how rapid the motion. It is then only when velocities approach that of light that such a perspective enters into experience, and then only indirectly as in the calculation of the change in mass of the particle shot out of the atom. But if we could see what is found in Eddington's suppositious airplane we should get the visual temporal perspective directly, for of course time slows down in proportion as spatial dimensions are foreshortened. The natural assumption would be that these temporal perspectives are to be regarded in the same light as are spatial perspectives. The real dimensions and the real temporal passage are what the passengers in the airplane find them to be, just as their distorted view of us is to be corrected by what we find to be about us and what we find to be going on about us.

It is at this point that the Larmor-Lorentz transformations and the negative results of the Michelson-Morley experiment enter. These transformations were worked out to indicate the mathematically stated conditions under which the Maxwell equations for electromagnetism would be invariant. The Newtonian equations are invariant within the field of Newtonian mechanics. That is, they hold whatever center of origin is taken as the center of reference and, in the case of the relative motion of systems with uniform velocity, whichever system is regarded as moving. It was found that to obtain invariance for the Maxwell equations it was necessary to affect the symbols referring to space, time and energy, including mass, with a coefficient $1/c$ in which c is the uniform velocity in a vacuum of the electro-magnetic wave, of which light is one form. The changes in spatial and temporal dimensions which this formula of transformation demands are those which the temporal perspectives, to which I have referred above, call for, and there is the same assumption of an absolute value for the velocity of light. Furthermore this transformation formula gives just the foreshortening of the earth's diameter in the direction of its motion in its orbit that accounts for the negative result of the Michelson-Morley experiment.

Apart from the striking coincidence in the results reached by means of the transformation formulae, Einstein's theory of relativity, and the result of the Michelson-Morley experiment, the outstanding fact is the common assumption of a constant velocity of light. In the case of the transformation formulae it is not surprising that the constant should be sought in so fundamental a character as the velocity of the electro-magnetic wave. In the case of relativity the possibility of measurement by light-signals in different time-space systems presupposes the uniformity of the velocity of light, and this is the explanation of the negative result in the Michelson-Morley experiment. "It means," I quote from Whitehead, "that waves or other influences advancing with velocity c as referred to the space of any consentient set of the Newtonian group will also advance with the same velocity c as referred to the space of any other such set."[2]

There should be added to the account of this conjunction the sweep of the atom out of the realm of mass mechanics into that of electro-magnetism, and the expression of energy-distribution in terms of fields. The importance of these changes lies in the change of reference of reality as between distance and contact experience. Formerly, there was a close correlation between mass mechanics and perceptual reality. The reality of what we saw was to be found in what we could get under our hands, and what we got under our hands accorded in imagination with mass as the quantity of matter. But the still more important point was that we felt the reality to lie in the volume itself in abstraction from its relations, that the reality of the thing could be there in advance of the system into which it entered. All the varieties of what I have called spatial perspectives of the same objects refer to identical objects found in the field of contact experience—of what we feel and see simultaneously—and this holds not only for our own perspectives but also for those of others. It finds its exact expression in congruence. What I have termed temporal perspectives do not occur in experience, except in such highly imaginative presentations as Eddington's airplane. But in perspectives which involve differences in simultaneities we seem to pass beyond the range of their perceptual resolution in the field of contact experience. We are compelled to bring them into accord by transformations. And this is just the situation which obtains in respect of the invariance of the Maxwell equations. The world from the standpoints of different space-time systems, with different values for the common units of space, time and energy, can only be assimilated by transformations. There is as close a parallelism between an electro-magnetic universe and the world of distance experience, that of visions, as between the world of mass mechanics and our contact experience.

However, there is a break in this complete correlation. As I have already indicated, the increase in mass of a moving body takes place in the space-time system within which it is moving, but the calculation of that increase in mass takes place by means of spatial and temporal units which belong to another space-time system, while the increase in mass is measured in the space-time system within which the motion is taking place. We actually find in measurement of our own pointer readings, with our own simultaneities, that the mass of the alpha particle has increased. We could discover that increase in mass without any use of

the apparatus of relativity, but we account for it by a theory which implies that a clock on the alpha particle will be running slower than our clock, and it is by a calculation that involves the time of the alpha particle that we reach the change in mass which we discover in our own time system. In other words, the correlation breaks down at the point at which it is brought to the test of an experimental finding, which must have a reality of its own or it could not test the hypothesis. We must be able to state the facts involved in our own apparatus, clocks, electrometers in terms which are independent of the Lorentz transformations and the Einsteinian relativity. And in this world of final adjudication of the apparatus, the building that contains it and the ground on which it stands and its surroundings, the ultimate reality is not what belongs to distance experience, but to what can be presented in the contact experience which this distance experience promises or threatens. If we are not to go back of the field of experience into a metaphysical world of Minkowski space-time, with its events and intervals, we must come back to the perceptual world of scientific findings.

Let me state the situation again. The changes that take place in the field of electro-magnetism cannot be stated in a set of equations that are invariant for space and time. It is necessary to assume a different spatio-temporal structure in the field in which the change is going on. The clocks are going slower and diameters of things in the direction of the motion are decreased, while the mass is increased. These are changes which theoretically are all registered in the field which is at rest and within which the motion is taking place. But the calculation of them implies a spatio-temporal ordering which does not belong to that field. It implies another center of reference. The perceptual reality to which these changes in the field of distance experience refer differs according as they are taken from the standpoint of one field of reference or from another. This brings out the other striking character of the situation, that things whose substance belongs to the field of electro-magnetism cannot be defined in terms that allow of their being isolated as perceptual findings. For such definition it is necessary that a reality can be recognized in the thing that can be given in the spatio-temporal features of the perception—in pointer readings for example. This is the characteristic of mass, as I have insisted. Though we can define mass only in terms of a system of bodies in motion with reference to each other, we can think of the substance of the massive thing as found within the volume which we see or imagine, and can then put it actually or in imagination into relation with other things. Electricity as the substance of an electron can only be thought of in terms of its field and of the relations of that field with the fields of other electrons. Faraday's tubes of force and ether as a stuff have been used for the purpose of providing such an independent content, and have disappeared within our fingers. The fact is that science has come back to a structure of things that can be stated only in terms of distant experience so far as perception is concerned. This offers no difficulty in the structure of our theories. We know the amount of energy in a system and we can allocate it to the different members of that system, which can be located in space and time; but we cannot, so to speak, take a separate element in our fingers and say of it that this has a certain amount of energy within it which constitutes the "what it is" of the object, and then relate it to other things with like contents. Energy is conceivable only in terms of a system that is already there for the thought that deals with the thing. For the purposes of scientific method, the importance of contact experience does not lie in the greater reality of tactual or resistance experience over that of color or of sound, but in the fact that observation and experiment do come back to distance experience which must be itself directly or indirectly referred to what we can actually or conceivably get our hands upon. This remains the test of the reality of the perception, and is therefore the test of the scientist's finding in observation and experiment, and it is the condition of holding on to the fact as real in itself in independence of the varied hypotheses that are set up to account for it.

It has been customary to find the reality of the perception in the experience of the individual, and there have arisen all the multiform difficulties in placing this individual experience in the reality of the world to which he belongs, especially when such experience is used to criticize theories about that world. The scientist has been satisfied to find the same spatial and temporal structure in the individual's experience that he finds in the world, and thus to locate the individual's observations within the surrounding world, with all the exactness which spatio-temporal measurement makes possible. Now relativity, with the electro-magnetic theory out of which it has so largely arisen, has not only vastly complicated the spatio-temporal theory of measurement, but it has also reversed what I may call the reality-reference. Instead of saying

that the reality of the perspectives of our distance experience is to be found in that contact experience which is firmly bedded in the geometry of a Euclidean space and the even flow of a uniform time, we must say that it is only as we can read over this seemingly Euclidean space of our contact world into perspectives dependent upon the motion of distance objects and discover transformation formulae between these that we can reach the reality of what we perceive. Furthermore we cannot proceed as we prefer to proceed, with perceptual models, and build up, say, a Bohr atom out of a number of protons and electrons welded into a nucleus around which we can set other electrons in planetary revolutions. The positive and negative electricity which we use as the stuff of these ultimate particles does not submit to such imaginative perceptual analysis. We may talk about the diameter of an electron or seek to locate its electrical charge, but the substantial character of electricity cannot be thus isolated, and the Bohr atom has broken down. In recent speculation it has been found convenient to deal with matter as a form of vibration, but there is no meaning in seeking for that which vibrates.

And yet the dependence of scientific theory upon perceptual findings was never more pronounced, and it is to this dependence that I would direct attention. As I have indicated the alternative seems to be a reference to a metaphysical world that can only be assumed, together with the assumption that the logical patterns which we find in our own world have correlates in this metaphysical world. In the meantime our experience becomes subjective except in so far as our thought relations may be guessed to transcend our frames of reference. In the prerelativity days the spatial and temporal structure of the observed fact was that of the universe. However relative to the observer the sense qualities of the observed object might be, its perceptual definition in space and time gave it fixed contour and location within the relational structure which for the scientist at least was the absolute structure of the world, and in mass mechanics the substantial content of any volume could be thought of as residing within that defined volume. Perception gave both the logical structure of reality and the defined habitat of substance. The earlier theory of gases and of heat as a form of motion is outstanding illustration of the simplicity of this situation. Now neither the relational structure of reality nor the locus of its substance is to be found in the perceptual situation. But since the scientist can never reach the metaphysical space-time with its events and intervals except by an assumption, and since he can never grasp the entire field of any energy content, he is obliged to test his hypotheses by placing himself both in his own perceptual situation of, say, a system at rest and also in that of the system which moves with reference to his own, and to compare the spatio-temporal structures of the two systems. He proceeds by transformations, but they are transformations which are possible only as the observer grasps that in his own situation which involves his placing himself in the situation of that which he observes. Although this is more complicated, it comes back in its findings to perceptual occasions. Now this is only possible if that sociality of thought in which we occupy the attitude of the other by taking our own divergent attitude is also a characteristic of nature. Newtonian relativity *permitted* the observer to transfer himself from one system to the other and to note that the relative positions of bodies in the two systems remained the same whichever system he occupied, and that the laws of mechanics were satisfied in either case. But electro-magnetic relativity exhibits results within our system which *compel* us to have recourse to the other system with its space-time structure in order to account for them. Under Newtonian relativity sociality was confined to thought. Given the two systems moving with reference to each other, the conditions of either will forever remain the same, uninfluenced by the motion or rest of the other. Under electromagnetic relativity the mass of the moving object increases in the system at rest, and this involves the different spatial and temporal coefficients of the other system. It is this break in what I have called the correlations between differences of space and time in different systems which reveals in the perceptual world that sociality in nature which has been generally confined to thought. The increased mass in the system at rest must also coincidentally be moving according to its own clock and in a space measured by its own yardstick, in order that there may be an increase in its mass within the other system. We have already seen that there is sociality in nature in so far as the emergence of novelty requires that objects be at once both in the old system and in that which arises with the new. Relativity reveals a situation within which the object must be contemporaneously in different systems to be what it is in either. The experimental proofs of relativity all come back to such situations.

I have pointed out that this is no novelty in science, though it has always implied an unsolved problem. We find it in teleology in biology and in consciousness in psychology. The animal species is in the mechanical system determined both by past conditions and also by tendencies to maintain itself in the future. The conduct of the conscious organism is determined both by a physiological system from behind and also by a consciousness which reaches into the future. This can of course take place only in a present in which both the conditioning past and the emergent future are to be found; but, as these problems indicate, what is further called for is the recognition that in the present the location of the object in one system places it in the others as well. It is this which I have called the sociality of the present. If we examine the situation from the standpoint of relativity, we see that the very motion that is taking place within the system at rest carries with it a different spatio-temporal structure, which is responsible for an increase of mass within the system at rest. If we translate this into the other two situations, we see a biochemical process arising which we call life, but which so changes the conditions under which it goes on that there arises in nature its environment; and we see living forms selecting those past conditions which lead to future maintenance of life and thus introducing values and later meanings into nature.

If we ask for the past that conditions the emergence of the present we can find no other formulation for it than this, that whatever emerges must be subject to the conditioning character of the present, and that it must be possible to state the emergent in terms of the conditioning past. In Newtonian relativity, in the case of unaccelerated motion of two systems with reference to each other, the conditioning past was summed up in the dictum of the same relative position of the bodies of the two systems and the same mechanical situation whichever system was regarded as in motion. In this situation there is no emergence. If into this Newtonian relativity we now introduce the Special Principle of relativity we have the emergence of new characters of the moving body in the system within which it moves, because of its motion. And if we describe the body under the old conditions we must reduce it to rest, which only can occur without loss of the reality which the emergent motion brings with it if we set in motion the other system with the emergent changes appearing in that system. In the case of General Relativity, Einstein undertook the task of formulating the universal conditions under which the changes in the spatio-temporal structure of the universe seem to take place—those changes which are due to motion, accelerated as well as unaccelerated. He has shown that these are also conditions for changes in mass, and is at work upon the task of showing that the same is true for electromagnetism.

Now the principle of sociality that I am attempting to enunciate is that in the present within which emergent change takes place the emergent object belongs to different systems in its passage from the old to the new because of its systematic relationship with other structures, and possesses the characters it has because of its membership in these different systems. While this principle has been evidenced most clearly in the doctrine of relativity as applied to physical theory, it is here least evident for our experience because the changes in mass, for example, due to the velocities with which we are familiar are so minute that the changes in Newton's law lie in the field of distant decimals. On the other hand electromagnetic relativity has succeeded in presenting the form of the emergent with great exactness. We know the type of changes that will take place if any velocity appears within a certain system. Here we deal simply with the relation of the structures of space and time to motion. If we turn to the other two examples of sociality I have adduced—that of life and that of consciousness—we find ourselves in highly complex situations that are but dimly comprehended. We find that what understanding we have of live involves a reference to the future in the maintenace of the form and of the species. We know the life process is a physico-chemical process, but what the exact character of the process is we do not know as we know the character of a velocity. We do know, however, that the life processes are not confined to the organism, but taken as wholes include interactions between the organism and its surroundings, and we call that surrounding world, in so far as it is involved in these processes, the environment of the form and its species. That is, we recognize that emergent life changes the character of the world just as emergent velocities change the character of masses. And we know that what we call conscious processes are physiological processes, and that those processes which we generally call behavior utilize their organized adjustments in order to select the objects to which they respond, and that as a result of this behavior things within the environment of these living conscious forms take

on values and meanings. We know that conscious processes are dependent upon a high development of an encephalon which is the outgrowth of the nervous mechanism of distance stimulation and of the delayed responses which distant stimuli make possible. The whole of such a nervous system provides both the field and the mechanism for selection with reference to distant futures, and this selection endows surrounding objects with the values and meanings which this future subtends. But what the physiological process is which puts at the disposal of the individual organism its highly organized responses for the purposes of discrimination and selection no one knows. There is, however, a great contrast between application of the principle of sociality in these different fields. In the field of physical relativity we know the process of motion with great exactness, but there are but three or four recondite experiments in which we can bring into our experience the effects which velocities have in changing the characters of things. On the other hand, the effects that result from living and conscious processes are evident on every side, while the nature of the processes has hitherto been shrouded in impenetrable obscurity. But in all three of these fields the principle of sociality nevertheless obtains. In all three there is emergence, and the character of this emergence is due to the presence in different systems of the same object or group of objects. Thus we find that in one system with certain space, time and energy characters, an object moving with a high velocity has an increased mass because it is characterized by different space, time and energy coefficients, and the whole physical system is thereby affected. In like manner, it is because an animal is both alive and a part of a physico-chemical world that life is an emergent and extends its influence to the environment about it. It is because the conscious individual is both an animal and is also able to look before and after that consciousness emerges with the meanings and values with which it informs the world.

NOTES

1. Eddington, "Space, Time, and Gravitation," page 22 ff. For a more balanced account of the relativist theory the reader may consult A. Metz, "Temps, Espace, Relativité."

2. "Principles of Natural Knowledge," 2nd ed., page 43.

Suggestions for Further Reading

Works by Mead

The Individual and the Social Self: Unpublished Works of George Herbert Mead. Edited, with an Introduction, by David L. Miller. Chicago: The University of Chicago Press, 1982.

Mind, Self, and Society: From the Standpoint of a Social Behaviorist. Edited, with an Introduction, by Charles W. Morris. Chicago: The University of Chicago Press, 1934.

Movements of Thought in the Nineteenth Century. Edited, with an Introduction, by Merritt A. Moore. Chicago: The University of Chicago Press, 1936.

The Philosophy of the Act. Edited, with an Introduction, by Charles W. Morris, in collaboration with John M. Brewster, Albert M. Dunham, and David L. Miller. Chicago: The University of Chicago Press, 1938.

The Philosophy of the Present. Edited, with an Introduction, by Arthur E. Murphy, with Prefatory Remarks by John Dewey. Chicago: Open Court, 1932.

Anthologies

Selected Writings of George Herbert Mead. Edited, with an Introduction, by Andrew Reck. Chicago: The University of Chicago Press, 1982.

The Social Psychology of George Herbert Mead. Edited, with an Introduction by Anselm Strauss. Chicago: The University of Chicago Press, 1956. (A revised and enlarged edition has been published under the title *George Herbert Mead on Social Psychology: Selected Papers.* Chicago: Phoenix Books, 1964.)

Essential Works on Mead

Walter Corti, editor. *The Philosophy of George Herbert Mead.* International copyright, Archiv fur genetische Philosophie. Winterhur, Switzerland.

Hans Joas. *G. H. Mead: A Contemporary Re-Examination of His Thought.* Translated by Raymond Meyer. Cambridge, U.K.: Polity Press, 1985.

Grace Chin Lee. *George Herbert Mead, Philosopher of the Social Individual.* New York: Kings Crown Press, 1945.

David L. Miller. *George Herbert Mead: Self, Language and the World.* Chicago: The University of Chicago Press, 1982.

Maurice Natanson. *The Social Dynamics of George Herbert Mead.* Washington D.C.: Public Affairs Press, 1956.

For a more extended bibliography, see David L. Miller, *George Herbert Mead: Self Language and the World,* listed above.